Robert M. Young

Historical Notices of Old Belfast and its Vicinity

A selection from the mss. collected by William Pinkerton, F.S.A., for his intended

history of Belfast, additional documents, letters, and ballads, O'Mellan's narrative

of the wars of 1641, biography

Robert M. Young

Historical Notices of Old Belfast and its Vicinity
A selection from the mss. collected by William Pinkerton, F.S.A., for his intended history of Belfast, additional documents, letters, and ballads, O'Mellan's narrative of the wars of 1641, biography

ISBN/EAN: 9783744789042

Printed in Europe, USA, Canada, Australia, Japan

Cover: Foto ©ninafisch / pixelio.de

More available books at **www.hansebooks.com**

HISTORICAL NOTICES

OF

OLD BELFAST

AND ITS VICINITY

A SELECTION FROM THE MSS. COLLECTED
BY WILLIAM PINKERTON, F.S.A., FOR HIS INTENDED HISTORY OF BELFAST,
ADDITIONAL DOCUMENTS, LETTERS, AND BALLADS,
O'MELLAN'S NARRATIVE OF THE WARS OF 1641,
BIOGRAPHY OF MARY ANN M'CRACKEN,
NOW FIRST PRINTED.

With Maps and Illustrations

EDITED, WITH NOTES,

BY

ROBERT M. YOUNG, B.A., J.P., M.R.I.A., F.R.S.A.

Hon. Sec. Belfast Natural History and Philosophical Society
Author of the "Town Book of the Corporation of Belfast;" "Ulster in '98"
Co-Editor of the "Ulster Journal of Archæology"

Συναγάγετε τὰ περισσεύσαντα κλάσματα, ἵνα μή τι ἀπόληται

BELFAST
MARCUS WARD & CO., LIMITED, ROYAL ULSTER WORKS
W. MULLAN & SON; OLLEY & CO., LD.
LONDON : ELLIOT STOCK.   DUBLIN : HODGES, FIGGIS & CO., LD.
1896

SIR SAMUEL BLACK,
Town Clerk of the City of Belfast.

EDITOR'S PREFACE.

 THE PUBLICATION OF THE "TOWN BOOK OF THE CORPORATION OF BELFAST," IN 1892, *would seem to have awakened fresh interest in its history, and the Editor has been favoured with many original documents relative to the Borough and its vicinity, of which a selection are printed in this present volume. The most important of these is the collection of MSS. made by the late eminent antiquary, William Pinkerton, F.S.A., for his long-contemplated work, "THE HISTORY OF THE TOWN AND CASTLE OF BELFAST, WITH NOTICES OF THE IRISH BRANCH OF THE CHICHESTER FAMILY," presented by his widow to the Editor in September, 1894, with the request that they might be used in whatever way he thought best. After a careful examination of these voluminous papers, it was considered most fitting to print a selection of the unpublished manuscripts, so that the public might be the judges of the amount of original research undertaken as preliminary to the composition of the intended book.*

This had been partially recognised by George Benn in the preface to his "History of Belfast," which is based to a large extent on the foregoing collection. It would appear, however, that in his natural desire to use as far as possible his own material, many important facts already available in the Pinkerton MSS. escaped his notice. It must also be remembered that he proposed to limit the scope of his work to the town of Belfast, whereas the historical notices gleaned by Pinkerton from every available source relate to no insignificant part of Ulster.

William Pinkerton was born in Belfast on 22nd January, 1809, at 22, Bridge Street, the residence of his father, Andrew Pinkerton, who had come from Paisley, his native town, some years before, and established a discount office, then a lucrative private business. He had married, shortly after setting up his office, the widow of Ebenezer Black, manager of the "Belfast News-Letter," at the time Alexander Mackay had acquired this valuable property. William Pinkerton was sent to the Belfast Academical Institution as a pupil of James Knowles, then English Master, and father of the famous James Sheridan Knowles. His education was continued at the Belfast Academy, where the Rev. William Bruce, D.D., was the Principal. Here he acquired a knowledge of classical literature, afterwards of great use in his historical researches. In 1822 the Principal gave his farewell address, and the only copy preserved was written by W. Pinkerton. After he left school, he followed for years a seafaring life, and settled for a time in Pennsyl-

vania. On his return he married Miss Susan Watson, daughter of Thomas Watson, Bark Place, Kensington, and took up his residence at Ham, near London, where he commenced literary work about 1850, to which he devoted the remainder of his life.

His rare critical acumen and unwearied faculty of research in the bye-ways of history quickly found appropriate expression in sundry contributions to " Chambers's Journal " and " Book of Days." To these were added " Notes and Queries," to which he contributed many valuable articles from 24th March, 1851 (Vol. III.), till 25th February, 1871 (4th S. VII.). An obituary notice of him appeared in the issue of 5th August, 1871 (4th S. VIII., p. 118). Amongst other periodicals, he contributed to " The Anthropological Review," " The Fisherman's Magazine," and " The Field." But it was in the " Ulster Journal of Archaeology " that his most valuable papers appeared. Robert S. Macadam started this magazine in January, 1853, as the result of the antiquarian loan collection shown in the Belfast Museum at the British Association, September, 1852. W. Pinkerton's name first appears as the contributor of a letter relative to the price of victuals when Schonberg was at Carrickfergus in 1689 (Vol. I. p. 133). It is evident from his correspondence with Robert S. Macadam that he spared neither trouble nor time when writing these articles, actuated by the strong regard he felt for the country where he was born, and the town in which he had passed his youth. He writes in 1859, " I have become a London-Irish Rifleman, yet I have not the slightest intention of deserting your colours" (Macadam MSS.).

For many years he had thought of writing an exhaustive history of Belfast ; but the first public intimation of his intention seems to have been in his favourite " Notes and Queries" (3rd S. III., p. 143). He adds, in a notice of Barnaby Googe—" In 1573 Walter Devereux, Earl of Essex, was induced to attempt the complete conquest of Ulster. This is not the place to allude to the court and private intrigues which led to such an impolitic and foolhardy undertaking. The writer will have to treat of these matters at large in his forthcoming history of the most important town of that Province."

, He wrote to a Dublin friend about this time—" I have been for the past few years endeavouring to collect material for a history of Belfast, my native town. And I have, as stated in ' Notes and Queries,' gone over all the ground of Reid's ' History.' "

Amongst the " Pinkerton MSS." is a slip of paper on which he has written—" Dec. 2, 1865. The History of the Town and Castle of Belfast, with notices of the Irish branch of the Chichester Family, by William Pinkerton, F.S.A. If there be anie which are desirous, &c. Of the period we know but little, and that is very useless for our purpose."

W. Pinkerton had all the qualities essential to the historian. Capable of infinite pains in searching for his material, he was able to use it to the fullest advantage, and express his thoughts in easy and accurate English.

Without prejudice, and caring only for the truth of things, he was free from the partizanship which disfigures the works of many Irish historians.

This can be in part explained by his long absence from Ireland, and the freedom of thought acquired by residence in the United States. He was on intimate terms with the leading Ulster antiquaries, as his letters testify, including the Revs. W. Reeves (afterwards Bishop) and Classon Porter, R. S. Macadam, E. Getty, J. W. Hanna, George and Edward Benn, and the Rev. J. O'Laverty, P.P., the latter still happily surviving. In the summer of 1864 he visited the North of Ireland, and made many enquiries for historical purposes.

His health, which had been long indifferent, showed symptoms of breakdown early in the sixties, and he had to relax his efforts, although he was anxious as ever to assist a friend, as the following extract from a letter, dated October 13, 1863, to R. S. Macadam shows :—"My colleague, Mr. Robert Chambers, broke down, and, much against my will, I had to go to the front. I felt it as a kind of point of honour under the circumstances, or I would not have risked my own health in doing so."

By the discontinuance of the " Ulster Journal of Archæology," owing to the death of R. S. Macadam's brother James, Pinkerton was free to give his undivided attention to his " History of Belfast." His last article in the "Journal" was entitled, " Some Notices of Sir Arthur Chichester, Baron of Belfast." Unfortunately for his posthumous fame, he had planned his proposed work on too vast a scale for one lifetime to execute, resembling in this respect two of his contemporaries, Bishop Reeves and Edmund Getty, both of whom left important works uncompleted.

When the material accumulated at such a sacrifice seemed ripe for the historian's purpose, and his ready pen had indited a few scattered episodes in the history of the town he loved so well, " municeps non ignotæ civitatis," the end came, not unexpectedly, on 30th July, 1871.

Soon after his lamented decease, the extensive collection of MSS. formed by him for his projected work were generously lent by his widow to his old friend, R. S. Macadam. From some correspondence in the Macadam MSS., it appears that George Benn took them to his house at Glenravel, Co. Antrim, in the autumn of 1872, where he made an inventory (given in the Appendix). He also wrote to R. S. Macadam—" I am sure I could, if agreeable to all interests, make up a moderate-sized volume from the papers by bestowing some time to extracting something more from the old ' Town Book,' if still in Mr. Torrens' possession, the ' Belfast News-Letter,' and some other easily obtainable sources."

The result of this proposal was the well-known "History of Belfast" by George Benn, published by Messrs. Marcus Ward & Co. in 1877, a work of sterling value, much of which it owes to the researches of W. Pinkerton.

After the "Pinkerton MSS." had been given to the Editor, and a careful collation made of them with the portions used by Benn, it was seen that a great deal of valuable matter had been omitted or passed over with brief mention.

Amongst the more notable items so treated are Monroe's Raid on

Newry ; Monroe in Belfast ; Meredith's Relation of Several Services ; the Commonwealth and the North of Ireland, including Cromwell's letters ; the Chichester Patents ; the unique extracts relative to King William III. and his Court at Belfast, including the text of his Proclamations in the North of Ireland ; the Island Magee Witches, and Molyneux's Journey to the North.

In preparing the volume for publication, the Editor considered it would increase its historical value if some other original matter relative to the history of Belfast and its vicinity was added, so as partly to fill up the unavoidable gaps in the Pinkerton papers, and thus afford additional materials for future historians.

Amongst these will be found some " State Paper" extracts ; the Ulster Assizes, 1615 ; Account of John Corry ; Diary of Col. Bellingham ; Correspondence of Robert Greene ; Letters of Mrs. M'Tier, and Biography of Mary Ann M'Cracken.

Friar O'Mellan's " Narrative of the Wars of 1641," translated by R. S. Macadam from the original Irish, is included in this volume, as an unpublished account of a most eventful period in the history of this country, and from the further circumstance that the translation was made by an accomplished Irish scholar, who shortly before his death had expressed keen interest in the present work, and had offered his valued assistance. After his decease, his surviving relative, Miss Anna Macadam, most kindly placed his literary MSS. in the Editor's hands.

The historical material contained in the present volume is arranged as far as possible in chronological order. It is believed that almost all of it is now first printed. The Editor has given, in his Notes, original extracts from MSS. in his possession and elsewhere, rather than quotations from printed works.

All the full-page and other illustrations by Messrs. John and J. W. Carey, of Messrs. Carey, Hanford & Carey, were drawn for this book from suggestions and information supplied by the Editor. The photo-engraving has been executed by Mr. Joseph Lewis with his accustomed skill.

The Editor's thanks are due to Messrs. Walpole Bros. ; R. Cochrane, F.S.A., Hon. Sec. R.S.A.I. ; and Prof. G. F. Savage-Armstrong, M.A., D.Lit., for kind permission to use the blocks on pp. 13, 154 ; 3, 46, 163 ; 23, 24, 139, 141, respectively.

He also takes this occasion of returning his sincere thanks for the original MSS., &c., kindly presented to him by Mrs. W. Pinkerton, Miss Anna Macadam, Miss Gordon, and Christopher Aitchison, Esq., J.P.

His acknowledgments are especially tendered to the Earl of Belmore, G.C.M.G., for the notice of John Corry, and illustrative blocks ; J. Ribton Garstin, Esq., D.L., V.P., R.I.A., for the diary of Col. Bellingham ; Mrs. Adam Duffin, Mrs. James Henry, and the Misses M'Cracken. His best thanks are hereby given to the Countess of Shaftesbury, the Baroness von Stieglitz, Lord O'Neill, William M'Cammond, Esq., J.P., Lord Mayor of Belfast ; Sir Samuel Black, Town Clerk ; Alderman Lavens M. Ewart, J.P., M.R.I.A. ; Alderman James Henderson, M.A., J.P. ; the President of Queen's College, Belfast ;

the Dean of Dromore ; Rev. Denis Murphy, S.J., LL.D.; Rev. W. Reynell, B.D.; Rev. G. Hill; Rev. C. Scott, M.A.; Rev. W. T. Latimer, B.A.; Rev. J. O'Laverty, P.P., M.R.I.A.; W. J. Fitzpatrick, Esq., LL.D., F.S.A.; T. H. Torrens, Esq., J.P.; John Salmon, Esq.; Classon Porter, Esq.; W. Swanston, Esq., F.G.S.; John Vinycomb, Esq., M.R.I.A.; E. H. Clarke, Esq.; H. W. Clarke, Esq., M.A.; W. H. Drennan, Esq.; F. B. Simms, Esq. ; Don Jorge O'Neill, Lisbon ; Marriot R. Dalway, J.P., Esq. ; James Logan, Esq. ; James Johnston, Esq. ; F. J. Bigger, Esq., M.R.I.A.; F. W. Moneypenny, Esq.; J. H. Bland, Esq.; James Graham, Esq.; A. H. Coates, Esq.; D. Keay, Esq.; the Librarians of British Museum, Lambeth Palace Library, Belfast Free Library, Linen Hall Library, and the other friends mentioned in the text.

ROBERT MAGILL YOUNG.

Rathvarna, Belfast, November, 1895.

WILLIAM PINKERTON, F.S.A., 1809—1871.

CONTENTS.

	PAGES
EDITOR'S PREFACE, containing some account of W. Pinkerton, F.S.A.	v—ix
Report by Robert Cowley, 1538 ...	1
Claneboy, December, 1542 ...	2, 3
Piers and Malbie to the Queen, 1567 ...	4-10
Irish Linen Yarns, 1572 ...	11-13
Lord Deputy and Council to the Queen, 1573 ...	14-16
Answer to Lord Treasurer's Objections, 1594 ...	16-18
Petition of Agents, &c., Carrickfergus, 1594 ...	18-20
Sir A. Chichester and Island Magee, 1601 ...	20, 21
Letter from Thomas Walker, Newry, 1601 ...	21, 22
Inquisition taken at Ardquin, 1605, and Smith's Grant ...	23-26
Timber in Ulster, 1608 ...	27, 28
The Plantation of Ulster. Chichester to Salisbury, 1610 ...	28-30
Assizes held in Ulster, 1615 ...	30-39
Order of the Exchequer, 1618 ...	39, 40
Commission on Waste of Woods, 1625 ...	41, 42
Customs, Excise, &c., in Ireland, 1637 ...	42-48
Monroe's Raid on Newry, 1643 ...	49-55
The Cessation, 1643. Account of Corn ...	55, 56
Monroe in Belfast, 1644 ...	56-64
The Parliament and Belfast, 1645. Belfast Trade, &c., 1646-48 ...	64-68
A Relation of Several Services by Major Meredith, 1649 ...	68-72
The Commonwealth and North of Ireland, 1651-60 ...	73-108
Account of John Corry, 1654, by Lord Belmore ...	109-116
Account of Stranmillis, Belfast ...	117-123
Certificate by Daniel O'Neill. Petition of P. Russel, 1663 ...	123, 124
Account of Sir George Rawdon ...	124-127
Confirmation of the Chichester Patents, 1669 ...	127-138
Description of Ardes Barony, 1683 ...	138-143
Proclamation of Schonberg, Belfast, 1689 ...	143
Diary of Colonel Bellingham at Belfast, 1690 ...	144-146
King William III. and his Court at Belfast, 1690 ...	148-152
Journey to the North by Dr. T. Molyneux, 1708 ...	152-160
Depositions, Island Magee Witches, 1710 ...	161-164
Correspondence of Robert Greene, 1725-26 ...	165-168
Mrs. M'Tier's Letters to Dr. W. Drennan, 1776-84 ...	169-173
Life of Mary Ann M'Cracken, 1770-1866 ...	175-197
Narrative of Wars of 1641, by Friar O'Mellan, 1641-47 ...	199-247
APPENDIX. Inventory of Pinkerton MSS. and List of Books ...	249-251
NOTES ...	252-283
INDEX ...	284-287

List of Illustrations.

SEPARATE FULL-PAGE ILLUSTRATIONS.

PAGE

Lawson's Map of Belfast Harbour, 1789 ... ... (*Frontispiece*)
Dedication Plate, Arms of City of Belfast, in Full Heraldic Colours
(*To face Title-page*)
The Belfast Corporation Address to King William, 1690 ... *To face page* 1
Sir Arthur Chichester presenting Charter to Corporation, 1613 ,, ,, 29
View of Belfast in 1805 ... ... ,, ,, 57
Attack on Belfast by Col. Venables, 1649 ... ... ,, ,, 72
Interior of Assembly Room, Old Exchange, 1793 ... ... ,, ,, 127
Burning of Belfast Castle, 1708 ... ... ,, ,, 155
T. M'Cabe denouncing proposed Slave Ship Company, 1786 ... ,, ,, 170
Execution of Henry Joy M'Cracken, 17th July, 1798 ... ... ,, ,, 187

FULL-PAGE ILLUSTRATIONS PRINTED WITH TEXT.

Portion of Mercator's Map of Ulster, 1594 43
Chart of Belfast Lough, 1693 147
Portrait of Mary Ann M'Cracken 174
Map of Site of White Linen Hall, 1783 198
Old Houses at Queen's Square, 1854 248

ILLUSTRATIONS IN TEXT.

	PAGE		PAGE
View of Belfast and Long Bridge, by		Covenanters tearing their Colours ...	60
G. Petrie, R.H.A. (*reverse of half-title*)		Ancient Seal of Londonderry ...	63
Sir Samuel Black, Town Clerk		Token of John Steward	65
(*reverse of title*)		Token of John Clugston	67
Old Town Seal	v	St. Lawrence's Gate, Drogheda ...	69
William Pinkerton, F.S.A.	ix	Cromwell in Ireland	70
Lord Mayor of Belfast	xii	Arms of Newry	72
The Ford of Belfast	1	Seal of Commonwealth	73
Carrickfergus Castle	2	Seal of Belturbet	74
Ancient Seal of Carrickfergus ...	3	Arms of Dublin	74
Queen Elizabeth	7	Arms of Kilkenny	77
Dunluce Castle	10	Gateway, Walls of Derry ...	85
Arms of Elizabeth, Trin. Coll., Dublin	11	Title-page, Venables' *Experienced Angler*	88
Weaving	12	Arms of Munster and Connaught ...	89
Irish Girl Spinning	13	Arms of Leinster	91
Walter Devereux, Earl of Essex ...	20	Arms of Waterford	94
Hugh O'Neill, Earl of Tyrone ...	22	Oliver Cromwell	98
Castle of Ardkeen, Co. Down ...	23	City of Galway and Arms ...	99
Arms of Savage of the Ards ...	24	Belfast Church made a Fort ...	102
Sir Thomas Smith	26	Arms of Cork	105
Coleraine	28	Silver Salver of Claudius Gilbert ...	108
Arthur Chichester, Baron of Belfast	29	John Corry's Coat of Arms ...	109
Village of Masareene	31	Token of John Corry, Belfast ...	110
Ancient Gallows, Carrickfergus ...	32	Silver Tankard of ditto ...	113
Arms of Enniskillen	32	Old Water Works, Stranmillis ...	117
Arms of Londonderry	34	Lock-keeper's House, do. ...	118
View of Londonderry	35	The Quern	120
Ancient Irish Sgian	36	Hillsborough Fort	122
Arms of Dungannon	36	Portmore Woods	126
Carrick-a-Rede	40	Arms of Donegall Family ...	127
Felling Oaks for Belfast Castle ...	41	White Abbey in 1800	129
Connswater Bridge, 1603	44	Enclosing Deer-park, Cave Hill ...	130
Ancient Bell of Bangor	45	Portaferry Castle	139
Seal of Customs, Carrickfergus ...	46	Ardkeen Church	141
Bust of Swift, Trinity College, Dublin	48	Schonberg crossing Long Bridge ...	144
View of Mourne Mountains ...	49	Old Belfast Castle	146
Mourne Mountains from Castlereagh	52	Gloves, &c., of King William III. ...	149
Arms of Dundalk	53	Signature of King William III. ...	151
Charles the First	56	Map of Battle of Boyne	153
The Library, Trinity College, Dublin	59	Waringstown	154

	PAGE		[PAGE
Lisburn	155	Old View of High Street	187
Shane's Castle	156	Belfast about 1780	189
Giant's Causeway	157	Battle of Antrim	194
Castlereagh	160	Old Exchange	196
Seal of Carrickfergus	163	Owen Roe O'Neill	199
View of Belfast Lough, 1750 ...	164	Benburb Castle	200
Collier Tomb, Belfast Old Church	166	Speed's Map of Ireland	201
Belfast from Cabin Hill ...	169	After the Battle of Benburb ...	. 247
William Drennan, M.D.	173	William Ware	251
Capt. J. M'Cracken and his Wife ...	176	Corporation Bellman	252
Hearts of Steel attacking Barracks ...	178	Book-plate of Earl Donegall ...	265
Shop in Castle Street, 1790	179	Belfast Book-plates	272
Thurot's Landing	182	Old Glass-House, Ballymacarrett ...	283
Autograph of Henry Joy M'Cracken	184	Cocky Bendy	284
Henry Joy M'Cracken	185	Black Sam	287

WILLIAM M'CAMMOND, ESQ., J.P., LORD MAYOR OF THE CITY OF BELFAST
1894 AND 1905.

THE BELFAST CORPORATION ADDRESS TO KING WILLIAM, 1690.

THE FORD OF BELFAST

OLD BELFAST.

Report by Robert Cowley, Master of the Rolls, on the State of Ireland, April, 1538.

ULSTER, which is in the North, bordering with Scotland, long after the Conquest descended to the King by the marriage of the daughter and heir of the Earl of Ulster, by which Earldom he might dispend yearly (as I remember) 32,000 marks, whereof I think at this day he hath nothing.

In this portion, being the greatest of the five except Munster, these Lords now inhabit, writing themselves princes, O'neill of Ulster, O'donell of Tyreconell, Felym Baccagh, lord of Claneboy, as great a man of strength as O'neill, besides these other great Lords, as Magwire, McMahon, Magennis, O'hanlan, O'chaan, McWillie (a Welshman of the English Conquest), Alexander Carragh McDonell, a captain of the Scots, which hath conquered lands beside Knockfergus, builded fortresses and there inhabiteth, Savage of the English Conquest—all these being disobedient to the law. *(Extract Irish Correspondence, State Paper Office.)*

A

Claneboy, Dec., 1342.

THE L. D. advised a grant of Claneboy to Niall Connalagh O'Neill (nephew to the Earl of Tyrone), reserving Carrickfergus, Olderfleet, and Coleraine. About the same time, a Sir John Travers, who in the following year was made Master of the Ordnance, one of the many political quacks that have from time to time attempted to cure what they did not understand, wrote "Devices for the Reformation of Ireland"

VIEW OF CARRICKFERGUS CASTLE.

(Vol. x., Art. 85), and in May, 1543, the Lo. D. let Claneboy to him instead of to Niall Connalagh.

Jan., 1562. L. L. Sussex exemplifies the expediency of granting Claneboy to Niall Connallagh.

Mar., 1569. Sir Brian McFelim's Castle in Claneboy, called Castlereagh, being from Knockfergus, in the way towards Dublin, about ten miles, and three miles or thereabouts from Belfast. (Vol. xxvii., Art. 40.)

Mar., 1570. A Sir Thomas Gerrard and companions offered to plant the Glynnes and part of Claneboy, if they were granted 100 horse and 400 foot, till the three first crops be gathered, and the Queen's ships for defence against the Scots. Also to have commission to levy soldiers, labourers, and artificers in the counties of York, Lancaster, and Cheshire. (Vol. xxx., Art. 22.)

Sep., 1570. Will. Pers petitions for some rembrance for Sir Brian McPhelim, and a garrison to be placed for the defence of the poor subjects of Claneboy.

Mar., 1571. Sir Brian McFelim to L. D., explaining his motive for agreing with Sorley Boy, by which means there are more ploughs going in Claneboy than there had been for one hundred years. The country too poor to bear more English.

July, 1571. Will. Pers to the Queen, requests that Sir B. McFelim have the ancient lands of Claneboy on both sides the Bann.

McFelim himself writes from Belfast to the Queen, same date, to confirm to him and his heirs the lands of old belonging to his ancestors, Lords of Claneboy, on both sides of the Bann. Recounts his services. (Vol. xxxiii., Art. 3.)

Enterprise to inhabit and fortify Claneboy for the use of the Crown. (See Mem. which notes that this paper was written before the arrival in Ireland of Smith and Essex.) (Vol. xxxiv., Art. 52.)

Captain Thos. Brown and Capt. Thos. Borrowe petition the Queen—for the Arde from the mouth of the river of Strangford to the river of Belfast, including Castlereagh, and the woods by east that river adjoining to Kylwarling, and to the Dufferin in fee farm. And answers to the objections to their suit. End 1571. (Vol. xxxiv., Art. 42, 43.) (*Pinkerton MSS.*)

ANCIENT SEAL OF CARRICKFERGUS.

Piers and Malbie to the Queen, Feb. 8th, 1567.

UR most humble duties unto your Honors remembered. Your Lordships' letters of the 18th of this Jan. we received the 27th of the same by a messenger of Mr. Marshall's, and with the same one letter unto me, Capt. Piers; and before that we also received one other from your Lordships of the 12th of this month, wherein your Honors do think good to send here Capt. Gilbert's and Capt. Horsey's bands for the hastening away of the Scots, which undoubtedly is very honorably considered of your Lordships; and although (as we have already advertised your Honors) that Carleboy is gone with some part of his men, yet, contrary to his promise (which we knew well would so fall out), he hath left of his men behind him, whereof the VIII score with Tirlagh O'neill be of them, III score with the Clanalesters which manure the land of Monery and Cary, and lx with Alexander oge McAlester Nary (*sic*). And notwithstanding our knowledge thereof, we thought it good to dissemble our understanding, to the end that first himself should depart, and then his company might be dispersed, whereby we might the better compass their overthrow, which we shall endeavour to do to the uttermost of our powers.

Presently upon Carleboy's departure (according to the opinion we had when we first agreed to include Alexander Oge in the peace with Carleboy for the consideration aforesaid), the said Alexander being sent to by us to come in to acknowledge his duty unto the Queen's Majesty, utterly refused so to do, whereupon we thought meet to leese (*sic*) no time, but, concluding that the Abbay of Glanarme was a place to annoy him most, we took it, and placed there Capt. Cheston with his whole band and xii horsemen, at which time, with a dozen of horsemen going before, we took 60 fat beofes of the rebels, which we left with Capt. Cheston, and have appointed to send him by boat six weeks of other victuals, which day if we had not taken it, it had been set on fire by them. This was the 26th of this month, and this day Capt. Cheston writ unto us that he sent unto him that so soon as he can get his son to put in pledge for his good behaviour (who flieth from him for fear thereof) he will come in ; and now he hath dispersed his creaghtes abroad, willing them to shift for themselves, and is in great perplexity, for the taking of this place doth break their hearts. We have also placed in the castle of Glenarme Randoll Oge McAlester Harry, who hath brought thither his creaghtes, and manureth the ground ; who hath assured us that all his brother's followers will come in unto him, and likewise all the Clanalesters, which be the only men which the Scots most trust unto, and this day their messenger is with the said Randall Oge; so that although there is no doubt of the utter expulsing of the Scots and overthrowing of this rebel, yet shall it not be amiss that, according to your Lordships' good consideration and device, the two bands make their repair hither, provided that provision of victuals for them may be sent, either before them or with them—we mean malt and meal. And if we may have your Lordships' consents, there is yet one other abbay, called the Market town, where we would place another band of footmen with some horsemen, which place being kept together with Glanarme, shall bring all these parties of the North as civil as the English Pale, as also to keep out the Scots for ever ; the rest of the country between this and the English pale is in very good quietness. We have fortified Belfast, and have placed there 15 horsemen, so that in this town we live as quietly as in Dublin, and yet may it do more good that the two bands be here, although they tarry not, to give a greater terror unto those that be wicked or intend to be.

And where your Honors have been informed that for 600 men there is daily allowance given out for 900, we have not known thereof, and can well discharge that if any be it is only in bread, which is employed sundry ways, as by journeys which we often make, by a larger allowance given to the horsemen which be forced to keep boys, by hireing of churls by the soldiers, which they be forced to do for fetching them wood for their relief (and all too little), whom for want of money they must pay in bread, and by other sundry accidents which grow by necessity ; and yet, God be praised, here is

wheat enough had we mills to grind, which Brydges hath
taken in hand to make ; but if he go no better to work than
yet he doth (and contrary to all men's opinions), here will be
no mills made by him these seven years, and so much the
worse in that his best workmen which he brought from
Dublin be run away from him, whose names we send unto
your Lordships here inclosed ; it may please your Honors to
reward them accordingly. The meal, as the victualer saith,
doth begin to scant, and yet will go near to stretch out the
time limited. It may please your Honors to appoint some
quantity thereof hither ; and touching this overplus expences
(if any be), it will turn to small gain to us that have the
charge of soldiers, and therefore it behoveth us most to look
to it, as we do and will ; and where, upon the examination of
the soldiers in this point, we were informed that in lieu of the
overplus in bread they have wanted of their allowance in the
rest, we did give order, and still do, that they shall not
exceed 4d. per diem, saving, as is said, to the horsemen.

And where, in your Lordships' last letter, your Honors
wish to be ascertained of the present state of these parts, your
Lordships may please to understand by this before written,
that all things is in good case, and hope shortly shall be per-
fected ; and if it shall please Her Majesty now to cut through,
it is easy to be done. And touching our opinion of Tirlagh
O'neill, we cannot think well of him ; that, contrary to his
faithful promise which he made unto our very good Lord the
L. Deputy in our hearing, both for the putting away of those
Scots which at that instant were with him, and for the expulsing of all others which after should invade these parts, hath
now entertained 800 of these lately landed ; and sure it is, if
your Lordships do not make sure work with him, as we know
your Honors will do, he will do as his predecessor did ; and
keeping him from his evil intents, we can warrant your Lordships for these parts within our government, the way is now
open for the establishing the good quiet of this country. God
grant it may be well followed. For the true certificate of the
soldiers and others being here in Her Majesty's pay, I, Capt.
Malbie, this day took musters, and find the bands all complete, but many soldiers very sick, and except your Lordships
stand our good Lords to remedy us, and to take order for the
staying of a great quantity of rotten malt wherewith our beer
is made (the example whereof we do send unto your Honors

by this bearer to be seen and considered), we shall be all
poisoned ; as by proof, when we went unto Glanarme, being
but 12 miles hence, half of our footmen tired by the way, and
lay all night in the open field, and yet not being sick, which,
as they all agree, groweth unto them by the infection of the
drink made with this malt, which we, in the voice of them

QUEEN ELIZABETH.

all, most humbly beseech your Lordships to remedy ; and
had not the quantity been so great as it is, we were agreed
with one whole consent to have paid for it not to have been
occupied, and to have drunk water rather than to stand to the
danger of the infection, whereof many of our soldiers be now
lying sick.   And I, Capt. Piers, appointed to have the muster-

ing of Capt. Malbie's band, do find it full complete, but divers
of them sick and on foot, whose horses be dead and spoiled
in service.   I, Capt. Malbie, cannot advertise your Lordships
of the seamen, for that they be not here ; but so soon as they
shall be come, I shall not fail to use my duty, and certify
your Honors accordingly.   The wards of Yland Sidney
being 10, besides the constable, I must advertise your Lordships by meer knowledge to be furnished, for that I cannot
go thither.   That of this castle being xxth I found this day
furnished.   The ward of Dunlysh, I am told this day by one
of the soldiers which came yesterday from thence, is furnished,
being eight, besides the constable, which we have appointed
in a fort not far from it called Dromure, which standeth to
great purpose, and especially for the victualling of Iland
Sidney.   Here be pensioners—William Baker, late Lieutenant to Capt. Browne, and Edw. Browne, late ensign-bearer
to him ; Christopher Blunt, late Lieutenant to Capt. Scryven ;
Jhon Cornwall, late Lieutenant to Gyles Cornwall; and
William Spencer, late ensign-bearer to Capt. Wilforde ; and
Robert Munchman, provost-marshal, and their men.

Sir Bryan McPhelym was lately with Bryan Caragh
McCormock, his father-in-law, who hath promised him to be
henceforth a good subject, and at that time did Hugh
McMoretagh likewise.   We intend to try them shortly as we
did Alexander Oge, and if it please, O'neill Bryan Caragh
dare not but be a good subject.   Sir Bryan hath since been
very sick, but, God be praised, is recovered.

We have to inform your Lordships that Bridges and
his men take their meat and drink out of Her Majesty's
store, and forasmuch as we find great unlikelihood of the
building of the mills by him, we have bargained with a
Manskeman here, who will set us up one within this month
to grind.

And where we had made bargain with certain of the
soldiers here to set upon the fortifying of this town presently,
and for want of money to have paid them in victuals, which
they were content withal, we do make stay now until we shall
hear from your Lordships for present provision of malt and
meal to be sent hither forthwith the rather for that purpose,
for which we humbly beseech your Honors, and for your
Honors' speedy answer in all the premises by this our messenger sent of purpose, for the soldiers will not work except

they may have their whole day's wages in victuals, which is double allowance.

We be advertised that Sarleboy doth fortify in the Raghlyns, and intendeth to inhabit there. He must needs be put from thence when time serveth. He is now gone into Scotland; some say he will return shortly. O'neill's messenger is with him, and so is a good spy of ours, by whom we shall shortly understand their whole enterprises, which we shall signify unto your Honors.

It may please your Lordships to send hither an alphabet in cypher, for that sometimes such matters may happen to be advertised as are not meet to be known, and by chance may be intercepted by mishap, which often fortuneth, and by a cipher is to be prevented.

We went this day to the brew-house to see this last brewing, and there we saw that the grains, being hot, is as rotten as anything can be, and that the wort would not run through it, it lieth so hard clumpered in the vessel; and yet is not that malt so ill as this which we send to your Lordships, which the victualer doth mind to occupy. We beseech your Honors to consider of it.

Very now came a letter unto us from our singular good lord, the L. Deputy, in which, among other matters, His L. doth find fault with us upon your Honors' letters sent unto him of our undutifulness towards your Lordships. We may not deny; but upon your Lordships' mistaking of our meaning in our said letters, your Honors might well judge of us otherwise than we intended; and, notwithstanding, if it might have pleased your Lordships to have given your own correction in anything that was done amiss, it had been punishmt. enough, and yet we repose that trust in your Lordships' goodness towards us, that if we have been otherwise than have becomed us your Lordships will salve it, and in our well-doings your Lordships will not let to further our credit, in which we most humbly beseech your Honors.

At this instant came a messenger from O'neill with this letter here enclosed, who saith that he hath sent away all his Scots; but we do think it but to be dissembling, all to win time.

It may please your Lordships to break the malt, whereby you shall see the goodness thereof; and if your Honors shall so think good, we would humbly beseech you (for your better satisfaction of this estate) to address hither some person of credit, that may by lively mouth certify your Lordships fully of the quiet state of this country, which your Honors shall presently perceive by his quiet passage hither. And where your Lordships sent hither a good number of broags, they be so evil that they will not last above 24^{ti} hours. We will conclude in advertising your Lordships that presently Capt. Cheston writ unto us, that Alexander Oge with his Scots gave him alarum, who, issuing out with part of his company and his horsemen, slew the captain of the Scots, called Donell McCane, and three more, and many hurt, who thereupon fled, and one of his horsemen and two of his footmen were hurt a little with arrows. Thus beseeching your Lordships to dispatch our messenger away with remembrance of our bounden duties, we most humbly take our leaves. From Cragfergus the 30th of January, 1567.

Your Lordships' most obedient,

WILLM. PIERS, NICHOLAS MALBIE.

For the Queen's most excellent Majesty.

(Irish Correspondence, State Paper Office.)

DUNLUCE.

Irish Linen Yarns.

ARTICLES FOR EXPORTING IRISH YARN, MARCH, 1572.

State Paper Office,
Ireland.

HE causes that maye move Her Matie. to graunte the lycence for transportinge of Iryse yarne from Irelande into Inglande.

Firste, because it hathe beene laufull, tyll of late that a restraint was made by an Acte of Parlement in Irelande, at the petition of the merchauntes of the same cuntrye, pretendinge that the yarne shulde be made into lynen cloth there, which pretence takith no effecte for lacke of weavers and other artificers in that realme.

Also, where upon the transportinge of the same yarne in tymes paste into the Counties of Chester and Lancaster, the poore people of the same cuntreies, especiallye aboute Manchester, were set on worke to the releife of 4,000 persons within that lordship only (as appereid by theire supplication redy to be exhibited this laste Parlement), the same poore people for lacke of worke are utterlye impoverished, living idely and redy to faule into miserable shiftes and ecctremityes.

Also, where as theire grewe unto Her Matie. a good revenue yerely by the custome of suche yarne, in Her Highnes portes of Chester and Lyerpoole, the same revenue is utterlie ecctinguished, whereof parte should be revived for so manie packes as shulde be contained within the lycence required.

Also it maye be provid that for lacke of laufull vent the makinge of that yarne is nowe decainge in Irelande, the people beinge naturallye gyven to idelnes, wyll leve of to manure theire grounde for flax, as hathe bene accustomed ; and lastely the merchantes there do ordinarily steale over the seid yarne into forreine realmes, at certayne havens and creekes in the Irishe cuntreis, where Her Matie. hath no offycers to demaunde her dueties.

Therefore, for as muche as this Acte in Irelande is but an innovation, not takinge the effecte for which it was ment, the cuntreis of Chessheire and Lankasheire impoverished, and by this lycence to be relevid, Her Maties. custome revived, the makinge of yarne in Irelande maynteined, and the Irishe merchauntes of theire unlawfull stelth prevented ; I hope your good Lordship wyll the rather upon theis reasonable causes perswade, that this lycence maye be graunted, ecctendinge onlie to 3,000 packes after 6 score to the 100th to be transported into Inglande within 5 yeres next folowinge, with libertie to attache and take all yarne that shall come over to be solde, not warraunted. And besides Her Maties. pitty to be ecctended to her poore subjectes before named, I shall alwayes be thankefull to Her Matie. for this releife to me, and thinke myselfe bounde to your Lordship as the menne for this benefit, and so humblie I rest [slightly torn at the end].

Weaving.

LORD DEPUTY AND COUNCIL TO THE QUEEN, 27TH JUNE, 1572.

State Paper Office,
Ireland.   [*Extract.*]

IT MAY PLEASE YOUR MOST EXCELLENT MAJESTIE,

I your Matues. Deputye receaved furthermore of late your Highnes letter wrytten in the matter of your Mates. lycense for transporting of yarne, graunted to Thomas Moore your servaunt and pensioner, who also shewed before us your Mates. letters patentes of the aforesaid graunte, which we have cawsed (as by your Mates. said letters we ar willed) to be recorded and enrolled in your Mates. Courte of Chaunceric here, and the rest of your Highnes Courtes of record, and have caused suche severall injunctyons also uppon those letters patentes to be passed and adwarded, as the said Thomas Moore to his furtherance and with his contentation, demaunded at our handes. And notwithstanding, some of the townes, as Dublin and Drogheda, chalenging by the statute which prohibiteth that transportation, a propertie in their townes custome, to theym due, as the statute apoynteth uppon those wares; the same Thomas Moore was empeched twyse, by arrest, for those custumes. Whereof we having understanding, released hym, and sending for the Mayour and some of the Aldermen of Drogheda which empeached hym, and the Sheriffes of Dublyn which lykewise theare arrested hym, to come before us, did committ theym to your Maties. castell of Dublyn, where for a space they weare deteyned for their contempt. So as we judge, albeit they styll cleave to the right of the statute wherby they presume, as that they may by the same (beeng not repealed) entitle them selves and demaunde the townes custome, as dewe to be paid unto theym, as by the said Acte ys lymited and reserved for eche quantitie of suche prohibited wares, notwithstanding eny lycense therefore to be graunted; that yet they will hensforth forbeare any further to molest the said Thomas Moore abowtes those cawses; but meane to make rather humble sewte to your Matie. to have consideration of their petition and clayme in this behalf to be exhibited, uppon which they may knowe your Mates. direction and resolution. And wheare, as your Majesty wryteth, your Highnes hath been infourmed, the passing of your lysense of that quantitie of yarne would smally prejudice the trafique used of that commoditie ; for that we acknowledge yt our dewties, for the trust your Matie. reposeth in us, to assertayne your Matie. of our opynions, we must affyrme to your Matie. howe the yarne steyed within this realme, ys not a thinge alonly commodyouse in many parties of this realme, whereby a nomber of loomes have been sett on wourck synce thordynaunce of the said statute, and dyverse persons relieved therby and put to labour in avoyding of ydlenes ; but moost of all, the same florysheng in th Englishe Pale, wherby having of our selfes sondry tymes seen dyverse of those loomes and the good and lardge size and workmanshipp of the lynnen clothe, of striped canvas, sackcloth, and suche lyke of greate breadthes redy woven, not afore put in use, the same hath offred good lykelehood and hoope of good and greate plentie thereof, to arryse, of commoditie of this common weale, throughe the contynuance of the same. And yet can we not denye the abuse of some, which have and do attempt withowt lycense, both to convey and otherwise also to steale owt of the realme, sondry quantities of the said yarne, to the disadvauntage of the weale publique, and offence of that your Highnes lawe : whereof many have been towched, and felt the smart of the statute for suche transportation, by forfeycting those goodes, and many of Dublyn presently indicted for lyke matter, and ar to abide their justification. Through which meanes contynued (as we entend to looke narrowly thereunto) yt ys lykely that hereafter theare will be both better obedience used, and also more care and feare (we trust) taken, as shoulde be, to avoyde the daunger of your Ma^{tes.} lawes in this behalf provyded. And thus having humbly opened to your Matie. the whole state of this matter, do leave the same to your moost graciouse consideration, as may be thought fytt to your Highnes for the benefytt of your subjectes here. In which cause, we have not ymparted of this our wryting to your Highnes, to eny of the subjectes of this land, otherwise then conferryng thereof emongest our selfes, which are here of your Maties. Privye Counsell.

From your Maties. Castell of Dublyn, the 27th of June, 1572.

 Your Maties. moost humble and faithfull subjectes and servauntes,

  (Signed) W. FYTZWYLLIAM. H. MIDEN.
        ROBERT WESTON, canc. LUCAS DILLON.
        ADAM DUBLIN. JO. PLUNKET.

To the Queene's most excellent Majestye.

From a Painting by F. W. Topham.

IRISH PEASANT GIRL SPINNING.

Lord Deputy and Council of Ireland to the Queen, May 23, 1573.

CCORDING to your Majesty's letters brought by me, your Treasurer, we are presently in hand, and mean to proceed for the manner of the government of Connaghe by Commission of Oyer and Terminer, wherein it hath pleased your Majesty to appoint me your Treasurer chief. For the accusations of the Earl of Clanricarde and me, each against other. As those exhibited by the Earl against me were examined and tried, so mine against him are for a time laid aside, and the lets thereof growing in such sort removed, as shall appear to your Majesty by the copy herewith sent of our action at council concerning that matter. By our last we signified unto your Majesty that we had sent down commissioners into the north to have speech with Tirlaghe Lenaghe, for some peaceable ways if it might be. They concluded on an abstinence until the 20th of this month, and now upon the expiration thereof we have sent down again to renew it, if it may be. But how unlikely it is shall appear to your Majesty by the copies sent herewith of his own letters, and sundry others from the Marshall, Justice Dowdall, and Dean of Armaghe, and Collo McBryan, declaring how he draweth and seeketh to draw force unto himself. O'donel having accorded with him, Sir Bryan McPhelim being joined in full confederacy with him, Magennys having already compounded with him, and Arte McDonnell with the Galloglaghes being very like to compound with him also. But for the better stay of Magennis and Arte, we have given order to the Marshal for taking of their pledges. And for the more animating of them in duty, wherein for want of competent force they seem to quail, as by the said letters may appear. But specially to withstand the malice of the enemy, and likewise not without great need to supply the wants of some parts of the borders of the Pale towards Lowthe (where all our travail, care, sundry commissions and often writings notwithstanding) how unready they are, though next the danger, shall plainly appear to your Majesty, by the copy herewith sent of the Sherif of that Counties letters, we have resolved to entertain 300 English footmen, whom we do and will put in pay, as fast as we may gather them. And yet not without great cause do we humbly renew our motion made by our last letters, for a supply of men defalking of the whole so many, as here we mean as we may to entertain. For, besides that the North is apparant ill, there be many other places of whose soundness we have good cause to doubt. And how Sir Brian hath lately burnt a great part of the town of Knockfergus, and what he more intendeth against it, and the abbaye, your Majesty's storehouse there, shall appear unto you by the copy herewith sent of that Major and his brethren's letters sent unto us. God hath taken your Majesty's late chancellor unto his mercy, and we, until your Majesty hath resolved upon another to succeed him, which we humbly pray to be with as convenient speed as may be, have appointed me the Archbishop of Dublin to be the keeper of the Great Seal of this your realm, &c. From your Majesty's Castle at Dublin, the 25th of May, 1573.

W. FITZWILLIAM,
(and the signatures of the Councillors.)

Inclosed in this dispatch is the following letter from Marshal Bagenal :—

"My humble duty considered. I have received your L. letters directed to Tirlaghe Lenaghe, and have accordingly sent them unto him. I have also received the copy of the Queen's Majesty's letters, and the copy of the peace, and a letter to Capt. Malbye, which I have sent unto him. Tirlaghe Lenaghe, as I was advertised, was yesternight at Benburbe with his power. I have also received your Lordships' letters counseling me, the barron's sons, Magennis and the Galloglasses, to entertain the late cashed soldiers for our better defence, who say they are not able to entertain so many as shall be able to defend them, nor will not agree to any such charge, except they be compelled by your L. and Council. I would have charged them with cess before this time if I had not had commandment to the contrary from your L. and council, but all would not have served against his force ; O'donell, the Scots, and Sir Bryan McPhelim, which be accounted to be the number of four thousand men.

I have charged myself with more men than my living and revenues will stretch to keep, and have been at more charge here than I think now well bestowed. And if I should be abandoned from this place, Her Majesty in short time should have no subject from Dundalke to Knockfergus, which I think I shall be driven of force unto, as I think all princes are bound to defend their subjects from rebels, and trust his Majesty will so do. And where your Lordship wrote unto me that you sent commandment to the Lords and gentlemen of the borders to be in a readiness there. I hear of none that be either at Ard or Dundalke. I have sent them warning of Tirlagh's coming. There be none of Captain Malby's men come unto me, for he saith he cannot well spare them." *(Irish Correspondence, State Paper Office.)*

Answer to the Lord Treasurer's Objections, July 23, 1594.

 HERE it seemeth good to your Lordship that a portion of land shall be reserved out of the ancient land belonging to the town of Carickfargus for the use of the garrison, and another portion for the use of the Queen's Castle. Our answer is that the same lands have been belonging to the town time out of mind, being never severed therefrom, nor any man able to make title thereunto. And as touching provision for Her Majesty's garrison, we are content that they shall have free grazing in the summer, with hay and winter provision for their horses and hackeneyes which they keep for Her Majesty's service.

Constable to have Grazing.

And for land to be laid to the Queen's Castle out of the same, we do also answer that the Constable for the time being shall have like allowance as before for the garrison; and he being also a freeman of the town by our Charter, shall have over and besides the said grasing and hay, &c., as large a portion of land as the best freeman or alderman of the town shall have, yielding for his share such duties and charges as other townsmen do for the like proportion and quantity.

We humbly beseech your Lordship to consider the premises, and to weigh the pitiful and distressed estate of that poor town; the innumerable killings, burnings, spoils, and stealths made upon them, with the often famine and misery which they have sustained for the defence and safe keeping of that Her Majesty's goole of the North : as also the great poverty which now of late they are brought unto by these late outrages, spoils, and stealths made upon them by their evil neighbours, which have lands enough of Her Majesty's lying near about us waste, by the space of 20 or 30 miles compass every way from our town lands, which in regard of them are but a handful, and therefore very hard to be taken from us.

We are further to inform your Honor, that we are at the yearly charge of 50li. ster. at the least, with the garrison, in finding them houseroom, fire, bedding, besides other necessaries. And now since February last we have been at more than 100li. charge in fortifying the town for the present defence of the same, and will cost us 20li. ster. by the year in repairing and maintaining the ditches and rampirs until the wall shall be built. *50li. by the year for the garrison.*

We do assure ourselves the entertainment which the Constable hath of Her Majesty may well maintain the Castle without seeking to take away for his own private use that which is the relief of many a poor creature, and if he shall allege the contrary we will undertake (if it shall stand with your Lordship's liking) that the town shall keep as many warders, as sufficient men, and as well furnished, as are now there, for half the pay he hath for the same. *for half the pay.*

And as touching Wodborne, which is 20 Irish acres, we desire to have the same at such rent as it is surveyed, viz., 15s. ster., and yet the same to remain to the use of the garrison, for that they cannot keep their horses and hackneyes in any other place safe from the enemy, especially in time of war, provided that in such troublesome times we may have some relief thereof. We did upon the same consideration give unto Mr. Eggerton 10li. ster., that he should not hold the same in severalty to himself, after he had procured a grant thereof, whereunto he did agree, for that he perceived how necessarily the same did lie for the safety of all our

B

goods; and the Constable hath, notwithstanding, as great
commodity and profit thereof as the whole town hath, and
for that part of the town's land which lieth west from Woodborne to the Earl's meadow, the garrison and constable have
the whole grasing and commodity thereof as well for summer
as winter provision for their horses and hackneyes.   The
said ten plough lands is no such great compass or circuit as
may perhaps seem to your Lordship, and we do now hold the
same in a manner with as great commodity as when the same
shall be alloted.   For our chief purpose in seeking to have
the same laid out, is to the end we may entrench and ditch
it about, leaving some few narrow passages for the enemy to
come in, by which means we hope to save our goods, which
oftentimes heretofore we have lost, for that the land is not
enclosed.

   We must acknowledge ourselves bound to your Lordship
for many favours, most humbly beseeching your Honor for
a good dispatch, and what good shall befal our town in these
their suits must of right be attributed to your Lordship, for
which they and their posterity shall to their uttermost for
ever rest thankful.

   Our answer to the L. Treasurer's objections touching the
lands.   *(Irish Correspondence, State Paper Office.)*

Petition of Agents for the Town of Carrickfergus, 25th July, 1594.

To the Right Honble. the Lord Burghley, Lord High Treasurer
of England.

OST humbly beseecheth your honorable Lordship, William
Lymsey and Humfrey Johnson, agents for the town of
Carrickfergus, to consider the substance of our demands,
consisting in these two points following:—First, to have
granted all the ancient land and common belonging to the
town, which have continued in the possession and maunrance
of the Corporation time out of mind ; the same being commanded by Her Highness to Sir Henry Syddney to allot and
appoint, which yet remains undone by reason of his revoca-
tion, as in our petition is more at large expressed.   The
like warrant we now crave to the Lord Deputy.   Together also with the land
belonging to the Abbey of Woodborn, adjoining to the town, which we now hold
by *concordatum* from Her Highness, the same being surveyed at 20 Irish acres,
which we are content shall be chiefly to the use of the garrison there resident, so

that in time of war we may have some relief thereof, for which we are content to pay the yearly rent reserved to Her Highness, being 15s. sterling. Secondly, that it wd. please Her Majesty to finish the walling of the town, and make up the Peare, as is specified in Her Highness's gracious letters patents to us granted, and now in force ; whereupon we do yield and agree to pay yearly £40 rent to Her Majesty, as in the said letters patents is mentioned.   If your Honor did know the often slaughters, burnings, preys, spoils, and stealths made upon us, it were most lamentable, the which we could in particular lay down but for troubling your Lordship.   And now of late since March last, upon bruit of the Earl of Tirone's going out, the country, taking that opportunity, did prey and spoil the most part of Her Majesty's subjects in those parts, and the garrison being then called away by him that had the command of them, the town left naked and open to the enemy.   Our Mayor then, with all the townsmen, were constrained to work all day and watch every night for their own safety and defence of Her Majesty's town, which, being walled, they might with some boldness have issued out and resisted the enemy, and saved their goods, as oftentimes they have done.   And the land being alloted, they would have ditched and entrenched the same, leaving some few and narrow passages to the enemy, whereby they should have been less able to do harm, and with more advantage be encountered, where now the townsmen durst not issue out for hazarding the town and their few goods in it.   Right Honorable, if the great extremities by famine and otherwise were thoroughly made known to Her Majesty, your Honor, and the rest of her honourable Council, no doubt Her Highness would think this too little, but would yield us much more than we now demand. And where it is enformed your Lordship the unreasonableness of our suit in seeking to take all from Her Majesty, as namely, the abbey or palace, albeit the same is contained within Her Highness's letters patents, yet we never hitherto made any penny profit thereof ; and if the granting of the same shall seem prejudicial to Her Majesty, we are ready (having authority from the town), upon the dispatch of our suit, to surrender the same, and to yield to any other thing which to your Honour shall seem reasonable.   Our town, in regard of your fatherly care of all Her Majesty's dominions and countries, did advise us especially both to acquaint and depend upon your Honour in all causes touching their suits.   Therefore we humbly beseech your Lordship not to believe any suggestion against us, for that we will inform your Honor nothing but truth, which we will maintain with the loss of our goods, liberties, and lives.   Wherefore, if anything seem to your Lordship to be unreasonable, we humbly crave to have the same delivered in particular, which done, we doubt not but to satisfy your Lordship with reason.   Thus craving pardon, with our hearty prayer to God for your Lordship's long-continued health to the relief of poor suitors, We most humbly take leave.

Indorsed.   The humble petition of Willm. Lymsey and Humfrey Johnson, agents for the town of Carrickfergus, in Ireland.

Note of the Bounds of the Town Lands, July 25th, 1594.

AT the west end of our ancient town standeth the Abbey of Woodborne, which hath belonging unto it 20 Irish acres of land, from the which land unto Earle's Meddow we esteem to be a mile, which is as far as the town's land reacheth in length westward ; and from the sea-side, being south to the great mountain northward, about three-quarters of a mile.

At the north-east end of the town standeth a spyttel-house, whereunto is belonging 4 or 5 Irish acres of land, from which land unto Copplande water is about some quarter of a mile, which is as far as the town's land extendeth that way in length.   And from the seaside northward in breadth up to the hills, upon which hills there is a Loughe called Loughmourne, of a mile in length northward, which runneth into the river of Copplande water ; and so westward from the Loughe above the hills there is moores, mosses, and heathy, bad ground as far as the end of the great hill called the Knockowe, whereunto adjoineth the Earle's meadow, by the separation of a river coming out of the end of that hill, which doth part the town's land and the Earle's meadow, upon which hills of moor and heathy ground we have, time out of mind, had comen (*sic*) of Turbarye heath and pasture in the summer-time, whereby our cattle in the heat of the day might be near the Lough for their refreshing.

The wall undertaken by Mr. Lackforde was 8 foot at the foundation in breadth, to be built 16 foot high, and to be at the height of the said 16 foot 6 foot broad, and thereupon a vannor of 4 ft. high and 2 ft. broad, which in the full height is 20 ft. The charge of every pearch of the same height and breadth will stand in the building thereof at the least 15li ster. And there is yet unbuilt 90 pearches, besides three towers and two gates, which must be built 4 ft. higher than the rest, with frestone for the gates, towers, and spikeholes ; as also 8 stancks of lime and stone, which must be made without the wall to keep the ditches full of water, which altogether will be above the number of 10 pearches. So the whole unbuilt is at the least 100 perches, which, after the rate aforesaid, doth amount to 1,500li ster., besides the charge of building up the keye or peare. (*Irish Correspondence, State Paper Office.*)

EARL OF ESSEX.

Sir A. Chichester and Island Magee, 1601.

ISLAND MAGEE was granted by Queen Elizabeth to Walter Earl of Essex, who died of dysentery in Dublin, the 22nd of September, 1576. After his son Robert Earl of Essex was beheaded on the 25th February, 1601, I find Sir Arthur Chichester writing from Knockfergus, April 6th, 1601, the following words to Sir Robert Cecil :—

"Att my last beinge in Englande, I dealte with one

Charles Ogle, servaunte to the Earle of Essexe, for a peece of land lyenge neere this towne, named the Ilande Magic, which was land of the said Earles, and by him geven to his servaunte Ogle for the terme of 21 yeeres, yt hath longe layn wast, and considering the traysons of those gentlemen I am doubtfull to deale anie further therein, and to bestowe anie charge upon hyt, unlesse I have some assurance from her Majestie for possessinge thereof. It is a thing of small valuer, if yt wyll please your honore to gett me the sead farme thereof I wyll bulde some fortes and castles upon hit, and keepe yt from annoyance of reables."

Of course, Essex being beheaded for treason his estates were confiscated, and there was no use in Chichester dealing with Ogle or any person else for them, when he might get a grant of them for nothing. Though so early in the field, it does not appear that Chichester obtained a grant of Island Magee until 1610. (*Pinkerton MSS.*)

Letter from Thomas Walker, close Prisoner at the Newry, Aug. 22nd, 1601.

To the Rt. Hon. the Lorde Mountjoye, Lorde Deputie of Ireland.

RIGHT HON.—

YOURE honor's pore petitioner, a prisoner till my truth have had her trial, which I trust in God will not be long. Since, I understand, your Lordshipe hathe sente into Inglande aboute me, doth beg, for his sake whoe hathe fashioned us to his owne similitude and likenesse, that your honor will not see me hunger for want of meanes. My goode Lorde, I speake this in all humilitie, for them I sent to for my meanes feares by sending to supplie my wants lest they be alsoe brought in troble for me ; that in the world's eie I seeme hardly thought one, when, had I had a souldier's harte, as I wanted not his forwarde minde, and not given place unto effeminate thoughtes, forgettinge how I promised to my God if it would please him to send his angell to conduct me safe, and give me favor in the presence of Terone, I would not feare to smite him, weare his garde about him, it had not bin so whith me as it is ; and to see Gode's mercie towardes me that daye, he had no garde to speak on, neither had he on a quilted coate, but only a blacke freese gerkin, which, being unbuttoned, I might see his naked brest. I havinge my armes redelivered me by his own commandement, he tooke me twice in that short time I was with him by the hande, sayinge I was welcom to him, and toulde me by those wordes I was the fortunatest man that ever came unto him, for had not my horsemen bin the honester, sayde he, they would have sore wounded thee, but

had my footmen met thee, thou hadest not never come alive before me. Thus before and after I was most mithily preserved by the Lorde, and persuade myselfe it is to some good end, wherefore his name be praysed whose mercie endureth for ever. And, my goode Lorde, when I am found an honest man towards my country, I will shew myselfe a true servant to your honor, in giving your Lordshipe to know what I have heard and seen in my travells; meanwhile, I will laye it up in my harte till I may have accesse unto your Lordship. Yet earnestly beseeching your honor, for Gode's sake, to shake offe by little and littel the hard conseate your Lordship with good reason hath of me, for God, that knows my hart, knows it is free of that maculated spott. I am a foole to speake thus much; but, alas! hath not the sillie asse, that is beaten for his stumblinge, sense to know in what he made his Lorde a faulte. A littel beare with me, goode my Lorde, for I have wrotte this in my teares, and whatsoever I have sayed or done, hereafter, God willinge, I will give a reason for it, but it will seem foolish for a time. Thus, fearinge to overlaye your honor's patience with copiousness of words, I will surcease, committinge your honor to the safe keepinge of the Allmightie, that his stronge arme may be ever with your good Lordship to your live's end. From the prison of the Newry, Satterday, the xxijth of August, 1601.

HUGH O'NEILL, EARL OF TYRONE.

CASTLE OF ARDKEEN.

Inquisition taken at Ardquin, 4th July, 1605.

N indented Inquisition taken at the town of Ardwhy in the County of Down, on the fourth day of July, & in the third year of our most illustrious prince & lord James, by the grace of God, King of England, Scotland, France & Ireland, & of Scotland the thirty-eighth, before William Parsons Esq. surveyor general of our said lord the King of his Kingdom of Ireland, Robert Barnewall Esq. & Lawrence Masterson Esq. by virtue of a commission of our said lord the King under his great seal of his Kingdom of Ireland directed to the same William, Robert, Lawrence & others by the oath of honest and lawful men of the county aforesaid whose names ensue.

John White Lord of the Dufferin Esq. Christ. Russell of Bright Esq. James Dowdall of Strangford, Gent. George Russell of Rathmullen Gent. John Russell of Killough, Gent. James Stackpoole of Ardglass, Gent. Simon Jordan of Ardglass, Gent. Robert Sword alias Crooley of Ballidonell, Gent. William Meriman of Ballineborgash, Gent. Sillernow Croney of Scrow, Gent. Patrick Russell of St. John's Point, Gent. Robert Hadsor of Cullevaile, Gent. Owen McRorie of Down, Gent. Simkin FitzWilliams of Grange, Gent. & Redmond Savage of Saul, Gent. After reciting the lands & boundaries of Clandeboy, Kilultagh &c. the Jurors aforesaid say further on their oaths that the said late queen Elizabeth

being seized of all & singular the premises as above, by her
Letters Patent bearing date at Westminster in England the
sixteenth November, in the thirteenth year of her reign
according to the intention, effect, & covenants of certain
indentures between the said lady the Queen on the one part,
& Thomas Smith Knight, & Thomas Smith son of the aforesaid Thomas, then one of the pensioners of the said late
Queen, within the said Kingdom of Ireland, of the other
part, passed under the Great Seal of England, bearing date
the fifth day of October in the thirteenth year of her reign
gave & granted, among other things, all & singular the
above recited premises, with their appurtenances by the
names in the said Letters Patent mentioned & specified
under certain conventions & provisions in the said LETTERS
PATENT, the tenor of which follows in these words.

CREST OF
SAVAGE (ancient).

ARMS OF SAVAGE OF ARDS.

CREST OF
SAVAGE OF ARDKEEN.

Translation of Smith's Grant.

LIZABETH, by the Grace of God, Queen of England,
France, & Ireland, Defender of the Faith &c. TO ALL
to whom these our present letters shall come greeting,
KNOW that we of our special grace of God, & of certain
knowledge & our mere notion, & in consideration of certain
covenants & articles of agreement on the part of our
well beloved & faithful counsellors Thomas Smith Knight,
& Thomas Smith son of the foresaid Thomas Smith
Knight, one of our pensioners within our Kingdom of
Ireland their heirs & assigns to be fulfilled executed as specified and declared
in certain indentures executed between us on the one part & the aforesaid
Thomas Smith Knight & Thomas Smith his son on the other part, bearing date
the fifth day of October in the thirteenth year of our reign We have given &
granted & by these presents for us our heirs & successors we give & grant to
the aforesaid Thomas Smith Knight & Thomas Smith his son all & singular
the manors lordships castles monasteries abbies priories chanteries free-chapels
rectories messuages houses edifices lands tenements meadows pastures woods
waste lands forests chases parks warrens lakes waters pools fish-ponds commons
moors marshes wastes furze briars quarries mines rents reversions services

advowsons of churches tithes wards marriages reliefs escheats commodities emoluments & hereditaments of ours whatsoever with all & singular their appurtenances in the great Ardes the lesser Ardes Claneybuy towards the south from the Castles called Castle Belfast, Castle Mowbray, and Castle Toome from the late Monastery or Priory of Masserine in Clandeboy parcel of our county of Ultonia or Ulster within our Kingdom of Ireland, And the aforesaid Castle of Belfast Castle Moubray and Castle Toome with their appurtenances And all that Monastery or Priory of Masserine with the appurtenances in Clandeboye aforesaid Likewise all & singular other manors, lordships, castles, messuages, lands, tenements, meadows, pastures, woods, moors, marshes, rents, services, advowsons of churches, tithes, natives male and female, & all others our profits, commodities, emoluments, & hereditaments whatsoever lyeing and being in Clandeboye, Tirone & other places continuously adjacent in our county of Ulster aforesaid which the said Thomas Smith Knight or Thomas Smith his son or their heirs or assigns can obtain possess or inhabit against the Irish, before the twenty-eighth day of March which shall be in the year of our Lord one thousand five hundred and seventy-nine, all mines or quarries of gold silver & copper being only reserved & excepted to us our heirs & successors TO HAVE HOLD & ENJOY all & singular the aforesaid manors, lordships, castles, monasteries, abbies, priories, messuages, lands, tenements, meadows, pastures, woods, moors, marshes, free warrens, chases, forests, lakes, waters, pools, fishings, furze, briars, quarries, mines, advowsons of churches, tithes, rents, reversions, services, wards, marriages, reliefs, escheats, And all & singular the premises with all & singular the appurtenances (except as before excepted) to the aforesaid Thomas Smith Knight & Thomas Smith his son and the heirs of the body of that Thomas Smith the son lawfully begotten And in defect of such issue to the right heirs of the said Thomas Smith Knight for ever. TO HOLD of us our heirs & successors as of our Castle of Knockfergus by the service of one Knight's fee RENDERING annually to us our heirs & successors after the feast of St. Michael the Archangel which will be in the year of our Lord one thousand five hundred & seventy-six for every carucate of the said land called in English a plow land containing one hundred & twenty acres of land of the measure in the said Indentures specified, twenty shillings of lawful money of Ireland at the feast of the Annunciation of the Blessed Virgin Mary & the feast of St. Michael by equal portions in our exchequer of Ireland, to be collected by our Sheriff there & to be annually paid by him at the hands of the Treasurer of our foresaid exchequer of Ireland into the hands of the receiver of our said exchequer there, the first payment thereof beginning at the feast of St. Michael which will be in the year of our Lord one thousand five hundred & seventy-six AND FURTHER of our more abundant special favour, we will grant for us our heirs and successors that the said Thomas Smith Knight & Thomas Smith his son their heirs & assigns tenants & residents shall be quiet & exonerated from all exactions called coyne & livery & from all other such like cesses whatsoever now used or which hereafter may be used or imposed within our foresaid Kingdom of Ireland during the term of seven years after the date of these presents AND FURTHER we have given & granted & by these presents we give & grant for us our heirs & successors to the aforesaid Thomas Smith Knight & Thomas Smith his son & their heirs court baron, leet & view of frank-pledge, assize of bread, wine & beer in all & singular the premises & in every parcel thereof AND FURTHER of our more abundant special grace for us our heirs & successors we give & grant to the aforesaid Thomas Smith the father & Thomas Smith the son, their heirs & assigns full license power & authority to alienate give & grant all & singular the premises to be held of the said Thomas Smith the father & Thomas Smith & their heirs for such & such like rents & services as to the said Thomas & Thomas & their heirs may be pleasing, provided however that such alienations or grants or the services or tenures to be thereupon reserved or any of them be not contrary to any condition declared or expressed in the Indentures aforesaid PROVIDED always that if the aforesaid Thomas Smith the father Thomas Smith the son or their heirs shall not obtain possess & divide all & singular the premises according to the true & right intention covenants & agreements in the said Indenture specified, that

then those our Letters Patent as far forth as all & singular the premises thus
not obtained possessed & divided shall be void & of no strength in law. And
nevertheless as to the residue of the premises they shall remain firm & stable in
their own strength, vigour, and effect. PROVIDED also further that if the
aforesaid Thomas Smith the father, & Thomas Smith the son, & their heirs, shall
not fulfill all & singular the covenants & agreements in said Indentures specified
on the part of them or either of them to be further fulfilled that thenceforth these
our Letters Patent shall be void & of no effect in law. And that thenceforth it
shall be lawful for us our heirs & successors to re enter into all & singular the
premises & to possess, enjoy, & hold the same in our former rights, anything in
these Letters Patent or in the Indenture aforesaid contained to the contrary
notwithstanding. In testimony of which fact we have made these our Letters
Patent. Witness myself at Westminster the sixteenth day of November in the
thirteenth year of our reign 1571.

As the Smiths did not do as proposed by them, the Queen granted the manor and
appurtenances of Castle Reogh to one Con McNeal Oge O Neale, Knight in consideration of
divers faithful & good services by letters patent dated Dublin 30th March in 29 year of her reign
all the lands except those belonging to the bishop of Down, with remainder to Hugh O Neale
the reputed son of the said Con. Con died at Castle Reogh 7 April 1589, without heir. Hugh
died 6 Jan 1588 at Down.

One Brian Fertogh O Neale was the owner levied cess &c. after Conn. *(Pinkerton MSS.)*

SIR THOMAS SMITH, 1512-1577.
(Fac-simile of the Portrait in his " Life." London, 1698.)

Timber in Ulster.

AM well acquainted with all partes of Ulster, in the Countie of Dunnagall I am sure ther is none at all, neither is ther anie in the countie of Colerayne both which counties lye upon the sea. But ther is good store in Glancomkeyne, Kylletra, & Braselowe w^h counties lye upon the loagh knowne by the name of loagh Eagh w^h loagh is navigable from each syde & end all over, the nearest place to the sea from thence is Knockfergus w^h is 12 good myles overland, but the river of the Bann runns from the loagh by the Castle of Toome to the Castle & abbaye of Colerayne wher it ebbs & flows from the sea. This passage by water is about thirtie myles (rather more than lesse) in w^h there are six or seven lepps & shotts, besydes this the harbore is so bard wth sholles that no shipp of buthen can com in at anie tyme, which togeather with hit lyenge too farre to the North makes me to conceive lyttle good is to be expected by that passadge, if anie be it must be made by carrienge thereof over land from the loagh syde to Knock-fergus w^h is a goodly harbore, & accessable, & a safe rode all weathers, but farre off to make a retourne for England, about Knockfergus there are no woods neere than Belfast w^c is eight myles off but lyenge upon the river w^h is portable, I have ther some wooken *(sic)* trees but so crooked & shrofed that no man fells them for tymber either for pipestaves or other use of buyldinge, but it maye be they wyll serve for some use for shippinge, such as they are, & all that is neere unto it shall be reserved untyll y^r lo^p appointe some man to see it, & I wys nothing more than that it maye prove for the use yor lo^p would have it. Kylultagh lyes on the one syde upon loage Eagh & on the other syde upon the river of the lagan w^h is the river that runes by Belfast to Knockfergus, in that countrie are good tymber trees, but the countrie is but small, & therfore the quantitie of tymber can not be great, this belonges to Sir Foulke Conwaye & as I

conceive a small charge wy'll clense that river (& so force it to
rune togeather where it is shallowe) as to make it portable of
tymbers of anie syce ther are other woods in Fermanagh but
they are of no great quantitie as I am informed. *(Pinkerton MSS.)*

COLERAINE.

The Plantation of Ulster. Lord Deputy Chichester to Lord Salisbury, 3rd October, 1610.

OR the instrumentes of the Plantation, I
meane the Brittysh Undertakers, those from
England are for the most part plaine countrie
gentlemen, who maye promise much, but
geve unto us small assurance or hope of
performinge what to a worke of such
moment doth appertaine. If they have monie they keepe
it cloase, for hitherto they have disbursed but lyttle,
and if I maye judge by the utter apparance, I conceive
that the least trouble or alteration of the tymes here
wyll scare most of them from us. It is sayd by themselves, that since the denomination of the parties att fyrst
by the Lords that were Undertakers, some have exchaunged
their portions, and others solde them outright. In one
precynct of those that have appeared, two are Churchmen
and one a youth of some 18 or 19 yeares olde, whose names
I have noted in the sedule sent by Sir Olever Lambert.

SIR ARTHUR CHICHESTER, BARON OF BELFAST, PRESENTING THE CHARTER OF INCORPORATION
TO THE SOVEREIGN AND BURGESSES IN CORN MARKET, 1613.

The Scottysh came with greater part and better accompanied and attended; but it maye be with lesse monie in their purses; for some of the princypall of them upon their first entrance into their precynctes were forthwith in hand

The Right Hon:ble Right Wise and Valiant ARTHUR LO: CHICHESTER, LO: Baron of Belfast Lo: High Treasurer of Ireland and some times Lo Deputy of that Kingdom 11 years & upward One of the Privy Counsell in ENGLAND.
The above Inscription is round the Oval of the Original.
Co Thomd'Unique Print in the Collection of Joseph Gulston Esq.

with the natives to supply their wantes, or att least their expenceis, and in recompence thereof do promise to gett lycense from His Matie. that they maye remayne upon their lands as tennantes unto them; which is so pleasinge to that people that they wyll strayne themselves to the uttermost to gratifie them; for they are content to become tennantes to anie man, rather than be removed from the place of their byrth and education, hopinge, as I conceive, att one tyme or

other to finde an opportunitie to cutt their landlords' throtes;
for sure I am they hate the Scottyshe deadly, and out of their
malice towards them they beginne to affect the Englysh better
than they have byne accustomed.

They sell awaye both corne and cattle, and when they are
demanded why they do so, their aunswer is that they know
not what else to do with them, nor to what place to carie
them, the portion of land assigned to each of them beinge too
lyttle to receive and feede the goods he hath for his owne
perticulare.

They seeke by all meanes to arme themselves, and have
undoubtedly some peecies in store, and more pikes, and
therof can make more dayly; but powder and lead is scarse
with them.   I wyll do my best to prevent their revolte, but
I greatly doubt yt, for they are infinitly discontented. . . .
We are now all of us become buylders and planters here,
and not wasters and destroyers as in our younger yeares, and
would gladly rest in quiett if our yll neighbours wyll permitt
us; and that makes us the more sudious to prevent their
revolt, and to settle peace and quietnes amonge them.

Assizes held in Ulster A.D. 1615.

ANTRYM.

GENERAL Session was held at the Castle of Carrickfergus on
the 16th of March, 12 James I. (1615), before Gerard Lother, Esq.,
one of the Judges of the Common Pleas, and John Beare, Esq.,
Sergeant-at-Law, under a Commission dated the 15th February in
the same year, and an Inquisition taken before the following Grand
Jurors :—

John Plunkett,	James Russell,
William Boyde,	Robert Hamell.
Hugh Magee,	Saunders Edmonston,
James Blare,	John M'Colloe,
Andrew Holme,	Gillduff M'Cawley,
Patrick Woods,	Rorie O'Morrey,
Archiebald Boyde,	Neil m'brian O'Neile.
William Stevenson,	

Who say that Murtagh O'Hanyll, of Stenement, yeoman, on the 2nd January, 1614,
at Whiteabby, stole 3 cows worth 20s. each, the property of Michael Newby,
gentleman. Guilty. To be executed.

That Ever McBrehon, of the Roote, yeoman, on the 20th Octr., 1614, at Strad-
ballythomas, stole a bridle [unum frenium] worth 5s., the property of Edward
Steward. Guilty. To be executed.

That Brian O'Gribben, of Edendufcarricke, yeoman, on the 27th Nov., 1614, there committed an assault upon Elise ny Lagan, the widow of William Toole, a faithful subject, and with "a cudgill" worth one halfpenny which he had in his right hand he struck her in the front of the head, giving her a mortal wound of 4 inches in length and one inch deep, of which she languished until the last day of the same month, when she died. Guilty. Says he is a Clerk. He is therefore, as is shewn in a former case, branded in the left hand and delivered to the Ordinary.

That Donald O'Mulchallen, of Killelaghe, yeoman, on the 1st April, 1614, at Bellfaste, stole "one nedge of Iron" worth 2s., a mantle (unum pallium anglicanum) worth 6s., and "a chizell" worth 8d., the property of James Hutton, of Bellfaste. Guilty. To be executed.

That Laghlin McEdmund O'Carr, of Ballenure, yeoman, on the 12th January, 1614, at "le Parke," stole "a sacke" worth 4s., "a bridle" worth 2s. 6d., and "a pillyn" worth 2s., the property of Brian Mcdudarragh Magill, of the Parke. Acquitted.

That Richy Bell, of Carrickfergus, yeoman, on the 4th February, 1614, at Strad-ballythomas, stole a black horse worth £3, the property of a person unknown. Guilty. To be executed.

That Firlagh McCan and Conchor McGraudy, of Enishelaghlyn, yeomen, on the 24th Decr., 1614, at Enselaghlin, between the hour of 11 and 12 at night, entered the mansion house of William Helton (or Belton), a true and faithful subject, with the intent of committing a burglary. Guilty. To be executed.

That Donald Magee, of Edendufcarick, yeoman, on the 7th February, 1614, at Masserine, stole a goose worth ( ) pence belonging to a person unknown. Guilty. That he be taken back to prison and his fetters taken off of him, and that he be then brought to the town of Masserine, and there whipt around the market and the folds thereof (circa forum et pliteas ejusdem).

THE VILLAGE OF MASAREENE, 1851.

That Cormuck mcFardorogh O'Neale, of Killmakevet, yeoman, on the 10th August, 1614, at Downsecas, stole 2 mares, one being of a grey colour and the other of a black colour, worth 50s. each, and two colts, one grey and the other brown, worth 20s. each, the property of Shane McCan. Acquitted.

That Shane roe O'Heale, of Glynarm, yeoman, on the 10th Decr., 1611, at Redbaie, stole a chestnut horse, a brown horse, and a grey horse, worth 40s. each, the property of Owen mcRobart. Acquitted.

That Cormuck O'Neale, of the Fues, yeoman, on the 10th Decr., 1614, at Cloghardury, stole a cow worth 20s., the property of Master Cambell, of the same place ; And that Gilbert mcLawry, of Aghneberaghe, yeoman, relieved him, and bought the cow from him.

That Jenken McQuyllin, of Moybluske, yeoman, on the 11th Decr., 1614, at Ungalle, stole a black cow worth 20s., belonging to Edward Steward. Guilty. Says he is a Clerk, whereupon Robert Openshawe, the Bishop's minister of that place, claims him, and being burnt in the left hand, he is delivered to the Ordinary.

That Hugh oge and Cahir O'Mullan, of Megerilehan, yeomen, on the 10th April, 1614, at Conyre, stole a kettle worth 10s., and "foure yeards of clothe" worth 40s., the property of Brian O'Cahan, of Conyr; and that Neale mcGillecholem, of Megerylehan, yeoman, aided him. No finding.

That Denis alias Donat Timpany and Owen O'Carr, of Handmagie, yeomen, on the 24th Decr., 1614, at Whitheade, stole 4 oxen and 4 cows worth 20s. each, the property of Thomas Bashford, of Carrickfergus ; and that he was relieved, &c., by Donald O'Carr, of the Cave, yeoman, on the 27th of December following. No finding.

That Rory Carragh O'Lawry, of Lissnegarvagh, yeoman, on the 10th July, 1614, between 11 and 12 at night, entered the mansion house of John Yeatts to commit burglary. Acquitted.

THE ANCIENT GALLOWS CALLED "THE THREE SISTERS," CARRICKFERGUS.

That James O'Hamyll, of Tullenscros, yeoman, on the last day of Septr., 1614, at Ballechackiner, stole a brown and a yellow cow worth 20s. each, belonging to Thomas Gralson, and was abetted by Donat oge O'Hamnell. No finding.

That Murtagh and Donogh O'Mulchallen, of Ballevickechone, Co. Tyrone, yeomen, on the 1st of April, 1614, at Conure, Co. Antrym, stole 3 cows worth 20s. each, the property of Thomas Meltunus, and were relieved, &c., by Hugh O'Mulchallen, of Edenduffecarick, yeoman, on the 4th of April following.

That [   ] O'Mollan, of Edenduffecarick, yeoman, on the 27th [   ], 1614, at Largie, stole 2 [   ] worth 20s. each, the property of Tibott Mc[   ] McQuyllyn, and was abetted by James [   ] Neefan, of Gregrebban, yeoman, and Neale mcGillehy [   ], at Mogheriligan. No finding.

ARMS OF ENNISKILLEN.

FERMANAGH.

An Inquisition taken at Eniskillin before Sir John Blenerhasset, Knight, one of the Barons of the Exchequer, and Sir Robert Oglethorpe, Knight, the second Baron of the same Court, on the 8th of March, 12 James I., under a Commission dated the 16th of February in the same year, upon the oaths of the following Grand Jury :—

> Launcelot Carlton, of Enistlare,　　⎫
> Thomas Crayton, of Knockneny,　　⎬ Esquires,
> 　　　　　　　　　　　　　　　　⎭

John Stokes, of Mountsedborrow,
Alexander Patteson, of Tooragh,
Thomas Cranston, of the same,
Gabriel Cunningham, of Cartnell,
} Gentlemen,

John Ogle, of Maglas,
Thomas King, of Magheriboy,
William Atkenson, of the same,
William Penant, of Knockneny,
} Yeomen,

Symon Presly, of Mountcalverte,
James Belfard, of Lisnaskeagh,
Walter Notly, of Lurg,
James Summerwell, of Turagh,
John Smythe, of Lisnaragh,
} Gentlemen,

Who say that Donnogh McArdell, of Dervick, yeoman, on the last day of March, 1612, stole 5s. 3d. cash in a purse (*in quadam crumena*), a pair of shoes worth 6d., and a coat (*unam tunicam*) worth 3s., the property of Patrick O'Goen, and a pair of "trusses" (*unum parum femoralium*) worth 2s., the property of Art McRolly. Guilty. He says he is a Clerk, whereupon John Barber, the minister of George, Bishop of "Cloher," claims him, and being branded in the left hand, he is delivered to the Ordinary.

That Tirlagh McIgerre, of Collpaghie, yeoman, on the 20th Novr., 1614, at Drommacklaras, stole a brown cow worth 20s., the property of Rorie O'Managhane. Acquitted.

That Hugh McPhillip and Hugh McManus, of Latryme; Donnell M'Hugh, McGilpatricke Magwyre, and Gilleduffe McMaghone, of Coole, yeomen, on the 24th Nov., 1614, at Aghlogherie, stole 2 horses worth 30s. each, and 5 cows each worth 20s., belonging to Robert Mongomerie, gentleman. Acquitted.

That Collo McArt oge McMaghowne, of Magherrony, yeoman, on the last day of May, 1612, at Clonkellie, stole 2 mares worth 30s. each, and a horse worth 20s., the property of James Gortagh Magwyre. He pleads a pardon, as appears by a ticket (*per ticketam*) under the hand of Sir Edward Blany, Knight, the which pardon is dated the 13th Nov., 1613, and is allowed.

That Cochonnaght M'Keon, of Colrane, Co. Londonderrie, yeoman, on the 4th Novr, 1610, at (Colfane) Co. Fermanagh, stole 30s. in money, and a sword worth 3s., belonging to John Harte, and "two shurts," worth 2s. 6d. each, the property of Teige O'Mady. No finding.

That Phealem McPhillip and Shane boy McQuine McMahowne, of Latryme, yeomen, on the 24th Novr., 1614, at Aghlogherne, stole 2 horses worth 30s. each, and 5 cows each worth 20s., the property of Robert Moungomerie, gentleman. No finding.

That Cormock mcRedmond Moyle Magwyre, of [Raiskilly], yeoman, on the 26th Octr., 1614, at Lattkerie, "in quendam Evelin ny Magwyre de Coole, spinster, insultum fecit et contra voluntatem suam felonice rapuit ac carnaliter cognovit." No finding.

That Tirlagh and Patrick McHugh, of Aghlony, yeomen, on the 20th Nov., 1602, at Bellaghbiane, insulted Thomas mcCollo McShane Magwyre with a sword, worth 2s., which they held in their right hands, giving him a mortal wound in the right breast (dextro pectore) of 3 inches long and 5 inches deep, and many other wounds, of which he instantly died. No finding.

That Redmund mcEncastall and Hugh Modderrie Magwyre, of Aghlorchie, and Owen McEurie, of Dronaghe, and Coll Magwyre, of Coole, yeomen, on the 20th of Novr., 1612, at Aghalnghane, stole 8 cowhides worth 5s. each, the property of Richard Lighterfoote, gentleman. No finding.

That Con Roe O'Connelly, of Mullagheglasse, yeoman, on the 20th Novr., 1614, at Dromeforde, stole a brown cow worth £3, the property of Edward Sibthorpe, gentleman, and was aided on the last day of the same month by Cnogher mcCafforrie and Neile O'Mullegan, of Mullaghglasse. No finding.

C

DONEGALL.

An Inquisition taken at Lifford before the same Judges, and by virtue of the same Commission, on the 15th of March, 12 James I., by the oaths of the following Grand Jury :—

John Kuningham, of Newton, Esq.
William Hamelton, of Lougheske,
Rowland Congall, of Coolobegg,
Andrew Kuningham, of Collomatreny,
Edward Cathrell, of Fyneforde,
Daniel Callchoo, of Corcagh,
David Paine, of Glanefyne,
Arthur Terrie, of the same,
John Fleming, of Lifford,   }   gentlemen,
Patrick Rooney, of Tirrewe,
Tirlagh Ballagh Boyle, of Boyla,
Thomas Symons, of Donegall,
Christopher Weste, of Lifford,
Francis Edmons, of Tirrewe,
Roger Hancocke, of Enishowen,

Who say that Margery Harison, of Lifford, spinster, on the 9th of January, 1614, at Congane, stole 50s. in a purse belonging to Robert Carttwright. Guilty. To be executed.

That Robert Woodes, of Eneskill, *clerk*, on the last day of September, 1614, at Tullaghmoore, insulted Sawe ny Boyle, spinster, and with a stick which he held in his right hand he gave her divers wounds and "bruses" in the head and belly, of which she languished until the 28th of Novr. following, when she died. Not guilty.

ARMS OF LONDONDERRY.

LONDONDERRIE.

An Inquisition taken at Londonderrie before the same Judges, and under the same Commission, on the 21st of March, 12 James I., by the oath of the following Grand Jury :—

Baptist Johns, of Salterston,   }   Esquires,
Manus O'Cane, of Lysnebehoone,

William Nesbett, of the parish of Tomlefenlecane,
Morries O'Cane, of the parish of Donboe,
Gorry mcShane, of Ballyaghery,
John Rosse, of Rathbride,   }   gentlemen,
Gawen Rosse, of Fakerins,
Lawrence Atkins, of the parish of Faghenvayle,
William Abrehall, of Salterston,

Nathaniell Carington, of Mollench,
Toole mcVagh, of Magherifelte,
John Cooke, of Lemevaddie,   }
Simon Berford, of Bamfelled,   } gentlemen,
William Harison, of Magherae,
William Green, of the parish of Enisteede,

Who say that Donell Oge McDonell Boy O'Neale, of the parish of Magharra, yeoman, on the 10th Decr., 1614, waged open war, and on the 10th of January in the same year was supported, &c., by Cooll mcShane boy O'Neile and James

VIEW OF LONDONDERRY.

Carragh O'Neale, of Magharra, and Neile O'Gribben, of Moyacole, yeomen. Said Coollo and James are found guilty and adjudged to death, "ac interiora et membra secreta," &c., as in former cases.

That Donell oge mcDonell boy, of Magharra, yeoman, on the 20th Decr., 1613, waged war, and was relieved by Artt oge mcffelome mcTirlagh O'Neale. The said Art is found guilty, and the sentence is the same as in the lastly above-mentioned case.

That Neale O'Develin, of Killoghterr, yeoman, on the 20th Novr., 1614, at Killelagh, stole 15 "swyne" worth 2s. each, the property of Teige O'Hagane, gentleman. Guilty. To be executed.

That Donell oge mcDonell Boy, of Magharra, yeoman [and another whose name is defaced], Patrick O'Molleave, of the same, yeoman, Rorie [   ], and many other associates, on the 10th Decr., 1613, levied open war [the remainder of the entry cannot be decyphered].

That Richard White, of Maghera, with a skeine worth 2d. which he had in his right hand, gave a mortal wound to Hugh Roe O'Swyne of 3 inches long and 4 inches deep under the right arm, of which he instantly died. Guilty. To be executed, "et membra secreta," &c., as in former cases.

That Thomas Coxe, of Caman, gentleman, on the 1st August, 1614, at Bally-rassan, stole 24 "salte samons" worth 4d. each, "one paire of sheets" worth 5s., "a caddowe" of a black colour worth 3s., and a hammer worth 6d., the property of John Rosse. Guilty. Says he is a clerk, and thereupon Edward Bomker, the minister of John, Bishop of Derry, having claimed him, he is branded in the left hand and delivered to the Ordinary.

AN ANCIENT IRISH SGIAN.

That Donell oge mcDonell boy O'Neale, of Maghara, yeoman, on the last day of Novr., 1614, levied war, and was relieved, &c., on the 10th Decr. following, at Dondonell, by James McFardaragh and Rorie oge O'Brollaghane, of (Tamlaght), yeomen. The said James and Rorie are found guilty, and are adjudged to death, "et membra secreta," &c., as in former cases.

That Art O'Hennery, of Monegrange, yeoman, on the 2nd January, 1614, stole 3½ hides of tanned leather, each worth 4s., the property of William Hoarde, a tanner. Acquitted.

That James McFerrdorragh O'Neale, of Magheragh, yeoman, on the 22nd August, 1614, insulted Hugh Roe O'Quine, and with a skeane worth 6d. gave him a mortal wound in the back of 2 inches broad and 4 inches deep, and another mortal wound in the back of 2 inches broad and 5 inches deep, of which he languished at Kilcrenaghan until the 28th of the same month, and then died; and that the murderer was abetted, &c., by Rorie oge O'Brillaghan, of Magheragh, who was present at the time. The said James is found guilty, and adjudged to death, "et membra secreta," &c., as in former cases. Rorie is acquitted.

That James mcFerdorragh O'Neale, of Killcrannaghane, yeoman, on the last day of Decr., 1614, gave Neale O'Doyle, clerk, with a sword worth 2s., a mortal wound in the back of 4 inches broad and 5 inches deep, and divers other wounds in divers other places, of which he then and there died. Guilty. To be executed, "et membra secreta," as in similar cases.

That Toole O'Mulchreene, Connor O'Mulchreene, and Donell oge mcDonell boy, of Desertmartin, yeomen, on the 20th Decr., 1614, stole a chestnut-coloured mare and a she colt worth £6, a grey mare worth £4, "a nagg" of a grey colour worth 40s., the property of Thomas Foster, gentleman, and a black-coloured gelding worth £4, the property of Thomas Thursoy, gentleman. Guilty. To be executed.

That Cale O'Devin, of Clondermott, yeoman, one of the sheriff's bailiffs, on the 20th Feby., 1614, forceably on the King's highway near the town of Comber, insulted Shane M'Lincie, yeoman, and took from him two barrels of beare malte worth 8s. No verdict.

ARMS OF DUNGANNON.

TYRONE.

An Inquisition taken at Dungannon, before the same Judges, and under the same Commission, on the 30th of March, 12 James I., by the oaths of the following Grand Jury :—

Robert Stewarde, of Donnaghenrye, Esq..

James Callvill, of Srabane,
William Stewarde, of Crewe,
Robert Orack, }
Gilbert Kenedy, } of the same,
Robert Edmonston, of Killaman,
Charles Brookes, of Dromore,
Francis Clerk, }
John Webb, } of the same, } gentlemen,
Robert Cootes, of Disertcreagh,
William Carmichell, of the same,
Conn boy mcDonell O'Neale, of Dromore,
Brian Crosse O'Neale, of the same
Arthur Greames, of Ergill,
Owin Roe O'Qwyne, of Dromore,

Who say that Dermott oge McDonn, of Agher, yeoman, on the 20th Nov., 1614, there stole "a Caddowe" worth 8s., the property of Katherine ny Brien, spinster. No verdict. Pardoned.

That William Allett and Jocky Tallon, alias Armestronge, of Galnegore, yeomen, on the 10th Decr., 1614, there stole 8 sheep, each worth 3s., the property of Patrick McRory. Wm. Allett is found guilty, and says he is a clerk, whereupon John Moony, the minister of Christopher, Archbishop of Armagh, appears, and Allett being branded in the left hand is delivered to him. Pardoned.

That Hobbie Allett, of Dongannon, yeoman, on the 20th Octr., 1614, at Omye, stole 2 horses, each worth £3, belonging to James McGillscnan, a mare worth 40s., the property of Brien O'Ferrenan, and a horse worth 40s., the property of David Smyth. Guilty. To be executed.

That Robert Erwin, of Cregill, yeoman, on the 10th Novr., 1613, at Clonha, stole 2 horses, each worth 40s., the property of Sorragh ny Neale, widow. Guilty. As a clerk, prays the benefit of clergy, and thereupon he is branded in the left hand and delivered to the above named John Mooney.

That Hugh McValdon, of Largy, yeoman, on the 24th of December, 1614, at Townaghmagradagh, stole a grey mare worth £3, and a bay horse worth 20s., belonging to Rorie oge McBrians, and another bay horse of the same value, the property of Donell McBrians. Guilty. To be executed.

That Artt McCormock O'Hagan, and Shane mcArtt mcCormocke O'Hagane, of Donoghenrie, gentlemen, on the 14th Octr., 1614, there entered the mansion house of James Baxter, clerk, between 11 and 12 at night, and insulted him and his servants, and with a sword worth 2s. which they held in their right hands they struck William Magy on the right side of his head, giving him a mortal wound of 5 inches long, 3 inches broad, and 4 inches deep, of which he instantly died. Art not guilty, and Shane guilty. The latter to be executed, "et membra secreta," &c., as in former cases.

That Manus O'Hoone, of Ellanenuckie, yeoman, on the last day of Decr., 1614, at Tooreagh, stole 24 sheep worth 2s. 6d. each, the property of Donnell oge McEnally, yeoman. Acquitted.

That Laghlin O'Cullen, Tirlagh McDavid O'Cullen, and Patrick Boy O'Cullen, of Blackwater, yeomen, on the 7th March, 1612, at Ballacullen, near the Blackwater, stole a bay mare worth £5, the property of Francis Caprone, and were abetted by Teige Akeaneene, of Tulemason, yeoman. Laghlin guilty, and to be executed. The others acquitted.

That George Sacheverell, of Dongannon, clerk, on the 5th of January, 1614, there entered the mansion house of Edward Barnett, gentleman, and stole 5s. 6d. out of "a truncke." Acquitted.

That James O'Hagan, of Arrater, yeoman, on the 15th February, 1613, at Tolloghagen, "in quandam Annam Clinton, spinster, &c., insultum fecit et contra voluntatem felonice rapuit." Guilty. To be executed.

That Fealome O'Mullen, of Shigrome, yeoman, on the 1st Nov., 1614, at Ballaclugin, stole 2 mares worth 40s. each, the property of Teige O'Corr. Acquitted.

That Tirlagh Mergagh McGillicullum, of Carrintealin, yeoman, on the 20th Septr., 1614, there stole a brown horse worth 40s., and another brown horse worth 30s., the property of Hugh Grome O'Quyn. Acquitted.

That Edmund O'Mullarcky, of Ballynecowly, clerk, on the 20th of August, 1613, levied open war, and on the last day of that month was relieved, &c., by Donogh and Teige mcGeanaght, yeomen. The two latter are found guilty and adjudged to death, " et membra secreta," &c., as before mentd.

That Connor O'Mullcrene, of Coollkeerin, yeoman, on the 3rd Decr., 1614, stole a bay mare with a colt worth £6, a grey mare worth £4, and a grey "nagge" worth 40s., the property of Thomas Foster, gentleman, and a black gelding worth £4, the property of Thomas Thursky, gentleman. Acquitted.

That Dermott oge McDoun, of Mullaghallorie, on the 20th Novr., 1614, published and declared these words, vizt. :—" *That he had two swords, and that he aid hope to have good use for them before Xpias (Christmas), for the Poope of Roome would send over O'Neale, the Earle of Tyrone, as a Kinge to governe th's kingdome with greate authoritie as he had in former times,*" seditiously and traitorously, to the great contempt of the King, against the peace, his crown, and dignity, and contrary to the form and effect of divers statutes. No verdict.

That Shane mcArtt mcCormock O'Hagan, of Donaghenrie, yeoman, on the 14th Oct., 1614, with a sword worth 2s., struck William Magie on the right side of his head, giving him a mortal wound of 3 inches broad, 5 inches long, and 4 inches deep, of which he instantly died, and that he was assisted, &c., by Tirlagh mcHenrie O'Hagan, of the same place, gentleman. Said Tirlagh is acquitted. Said Shane is further stated to have been aided by Hugh Grome O'Quine, of Killmackmorrchie, yeoman, who is also tried and acquitted.

That Manus and Morragh O'Mongan, of Tamplemagra, yeomen, on the 20th Novr., 1614, at Maghenekeeragh, between 2 and 3 at night, entered the mansion house of John Roberts, gentleman, putting Sawe ny Feake, spinster, in bodily fear of her life, and stole therefrom a brown cow worth 20s., the property of a person unknown then in the house, as a distress, and also stole a rope *(funem)* worth 3d., the property of said John Roberts. Guilty. They say they are clerks, and they are therefore branded in their left hands and delivered to the above-named minister, John Moony.

That Edmund oge McEgerr, Patrick oge McEgerr, Shane McQuyne O'Neale, Tirlagh O'Groome McEgerr, Owen McMahawne, Edmund Duffe McEgerr, Tirlagh oge McEgerr, Neale Modder O'Neale, Hugh O'Neale mcCormocke, Enies Duffe McEgerr, and Edmund Echaggie, of Clogher, yeomen, on the 10th of January, 1614, there waged open war, &c. No verdict.

That Patrick Modder O'Maghane, of Termoumeaghan, yeoman, on the 4th January, 1614, at Curraghroe, wounded and ill-treated Saue ny Harae. No verdict.

That Thomas Goodlucke, gentleman ; George Allexander, yeoman ; David Ecklies, "Tailor ;" John Cauder, "weaver ;" and George Straughan and Thomas Stephinston, yeomen, all of Derregellie, on the last day of November, 1614, at Cavangarvane, riotously assembled together and entered the dwelling-house of William Darragh, clerk, who had been in the quiet possession thereof for a term of years, and expelled him and his servants therefrom. Thomas Goodlucke is tried and acquitted.

That Owin Magwyre, of Dongannon, yeoman, on the 25th March, 1610, at Ballinseggarde, stole a black horse worth £12, the property of Shane O'Neale, yeoman. No verdict.

That Owin mcFardorogh boy Magwyre, of Agher, yeoman, on the 3d March, 1614, published and declared the following seditious words, viz. :—" *That he would kill Emanuell Ley, and throwe his heade out of the windowe of his own castle, for that the Earle of Tyrone shoulde come with the King of Spaine his forces, and come to Mounaghan, Dondalke, Drogheda, and Dublin, and that the Earle of Tyrone sholde be King in Ireland, and woulde kill all the Scotts and Englishmen in the Kingdome.*" No verdict.

That Dermott oge mcDoun, of Agher, yeoman, on the 20th of November, 1614, there spoke, published, and declared these malicious words, viz. :—" *I woulde God I hadd fortie Soulders in armes in everie Castle within this Kingdome of*

Ireland, and a good store of others sufficient men at my commaunde within the Castle of Dublin, and the Kinge of England allso with me there, whereby I might make the said King of England (meaning the now King James) to kisse the Poape his showe." No verdict.

That Hugh mcDonell O'Neale, of Ballylaghnegue, gentleman, on the last day of Decr., 1613, there spoke, &c., these seditious words, viz. :—" *That the King of England was but a veric poore fellow, when he was a scoller learninge the languages, and that he did much woonder that he shoulde be King of England, for if it shold be tried by historics or crounicles, himselfe had as much right to be King as hee*" (*meaning the now King James*). Acquitted.

Order of the Excbequer

DEPOSITED IN THE EXCHEQUER RECORD OFFICE, FOUR COURTS, DUBLIN.

xxxmo. die Aprilis, 1618.

MEMORANDUM. Whereas the King's most excellent Majestie that nowe is, by his letters pattents dated the vjth daie of July, in the second yere of his raigne of England, &c., did graunte to Sir Randall mcDonnell, knight, and the heirs males of his bodie, wth remainders over the countrie called the Route, in the countie of Antrime, containeing ix Toughes, the country called the Glynns, in the said countie, containeing 7 Toughes, the Iland of Rathlynns, parcell of the Glynns, and the foure townes called the Creggs, parcell of the Route, to be holden of his Matie, his heires and successors, by the service of sixe Knights' ffees, in capite. And graunted alsoe other letters pattents, dated the xijth daie of Maye, in the fourth yere of his reigne, to Shaune mcBrien O'Nealle and his heirs, the toughes of Minter Rindie, Toughenesinghe, Toughe Muntercallie, Toughe Knockeboynabarde, and Toughe Muntermurigan, in the said Countie, to be holden of his Majestie, his heirs and successors, in capite by the tenneth parte of a Knight's ffee. And alsoe graunted by other letters patents, dated the xth daie of March, in the fift yere of his highnes raigne, to Rorie oge mcQuillene and his heirs, the toughe of Clynahartie, in the said countie, to be holden of his Majestie, his heirs and successors, in capite by the xxth parte of a Knight's ffee, and alsoe graunted by other letters pattents, dated the xxvjth of June, in the fourth yere of his highnes raigne, unto Chahill O'Harrae and his heirs, the Toughe of Keart, in the said countie, to be holden of his highnes, his heirs and successors, in capite by the service of the xxth parte of a Knight's ffee. And alsoe graunted by othere letters pattents, dated the xxvjth of May, in the fourth yere of his Maties raigne, to oge Neille mcNeille, and Hugh o'Neile, the territorie or toughe of Kilmacherett, and the toughe of Killelaghe, in the said county, to be holden of his highnes, his heirs and successors, in capite by the service of the xxth parte of one Knight's ffee. And whereas processe of distringas yssued out of this court retornable this Terme against the before named parties, and the tennants of the forsaid severall Toughes, to cause them to doe their severall homages due to his highnes for the said Toughes, by vertue of their said severall Tenures, ffor respittinge of wch service of homadge a ffynne is usually accostomed to be paid to his Matie, and that sometimes more or lesse accordinge as the lands soe holden are valued ; and forasmuch as it is sufficiently knowne to this court that the forsaid Toughes are scituated and beinge in the north parts of this Kingdome, wch is intended shortlie to be planted wth collonies and undertakers, soe as at this present the said Toughes, being for the most part wast and unhabited, are as yett of litle annuall value. And forasmuch alsoe as the right honnorable the nowe Lo: Deputie hath this daie under his hande signified to this courte as followeth :—I knowe much of the lande w^{thin} menconed is wast (meaninge the before named Toughes), and noe parte of it improved by any maner of husbandry other than in grasseinge of cattle and in soweinge of litle oates, and the propriators of the lande to be for the most parte very poore and needie, and the twoe childrenn of Neile mcHughe to be yett under age, wherefore I thinke it fitte that the Court of Excheaquor should consider thereof, and to rate the respitte of homadge accordinglie for a time untill the country be better inhabited, and these men made to understande that it is not an imposition but a lawefull duetie and paiement due to his Matie, this is my advise and opinion for the present. xxxth of Aprill, 1610. Arthure Chichester. It

CARRICK-A-REDE.

is therefore ordred, upon mature and deliberate consideracon hade by the Barrons of this his Ma^{ts} court of Exchequor, as well of the state of the wasts of the said northeren parts of the nature and disposicon of the natives there resideing, as alsoe of his honnor's said advise, that every of the before-named parties shall nowe paic to his Majestie as a fine for respitteinge of their severall homadges for everie Toughe they hold as aforsaid yerelie from the date of their said letters pattents, for and untill the feast of Easter last past, 1610, the somme of foure pence, togither wth such fees as is due to the second Remembrauncer of this Court, for makeinge their acquittances and warrants of atturney : and henceforth as civilitie and habitacon shall increase in the forsaid parts, and as there said lands hereafter shall be improved and manured, soe this Courte answerablie will consider and advise to augment their fines to be due to his highnes, his heirs and successors, for the respitteinge of their severall homadges for there severall Toughes aforesaid.

JO. DENHAM.

FELLING OAKS FOR BELFAST CASTLE IN KILWARLIN, 1611.

SUIT in chancery in 1625, between Hugh, Lord Viscount Montgomery of the Ardes & Dame Amy Conway widow & administratrix of Sir Foulke Conway deceased, the decision decreed to the Lady Amy permission to cut trees & woods, mentioned in a certain order of the court, for the use of her iron works, & all manner of woods & underwoods growing on the lands of Slutt M'Neale ; except only the bodies & butts of great and young oak & ash which are not already dead or hollowed, & except such boughs and branches of oak as are fit for pipe boards, mill timber ; house timber, or ship timber ; the exception or restraint to continue only untill a division of the woods shall take place, & for this purpose it is ordered that a commission issue to the Bishop of Dromore, Sir Edward Trevor, Sir Henry O'Neill, Nicholas Ward, and Richard West, to inquire on oath what waste had been committed in the woods since the 22nd August in the fourth year of the late King James.

The commission was issued on the 18 of June, & they immediately impannelled a jury "some of whom were carpenters well versed in timber works." They found that there were standing on the lands of the size of six inches at the butt 8,883 trees ; & that there had been cut, of the same size, 11,631. They also find that there had been cut for the use of Lord Chichester, for the building of his houses at Carrickfergus & Belfast, no less than 500 oak trees. One Adam Montgomery had with four workmen cut a great number of trees.

Mr. Dalway cut three score of trees. Anthony Coslet tenant of Sir Moses Hill cut 127 trees at Blairis ; & all were cut without leave of the lord Clandeboy, the Lord of Ardes, Sir Foulke Conway, his Lady or any of their agents. The Commissioners further state that the roofs of the churches of Grey Abbey, & Cumber, a store of timber for the Lord of Ardes buildings at Newton & Donaghadee had been taken from the woods in question, besides a great store for the manufacture of pipe staves, hogshead staves, barrel staves, Keeve staves & spokes for carts. And they conclude with dividing the woods into two parts, one for Lord Claneboy, the other for the Lord of Ardes. *(Pinkerton MSS.)*

Customs, Excise, &c., in Ireland, A.D. 1637.

The following extracts are taken from a report on the state of the Customs, written by Charles Moncke, Surveyor-General to Sir George Ratcliffe, in 1637. (From Harleian, No. 2138.)

" HE merchants and pedlars discharge at Glenarm, where there is no waiter, and fill the country full of commodities whereof none appear in the books. The pedlars out of Scotland take advantage of such unguarded creeks, and swarm about the country in great numbers, and sell all manner of wares, which they may afford at easier rates than poor shopkeepers that live in corporations, bear offices, pay cess and all charges, and their due customs, and are beggared by these Runagadoes, who have no residence or place of abode in the kingdom, but bring over wares, steal the custom, and convey the money over in specie, and that to no small value, which journeys deserve a careful and speedy prevention."

" There is a place called Conn's water, within two miles of Belfast, and another place called Garmoyle, part of the port of Bangor, in both which places the officers of Carrickfergus receive a benefit of the third part of the customs for wines or other goods discharged there, whereas, if they entered in Bangor, the King receives the whole. The farthest of these creeks is not above three miles from Hollywood, where the waiter is resident, and can come at low water to the ships' sides. I

PORTION OF MERCATOR'S MAP OF ULSTER, 1594. (FAC-SIMILE OF ORIGINAL.)

gave charge to the waiter of Hollywood to take charge of them, that
no goods should be shipped or discharged there but he should be
present with the officers of Carrickfergus, it being unfit that wines and
goods of value should be discharged there without them both.

"There wanted a boat at Hollywood, which I gave orders to buy,
and to give Boulton, the waiter, fifty shillings per annum to keep in
repair.

"John Boulton was waiter at Hollywood, being a creek of Bangor,
by deputation for per ann. £20.

"There was no beam, scales, weights, or storehouse at Hollywood,
so the goods seized, being put in weak places, have been stolen away.
I gave order for supplying these defects."

CONNSWATER BRIDGE, 1603.

BANGOR.—"There is a fair custom-house built but not finished by the
Lord of Claneboy, who hath received between two and three hundred
pounds of the King towards it, and hath bestowed at least six hundred
pounds already, and two hundred pounds more will hardly finish it. It
is a large pile of stones made with flankers, and might serve as well for
defence of the harbour. There are very large storehouses, lodging
chambers for officers, with chimneys, studdys, and places to lay all
sorts of commodities in, with as much convenience as may be. If it
were finished it were the best custom-house in Ireland, and stands as
convenient as it can be placed to the ground given by his Lp. for a
wharf and crane, which he hath granted under his hand and seal, and
was himself present at the setting of it forth, and is most forward upon
all occasions to give the officers countenance and furtherance ; and it
is a pity but either the King's Majesty or his Lp. should finish that
work so happily began by his Lp. of the custom-house."

He notices no establishment at Belfast ; but among the officials at
Carrickfergus he mentions John Sande, waiter at Belfast, £20 fee per
annum.

" At Carrickfergus, the custom-house and storehouse are very fair, well situated, and strong, being an old castle repaired, wherein are many convenient rooms for lodging chambers, studies for officers, and all things necessary. It is almost finished, and, being fully repaired, is

ANCIENT BELL OF BANGOR.

the fittest place can be chosen. It is well floored, wainscotted, and glazed, and hath provided the King's arms very decently to be on the outside of it.

" Two boatmen at Carrickfergus deserve their salary if they be honest, trusty, and always have their boat afloat and ready; but I suspect them, being Scotchmen, to be hardly indifferent against their countrymen who altogether trade in that place.

" John Hornby, the waiter of Carrickfergus, gave a let pass for two tuns of French wine to be discharged at Garmoyle out of a ship of Belfast, the first of June, 1637, which was more than a waiter ought to do, although it had paid custom, it being their duties to execute warrants and make none. Of this and some other miscarriages I did admonish him, and I verily believe that it will not be long before he give further occasion, he being somewhat extravagant in his ways, and debauched and idle.

" Andrew Edmonds, waiter at Bangor, salary £15 per ann. A man of evil fame, debauched, and dangerous to his nearest and dearest friends, having, as it is known, offered violence to his own mother, and drawn her blood to the danger of her life. He used many exorbitant and strange extortions, and was so peremptory in them, that he boasted that he . . . . . but to get at least 20 shillings a-week by them, as if he had a warrant to receive bribes or extort."

From Drogheda to Derry, dreads his journey home.

Speaking of the London Companies' possessions in Co. Derry, he says :—

" The country is spacious, the soil for the most part good, and yielding commodities of the best value; but, alas! I find that the English there are but weak and few in number, there being not forty houses in Londonderry of English of any note, who for the most part only live. The Scots, being many in number, and twenty to one for the English, having privy trade in the town and country, thrive and grow rich, and the Irish for the most part beg, being the reward of their idleness."

SEAL OF THE CUSTOMS AND PORT OF CARRICKFERGUS, 1605.

The difficulties, mountains and deep ways. Never went a worse Journey in his life ; 3 score and ten days.

Carrick. The customs there inwards and outwards to the 24 Septr. was £1,137 3s. 9d. Bangor, from Lady Day to 17 Septr., inwards, £71 9s. 11d. ; out., £920 16s. 8d.

It might be as well to describe the mode of taxation at the time.

The Customs Inwards and Outwards were settled on the Crown by the Act of Subsidy of Poundage and Tonnage passed in the 14th and 15th year of Charles II., whereby one shilling in the pound, or 5 per cent., was decreed to be paid for all goods and merchandise (wines and oils excepted) imported and exported by natives, according to the value as rated in the book of rates, or affirmed by oath of the merchant.

Goods imported or exported by aliens paid double the customs payable by natives.

French wine paid £3 10s. per tun if imported by a native, but £4 13s. 4d. if by an alien.

Salad oil was liable to a duty of £3 3s. if imported by a native, but if by an alien, £3 18s. 9d.

The Imported Excise settled by the same Act was a duty granted to the Crown, whereby all drugs imported were to pay 10 per cent., or two shillings in the pound.

The Inland Excise, by the same Act, was a duty of 2s. 6d. on every 32 gallons of strong beer brewed by common brewers, and also on every other person who should tap or sell the same publickly or privately.

Every 32 gallons of small beer brewed or sold was liable to a duty of six-pence.

All Aquavitæ, or strong waters, made or distilled for sale, paid 4d. for each gallon.

ALE LICENCES, a duty settled on the Crown by the same Act, whereby no person may sell ale or beer by retail without a license, the cost of which was twenty shillings (and one shilling to the collector) for each licence yearly.

WINE AND STRONG WATER LICENCES were settled on the Crown by the Statute 17 and 18 Charles II. There was no certain rate for these licenses, the duty being "compounded and agreed for yearly, according as the circumstances of trade and times do offer and give encouragement," paying two shillings for each wine and one shilling for each strong water license to the Collector.

FINES AND SEIZURES were levied and made for infringements of the Customs and Revenue Acts.

PLANTATION DUTY was the English duty received and secured with the exchange of money (over and above the usual duties payable inwards) for commodities of the growth and production of the English plantations brought directly thence and bound for England, and only landed in Ireland upon very urgent and extra ordinary occasions. As in case of shipwreck, or a vessel in want of provisions, so much was admitted entry as would enable the captain to pay for supplies. The said duty on being received was transmitted by bills without charge to the Receiver-General of the Customs in England.

QUIT RENTS were payable to the Crown by the Acts of Settlement and Explanation out of the estates forfeited by the rebellion in the year 1641.

CROWN RENTS were ancient yearly rents reserved to the Crown on land granted by favour since the conquest of Ireland.

In the Inland Excise were also included Hearth Money by the above-mentioned Act, according to which every fire-hearth, stove, publick oven, or kiln, paid two shillings annually. A fire-place unfixed or without a chimney paid four shillings.

There were other ancient duties then collected, as PRISAGE, belonging to the Dukes of Ormond as the King's hereditary butlers. Every ship importing more than nine and less than 18 tuns of wine paid a tun in kind, and every vessel importing more than 18 tuns paid two tuns and no more, which was collected for his Grace by his agent.

When on this subject, I may add that the Lord Deputy, the Lord Chancellor, the Privy Councillors, the Serjeants-at-Law, the Attorney-General, the Solicitor-General, and the Clerk of the Council, were allowed to import each a certain quantity of wine duty free. This, however, in 1693, or earlier, was commuted into a money payment, the Collector of the Port of Dublin paying in lieu thereof—

To the Lord Lieutenant, £76 10s.; to the Lord Chancellor, £15 12s.; to every Privy Councillor, £11 14s.; and to the Serjeants-at-law, Attorney-General, Solicitor-General, and Clerk of the Council, the sum of £5 17s. each.

An excellent account of the Irish Revenue for five years, from the landing of Duke Schomberg in August, 1689, to Christmas, 1693, in the handwriting of Bartholomew Van Homrigh, Commissioner of the Revenue, and the father of Dean Swift's unfortunate Vanessa. He was appointed Commissioner by patent dated 15th July, 1690 and held the office till his death, 29th December, 1703. (*Pinkerton MSS.*)

DEAN SWIFT, 1667-1745.

VIEW OF MOURNE MOUNTAINS.

Monroe's Raid on Newry, 1643.

A Dispatch by an Unknown Officer.

HE 26th of Septemb., 1643, was appointed for the meeting of all the forces at Lisnagarvy. This meeting should have been much sooner, but that some things did hinder, whereof one was an offer made by divers Rebells of comming in, if they might have protection, and offering to doe service against the Rebells. It was tought fitt to receave them, but upon the assurance that they should doe some such service by killing some of the Rebells as should make themselves irreconcileable to them. The Cannon allso came at that time out of Scotland, and the Earle of Leaven did intend to take some pieces with him, having an intention to goe to Charlemont, for without them wee did not think it fitt to go thither, and wee could onely have destroyed the Corne. This Expedition it was hoped would have relieved Dungannon, which the Rebells did hold besieged, and it was most certayne that it would, for if that provision of victualls for 20 dayes were brought which was commanded, the army must of necessitie have passed so neere to Dungannon, either in besieging of Charlemont or destroying of Corne, that it would have been relieved without all doubt. But, first, there could bee but 14 dayes' provision of victualls gotten, a very small proportion, for the goeing to Charlemont from Carrickfergus would bee six dayes' march. Another hinderance from goeing to

E

Charlemont was want of carriage, for there were not beasts enough to carry the Canon and the ammunition. Another let there was, that when the Scotts army came to Bellfast, it rained so extreamely for two nights and a daye that it made the wayes extreameldy bad and the rivers very high, so that the Army, consisting of Eight halfe Regiments of Scotts, with all theyr horse, and 1,000 foote of English forces, and 3 troopes of horse and some field pieces, marched first to Loughbricklen. There being some forces of the Rebells, they went to Tanderogee. Some little encounter they had, and if the Rebells had bin willing they might then have fought, for there were all theyr forces, but they had no will to it and retired, and the Scotts army, not having had anie intention for to goe further, contented themselves with destroying the Corne about Tanderogee, and from thence marched to the Newry, where more men were left, so that that garrison is now 1,200 strong in foote and a troope of horse. One end of the Towne hath a hill that overlooks it, and on it the Church, which formerly had been made for a defence for the Towne. I have repared all these things which age and neglect had decayed, which might serve for the defence of the place, and at the other end of the Towne next the river order was given for the making of a worke which might defend that part and make the Towne tenable, which without that it would hardly bee. In the time that the Army stayed there, what Corne could be gotten was brought into the Towne. In the returne from hence some parties were sent into the mountaines of Morne ; all the Corne where they came to was destroyed, and all the Irish houses burnt. There was a party also sent into McCartan's woods. There Lievtenand Colonell Hamilton, of the Lo: Claneboye's Regiment, having with him 24 files of musketiers of 6 to a file, having taken a prey of Cowes, and coming through the woods with, the Rebells having made a barricade crosse the way with pieces of trees, they suffered them to breake up one barricade without molestation ; and when they had gone a little further and met with another barricade, beginning to undoe it, the Rebells set upon them. At the first, or allmost at the first charge the Lievtenand Colonell was shott through the bellie, which did so dishearten the soaldiers that they were within very little of routing ; but it hapned that there was a gentleman ther, a good gallant man, one that had been a commander, but then without command, and onely a voluntier, spake so to them, and behaved him-selfe so well with them, that he did reassure them. But the Enemy pressed them so hard, that hee would not have had leave to have given them assurance if that Major Ballindin, who commands the Generall's Guard of horse, and was there with that troope and another, had not caused them to close on one side, and hee charged the Enemy, which hee did very well and resolutely.

This skirmish (wherein some officers were hurt and about 140 soaldiers killed) lost them some of theyr cowes, but they brought 2 or 300 to the Army, which upon the returne of the Parties that went into McCartan's woods marched to theyr several quarters. Now they are providing for theyr winter quarters. The Lo: Conwaye's Regi-

ment lyes at Lisnagarvy and at 4 fortes which are made at Kilulta.
Mr. Chichester's Regiment lyes in Bellfast and in Malone, where a
fort is making.   Sr. John Clotworthy's Regiment lyes at Antrim, at
Montjoy, which is likely the Rebells will now attempt, for they have
nothing now to trouble them, Dungannon being given up to them
after they had endured great extreamitie for want of victualls, living
divers weeks without any bread at all, and having nothing to eat but
the hides and tallow of the beasts.   The keeping of Dungannon would
have been of good importance, but things hapning out so as that the
Scotts did not goe, the Lo: Conway stayed for to make triall, if it
were possible to relieve Dungannon.

To that end he went to Antrim, and took order for the sending of
men over the lough, but gave them order to gett intelligence of the
state and condition of the Rebells, and wether they were strong about
Dungannon or no, for it was thought that the Rebells would draw all
theyr forces to attend on the Scotts Army, and therefore would have
none or very few men about Dungannon, and because that this was
likely, and he knew how little a while they would have occasion
to attend upon what the Scotts Army would doe, and therefore that
they would return quickly to Dungannon againe.   Therefore, so soone
as hee knew that the Scotts would not march towards Dungannon,
he did immediately sent away a drumme over the Lough with a
message to Sr Phillemy O'Neille, but with a command for to see
wether it were possible to get into Dungannon, and then hee was to
deliver a letter to Captaine Jones, wherein he was commanded to
quitt Dungannon & to blow up the Fort because it was impossible to
supply them with victualls.   If this could have been done, there
would have been done as much by that single drumme as could have
been done by all the men wee could have sent, but the windes being
contrary, no boate could passe in divers dayes, and our men going
over, they heard that the Rebells were about Dungannon ; and the
last did receive certain intelligence that the Rebells were very strong
about Dungannon, that they had intelligence of theyr coming over the
Lough, and that they had prepared an ambuscade, for they knew
theyr number.   It hapned that the day before they came Dungannon
was delivered upon very good conditions, and they were brought by
Sr. Phillemie O'Neille in safetie to Montjoy.

Captaine Jones (who commanded in Dungannon) behaved himself
as well as it was possible for any man to doe, and the Rebells themselves doe give him a very good testimony, and because that Montjoy
is now next in danger, the Lord Conway had sent order for 300 men
out of the Regiments of the Lo: Claneboy and the Lo: Montgomery
and Sr. James Montgomery that wee may keepe it if it be possible ;
the whole care of keeping it lying upon the English.   The Regiments
of the Lo: Claneboy and the Lord Montgomery doe lye upon theyr
owne lands.   The Regiment of Sr. James Montgomerie lye in the little
Ards as yet : the Scotts Army lyes at Carrickfergus, thereabout, in
the Ards and Claneboyes, upon the Ban's side from Toome to Coll-
rane, and in the Newry.   The yeare hath been very wett, which had

made the harvest very backward : it is now the 9ᵗ of Octob : and the Harvest is not yet in : the Rebells doe what they can to gett the Corne. Because they should not bee neighbours to us, all is done that possiblic can bee to destroy theyr corne, and to that end parties are sent out by the Lo : Conway, whereof some are now abroad. (*Pinkerton MSS.*)

A FURTHER DISPATCH.

HE Scottish Army, or partie, as they call it, which did consist of 3,600 foote, and 3 troopes of horse, and 4 field pieces, did march about the 7th of this month to Charlemont, and I believe might have taken it without any great loss, but they sent to the Newry the next day after they came thither, 100 men upon soe manie of their baggage horses for meale, and the same day they sent out their horse with 200 musketiers one baggage horses into the Countrie to understand what the Rebells did prepare to do, and what prey of cowes they would get to bring to the armie : they met with very ill wayes, and so disadvantageous that they brought little or nothing from the Rebells. About 40 of the musketeers, as I have heard, were lost by apprehending the disadvantage of the ground and the thought of the enemy too much, although he that commanded them did all that was possible for him to doe ; by some entelligence they got that day, it was doubted the Rebells would make an attempt upon the partie which was to come from the Newry with meale, which although they were 400 musketiers with those that were sent and those that came from the Newry, yet was it thought there might be danger, the Rebells being reported to bee 3 or 4 thousand, and if they should be beaten the army would bee lost, for all the victualls were spent, so that Charlemont was quitted, and the Army marched to meet there partie from the Newrie, which they did in good time, the soaldiers having had nothing to eat in a day or two before. A little before there marching the Rebells in the woodes between Portadowne and Charlemont made a show upon a hill with 3 Coloures, and all their women, horses, and

Cowes, and Goates, to make a great bodie, and at their coming away a peece was shott from the Castle which strook of a soaldier's arme, and hurt another. They did it in a bravadoe, having onely shott that peece all the coming and going ; some few soaldiers were killed there, and Colonell Hume was shott in the heele, the day after that the partie from the Newry was met, was spent in giveing of meale to the soaldiers. The next day another partie was sent into the mountaines, and a place appointed for them to meet with the maine bodie, which marched another way into the mountaines passable for the Cannon. At night they met, and the partie brought in many cowes and Killed about 40 men or more and many women and children, in all (some say) 500, some say 700 ; of the Scottish soaldiers few were lost ; diverse of these who came without command in hope of gain, and are here called plunderers, an ill race of people, and very hurtfull to an armie, were lost. The Rebells made no fight at all, they had not anie powder in that place, yet they did endeavour to drive back their Cowes. Some of them came neere to the Place where the maine bodie of the Scotts was, from which a partie of 100 musketiers was sent out and mett with them ; upon notice given to the Gennerall Maior he went with about 2 third partes of his men, and sending some commended men before, they met with the armie sent out in morning. They took each other for the enemy, some shott were given, but they quickly found there mistake. The next day, the bodie of the armie went to the Newry by the way that the cannon might goe. A partie was sent by the hills that came at night to the Newry, and brought great store of . . . .

ARMS OF DUNDALK.

but the Irish fledd, and by reason of that chaseing of the enemy from place to place with there catle, they were forced nearer Dundalke than usuall, whereof that Garrison having notice sent out men and took from them a great prey of 2,000 Cowes and very many sheep. 2 dayes after, the weather being fowle, parties were sent out unto the mountaines between Carlingford and Dundalke, whence they brought home manie Cowes and Sheep ; allsoe the whole division of the prey att their returne was 2,700 Cowes. It is sayd that there was lost and killed in this expedition of the plunderers and soaldiers about 400 men. I will not report it for certaine, although I hard some Scottsmen themselves say soe, because the most parte of them were lost scatteringlye, and being under no government it could not be discerned when they were lost. In the absence of the Scotts Armie, I had commanded that parties of my Regiment should be sent out into the woods and imployed in makeing workes for keeping small garrisons to cleare the countrie of the Rebells, and upon the 9 of this month 300 Musketiers and 40 horse, commanded by Captn. Rawden, lighted upon some of the Rebells that were returned into the woods and bogges of Kilullta and Kilmore, to divyd the Scottishe armie, and killed divers of them, drove some of them into Loghneagh, where they were drowned, and the rest fledd over the Bann. They tooke from them 260 Cowes and manie mares and Coltes; and in a few daies after, upon the comeing back of the Scotts, Captn. Rawden, beleeveing the Rebells would for there safeguard' betake themselves again into the woods of Kilmore and Clanbrassell, sent out 10 horse from a worke he was att in Killulta to discover: who assured him that diverse of the Rebells were come back with their goods over the Ban, and that about 20 of them shewed themselves in the woods and marched towards them, but the horse charged them, and as soone as they had given fire upon them were rid of their Companie. Upon that intelligence, 400 foote and about 90 horse went out under the Captn. Rawden and marched to the Ban side in severall parties and wings, cleared the woods between Kilulta and the Ban; but the Rebell scouts, discovering some of our horse upon the side of the woods, they gott both their cattle and themselves over the River, notwithstanding 2 of Sr. John Clottworthy's boates by appointment were come with musketiers to the mouth of the Ban to prevent it, that being the onlie place fordable in 10 miles; but they have acquainted themselves and there cattle with takeing the River, that they doe it as readily as duckes. The next day some horsemen were sent back with orders to fire the Cabbins mongst the woods in there way to the Lurgan to amaze the Enemie, and make them believe the whole partie was defeated, which took good effect, and that made the Rebells secure on the other side, and that evening the whole partie marched without anie noyse up the woods neere Knockbridge, where there is a deep foard, and quartered within halfe-a-mile that night, and by dawne in the morning marched away to the foord, where a 100 men were left to make good the passe, and all the baggage and horse by command took up the rest of the foote and carried them over att 3 turnes behind them. The enemie had scouts that discovered them, whereupon they run all with their goods to the highway to Charlemont. A few troope of 30 horse was sent awaie, and the rest marched after, and the foote were commanded to goe 4 miles to Battle hill, and there to stand to make good the retreat of the horse. After 2 miles' march the Horse came to a worke of the enemie, which they quitt without once giving fire upon them; butt the filling it upp with sodds to passe over gave them halfe-an-houre's Interruption. After they made great hast to overtake the Rebells, who fledd towardes Charlemont, and to make good rest there, Carriages, cattle, mantles, and what else troubled them.

There was standing corne in diverse places by the way side, which saved manie of them. The Horse pursued many of them to the

Black-water side, where manie of them were drowned. Manie were
killed in their way, and much more execution had been done
if the Horse had not bene tyred; there was not 12 that could
come upp to the end of the Chase. They brought back about
700 Cowes, and if they could have carried it, and had time to doe it,
abundance of meale and butter and other thinges had bene brought
away which was left. The same night the Horse and foote and
all they had gotten were by great diligence gotten safe back
over the Band. Some 4 Musketiers had stolen out contrary to
express command to plunder in the woods, where they were killed
that night. Some of the Rebells were come back after them, and
made manie showes in the night from the farther side of the River
upon the buy *(sic)* guard att the foorde and broken bridge, but being
deceived by false fires and lighted matches that the centeries had
order to lay, did no harme, so that the next day they all marched
home through the woods very safely with there prey. *(Pinkerton
MSS.)*

The Cessation, 1643—Account of Corn.

Corn left at the Right Honble. the Lo: Blayney his quarter, and taken away by
the Irish, 5th October, 1643, in O'Neiland. Of Barley dressed, 3 br. bar. ; more
120 Stookes of Barley estimated to brs., 40 br. bar. ; of Burnt Oates, 60 br. bar. ;
more 290 Stookes, estimat. 90 br. bar.

Corne taken then by the Irish out of Capt: Patterson's quarter. Of Barley,
100 stooks, estim. 33 br. bars. ; of oats, 600 stooks, estimat. 200 br. bars.

Corne left at Capt. Parratt's quarter, in Oriell, and taken by them. Of oats,
ready dressed, 66 br. bars. Totall of the oats taken away belonging to ye Lo:
Conway's Regt., 765 br. bars, which at 6s. a bar. comes to £229 10s.

A note of Corne taken up by the Irish from the officers and soaldiers of
Colonell Chichester's Regiment. At Maghulacon, oates, 52 br. bars. ; at Legar-
lorry, oates, 22 br. bar. ; at Leganory, shilling barley, 3 br. bar. ; at Legarrory,
shilling barley, 10 br. bar. Total, 87 br. bar.

And neere Tollbridge, as much oates as 20 men stokt and reapt in one day ;
this did belong to Major Chichester.

Corne belonging to Capt. Lyndon, Burnt Cornes, 20 br. bar. ; also 60 stooks
oates estimat. 20 br. bar.

Corne belonging to Captn. Ellis, Shilling, 40 ; Burnt oates, 100 ; Seede oates,
10 ; barley, 16 ; meale, 6 ; barley in stooks, 80. At Castlecope, seven score stooks
by estima. 42 bar.

Corn taken by them belonging to Capt. John Michaell and his company in
O'Neiland, 5th October, 1643. Of oates, thrashed and cleansed, 140 ; of wheat, 4 ;
of barley, 3 ; of seede oates in stooks, about 60 ; besides the soldiers' corne and
meale, estimated nearly 100.

Corne taken then belonging to Capt. Trusdall's Company. Of barley, dressed,
24 br. bar. ; more 100 stooks barley, 33 br. bar. ; of oates, 39 br. bar. ; more 30
stooks of oates, 10 br. bar. The totall barley, 140, which at 15s. a bar. comes to
£105. Summa totalis, £334 10s., of all which we desire present satisfaction.

Corne belonging to Capt. McAdam. Of oates in stook, estimat. 60 ; burnt
oates, 20 ; barley in stook, estimat. 20.

Corne belonging to Capt. Martin, neere Hamilton's barony, oates, 60 ; at
Molaghdroy, oates, 30 ; Shilling at Mulaghdroy, oates, 2 ; and as much corn neere
Mulaghdroy as 70 men could reap and stook in one day.

More Corne belonging to Captain Ellis. Burnt oates at his old qrtrs., 7 ;

barley, 3 ; at his new qrtrs., oates in stook, estimat. 15 br. bar. ; barley, 7 br. bar. ; at another place, 6 stooks and 5 stooks of oates, and 2 stooks of barley, by Estimation, 40 bar. The totall of all the oates taken away belonging to Coll. Chichester's Regmt. being 458 br. bar., which at 6s. a bar. comes to £137 8s. The Totall of Barley, Shillings, and Meale, 192 bar., which at 15s. a bar. comes to £144. Summa Totalis, £281 8s., of all which we desire present satisfaction. (*Pinkerton MSS.*)

CHARLES THE FIRST.

Monroe in Belfast, 1644.

BY W. PINKERTON, F.S.A.

ONROE, on the 27th of April, 1644, received a commission from the English Parliament to be commander-in-chief of all the English and Scotch forces in Ulster. Sir James Montgomery, having notice of this commission, sent to desire the rest of the British Colonels to meet him at Belfast to consider of an unanimous answer to be given to Monroe when he would assume their command. On Monday, May 13, the officers met, including Sir James himself, Lord Montgomery, Lord Blaney, Colonel Hill, Major Rawdon, Sir Theophilus Jones, Major Gore, and Colonel Chichester, who commanded Belfast. They met in the evening, and adjourning their consultation to the next morning, had retired to their lodgings, when a soldier of Colonel Chichester's regiment, coming from Carrickfergus, brought advices that Monroe had given orders for the garrison of that place, Colonel Home's, and other Scotch regiments to be ready to march at two of the clock the next morning towards Belfast. The guards hereupon were strengthened, and every officer, as well those of the field as others, ordered upon duty. This being done, some horses were sent as scouts to make discoveries, who, returning at six in the morning,

VIEW OF BELFAST FROM RITCHIE'S DOCK, 1805.

(From a water-colour drawing by D. Stewart, in possession of E. H. Clarke, Esq.)

positively affirmed that they had been within three miles of Carrickfergus, and that the whole country was clear, without a man to be seen.
Upon this advice the guards were all discharged except the ordinary
watch, and the officers, who had been up all night upon duty, retired
to their rest. About an hour after, Monroe was descried within half-
a-mile of the town, advancing with great speed towards one of the
gates, which, before the drums could beat and the garrison be drawn
together to make opposition, was opened to him by a sergeant of
Captain MacAdam's and the soldiers of the guard, so that he
marched orderly through the place till he came to the opposite
or south gate leading to Lisnagarvey, and then directed his men in
several parties to possess themselves of the bulwark, cannon, and
guards. Colonel Chichester prevailed with the other Colonels to
repair to Monroe, and ask what he meant by surprising the town. He
replied that as Colonel Chichester had published a proclamation
against the Covenant, by which such as had taken it conceived themselves to be declared traitors, discountenanced his officers and the
townsmen who offered to take it, and had formerly refused some of
the Scotch to garrison there, he did not think himself safe without
having a garrison of his own in the place ; and so ordered Colonel
Chichester's men to depart, except such as he would leave as a guard
to his house. Thus was Belfast lost by the treachery of the scouts, who,
meeting Monroe, had been ordered by him to return and carry that
false intelligence of there being no forces to be seen in the country.

The treacherous action of Monroe overawed the British Colonels,
and induced them, without much further hesitation, to place themselves under his command, and co-operate with him in opposing the
Irish. But the act of hostility was reported at once to the English
Parliament, who required an explanation from the Committee of
Scotch Estates in Edinburgh, and they returned by the Scotch Commissioners at London the following account of the proceeding,
probably as delivered to them by Monroe :—

> According to the direction of the Committee of Estates of the Kingdom
> of Scotland, we do return this answer following to the desire of the honble.
> Houses of Parliament concerning the surrender of Belfast.
> That Col. A. Chichester, contrary to the declaration of both houses
> 1 November, 1643, did agree to the Cessation made with the Irish.
> That upon his agreement to the Cessation £3,000 sterling was promised
> to him out of the Cessation money, whereof he received £500 sterlg.
> That he kept constant correspondence with the Lord of Ormond by letters
> and other ways after the Cessation.
> That he conveyed Adjutant Stuart and Col. Seyton, then come from the
> King's army in England, from Belfast to Dublin, there to negotiate with the
> rebells.
> That upon orders from the Lord of Ormond he caused proclaim all those
> that joined with the Covenant traitors and rebels, and administered an oath to
> his Regiment and Inhabitants for opposing the Covenant.
> That he cashiered all such as had taken the Covenant, or refused to take
> the oath against it.
> That from the time of the first landing of the Scottish Army in Ireland
> there was always a part of the Scottish forces quartered in Belfast until the
> 17th of March, 1644 ; that Col. Cambel's Regiment went into Scotland. And
> the said town was only a place for quarters, and not fortified till, after the

removal of the Scottish forces, Col. Chichester brought his Regiment and Troops which were quartered in the country into the town, and by order from the Earl of Ormond fortified the same, planted cannon on the works, and did begin to cut off the highway that enters Carrickfergus port. Whereupon Gen.-Major Monroe, being advertised on the 12th of May, 1644, that the Earl of Ormond and Council in Dublin had resolved to convey 1,500 men into Belfast for the further strengthening of that garrison, did, upon the 14th of May, in the morning, surprise the forces under command of Col. Chichester, and possessed himself of the town of Belfast before they could be in readiness to make opposition. Whereupon the said Col. Chichester went to Dublin, and his forces to the rebels, and the Lord of Ormond and Council, then finding themselves disappointed in their designs, wrote a letter to Major-General Monroe within three days after the town was taken, requiring him to restore to Col. Chichester the said town of Belfast, with all the ordnance, arms, ammunition, &c., as may appear by the said letter herewith presented. Now, forasmuch as the said Col. Chichester and his Regiment had agreed to the Cessation, and joined with the Rebells in their Councils and actions, and so continued in avowed opposition and open rebellion against the parliament of England for the space of six months after the declaration of the honble. houses, the Commander-in-Chief of the Scottish army was obliged by his commission and instructions to endeavour the reducing of that garrison, and having recovered the same out of the hands of the rebels, the said town or garrison of Belfast ought to be at the disposal of the commanders thereof during their abode for that service in those parts, where such towns and places are, according to the tenth article of the treaty between the Kingdoms of the sixth of August, 1642, especially since it is so necessary for quartering of the Scottish forces there, who otherwise are not able to subsist, no care being taken for their entertainment.

And as the said garrison, since it was in the power of the Scottish army, hath always been patient to any having authority from the honble. houses for magazine and other uses, so shall it be for the future on all occasions.

It will be observed how the Scottish Commissioners term this treacherous surprisal "the surrender of Belfast;" nor is the rest of their communication distinguished by greater truth. It was not until a year after the rebellion broke out that Scotch troops were quartered in Belfast. A part of Colonel Campbel's regiment were the first of them quartered in that town, about seven months after the Scotch army had arrived in Ireland. Adjutant Stuart and Colonel Seaton were allowed to pass through the Scotch army, as well as the regiment of Colonel Chichester. And the Commissioners of the Parliament, writing from Belfast on the 16th December, 1646, to the Estates of Scotland, further state—

That there never was any oath administered by Colonel Chichester either to his regiment or the inhabitants for opposing of the Covenant, and though divers of his regiment had formerly taken the Covenant, he never cashiered any for so doing, nor was any oath against it proposed, neither did any quit his regiment upon the publication of the proclamation issued by the Earl of Ormond against the Covenant, save one, Lieut. McAdam, who took occasion thereupon to repair into Scotland, though he was earnestly desired by Colonel Chichester to stay, and was promised a company for so doing.

And though we take not on us to excuse or extenuate any of the miscarriages of Colonel Chichester, yet as any thing is suggested to fortify the reason of detaining this town (so properly and entirely belonging to the disposal of the Parliamt. of England) we conceive it our parts to endeavour the rectifying of any mistake in that kind, and rest assured that whatever consequence is drawn from the reports of Col. Chichester agreeing to the Cessation with the Irish rebels, contrary to the Declaration of the Parliamt. of England, is so fully known to be ill-grounded, that nothing is more manifest than that his regiment was one of those that were before Charlemont, when the news of the Cessation came to that Army, that they continued with the longest that time in the field, and that he sent on all occasions after that time part of his Regiment with the other forces when they went abroad, partaking also in the dividend of the cattle gotten from the rebel, as others did that attended that service. And all this was constantly done after the Cessation, and untill the town was possessed by Major-General Monro, Col. Chichester being then only permitted to stay in the Castle with one hundred of his regiment, and the rest of them at that time designed quarters in the parts near the town. And truly though Col. Chichester had submitted to the Cessation contrary to the directions of Parliament, yet why he should be therefore conceived as one that is in the condition of an Irish rebel, and so to bring the place taken from him within compass of the 10th article of the treaty of the 6th of Aug., 1642, we understand not. And certainly his fault at the time of taking this town from him, either was not apprehended so heinous, as some do since call it, or the indulgence great which was used towards him in permitting him to abide in the Castle with one hundred of his men, in quartering the rest of his regimt. near Belfast, and suffering him to dispose of his stock without contradiction. And when he would remove, in allowing him to depart hence to Dublin avowedly when he made no such condition for himself, but was at the pleasure of those that had both him and the town in their possession. We cannot but observe that this gentleness was more by many degrees than is usually afforded to rebels ; or otherwise, that his offence at that time was not such as to be a sufficient ground or colour for taking, much less for keeping, the town, and making such conclusions as are now drawn from thence.

LIBRARY, TRINITY COLLEGE, DUBLIN.

And the Commissioners conclude their paper by excusing Col. Chichester, saying that if he did go to Dublin and join with Ormond, that it ought to be considered how that his own town was wrested from him, and how badly and treacherously he had been treated.

There was, however, a Captain John MacAdam in Colonel Chichester's regiment, and his description of the capture of Belfast, as given on oath on the 14th June, 1644, is preserved in the Library of Trinity College, Dublin. It is entitled—

THE examination of Captain John MacAdam, aged about 28 years or thereabouts, taken before the Right Honourable James, Earl of Roscommon, and Sir James Ware, Knt., &c., upon oath ministered by the Clerk of the Council the 14 day of June, 1644.

The said Captn. John MacAdam being duly sworn and examined sayeth, that in the month of May last the foot company then commanded by the

examinant in Col. Arthur Chichester's regiment, being then quartered at
Stranmilles, within less than a mile of Belfast, and the examinant having
necessary occasion to repair to Belfast, left the charge of his company with one of
his sergeants, James [illegible], and he, the examinant, went to Belfast, where he
lodged that night. And he sayeth that early the next morning, one John Plunket,
a gentleman, then of the examinant's foot company, came to the examinant's
chamber and told him that the foot company were broken, and that many of them
that were Covenanters had, by order of Major-General Monro, marched that morning from Stranmilles to Belfast, with drums and colours flying, and that by like
orders from Major-General Monro they had that morning torn in pieces their
colours in the Market Place of Belfast. Whereupon the examinant, his chamber
window looking into the Market Place, ran immediately to his chamber window, and,
looking out and seeing one Captn. Kennedy, Captain of the Watch, in the Market
Place, the examinant called to the said Captn. Kennedy, and taking notice to him
of the mutinous and disordered carriage of the examinant's said company, desired
the said Captn. Kennedy to stay there until the examinant could get ready and go

THE COVENANTERS TEARING THEIR COLOURS, BELFAST, 1644.

to him. Whereupon the said Captn. Kennedy answered that it was to no purpose,
and that he would not do it, for that the said company had done so by order of
Major-General Monro, and that he, the same Captn. Kennedy, had seen and read
the said order under the hand of Major-General Monro, whereby it was appointed
that the said company should march with colours and drums as they did to Belfast,
and there openly in the Market Place to tear the colours of the examinant as
Captn. of the said company in Colonel Chichester's regiment. And that done, to
march immediately with the said company to Carrickfergus; and, as the said
Captn. Kennedy then told the examinant, there was in the said order, signed by
Major-Genl. Monro, a clause requiring Colonel Home, who commanded the
garrison at Belfast, to be aiding and assistant to the operation of the said order.

Monroe immediately after made a similar attempt to capture the
town of Lisnegarvy; but finding that garrison on its guard, he
demanded a conference with Lieut.-Colonel Jones, then commanding

there. Being firmly refused admittance except by main force, he first blustered about his authority from England, then threatened to seize all their cattle; but at last, cooling down, he satirically wished the garrison joy of their determination, and marched back to Belfast.

On the fifteenth of August, 1646, Mr. Tobias Norrice was appointed, by the Committee, Comissary at Belfast, and directed to proceed to Chester with all speed, take possession of the arms and stores there, and ship them to Belfast. His instructions from the Committee say that he is—

> To receive all arms, ammunition, clothes, and victuals which shall be sent out of this Kingdom for relief of the British Army in Ulster, and consigned to you, or otherwise brought to the stores there; and to lay up, preserve, and keep the same in safe storehouses and in good condition for the use of the said Army. To issue out and deliver such arms, &c., to such persons and in such quantities as the Commissioners of Parliament in the Province of Ulster may direct.

The Commissioners for Ireland write to the Committee at Derby House, from Dublin, on the 23rd of November, stating that the Earl of Ormond had positively refused to treat on their terms, and that they would now send on the ships, with a quorum of the Commissioners, viz.:—Sir Robert King, Sir John Clotworthy, and Robert Meredith, to Belfast, in charge of the forces, with £3,500, part of the £5,000 with which they had been entrusted for the public service. They also write to Holyhead and Chester, ordering the troops there to be sent on to Belfast instead of Dublin.

The Commissioners arrived in Belfast Lough in the latter end of November, and landed part of their men at Groomsport, part on the Antrim side, and some, at first, they left on ship-board; for the Scotch absolutely refused to allow a man of the English army to enter Belfast, but they did not dare to refuse entrance to the Commissioners. On the first of December they write to Major-General Monroe, then commanding at Carrickfergus, of their arrival after a very severe and stormy passage, detail the sufferings of their men in the open fields, and demand quarters for them in Belfast. Monroe, writing back the same day, says:—

> Touching quartering at Belfast, if you have an order from the Committee of both Kingdoms for that effect to the commander-in-chief of that garrison, I do not doubt but it will be readily obeyed by him, who must answer for his deportment to the General of the Army, the Earl of Leven, if otherwise that be wanting. I believe the Colonel will be loath to part with his garrison till such time as he know of his Excellency's pleasure. For my part, be pleased to know that my command over Col. Home's garrison cannot reach so far as to put him from it, unless I were acquainted with the General's pleasure, being more than I would answer for on my life and credit.

The Commissioners again write to Monroe, stating that their want of horses alone prevents them from waiting on him in person, and telling him how unsatisfactory it must be for Parliament if the forces which they have sent hither should perish with cold for want of harbour in any town, being kept from the same by persons serving in the same cause.

Monroe replies that he is exceedingly sorry for the hardships of the troops; but "touching Belfast," he adds, " I protest to God I cannot vary from what I have already declared without an express command from the Earl of Leven, General to the Scotch Army in Ireland, for it being contrary to the treaty that we should mix in quartering (if any inconvenience should happen thereby, as the Lord forbid), the General would call me to an account for the same, as he may do if I consent to give up any of our garrisons without his knowledge. I intreat you to rest satisfied, and not press me beyond my power." He thinks, however, that the Commissioners may accommodate the soldiers with such shelter as the poor country can afford among the British regiments; and adds that dispute and controversy will not fail to break out and ensue if the forces are mixed with the Scotch regiments, who will not willingly part with their quarters.

The Commissioners then, finding that they can do nothing with Monroe, write to Col. Home, forwarding the letter by their own secretary, as follows :—

At Belfast, 7th December, 1646.

We, the Commissioners sent from the Parliament of England, according to our Commission of the 16th of November, being commanded to direct the forces to Belfast, and having upon our arrival acquainted Major-General Monro with their being come to quarters in this place, that so the Parliamt. might receive satisfaction, and their forces convenient shelter and accommodation necessary for the preservation of their lives in this winter season, and finding the answer returned to us in his letters unsatisfactory, withall importing that his command over you in this place could not reach so far as to put you from the same, We do therefore, by this, desire to know from you by whose authority you have garrisoned this town, and that we may see what order you have for keeping the same, and know your positive resolution whether or no you will allow the forces directed hither by the Parliament, and now landed, to be garrisoned in this town of Belfast, according to the directions of the Parliament of England. To which we desire your present answer in writing signed by you.

On the 9th of December Col. Home replies to the Commissioners, humbly craving their patience, and stating that he is but a servant of the public sent hither by commission from his Majesty and the Commissioners of both Kingdoms, and concludes thus :—" So being entrusted with the keeping of the place, I cannot take upon me to garrison any forces therein until I acquaint the State of Scotland, the which I shall do with all possible diligence."

The Commissioners then draw up a _resumé_ of the whole proceedings respecting the surprisal of Belfast, and send it express by Lt.-Col. Conelly to the Parliament and Estates of Scotland and the Earl of Leven, Lord General of the Scotch Army. Connelly is instructed to explain anything that might be required of him, and ordered to stop no longer in Scotland than six days.

The Commissioners had landed three companies of Lord Foliot's regiment, which they wished to march at once to Londonderry. Having obtained promises of aid and assistance from Monroe during their march wherever Scotch troops were quartered, the three companies, under command of a Lieut.-Col. Welton, set out on the 9th of December. Besides their letters of public import, the Commissioners send private letters by Lt.-Col. Welton, introducing him to Thornton, Mayor of Derry, as a gentleman in whom they have every confidence. But on the 16th of the same month they write again to Thornton, ordering him immediately to make Lt.-Col. Welton, Capt. Cook, Gabriel Leake, and an Elizabeth Hutchin prisoners, and to send them to Belfast. They were also to procure testimony of Col. Welton being married to Elizabeth Hutchin, or what else they can discover touching his familiarity on the occasion of his bringing her into Ireland, which, he being already married in London, is a great scandal to the professors of religion.

ANCIENT SEAL OF LONDONDERRY.

Hook, Leake, and Hutchin receive passes to go to England on the 1 of January, 1647, but Lt.-Col. Welton is still retained in prison, and on the 8th a widow More and her servants at Bangor are examined as a fresh evidence against him.

The Scotch being determined not to let the English troops into Belfast, offered to surrender their quarters in Lecale, then held by a Col. Hamilton, and the Commissioners were obliged to accept the offer, agreeing to pay in victuals £25 per month to Col. Hamilton, being the money he received from the quarters ; and to pay for hay, straw, corn, repairs of houses, huts, and to the Scotch regiment as Bernard Ward, John Echlin, and A. Stainton might appoint, Col. Home engaging to respect and give the English constant communication with their storehouses in Belfast. And on the 20th orders were sent to the English troops to march to and take possession of Lecale, and quarter themselves there in the most advantageous manner that they can.

The Commissioners write off to Chester for spade shovels, pick-axes, and other intrenching tools for Lecale, and ask Monroe for some that he had been supplied with ; but he states that after the battle of Benburb there was such a mania for making intrenchments that all his tools were used up, and that, besides, they were very bad. They also order the ship *Rebecca* to take round some iron guns to Strangford, and to cruise off that place for the future, so that she may be in constant communication with the forces at Lecale.

On the 31 of Decr. they also write a polite letter to Lady Claneboy at Killileagh, requesting that his Lordship's troop would give up Dundrum Castle, as it was necessary for the security of the quarters in Lecale that it should be held by the English.

On the 8 of January an answer was received from the Scotch Estates. It had been delivered to Col. Connelly on the last day of December, but he did not arrive in Belfast till ten o'clock on the night of the eighth. They say that as their Commissioners are now at London treating for the surrender of Belfast, they cannot stultify them by giving up the town now; but they have written to Monro to quarter his army as closely as possible for the accommodation of the English forces, and to allow them the use of houses in the town for stores and magazines.

On the same day they gave an authority to Lieut.-Col. John Hewetson to take possession of the manor or lordship of Newcastle, in the County of Down, lately belonging to Sir Connor Magenis, now in actual rebellion, and to hold it *in custodiam* under the parliament of England, paying £4 yearly for the same, and all the usual assessments and taxes. (*Pinkerton MSS.*)

The Parliament and Belfast, 1645.

SIR ROBT. KING, ONE OF THE COMMISSIONERS OF ULSTER, PRESENTED THIS PAPER TO THE COMMITTEE FROM THE REST OF THE COMMISSIONERS, PRESENTED TO THEM, 6TH NOVEMBER, 1645.

In the beginning of the Rebellion, Sir James Montgomery quartered himself and regiment with his troop in Lecale, which was able to have entertained two regiments if it had been well governed. But the said Sir James, not minding the manage of the work, procured secretly quarters upon my lord Claneboy's lands, and made the country believe that there was such necessity of his regiment in the Ardes, and other places thereabouts, and that my Lord of Ards had written for him and his regiment, who did so indeed, but by the said Sir James' procurement, which will appear by the testimony of Capt. Maxwell if you call him to it, and so left Lecale to the benefit of the rebels and the out-running of the inhabitants. The said Sir James thereafter went to Parliament for arrears to his regiment, but what he received for his regiment he converted to his own use, save only clothes, who, when he returned home, the army being upon the field, who both had done good service, and was going on the same, he so devised and withdrew my Lord Montgomery and Sir William Stewart, and Sir Robert Stuart and others of the Colonels, from the service, and went to Dublin and joined in a Cessation with the rebels, and at his return commanded his regiment to join in the same, who refused and would not adhere to him, notwithstanding of many threatening, and not long after some of his Captains being in Downpatrick perceived a stranger, and asked what was his name, from whence he came, who would not give any perfect answer, and they hearing that he spent much and appeared to be a suspected person, did take him, and brought him to Portaferry, and there Sir James conferred with him secretly, and when he was commanded with a keeper, Sir James desired to let him go; but they refused and sent him to the General Major, who could have no evidence against him, but afterwards Sir James being with his Lieut. Col. and others of his officers, told them that his name was M'Donnell, and that he was carrying a commission from the King and the rebels to Montrose for the setting of the bloody wars afoot in Scotland, and said he knew who carried the Commission over. This you may have upon the testimony of Capt. Maxwell, and Capt. Wachop and others of the Captains, viz., Major Keeth and Capt. Wachop, by also about the time the Covenant was sworn in Ireland.

Belfast Trade, &c., 1646=48.

The Committee, on the 6th of August, 1646, license one Thomas Limburner to export to Carrickfergus, free of duty, cloth, serge, stockings, whalebone, bodices, silk, ribbons, black & coloured hats, hoods, buttons, points, haberdasher's ware, to the value of £300 or thereabouts, to be sold for the use of the army & the poor inhabitants in that wasted country.

On the 17th of September they also license John Stewart & Archibald Moor, merchants of Belfast, to import from Liverpool, free of duty, several trunks of haberdashery ware, with silks, buttons, & trimmings for suits of clothes; two fardels containing hardwares,

skins, & pasteboard; 8 bags of hops, one box of drugs, one runlet of oil, 1 cwt of cotton for candle-wicks, 12 hats, and 4 dozen pound of whalebone; two fardels of wool cards, 16 ells of hollands, & six pieces of buckram, for the use of the army and the poor inhabitants in that wasted country.

On the same day they also license one James Maxwell to transport from Liverpool, to Carrickfergus, Belfast, or Bangor, duty free, 25 bags of hops, 8 pieces of cloth, 12 pieces of stuff, & £30 worth of haberdashery ware for trimming suits of clothes for the use of the army and the poor inhabitants of that wasted country.

INSTRUCTIONS TO MR. NORRIS, COMMISSARY AT BELFAST, TO PROCEED TO WEST CHESTER WITH ALL HASTE, AND TAKE POSSESSION OF THE ARMS, &C., AND SHIP THEM TO BELFAST. *15 August, 1646.*

You are to receive all arms, ammunition, clothes, and victuals which shall be sent out of this Kingdom for relief of the British Army in Ulster and consigned unto you, or shall otherwise be brought to the Stores there, and you are to lay up, preserve, and keep the same in safe store houses and in good condition for the use of the said Army. And you are to return certificates from time to time unto such Commissaries or other persons as shall consign such arms, ammunition, clothes, victual, or other provisions unto you with the contents and conditions in which you received them. And you are to send duplicates of such your certificates to this Committee, that a true account may be kept of what is applied to the Army, by whom, and in what manner.

You are to issue out and deliver such arms, ammunition, clothes, victual, and other provisions as shall come within your charge and custody, unto such persons and in such quantities and proportions for the use of the Army or any particular regiments, companies, troops, officers, or soldiers thereof as the Commissioners of Parliament now residing in the Province of Ulster, or any two of them, shall by their warrants direct during their residence as Commissioners in those parts, or as you shall receive further directions from the Lord Lieutenant of Ireland, or any other appointed by the Parliament of England to have the government of the military affairs in that Province.

You are to observe and follow all other instructions and directions which shall be given you by this Committee for the well managing of the trust reposed in you and discharge thereof. And to give such advertisements from time to time of the state of the stores under your charge as may be for the providing of new supplies when occasion shall require in the particulars that shall be requisite.

Signed by Sir Jo. Temple, Sir J. Clotworthy, Sir Greg. Norton, Sir Walter Earl.

A CONFIRMAT. OF A DIVISION BY THE COMMITTEE'S ORDERS OF 23 JULY LAST.

The proportion of arms and clothes sent to Ulster are to be distributed amongst the 10 Regiments of foot and 17 troops of horse of the British Army. *19th October, 1646.*

To each regiment.		To each regiment.	
Matchlock musquets ...	240	Barrels of powder ...	10
Firelock musquets ...	60	To each troop.	
Pikes	120	Barrels of pistol powder	2
Swords and belts ...	240	To each regiment.	
To each troop.		Tons of match	2
Pair of pistols with holster	17	To each troop	1
Saddles and furniture ...	14	To each regiment.	
Swords and belts ...	29	1 ton of musket bullets.	
		To each troop, 111 lb. wt. pistol bullets.	

F

Beside the above division by equal proportions, there were distributed among the 4 regiments of foot that were at Benburb—

Ld. Ards' reg. of foot, Ld. Claneboy's, Col. Conway's, and Sir James Montgomery.

Matchlock musquets	...	...	200	Pikes	...	...	100
Firelocks	...	...	50	Swords and belts	...	...	200

The 10 foot regiments are :—

Ld. of Ards.	Sir Wm. Stuart.
Claneboy's.	Sir R. Stuart.
Col. Conway	Ld. Foliot.
Sir J. Mongomery.	Col. Mervyn.
Sir J. Clotworthy.	Sir Wm. Cole's.

17 troops are :—

Col. Hill's reg. consisting of 5 troops.	Sir W. Cole's.
Col. Conway's troop.	Sir R. Adare's.
Ld. Ards' troop.	Sir R. Stuart's.
Claneboy's.	Sir W. Stuart's.
Sir J. Montgomery.	Cap. Geo. Montgomery's.
Sir J. Clotworthy's.	Cap. Dudly Phillips'
Capt. Clotworthy's.	

The provisions to be delivered to the forces by the Commissioner at Belfast as they shall think best for the service, having regard to the necessity of the place where quartered and preservation of the country.

Tons of Salt,   33½.
Bows of Meal, 6,666⅔.
Suits of Clothes, 4,615.

19th October, 1646.

Agreed and divided by Will Cole, Ja. Trayle, Arthur Hill, and Geo. Rawdon ; Ja. Claneboy, Ro. Hannay, Robt. King, Gentlemen of Ulster.

ORDER FOR MR. NORRIS, COMMISSIONER, TO RECEIVE.

By the Commissioners' Government of Ulster, the Customs of several ports in Ulster to defray public charges.

"These are to authorise you to receive the customs of the several ports of Carrickfergus, Belfast (not as yet disposed of by us), Bangor, Donaghadee, and Strangford, together with what they are in arrears at Michaelmas last, to empower your occasions about the public stores and to continue the receiving of the same until you shall have further order to the contrary, keeping a just account thereof in writing, that you may be answerable for the same to those the Parliament shall intrust ; and the officers of the customs of the said ports are hereby required to pay the same unto you every quarter as they were accustomed, of which they may not fail at their perils. And for so doing this shall be your warrant. Given at Belfast, *23 of October 1646.*   "ARTHUR ANNESLEY.
"To Tobias Norris, Gent., William Beale."

By the Commissioners for Ireland.

"Whereas the Commissioners formerly in this Province had given power to Mr. Tobias Norris for receiving the customs of the several ports abovementioned for the use of the public service intrusted with him, commanding the officers of the said customs to make payment every quarter unto him, We do hereby confirm the same, and do strictly require the said officers to make due payment thereof accordingly as they will answer the contrary at their perils. Given at Belfast, *30 Decr., 1646.*

"ROB. MEREDITH, ROBT. KING, JNO. CLOTWORTHY."

James Maxwell, of Carrickfergus, *May, 1647*,
Had license to embark from the ports of Chester or Liverpool to Belfast or Carrickfergus for the use of the Army there, Twelve pieces of cloth, thirty pieces of stuff with haberdasher's ware fitting for trimmings, Twenty dozen of scythes, three score dozen of sickles, one barrel of nails, and twenty bags of hops, custom free.

John Clugston, merchant, had license to export to Belfast, Twelve bags of hops, Two packs of broad cloth, Two packs of stuff, Two packs of small ware, 10 Dozen of hats, and a bundle of bridle reins, to the value of £300.

Patrick Smith, 6 bags of hops, one fardel of stuffs, one fardel of bridles and other furniture for horses, one fardel of small ware as haberdasher's ware, two dozen of hats, one box with combs, and a small cask of tobacco, in the ship the Jonas of Kirkaldy.

Gilbert Eccles, from London to Carrickfergus, 1648, four packs of clothes and stuffs containing also buttons, silk, buckram, bays, taffeta, hollands, stockings, laces, paper, pasteboard, gloves, four barrells raisins and glasses, Ten bags hops, six boxes of tobacco pipes, a small cask of cards for wool, two chests with glasses, two hampers of hats, and some Crooked lane ware, six doz. of scythes, two packs of sickles, two barrells of rice, and a bundle, of value of £300 or thereabouts.

GEORGE BOOTH'S REMONSTRANCE ABOUT THE WANT OF CARTS FOR THE ARMY IN 1647.

I am given to understand that there is provision of carts made to come over here. God grant they prove, not useless here when they come, for I fear they will prove too heavy of themselves without any load for our small garrons. My Ld. of Strafford sent some store of them over here, but we could never make use of them, but of the irons of them. Therefore, except there be good strong draught horses or oxen provided for them, & skilful men to drive, they will be endangered to be lost with the provisions in them.

FIRST ESTABLISHMENT OF A POST TO SCOTLAND AND ENGLAND, 1648.

The sending of forces from Scotland created a new & increased intercourse with Ireland & the exigencies of the rebellion demanding a quick & continual means of intelligence, led to the establishment of a post between the north of Ireland, Edinburgh, & London. England being more interested in the matter than Scotland agreed to bear all the extra expense, & the English Parliament and Scotch Commissioners concluded to make Carlisle the starting-point from the English side. From Carlisle the route and postmasters were—Annan, twelve miles, Mark Lock ; Dumfries, twelve miles, Robert Glencorse ; Steps of Or, twelve miles, Andrew M'Min ; Gatehouse of Fleet, twelve miles, Ninian Mure ; Pesthouse, eleven miles, George Bell ; Kirk of Glenluce, thirteen miles, John Baillie ; & from thence to Portpatrick, ten miles, John M'Caig. The persons named were considered the only ones fit for the employment "as being inn-keepers and of approved honesty in those parts." Every thing being ready, on the 27th September, 1648, the English Parliament was called upon to ratify the arrangements & supply "John McCaig, postmaster in Portpatrick," with a post boat, and the demand was at once complied with. The intermediate stations between Portpatrick and Edinburgh were Ballantrae, Drumbeg, Ayr, Kilmarnock, Glasgow, Kilsyth, Linlithgow.

THE COMMITTEE AT DERBY HOUSE.

"To Colonel Monk,

"We have formerly written you concerning Belfast, which the Scots ought not to have had at all. And we again desire you to use all the means in your power to put the sd. town of Belfast in the possession of the Parlmt. of England, and you will take care that none land in Ireland out of Scotland, or any of those that are in England in arms against the Comonwealth may come over hither. We have written to Capt. Clark to ply up and down the coast to prevent them. *29 Aug., 1648.*"

They write on 5 Septr.—Heard of the overthrow given to the Duke of Hamilton, want to know what Scotch regiments in Ireland were concerned with it. Monk to inspect and inquire.

To Col. Monk,—They have not a cypher; have written of the whole affair to Col. Jones; please give him a meeting, and consult on the matter together. *22 Septr., 1648.*

Col. Monk appointed Governor of Carrickfergus; great praise for taking the towns from the Scots, 4 October, 1648; beg of him to recommend a fit person to be governor of Belfast, and return us your opinion by the first opportunity.

Write to Coot and Monk stating that many under them in the service of the Parliament had treacherously invaded England under Hamilton, to be careful casting officers. "We shall only add this caution, that in the exertion of his power you will be careful to do it so that when you attempt it you may be able to carry it through without afront."

Some advantage might be made by giving the Irish protection to sow and plow within his quarters. *18 Novr., 1648.*

THE WEEKLY CONVEYANCE OF LETTERS FROM IRELAND, 1648.

On every Monday, precisely at noon, a post shall go hence from Dublin, to be at Groomesport on Thursday, where the passage shall be always ready, the wind serving, to depart with the morning's tide, to be at Edinburgh by Monday noon following, which shall be the time of departure of the post from thence for London by way of York, and precisely to be at London on Saturday at night. And from London back again on the same days. To wit—on Monday at noon from London by York, to be at Edinburgh on the Saturday evening. And on Monday noon from Edinburgh to Dublin, if the weather hinder not, before the next Monday following.

The deliverer of the letter or letters in Dublin payeth nothing, but the receiver in England or Scotland is to pay nine pence per letter, or two shillings and sixpence per ounce if packets.

The deliverer of the letter or letters in England or Scotland is to pay three pence per letter, and the receiver in Ireland sixpence. And if packets, proportionably ⅓ of two shillings and sixpence an ounce in England and Scotland, and the rest in Ireland by the receiver.

Four posts or messengers shall be appointed to go betwixt Dublin and Edinburgh on foot and horse as they can conveniently, and from Edinburgh to London by the ordinary way of the post night and day.

Mr. Friswell's propositions for the settlement of the weekly conveyance
of letters to and from this Kingdom. (Pinkerton MSS.)

A Relation of several Services,

At the which I was present in the Wars of Ireland, from the year 1649 until
1653. By MAJOR MEREDITH.

ABOUT two days after the storming & taking of Drogheda in the year 1649, the Lord Lieut. sent Col. Chidley Coote, with his own & Lieut. General Jones's Regiment of Horse & Col. Castle's Regiment of Foot, to possess Dundalk. Those Regiments, having marched all night, arrived at Dundalk the next morning, which they found the enemy had newly quitted, so that, without farther trouble, there was left there as Governor Col. Ponsonby [the Major to Col. Coote] with his troop & some few foot, and the Regiments, both Horse and Foot, marched immediately that day back to the Camp, which was then in the fields near Drogheda. About a day or two after, the same party, together with Col. Venables' Regiment of Foot & two troops of Dragoons, were sent under the command of Col. Venables to reduce some part of the North, and for that purpose guns for battering, & victuals, were sent to attend him by sea in a Man of War. The first place they marched to was Carlingford, and the same day the party came thither the ships came into the Harbour, and passed the Fort, which lies in the mouth of it, without any prejudice, though they made several shots at her as she passed. That night we encamped on the South side of the town in fields near adjoining, & the ship cast anchor near the Castle. The next day preparations were made to land our Guns, & to raise a battery, in order to which guards were placed near the Castle; but before we either landed Guns, or made our battery, the enemy came to a parley, and the Castle was surrendered unto us on Articles.

ST. LAWRENCE'S GATE, DROGHEDA.

The next day after the surrender of Carlingford, Col. Venables took Lieut. General Jones's Regiment of Horse, and marched by the water-side under the mountains unto the Newry, to summons that place. We passed the River at a Ford about a mile below the Newry; the remainder of the party were left with Col. Coote to come the other side of the Mountains with the carriages, the way we marched not being passable for carriages. The same evening, we came to the Newry and faced it, the Governor came out and treated, & so we concluded that the Horse were admitted into the town, and marched through it to pass the bridge, to quarters on the other side of the water where was most conveniency, & the next day the Castle was surrendered on Articles.

We rested at the Newry till the rest of the party came up, which was three days after, in which time there came a Cornet, & two or three more from Lisnegarvie, who assured us that if we could advance we should have that place surrendered unto us. Upon which invitation, by advice of the officers, we advanced from the Newry, having left an Ensign & some few men in the Castle. The first night we lay

at Dromore, sixteen miles from the Newry, and encamped in a field
South-west of the said town, by the highway side, well enclosed with
hedges, not having any intelligence of any enemy being near us.   But
about three hours after we were encamped, there came advertisement
from Dundalk that Col. Trevor was attending us with a considerable
party of Horse, and resolved to fall on us before we got to the Newry.
Upon which intelligence, orders were sent that the Horse should draw

CROMWELL IN IRELAND.

into the Foot quarters, which was a field on the outside of which the
Horse lay; but the orders being cursorily given, & no alarum general
in the Camp, there was but little notice taken of them.   For I cannot
tell, whether through the negligence of him that carried the orders, or
those that gave them, but certain truth it is that they were never
known to half the Horse [& the Dragoons never heard of it at all],
which omission had like to have been our total ruin, & was the only
cause of the greater part of the loss we afterwards sustained.   The
enemy, according to the intelligence, having coasted us all that day

on the left hand, had by their scouts, which they kept on the tops of
the hills [whilst their party kept the bottoms], certain intelligence of
our motions, & were so confident [as I have since heard] that some
of them came into the outside of the quarter & viewed the order of
our quartering, & afterwards returned & gave an account of it to their
party. Upon which the enemy resolved to attempt our quarters,
which accordingly they did, an hour before day, the next morning, &
we having scouts abroad [the strength of our guard being in the
quarters] the enemy found no resistance, but followed the scouts into
the guard, who at once had received the alarum, & the enemy, they
pursuing the scouts so close that they came to the guard as soon as
the scouts. So that with very small or no dispute they routed the
guard & pursued them through the quarter, which so sudden rout of
the guard had the like influence on all the Camp, being in no order to
receive an enemy or defend themselves, judged of their own condition
by that of their fellows, and fell to a total rout. Which had never
been recovered, had it not pleased God that the situation of the place
was such, being surrounded with a very strong hedge on most parts,
& a bog behind it, that our men could not readily find how to get
away, the morning proving extraordinary dark, by which means
likewise it pleased the Lord that the enemy were not sensible of their
own advantage, but stood with the gross of their Horse, which was
about 400, on a hill near. They, judging by the small resistance
which they had heard made, that we had been totally routed by their
first party, & that those parties would keep us from rallying, that they
should have nothing to do when it was day but to pick up a scattered
party wholly strangers to the country. And this I know to have been
their opinion of us by the relation of some of their chief officers since.
But the same Providence that guided and guarded us, misguided
them. For the former party, who were ordered in case they got in to
the quarters to stay there & not pursue, but to keep us from rallying,
contrary to their orders followed the pursuit of the guard, & so left
us, though all dispersed, to recollect ourselves, & the day breaking, we
sooner were sensible of our own miscarriages than the enemy could
be, who were some distance from us, sounding levitts for joy of their
supposed victory. We, perceiving ourselves in great disorder, made
the greater haste to unite again. Very suddenly we had rallied about
40 or 50 horse, which being drawn up on a small rising ground which
was in the field, those that had before hid themselves in holes and
ditches immediately took up their arms again & repaired to us. And
before it was so light as the enemy could discern what we were, we
had rallied 4 or 5 more small bodies of Horse, & a handsome body of
400 Foot. And as if every one had been ashamed of what was before
done, there was no other voice among the soldiers but to redeem their
past miscarriage by presently fighting, which forwardness of theirs, I
confess, was a good argument to engage the enemy, & therefore
went to the Commander in Chief, & declared unto him the probability
of good success if we went out & fought, but I was answered he
would not engage but on the ground we stood, with which answer I

returned to my charge, & the soldiers still desiring very much an engagement, I went again to the Commander in Chief, and desired, at least, he would permit me to take a small party of Horse & advance towards the enemy, to search a tent of Major Villers, wherein there was a fortnight's pay for the Lieut. General's Regiment ; telling him besides it would be a countenance to some who lay hid between us & the enemy to repair to us.   Upon which I was permitted to take 40 or 50 Horse & advance towards the enemy, which I did, & was no sooner within half musket shot of them, where we drew up, but they immediately sent a good party to charge us.   But it pleased God to order that business so, that after a long and sharp dispute between these two parties only, that we routed them, & followed them so close that their main body took the rout likewise, so that that party, together with some more of the Lieut. General's Regiment, which came with Capt. Casack & Lieutenant Thomson, we had the pursuit of them unto the Bann water towards Newry, being 7 miles.   In the pursuit we recovered all our prisoners & two standards which they had taken of ours, killed many of them, & took many prisoners, among whom were two Captains of Horse & other inferior officers. The rest of the Horse were employed in the pursuit of one Major Chatfield, who was drawn up in the town with 100 Horse, & had prisoner with him Major Viller and Captain Usher, both of whom in the pursuit were recovered, & the officer that had the charge of them, a Cornet, came into us.   Thus it pleased the Lord to disperse that cloud which threatened us with so great a storm, with which undoubtedly we had been destroyed, had not God been our mighty helper & defender.

As soon as we returned from the pursuit, the party began their march unto Lisnegarvie, into which they were very welcomely received that night, the party quartering in the fields near to it.   And next day, with the addition of one troop of horse, which were of that country, & there joined with us under the command of Major Bruffe, we marched unto Belfast, & faced that place, which was within 3 or 4 days surrendered to us on Articles.   About ten days after the surrender of the town, Lieut. General Jones's Regiment marched back unto Dublin, & what afterwards was done in those parts Sir Theophilus Jones can best give you an account of, being there with his Regiment from a little while after we came away, until all action was finished in those parts.

(In a letter from Wm. Meredyth to Dr. Henry Jones giving an account of his services, June, 1656, Jones, it seems, being about to publish an account of the rebellion.) (*Pinkerton MSS.*)

ARMS OF NEWRY.

ATTACK ON THE NORTH GATE OF BELFAST BY COL. VENABLES, 1649.

SEAL OF THE COMMONWEALTH.

The Commonwealth and the North of Ireland.

CORRESPONDENCE WITH THE PRIVY COUNCIL, DUBLIN, &c., 1651–1660.

(Copied from MSS. Bermingham Tower, and Trinity College, Dublin, by W. Pinkerton.)

Letter from the Commissioners at Belfast to Lieut. Gen. Ludlow, 2 Aug., 1651.

" HONOURED SIRS,

"The Lord in mercy gives us every day new occasions to praise his name for his manifold appearances with his servants in their undertakings to carry on the great work he hath called them unto. The experiences thereof which you have been partakers of in your own person doth much rejoice us. It hath pleased God to open a way for our forces in Scotland to pass over the water into Fife. About 500 horse and foot of them went over about the 17th of July, and on the 20th engaged with Sir John Browne's Brigade, where, after a sharp encounter, the Lord gave the enemy a defeat, about 2,000 slain. Sir John Browne, their Major General, and many other commanders and 700 soldiers taken prisoners and 50 colours taken. The Lord endue us with a frame of spirit suitable to his doings towards us. Mr. Lour (?) is sentenced to lose his head, but reprieved by the Parliament upon the ministers' petition on his behalf till the 15th of this month. Some small disasters the Lord is pleased to mix with these great mercies to teach us to know where our strength lies. The *Hinde* frigate is cast away near Carrickfergus. Capt. Sherwine that commanded it and 52 of his men escaped and about 12 perished. We hope the guns and tackling will be recovered. Forty foot and ten horse in convoying bread to Capt. Venables were, at the Moyrie, between Dundalk and the Newry, this week cut off by the Tories which keep in the Fews. Truly, Sir, your company is much longed for by your servants."

Belfast, 2 August, 1651.

Venables was then in the field, 1,300 foot and 500 horse, with the intention to capturing the strong fort of Ballinecary in Cavan, and to settle some garrisons in the bowels of the enemy at Belturbet and other places.

SEAL OF BELTURBET.

A depot of provisions made for Venables at Trim, Dundalk being visited with the plague.

Privy Council, writing to Venables, Sept., 1651, say:—

"We have gotten a very good minister, lately come out of England, whom we have agreed to send unto your quarters about Lisnegarvy and Belfast ; his name is Mr. Weekes ; we do believe you will be pleased with him."

THE COUNCIL AT DUBLIN.

To Col. Venables, Col. Barrow, and Mr. Timothy Taylor.

"GENT.,

"We have sent Mr. Wyke, a minister of the Gospel and a man of meek spirit, so far as we can discern, to preach the Gospel in the North. To whom we desire you to give all due encouragement, so far as you find him useful in the work of the Gospel. And because there is a great scarcity of persons fitly qualified to be sent out to preach to the people, we desire you to countenance and encourage frequent Christian meetings both publickly and privately to confer with each other about Gospel duties, and to declare unto one another their experience of the Lord's love and gracious dealings to them, to exercise their gifts in prayers and exhortations for the refreshing and edifying one another in love and in knowledge of the Lord Jesus, avoiding vain and unnecessary questions and disputations which administer strife, that the Lord Jesus may thereby be glorified, his name be exalted, and the present defect of instruments in some measure supplied. All which we leave to your Christian consideration to practise as the Lord shall lead out your spirits. *4 October, 1651.*"

ARMS OF DUBLIN.

Dublin, 4 October, 1651.—County Antrim charged with a monthly assessment of £1,500 ; Down, £1,250. To maintain the army and forces there.

THE ASSESSMENT FOR ULSTER.

The whole Province of Ulster, with the County of Louth, excepting the Barony of Farran, assessed for a monthly tax of £5,430 in these proportions :—

Antrim	...	£1,500	County Louth	...	£330
Down	...	1,250	Londonderry	...	250
Donegal	...	700	Fermanagh	...	150
Armagh	...	350	Tyrone	...	100
Cavan	...	800	Monahan	...	200

for 6 months, counting 28 days to the month, on all persons in cities and country according to their estates, stocks, &c., all property ; defaults levyed off the whole barony.

11 Nov., 1651.—To Col. Hill on asking advice.

"We usually allow the wives and children of delinquents some part of the sequestrated estate, not exceeding a fifth part, provided that they be under protection, and that their portion be liable to contribution equally with others, and we leave it free with you to grant the same allowances where you shall find just and reasonable grounds for it. As for the particular persons you mention, whose necessitous conditions require the like relief, we are willing they and their families should be looked upon as capable thereof, whether they leave wives or not. But in all cases where sequestrations are actually made, the personal estates of delinquents as well as the real ought to be sequestrated. For Col. Conway's estate, we shall do him right on his petition, when he appears before us ; but in the meantime the sequestration of the Lord Conway's estate is to be prosecuted. As for those that plead particular articles for exemption from common charges and contributions (as Col. Trevor does), we desire you to examine them and certify as how you find them. As to the supplying of defects of contributions of wasted Counties out of Counties that are solvent, our meaning is very much misunderstood therein to our prejudice. The thing we had in our eye, and most immediately in our care, was the making of a certain provision for the forces, without which the British quarters cannot subsist, and not favouring the Irish ; which may easily appear by the power given to the Commissioners of the Revenue to assess and levy what is assessed upon the Irish quarters so far as the same can be levied. And we conceive that those defects of the Irish counties with the increase of the assessment will not amount to so much upon the British as the ease they have by taking off dry quarter and other irregular taxes. We pity the nakedness of the soldiers, but they have clothes coming over from England, as we are assured by Mr. Rowe's last letter, and yet in the meantime you shall do well to furnish them with shoes and stockings during their instant necessity, which must be defrayed by the excise or some other way. We have no more at present, but remain."

Dublin, 28 Oct., 1651.

The Council, writing to Col. Barrow, one of the Commissioners of Revenue at Belfast, say:—

"Since you yourself and Col. Venables are in the Commission with the rest, it will be much in your own power to see that the contributions be as well paid in Ulster as it is in other Provinces, and that the forces be in equal condition with others ; so that no discouragement ought to arise to you or the soldiers under your command in that respect. Col. Venables proposed to us the destroying and burning of that corn which the enemy in Cavan and other places have reserved for seed the next year, and he offers it as a fit means to distress and so force the enemy from his bogs and fastnesses. But indeed we dare not at this distance interpose our advice in matters of that nature, nor will we give any order in it. You best understand how feasible the business is, and how little hazard there will be wasting your men, or exposing your other quarters to the incursions of the enemy in attempting it, and therefore to your further deliberations we must leave it."

Dublin, 11 Nov., 1651.

In a letter to the Commissioners of Revenue at Belfast the Council say:—

"For the nameless superannuated Scotch minister you write of, who had £20 allowed him the last year, if the man be Godly, and you apprehend him a fit object of charity, it is left to you to allow him for this year what you shall conceive fitting."

9 Decr., 1651, Dublin.

Arms of Ulster.

17 Decr., 1651.   To Commissioners at Belfast on complaints of Colonels and want of forage.

"We think fit to let you know that Ulster must bear its own burthen, and if the forces there be more than you can pay, a fewer number must serve for the defence of that country and carrying on the publick service.

"E. LUDLOW.

"Miles Corbet.   Joseph Jones.   John Weaver."

Council of State write to Commissioners of Revenue at Belfast, 12 Feb., 1652.

"The Isle of Man being now in the obedience of the Parliament, and such parts of Scotland as are in possession of the Parliamentary forces, may be freely traded to in all lawful commodities ; but in regard of the present scarcity, no wheat or other sort of grain or victual must be exported.   To be careful of suspicious persons with defective passes from Scotland, but to have a special regard to preserve any articles made by any person in command for the service of the Commonwealth of England.   The capitulation made with Balcarras can scarcely extend to leave to come to Ireland."

To carry on the next summer's campaign in Ulster, there are required—

154	Tons Meal.
50	Tons Cheese.
4000	Complete suits, consisting of cassocks, breeches, shirts, shoes, and stockings.
400	Tents.
1000	Bibles.
100	Barrels of powder.
15	Tons of match.
5	Tons of bullets.
1000	Pikes.
200	Pistols.
300	Firelocks.
600	Muskets.
200	Carabines.
100	Hand Grenadoes.
100	Spades.
50	Shovels.
50	Pickaxes.
12	Iron Crows.
4	Iron Tunnes.
2	Ropes to mount ordnance.
600	Sacks.
200	Kettles.

The pay of the forces for Ulster was £700 per month, the revenue only bringing in £240 ; the balance of £460 was respited in the soldiers' pay, till Cavan, Monaghan, and Tyrone be reduced and brought under contribution.   In Ulster—Tyrone, Monaghan, Fermanagh, and Armagh wholly waste, yielding no contribution or profit.

"It is ordered that the Commissioners of Revenue in the Province of Ulster do take care that no Minister within the said Province, except such as have or shall take the Engagement enjoined by the Parliament, be permitted to enjoy the benefit of any tithes or of any ecclesiastical promotions or maintenance from the State."   *18 Aug., 1652.*

N.B.—The Engagement was simply—To be true and faithful to the Commonwealth of England, as the same is now established, without a King or a House of Lords.

4th Sep., 1652.

"We are creditably informed that one Cunningham, a minister at Broad Island, hath been observed to use a passage in his prayer to this effect—'Lord, wilt thou be pleased to give the whip into our hands again, and thou shalt see how we will scourge these enemies of thy people.'   And that the Scotch Ministers do preach as violently against the Parliament as ever.   And likewise that their gentry do meet together in great numbers, and are very close in their consultations.   We earnestly desire you would look narrowly into these things, and you will use some course for the timely prevention of such numerous and tumultuous assemblies of disaffected and discontented people.   The Scotch gentry have their meetings by 50 or 60 at a time, sometimes under the pretence of hunting.   There was lately a great meeting of them at Ballymena, where they were quickly housed and not one to be seen in the streets."

To the Commissioners of Ulster.　Dated Kilkenny, 30th October, 1652.

" You are to allow every soldier 2s. 6d. in money and seven pounds of oatmeal or six pounds of biscuit weekly, or, for want of oatmeal and biscuit, eight pounds of bread.　And what the oatmeal, biscuit, or bread costs the State over and above nine pence weekly, the first penny, adding thereunto the charge of freight, carriage to the stores, field, or garrisons, or any kind of waste, you are to charge it on the soldiers' arrears, that the same may be discounted accordingly.　And if the soldier provides his own bread, you may, instead of his weekly allowance, pay him nine pence per week, if you consider it to be to the advantage of the service.

ARMS OF KILKENNY.

" You may, notwithstanding the late proclamation prohibiting the exportation of cattle, &c., give licenses for the exportation of hides into England only, and butter, tallow, salmon, herrings, and all sorts of fish into England, or any other place, having always regard that thereby those commodities be not heightened in their prices to the prejudice of the soldiers and the poor inhabitants.

" All goods exported into England or Scotland must pay excise, salmon and all other fish only excepted.

" You are not to set the Commonwealth lands for above one year, without special order from us.

" You are to proceed against Popish priests and schoolmasters according to such directions as you will find in the qualifications.

" As to the directions formerly given you concerning the Scottish Ministers, and such as principle the people against the present government, we can give you no other rules than what we sent you therein, unless there be some proof against them.

" You are not to suffer any of the officers of the Scottish nation that have borne arms against the Parliament, and refuse to subscribe the Engagement, to live within your quarters, and that none be permitted to be of Jurys but such as are willing to subscribe the Engagement.

" The persons that have been preyed upon by the Irish are not to be permitted to sue for reparation before they subscribe the Engagement.

" Whereas you desire to know whether the protected Irish, that have lived within your Passes these three or four years past, and paid contributions, should be liable to make restitution for the robberies committed by their kindred in other counties ; we must and do reserve the determination of such cases to the Commissioners for Administration of Justice to proceed therein according to Rules of Justice.

" You are to allow all Prisoners that are not able to provide for themselves three pence per day out of the Treasury.

" We have not leisure to send you the Rules for repairing of British losses, with such other laws and declarations as have been made for the Settlement of this Dominion ; but as God affords us opportunity, you may expect resolutions to these things.　But conceiving it to be of importance to the settlement of the country, we have sent you enclosed powers to unhead the Creaghts, wherein we pray your particular care in putting the same into execution, as you shall find most conduceable to the service."

THE SCHEME TO TRANSPLANT THE SCOTS FROM ULSTER, 1653.

LETTERS BETWEEN THE COMMISSIONERS IN ULSTER AND THE GOVERNMENT IN DUBLIN.

N Friday, the 1st instant (April, 1653), we came to Belfast, where we met Col. Hill, and that day issued a summons for all such as had borne arms against the Parliament in England, Scotland, or Ireland, and lived within our quarters in that part of Ulster, to appear before us at Carrickfergus on Wednesday following, to render an account of their so living within the Parliamentary quarters, and of their affections and fidelities to the present Government.

On Saturday, the 2nd instant, being then at Carrickfergus, considering what to do with those who were to appear before us on Wednesday following. Resolving, in regard of their great number, not to commit any to prison, the several experiments which had been fruitless in that kind, but to use all ways of gentleness and meekness towards them : we concluding and unanimously agreeing, that there is no visible expedient to preserve these parts in safety but by transplanting all popular Scots into some other part of Ireland, and that it was necessary immediately to put this in execution as to the most dangerous of them ; and finding them sufficiently averse from the Irish, we thought it would as well strengthen your hands against the common enemy there as weaken your fears and lessen your charge in these parts ; nevertheless, because we had no power to make such a resolution but by the last article of our instructions, and because it was necessary, if this be practised, that yourselves appoint the place to which they should be so transplanted, we did not think fit to publish our thoughts in this till we should receive your honour's approbation and direction concerning it, which we humbly beg with what speed your greater affairs will admit. In the meantime, we have heard what they could offer us towards full satisfaction concerning their fidelity and peaceable demeanour for time to come, and find them all desirous we should trust to security by bond, which we can not think sufficient, in regard that if they give us our friends to be bound for them, they will not scruple to leave them to be destroyed by us ; if our enemies, we suppose such will revolt with them. So then we rather chose for present security, till your pleasures might be known concerning transplanting the most dangerous, to tender them the engagement, which the greatest part of them have signed, but we cannot say out of conscientious grounds ; the rest have part of them signed a negative paper, which we send enclosed ; some others refuse that and this, and will neither promise nor give bond not to disturb the present Government; but we have not imprisoned them, in regard we do not at present fear their power, and are not willing to let the rest (towards Derry whom we have not yet called) see how far we mean to go.

In our observation of the temper of this people, we find that they are more or less perverse, according to the temper of their respective ministers, and their being planted all together or mixed among English and Irish, which are also further arguments to us for their transplantation.

Touching the prevention of correspondence, we thought it necessary, before we could make any resolutions thereupon, to view the sea coast, which we have already done as far as Cushendun, near Fair Foreland, the North East point of Ireland, and find that there are landing-places all along the coast, though not one good harbour, except Olderfleet haven (which is as good as any in Ireland), and that in two hours they may pass betwixt the headland of Cantyre and the coast of Ireland between Glenarm and Fair Foreland, so that we judge it impossible to prevent correspondence while the Scots are suffered to live along the sea coast ; nevertheless, that we might do something towards it, we have sent Captain Finicke's company to seize all the boats upon the coast, as also to discover and intercept correspondences, likewise sent a letter into Scotland to the Governor of Air for his advice and concurrence in this matter, and also given some other intimations which we send enclosed.

We intend on Monday our journey towards Derry to try the temper of men in those parts that so we may be fitted to give a judgment on the whole, which we intend to do in all parts at one time, according to the several capacities in which we find persons to be, in order to the effectual doing of which, we humbly conceive it requisite that those forces about Antrim, bordering on these parts, be in readiness to attend anything that may occasionally fall out upon such alterations, which may prove to be very little if the business be secretly carried, but privacy in your debates of these things, and the like care in the sure conveyance of your resolutions to us, will much facilitate this work, which if discovered may probably cause great disturbance, if not frustrate this whole work.

We conceive here are at least 300 serviceable saddle horses, besides a greater proportion of draught horses, also fit for service, which are in persons' hands not fit to be trusted with them, although the respective owners have given security to have them forthcoming, which we can not take out of their hands, in regard we have not money to pay for them, nor know how to keep them for want of forage if we take them into our hands, and therefore desire your commands concerning them. And all things else we may serve you with shall be faithfully obeyed by your honours' humble and faithful servants.

Carrickfergus, the 9th of April, 1653.

The Commissioners who wrote this letter were Dr. Henry Jones, afterwards Bishop of Meath, Colonel Arthur Hill, Col. Venables, and Major, afterwards Sir Anthony Morgan. The Government in Dublin immediately had a copy of the proclamation printed, with a list of the names of the persons intended to be transported, and sent it down to the Commissioners in the North.

A LIST OF THE SCOTS TO BE TRANSPLANTED FROM THE COUNTIES OF ANTRIM AND DOWN.

BELFAST AND MALONE QUARTERS.

Lieut. Thomas Cranston.
Corporal Thomas M'Cormack.
Hugh Doke.
Robert Clugston.

George Martin.
Alexander Lockard.
Robert King.
Quintine Caterwood.

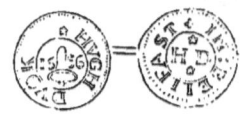

WEST QUARTERS OF CARRICKFERGUS.

John Murrey.
John Russell.
John Reade.
Thos. Young, of Ballynehery.
John Donelson.
John Hanna.
James Reade.
James Patterson.
Wm. Biggard.
George Russell.
John Homes.

George Gibson.
Robert Dickie.
John Clarke, senior.
Patrick Martine.
Richard Cambell.
Andrew Reade, junior.
Quarter-Master Archibald Crafford
Robt. Archball.
Andrew Wilson.
Alexander Miller.

BROAD ISLAND AND EAST QUARTER OF CARRICKFERGUS.

Hugh Donellson.
Captain Edmonstone.
Ensign David Macley.
Robert Gardner.
David Harper.

William Miller.
John McKergor.
John Dowgell.
Matthew Logan.

ISLAND MAGEE, MAGHERAMORNE, AND BALLYNURE.

Capt. Robt. Kinkede.
James Browne.
Ensign Willm. Stephenson.
Capt. James M'Cullogh.

John Blare.
Willm. Agnew.
John Agnew.

SIX MILE WATER QUARTERS.

Capt. George Welch.
Thomas Wyneam.
Capt. Ferguson.
Lieut. Hewston.
Lieut. Robt. Ferguson.
Alexander Pingle.
Andrew Taggart.

Quintine Kenedy.
James Cuthberd.
John Cowtard.
Robert Gragham.
John Cowan.
Thomas Rea.

EARL OF ARDES' QUARTERS.

Lord of Ardes.
Capt. James Cambell.
Capt. Willm. Buchannon.
Teige O'Monney.
Willm. Crafford.
John Crafford.
Brice Crafford.
John Crafford.

Mr. Francis Shaw.
Gilbert McNeile.
Willm. Sloane.
George Young.
John Wilson.
Peter Young.
Mr. Arthur Upton.

ANTRIM QUARTERS.

Capt. Henry Sibbalds.
John Davison.
Capt. John Williams.
Capt. John Fisher.
Capt. John McBride.
Quarter-Master Mitchell.
Major Clotworthy.
David Mitchell.
Ensign John M'Cornett.

John Wagh, merchant.
Robert Shannon.
John Whyte.
Quarter-Master Ferguson.
Capt. James Collvill.
Lieut. James Lynsey.
Lieut. James McAddams.
Gilbert Eikles.

SHANE'S CASTLE, LARGEE, AND TOOME QUARTERS.

Lieut.-Col. Walter Stewart.
Lieut. Andrew Adayre.
Henry Vernor.
Willm. McCullough.
Lieut. James Dobbins.
Ensign John Bryen.
Thomas Bollock.
Matthew Hamele, Leard of Raugh-
    wood.

Captain Robert Hewston.
Lieut. Robt. Carr.
Lieut. James Pont.
Lieut. Hamill.
Lieut. Greenshields.
Ensign Dobbin.
Lieut. Alexander Cunningham.
Ensign Robt. Cunningham.
Lieut. Martine.

BRAID AND KEART AND CLENOGHORTI QUARTERS.

Thomas Adair.
Corporal James M'Cullogh.
Willm. Hamilton.
John Sprule.
Lieut. Paul Cunningham.
Capt. Willm. Hewston.
Capt. Thom. Fawebarne.
Capt. David Johnston.
James Ewart.

Nimion Dunbare.
Halbert Gledstone.
Lieut. Arthur Aghmuti.
Lieut. Willm. Johnstone.
Major Alexander Adaire.
Cornet James Browne.
Cornet John Stewart.
Adam Johnstone.

KILLELOGH AND KILMACKUETT QUARTERS.

David Kenedy.
Lieut. Hugh Cambell.
George (if not John) Gordon, of
    Bowskeagh.
Lieut. Erwine.
Lieut. Anthony Ellis.

Lieut. McIlroy.
Capt. Hercules Longford.
Willm. Norris.
Willm. Cunningham.
George Cambell.

GLENARM BARONY.

Mr. James Shaw.
Capt. John Shaw.
Mr. Donnelson.
Capt. John Agnew.
Willm. Greige.
Randall Bushell.
James Donellson.

Capt. Lieut. John Hume.
James Fenton.
John Mount Gomery.
John Shaw.
James Cruny.
Francis Agnew.

G

ROOTE QUARTERS.

Major John Stewart.
Lieut.-Col. Robt. Kenedy.
Capt. Alexr. Stewart.
Fergus McDougall.
John Boyle.
John Getty.
Alexander Stewart, senr.
James Maxwell.
Capt. Marmaduke Shawe.
John Henery.
Cornet Robert Knole
Willm. Hutchin.
Alexander Scott.
Donnel M'Cay.
Lieut. James Moncrief.
Robt. Harvey.
Willm. Spherling.

Thos. Boyd.
Sam. Dunbarr.
Alexr. Dunlapp.
Adam Dunlap.
Patrick Glen.
Major Hugh Mount Gomery.
Andrew Rowan.
Angus Cambell.
Cornet John Gordon.
Captain John Hewston.
Lieut.-Col. Cunningham.
John Kidd.
Lieut. Arch. Cambell.
Mr. John Peebles.
Mr. Cartaret.
Capt. John Robbinson.
Quarter-Master Robt. Stewart.

COLERAINE QUARTERS.

John Johnstone.
Thos. Abernethy.
James Carr, of Arteslone.
James Johnston.

David Wilson.
Robert Fulton.
Andrew White.

CASTLEREAGH, KILIORHNI, AND LISNEGARVY QUARTERS.

Corporal Gilbert Matthews.
John Streane.
John Cowtard.

James Gragham.
John Cowan.
Thomas Rea.

LORD OF ARDES' QUARTERS.

Lord of Ardes.
Capt. James Cambell.
Capt. Willm. Buchannon.
Lieut. Hugh Dundas.
Capt. John Keath.
John Mountgomery, of Movill.
James Mowell.
James McConchy.

Willm. Catterwood.
Mr. Willm. Shaw.
Fergus Kenedy.
Capt. Hugh McGomery.
Mr. Hugh Mountgomery.
Lieut. John Wilson.
Lieut. Andrew Cunningham.
Lieut. McDowell, of Comber.

LITTLE ARDES, GRAY ABBEY, AND LISBOROUGH QUARTERS.

Capt. Magill.
Gilbert Harran.
Robt. Rosse.

John Parke.
Lieut. John Mumpeny.
James Maxwell.

LORD CLANEBOYE'S QUARTERS.

Lord Claneboy.
Lieut. Gawen Hamilton.
Capt. John Bayly.
Lieut. Hugh Wallas.
James Ross, senior.
Wm. Hamilton, of the Rowe.
Mr. George Rosse.
James Hamilton, of Ballyme-
gonnan.
Patrick Allen.
James Rosse, junior.
Gawen Hamilton.
Capt. Alexander Stewart.
Wm. Hamilton, junior.

John Steephenson.
Ximion Pate.
Lieut. Edward Baylye.
Francis Purdy.
Capt. John Steephenson.
John Barkley.
Quarter-Master Edwd. McKee.
Ensign James Cooper.
Lieut. Robt. Cunningham.
Lieut. Carre.
Captain Mathew Hamilton.
Capt. Collin Maxwell.
David Williamson.

LECALE QUARTERS.

Lieut. Hugh Mountgomery.
Lieut. Launcelot Greere.
Lieut. Thomas Lynsey.
Lieut. Wodney.
Lieut. John Reynolds.
Capt. John Wool.

James Stewart.
John Dunbarr.
John Tennent.
James Porter.
Stephen Major.
John McDowell.

A List of the persons delivered by the Scottish Agents for the Counties of Down and Antrim, and desired to be dispensed with for their removing.

BELFAST QUARTERS.

Quintine Caterwood.

Alexander Lockard.

BROAD ISLAND QUARTERS.

John McKergor.

David McLay.

SIX MILE WATER QUARTERS.

Capt. Geo. Welch.

Lieut. Hewston.

ANTRIM QUARTERS.

Capt. John Williams.
Capt. John McBride.

Ensign McCormack.
John Wagh.

SHANE'S CASTLE QUARTERS.
Capt. Robt. Hewston.

KILLELEAGH AND KILMAKEWET QUARTERS.

David Kennedy.
Lieut. Cambell.

John Gordon.

GLENARM QUARTERS.
John Shaw.

ROOT QUARTERS.

John Boyle.
John Getty.
Alexr. Scott.

Anth. Kennedy.
Andr. Kenan.
Mr. Carcart.

LORD OF ARDES' QUARTERS.

James McConchy.
John Montgomery.
Capt. Willm. Buchanan.

Lieut. Hugh Dundas.
Lieut. Geo. Nowell.
Lieut. Andrew Cunningham.

LITTLE ARDES QUARTERS.

Gilbert Haron.
Robt. Maxwell.

Lieut. John Mompeny.
Lieut. John Wilson.

LORD CLANEBOVE'S QUARTERS.

Lieut. Gawin Hamilton.
Lieut. Hugh Wallace.
Quarter-Master McKee.
Capt. Math. Hamilton.

David Williamson.
Lieut. Andw. Carre.
Lieut. Robt. Cunningham.

LECALE QUARTER.
Lieut. Thomas Lyndsay.

THE REPLY OF THE COUNCIL OF STATE TO THE COMMISSIONERS, 13 APRIL, 1653.

The first thing you propound is the transplanting of such popular men in those parts, of whose dutiful and peaceable demeanours you have no assurance, unto some other part of Ireland where their influence may not be prejudicial to the Commonwealth. Wherein, after serious consideration, we do fully agree with you that the thing is desirable, if you judge it may be done without such disturbance in the country as may raise the expectation of the Irish for some issue to their advantage.

The places into which we conceive they may with safety to the Commonwealth, and advantage to themselves, be removed are parts of the Counties of Kilkenny, Tipperary, and Waterford. The Decies, in the County of Waterford, and such other parts of that county where they may with security inhabit. How this may effectually be put into execution, we leave to you to determine and prosecute as you shall apprehend to be most practicable with least noises. We cannot see but it must be either by securing the persons of the men until their families and stocks be removed, or by taking security by bonds from them to remove by a day appointed. And to the end they may not apprehend their removal to be of prejudice to them, you may give them assurance that they shall enjoy the benefits of their estates and farms from whence they remove for this year to come, they employing persons to manage the same of whose fidelity to the Commonwealth you receive assurance.

To this the Commissioners for settling Ulster write from Derry, *24th April, 1653.*

We entered into the consideration of Conditions to be held forth to such as should be transplanted which might induce them to undertake the thing willingly, and so prevent all occasions of disturbances, and thought it adviseable to offer. First, That valuable consideration might be allowed in land for the lands, leases, and houses of such as should be transplanted, according to their respective interests.

Second, That they may hold such lands till this time two years without cess or contribution, and be allowed what timber is necessary either for building or repairing old houses.
The same to be allowed out of the Commonwealth's Woods.

Third, That they may enjoy by their agents the profits of their lands they now possess here till November next.
Approved of.

Fourth, That we engage, if they require it, to take off all their corn now upon the ground, being made into meal and delivered into the store at the market price, and pay the money to them where they shall desire.
Approved of.

Fifth, That convoys be allowed to them, and licences to keep arms for their defence.

Sixth, That they may choose their own ministers, provided they be such as are peaceably minded towards those they live under, and not scandalous.

Approved of.

Seventh, That such as have not titles to land shall have leases of so much as they can stock at a valueable rent.

Approved of.

Now in regard of the great weight of this affair, we resolved not to declare these conditions, or proceed in it any farther, till we should receive your Honours' approbation of these, or directions concerning other conditions, which we humbly beg with all possible speed, in regard of the nearness of the expiration of our commission.

We have here met with one Lieut. Hamilton (who formerly took the Engagement, and was since in arms against you at Worcester), whom we have secured and intend to send him to Dublin, together with one Major Graham (who formerly betrayed a Castle of ours to the enemy), to be disposed of as your Honours shall think fit. We find this town a place of very great strength, and might easily be made well nigh impregnable. We have some thoughts of transplanting some of the Scotch inhabitants into some of the towns of the South, if we can find fit grounds to hold out for their removal, their number being at present almost equal with the English, which we judge very dangerous to be allowed. In which we also crave your further directions, and humbly remain

Your Honours' humble and faithful servants,

ROBT. VENABLES, ARTHUR HILL, HENRY JONES,
WILLM. ALLON, ANTHONY MORGAN.

Londonderry, 24 April, 1653.

GATEWAY, WALLS OF DERRY.

(The Parliamentary Commissioners in Dublin then printed a proclamation, dated at Carrickfergus 23rd May, 1653 ; omitted here, as it is given in Reid's *History of the Presbyterian Church in Ireland,* 2nd ed., vol. ii., p. 178.)

LETTER OF THE ULSTER COMMISSIONERS.

RIGHT HONOURABLE,

In pursuance of what was formerly presented unto you, our Commission being determined to give you by one of our number this following account of our actings, in the further observance of your instructions for the settling of Ulster.

Upon Adjutant-General Allen and Major Morgan's departure (finding that some time would be elapsed before the Declaration could be printed and sent to us) the enclosed paper was agreed upon and signed by us all, to be sent by us that stayed here with all speed into the several Quarters, to the end that no time might be lost in hastening the transplanted to make choice of their Agents to attend yours in order to their future removal, which was accordingly executed, and the transplanted met at the place appointed before the Declaration came to us, which we received the 5th instant, upon consideration whereof it was not thought fit to publish the same for these ensuing reasons.

First, Because of the great mistake of the printing the names.

Secondly, Because we would take all occasion from any [by variation or transposition of matter from that which we had formerly held forth unto them] to suggest unto the rest [who are too ready to lay hold on any colourable pretence to misrepresent our actions] that we had in the least differed from our former papers.

Thirdly, Because if the Declarations had been issued as soon as received they would have added nothing in furtherance of the work intended, being they contain no new matter save only the preamble.

Fourthly, Because they could not be sent and divulged into the several Quarters before the day appointed for the return of their final answer in choosing and instructing of their Agents for the purpose aforesaid, which was appointed to be the 7th.

Lastly, Because we had received some information from their meetings of their averseness to remove, to which we had formerly hopes they would have been more pliable, and so conceived that they might give occasion to make some alteration in what was already intended to be declared. Upon the 7th and 8th instant, the Agents of both Counties attended us for passes, which we accordingly granted them.

Those of the County of Antrim gave us to understand that they could not possibly take their journey for want of money in regard the Transplanteds left them before a collection could be made: Wherefore to further their despatch we were necessitated to borrow £40, which we have delivered unto them, and humbly desire that you would be pleased to issue your warrant to the Commissioners of the Revenue to levy the same equally upon the Transplanteds that the same be repaid accordingly to Col. Venables' orders, that so we may be discharged of our engagement for the same.

During the time these Agents attended us, some gentlemen of both Counties [being more desirous to choose and conclude for themselves than by Agents] desired passes from us to attend you to that purpose, which we accordingly granted them. Their names and petitions signed will be delivered with this unto you. If more shall desire the same we shall readily agree to afford them passes, because we conceive it may much further the work intended by begetting a better understanding in those that are left behind in your good intentions towards them, when they shall perceive others beside their Agents return satisfied, and fully agreed with you for their future residence. By all that hitherto we can see, either into the humours of these people or the issue of this business, we do not yet find that there will need much force or further threatening to render them conformable, so they may be satisfied in the ensuing propositions.

First, That the places they go to inhabit be free from infection, and probably secure from Tories and enemies.

Secondly, In regard that many of them are of mean conditions, they desire they may be left to choose their own landlords in any of the two provinces, by whose just dealing and countenance they may have hopes to live with the less oppression and disturbance.

Thirdly, That if they contract for the State's lands their Contribution may be included in their Rent, that so they may be at a certainty.

Fourthly, That they may have such terms for years of the places that they go to possess as may probably render them and their posterity gainers for the present hazard and great charge they are at in removing, and planting of the waste they go to possess.

Fifthly, That those that have free holds or considerable leases of value may not be forced to surrender their evidences or transfer their rights until they have legal assurances made unto them of what they receive in exchange.

Sixthly, That they may enjoy the profits of their estates that they leave behind [paying contribution out of them as they now do] until the places exchanged with them be so planted as may render them a future livelihood, which is conceived cannot be less than one year after November next.

These things being accidentally discoursed with us by several of them, and considering that these being added to what are formerly proposed, they are but what we should propose for ourselves if we were in their case. We have presumed to offer them to your consideration, believing that if you find them fitting to be consented to, and reserve them as concessions of favour from yourselves, with what other things of that kind may occur, all obstructions will be removed as to the general transplanting. Except in some few particular cases, which, by reason of age, sickness, or other necessary impediments, cannot remove without apparent ruin to their persons or fortunes.

And further, you will beget in the hearts of these people such an understanding of your good intentions towards them, beyond all what they have heard or thought of you, as that we are persuaded you will within a twelvemonth more leave few here that will not be willing to go faster (it may be) than you would have them. We have one thing more to add for their encouragement, and also the State's advantage (as we conceive), which is, that all the land that is set them be set by the acre, that if you include the contribution in the rent, you do (after the first year's freedom) the next year reserve very little more than the contribution comes to, and so increase your rent yearly for two or three years after until you come to such a rent as you find fit for the State to receive for their whole time, and them to pay with respect to their future comfortable subsistence and well-being.

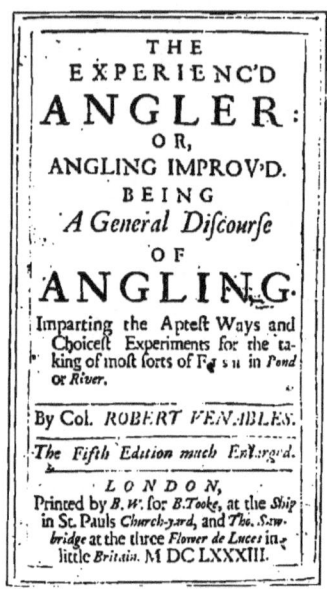

THE
EXPERIENC'D
ANGLER:
OR,
ANGLING IMPROV'D.
BEING
A General Discourse
OF
ANGLING.
Imparting the Aptest Ways and Choicest Experiments for the taking of most sorts of F su in *Pond* or *River*.

By Col. ROBERT VENABLES.

The Fifth Edition much Enlarg'd.

LONDON,
Printed by *B. W.* for *B. Tooke*, at the Ship in St. Pauls *Church-yard*, and *Tho. Sawbridge* at the three *Flower de Luces* in little *Britain.* M DC LXXXIII.

FAC-SIMILE OF TITLE-PAGE OF "THE EXPERIENCED ANGLER," BY COLONEL ROBERT VENABLES.

This business is in our thoughts of that weight (and presume in yours also) in respect of the future planting of these parts with English, and thereby securing of the same, that we cannot pass by the convenience that may ensue upon the premises if the ends aforesaid be obtained by them.

First, You displant these here without noise or clamour.

Secondly, their ministers will probably follow.

Thirdly, Whereas you have proposed these certain places to dwell in, neare and in a manner contiguous, you disperse them further asunder by giving them way to settle in any places in the said Provinces as aforesaid, and so render their conjunctions less powerful in opposition at any time against the State.

Fourthly, You will assuredly find after the first year profit by their removal, for they will then in rent and contribution be content, according to the goodness of the land, to pay yearly for their wastes (which it may be in 7 years would not be inhabited) much more than the contribution they paid here comes to.

But, If these people [notwithstanding the concessions afforded] shall still prove refractory, we conceive then no other means but force will render them comformable. In order to which we humbly offer that whom you think fit may be empowered, upon the return of their

ARMS OF MUNSTER.

Agents, to call all these Transplanteds to one place, that there it be demanded who are willing to remove by a time prefixed and who not. That those that signify their consents give assurance of performance by a prefixed time ; that those that refuse be imprisoned, and sent into Leinster and Munster to be secured, without disturbance to their families or prejudice to their estates, that so all may see that nothing is intended by their removal but present and future security.

As these parts suffer very much by closing of the ports, in order to their trade with Scotland, which we conceive cannot with safety to your affairs here be opened until these things be brought to an issue one way or another, for the trade into England and alongst the Coast also is exceedingly obstructed by some Pirates which lye upon these harbours.

They came lately into this Road, and soon after took two vessels loaden with corn and meal, bound for Connaught, out of the harbour

ARMS OF CONNAUGHT.

of Oulderfleet, which by composition [upon licence granted to the purpose] were rescued again. A third was taken coming from Colraine, and a fourth, being one of the poor men's barques that was recovered in Donegal, and laded with meal for Ballyshannon, was taken and sunk by them because she had no lading in her, so that if your Honours do not speedily cause some swift vessell of good force to come into these parts, to secure the passage betwixt England and this place, trade will be utterly at a stand. Riche's vessel is now at Ayr, and if she were here she is too small to deal with these, and, indeed, if they have courage to set upon her, and have sail enough to reach her, she will be in hazard of taking.

In order to your commands of the 14th of May orders are issued for the listing and appraising of all serviceable horse ; it will be a work of time before it be exactly done ; as soon as it is effected, care will be taken to return you a perfect list, according to instructions. There were some gentlemen nominated and sworn for the appraising of the horses lately bought in these parts, who have petitioned to be satisfied for their pains and expence in attending that service, and in regard we have no command of the Treasury here, we beseech your directions concerning the same to the Commissioners of the Revenue. We make bold to remind you of what had been formerly offered concerning a Packet Boat between these parts and Soctland ; with what hath been herein presented we leave to your consideration, and rest

> Your Honours'
> Most humble and faithful servants,
> R. VENABLES, ART. HILL, H. JONES.
> (Trin. Coll. Dub. F. 3. 18.)

Carrickfergus, June 14, 1653.

The next that we find upon the subject is the following letter from the Government at Dublin to the Commissioners in Ulster :—

RIGHT HONOURABLE,

In obedience to the order of reference of the 21st inst. to us and others directed for receiving and debating such papers and proposals as should be offered concerning the Scotts, or by the Scottish Agents concerning the intended transplantation of the Scotts out of Ulster, and in order to the settling and securing of that Province, and for reporting of the same to your Honours with our opinions there-upon : Upon considerations had of the whole matter we humbly offer the proceedings, and our sense therein as followeth. That the necessity of that work of transplantation appearing, we confine our-selves to the debate of the manner how it was to be effected. Particularly with respect had to the places whither, the time when, the persons who, and the conditions under which those were to be removed. The Agents for the Counties of Antrim and Down being called before us, and we having heard what was by them offered concerning every of these particulars.

First, For the place whither they were to be transported the said Agents excepting the County of Waterford as over remote, and in general to the places mentioned in the former proposals as over much limited, desiring rather to be therein left at large, and to their own choice : Upon debate it was concluded—

Firstly, That of the Counties formerly proposed the County of Waterford should be excluded in favour to the transplanted, yet in further favour to them (and at the request of the said Agents) reserving to any of the Scotch merchants of the transplanted (who should require it) liberty to reside in and trade in the City of Waterford.

Secondly, That such of those who are to be transplanted and provided for on the account of the Commonwealth, according to the former proposals, shall be disposed of in the County of Kilkenny and Tipperary according to the said proposals.

Thirdly, That all of those who are not to be provided for by the Commonwealth as aforesaid, and to be transplanted, should be left to their liberty for taking land from any proprietor in the respective Counties of the Province of Leinster, respect being had to their numbers in every said County.

ARMS OF LEINSTER.

Second, For the time when to be transplanted. It being insisted upon by the Agents that it should be deferred until the next year, the season of the year for such a work being now (as they said) elapsed. And it being debated and considered that the giving them the time desired was to give opportunity and time for their designs in the *interim* as occasion should be offered, and that therein they might have the opportunity for disappointing the intended security of the Province of Ulster, consisting (probably) in their removal. And if what was to be herein done were not speedily effected, the season of the year would be altogether elapsed as to their accommodations.

It was therefore concluded :—

Firstly, That the 15th of August next shall be the time limited for the removal of the persons in Ulster thereunto nominated.

Secondly, That the families of those persons so removed as aforesaid shall also remove out of Ulster to the places appointed them in Kilkenny and Tipperary, or to the places chosen by them in Leinster as aforesaid, by the first of November next following.

Thirdly, As to the persons who should be removed. The said Agents offered the names and petitions of several whom they conceived not fit to be removed, which, being taken into consideration, it was resolved :—That the names of the list last sent by the Commissioners for the settling of Ulster should stand for the present, and that the persons mentioned in the papers delivered by the said Agents of Down and Antrim, together with the petitioners mentioned, should be referred to Col. Venables, and to such as he shall think fit to consult withal, who are to consider what is to be done therein according to the rules to be given them in it. This to be expressed in a letter to Col. Venables to that purpose. Also, on the reading of the Lord of Clandeboy's petition concerning his not removing, it was resolved that nothing therein appeared for altering that formerly ordered for his removal out of Ulster. As to the conditions on which those persons were to be removed : It was resolved that their concessions in the printed paper of the 23rd of May, 1653, should be insisted upon as to the matter, yet leaving to the said Agents the liberty of offering in writing, which they further desired in pursuance of the former, who thereupon tendered their following proposals :—

First Proposal. We desire that, instead of exchanging our estates with any in this country, we may have liberty to dispose of them to well-affected English in the North, and may have freedom to chuse lands here where we can bargain with greatest advantage. Considering which, the first head in this proposal is granted, provided that the persons to whom the lands in Ulster shall be so disposed be such as shall be approved by Commissioners of the Commonwealth, or whom they shall appoint. The next head in this proposal, concerning liberty for the making choice of lands in Leinster, was formerly granted.

Second Proposal. We humbly desire two years' freedom from contributions from May next, being the soonest we can enter into the country husbandry. Concerning this, resolved : That it be offered to the Commissioners of the Commonwealth that two years' freedom from contribution be given, beginning from May last past.

Third Proposal. We desire freedom from subscriptions and oaths for ourselves and ministers. To this is answered : That it is not our practice to force engagements upon any contrary to their consciences.

Fourth Proposal. That our wives and families may enjoy half our houses till May next, with liberty to dispose of corn and fodder for the wintering of cattle. For this we referred ourselves to that before resolved concerning the time of removal.

Fifth Proposal. That we may have liberty to assign our debts warrantably to some who have taken the engagement, that they may be recovered for our enablement to plant in this country. In this they are referred to the practices in England in such cases.

Sixth Proposal. We do desire that we may have the use of this year's fallows and dunged lands we have in the North, paying by the acre for them at the rate of the rest of the land. This is granted.

Seventh Proposal. That our horses shall not be taken from us. Granted equal freedom with the English.

Eighth Proposal. That those of our number resolved to drive trades by land or sea, we may have all the freedom and immunities other subjects have. This granted in respect to trade.

Ninth Proposal. That we be provided in arms for our necessary defence in the places we come to, and that the protectors bordering upon our plantations may make up what goods shall be taken from us by robbers or stealth. For this they shall be allowed their arms, and the same care shall be taken of them as of the Protestant English.

Tenth Proposal. That after November next no quartering of soldiers be upon our families. For this they shall be in the same condition as other English Protestants.

Eleventh Proposal. We are likewise required by our instructions to desire that so many servants and tradesmen whom we can persuade to come along with us may have the benefit of the conditions granted to ourselves. And our servants to be compelled to come along with us. This granted.

All which the before-mentioned, being the substance of our debates with the said Agents in this thing and our sense in it, we humbly offer to your Honours, with this our further opinion in the whole matter.

That such of those who are to be transplanted as aforesaid who shall refuse to remove contrary to orders therein given shall be declared delinquents, and be proceeded against accordingly to the securing of their persons, and sequestrating and confiscating their estates. *Dated 30th of June, 1653.*

Charles Coote, Hierome Sankey, Anthony Morgan, Wm. Allen, Hen. Jones, Phil. Carteret, Rich. Lawrence.

Order touching the Scotts in Ulster.

Upon consideration had of the reports made unto us the 30th day of June, 1653. By virtue of reference of the 22nd of the same month to Sir Hardress Waller, Knt.; Sir Charles Coote, Knt. and Bart.; Col. Hierome Sankey, Col. Richard Lawrence, Col. Daniel Axtell, Col. Robt. Barrowe, Dr. Henry Jones, Col. Sadleir, Adjutant-General Allen, Major Morgan, and James Standish, Esq., or any four or more of them, for receiving and debating such papers and proposals as should be offered concerning the Scotts, or by the Scottish Agents concerning the intended transplantation of the Scotts out of Ulster, and in order to the settling and securing of the Province, and for reporting the same unto us, with their opinions thereupon, which they having done accordingly, with respect had to the places whither, the times when, the persons who, and the conditions on which these persons were to be removed.

It is ordered (First) for the places whither they are to be trans-planted. That of the Counties formerly proposed, the County of Waterford shall be omitted in favour to the transplanted, yet, in further favour to them, reserving to any of the Scottish merchants of the transplanted who shall require, a liberty to reside and trade in the City of Waterford, they first promising under their hands in writing that they shall not act nor do anything to the prejudice of the Commonwealth of England : And that such of those who are to be transplanted and provided for on the account of the Commonwealth, according to the premised proposals made at Carrickfergus the 23rd May, 1653, by the Commissioners appointed for the settling and securing of Ulster shall be disposed of in the Counties of Kilkenny and

ARMS OF CITY OF WATERFORD.

Tipperary according to the said proposals, and all others who are not to be provided for by the Commonwealth as aforesaid, and are to be transplanted, shall be left to their liberty for taking land from any proprietors in the respective Counties of the Province of Leinster, respect being had to their numbers in every of the said Counties.

Secondly, That the times for the persons named in the list for to be removed out of Ulster into the places before-mentioned shall be at or before the first of November next : And that the respective families of those persons so removed as aforesaid shall also remove out of Ulster to the places appointed in the Counties of Kilkenny and Tipperary, or to the places chosen by them in Leinster as aforesaid, at or before the 15th of April now next ensuing.

Thirdly, That as to the persons who shall be removed, the names in the lists hereunto annexed, last sent by the Commissioners for settling of Ulster, shall stand. And that the persons mentioned in the papers now delivered by the Scottish Agents for the Counties of Down and Antrim, together with the petitions concerning persons not to be removed : And the consideration of any other persons in the said list mentioned shall be referred to Col. Robert Barrowe, Col. Robert Venables, Major Francis Bolton, Major Daniel Redman, and Capt. Bickerstaffe, or any two or more of them, who shall be and are hereby authorised to dispense with the removal of such persons in the said papers, petitions, or list mentioned as they or any two or more of them shall judge to be unfit to be removed in regard of age, sickness, or other impotency of body, and of such other persons in the list mentioned as they or any two or more of them shall judge fitting to be dispensed withal for their removing aforesaid. Provided that the said dispensation be not extended to any person or persons that contrived, counselled, aided, or assisted the siege of Londonderry, then defended by the English forces under the command of Sir Charles

Coote, now Lord President of Connaught, nor to any person or persons that counselled, acted, aided, or assisted the removal of Col. Monk from his command in the County of Louth or the Province of Ulster. Nor to any person or persons that have acted, councelled, aided, or assisted in the war against the Parliament of England, their army or forces.

Fourthly, As to the conditions on which those persons are to be removed. It is ordered that the Commissioners, in the printed paper of the 23 of May, 1653, held out by the said Commissioners for the settling of the Province of Ulster, shall be and are hereby ratified and confirmed : And in further favour to the persons to be transplanted, and in answer to the proposals delivered by the Agents aforesaid, it is also ordered :—

First, That they may have liberty to dispose of their respective estates in the Counties of Down and Antrim, respect being had to the qualifications under which they do fall in the Act, entituled an Act for the Settling of Ireland : Provided that the persons to whom the lands in Ulster shall be disposed, and the conditions on which the said lands shall be disposed, be such as shall be approved by us, or whom we shall appoint.

Second, That from May last past they shall have two years' freedom from contributions for the waste lands on which they shall plant.

Third, To that by them desired, that they be freed from subscriptions and oaths, we declare it is our principle, and (we trust) the Lord will enable us to make it our practice, to use all tenderness to tender consciences.

Fourth, That the wives and families of those who are to be transplanted as aforesaid shall enjoy the benefit of their houses wherein they now are until the 15th of April next ensuing, and to dispose of their corn and fodder for the wintering of their cattle.

Fifth, As to their desire for the recovery of their debts. Those that do actually remove shall have liberty to receive their just debts, notwithstanding their not taking the Engagement, such persons first obtaining a license from Col. Venables, under his hand, to dispense with the taking the Engagement in order to their suing for their debts.

Sixth, For such lands as are fallowed and dunged this year. The benefit whereof shall be granted for the next crop.

Seventh, Whereas they desire that their horses may not be taken from them. They shall be therein in the same condition with the other English.

Eighth, That such of the persons to be removed as aforesaid who shall trade by sea or land shall have, in relation to trade, the same freedom and immunities with other English, they first promising, under their hands in writing, that they shall not act or do anything to the prejudice of the Commonwealth of England.

Ninth, Whereas they desire that arms be allowed them in the places to which they remove, and that the protected Irish bordering upon them may make up what goods shall be taken from them by robbery or stealth. It is declared that the same care shall be taken of them as of English Protestants.

Tenth, To that desire of theirs, that after November next there should be no quartering of soldiers on their families. They shall be for that in the same condition with the English Protestants.

Eleventh, As to the tenants of the persons so removing, and to tradesmen who shall be willing to go along with them. Such shall have the benefit of the same conditions granted to the persons in the same qualification with them respectively : And as for compelling their servants to remove with them (which they desire), they are therein left to the law in such cases. *Dublin, the 13th July, 1653.*

C F. E L. M C. J J. (Charles Fleetwood, Edmund Ludlow, Miles Corbett, John Jones.)

(Order Book. A. 84. Bermingham Tower.)

REPLY TO SIR ROBERT ADAIR'S PETITION, 12 JULY, 1653.

"PON reading the petition of Sir Robt. Adaire, Knt., setting forth his good and faithful services in England and Ireland, and desiring the benefit of his estate in Ireland, and that the same might be freed from sequestration, according to the favour held forth in the Parliament's declaration unto such who have since the Battle of Dunbar, on the 3d of September, 1650, deserted Charles Stuart, and not borne arms since against the Parliament. And upon a perusal of a certificate from the Commissioners lately appointed for the settling and securing of Ulster, to whom the examination of the Petitioner's allegations and delinquencys was formerly referred. It appearing that the said Sir Robt. Adair hath been very serviceable formerly to the Commonwealth of England, and suffered much for his faithfulness and affections to the same. And further, that he was a Colonel in the Scotch army at the time of the engagement at Dunbar with the English forces, but by reason of some indisposition of body was not at that fight, nor did serve afterwards amongst them, but his regiment was then given unto Major-General Massey; and that he hath ever since, for ought appeared unto them, lived peaceably without acting any thing to the prejudice of the Commonwealth. It is upon consideration of the whole matter thought fit and ordered That the said Robt. Adaire be and is hereby permitted to enjoy his said estate in Ireland, and to receive the rents, issues, and profits thereof until further order, paying contribution and other publick duties : and the Commissioners of the Revenue where the said estate lyeth are to see this order duly observed and made good unto him accordingly. Whereof they and all others whom it may concern are to take notice."

Dublin, 12 July, 1653.

C. F: E. L: M. C: (Charles Fleetwood, Edmund Ludlow, Miles Corbet), Parliamentary Commissioners for managing affairs in Ireland.

Dublin, 13th July, 1653.

"Ordered, that a packet boat be settled for the conveying of intelligence betwixt the Province of Ulster in Ireland and the Town of Ayr in Scotland, and that Col. Robt. Venables and the rest of the Commissioners of Revenue at Belfast do order the same, as may be most for the advantage of the public."

"It is ordered that it be referred to Col. Robt. Venables and Col. Robt. Brown, jointly and severally, to consider how trade in the small ports between Ulster and Scotland may be opened without prejudice to the publick, and likewise of fit persons to be by them appointed, who are hereby authorized to give Licenses unto such persons as they shall conceive to be of honesty and integrity to trade with their ships and goods between any port of Ulster and Scotland, and to pass and repass without molestation.   Such persons so trading to give good security to land their goods and merchandise in some of the Parliament's Garrisons and not elsewhere, and to return certificates from the Governors of the Garrisons where the goods are landed."

5 August, 1653.

In Aug., 1653, the Council write to Venables and Col. Barron, desiring them to consider the various ministers in Ulster, to certify the names of such as may be peaceable and well affected to the Commonwealth, what maintenance they receive and from whom, where they reside, so that the Government may dispose of them equally for the most advantage of the Gospel, and that fitting encouragement and allowance may be settled upon them for their pains.

The Council of State, writing to the Commissioners of Revenue in Ulster, Sept., 1652 :—

"The wild course of life which the Irish practice in Creats which doth yield most relief to the enemy, we therefore desire that all Creats may be broke, and fixed in families living apart in convenient quarters where they may till the ground, &c."

To Col. Venables.   Dublin, 21 October, 1653.

"We desire you, with all convenient speed, to send up the Original Surveys of Cavan, Fermanagh, Donegal, Tyrone, and Antrim (you so happily met with) by some trusty hand, close sealed or locked up.   And in ye meantime that you keep them as private as you may, and suffer no copies to be taken of them.   And as often as you shall meet with any papers of that nature we think fit they should be immediately conveyed unto us : for such papers were collected at publick charge, and are most useful to the Commonwealth."

C F.   E L.   M C.   J J.   (Charles Fleetwood, Edmund Ludlow, Miles Corbett, John Jones), Council of State Privy Council.

LETTER FROM THE LORD GENERAL CROMWELL.

To the Rt. Houble. the Lord Deputy and Council in Ireland.

MY LORD AND GENTLEMEN,

We having taken into consideration the inclosed petition of Sir Robert Adaire, with the certificate of General Monk concerning his faithful adhering to the Parliament and his good service in Ireland, we do think fit that the accounts of the arrears of the said Sir Robert for his service in Ireland be stated, and debentures given him for the same.   And we desire you to give order for the speedy doing thereof accordingly, That so he may be put into an equal capacity and forwardness to receive satisfaction out of the lands in Ireland with others who served in the same service.

We rest

Your loving friend,

OLIVER P.

Whitehall, March 22, 1654.   *(No. 46, f. 104, Bermingham Tower.)*

II

OLIVER CROMWELL, 1599-1658.

ANSWER TO THE PRECEDING LETTER.　DUBLIN CASTLE, 6 FEB., 1655.

The answer is perhaps too long to copy out in full : it acknowledges the receipt of Cromwell's letter, and says the Council referred it, with Adair's petition, to the Commissioner of Accounts, who replied that Adair's delinquency in fighting against the Parliament at the battle of Dunbar obstructed the payment of the debenture, which amounted to the large sum of £1,968, equivalent to 9,843 acres of land in Ulster ; and as the lands of Ulster will scarcely satisfy the claims of the army, the Council consider that the debt is postponed by Adaire's act of delinquency, and they therefore respite the delivery of the debenture till they shall receive his Highness's further pleasure.

(From entries of Letters to the Lord Deputy and Council. No. 21. A. 30.)

To the Right Honourable the Commissioners of the Commonwealth in Ireland.

GENTLEMEN,

·　　　We formerly recommended unto you the case of Major-General Monroe, that the sequestration might be taken off his lady's jointure in Ireland, and that he might be permitted to enjoy the same. But he hath represented unto us that the sequestration is still continued, and himself detained at Dublin, to his great charge and prejudice. These are to signify to you that we have received such good satisfaction concerning him, and his resolution to live peaceably and to be true and faithful in the interest of the Commonwealth, that we could not but tender his present condition, and do therefore think fit that the sequestration be forthwith taken off from his wife's jointure, and he permitted to enjoy the same without any restraint of his liberty, and remain

Your loving friend,

Whitehall, 18 April, 1654.　　　　　　　　　　　　OLIVER P.

ARMS OF GALWAY.

ORDER TO COMMISSIONERS AT BELFAST, *May, 1654.*

"Whereas there is an occasion for the landing of provisions by sea for the supply of the forces in the precinct of Galway, It is therefore ordered that the Commissioners of the Revenue at Belfast do forthwith appoint such person or persons as they shall think fit to impress such vessels as shall be sufficient to perform the aforesaid service, allowing for the same the usual rate of State's pay. And all officers of the Admiralty, and all other officers military and civil, to be aiding therein. *Dublin, 5th May, 1654.*"

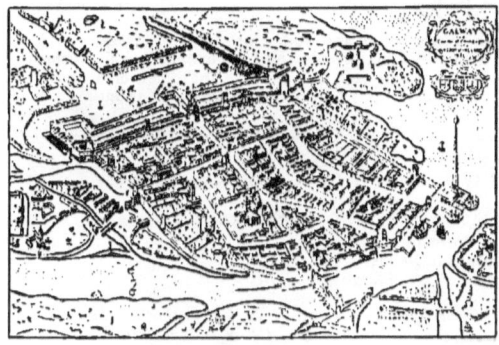

CITY OF GALWAY, 1651

GENERAL MONROE'S PETITION, *May, 1654.*

The Council to Commissioners at Belfast, the Lord Protector having written to the Council in favour of Major-General Monro in regard of the estate he claims in right of his wife, sequestrated, demand to know why and wherefore, so that they may reply to Oliver P. *18 May, 1654.*

Write on same date to General Monk, stating they had received an order from Cromwell.

"Which order is of so public concernment, that albeit we are ready to give it all due observance, nevertheless, having reasons to believe it was obtained through undue suggestions, and assuring ourselves that your employment in Ulster and engagements against the Scotts renders you capable of a fuller understanding of the demerits of the Major-General, and of his acting against the Commonwealth's interest in Ireland (which probably occasioned his sequestration), we desire you, in order to publick good, to certify unto us your knowledge concerning the Major-General aforesaid, that we may be able to undeceive where it is likely his delinquency has been misrepresented, and so proceed further thereupon as shall agree with public justice."

Dublin, 18 May, 1654.

Commissioners of Surveys of lands to return the Crown lands, bishops' lands, and in the Precinct of Belfast, comprising the Counties of Down, Antrim, and Armagh, were Col. Arthur Hill, James Quayle, Richard Bickerstaffe, Tobias Norris, Hugh Lloyd, Wm. Cunningham, Richard Francklin, and Hugh Harrison, Esqs.

Ordered that Mr. Jeremy O'Quin do forthwith repair to the town of Athy, and do exercise his gifts in the work of the ministry there, and at such places adjacent where he shall judge his pains may tend most to the advancement of the Gospel. And that he do examine and inform himself of the progress of the Word in those parts, and after some time return an account of his proceedings therein. *May 31, 1654.*

Ordered the Commissioners of Revenue at Belfast are to assign and let out to Mr. Wyke, minister, a portion of the lands of Dromore, formerly the demesne of the late Bishop of Dromore, not exceeding one hundred acres, and to make a lease thereof to him for the term of seven years. *Aug. 2, 1654.*

In Commission of the Peace for the County of Antrim :—

Arthur Lord Chichester.	Arthur Hill.
Sir J. Clotworthy, Kt.	Philip Pincheon.
Robt. Venables.	The Mayor of Carrickfergus.
Robert Barrow.	George Rawdon.

The oath sworn before the Judge or Clerk of Assize :—I, A. B., do, in the presence of Almighty God, promise and swear that I shall, according to my best skill and knowledge, well and truly execute the office of a Justice of the Peace within the County of   during the time I shall be continued in the said office. So help, &c.

1655. (*Orders and Commissions. A. 26.*)

PARLIAMENTARY CIVIL LIST, 1655.—BELFAST DISTRICT.

Schoolmasters.

Thomas Hasleam, Lisnegarvey,	...	£40
John Cornwall, Belfast,	...	20
John Smith, Carrickfergus,	...	20

Civil Officers, Precinct of Belfast, including the Counties of Armagh, Down, and Antrim.

John Tuttle, Receiver of the Revenue,	...	...	£110
His Clerk,	...	...	30
John Leithes, Storekeeper at Charlemount, Trooper's Pay.			
Daniel Boote, Storekeeper at Carrickfergus,		...	40
Mr. Thomas Morrice, Muster Master,	...	...	127 8
Tobias Norrice, General Charge of Stores,	...	...	100
John Preston, Master of the Packet boat,	...	...	100

Elizabeth Mulcaster, Nurse to the Hospital at Belfast, one
shilling per day.
John Daniel Shonbul, Surgeon, 4s. per day.

Custom Officers.

Roger Lindon, Collector at Carrickfergus,			£60		
Willm. Hill, Checque,	...		40		
Edwd. Grant, Surveyor,	...		30		
Hercules Hillman, Waiter,	...		18	5	0
Willm. Bennet, Waiter,	...		18	5	0
Robt. Brerely, Collector at Donaghadee,			30		
Roger Crimble, Checque,	...		20		
Anthony Ballard, Waiter, Larne,			18		
Edward Sanders, Waiter at Glenarm,			18		
Jas. Bickerstaff, Waiter at Roote,			18		
Willm. Aplin, Waiter, Groomsport,			18		
Henry Davis, Waiter, Strangford,			18		
Simon Spier, Waiter at Belfast,			18		

Pensioners. Precinct of Belfast.

Elinor Atkinson, per week,	...	...		10s.	
John Cooley,	...	...	...	2	6
Arthur and Martha Connely,	...	...	£1	0	0
Thomas Rogers,	...	...	...	2	
Kath. Cosbrooke.	...	...	...	2	
Elizabeth Hudson,	...	...	...	2	6
Isabel Sumervil,	...	...	...	10	
Grizel Shepley,	...	...	...	2	
Eliz. Kingley,	...	...	...	2	
Amabell Higgins,	...	...	...	2	
Eliz. M'Laughlin,	...	...	...	3	6
Francis Hooper,	...	...	...	2	6
Turlogh O'Lon, £5 per annum.					

TEIG O'HARA'S CASE, 9th March, 1655.

Teig O'Hara, Esq., took advantage of an Ordinance of the Lord Protector,
dated the 2 of September, 1654, admitting Protestant delinquents to compound for
their estates, and the lands, amounting to 1,850 acres, worth £269 yearly in 1640,
deducting chief rents, amounting to £23 6 8. £245 13 4 allowed to compound at
two years and six months' purchase, amounting to £614 3 4. For his personal
estate, valued at £38, he is allowed to compound for £8, the whole amount of his
composition being £622 3 4, to be paid in the manner following :—£207 7 9 in
May, 1655, and the like sum on 2nd March, 1656 ; on 12 August of the same year,
£207 7 10 ; the last sum and such sums being paid, the estate " shall be from
henceforth freed and discharged of and from all manner of sequestrations, confiscation, or forfeiture for and in respect of any delinquency in the same Teig O'Hara."
9th March, 1655.

Col. Barrow, Col. Trayle, and Mr. Timothy Taylor appointed to receive the
names of such as may be presented to them as persons qualified to preach the
Gospel, and being satisfied that they are pious, holy, gracious men, fitly qualified
for publishing the truth of the Gospel, and of sober, peaceable spirits, they are to
return the names to the Council, and if approved of, such ministers shall be
provided with a comfortable and sufficient maintenance. 9 May, 1655.

SCOTCH MINISTERS RETURNED BY COLONEL TRAYLE. 20 Nov., 1655.

Upon consideration had of the return by Lt. Col. Trayle and Mr. Timothy
Taylor, minister, touching the Scotch ministers in the Province of Ulster, and of

the report made of the chief officers of the army thereupon : It is thought fit and ordered that the allowance of Fifty Pounds be paid out of the Publick Treasure to the respective ministers, mentioned in the annexed schedule, on the 25th of December and 25th of March next.

James Gordon.	William Richardson.
John Drisdaile.	Andrew Steward.
Patrick Adaire.	Gabriel Cornwall.
Robert Cunningham.	Thomas Hall.
John Gregg.	Gilbert Simpson.
Gilbert Ramsay.	William M'Cormick.
Thomas Peebles.	William Jack.

Being in all the number of fourteen, and living in the Counties of Down and Antrim.

Commissioners of Revenue at Belfast are to take notice and prepare warrants accordingly.

20 Novr., 1655.

THE CONVERSION OF THE OLD CHURCH IN HIGH ST. INTO THE "GRAND CITADEL," 1651.

Feby., 1656.

The Council having recd. a communication from Col. Cooper commanding at Belft., and the petition of Love Bure, &c., of Belfast, referred all the papers to his Ex. Lord Henry Cromwell, Commander-in-Chief of his Highness' forces in this Nation, to act as he shall think meet in giving orders about sleighting the fort in Belfast, and restoring the meeting place to the inhabitants there.

FROM ENTRIES OF ORDERS OF REFERENCES UPON PETITIONS. *(A. 11.)*

Upon reading the petition of Archibald Adaire, praying the orders of this board to require the Registrar General to deliver unto the petitioner a debenture in his custody, which he obtained for the arrears of his deceased father, Sir Robert Adaire, Kt., for his service in Ireland. And upon consideration had thereon, and of a letter of his Highness, and the former orders of this Board in the case : forasmuch as it appears that the said Sir Robert Adaire was actually in arms and engaged against the Commonwealth at the fight in Dunbar in Scotland, and by the rule of the Act for stating the arrears for services in Ireland—It is provided that such as have revolted from the Parliament and turned to the enemy shall lose the benefit of their arrears due before such revolt, and for that the said debenture was respited in the hands of the Clerk of the Council, by order of this Board, for the reason aforesaid. It is though fit and ordered, That the Clerk of the Council do forthwith cancel the said debenture, and certify the same into the office of the Commissioners of Accounts, that notice may be taken thereof accordingly. Dated at the Council Chamber in Dublin *2 February, 1656.*

T. H., C.C. (Thomas Herbert, Clerk of the Council.)

The Council write to Col. Arthur Hill and Major Rawdon and Timothy Taylor, minister of Carrickfergus, stating that the 27 Feb. had been appointed to be solemnly kept as a publick day of thanksgiving throughout the nation on account of the Protector's escape from assassination, and that the day was very slightly observed by the Scotch ministers in Ulster, though at present under salary from the Civil list; to inquire who those ministers were, and the places where settled, and certify the same to the Council. Date *24 March, 1656.*

"Ordered, that the respective ministers hereunder named, being fifteen in number, are appointed to preach the gospel in the precincts of Londonderry and Belfast, in the several and distinct places as to their several names hereunder is annexed, or elsewhere, in any other vacant place in the said precincts, where they may respectively conceive their labours may be most conducive to the advancement of the Gospel; and for their pains and care therein to receive the yearly salary of one hundred pounds a-year, to commence from the 25 of March last, and to continue till further order. Whereof the Clerk of the Council is to take notice and cause their names to be entered in the Civil List." *Dublin Castle, 13th May, 1656.*

James Gordon,	at Comber.	Pat Adair,	at Carncastle,
Jno. Drysdale,	Portaferry.		Garden.
Jno. Gregg,	Newtown.	Rob. Cunningham,	Braid.
Gilbert Ramsey,	Bangor.	Gab. Cornewall,	Balliwoolen.
Thos. Peeble,	Kirkdonnell.	Thos. Hall,	Larne.
Wm. Richardson,	Killileagh.	Gilbert Simpson,	Ballyclare.
Andw. Steward,	Donaghadee.	Wm. Jack,	Aghadowey.
Andw. McCormick,	Magheralin.	Donald Richmond,	Hollywood.

Ordered that the sum of £10 be allowed for and towards the demolishing the fort at Belfast, and bringing the guns and other provisions thence to the Castle of Carrickfergus. *28 May, 1656.*

The quarter's salary for Belfast ministers, appointed to be paid by Thos. Tuttle, the Collector, due 20th June, 1656.

Timoth. Taylor, Carrickfergus,	£50	0 0
Essex Digby, } Belfast,	30	
Willm. Dix,	30	
Andrew Wike, Lisnegarvey,	37	10
James Kerr, Ballymoney,	30	
Thos. Johnson, Dromore,	25	
Jeremy O'Quin, Billy,	25	
Thos. Skelston, Newry,	25	
Pat Duncan, Hillsborough,	20	
Willm. Fullerton,	20	
Dan. M'Neile, Ballycastle,	20	
Robt. Ecklin, Strangford,	20	
Willm. Moore, Knock and Breda,	12	10
James Watson, ...	12	10
John Walwood, Glenavy, ...	10	
Hugh Graffan, ...	6	5
Andrew Law, Dundrum, ...	12	10
James Gordon, Comber, ...	25	
John Drisdaile, Portaferry,	25	
John Gregg, Newtoune, ...	25	
Ant. Buckworth, Magheralin,	15	
Gilbert Ramsey, Bangor,	25	
Thom. Peebles, Kirkdonnell,	25	
Will. Richardson, Killileagh,	25	
And. Stewart, Donaghadee,	25	

And. M'Cormick, Magheraly,	...	...	£25
Pat Adaire, Garden Castle,	...	...	25
Robt. Cunningham, Broad Island,	...	...	25
Gabriel Cornwall, Ballywoollen,	...	...	25
Thos. Hall, Larne,	...	...	25
Gilbert Simpson, Ballyclare,	...	...	25
Will. Jack, Aghadowey,	...	...	25
Donald Richmond, Holywood,	...	...	25
Ministers' Widows, half a-year's salary.			

ORDER OF REFERENCES ON PETITIONS.

Upon reading the petition of Arthur Lord Viscount Chichester, setting forth that by means of the late Rebellion the woods near his residence have been destroyed, that through the many garrisons which have been continually on his estate most of his buildings have been demolished, and therefore prays a quantity of timber out of the Commonwealth woods to rebuild his houses withal. It is thought fit and ordered that the petitioner be hereby permitted to have a portion of timber out of the woods in the County of Londonderry as belong unto the Commonwealth for the aforesaid use, provided the same exceed not one hundred trees.

Col. Newbrough appointed to see the same. No timber near a navigable river useful for shipping be taken. Lord Chichester paying for the trees such prices as Col. shall conceive them to be worth. Council Chamber, Dublin, _15 July, 1656._

For our right trustie and right well beloved our Councel in Ireland.

RIGHT TRUSTIE AND WELBELOVED,

A peticion hath been exhibited unto us by William Spencer, setting forth that being but seaven yeares old att the beginning of the Rebellion in Ireland, hee repaired with his mother (his ffather being then dead) to the Citty of Corke, and dureing the Rebellion continued in the English Quarters. That he never bore Armes or acted against ye Common Wealth of England ; that his Grandfather, Edmond Spencer, and his ffather were both Protestants, from whom an estate of Lands in the Barony of ffermoy and County of Corke Descended on him, wch. dureing ye Rebellion yielded him Little or nothing towards his releife. That ye s^d. Estate hath been lately given out to the Souldiers in satisfaction of their Arreares onely upon the accompt of his p'fessing the Popish Religion, wch. since his comeing to yeares of discretion hee hath as hee professes utterly renounced. That his Grandfather was that Spencer whoe by his writings touching ye reduction of ye Irish to Civilitie brought on him the odium of that Nacon, and for those Workes and his other good Services Queene Elizabeth conferred on him y^t Estate, wch. y^? said Wm. Spencer now claimes. Wee have alsoe been informed y^t ye Gentl is of a civill conversacon, and y^t the extremitie his Wants have brought him to have not p'vailed over him to put him upon indirect or evill practices for a lively hood. And if upon inquiry yo^u shall finde his case to be such, Wee judge it just and reasonable, and doe therfore desire and authorize you y^t hee be forthw^th resstored to his estate, and that Reprisall Lands be given to ye Sould^rs elsewhere. In ye doeing wherof Our satisfaccon wilbe ye greater by y^e continuacon of that estate to y^e yssue of his Grandfather, for whose eminent deserts and services to y^e Common Wealth y^t Estate was first given him. We rest

Your loveing Freind,

OLIVER P.

Whitehall, 27th March, 1657.

ARMS OF CORK.

FROM THE CIVIL LIST OF IRELAND, 1657. (*A. 2060.*)

Precinct of Belfast. Ministers.

Gilbert Simpson, Ballyclare,	...	£100
William Jack, Aghadowey,	...	100
Donald Richmond, Hollywood,	...	100
Barnham West, Kilwarlin,	...	120
James Thelfall, Kilmore,	...	100
Cuthbert Harrison, Shankill-cum-Lurgan,	...	100
Thos. Crawford, Donegore,	...	100
John Barnes, Dromcree,	...	100
Robt. Hamilton, Killead, upon Sir John Clotworthy's presentation being allowed of,		100
Clinton Maud, Antrim, upon the like presentation,	...	100
John Jones, Seago,	...	80
Robt. Huetson, Rathfriland,	...	120
Henry Levingston, Drumbo,	...	100
David Fearfull, Drumkad,	...	50
Robt. Hogsyeard, Ballirashane,	...	100
David Buthel, Ballymena,	...	100
Anthony Kennedy, Templepatrick,	...	100
John Douglas, Braid,	...	100
John Fleming, Bally,	...	100
John Ayton, Tynan, Co. Armagh,	...	100
James Shaw, Carnmoney,	...	100
Willm. Milne, Isle of Magee,	...	100
Francis Reddington, Upper Fengh,	...	100
Anthony Shaw, Ballywalter,	...	100
Michael Bruce, Killinchy,	...	100
John Shaw, Machrishohell,	...	100
James Fleming, Glenarm,	...	100
Robert Denner, Connor,	...	100
Willm. Swalden, Carlingford,	...	100
Edward How, Charlemount,	...	80

31 at £100 each for the precinct of Derry.

Schoolmasters.

Thomas Hasleam, Lisnegarvey,	£40
John Cornewall, Belfast,	30
John Smith, Carrickfergus,	30
John Newtone, Downpatrick,	20
Ralph Davenport, Antrim,	30
Lawrence Swarbreake, Lurgan,	20
Donnagh O'Dowda, Ballycastle,	20
George Savage, Armagh,	30

Civil Officers.

Robert Bridges, Collector of Revenue for the Counties of Down, Antrim, and Armagh,	...	...	£100
Thomas Norris, Muster Master,	...	...	127 8
John Preston, Master of Packet Boat,	...	...	60
Rich. Johnson, Storekeeper at Carrickfergus,	...	40

Officers of Customs. Belfast.

Simon Spier, Waiter,	...	£18
Thomas Hodgkinson,	...	18

Pensioners.

Elinor Atkinson,	...	10s per week,	...	£26	
John Cooley,	...	2 6	...	6	10
Thos. Rogers,	...	2	...	5	4
Arthur and Martha Connolly, 20 between them,	...	52		
Izabell Sommervill,	...	10	...	26	
Elizabeth Kingley,	...	2	...	5	4
Hanniball Higgins,	...	2	...	5	4
Eliz. M'Laughlin,	...	3 6	...	9	2
Turlogh O'Lon,	...	...	...	5	
John Dan. Shonbull,	...	10	...	26	
George Portus during his continuance at Ballyhurbert,		30	
Robert Montgomerie,	...	...	12	

" *To our Right Trusty and dearly beloved Brother Henry, our Lord Lieutenant of Ireland.*

"Right trusty and dearly beloved brother and Councellor, our Lord Lieut. of our Realm of Ireland, we greet you well.   Whereas humble suit hath been made to us by Sir Timothy Tyrrill, who married the daughter of the late Archbishop of Armagh, for a lease of lands in Ireland, a matter sometime depending before our late deceased father of blessed memory.   We having taken the same into consideration, with the regard we have to the memory of the said learned Archbishop, we think fit, and do accordingly require you to suspend in the hands of the said Sir Timothy Tyrrill the two next gales of rent for the lands he holds of us in Ireland.   And for your so doing this our Letters shall be to you a sufficient warrant and discharge in that behalf.   Given at our Court at Whitehall the *first of March, 1658.*

"Your affectionate brother,

"RICHARD P."

The Lord Deputy and Council having taken Mr. James Shaw's petition into consideration, therein setting forth that he hath exercised his ministry in Carn-money, in the County of Antrim, for two years past, and praying a competent maintenance while he preaches the word there, as also the certificate of Mr. John Hart and Mr. John Drisdaile, ministers of the Gospel, who represent that the said

Mr. James Shaw hath been tried by his brethren of the ministry, and is found to be well qualified, not only in respect of his learning, but of piety and sobriety as becomes a minister of the Gospel. It is thought fit and ordered that Mr. Shaw may have salary of £100 per ann. as long as he continues to preach to the inhabitants of Carnmoney. *17 March, 1658.*

In the petition of Col. Arthur Hill in the behalf of the Lord Chichester and himself, praying leave to transport (import) thirteen tons of lead, duty free, for their own use. It is ordered that, pursuant to an Ordinance for the encouragement of Adventurers to plant in Ireland, Col. Arthur Hill is permitted to transport the quantity of thirteen tons of lead, the same being to be landed together at Carrickfergus without paying any customs or other publick duty.
Dublin, March, 1658.

WM. PETTY, Clerk of Council.

REFERENCE UPON PETITIONS. *(A. 15.)*

"LORD DEPUTY AND COUNCIL,

"Upon consideration of the petition of the merchants and inhabitants of Belfast, praying relief against the irregular and undue practices of the officers there employed by the Farmers of the Customs. Ordered that the said Farmers now in Dublin have a sight of the petition, and they are to take the matter complained of into consideration, and to take care that the petitioners have every redress therein as shall appear to be just and meet. And the said Farmers are likewise to have regard that for the future the petitioners receive no needless disturbance or any just cause of complaint." *Dated 25 June, 1658.*

THOMAS HERBERT, Clerk of the Council.

Upon consideration had of the humble petition of Mr. John Drisdaile, of Portaferry, in the County of Down, and Mr. Robert Cunningham, minister at Broad Island, in the County of Antrim, setting forth that the five ministers hereunder named are tried and approved of for holiness, and of conversation and abilities to discharge the work of the ministry in a good measure, as also are men of a peaceable disposition, and therefore praying that for their encouragement in the Lord's work they may be received into salary. They are ordered to receive £100 a-year each, and to be placed in the following places :—

Anthony Shaw, Ballywalter, Down.	James Fleming, Glenarm, Antrim.
Michael Bruce, Killinshy, Down.	Robt. Denner, Connor, Antrim.
John Shaw, Machrisohell, Antrim.	
30 June, 1658.	*(A. 91. Bermingham Tower.)*

The Comns. of Revenue to provide a house for Claudius Gilbert while preaching in Dublin. *1659, February.*

Essex Digby. It is referred to the Committee for approbation of Ministers to appoint one for Belfast in room of Essex Digby, removing to the parishes of Gheashill and Ballycoman, in the King's County. *18 March, 1659.*

ORDERS IN COUNCIL, *30 Novr., 1659.*

Quaker books consigned to one Samuel Claridge found on perusal to have an erroneous untoward spirit, denying external reverence to magistrates, contemning and disgracing ministers as antichristian, not ministers of Christ, but dumb dogs, priests, and hirelings ; expressing much bitterness against learning, maintaining perfection and freedom from sin in this life, also Popish and other tenets contrary to sound doctrine. Books to be detained, not suffered to be dispersed.

BY THE COUNCIL FOR THE GOVERNMENT AND MANAGEMENT OF AFFAIRS
IN IRELAND.

Upon consideration of the petition of Patrick Adaire, Minister of the Gospel, and the certificate of Dr. Dudley Loftus, whereby it appears that the said Patrick Adair, incumbent of the Parish of Cairnecastle, hath no more left unto him for his maintainance, according to the valuation made on the return of the Commissioners for visiting of parishes in the County of Antrim, than sixty-three pounds per ann. And for it appears by certificate of James Standish, Esq., that there was paid to the said Mr. Adaire the sum of nine pounds, and no more, as addition to his allowance for the year ending the first of May, 1659, so as there remains due to Mr. Adair the sum of twenty-eight pounds to complete his salary of one hundred pounds for the said year, and also thirty-seven pounds for the year ended the first of May, 1660, making in all three score and five pounds. It is therefore ordered that John Price, Receiver, do issue and pay unto the said Patrick Adair the sum of sixty-five pounds. And for so doing, this, together with his acquittance, shall be sufficient warrant; and for the future the salary of the parish of Carnecastle must be made up one hundred pounds, the yearly salary allowed to Patrick Adaire. *Dated at Dublin the 19th day of May, 1660.*

BROGHILL, CHARLES COOTE, WM. BURY.

SILVER SALVER, TRINITY COLLEGE, DUBLIN, THE GIFT OF CLAUDIUS GILBERT THE YOUNGER.

Account of John Corry, Freeman of Belfast, 1654.

BY THE RIGHT HON. THE EARL OF BELMORE, G.C.M.G., &c.

JOHN CORRY, who was admitted on the 1st July, 1654, as a " mᵗ ffree of the staple" of Belfast on the payment of a fee of £2 os. od., is believed to have been an immigrant into Ireland from Scotland, but at what period is not known. In an old MS. (from Sir W. Betham's collection) entitled, *History of the Co. Fermanagh, with the antient families of the same*, written 1718–19, &c.,* now at Thirlestane House, Cheltenham (in the catalogue at p. 238, No. 13,293, *Betham MSS.*), we find it stated that—

"The family of Corry was formerly remarkable in Scotland for their vallour, by yᵉ frequent wars, which sometimes happened betweene England and Scotland ; and beareth in their Coate of Arms, ' *Argent a saltire Couped, Gules, etc.* ' "

In *The Historical Families of Dumfriesshire and the Border Wars*, by C. L. Johnstone, it is said, at pages 5 and 6—" The second son of Sir William de Carlile and Margaret Bruce was killed at the battle of Durham in 1346, leaving one child, Susanna, who was afterwards married to Robert Corrie. A charter in favour of his brother, William de Carlile, from Robert Bruce, styles him the King's sister's son ; and another, dated at Melrose, 1363, from David II., in favour of Susanna Carlile and her husband Robert Corrie, calls the deceased Thomas Carlile the King's blood relation, and grants to his daughter and her spouse the lands along the southern coast of Dumfriesshire, which had belonged to her grandfather. The Corries (the name is Celtic for hollow) were the hereditary keepers of the castle of Lough Doon in 1306, and a little later, owing to the marriage above named, added greatly to their possessions in Dumfriesshire, &c.,

---

* This MS. is limited to "British families." It is supposed to have been Notes for a History, which Dr. Samuel Madden, F.T.C.D., and a Fermanagh Landowner, intended to write.

&c." Their estates, which included Gretna, and the ruins of the
ancient Redkirk and the celebrated Lochmaben Stone, where treaties
were signed with the English, extended into Cumberland. "But
during the fifteenth century the rebellion of the Douglases involved
Dumfriesshire in a civil war. In 1484 George Corrie took the side of
the insurgents, and when they were defeated he was outlawed, and
part of his estates transferred to Thomas Carruthers, a loyal freeman
of Annandale. His brothers, Thomas and William Corry, for some
time retained a portion of the family lands, but subject to constant
forays on the part of their neighbours ; and in spite of numerous
lawsuits they could get no redress. Yet Thomas Corrie, of Kildwood
and Newbie, was of sufficient importance to be appointed in 1529,
with the King's treasurer and two Scottish knights, an arbiter in a
family matter between the Earls of Eglington and Glencairn. He
married a daughter of Lord Herriot."

In the long run the Corrys appear to have lost or parted with their
landed possessions, and probably took to commerce. In 1639 one
" John Corrie " was the Provost of Dumfries. He may possibly have
been the father of the subject of this note.

As far as any record remains, John Corry, the merchant of Belfast,
had an only child James, who, as he was in his 62nd year in 1695
(the date on a picture of him by Pooley, now at Castlecoole),
must have been born in 1633 or 1634. John Corry's wife's name was
Blanch, as shown by a Chancery Bill of 1656—Jennett Petilla *alias*
M'Cully *v.* John Corry and wife, and Hugh Eccles and wife ; entered
29th August—and it is said in the above-mentioned *Betham MSS.*
that " Coll^ James Corryes mother was of the family of Johnston,
who derive themselves from the Marquess of Annandale in Scotland"
(*i.e.*, from his ancestors). From the allegations of the Chancery Bill, it
appears that the plaintiff's son, one Archibald Moore, deceased, had
been of Lisnegarvy, now Lisburn, and that John Corry and his wife
had been " of a long and familiar acquaintance with her son" (whose
widow had married Hugh Eccles).* This makes it appear probable
that John Corry had originally settled at Lisburn.

There is an entry in *The Town Book of Belfast*, p. 77, without date,
but probably of 1656, which shows that John Corry was residing there
at that time ; and this is followed by an engraving of his penny
token.

In 1656 he purchased an estate known as the Manor of Coole,
in the Co. Fermanagh, from the representatives of an Englishman,
Mr. Arthur Champion, M.P. for Enniskillen, who had lost his life in
the Rebellion of 1641, and who had purchased the property in 1639

* *Vide* History of the Corry Family, by the Earl of Belmore, pp. 10, 11, 12.

from Captain Roger Atkinson, the original Patentee, subject, however, to a lease of it to Atkinson and Edith his wife, for the lives of both and of the longest liver of them.

John Corry appears to have come to reside in Fermanagh soon after acquiring his estate there. He had purchased with a defective title, and disputes had twice to be compromised ; once with an English creditor named Pembridge ; and again with a nephew of Arthur Champion, of the same name. Mr. Corry was appointed a Commissioner for levying subsidies in Fermanagh 8 November, 1662, and on the 14 November, 1662, a Justice of the Peace for the Counties of Fermanagh and Cavan. He served as High Sheriff for Fermanagh in 1666.

It is supposed that Mr. Corry settled some of his relations about him. A Mr. Laurence Crawford was, according to the *Betham MSS.*, his nephew. This gentleman, whose name appears amongst those inhabitants of Fermanagh who were attainted by King James II.'s Parliament of 1689, resided close to Castlecoole until 1731, successively at Cavancarragh, Bonnybrooke, and Carrowmacmea, or possibly in that part of the old townland of that name now known as Cloghtate. It is not certainly known who his father was ; but there seems to be grounds for supposing that he was the son of William Crawford, of Ballymenagh, Co. Antrim, gent., of whose effects Mr. Corry took out Letters of Administration in 1661, for the benefit of his widow, Ann Pibles, *alias* Crawford, and her children. If this Ann were John Corry's sister, she must have had a former husband. Mr. Crawford himself appears to have been a gentleman-freeholder on a very moderate scale. But of his descendants (Crawfords) eight have been High Sheriffs of Fermanagh.

Besides the Crawford family, there was another family of Corry settled in Carrowmacmea. There is an unexecuted counterpart of a lease of that townland at Castlecoole from John Corry, gent., to James Corry, gent., dated 1662. Whether James and John were brothers, or more distant relatives, cannot now be determined. But there is every reason to suppose that they were related. The site of James's house has been included in Castlecoole demesne since 1763. James had a son John, who died in 1703, and who had three sons, mentioned in his will, dated 13 November, 1701, viz., Alexander, James, and Charles. Alexander had gone in His Majesty's service to Jamaica, and does not appear to have ever returned ; James married, 8 April, 1711, Margaret, one of the daughters of Laurence Crawford before-mentioned, and had John, b. 1711-2 ; Laurence, b. 1713-4, who having m. Ann Welsh, d. 1799—leaving James (who was probably the person who, by his wife Sarah, had Laurence, b. 1794), and Alexander (of Carrowmacmea), who d. 1831, aged 76, leaving Alexander, who emigrated to America about Anno domini, 1835 ; Robert, b. 1715 ; Alexander, b. 1716, who was probably father of Alexander, of Killynure, who d. 1834, aged 62 ; Leslie, b. 1719 ; and another child, b. 1720. Charles may have been the father of Charles and William Corry, to whom Col. John Corry, of Castlecoole, made bequests in 1721. John

Corry, of Carrowmacmea, had a daughter Ann (who married William Nixon, 22 April, 1701). He himself married Ann Irwin, "a widdow," on the 14 April, 1697.* Probably Captain Robert Corry, who was killed at the battle of Newtownbutler, was his brother. It seems more likely that he and his father,† or perhaps a brother, were the James and John Corry who, in 1689, signed the address from Enniskillen which the Rev. Andrew Hamilton took over to King William and Queen Mary, than Capt. James of Castlecoole and his son John ; as Captain James, at any rate, was apparently in England in July and August, 1689 ; though it is possible that his son either remained in Ireland or soon returned to it ;‡ whilst John of Carrowmacmea, in his will, bequeaths arrears of pay due to him by the King, which looks as if he had been in the garrison at Enniskillen. His will is witnessed by John Corry the younger of Castlecoole, and William Crawford, which points to a relationship of the parties.

To return to John Corry of Castlecoole. It is not known when his wife died ; but no mention of her is found after 1656. His son James married Sarah, daughter of Oliver Anketill, Esq., of Co. Monaghan, in or about 1663-4, being then about thirty years of age. He had at least four children by her, viz., Sarah [whether baptised or buried is obliterated], 25 Nov., 1666; John, whose baptismal entry in the Enniskillen Vestry-book runs thus :—" 1667. 8 Janry. Jo: son to Capt. James Corry. Bapt:"; Rebecca, married in 1698 to James Moutray, M.P. for Augher ; and Elizabeth, married, probably in 1700, to James Auchenleck, who had been attainted by the Parliament of 1689. It is supposed that at one time Captain Corry resided in Enniskillen, very likely in a house next to the Market-house, which Michael Cole (afterwards Sir Michael) had leased, 4 Oct., 1664, to James Reyd, merchant, for 50 years, at 40 shillings a-year, and a fine of £15 ; which lease is now at Castlecoole. This James Read was admitted, on the 21st November, 1663, " a free commoner and march¹ of the Staple " of Belfast.§ He issued a penny token at Enniskillen, the inscription on which is given in Canon Bradshaw's *Enniskillen Long Ago,* as published in the *Historical and Archæological Journal, 1872.*‖

James Corry seems to have had a good deal to do with the management of the estates (for there was one also in Monaghan) in his father's lifetime, and to have had part of them settled on himself in 1674, and again as to a moiety in 1679. His father covenanted not

---

* The Vestry-book of Iniskeene (Enniskillen) parish, in P.R.O., is the authority for most of the dates. The Visitation Returns for Derryvullan is that for the dates of the burials of the two Alexander Corrys.

† The original James was elected a churchwarden of Enniskillen parish on Easter Tuesday, 21 April, 1674, as James Corry, the elder, of Carrowmacmea.

‡ In a MS. in Trin. Coll., Dub., F. 4, 3, being a list of "such Protestants of Irl: as are lately fled out of yᵉ kingd: &c.," we find " Curry: Ja: fermanagh, W. 3. ch.: £800." If three daughters of Captain Corry were living in 1689, and accompanied him to England, then we may assume that his son John remained in Ireland, as he served their Majesties during the war, as will be seen below.

§ See *The Town Book of Belfast,* p. 262.

‖ On *obverse* side—JAMES. Reid. MarcHANT, with a bell as the symb. *Reverse*—IN. INeskilLin. 1663. with J. R. in centre.

to dispose of more than £50 by will, which accounts for there being no trace of a Will or Administration. It is not therefore known when John Corry died. A silver tankard, bearing his arms, has the hall-

SILVER TANKARD OF JOHN CORRY, 1681.

mark of 1681. At this time there was "a chief or" to the coat, which shows that John was a cadet of some family, and which was discontinued in the next century when the connection had become remote. James Corry, who had received a commission of Captain from the Duke of Ormonde, July 11th, 1666, married again in Dec., 1683. The Consistorial Court marriage license for "James Corry, Esq., of Dublin, and Lucy Mervin, Sp⁻⁰" is dated Decr. 3rd. The lady was daughter of Henry Mervyn, of Trillick, and granddaughter of Sir Audley Mervyn. In the marriage settlement, John Corry is referred to as having reserved power to make a settlement on another wife. In a Chancery Bill of 28 May, 1686, he is referred to as deceased.

At the beginning of the Revolution of 1688, Captain Corry was living at Castlecoole. He was a magistrate of the County Fermanagh. When King James's Government resolved to place a garrison in Enniskillen, the inhabitants became very uneasy; and five of them, named William Browning, Robert Clarke, William MacCarmick, James Ewart, and Allen Cathcart* (afterwards Captain), resolved to refuse admittance to the troops, and set carpenters to work on the drawbridge. They sent notice of their determination to the surrounding country. Captain Corry, "and indeed most of the inhabitants, were

---

* The *Betham MS.* (1719-20) at Cheltenham says that Allan Cathcart had been a rich merchant at Enniskillen. He was High Sheriff of Fermanagh, 1704. He was buried at Enniskillen, 1720.

I

in favour of admitting the soldiers."* M'Carmick went, on Dec. 13th, to consult Gustavus Hamilton, of Monea. On his return, he was met by a messenger from the Provost, Paul Dane, saying that "Mr. Latournall came just now from Captain Corry," and had commanded the carpenters to leave off working at the drawbridge, and begged that he should send for his brethren, and dissuade them from denying the soldiers entrance, and to provide them quarters. The whole matter was debated over again. Mr. Hamilton gave his influence for defending the town, and preparations for doing so were made, in spite of Captain Corry. The latter appears, on the 17th, with Sir Gerard Irvine (another magistrate), to have seen Mr. Browning riding into the town at the head of a party of horse, to have had him seized, and to have threatened to put him in gaol on a charge of bearing arms against the Government. This was forcibly resisted by the towns-people, who gave the magistrates notice to leave the town, under a threat of being put in gaol themselves. Subsequently the latter were willing to join in the defence, provided that Sir Gerard Irvine was made Colonel of Horse, with Hamilton (who had been elected Governor on the 13th) as his Lieutenant-Colonel, and Captain Corry, Colonel of Foot, which would have made him Governor of the town, with Thomas Lloyd as Lieutenant-Colonel. This proposal was rejected, and, according to Professor Witherow, Capt. Corry soon went to England. Probably out of this incident was manufactured a charge against him in the 49th paragraph of the Report of the Chichester House Commissioners, on the forfeitures in Ireland and King William's grants, as follows :—" Butt Inquiring into ye merrits of this gentleman, It appears to us y^t he gave no assistance to the Garrison of Iniskillen, that in the town of Inniskillin he Publiquely declared he hoped to see all those hanged that tooke up Arms for ye Prince of Orange, and his house was burned in the said Garrison." When this appeared he met it by obtaining a certificate, under the corporation seal, and the hands of Mr. Letournall, Provost, and Messrs. D. Rynd, Jason Hassard, Robert Clarke,† Hall, Roscrow, Paul Dane, and John Rynd, that he had been very diligent in arming men for his late Majestie's service ; that he had raised a very good troop of horse and foot company, and mounted and armed many of them at his own expence ; that by his encouragement several of his Relations and friends followed his example ; that he had furnished the garrison with considerable quantities of supplies ; that his house in the garrison was not burnt, but still continued in good repair ; that his house at Castlecoole was burnt‡ by the Governor's order, to prevent the Duke of Berwick from posting himself there ; that they believed that the words alleged to have been spoken by him " were never spoke by him, for yt wee never heard him charged with ye same till by the said Report, nor doe we believe his principales lead him to any such expressions, having always and upon all occasions showed himselfe forward to serve their

* Professor Witherow.
† This name is that of one of the original five defenders of the town.
‡ In July, 1689.

late Majesties, and to Incourage his friends & relations to doe ye same ;" that his only son had served their Majesties throughout the late war both in Ireland and Flanders ; that several of his relations had lost their lives in the said service ; and that, if he had publicly used such expressions, some of them must have heard him, or at least heard of it afterwards.

This reply to the Commissioners' Report is supported by the fact that, after the Report was printed in Dublin, the Irish House of Commons, on the 78th paragraph being read to the House, resolved, *nemine contradicente*, "That all the Protestant freeholders of the kingdom have been falsely and maliciously misrepresented, traduced, and abused in a representation made of them in the said book. . . . And that such misrepresentment hath been one of the great causes of the misery of this kingdom." On the 28 September one of the Commissioners, who was a member of the House, having been heard in his place on a charge of being one of the authors of the paragraph, and he having prayed the House to excuse him from making any answer thereunto, it was ordered that he "be expelled this House." On the 2 Oct. two other of his colleagues were censured. A third being dead, "The House thought not fit to put any further question on him."* The original Report is in the Public Record Office in Dublin ; but no evidence is forthcoming there. James Corry had received two grants in compensation for his losses. One was of a heavily incumbered estate in his own neighbourhood. This grant was voided on the ground that the former owner, Cucconagh Maguire (who was killed at the battle of Aughrim) had had only a life estate in it, and that the estate was not vested in the Crown. This claim being admitted, it was restored to his son Bryan. The other grant was of a mortgage of £2,000 on lands in the County Wicklow. This James Corry retained, but compromised it for £1,000. His losses had been proved on oath to have been £3,000 and upwards.† His estate was worth £800 or (as he himself put it) £1,000 a-year.

After the war, James Corry lived for a time in apparently straitened circumstances in England. His second wife appears to have died there ; for in 1692 he re-married Elizabeth Harryman, who possessed two tenements in London. They executed a deed of separation in 1695. In 1692 James Corry was appointed Colonel of a regiment of Horse Militia to be raised in Fermanagh, which county he represented in the Parliaments of 1692, 1695, 1703, 1713, and 1715 to his death in 1718, and at first seems to have been an active member. His name appears in the list of persons attainted in 1689 both as of Fermanagh and of Monaghan. He was High Sheriff of Fermanagh in 1671, and of Monaghan in 1677.‡ In 1696 he was appointed a Deputy Governor of Fermanagh ; and Governor in 1705.

---

* *Commons Journals.*

† A full account will be found in *The History of the Manors of Finagh and Coole*, by the Earl of Belmore, pp. 131-9.

‡ There was another family of Corry in Monaghan at the time, but no "James" amongst them. *Vide* Mr. Shirley's *History of Monaghan* (Corry of Rockcorry).

His name is included in the *Commission of Array of the Militia of Fermanagh* in 1702. After a disastrous fire in Enniskillen on the 2nd June, 1705, he was appointed by the Corporation, and other sufferers, their agent for managing and obtaining what money might be collected, as well by the Lord Lieutenant's brief as by voluntary subscriptions, upon their behalf. He appears, by a letter from William King, Archbishop of Dublin, to Sir Michael Cole, dated from Tunbridge Wells, Aug. 12, 1705, to have pressed the Duke of Ormond much on the subject, and the latter "had spoke to the Queen about the affair, and was in hopes to obtain a brief in England." Colonel Corry was himself a burgess of Enniskillen, having been sworn 2 Oct., 1694, and served as Provost in 1697. He held the office of "Master of the Game." He built a new house at Castlecoole adjoining the old one about 1709 or 1710, and died an octogenarian at Castlecoole, 1 May, 1718.

He was succeeded by his only son, John, who had entered Trinity College as a Fellow Commoner 3 May, 1685, but did not graduate, and who sat (as Captain Corry) in the House of Commons for Enniskillen in the Parliament of 1703-13. He served as High Sheriff of Fermanagh in 1711. In 1715 he was appointed Colonel of a Regiment of Foot Militia in Fermanagh, his father on the same day receiving a fresh commission as Colonel of a Horse Militia Regiment. He succeeded his father as member for the county in 1719. In 1701-2 he married Sarah, one of the co-heiresses of William Leslie, M.P., of Prospect, County Antrim, a cadet of the house of Rothes,* and died 11 Nov., 1726. He was succeeded by his third but only surviving son Leslie, then a minor. Leslie Corry was born on or about Oct. 15, 1712, at Castlecoole, and entered Trinity College, Oct. 11, 1728, as a Fellow Commoner. He graduated B.A. in 1732. He was High Sheriff of Fermanagh in 1737, and M.P. for Killybegs 1739-40-41. He was appointed Colonel of the Fermanagh Militia, in room of his father, 11 April, 1740, and on May 17 a Deputy Governor of the County. He died unmarried on or about Feb. 20, 1740-1, aged 28, when his landed property was divided between his eldest sister, Martha, the wife of Edmund Leslie (afterwards M.P. for Newtownlimavady, who took the name of Corry after Leslie, until his wife's death about 1764), and Galbraith Lowry (afterwards M.P. for Tyrone), the husband of his sister Sarah, and Margetson Armar the husband of his sister Mary, who got Castlecoole. It was, however, all reunited in 1779 in the person of Armar Lowry Corry, Sarah's only surviving son, who in 1797 was created Earl of Belmore, and was great-grandfather of the present holder of the title, who thus is seventh in descent from John Corry, the freeman of Belfast.

* William Leslie was third son of Henry Leslie, Bishop, 1st of Down and Connor, and afterwards of Meath, who was grandson of the 4th Earl of Rothes.

FAC-SIMILE OF JOHN CORRY'S SIGNATURE.

OLD WATERWORKS, STRANMILLIS.

Account of Stranmillis, Belfast.

By WILLIAM PINKERTON, F.S.A.

R. EVELYN PHILIP SHIRLEY, in his *Account of the Territory or Dominion of Farney* (London, 1845), erroneously thinks that this is the place thus mentioned, under the date of 1635, in the manuscript of Sir Wm. Brereton, published by the Chetham Society. Brereton is clearly and evidently speaking of Belfast, and he continues as follows :—

"Near hereunto Mr. Arthur Hill, son and heir to Sir Moses Hill, hath a brave plantation, which he holds by lease, which still is for thirty years to come ; the land is my Lord Chichester's, and the lease was made for sixty years to Sir Moyses Hill by the old Lord Chichester. This plantation is said doth yield him a £1000 per annum. Many Lancashire and Cheshire men are here planted, with some of them I conversed. They sit upon a rack rent, and pay 5s. or 6s. an acre for good ploughing land, which is now clothed with excellent corn."

Brereton seems to have been indefatigable in obtaining information when in Ireland ; but he falls into a slight error here. Arthur Hill was a younger son, Peter was the name of the son and heir of Sir Moyses. In the "*Report of Works done*" I find that the Commissioners, after "leaving Lisnegarvey, and approaching nearer to Carrickfergus," thus describe the "brave plantation" made by Sir Moyses Hill in 1611 :—

"Came by a strong fort built upon a passage on the plains of Moylon, with a strong palisade and a drawbridge, called Hilsborowe.
Within it is a fair timber house, walled with bricks, and a tower slated.
Some other houses are built without it, wherein are some families of English and Irish settled. This fort was built by Moyses Hill, who hath a lease for sixty-one years of the same, with a good scope of land, from Sir Arthur Chichester."

When afterwards, during the Protectorate, Colonel Arthur Hill, then the head of his family by the death of his elder brother Peter, built a fort at Kilwarlin, he called it Hillsborough. The Commissioners continue their report thus :—

"Within about a mile of Hilsborowe, by the river of Lagan, where the sea ebbs and flows, in a place called Strandmellis, we found the said Moyses Hill in hand with building of a strong house of stone, fifty-six feet long ; and he intends to make it two stories and a half high, it being already about the height of one story, and to build a good bawn of lime and stone about ; which lands are held by like lease as Hilsborowe aforesaid."

A copy of this lease is in my possession. It is headed—" In the Lower Claneboys, County of Antrim," and purports to be made the eighteenth of April, 1606, between Sir Arthur Chichester, Lord Deputy, and Moyses Hill of Hilsborowe, County Antrim, whereby Sir Arthur demised to the said Moyses, his heirs and assigns, all that and those the towns and villages or hamlets in the Territory or Tuogh called Tuogh Nefall, alias Tuogh Fall, and Myloune, viz. :—

Ballicollo, Ballydownmory, Ballindollaghan, Finahie, Ballyodrain, Ballivally, Ballicromage, Ballimurchane, Ballinrisk, Ballimeighmorey, Ballydownefin *alias* Ballinafeighan, Ballingarrie, Ballyminraher, and Ballymister.

LOCK-KEEPER'S HOUSE ON THE LAGAN.
(From painting by Dobie, in possession of F. W. MONEYPENNY, ESQ.*)*

The parcels of lands, or halftowns, or villages, of Millicton, Tulli-manan, Balliogman, Ardoine, Balliardsallagh, and Balliallyc. And all other lands within the said territory, whose bounds and limits are, on the South the main Bay of Knockfergus, and part of the Lagan river falling into that Bay. On the East runs into the said Bay a small stream from Altcomogh, between this Tuogh and the Tuogh Tinament, and thence the meares are directly about half a mile between its lands and Tuogh Killelagh unto the very top of Slewtermore, and thence about another half mile unto and through the Glyn of Barrattnagarrane, which is a meare between this Tuogh and Clandermot, and thence about another half mile directly by the top of the Glyn of Altmakeigh, and thence about another half mile directly to a little mount near

Kanebeg Church, which is a meare between Tuogh Fall and Derry-volgie, from which mount runs a small stream through or near the bog Fowerglasse, and so directly into the Lagan river.

Also all those fishings and weirs of all kinds of fish in that part of the Lagan river, lying from the point of land towards the sea, whereon the little Fort of Mount Essex stands, westward so far as the river extends in or by any of his lands.

Excepting all lands belonging to any Abbey, or other religious houses, all Churches, Rectories, Chapels, or Vicarages, and the glebes thereof; all timber and underwoods, hawks, advowsons, and mines whatever.

To hold from the Feast of the Annunciation last past, for the term of sixty-one years, at the rent of Ten pounds, English. Several duties of salmon, &c., are to be also paid. And Mr. Hill is to be Seneschal during the term of his lease within the said territory.

The boundaries of the lease are easily traced, the names of the townlands have almost the same spelling as they are laid down in the Ordnance Survey of the present day, and they formed the south-eastern portion of the lands of Sir Arthur Chichester in Antrim. The "small stream" was the Blackstaff, which with its affluent the Clowney runs up into Altcomogh, the glen between the Wolf Hill and Devis. Lendrick, in his map of Antrim, published in 1790, says that the manner of spelling the names of townlands is quite arbitrary, and depends on a variety of unfavourable circumstances, but we may readily trace out the most of those. Ballicollo, Dunmurry, Bally-dolaghan, Ballyfinaghy, Ballydrain, Cromac, Ballymurphy, Ballydown-fin, are all well known at present. The names of all the townlands next the hills have suffered little change, but those lower down next the river have been swallowed up in the modern denominations of Upper and Lower Malone. There is still an Ardoyne, and Balliard-sallagh in the same district is most probably the modern Ballysillan.

We do not know when or by what bargain this lease came to a termination. In 1635, when we last hear of it by Brereton, it had then thirty-two years to run, but it must have been revoked soon afterwards. For in 1639 an order of composition and agreement was made between the Commissioners for Defective Titles on the King's behalf, and Edward Lord Viscount Chichester, and Arthur his son and heir apparent, whereby it being expressed that his Lordship and son should have a good and sufficient estate granted unto them, their heirs and assigns, for ever of the Manor of Belfast, they and Arthur Hill, Esq., surrendered all their grants, titles, and leases to Sir William Wraye, Bart., and Henry le Squire, Esq., who were empowered to receive the same by the King. And Henry le Squire, Esq., agent to Lord Chichester, having compounded with the Lord Deputy and the Commissioners for remedy of defective Titles, and paid the fine of £467 17s. 6d., received a new grant from King Charles the First, dated at Westminster, 20th of March, in the fifteenth year of his reign (1640). In this grant I find—

"The capital messuage and demesne lands of Stronemellis, and two Corn Mills upon the Lagan."

It is generally but erroneously supposed that Stranmillis took its name from those mills—the mills on the strand—which is, as things go, a very good derivation. But when Moyses Hill commenced to build a house there, which he called Strandmellis, there was in all probability not a mill in all Ireland, saving a quern or hand-mill. My friend, the eminent Irish scholar, Mr. Robert MacAdam, of Belfast, informs me that he has no doubt the name Stran-millis, or Stron-millis (as usually pronounced), is merely a slight variation of the Irish *Sruthan-milis*, signifying "sweet stream." And I am confirmed in the opinion that this is a correct derivation from a passage in the above grant, where, describing the Eastern boundary of the Chichester estates, it mentions "a small river called Shroghanmellie, *alias* Shroanemellis, *alias* Strandmellis."

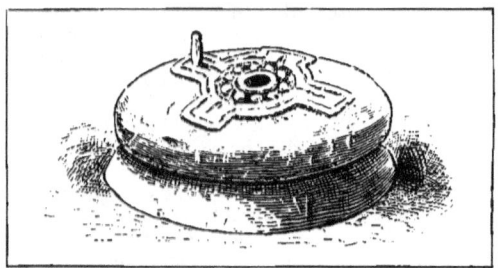

THE QUERN.

Arthur Hill was the immediate founder of the large estates now enjoyed by the present Marquis of Hillsborough, and the younger son of Moyses Hill, who built Strandmellis. Lodge, in his *Peerage of Ireland*, an immense and praiseworthy undertaking, the usefulness of which is partly destroyed by its many gross inaccuracies, probably inseparable from such a work, tells us that a

"Sir Robert Chichester, nephew to Arthur, Lord Deputy, being married to a daughter of this family (the Hills of Devonshire), we may reasonably presume that Moyses Hill, ancestor to the Earl of Hillsborough, was introduced into this Kingdom by that noble Lord in a military capacity, and was, during the course of O'Neill's rebellion in the North, one of those gentlemen who, in 1573, were associated under Walter Devereux, Earl of Essex, to suppress it."

Now there were a considerable number of O'Neill's rebellions in the latter part of the sixteenth century. The leaders of that distinguished family, being generally styled Princes of Ulster, on the *lucus a non lucendo* principle, just as we speak of the King of Bonny now-a-days, seem to have passed their lives either in making abject submissions, or in open defiant rebellion to the Kings and Queen of England ; but Walter Devereux, Earl of Essex, was never employed to suppress one of them. And the ridiculous absurdity of the passage is rendered still more palpable when it is recollected that Sir Arthur

Chichester, afterwards Lord Deputy, did not make his appearance in Ireland till the year 1599.

Colonel Arthur Hill had the command of the Regiment of Horse, consisting of 600 men, raised by Charles I., in 1641, to serve against the rebels in the North of Ireland. After the Kingdom had been compelled to submit to the Parliament, he entered their service, and was appointed a Commissioner of Revenue for the Precinct of Belfast, and very ably he fulfilled that duty, both under the Parliamentary and Protectorate Governments, until the Restoration. A letter from the Council at Dublin to Colonel Arthur Hill, their Commissioner at Belfast, is so characteristic of the period and the men, that I feel I may make no apology for introducing it here.

"Dublin, 23 December, 1652.

"To Colonel Arthur Hill, to be communicated to the rest of our Christian friends within his Precinct.

"Those unto whom the Lord hath in any measure, through grace, made known his free, eternal, and unchangeable love, cannot but be sensible how He hath of late manifested some displeasure against us, by continuing the pestilence in very many of our quarters and garrisons, and stirring a vanquished and dispersed enemy to an unusual resolution of attempting the surprisal of the fort and isle of Arran, and therein to prevail, not by strength, but by reason of a strange spirit of despondency which possessed him that commanded that place far unsuitable to his accustomed temper in the judgment of those that knew him. Upon serious consideration of those sad reproofs, we conceive it a duty incumbent upon us to mind those that fear the Lord in this land to be frequent in prayer, and earnest with Him to reveal his will unto his servants, what those failings in them are which He so sharply witnesses against. And that the Lord would renew unto his people a spirit of prayer and supplication, a spirit of prevailing with the Lord, and of dependance upon Him : That we may be delivered from a spirit of compliance with the enemies of God, and that our hearts may not be captivated in the snares which they spread for us, lest the anger of the Lord kindle against us.—Numbers xxv. 3. That we who in great mercy are hitherto spared may cleave unto the Lord, and keep his Statutes and Judgements, this being the wisdom and strength of God's people in the sight of the Nations.—Deuteronomy iv. 45. That the Lord may not give us over to a spirit of slothfulness and security in the management of the trust reposed in us, and that we may take heed to ourselves, and keep our souls diligently, lest we forget the out-goings of the Lord with us in England, Scotland, and Ireland. Those great things which our eyes have seen God do for His people, and lest they should depart from our hearts.—Deuteronomy iv. 9. Deadness of spirit, worldly mindedness, forget-fulness of what the Lord hath done for us in the day of our affliction, and attribut-ing much to the arm of flesh and wisdom of man, are sins that easily beset the Saints and servants of God in the time of their prosperity, when their enemies are scattered, and the powers of the earth laid down before them, and may be those failings for which our merciful Father holdeth His rods of correction over us. And therefore the better to stir up our hearts to this duty, we have thought convenient to recommend the 30th day of this month to be observed in the duties and exercises of fasting, humiliation, and prayer before the Lord, for the reasons and ends afore-said, by all those whose hearts He shall draw forth for that duty, whereof we have thought fit to give you this notice, and desire that all those that fear the Lord within your Precinct may have notice hereof, and do what He shall put upon their hearts in order to the solemn and serious working of Him upon that day or any other time, that we may not despise the chastening of the Almighty, but hearken unto His rod, and embrace His fatherly correction.

"MILES CORBET.
"CHARLES HERBERT.
"JOHN JONES."

The usurpers, however, were not by any means bad paymasters. In 1650 the Parliament granted Col. A. Hill, "in recompence of his many eminent services in Ireland," the sum of £5,000. Again, in 1656, the Parliament, "in consideration of his many public and eminent services to the great furtherance and advancement of the public interest," granted him a further sum of £1,000 ; they, however, added that it was to be "a full satisfaction." He sat in the very same Parliament for the Counties of Down, Antrim, and Armagh—a Parliament, by the way, the members of which were called and chosen by Cromwell alone to represent the three Kingdoms of England, Scotland, and Ireland. Moreover, in the same year, the Protector and his Council, by letters dated Whitehall, 29th of April, granted him in trust for his younger son, Arthur, about three thousand acres of

HILLSBOROUGH FORT.

profitable land, with some wood and bog, in the territory of Kilwarlin, in the County of Down. And Colonel Hill, being previously seized of divers other lands in that territory, they were all erected into the Manor of Hillsborough & Growde, with liberty to impark one thousand acres in each, with power to hold fairs and markets, and all other jurisdictions and privileges. One would reasonably have supposed that, at least, those lands would have been taken from him at the Restoration, but that was not the way affairs were managed then. Though these were lands forfeited by men who, as they said, fought for their King against the zealots who put him to a disgraceful death, they also fought for their lives and the religion of their country against the Scottish Covenanters, who, in the height of their cursed intolerance, had solemnly sworn to extirpate them.

In March, 1660, he was appointed one of the Commissioners of the Court of Claims, for putting into execution His Majesty's Declaration for the Settlement of Ireland ; and, " being eminently active to the hazard of his life and estate in his endeavours to restore the King," he was sworn a member of His Majesty's Privy Council, and had a pardon, dated at Westminster, for all the crimes committed by him during the course of the rebellion. And Colonel Hill, having built within a few years, at his own charge, and upon his own lands, during the rebellion, for encouragement of an English plantation and security of the country, a considerable place of strength called Hillsborough, fortified with four bastions, or flankers, commanding the chief roads in the County of Down leading from Dublin to Belfast and Carrickfergus ; His Majesty was pleased to consider that the surprise thereof, upon any insurrection, might prove very prejudicial to his service, and how much it would conduce to His Majesty's service and the safety of the country that a guard should be placed in that fort for the security thereof ; he therefore granted a patent at Westminster for erecting it into a royal garrison by the name of Hillsborough Fort, with a Constable and officers to command it, to be called and known by the name of Constable of Hillsborough Fort, and twenty warders to be nominated and chosen by him ; the Constable to have the allowance of 3s. 4d. a day, and the warders 6d. each ; and this office was granted to him, his heirs and assigns, for ever.

Certificate written by Daniel O'Neill, 1663.

"These are to certify unto whom it may concern that Cap. Conn. Magneisse, of Culcany, in the County of Down, to my knowledge (I being the Governour of the Towne of Trim), by vertue of a power from his Grace the Duke of Ormond (the Ld. Luetent. of Ireland), upon the sevent day of August, or there about, in the year 1649, have seen the said Cap. Conn. Magneise, having then a foot company, march with the said company through the Town of Trim aforesaid, unto the Randezvous of the said L. Lt., as witnesseth my hand the *13th of October, 1663*.
"D. NEILLE."

Petition of Patrick Russell, 1663.

"*To his Grace James Duke of Ormonde, Lord Lieutenant General and General Governor of Ireland.*

"The humble petition of Patrick Russell, of Coniamstown, in the County of Down,

"In most humble manner sheweth that in the year 1641, when the rebellion began in Ireland, your petitioner did unanimously adhere and contribute, to the utmost of his power, to the British forces then in the County of Down, and continued so for some months there after. At which time, being oppressed and not able to live in his place of abode, he, being no military man, was forced to desert his dwelling for safeguard of his life, and lived in a sad and disconsolate condition until the year 1649. At which time your Grace laid siege to Dublin, where your petitioner was with your Grace, and from your Grace making manifest his constant loyalty in that service, obtained the annexed order, to be settled in his estate of 300 acres of land ; by virtue of which order he was put in possession thereof by the Right Honble. the Earl of Ardglass, then Governor of Lecale and Kinalerty, in the County of Down, and ever since continued so possessed. In regard he made appear before the Commissioners of the Revenue at Belfast, in the usurper's time, that he performed many good offices for the English and the Scotch in the first year of the said rebellion, in saving their lives and goods to the number of sixteen persons, who are now living, and ready to attest the same. That your petitioner having put in his claim before the Honourable Commissioners of the Court of Chancery, the same could not for want of time be heard, whereby his innocency might be made appear.

> "Wherefore your petitioner most humbly beseeches your Grace that you will be pleased to favour your petitioner with your Grace's certificate in his behalf for obtaining his pardon from his Majesty.
>
> "And he will ever pray, &c., &c."

"*Dublin Castle, December 5th, 1663.*

"We have duly considered the above petition, the reasons therein mentioned, and our order of the 30 of July, 1649, which, upon good inducements, we then granted to the petitioner's behalfe : and upon the whole do conceive him to be a person capable of deserving his Majestie's gracious pardon.

"ORMONDE."

Vera copia.
W. GODOLPHIN.   (*Pinkerton MSS.*)

Account of Sir George Rawdon.

BY W. PINKERTON, F.S.A.

SIR GEORGE RAWDON was the only son of Francis Rawdon, and was born at Rawdon, near Leeds. Early in life he became secretary to Edward Lord Conway, principal Secretary of State, and by him he was employed as an agent on his Irish estates. In 1639 he was Member of Parliament for the town of Belfast, and in November, 1641, being Major of Lord Conway's regiment of horse, he successfully defended the town of Lisnegarvey, or Lisburn, against Phelim O'Neill and 8,000 Irish rebels. After serving with distinction during the war of the Rebellion, when Ireland was completely subdued by the Parliament, he took office under it as one of the Commissioners of Revenue of Ulster, and, in that capacity, he was exceedingly useful in reducing, as far as he could, the Parliamentary Composition imposed upon Lord Conway's estate.

A great number of very interesting letters of his to Lord Conway are in the Record Office. After Cromwell died he prudently turned towards the rising sun of the Restoration, and, in 1660, he was appointed one of the Commissioners for executing his Majesty's Declaration for the Settlement of Ireland. In 1665 he was created a Baronet of England, under the title of Moira, in the County of Down. Not a syllable of his service to the usurpers is hinted in the accurate peerage book of Lodge, but it says that "as he had the strongest disposition to be as useful as possible to his country, so he had an ample fortune which enabled him to show it, whereby he gained the greatest respect and esteem."

He does not seem to have been so lucky under the Protectorate as his brother Commissioner, Col. Hill ; though he performed his duty well and ably, he does not appear to have received any more than the mere salary of his office. But at the Restoration he received many grants under the different Acts of Settlement, in the counties of Down, Dublin, Louth, and Meath ; and, for the sum of £200, he was allowed to pass patent of 2,078 acres in the barony of Upper-Iveagh, in the county of Down. It is thus set forth in the patent of date 1681 : "King James I., out of his great desire and care to plant the province of Ulster, was graciously pleased, in the eighth year of his reign, to grant letters patent, under the great seal of Ireland, for the passing of all the lands lying within the country, then commonly known by the name of Iveagh, and for the dividing, settling, and planting thereof, to several freeholders of the Irish nation, in hopes the said lands might thereby be manured, and better inhabited ; and did, among other grants, pass by letters patent, bearing date the same year, fourteen sessioughs, or half towns, within the territory of Moira, in the country of Iveagh, to Murtagh Mac-Terlagh O'Lavery of Moira : but notwithstanding that he and his grandson, Hugh O'Lavery, enjoyed the same, yet neither of them made any considerable plantation thereupon ; and in 1639, Hugh conveyed a great part thereof to several persons, and in 1641 forfeited the rest by rebellion, which, by the commissioners of claims for satisfaction of arrears of pay to officers and soldiers, were sold (as above) to Sir George Rawdon ; being a person that had performed very loyal and acceptable services to the crown, and had bestowed much costs and pains to improve and plant the said lands, had built a market town thereupon at Moira, which was inhabited with conformable Protestants, and having been decreed to, and purchased many other lands, they were erected, at his suit, into the manor of Moira, where he had obtained a licence, in 1669, to hold a Thursday market, and four yearly fairs on the Thursdays in Easter week, after 24th of June, after the 1st of August, and after the 29th of September.—And whereas he had purchased divers towns and lands in the territory of Kinelearty, within the said county, and for that some of these lands were mountainous, and others much encumbered with rocks, underwoods, and bogs, whereby the Irish in the rebellion, and thieves and tories, did in former times frequently harbour there ; and that of late, those lands, by his care and cost, were become well inhabited and planted, he having built two mills there, put the parish church in repair, erected a considerable town, and in the middle thereof had set out a large market place, which was paved, and made fit for market and fairs to be kept there, and which new-built town was situate in the very centre of the county ; the king therefore created the premises into the manor of Kinelearty, with a demesne of one thousand acres – liberty to empark the like quantity ; to keep courts, appoint seneschals, hold a Thursday market, and two fairs at the town of Ballinehinch on first February and twenty-ninth of June, to continue three days each, and many other privileges."

He died in the eightieth year of his age, in August, 1684, and was buried with great magnificence at Lisburn. Sir John Rawdon, the fourth baronet and great grandson of Sir George, was, in 1750, advanced to the peerage by the style and title of Baron Rawdon of Moira ; and he was further advanced to the dignity of Earl of Moira in 1762.

In the print room of the British Museum is a small engraving of Sir George Rawdon, with the following inscription :—"The true and lively pourtraiture of that valliant and worthy patriot and captaine, Sr George Rawdon, knight and barronet, Ætatis suæ 63." R. White, delin. et sculp. The armorial bearings used by the elder branch of the family are placed within an oval beneath the portrait. They are :—Quarterly, 1. Argent, a fess between three pheons sable, Rawdon ; 2. Argent, a fess between two lions passant regardant sable, Folifoot ; 3. Argent, a chevron between three hinds' heads erased gules, Beckwith ; 4. On a fess three escallops, a canton ermine. On an inescutcheon the badge of a baronet of England. Crest, a pheon. Motto—"Nisi Dominus frustra."

EXTRACTS FROM LETTERS OF GEORGE RAWDON, 1666.

George Rawdon, writing to Lord Conway from Dublin, 12 May, 1666 :—

"Another sad fate is befallen in the North. I believe the one half of the cattle in Antrim and Down are dead of the murrain ; corn double the price it was a month past, and no milk."

The same, 18 of May. All in the way of beggary. Murrain ; no trade, &c.

He writes—"I had letters to-day from my wife, who is well, with all the children. The great race at Lambeg for the plate was run the last week by the Earl of Donegall's Barb, Will Hill's Blink, and Major Richardson's Wingfield, who came first and the Barb next and Blink last ; the Lo. Massareene was there, but did not put in his horse Tangier."

The same, 1 June, Lisburn.

"I gave your Lordship notice in my last of the great mutiny, or rather rebellion of the garrison at Carrickfergus, which my Lord Lieutenant apprehended to be of such dangerous example that he on the sudden took a resolution to come himself in person to reduce the mutineers, and shipped away 400 of the Royal

Regiment with the Earl of Arran and Sir Wm. Flower, which had so quick a passage by sea that they were at Carrickfergus before his Grace reached Hillsborough by land. He came the first night to Dundalk, and on Sunday evening last to Hillsborough, being his second day. As we were ready for church, Will Hill, who rode all night, came to me and told me the news ; so I made what preparation I could in 3 hours' time, and met his Grace at Dromore with full 200 horse of our neighbours, which were many of them well mounted, and being orderly drawn up made a great show, and were very much spoken of by the company, and his Grace has since often mentioned them, and asked me if they were Killulta men. There came with him the Earls of Drogheda and Fingall, Viscts. Dungannon, Dangan, Taafe, and several Knights and Gentlemen, and the lifeguard of horse, and all the troops in his   were ordered thither. The Earl of Donegall's and Capt. Hill's were lying about Carrickfergus before. The Marquis of Antrim, the Earl of Clanbrassil, and Bishop of Down came hither to meet him.

"His Grace came from Hillsborough on Monday morning, and passed through this town to dinner to Belfast : whither I went after him and the company that were here with me, and that evening the Earl of Arran came up to Belfast and gave account of these passages. On Tuesday the Lord Lieutenant and all his train went to Carrickfergus, and being the king's day, after solemnity in the church and dinner past, his Grace directed me and the Judge Advocate to take the pains to take examinations of all particular passages, and of the ringleader especially, to

THE KEEPER IN PORTMORE WOODS, 1666.

prepare them for a martial court the next morning, which was done, and by commission from his Grace the Court was held, the Earl of Donegall being president, in his Lordship's house, and the mutineers brought bound, two together, and heard their charge drawn up by the Judge Advocate, Doctor Cook, and confessed their guilt and begged mercy on their knees, and after they were withdrawn into the court the Court voted them all guilty of death for breach of several Articles of War, and considered the examinations taken the day before, and picked out 10 that were the chief   and actors, and voted that the Earl of Donegall and Arran might be pleased to interceed with his Grace for sparing the lives of all the rest, except those 10, which he granted, and all the rest are, or will be, shipped in 2 or 3 frigates here and sent to the West Indies, and I suppose the 10 were hanged yesterday. The four Captains—Col. Mayart, Fortescue, Butler, and Reversham—are without companies ; they were much blamed, being all absent but Capt. Butler, and the 4 Companies are still in Carrickfergus till others be ordered thither.

"After, on Tuesday, his Grace and all his train came hither, about 8 of the clock, where they found supper ready ; 2 long tables in both dining-rooms, and all the chambers ready for lodging, and good wine of all sorts ; and were all well accomo-

INTERIOR OF ASSEMBLY ROOM IN EXCHANGE, OLD BELFAST, 1793.
(*From a contemporary engraving in possession of Mrs. W. Pinkerton.*)

dated here in good chambers in town and seemed well pleased with their entertainment, and my Lord Lieutenant, at breakfast, drank your lops. health in a great glass of claret, and commanded me to tell you so.

"But my disappointment of venison was so great that I cannot forgive the keeper; he had orders on Monday morning to kill a buck at [Portmore], they being very fat there, and shot and hurt one and lost it, and shot again another and missed, so that their great expectations of fat venison was disappointed, and especially his Grace that had none this year at Dublin. I am so ill pleased with this knave, to take upon him to be so good a woodman, that if your lp. had not sent him over I would presently give him his pass. I waited on his Grace and the company beyond Moyherelin, and upon the way hither (which is here very good roadway) his Grace expressed his delight to see such a country, and was well pleased and all his train."

Ormond writes from Dublin, 6 June :—

"After my departure from Carrickfergus nine of the mutineers were executed.

"Their officers also and all others will hereafter be more carefull in the government of their companies by the inconvenience befallen these, their companies being for the present disbanded. They are men of unquestionably good affections, and were only unfortunate in having worse men than others, and being absent all (but Capt. Butler) when the mutiny began by leave from the Earl of Donegall, Governor of the place."

In a communication that the Earl of Donegall makes, he says that one Proctor Dillon and one Williams were the ringleaders. Dillon was killed. *(Pinkerton MSS.)*

ARMS OF DONEGALL FAMILY.

Confirmation of the Chichester Patents,
Inrolled 1669.

GRANT from King Charles I., in virtue of the Commission for remedy of defective Titles, dated at Westminster 20th March, 15" Car. I., and for the fine of £467 17s. 6d., paid by Edward Viscount Chichester of Carrickfergus, and Arthur Chichester, his son and heir apparent. In consideration also of the many good, true, faithful, and acceptable services to the Crown, performed by them and by Arthur Lord Chichester of Belfast, deceased brother of the said Lord Edward, and of their surrender of Lough Neagh, *alias* Lough Sidney, *alias* Lough Chichester, with the soil and fishing thereof, and the Wears and Fishings in the River of Bann, near Toome, Co. Antrim, and of the Advowson of the Church of Magherahohill, and the Rectory and Advowson of the Church of Ballyprior, in

Island Magee, said County, to the King, his heirs and successors. And pursuant to Privy Signet, dated at Hampton Court, 24th September, 1638, which sets forth that Lough Neagh, *alias* Lough Chichester, which had been granted by King James to Lord Chichester, was so commodious for upholding the Fishing of the Bann, that the Governors and Committees of the London Plantation there were necessitated to farm the same at £100 by the year, which Fishing of the Bann was now come to his Majesty's hands. And the Lord Chichester, by Henry Le Squire, Esq., his Agent, having compounded with the Lord Deputy and the Commissioners for remedy of defective Titles to make the surrender, his Majesty directed that surrender to be taken, and this grant to pass of all other the Estate whatever belonging to his Lordship and his son Captain Arthur Chichester, as also the Rectorial Tithes of the Parish of Shankhill, *alias* Belfast, with the Advowson of the Vicarage of the same Church in lieu of the said surrenders ; and likewise an Annuity, Pension, or yearly Rent Charge of £40 English, reserving to them and their heirs liberty to fish for and take Salmon in and upon the said Lough for the provision of their house or houses; and also excepting to them and their heirs all the Eel Wears and Eel Fishings, or places to take eels in, at, or near Toome, which formerly were not demised or granted to the City of London ; yet so as such Orders, Laws, and Rules as shall be from time to time prescribed and set down generally on the King's behalf for the Fishing of the Bann be observed by them and their heirs both in their Salmon and Eel Fishings. And, lastly, that the whole Island Magee be united into one Parish, and all the Rectorial Tithes within the Island disposed of some way for the benefit and behoof of that Church and the College there, for bettering the means of the Vicar and the finding of Lectures, as should seem most meet.

Co. Antrim.—There is therefore Granted to the said Lord Edward and Arthur, and to the Heirs and Assignes of the said Arthur, for ever, of the entire Castle or Mansion House, Park, Demeasne, Buildings, Site, Mills, Manor, Town, and other the Hereditaments of Belfast, All Manors, Castles, Towns, and Lands of and in the Territories and Precincts of Lands of Toughnefalle, Toughmoylone *alias* Mylone *alias* Malone, Tough-Tinament, Carnenony *alias* Carnemony, Carnetall, Monkesland, and Ballyhone, as followeth.

The capital Messuage and Demeasne Lands of Stronemellis, and two Corn Mills upon the Lagan.

The Towns, Lands, and Hereditaments of Ballycollo, Ballydownemorric *alias* Ballydownemurrie, with a Corn Mill there ; Ballydollaghane *alias* Ballydollaghane, Fumanghie *alias* Ballyfinagie, Ballyrodrane, Ballinvalley, Ballycromage *alias* Ballycromoge, Ballyamarchane *alias* Ballymurfey, Ballinofeagh *alias* Ballynefey, with a Water Mill and a Fulling Mill there ; Ballinriske, Ballymeighmonie *alias* Ballymonie, Ballydownefin *alias* Ballydownefeyne *alias* Ballynafeighe, Ballengarric, Ballygarmartine, Ballinrahane *alias* Ballyvallyenerasure, Ballymister *alias* Ballyvister, Killyetan *alias* Ballyetan *alias* Ballyetigan, Tulloghmanane, Ballyogaman *alias* Ballygaman, Ballyquoite, Ardoyne *alias* Ballyardone *alias* Ardun, with a new Forge there ; Ballyardsallagh, Ballyvallie *alias* Ballynvallic *alias* Toughmanagh, Clownie and Cullantrie in Toughnefall and Toughmoloyne.

Co. Antrim.—The Towns and Lands of Ballycoolegalgic *alias* Ballycoolegallagie *alias* Ballyroculgalgalgie, Ballycloyne, Ballycullantrie, Ballingallinie, Ballyfoughnamonie, Ballynaneigure *alias* Ballyneginure *alias* Ballinegwire, Ballymullaghimanye, Ballymissilane *alias* Ballysillane, Ballylegaile *alias* Ballyleganile *alias* Legeneile, Ballycrosse, Itinicester *alias* Itiniskall *alias* Oughtmarakneskall, Oughterard 3 Qr. Ballioghagane, Ballysteigheoghe-Inerle *alias* Ballyskeigh-Inerle *alias* Skeoganerle, Ballylissitollard *alias* Lissitillard, Ballyedenderry and the Fort, Gallynaghe, Ballylissegalrome, Ballyircustillie *alias* Ballycloghnacastallie *alias* Cloghcastle, Ballingowlane *alias* Ballygolane, Ballykeile *alias* Ballyceele, Ballylishigalriea *alias* Ballygalryan, Ballygorinward *alias* Ballygallyneward, Ballyglangoromelie *alias* Ballygormelie, Ballyarfekille and Ballyvardinue *alias* Ballyvardune *alias* Ballyvaston *alias* Ballyvastony, in the Tuogh-Tinament.

Co. Antrim.—The Towns and Lands of Ballyvincollard *alias* Ballyrincollard *alias* Ballyrancollard, White Abbey, Le Coole *alias* Ballycoole, Cloghnycastallie, Ballyvasconine, Gallynagh, Drommore *alias* Dromore, Ballydownanine *alias* Dunany *alias* Downany, Ballycoole, Ballyardnesoole *alias* Ballyardnesole *alias* Ballynecreggy, Ballyhenry, Ballymulduffe *alias* Bally-Imulduffe, Ballymesine *alias* Ballyvesey, Ballylaghline *alias* Carrickferne, Ballycurraghfarney *alias* Bally-chone *alias* Ballyhone, Le Earle's Meadow *alias* The Earl's Mosse, Ballynemanagh *alias* Le Grange of Ballynemanagh, Cloghloghortie, Ballykeile, Carnecall and Bally Jordan *alias* Jordanstowne in Carnemonie, Carnecall, Monkesland, and Ballyhone *alias* Bally-John.

VIEW OF WHITEABBEY IN 1800.
(From McSkimin MSS.)

The Rectory of the Church or Chapel, and the Advowson, Presentation, and Patronage of the Vicarage of Senekill, *alias* Shankill, *alias* Albedevade, *alias* Belfast, parcel of the possessions of the late Monastery or Abbey of St. Patrick of Down. With all other Hereditaments, spiritual and temporal, within the said Territories or Tuoghs, whose bounds are described in the Patent, viz. : -

Towards the entire South part of the said Territories lye the Bay of Carrick-fergus and the River Lagan ; and to the East part of the said Territories or parcels of Land thereof, and the Lands of Carrickfergus, runs a small River beginning near the water-fall Fasermeagh, and running by or near the old stone House called Cloghanoghertie towards the West from the same, and also from another small River called Silver Stream towards the East, and from Faser-meagh aforesaid the Meares extend directly between the said Territories and the Tuogh of Ballynlynny about quarter of a mile near the top of the Glynne of Altballymanagh, and so by the midst of a small Bogg there ; and from thence about half a mile between the said Territories directly to the top of Carneshalgagh Hill ; and thence about quarter of a mile directly to a small Bogg at the top of the Glynne of Altonbreedagh, and so through the middle of the small Bogg there ; and thence about quarter of a mile to the top of Lisselinch Hill, and thence through the middle of the Bogg or Wood of Moymerlagh, near said Lisselinch ; and from thence about quarter of a mile to an old Stone called Ballyrobart, and thence for about quarter of a mile directly through the midst of the Bogg called Monymulligine by the Ford of Aughballymestine ; and from thence about half a mile directly by the middle of the Bogg of Monarhohill ; and so between the said Territories and Ballinlynny aforesaid the Meares extend to the old foundation Stone called Cloghballybascon *alias* Ballyvaston ; and from thence about half a mile directly to the Fall of the River called Assdermott ; and thence about half a mile directly through the Ford of Annaghdullagh ; and thence about half a mile

K

between the said Territories and the Tuogh of Killelagh directly by the top of Altomagh Glynne ; and thence about half a mile by the upper part of the Mountain Marsh to the top of the Hill of Slughtmermore ; and thence about half a mile between the said Territories and the Tynament of Clandermott directly over the Plaines and through the middle of the Glynne of Ballyaltnagarran *alias* Barraltnaragan ; and from thence about half a mile directly to the top of another Glynne called Altmakeigh ; and thence about half a mile over the Hill to and by the Highway of Ballymogerlie ; and thence about another half-mile between the said Territories and Derryvologie *alias* Fealoagh directly to the Mountain of Cooleanbeg, leaving the Glynne of Alchorane in the said Territories and parcels of Land ; and from the said Hill runs a small River, called Shroghanemellie *alias* Shroanmellis *alias* Strandmellis, and runs between the said Territories and the Tynament of Derryvologie aforesaid, till it falls into the Moor or Bogg of Fooreglasse, and so through the midst and from the South part of the Bogg issues

CAVE HILL—ENCLOSING THE DEER-PARK.

another small River, which runs between the said Territories and Tynament into the Lagan, which River of the Bay of Carrickfergus are the South Boundaries and Meares of the said Territories and Parcels of Land. All the foregoing Premisses created into the Manor of Belfast, with Courts Leet and Baron.

Also the entire Fishing of the River Lagan, the Soil, Wears, Customs, and Duties of the said River. The Ferry of Belfast.

Co. Antrim.—The impropriate Rectory of Entroya *alias* Antrym, which consists *inter alia* of two parts of all the Tithes of Corn and Hay of the Towns and Hamlets of Ballygallantrim, Ballycregiddery, Ballyconmagh, Ballywanly *alias* Ballywinonise *alias* Ballyaltahunching, Ballynecrigie, Ballyberan, Ballyrannell, Ballyrathbegg, Ballymullen, Ballycroskenan, Ballycallynordolly, Ballyaltwonisie *alias* Ballyattywonisy, Ballyantrym, Ballykeile, Ballynormullen, and Ballynclasonbegg, with the Advowson and Presentation of the Vicarage thereof. The Estate of the late Abbey or Monastery of Woodburne *alias* Goodborne.

Co. Antrim.—The Church or impropriate Rectory of Ballynlinny in Tuogh-Ballynlinny, which consists of two parts of the Tithes of Corn and Hay, within nine Townlands in the County of Antrim, with the Advowson and Presentation of the Vicarage. The Estate of said Abbey. The Towns and Lands of Ballinmullie, Killgreelie *alias* Killgrill, Ballinlinny, Lisnelinsenem *alias* Lisnelinchie *alias* Lisneseven, Ballivalter *alias* Ballywalter, Ballyalgakie *alias* Ballycogegy *alias* Ballygagy, Cloghballyrobert *alias* Ballyrobert, Ballynephellitt *alias* Ballynepellodie, Ballyhartway *alias* Ballyhartfield, Ballytemple, Ballypatrick *alias* Templetowne *alias* Templepatrick, Ballyrickmore *alias* Rickamond, Ballyturbvernegno *alias* Tubbenegnowe, Ballykillm'kee, Ballycoosen *alias* Ballychoosin, Ballymullaghbritt *alias* Mullaghbritt, Ballychone *alias* Bally-John, Ballygeolagh, Ballyonemegaile *alias* Ballyvingell *alias* Vingall *alias* Stomgall, Ballyvoage *alias* Ballycasland, Ballyshradinmarish, Stradnemorsligh *alias* Stradenemollyshagh, Ballyneelogh *alias* Ballyneglogh *alias* Stradenomemyagh *alias* Stradenemoynagh, Ballyotoge, Carnegraine, Carnenanie, Ballybarnes, Barnish *alias* Ballybarnesse, Brusk *alias* Bruslee, Moyvliske, Ballymartin and Ballyclocarduffe *alias* Ballyclocanduffe *alias* Cloghanduffe, with all their Appurtenances in the Territory or Tuogh of Ballynlinny, and also that entire Territory, with all the Members and Hereditaments therein. All these Premises, from the Rectory of Ballynlinny inclusive, and the Rectories of Templepatrick, and Moyvliske, created the Manor of Ballynlinny, with Courts Leet and Baron.

Co. Antrim.—The Towns and Lands of Ballynehowlane, Bally-Edward, Ballyhone, Ballynelige, Ballymullaghfenro, Ballycregenconboy, Ballynenowlane, Ballymullnemossagh, Ballyrollo, Ballyrickard, Ballylissetlady, Ballycugelie, Ballyfollard, and Ballyglin, within the Territory or Tuogh of Magheramorne, with that entire Territory, and all the Members and Hereditaments thereof.

Co. Antrim.—The Towns and Lands of Ballyistin, Ballynarranic, Ballynowe *alias* Ballynue, Ballydowaghe, Ballyardmagh, Ballyardmaghbreegie *alias* Ballyarducabreegy, Ballyodowennewe *alias* Ballydowemowe, Ballyloghanmore, Ballydownedrewe *alias* Ballydonedrou *alias* Ballydowndren, Ballycorra, Ballynevalla *alias* Hillynevely *alias* Ballyneboly, Ballynebantro, Ballycollan, Ballylissenuskie *alias* Lissneliskie, Ballydrumneddarogh, and Ballyboy *alias* Ballyvoy, with a Fulling Mill and a Corn Mill there ; Ballylathnalarke, Ballybraconside, Ballyaltwicke, Ballytressnaitt *alias* Ballytrassnaiott, Ballynesheale, Ballymoden *alias* Ballymoieden, Ballynealbanagh, Ballyclogher, Ballynesavage *alias* Ballysavage, Ballynemeragh, Tubbernegill *alias* Ballytubbergill, Ballynewooddoge, Ballyclewarde, Ballymoy, Ballyhowell, BallyKilbride *alias* Kilbride, Ballyrashee *alias* Rashee, Ballyrashymore, Ballyrashybegg, Ballygoghry *alias* Ballygogie *alias* Ballycogie, Ballybealaghclare *alias* Ballyclare, and a Corn Mill; Ballyslowgromagh *alias* Ballyslowcronagh, Rathmore *alias* Ramore, Bally-Handragh *alias* Handreagh, Ballygallantrim *alias* Ballygallantrem, Ballycreighderry *alias* Ballycregyderry, Ballycomagh *alias* Ballycomna, Ballygonie *alias* Ballygowen, Ballynememis, Ballynecreggie *alias* Ballynecreigh, Ballyberom *alias* Ballyberran, Ballydownedrim, Ballyrannell, Ballyrathbegg *alias* Rabeg *alias* Dromagolgan, Ballymullen, Ballycroskennan, Ballytollynardolly *alias* Ballytullynardullie, Ballyaltinvinley *alias* Ballyaltinvinsey *alias* Altahunshinagh, Ballyantrym *alias* Balliantrim, Ballykeile *alias* Ballykeele, Ballynormullen, Ballynelossanbegg *alias* Ballynelassanbegg, Ballycuggerie, Ballyardmoydoiegmore *alias* Ballyardmoydeegmore, Ballyardmoydeigbegg *alias* Downagur, with a Fulling Mill and a Corn Mill there ; all in the Territory or Tough of Moylinnie, and that entire Territory.

Co. Antrim.—The Towns and Lands of Ballyhulruske *alias* Ballytulruske *alias* Tullaruske, Ballym'award, Ballygennenagroath *alias* Ballydromnegreagh, Ballydonnaghie, Ballykillerodan, Ballyboddar, and Ballyknockneferren, all within the Territory or Tinament of Clandermott, and that entire Territory.

Co. Antrim.—The Rectory, Church, or Chapel of Glynne, and the Advowson, Presentation, and Right of Patronage of the same Church in the

Territory of Magheramorne. These Premises, with the Rectory of Antrim previously mentioned, the Abbey of Disert, the Rectories of Duryen and Dromald on the other side, created the Manor of Moylinny, with Courts Leet and Baron.

The Rectory or Chapel of Moyvlusk, containing two third parts of the Tithes thereof. The Rectory of Templeton *alias* Templepatricke, containing two thirds of the Tithes thereof. The Estate of the late Priory or Hospital of St. John of Jerusalem. The Advowson and Presentation to the said Church of Temple-patricke.

An old religious House called the Friery of Masserine, with the Site and Appurtenances thereof, and the Town and Lands of Ballydonaghy in Ederdaowen upon the Six-Mile Water belonging to Masserine.

A parcel of Land, situate on the South Bank of the River Owenviewe *alias* Six-Mile Water, near the House of Massarine and thereto belonging, late occupied by the Garrison there, and is near surrounded by an old Foss or Ditch, extending from Loughneagh near Owenviewe. The Abbey or Monastery of the Virgin Mary of Disert *alias* Kells, with the Site, Edifices, Orchards, Gardens, &c., thereto belonging.

The Towns and Lands of Ballytocallymullen *alias* Ballycullymullan *alias* Kells, Ballym^cEvagh, Ballickneldrome *alias* Ballickneldrone *alias* Kildrome *alias* Kells, Ballyfuguske *alias* Ballyfugask *alias* Ballyfuguskie, Ballycreagh *alias* Creagh *alias* Ballynecreggie, Carwacke, Ballyvillie, Hanultie *alias* Hamlete *alias* Avultie *alias* Ballylisnaquingally *alias* Lissneguggie, and Ballyferrnsures *alias* Ballynesures *alias* Ballyferensure, with all the Tithes of these Lands.

The Rectories and Advowsons of the Vicarages of the Churches or Chapels of Duryen *alias* Dunyne and Dromald or Dromard *alias* Dromawlagh, in the Fuigh *alias* the Fyvagh *alias* Tuoghfuigh.*

The Rectory or Chapel of Dough-Connor *alias* Connor. The Rectory or Chapel of Killwigh *alias* Killroote in Tuogh Braden-Island.

The Church or Chapel of Ballynemeannagh. The Advowson and Patronage of the Vicarage of the said Church.

All the Tithes belonging to the aforesaid Rectories, in which are included those of Templeoughtragh, in or near Glanarme, and of Kilkeevan, in the Island of Maguy.

The Advowson, Presentation, and Right of Patronage of the Churches and Chapels of Dough-Connor *alias* Connor, and Kilwigh *alias* Kilroote. The Estate of said Abbey of Kells, with all other the Possessions thereof.

The Towns and Lands of Ballydun and Ballymenihan, with their Tithes, parcel of the Preceptory of Ards, and the estate of the Hospital of St. John of Jerusalem. The Chapel or Grange of Templenelafyn in Island Maguy, with all the Tithes of the four Towns of Mullaskee, Mullastee the estate of the Monastery of Comber, the Church or Chapel and Tithes of Cranoge in Tuoghfall, the estate of the late Abbey of Bangor.

The Advowson, Presentation, and Right of Patronage of the Rectories and Vicarages of Cramechill in Tuoghfuigh, Squirria *alias* Skerris in Knockboynabrady, and Rathkavan in Tuogh-Muntermurregan, in the Lower Clandeboy.

The Impropriate Rectory and the Advowson and Presentation of the Vicarage of Cueill *alias* Coole in Carnemonie, which Rectory consists *inter alia* of two third parts of the Tithes of Corn and Hay of the Town and Lands of Carnemony *alias* Carmony, the estate of the Abbey of Woodburne.

The Towns, Lands, and Tithes of Garrymore and Ballygreenlawy *alias* Ballygreenlawye in Tuoghlearne, and Ferry from Island-Magee to Oulderfleete.

The late Abbey, Church, or House of Cistercian Friers of St. Augustine's Order of Inver, with the Site, &c. The Towns and Lands of Carneduffe. Bally-shagg *alias* Ballyhagg and Brundod, with the Tithes in Tuogh-Magherimorne in the Lower Clandeboy, and all other the estate of the said Abbey.

The Abbey or Monastery of Woodborne, or Goodborne, with all the estate thereof [among which is the Church or Rectory impropriate of Killaloige *alias* Kildalog in the Rowte, mentioned in the Patent of 1621]. [Except the Rectories of Killprioragh, Balydun, Kilkewan, and Templenclafine.]

* In the Patent of 1621 here were added the Rectories of Dundermot and Rolswilike in the Rowte.

The Castle, Town, and Lands of Oulderfleete *alias* the Curran, containing Three Quarters, containing one hundred and eighty Acres English Measure. A parcel of Land adjoining or belonging to the late Church of Friers, called Clondumalles *alias* Dunmallis, near the Lands of Oulderfleete, North, and the Town of Larne, South, containing Fifteen Acres English Measure. All the Tithes of Oulderfleete, Blackan *alias* Blackhave, and Grillanchill *alias* Grilbanchill belonging to the said Church.

The Castle, Town, &c., of Portmucke.

The Castle, Town, and Lands of Castle-Chichester.

The House, Manor, Territory, and Lands of McGuiye's Island *alias* Magees-Island *alias* Ilandmagee, with all the Hereditaments thereof, Spiritual and Temporal.

The aforesaid Premises of Olderfleete, Portmuck, Castle-Chichester, Island-Magee, Dunmallis, the Abbey of Inver, the Rectory of Glynne, the Lands of Carnduffe, Ballyshagg, and Brendodd, created the Manor of Castle-Chichester, with Courts Leet and Baron.

The total Rent to be paid for the above estates in the County of Antrim, £32 1s. 8½d.

Co. of the Town of Carrickfergus.—The Castle or Mansion-House of his Lordship, now called Joymount, and lately called the Pallace *alias* the Storehouse, with all the Buildings, Gardens, Orchards, &c., in or near Carrickfergus.

The late Abbey, Monastery, or Priory of Carrickfergus, called St. Francis Fryorie, and lately named the Pallace, with the Site and all the Estate thereof in the County of Carrickfergus.

A Piece of Ground on which Four Tenements were lately built in Water Street, surrounded with a Wall, and made part of the Court-yard of Joymount-House, containing in length from Spittlegate by the street, towards the said House, One hundred and forty-five feet or thereabouts, and backwards in breadth to the North about twenty-one feet. A Piece of Land, lying North of the said Four Tenements, on which his Lordship's Stables are built, belonging to said House.

Two Watermills, called Chichester-Terrott's Mills, North-east of Carrickfergus. Seven Tenements on the Hill leading to the Scottish Quarter of the said Town. A Piece of Land near the said Mills, called Leadeland, and Raven's Acre. All the Messuages, Tenements, and Buildings without the Walls of Carrickfergus to the East, and bounded on the east by the River running along near the House late belonging to Robert Ellis ; on the South by the Sea ; on the North by the Orchard Wall of Joymount ; and on the West by the Town Wall, with the Backsides, &c., thereof. All the Ground, Soil, or Land which Arthur late Lord Chichester had, or which the Lord Edward and the said Arthur his Son, or his Heirs, should recover from the Sea. A Messuage or Tenement called the Hospital of St. Brigid in Carrickfergus. A Stone House and an Acre of Land, more or less, late belonging to John White, Burgess, bounded South by the Land of said John White and Richard Sendall ; North by the old Rampier of the Town ; West by St. Nicholas's Church-Yard ; and East by the Stone House formerly occupied by Egidius or Gyles Cornewall, deceased, and now by his Lordship. A House or Tenement, called Sendall's-Hall, *alias* Sendall's Old Stone, with a parcel of Land adjoining and therewith used.

The moiety of a Burgage of Land, with the buildings thereon, in West Street, called Taaffe's half Burgage, containing in breadth next the Street Forty-two feet, and running back to the Church-Yard. Another half Burgage on the North side of West Street, between the aforesaid half Burgage, East, and Alderman T. Cooper's House and Land, West, containing in length to the Street Forty-two feet, and back to the Church-Yard, North. A Piece of Land, where the East-Mills, called the Double-Mills, lately stood, enclosed now with the Walls of Joymount Garden and the Town, with all the buildings thereon and the West-Mills.

The Site, &c., of the Monastery of Woodborne *alias* Goodborne, with a parcel of land adjoining and the Tithes thereof. A parcel of Land, called Downemallerewe, lying on the West of Woodborne. Two parcels of Land in the Field on the West side of the River of Woodborne. A parcél of Land in the Town and Fields of Carrickfergus, the reputed property of Nichs. Dobbin, Burgess, deceased, meared West by the Road to Glanarme; North by Anthony Dobbin's Land, and by his Lordship's Land, East. Two parcels of Land, called Bridewell-Park, Greenemount, and Spittle-Park, between Glanarme-Way or Glanarumway and Copeland-Water, bounding on the lands of John Carne, East; on the East-Mill Water Course, South; by two parcels of Land belonging to Nichs. and Anth. Dobbin, West; and by late J. Skullie's, North. A parcel of Land, lying South of the last parcel, about Twenty Perches long and Six broad, enclosed by a Ditch, and lately purchased by his Lordship of Sir Hercules Langford, Knt.

A parcel of Land on the West side of the River Woodborne, bounded by the Road near Woodborne Abbey leading to the Garrison Pasture, East; by the Lands assigned to Richd. Conlan and others, West; by the High Road not far from the Sea, South; and North, for the space of about Two hundred Perches, by the Garrison Pasture, 530 Acres English.

A parcel of Land meared on the South by the Garrison Pasture; on the North by Lands assigned to the Bishop of Down and others; on the East by a High Road for about Two hundred Perches westerly in length to the Mountain of Knocka, and granted by the Corporation of Carrickfergus to Sir Arthur Chichester by Indenture dated 28 October, 1606, 105 Acres English.

The entire Circuit and Precinct of Land, arable, meadow, pasture, turbary, mountain, and bog, within the County of the Town of Knockfergus, lying between the Deer's Lane and Bruslee Ford, near Lurganreagh. And also two Aldermen's Shares in the Fields of Carrickfergus, between Glanarme and Copeland Water, lately purchased by his Lordship from Sir Thos. Hibbots, Knt., deceased.

The Castle or Hall called Birlett-Hall or Castle, sometime in the possession of Sir Moses Hill, Knt., deceased, and after of Alderman T. Witter. The Castle, called Dobbin's Castle, and the Castle or Mansion House adjoining. A parcel of Land, Seventy Perches long and Thirty-eight broad. Another parcel One hundred and fourteen Perches long. Another parcel containing Twenty-four Acres. Another parcel Two hundred Perches long and Sixty-eight broad.

A Messuage and a parcel of Land on the West side of the suburbs of Carrickfergus. The Castle or Messuage in High Street, lately purchased from Francis Hill, Esq., and Mary Russell. A Messuage in said Street purchased from Michl. Newby. A ruinous Tenement in said Street, late occupied by M. Savage. A Messuage in said Street bought from Phelim Roe McGee. A Messuage next to that bought from Rd. Spearpointe. A parcel of Land near Joymount, now converted into a Backside or Bawne, bought from Mary Russell. A parcel near the Brew-House, and purchased from the Corporation.

A parcel where a Messuage is built, late occupied by Thomas Kirkpatrick. A parcel of Land adjoining. A piece of Ground called the Widow Bird's Garden. A Messuage, bounded by the Church-Yard, inhabited by Robert Walsham.

The Town and Lands of Marshalstowne.

A parcel of Land near Woodborne, called Scoute's-Bush, *alias* Lettice-Land, bounded by the Sea, South-west, and by the Road to the Knocka, North.

The Total Rent to be paid for the above Estates in the County of the Town of Carrickfergus, £2 7s. 7½d. p. Ann., subject to a fine of £10 whenever the Crown should build the Walls of Carrickfergus.

County Downe.—The Town and Lands of Ballynefeighe, at a yearly rent of £0 7s. 9d.

All the Premises in the County of the Town of Carrickfergus, and the County of Down, created the Manor of Joymount, with Courts Leet and Baron.

County of Donegall.—CITY AND LIBERTIES OF DERRY, AND COUNTY OF DERRY.—The entire Barony, Territory, and Circuit of Land of Inishowen and O'Dogherty's Country, with all the Rights, Members, and Appurtenances thereof, Spiritual and Temporal. All the Lands within Loughswilly and Loughfoyle, or elsewhere in the Sea, Bays, and Creeks within or near the said Territory.

The Castle, Manor, or House and Tuogh of Ellagh, and all the Castles, Towns, and Quarters of Lands of Ellaghmore, Drumdryne *alias* Drumadrene *alias* Dundreane, Ellaghbegg, and Ballynegalleagh *alias* Ballynecalleagh.

The Towns and Lands of Magherenicarr *alias* Magherencar, Bonemayne, Coskeyne, Mastimelan, Ballym^crowertie *alias* Ballym^cgrowertie, Lisfannon, Skyoge, Tomoge, Skygaden, Carrowreagh, Carnesanocke *alias* Carroneshenagh, Ballyderdaowen *alias* Ballyederdaowen, Killm^cKillaveny *alias* Killm^cKillveny, Garvey *alias* Garvegerry, Tullywonyn *alias* Tullywasinn, Ballyena, Gortcarmagan, Derryvaughan *alias* Derryvaine *alias* Crossihowell, Soppock, Drumhegerty, Carnamoyle, Uskeheyne *alias* Uskeyheyne, Ardmore, Creigh *alias* Creigg, Ballyarnell, Mough *alias* Muffe, Dromskallon, Ture, Aughte, Ardocryne, Trometragh, Caroncule, Cabragh, Crehenan, Minbaltony, The House called White-Castle, Rowskey, Carronmore in Glantagher, Carronvleigh *alias* Carronbleagh, Cearrhan, Altoughan, Gallywelly *alias* Galboyly, Cashell in Glantagher, Ballyvloske *alias* Ballybloskie, Carrick-Iwoden *alias* Carrick-Iwhoden in Glannygannon, Tullanree *alias* Tullaghnaree, Magherynedroman, Carronreagh in Glannygannon, Clare *alias* Claremore, Ballyratton, Tullynavin, Tavynegallon *alias* Tavenaghgallon, Tullyalla *alias* Tavenenogla, Two Townlands, The Mountains of Evasabreedy and Minnemarragh, Sorne, Mynaneagh, Sallgillanow, Slewsnaght, Mynabroughtduffe, Glanardgavenagh, Myneauly, The Shell-Islands in Loughfoile. The Premises thus far created Manor of Ellagh, with Courts Leet and Baron.

Co. of Donegall.—BARONY ENISHOWEN.—The Castle, Manor, Lordship, Tuogh, Lands, and Hereditaments of Greene-Castle *alias* Newcastle.

The Towns and Lands of Ballym^cArthur *alias* Ballym^cArthull, Fardrome, Crehue *alias* Crehugh, Ballyelehan *alias* Ballyeaghan, Carrontrassan *alias* Carrontrasnah, Shrone, with the Port or Creek of Portsallagh *alias* Enversallagh and Shrone. The Castle called Redcastle, *alias* Carrickm^cquivellen. The Town and third part of Cloncroe, Ballyargus, Dronge *alias* Drunge, and Ballylane. The Towns and Lands of Culladoe *alias* Culladowe *alias* Ballywoggery, Bradeaughlin *alias* Tirrowe, Ballynally, Carrongarrowe *alias* Carnegarve, Ballybracke, Dromwyre *alias* Dromawyer, Glanygovenagh, Masoaglin *alias* Glanganvyn and Minlitterbeale. The Mountain of Creggnamaddie. The Town and Lands of Carronbegg, Ballym^cgarronie, and Carronvleigh in Turmone. The Hamlets of Leckemy, Ballybrinn, and Dromley *alias* Drumiley. The Towns and Lands of Carronmenagh *alias* Carronmanagh. The Mountain of Carrahenshefeigh. The Towns and Lands of Leotrim-O'Cullenan, Ballycarry, Tirm^ccowra *alias* Tirm^ccrowra, Dunagreynan, Kindroyde *alias* Kinderhed *alias* Kindroghed, Dristernan, Aughatubritt *alias* Aughatubridd, Monadoragh *alias* Monadragh, Aughagalasson *alias* Aughaglasson, Wort *alias* Woart, Waskill, Caronmore in Glanyla *alias* Glandecin, Cashel in Glanyla. The Island of Enistrahull *alias* Enistrahell in the Sea. The Premises thus far created the Manor of Greenecastle, with Courts Leet and Baron.

Co. Donegall.—BARONY OF ENYSHOWEN.—The Castle, Manor, or Lordship, Town, and Tuogh of Boncranagh.

The Towns and Lands of Ballyenry *alias* Ballyencery and Tullyarvill *alias* Tullyarvelly. The Mountain of Duntersen, reputed parcel of Tullyarvill. The Towns and Lands of Slydran and Ballym^cganny. The Half-Towns and Lands of Toneregee, Ballym^ccarry, Tullydush, and Aughachullie *alias* Aughachillie. The Towns and Lands of Arderayman, and the Mountain of Cregcumber, reputed parcel thereof. The Towns and Lands of Monyworo *alias* Monygworry, and Granygoagh *alias* Gransheag *alias* Grange, and the Mountain of Myndecallagh *alias* Mintecalleagh. The Towns and Lands of Luddan *alias* Sluddan, Trillagee, Clonm^cgee *alias* Clum^ckee, Glassault, Altosheyne, Carne, Rosscyeny *alias* Rasheny, Caronreagh, Ballym^cgeene, Maherenale *alias* Cregnamullen, Fugarte, Laggacurrie, Carrickbrackle *alias* Carnebraghey, Ballym^cmurierhe *alias* Ballym^cmorierhe, Tullynabrattie, Dowygillen, Ardaghee, Ballylovrin *alias* Ballyluffin, Cloagh, Monyclohine *alias* Monyclogheyne, Altehalle *alias* Altoghallagh, Rouskie, Dunally, Cressconnell, Rosemagh *alias* Rosemagha, Downane *alias* Downafie, Litter *alias* Letter, Crishmanagh, Lynan in Erris, Inver *alias* Dunreigh, Lethderrigg *alias* Laghbun,

Monagh *alias* Munagh, Monaloobane *alias* Monaloovane, Lislyn *alias* Lisloyne, Lyowen, and Gortearagan. The Towns or Half Quarters of Moughkinnagowa, Toughanakinnagowa, Connackinnagowa, and Fillaskie *alias* Ardagh-Ikinnagowa. The West part of the Mountain of Sleancmayne, reputed parcel of Fillaskie. The Towns and Lands of Crislecoule *alias* Crislocule, Crisloghmore, Tubbanecarrowe *alias* Tubbanecarrogh, Carronamaddy, Monespinoge, Castlecoule *alias* Cashellcoallie, Macullenbegg *alias* Maghcullenbegg, Macullenmore, Moynassee *alias* Mughnassee, Moughlena *alias* Mullena, Dromgovan *alias* Dromgowan, Grahgeagh *alias* Grange *alias* Ballymannagh in Birt, Mullovirt *alias* Mullagbirt, and Tullade *alias* Tullaghade. The Mountains of Ellacs, Sorne, and Mintoulogh. The Island of Inch *alias* Inishneostree *alias* Inishneostrey, containing Eight Quarters in Lough Swillie. The Island or Rock called Seal-Island *alias* Glashyedie in the Sea, near the Quarter of Land of Carrickeybrackey, with the Fishing for Seals there. The Premises thus far created the Manor of Boncranagh, with Courts Leet and Baron.

Co. Donegall.—BARONY OF ENVSHOWEN.—The Castle, Manor, and Lordship or Circuit of Malyne *alias* Maulyn.

The Towns and Lands of Ballycarran, Glangadd, Ballyhaneitragh *alias* Ballyeighan-Itragh, Ballyeighanwotrath *alias* Ballyhannowtrath, Dromcarbett, Carronmore *alias* Carrowmore in Malyne, Ballyellihane, Ballagh, Norrira *alias* Forrira, Cranegeny-Forrira, Carronvleigh in Malyne, Drunge, Cullin, Tullaugh *alias* Anisnager, Ballyeddidy *alias* Ballyedogie, Knocknamany, Knockglasse, Downane, Coronobate *alias* Coronbate, Colewart *alias* Grange of Colewart, known and called Coolewart-Itragh and Coolewart-oughtragh, Kenaght *alias* Kenaugh, Ballykenny, Ballyknawsie, Drumaskeagh *alias* Anisnager, Goorie, Vrigh *alias* Brigh, and a Rock called Stuckeruden, reputed parcel thereof. Ardmalyne *alias* Ardmanlyne, and the Rocks of Rowemanlyne and the Creek or Port of Porterrownan being parcels thereof. Ballygorman and the Rocks of Garue-Iland, with the Seal Fishing there, and an ancient Chapel, called Templemurgalla, reputed parcel of Ballygorman. The Ferry over the River or Arm of the Sea, called Loughfoile, from Greenecastle, Co. of Donegal, to Termonmaggillegan, Co. of Derry, with one or more Boats—To take for the passage of every Man, 3d. ; every Horse, Ox, or Cow, 6d. ; every horse-load, 2d. ; every Sheep, 1d., and so rateably for all other beasts, by Patent 20 Nov., 1621.

The Premises thus far created the Manor of Maulyn, with Courts Leet and Baron.

Co. Donegall.—BARONY OF ENVSHOWEN.—All the Rights of Patronage, Presentations, and Advowsons of the Churches, Rectories, and Vicarages of Cuklagh *alias* Culdafgha, Clonca *alias* Cloncagha, Donnaghelantaghe *alias* Dounaghelancagher, Clonmony *alias* Clonmanny, and Desertegney *alias* Dristerteigney, Fathen *alias* Fawen, and all other Churches, Chapels. &c., within Inishowen *alias* O'Dogherty's Country in the Patent of 1621. Four Salmons every day for ever out of the Salmon Fishing at Cullmore, or near Cullmore Fort, in Loughfoyle, during the Fishing Season. The Fishings of Boncranagh and Strabreage *alias* Traybreage. All Waifs, Estrays, Mines, Quarries, Wrecks, Courts, Free Warren, and Liberty to impark any quantity of Land, of and in the Manors aforesaid in Co. Donegal.

The Total Rents for the aforesaid Lands in the Counties of Donegal and Londonderry, £36 14s. 11d.

Co. Tyrone.—BARONY OF DONGANNON.—The Entire Manor, Fort, and Castle of Dongannon. The Town and Lands of Dongannon *alias* Dromcowe *alias* Killm'Cullen, and a Watermill on the Lands of Brough, near Dungannon. The Towns and Lands of Kenemeale, Carroghelmallcrosse *alias* Gortnaganinebrough, Dungorman *alias* Dromgorman *alias* Moyvall *alias* Dungarman, Killequinn *alias* Killaquin, Clontemolke, Colehill *alias* Coolehills Gortmarren *alias* Portmarren, Moycashall *alias* Moyegeshell, Lism'dermott, Knocksallagh, Killaurfey, Mullaterrory, Lisganine *alias* Lisgane, Mullareagh *alias* Lismullareagh,

Mulleoran, Dromlee, Lissamenan, Donatade *alias* Donadeade *alias* Dromastrade, Derrycreevy, Coolecloish *alias* Cooleclosh *alias* Coolecosh *alias* Strangmore, Droghvane *alias* Droghneboaghie *alias* Lisboy, Dromenehugh *alias* Lemoneheltan, Droghill *alias* Drean *alias* Droan *alias* Aughanacloagh, Tempane *alias* Tempaneroe, Cooleneknough *alias* Coolenegnughe, Dromeagh *alias* Altenovenoge *alias* Broaghderge *alias* The Red Foorde, Derrymeene *alias* Derryveene, Heskeragh *alias* Killcarragh *alias* Knockequinn, Call *alias* Lislaquith, Killedan *alias* Killedoone *alias* Cooleacurragh, Mullaghmore, Ardoliske *alias* Ardoluske *alias* Dromederdalogh, Tereneskill *alias* Terenekeilmore *alias* Terenekeilbegg, Clonduffe *alias* Cloneduske, Mulletedoone *alias* Mullaghedon *alias* Clonkinshan, and Cessaghbuey.

Co. of Tyrone.—BARONY OF DUNGANNON.

—The dissolved House of Franciscan Friers near Dungannon, with the Site thereof, and the Towns and Lands of Mullanehaye *alias* Mullanahath *alias* Mullaghdrolley, Tanagh *alias* Anagh *alias* Annagh *alias* Annaghbegg, Moylaboy *alias* Mullaboy *alias* Mulbuy *alias* Dromyntum *alias* Dooregarmuly, Killnemaddie *alias* Killamaddy *alias* Knockaboney *alias* Mullaghloghernagh. The Estate of said Friery. All these Lands created the Manor of Dungannon, with Courts Leet and Baron, Waifs, Estrays, Mines, Free Warren, and liberty to impark any quantity of Land within the Manor of Dungannon.

Total Rents of Lands in County of Tyrone, £18 14s. 6d.

City of Dublin.

—A Water-Mill and Pond and a Horse-Mill, parcel of St. Mary's Abbey in or near Dublin. To pay the Rent of Ten Shillings after the end of a Lease made 28 August, 17 anno Eliz. to T. Earl of Ormond, £0 10s. 0d.

Liberty to hold Two hundred Acres or thereabouts in Demesne in the several Manors of Dungannon, Ellagh, Greencastle, Boncranagh, and Maulyn. Power to create Freeholders in all the Manors. Licence to make Parks, with Free Warren and Chace. Dated *22 Septr., 1640.* Inrolled *16 Septr., 1667.*

Whereas King James I., by Patent dated 20 Nov., 1621, amongst divers other things, granted to Arthur Lord Chichester and his Heirs, for ever, Loughneagh *alias* Lough Chichester, &c. And whereas Edwd. Visct. Chichester and his son Arthur, now Earl of Donegal, according to the letters of King Charles I. dated 24 Septr., 1638, did, to comply with his Majesty's occasions, surrender the same, and in consideration thereof was to have a Pension (to them both for life) or Rent-Charge of £40 a-year, with liberty to fish for their own Provisions upon the said Lough, and with Eel Fishings at, in, or near Toome. And whereas finding John Visct. Massereene possessed of the Premises, and having made a lease to him thereof, at the Rent of £40 for the first Seven years and £50 for the remainder, the King (pursuant to Privy Seal, dated at Whitehall 28 Feb., 1660) granted and confirmed to Arthur Earl of Donegal and his heirs, for ever, all the said Fishings and Fishing Places of what kind soever in the said Loughneagh and Toome *alias* Lough-Sidney *alias* Lough-Chichester, and in the River of the Bann, with all the Soils and Islands within the same, from the said Lough unto the Rock or fall of Water called the Salmon Leap in the said River, together with certain Eel Wears in and upon the Bann. To hold the same as they had been granted by King James I., and also all Rents reserved, due, or payable out of the Premises, upon any Lease or Leases heretofore made to the said John Visct, Massareene. *3d July, 1661.*

King James I. having, by two different Patents bearing date 20 Nov., 1621, granted to Arthur Lord Chichester, Baron of Belfast, and to his Heirs, divers Lands in the Counties of Antrim, Tyrone, Londonderry, Donegal, and Co. of the Town of Carrickfergus, which were created into several Manors, with power to hold a Law-Day or Court of Record once in every three weeks before Seneschals of his and their appointing, and therein to hold Pleas of all Actions of Debt, Trespass, &c., not exceeding £20, and to receive the Fines of the said Courts ; to appoint Prisons, Bailiffs and other Officers, and to have the executing and returning of all Writs within the said Manors, and a Liberty to hold divers Markets and Fairs, as in the said Patents expressed ; to build Tan-Houses and to tan Leather, and to appoint a Say-Master and Clerk of the Market. And the said

Markets, Fairs, and Privileges having been omitted to be inserted in the Letters Patent of King Charles I. granting and confirming all the said Lands, under the Commission for remedy of defective Titles, and the Lands of Ballynefeigh in Co. Down being thereby made part of the Manor of Joymount, Arthur Earl of Donegal applied to the King for a new Grant to him and his Heirs of all the aforesaid Markets, Fairs, Courts, and other Privileges, and that the said Lands of Ballynefeigh might be made part of the Manor of Belfast, being situated near and more convenient to the parcel thereof, and grant the like Privileges to the new created Manor of Joymount as had been annexed to the other Manors by the Patents of King James. All which the King, by Privy Seal, dated at Whitehall 7 August, 1668, directed to be done, which was accordingly performed by this Patent, separating the said Lands from Joymount and annexing them to the Manor of Belfast ; granting to him and his Heirs to hold the said Law-Day or Court of Record within the Manors of Belfast, Ballinlinny, Moylinny, and Castle-Chichester ; to hold a Thursday Market and a fair 1 Septr., and the day after, at Antrim ; a Friday Market and two Fairs on 1 August, and the Feast of St. Simon and St. Jude, and the day after each, at Belfast ; to build a Tan-House in every of the said Manors, and tan Leather ; to appoint a Say-Master and Clerk of the Market in every of the said Manors ; to hold a Thursday Market and two Fairs on Monday next after the Feast of Saints Philip and Jacob, and on Monday next after Michaelmas Day and the day after each, at Dungannon ; a Market and two Fairs on 1 Augt. and 2 Novr., and the day after each at Cloncroe or Cloneroe near Red-Castle in Inishowen ; a Friday Market and two Fairs on 31 Augt. and 30 April, and the day after each, at Boncrannagh. A Law-Day or Court of Record, with all the aforesaid Privileges annexed to the Manor of Joymount, with Free Warren, &c., &c. Inrolled *12 July, 1669.* (*Pinkerton MSS.*)

Description of Ardes Barony, in the County of Down, 1683.

By WILLIAM MONTGOMERY.

THE Barony of Ardes is thick and well peopled, being above Seventeen miles long and three broad, is separated (on the South end thereof) from Lecahill by a great Flux and reflux of the sea (thence called Strong Ford River) a musket Shot over, in which, near the Ardes side, under an hill (by the Irish called banckmore) there is a whirle-poole or eddy of the returning Tides, called by the Scotch the rowling weele from the Loud Sound it sometimes makes, near to which if small boats come (except about full sea, when the water is smelt), it is said they will be suckt in and swallowed up, and that a great Vessell with a Topsaill gale doth pass through it hardly without being laid about : yet in this last century we have not heard of one boat or person lost by it : from thence in a quarter of a League stands the market town of Portaferry, where great barks do anchor, and at low ebb lye dry, and as much sea further brings great ships up to a Land's end (which from an hill that runs into the said river is) called Ballyhendrypoint, giving them under shelter thereof a spacious harbour, safe from the North and East winds' fury. Some pretenders have offered to find good coal here, but their want of money and incouragement hath hindered the tryal thereof. There is another harbour just opposite thereunto, on Lacahill side (called from a castle above it) Audley's Road, belonging to Nicholas Ward, of Castle Ward, Esqr., who hath a pleasant seat, buildings and plantations near unto it. And over against Portaferry there is a good Creek or Bay for barks, where they lie at Anchor in five fathoms at the Lowest ebb. This is beneath Strongford town, where is the residence and office of the Collector and Customer for ports adjacent. Moon at due South causeth high water at the Bar of the said River of Strongford. This Barony is divided in lower and upper, otherwise called the little and great Ardes, the first whereof, next Lacahill, send every winter great store of good

Wheat, Bear, Oats, and Barley to Dublin and elsewhere, and all the Eastern coasts thereof abounds with fishes, as herrins in harvest ; also Cod, Ling, Graylords (which are near as big as Cod), whiteings, Bavins, large dog fish, Haddocks, Mackrells, Lithes, Blockans, Lobsters, and crabs, and hath good cattle, especially sheep, which feeding on ye onre, keep wholesome and fat all winter and spring time ; within the Land are divers Loughs in which are store of Pike and Eels, Ducks, teel and widgion, and Swans ; the Hills whereof, some be craggy and full of Furs and heath, and the Fern and pasture fields afford Partridge, Quails, Curliw, and Plover of both sorts, and some store of rabbets. This whole Territory doth much want fuell, for with great paines they make it of Bogg mud, claped together and formed with hands, and turned often to dry in the Sun ; but the gentry supply themselfs with Coals from England and Scotland. This lower half Barony was planted by a collony and recruits of the English, when de Courcy pierced into these parts of Ulster and sackt down Patrick. The chief name and commander of that collony is Savage, who, with the Assistance of the Russells, Fitzsymons, Audleys, Jordans, and the Welshes of Lecahill, and the Whites and others of the County of Antrim (many of which Familys depended on and were followers to the Savages), have hitherto kept their ground ag^t all the incursions of the Oneals and divers clans, their vassalls, altho the York and Lancastrian broils drew many of their people to take

RUINS OF PORTAFERRY CASTLE.

the part they wished best to which was the York side. The chief of those Savages was stiled in Grants from Queen Elizabeth Lord of the little Ardes ; his Castle is that of Portaferry aforesaid, the Largest Pile of them all, and a fair slated house, anno 1635, is added thereunto, the chief (then being) having married a Daughter of the first Lord Viscount Montgomery of the great Ardes, a Second and an Antient Family of the same Savages is that of Arkin, it is of good account and hath also another Castle called Seatrick, both are very tenable for war if fortifyed and repaired, of whose Family one Cadet, Rowland Savage, since King James his Entry to England, hath built the two Castles of Ballygalgot and Kirkestown, being high Square piles as are usuall in Ireland, and gave the Same with Lands adjoyning to two of his Sons, about which are divers Irish papist housholds (but inconsiderable) mingled with the british near Portiferry. Northwestward is the old Abbey of Arquin, with Seven Towns (the Bishop's Lands) leased to John Echlin, Esq., whose father was the Grandson of one of the Same Sirname ; Bishop of Down at the beginning of the British plantation under King James aforesaid. These Lands are Said to be given to the Church by Savage of Portiferry, in an expiatory devotion or penitentiary benevolence when all Ireland was popish. The Said Mr. Echlin hath alsoe Severall Townlands in free-hold belonging to a great ruinous Pyle called Castleboy, once the Seat of the Pryor of St. John's in the Ardes, which hath a mannor Court also, there is likewise on the Eastern Shore (one league and an half from the Said Bar) Quintinbay Castle, with an house adjoyning thereto in good repair, with a Stone walled Court or Bawn and Flankers, all which (except the Pyle) Sr. James Montgomery, Knt. (who purchased the same and Lands thereunto belonging from Smith a defender of the Late Chief Savage), and his Son and Heir William, built and repaired. It commands the Bay, which can receive a Bark of fifty Tuns burthen. Near it is a ruinouse pyle called New Castle, which, with divers town Lands adjoyning, belong to James Hamilton, Esq., thence, on the Same Coast, three miles northward, stands Kirkestown Castle (which, and Quintinbay, are the only pyles in repair in this half Barony), whose late erected Garden Walls are washed with a pleasant fresh Lough near the Sea and opposite to the South rock. This James McGill of Ballymonestragh, Esqr., hath improved much by building walls and houses, and repairing in and about it. He lately purchased the Same and Some Townlands adjoyning from the Grandson of the Said Cadet of Arkin, and hath also built a windmill which is Seen far of at Sea and Serves (in day time) in good steed as a land mark for Saylors to avoid ye North and South Rocks aforesaid— Noted in all maps for the misfortunes that ships, Especially forreigners, have had on them in Stormy and dark weather, So that it were to be wished a light house were maintained there. Next lyes a Small Island called green Isle, and a Lesser patch of Rocky Land called buriall, which are the most Easterly parts of Ireland, being a place where vessells often ly at Anchor, expecting the desired wind to run their begun Course. This is the furthest north Extent of this lower half Barony, which hath in it the Small parishes hereafter named (vizt.), Bally-phillip, B'trustan, Slane, Woughtercastleboy, Arquin and Arkin, All which are now Served but in two places, to Witt, at Arkin and Portferry, which last only hath a Large Church in good repair, the rest are unroofed. I conclude the description of the Said Territorys with a brief Remark on ye Savages aforesaid, that they have always been a Stout and Warlike people, Loyall to the Crown of England, who, however they might have had Some Civil broyles amongst themselves, and became (as many noble English Families in Leinster, Munster, and Connaught) too much addicted to the Irish Customes and exactions, yet they are now as much civillized as the british, and doe live decently and conformably to the Church, and enjoy houses, Orchards, and inclosed fields, and hold all the possession they had at the entry of King James aforesaid (except Kirkestown and the Lands adjoyning, before mentioned, which, nevertheless, of the late purchase made thereof, doth pay chiefree to the Castle of Arkin) and doe Suite to the Courts Leet and Baron of the Mannor thereof, they having renew'd their pattents pursuant to the commission of Grace for defective Titles granted in ye reign of his Late Majtie of Glorious Memory. Then next to the Lower half Barony, mearing on the North, is the great Ardes, wherein are B. Halbert and B. Walter parishes (in the last is a Small Village, a slate quarrey, a creek for small boats, and a place very fitt for a great Harbour, both lately belonging to the last Earl of Clanbrazill, if a Key, as was intended by the said Earle, were built there. In these parishes are handsom slated houses lately built by John Bayly, Hugh Montgomery, and Hugh Hamill, Esqrs., Justices of the Peace, raised from the ground on their respective fee-farms, all within prospect of the firth between Scotland and Ireland. Contiguous and a little more Northerly, on the west side of this half Barony, is Gray Abbey parish, half whereof by Pattent from the Late King Charles (of Glorious Memory) belongs to William the Son and heir of Sr. James Montgomery aforesaid, in which is a double-roofed house with four flankers, Stables, and all needfull office houses, all Slated and built after the foreign and English manner with outer and inner courts walled about and surrounded with pleasant Gardens, Orchards, meadows and pasture inclosures under view of the said house (called Rosemount, from which the manor thereof taketh name). The same was finished by the said Sr. James Ano 1634, only some small convenient additions of building and orchards are lately made by his said Son. King James granted a Port to be at Gray Abbey Island, with Pilotage, Anchorage, Keelage and other advantages and priviledges to the same, and licenced Exportation of all native comoditys thereout except Irish Yarn ; but there is no trade there at this time. Near and in view of Rosemount-house are the walls of a Large Abbey of curious work, ruinated in Tyrone's Rebellion ; it is called in inquisitions and Pattents Abathium de Jugo dei ; in Irish, Monestrelea ; in English, Gray or hoar Abby, from the order of Fryers who enjoyed it, and had belonging to thereunto all its one parish in temporalibus et spiritualibus, and also diverse lands in the County of Antrim with Tythes there and in the lower Ardes, in Lecahill, the Isle of Man, and high lands of Scotland. Near it is a spring of excellent water. Campion reports that ye first donation of lands to it was Ano 1189 or 1190, which was in de Courcy aforesaid his time : the Church thereof was new roofed, slated, and reedifyed, and a yard thereunto walled about, and a competent stipend given for a Curat by ye said first Lord Montgomery ; about a mile thence is a small ruined Abbey, with some lands adjoyning, called black Abbey, from Fryars of that coloured habit belonging to the Lord Primate in right of his See of Ardmagh ; the rest of his parish, being 1,000 acres at 19 foot to yᵉ pearch, belongs to Sʳ Robert Collvell, Knight, by late purchase. Then is the parish of Donnoghadee—a Large Manor belonging to the Earl of Mont Alexander—wherein is a fair slated Church in shape of St. Geo. Cross, having four roofs meeting in the middle, and a Bell Tower ; here is a Large Key, a great work, all built by the said first Lord Montgomery, and an handsome market Town of the same Name with the parish, which is the usuall Port for transportation of horses and cattle to England, and is the nearest to Port Patrick in Scotland. About a mile and half from the Town Southward is Patrick Montgomery, Esq., his house of Creboy slated, seen far at sea, having Orchards and inclosures about it, and within a mile and a-half are quarreys of slate, which are used at Belfast, Carrickfergus, and elsewhere. Then abᵗ two miles northwards from the said Town is James Ross, of Portavo, Esq., his great house and large office-houses all of stone, brick, and lime, slated ; gardens walled in, and many well-fenced pastures, all his own erection, since his majᵗⁱᵉˢ happy restoration. In view thereof Copland Isles, part of his Estate, convenient places for a Deer Park, a warren, and other chases. About a mile more northerly is Graham's Port, a Key and harbour for small boats ; these two last-mentioned places are in Bangor Parish, which

ARDKEEN CHURCH.

belonged to the said last Earl of Clanbrazill. And from thence the next considerable is the Town corporate (a market one) of the same name with the parish ; it hath a Provost. 12 burgesses (and freemen made so by them), it sends two men (who are chosen by the burgesses and Provost) to sit in Parliamᵗ, it hath Denomination from an eminent Monastery (whereof some walls yet stand) believed to be the mother, at least the Eldest Daughter of Banchor in Wales ; there is a Large Church and a Bell Tower which were in part of the Monkish buildings, but raised out of its rubbage much reedifyed, and wholly roofed and slated, by James, first Lord Claneboys, who also built a great stable and other houses, and planted Orchards, and fenced in ground near unto the same, and is a noble seat capable of Improvements. In the middle of this Town is a large lofted, slated house, which serves a master which teacheth Latin for a dwelling and the Scholars for a School. At the end of the Town is a small Bay for barks, and on it a large slated house, double lofted, intended at first for a Custom house, both built by the said Lord Claneboy, from hence is the usuall passage over the Lough to Carrickfergus. And now, having traced all the North-east Coast of the whole Barony, let us note that all along from hence to the Bar of Strongford River the inhabitants

do manure and dung the Land with Sea Oar, by them called Tangle, which being spread
on it and plowed down makes Winter Grain and Summer Barley grow in abundance, and
clean, without weeds, cocles, or tares. The roads are pleasant and smooth in depth of
Winter. Now returning to Gray Abbey, which is the center, and on the West side of this
Barony, we come next to view newtown Parish, which is a large mannor. The Town of the
same name, called in Irish Ballynoit, is five miles of good smooth way distant from Gray
Abbey. It hath a weekly good market and is incorporated, and sends men to Parliament, &c.,
as Bangor doth. Here is a fair neat circular building, octagonall, all hewn free stone, carved,
painted, and guilded, with a small door and Stayres ascending to a battlement (which is breast
high from the Vault) within it, and from the Pavement of the said Vault issue divers spouts,
carved with severall Antiqz heads, which at the Coronation and Nativity days of our King
disembogue wine to the glad and-merry multitude. In the middle of this Fabrick, and upon
the Vault aforesaid, stands a pillar of hewn Stone of Eight squares, 20 feet high, with a Lyon
Syant on the Top. This piece of work is called the Market Cross, whence are made publick
(with the Town Solemnities) all proclamations that come from the Chief Governour of this
Kingdome. The body of this Fabrick, which is seen of four Streets, hath the King's Arms
fronting to the great Street, and the Town Armes on another Square thereof, thus, blazoned
Azure, a Crescent with both horns upward proper, from the nombrill whereof riseth a dexter,
arm and hand Armed, holding a flower de luce, reaching to the chiefe of the coat or ; also
other Shields armoriall belonging to the said first Lord Montgomery, and to his Matches and
Allies, with the badges of these Kingdoms are on the rest of the Squares aforesaid.
In this Town (which hath good Springs and Pump Wells, and a brook or bawn at each end
of the great Street) there is a Free Schoole, with good incouragement for a master to teach
Latin, Greek, and Logick, given by the said Sr Robert Colvill, who is purchaser and
Proprietor of the said Town and all the Lands in the parish. There is also a fair long
Church, part whereof were the walls of a priory which stood there ; but new walls were
erected and a new Church (which hath a Square Tower five Storys high, and a great bell in
it, joyned without any partition but large freestone Pillars and Arches), all which were roofed,
slated, and made by the said first Lord Montgomery in his lifetime, and by his order after his
death ; and contiguous to the old church walls, where stood the said Lord's house that was
accidentally burned Anno 1664, Sr Robert Colvill aforesaid hath in few years, from the
foundation, built up a large double-roofed house, stables, coach-houses, and all other
necessary or convenient edifices, with inner, outward, and back courts, and spacious well-
planted olitory, fruit, and pleasure Gardens, which have Fish Ponds, Spring Well, long and
broad Sanded Walks, and Bowling Green, all thereof walled about and reared (with divers
curious hewn stone Gates, uniformly regarding one another in a regular and comely manner) ;
the whole considered, there is few such, and so much work to be seen any one dwelling in
Ireland, nor any so great done by a Gentleman at his own expence. Near Newtown is a
piece of ground called Killtonga, in which hath been the cell of some devout person, but few
remains thereof are now to be seen. This lyes on the North side, but towards the South of the
Town stands the ruinous walls of the Church of an Antient Abbey, called Movilla, which had
large revenues Scatered at distance from it ; now it is inclosed with an old wall, which serves
for a cemetary to the whole Parish and Town. None but persons of the best sort being buried
in the said new-built Church, which was parcell of the Priory aforesaid. The said house,
Gardens, and Church Stand on a levell, and on the head of Lough coan, which is salt water.
13 mile long and five broad at some places, which washeth all the West side and South end of
this Barony, and hath in it many Islands, whereof some are accessible at low water, for it
ebbs above two miles and more downwards from Newtown, leaving a Large Strand ; and
hath also in it oysters, which are dregged in deep water, and some gathered from rocks on
which they grow, and from of the banks within the sea, which are thrown thereon after great
South and West winds, being left bare at low ebbs, and are good as well in Summer as
Winter. There be in this lough also store of mullets, plaice, Sand eels, Strand Cockles, and
in harvest time (some years) herrings are taken, and everywhere on the Western Coast of the
said Barony are abundance of wild fowle of all sorts, especially Swans, whereof a tame breed
are yearly kept at the fresh Lough of Ballygalgot Castle aforesaid, and Barnicles, Wild Gees,
Scapys, Cormorants, Sea Larks, Red Shanks, and those other before-named in the lower
Barony. And within the Land from Bangor to Kirkstown aforesaid is a long red bog which
gives passage by Land (from the said Lough Coan to the Main Sea) but at five or six places.
All this Bogg over it affords the great harrow Goose, Land Barnacles, Grove Snipes, and in
season, woodcocks ; also Hares and Foxes for Game. The Corn and Grass-fields have
Partridge, Quailes, and larks, the Trees and Hedges yield many black birds, thrushes,
Feltifares (about one bigness), Linnets, Goldfinch, and other Melodious Birds in plenty ; as
elsewhere in the said Barony, this part, called the great Ards as aforesaid, hath good Grain of
all sorts, and abundance of fuell cut by the spade) and dryed in the Sun. Out of the said
boggs are digged up (many times) long and great firr trees and black oak without branches,

which are fresh and good timber. The Oak serves for great beams for floors, and so doth the fir, wch will also affords Deals.

Lastly, as appurtenances to the said Mannor of Newtown is the high hill called Scrabo, formerly and now intended for a Deer Park, and therein is the quarrey of the best freestone that may be seen anywhere, if either durableness or smoothness and variety of green veins therein (when pollished) be considered, ye stones whereof are well known in Dublin, and taken thither and elsewhere in great abundance; also, within the Liberty of the said Town is a Large Salt Marsh full of medicinal herbs, the Grass wholesom for diseased horses and cattle, for which the netherland Dutch (before they had well learned or practised navigation to the East and West Indies, offered above £2,000 fine and £50 per ann. rent to have it for 61 years in Lease from the said first Lord Montgomery; but his L^dship being tyed to a brittish plantation, and (if that had been dispenced with) fearing the Trade of the brittish might be absurped in ye Dutch industry, and the Town of Newtown and those of Cumber and Bangor, which are at furthest but 3 miles from the said Marsh, hindered or discouraged in their building, that proposall was not accepted. I conclude with two or three Remarks more, vizt :—That from the great bogg issue many rills and Streams which makes small brooks sometimes almost dry in Summer to the Sea on each side the upper half of the Barony. And on them each plowland almost hath had a mill for grinding Oats dryed in Potts, or singed and leased in the Straw, which was the old Irish custome, the meal whereof was called Graden, very course. The mills are called Danish or Ladle Mills; the Axle tree stood upright, and the small stones or querns on the Top thereof; the water wheel was at the lower end of the Axle tree, and did run horizontally amongst the water, small force driving it; the same waters or Brooks being inclosed in Walls of loose Stones on the Strand of the Lough Coyn in little bays made wares or fish yards, which walls did suffer the tides to come insensibly through them till four hours' flood which (for the last two hours) flowed over the wall; y^n did the sea run strong, and the fishes followed the stream, and, finding food brought down thither by the fresh water brook, and yet the bay was calme; the fish remained there till first the ebb left the wall to appear, and then shuck through, as it came in insensibly, so that the fish, not getting back through the wall, were taken; but since fish days were neglected, those yards decay'd.

Sr.,—This is for your diversion at a Leasure hour. What is worth your noting you may cull out for truth on the credit of your Servant,

WM. MONTGOMERY.

Dublin, the 21st of July, 1683.

(Pinkerton MSS.)   *(MS. I. 1. 2. Library, Trinity Coll., Dublin.)*

Proclamation by the Duke of Schonberg, Belfast, September, 1689.

 HEREAS divers loose and idle people have of late committed several robberies, and daily continue them, under pretence of following the army. Therefore we have thought fit hereby to declare that none do presume to follow the army, and, under that pretence, rob and plunder the country through which we pass. And all such who shall, notwithstanding this our proclamation, follow the army (suttlers and such as are hired excepted) shall be deemed and punished as robbers. And we shall further order and direct the provost marshall and his men to seize and apprehend them as such, that they may be accordingly punished.   SCHONBERG.

Given at our Head Quarters at Belfast the 1st day of September, 1689.

(Pinkerton MSS.)

SCHONBERG'S TROOPS CROSSING THE LONG BRIDGE, BELFAST, 1689.

Diary of Col. Thomas Bellingham when at Belfast, June, 1690.

HERE is in the possession of Sir Henry Bellingham, Bart., of Castle-Bellingham, Co. Louth, the original Manuscript Journal of his Ancestor, Colonel Thomas Bellingham, kept during the years 1688-90, including the whole of King William's Campaign in Ireland during the last year, when Colonel Bellingham attended the King and acted as Guide to the Army till after the Battle of the Boyne.

With the exception of the portion relating to that battle (which is quoted in Macaulay's *History*) this Journal has not been published, but a careful transcript has been made from the original by Mr. Garstin, F.S.A., V.P.R.I.A., who has kindly supplied the following extracts (additions being enclosed in brackets):—

[May] ye 28th [1690]

Raine in ye morning. We went to Hyle lake [Hoylake] and ship't our horses early and sayl'd about 3 in ye after noon. We came att night in sight of the Isle of Man. Our ship ye Betty of Biddiford, Tho: Marshal, mr. [Master].

ye 29th

A fayr gale in ye morning, but calm about nine. We lay most of ye day near ye Mull of Galloway, and att evening came to an anchor near ye Copeland Islands.

ye 30th

Some showers. About 3 this morning we came to an anchor at ye White house. I went with mr. King to Carrigfergus, saw Dean Ward, and mr. King heard yt Kirke was displeas'd att him. About 12 I came by boat to Belfast. Din'd att mr. m'Cartny's, and sup't with mr. Twigg and lay that night wth him. I wrote to Nabby [his wife, Abigail (Hancock), at Preston, in Lancashire].

ye 31th [*sic*, not "st," and so throughout]

Some raine. I came to Lisburn. Waited on Ma: Gen: Kirk. Was with ye Duke [Schomberg], who was very obleiging. I din'd wth ye Earl of Meath, and came to Jo: White's.

June ye 1st [Sunday]

Much raine. I went to Magherelin. Heard mr. Cubbidge preach. Din'd att his house wth ye Coll. of the Brandenburgh Regiment, and was after with major Williams and Capt: Brereton att mrs. Kelly's. Ye Lord Drogheda pass't by.

ye 2^d

Severall showers. Some Quakers came to see me. I walk't in ye afternoon to Moyragh. Saw Sr Arthur Rawden's house, and walk^t wth Capt. Ross to ye Conservatory. The house and much of ye goods are well preserv'd.

ye 3^d

A fayr day. I went to ye mill. In ye afternoon I went to Drummore, and was treated by Capt. Brereton.

ye 4th

A fayr morning. Some showers in ye afternoon. I went to Lisbourn, waited on M.G. [Major-General] Kirke, deliver'd him his letter, din'd wth mr. Aleway, and was wth ye Duke. Some French horse came in. I saw cousen Purcell. I wrote to Nabby and Dan by ye poast, and came home in good time.

ye 5th

Abundance of rain. J. Shepheard came hither and brought news of ye K.[ing] leaving london yesterday.

ye 6th

High wind and some showers. Shepheard stayes still here. We have an account of a prey being taken by ye soldiers of Bellturbet, and part of them being brought into these quarters to be sold.

ye 7th

Wind and some showers. Shepheard went hence this morning. We hear ye enemy are advancing.

ye 8th [Sunday]

Very much raine. I receiv'd ye Sacram.[ent] at Macherelin, where mr. Cubbidge preach'd a very suitable sermon for ye day. I din'd wth him and was wth mr. John Disny. Capt. Lowry came hither and stay'd all night.

ye 9th

Still wet weather. Lowry went hence this morning. I designed for Hillsborough, but ye raine prevented me. John White pay'd Gillett his rent for grazing. [Last paragraph not contemporary.]

A fayr day. I went to Lisburn, but ye D.[uke] was gone to Bellfast, thinking to meet ye K.[ing], but return'd. I came wth Capt. Powell and stay'd some time with mr. Moore att Hillsborough, wch is preparing for ye King's reception. Y^enight there were severall bonefires made is [*sic*] beleiving ye K. was landed, but it prov'd an *ignis fatuus*. Severall Regiments are on theyr march towards a rendezvous near Ardmagh and Legachory. C. G. [Commissary-General] Douglas commands them.

ye 11th

A very hott day. We wash'd our sheep. I din'd wth Capt. Powell at Drummore. Some french challenged some horses in theyr parkes, but ye Major and Capt. Powell sent them to ye Gaurd. There were more bonefires made this night.

ye 12th

Very hott. I went to Moyragh. I saw Jewell's Regiment of horse, wch is a very good one, but ye Danish Regiment of Gaurds is ye best I ever saw. They are an orange coulour'd livery fac'd wth crimson velvett. I din'd at Moyragh and saw Mr. Sb[t or h?]eeres, Capt. Hamilton and Lieut. Hamilton, who was att Gernonstown [now Castle-Bellingham, Co. Louth]. Eben Loe [Ebenezer Lowe] was wth me.

ye 13th

Very hott. I went to Moyragh. Saw one Hatch who came a week ago from Drogheda. He call'd at Gernonstowne, and sayes things are very well there, and

L

that there is much corne growing thereabouts. He sayes K. James his army is in an ill condition for want of most necessaryes. There are about 7,000 of them encamp'd near Ardee. There are 3 Regiments in Dundalk and 3 in Drogheda, to which they have added no fortifications more than what were last summer. I saw Capt. Wm. Ponsonby att Moyragh and Lieut. Coll. Peirce.

yᵉ 14ᵗʰ

A great shower of raine after dinner, about wᶜʰ time we fancy'd we heard some great guns off from Bellfast, wᶜʰ we hope are for yᵉ K. landing. Here came James Hunter, yᵉ Quaker, and a quarter master of Levison's Dragoons. Yᵉ K. landed at Carrigfergus [written over "Donaghadee"].

yᵉ 15ᵗʰ [Sunday]

A fayr day. I went to Church, and din'd wᵗʰ mr. Cubbidge. Heyford's dragoons are quartered at Macharelin.

yᵉ 16ᵗʰ

A hott close day. I was sent for by 2 this morning, and before 6 I came to Bellfast. I was kindly received by yᵉ D. and Kirke, and favourably recommended to yᵉ K., whose hand I kiss't, and he promised to remember me. I was most of yᵉ afternoon wᵗʰ yᵉ Secretary. Yᵉ K. road out in yᵉ evening. I lay wᵗʰ mr. Mason. I this day wrote letters for England to Nabby, etc.

yᵉ 17ᵗʰ

A hott day. I gave yᵉ K. a petition. Din'd at Rourke's with mr. Aleway and others, and came home late. We mett with some french theives.

yᵉ 18ᵗʰ

Very hott. I sent Art away early this morning wᵗʰ letters. I had an answear from Toby Purcell. Mr. Loe was here.

yᵉ 19ᵗʰ

Very hott. I walked to yᵉ Mill and wash'd there.

yᵉ 20ᵗʰ

Very great showers. I went to Hillsborough, saw yᵉ K., and dranke of his wine. A messenger came from yᵉ Lᵈ Dover to desire leave to transport himselfe and family to Ostend. 2 dragoons were brought in prisoners. I was wᵗʰ my Lᵈ Meath and mr. Aleway att theyr tents, and brought Hunter yᵉ quaker's wife behind me home.

OLD BELFAST CASTLE IN 1690.

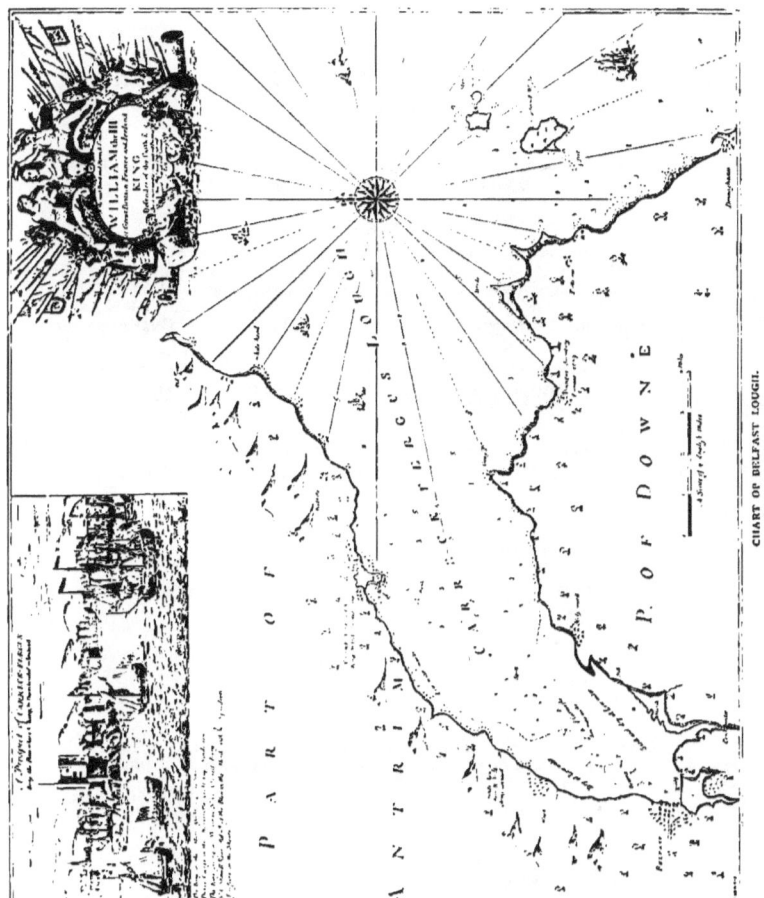

CHART OF BELFAST LOUGH.
Reduced from Greenville Collins's "Great Britain's Coasting Pilot," 1693.

𝕶ing 𝖂illiam the 𝕿hird and his 𝕮ourt at 𝕭elfast, June, 1690.

Extracts from Correspondence, &c., of George Clarke (Secretary for War), in Trinity College, Dublin, made by William Pinkerton, F.S.A.

June 18th, 1690. List of the General Officers at Belfast.

The Duke of Schonberg, The Count de Solms, The Count de Schonberg, The Earl of Oxford, The Duke of Wirtemberg, The General Ginckell, Lieutenant-General Douglas, Major-General Scravenmore, Sir John Lanier, Major-General Kirk, Marquis la Fourse, Major-General Tettan, Lord Sidney, Earl of Nassau, The Treasurer, The Secretary at War, Col. du Camelon Cambon, Quartermaster of Ireland.

The Fiscalls, 2 ; Commissary of the Provisions, 2 ; Provosts Marshalls, 3 ; two Commissaries of the Musters, one Waggon Master, Hospitall.

GEORGE CLARKE.

It is ordered that Du Perron, Captain of the Waggons, will observe, and cause to be observed, on the march, the household of his majesty in the following order :

TENT DU ROI.

3 Chariots des Cusines *(sic)*.
1 De la Boucherie.
2 De la Boulongerie.
3 De la Pouillerier.
6 Du Garde Mange.
8 De la Cave.
5 Conveniers de Table avec linges vessels, &c.
2 Confiturier.
4 Avec les sents.
1 Du clerk Coffereux.
2 De la Blanchiseuse.

The other waggons will follow in the order according to the list regulated by his Majesty. Made at the quarters of the Court at Belfast, 1690, 18th June.

AUVERQUERK.

RULES AND ORDERS TO BE OBSERVED IN THE MARCH OF THE ARMY.

IN the Quarters, where the Court shall have its apartments, the houses in the quarters shall be divided according to the quantity there shall be,—The Duke of Schonberg having choice the first, Count Solmes the second, Count Schonberg the third, and the rest of the Generals as they are on the list, without giving a house to any person whatsoever before those on the list be quartered. No one shall take any quarters unless it be marked by the Quartermaster-General or his Adjutant, and if any be found who marks or rubs out the chalk which was marked by the Quartermaster-General shall be punished.

No one shall march before the guards of the quarters, and shall all place themselves according to the orders given by the Quartermaster-General.

When the baggage shall march, the King shall have at the head of all, before the Artillery itself, six wagons, Duke Schonberg three, and the rest of the Generals one.   After that, the rest of the King's baggage, with all those of the Court, shall follow the Artillery, according to the list herewith appended, and the rest of the baggage of the Generals after, and then shall follow the baggage of each brigade, as they shall march.   If they march in two or three lines, and if the baggage can follow the lines, they shall.

The Guard being once placed, no one whatsoever of the Army shall pass, on pain of Death, without the King's express order.   All Waggon Masters obliged to come to the Waggon Master General every evening to receive his orders.

June 19, 1690.   GEO. CLARKE.

From a Photo. by W. SWANSTON, F.G.S.

THE GLOVES, STIRRUPS, AND HORSE-TRAPPINGS OF KING WILLIAM AT BATTLE OF THE BOYNE.
(In possession of THE BARONESS VON STIEGLITZ, *Carrickblacker, Co. Armagh.)*

Proclamation issued by William the Third when in Belfast.

WILLIAM R.

UR chief intention and design in this our Royal Expedition being to reduce our Kingdom of Ireland to such a state that all who behave themselves as becomes dutiful and loyal subjects may enjoy their Liberties and Possessions under a just and equal Government, and to the end that all our loving subjects who at present are in our obedience may find the good effects of Our Protection, and as much as possible in the distractions of War feel the benefit and advantage of continuing under the care of Our Power, Our Will and Pleasure is that all officers, soldiers, and others belonging to our Army do so carry themselves, both in Garrison, Quarters, and wheresoever they shall march, as persons ought to do who are under Military Discipline, and that they do not presume on any account to spoil or rob any Parks or Warrens, Plunder the Houses, do violence to or extort or take any horses, cows, or other Cattle from the Inhabitants of the Towns or Quarters where they are or shall be, but that they duly pay such reasonable Rates for those Provisions and necessaries they have or shall have occasion to make use of as is or shall be appointed by us, with proportion to the pay and entertainment they receive: And we do strictly charge all officers, soldiers, and persons whatsoever to observe and obey these Our Rules and Orders, and behave themselves accordingly: And all Colonells, Captains, and other officers are hereby Required not only to keep themselves within these due bounds and limits, but to see that their respective soldiers do the same, as they will answer the contrary at their Peril, it being Our Resolution, upon Complaint made to Us by any person aggrieved, to punish all such as in anywise offend against and act contrary to these Our Orders. And that no one may plead or pretend ignorance of this Our Royal Will and Pleasure, We do hereby direct and command that these Orders be published in all the Quarters of Our Army, and that one Comissary of the Musters do Publicly read them at

the head of each Regiment so often as they shall muster the same.

Given at Our Court at Belfast, the 19th day of June, 1690, in the Second Year of our Reign,

By his Maties. Command,

A True Copie.   GEO. CLARKE.

FAC-SIMILE OF WILLIAM'S SIGNATURE.

LETTER TO THE KING FROM GENERAL KIRKE.

MAY IT PLEASE YOUR MAJESTY,

According to your Matie's comandes I have ordred the troopes to march to the Newrey, who will be all there to morho *(sic)* night.   The enclosed came from thence by the bearer, who told me a Drumer of the Enemeye's had brought a letter for me, which maid me open the letters Directed to Lieut.-Col. Pursell.   I do not know the meaning of my Lord Dover's letter, except 'tis to know the sarienty of yor matie being hear. Yor matie will therfore be pleased to order me what answer I shall send, or whether I shall keep the Drumer.

May it please yor matie,

Your matie's most dutiffull servt.,

Drumore, June 19th, 1690.   KIRKE.

Drumore, June the 19, att 12 a clock night.

SIR,

This inclosed, coming from the Newry, I thought itt my duty to send his Matie, which I desire you to Deliver, and send me his Matie's commands.

Sir,

Mr. Clarke, Secretary at Warr.   Your most humble servt.,

KIRKE.

Proclamation issued at Hillsborough.

WILLIAM R.

HEREAS Complaint has been made to Us of great Disorders committed by the officers and soldiers of Our Army by the Liberty they assume of Pressing Horses and Carts, to the great Prejudice of Our Service, and Loss and Damage of Our Loving Subjects who are owners of the same : Our Will and Pleasure is that no officer or soldier within Our pay and entertainment, or other person whatsoever, do presume to press any horse or cart belonging to any of Our Subjects without leave and order first had under our Royal Sign Manual: And that whosoever shall dare, without leave and order as aforesaid, to press any horse or cart, if he be an Officer, he shall be dismissed Our Service; if a Trooper, he shall stand three several times on the Picquett; and if a Dragooner or Foot Soldier, he shall run the Gauntlope thrice through the whole Regiment. And we do strictly charge and command all persons that shall have leave and order to press, as aforesaid, only to pay such rates as they shall agree for with the owners, under the penalties afore-mentioned. And that no Person may pretend ignorance, We hereby direct and command that these Our Orders be forthwith published at the Head of every Regiment.

Given at Our Court at Hillsborough, the 20th day of June, 1690, in the Second Year of Our Reign,

By His Majesty's Command,

GEO. CLARKE.

I have left at Kilrea, Antrim, Belfast, Magharafelt, Armagh, &c., several sick men, to the number of above three score, most of which, I am informed by letter, are in a condition to come up and serve. But for those who are as yet very weak, it will be necessary to press horses for them from place to place. I humbly desire you therefore, sir, to get an order from the King, for the officer of my regiment, which I am sending down, to press horses upon the road at any place between the aforesaid places, and the army where we shall be, not exceeding the number of thirty; without it, I shall be forced to leave several of my best men behind, and lose some.

(Not dated.)   GENERAL CUTES (OR CUSTES).

Journey to ye North, August 7th, 1708.

BY DR. THOMAS MOLYNEUX.

LEFT Dublin, and came in 3 hours and ¼ to Bellough, a small village, thro' a very flat, open corn Countrey, good causey Roads, passing thro' Santry and Swords, which Last is a Borough, and seems to have been a place of some Antiquity, for severall old Ruins that are here, and, among others, of one of the old round Steeples, which stands near the church. Having dined at Bellough, we went on thro' the same kind of Countrey, and much about the same time thro' Balruddery, Julianstown, Bridge on the Nanny water (which bounds the County of Meath from Dublin) to Droghedagh. Droghedagh is a pretty Large town, Larger Houses, and every way liker Dublin than any one I have Seen in Ireland. It stands on the famous River Boyne, which is navigable within Walls to Boats of 40 or 50 ton. Its Walls and Fortifications are very old and out of Repair, having suffered much, as have also most of the Houses then standing, in its Siege by O. Cromwel. Here is, on the South side the River, on a height wᶜʰ comands the Town, and from whence you have a fair Prospect of it, a remarkable Danes' Mount, as it seems to have been, but to which there are now built 5 or 6 half Bastions of Stone Work, with a Ditch round it, by Cromwel, as they Relate. From Drougheda we went up the River Boyne, on the North side, to Nouth in two hours. About half way up you pass by yᵉ Remarkable Foard where was performed the Famous Pass of the Boyne. Here yet remains a broad Foard or two ; and on t'other side the River the Ruins of the Irish Battery, which, with a few Sculls, are the only marks of this happy place of action.

SUNDAY.

Having spent the morning at Knouth, after Dinner Cosⁿ: S. Dopping and I went on cross the countrey, in about three hours, to Ardee. The way is mostly in the County of Louth, fine open sheep-walk, all hills and Dales, making from a height a most pleasant prospect, such variety of fine risings, with some few scattered inclosures and Gentlemen's

MAP OF BATTLE OF THE BOYNE.

Houses everywhere presenting themselves. Ardee is a compact little Town—A Burrough—and seems to have been once a place of Good strength, for the many strong old castles and Double Walls that it has. From hence, three hours more Brought us to Dundalk, an ugly Town, and, I think, remarkable in nothing but for an extraordinary good Inn here, as good as most in England.

MONDAY.

We designed for Ardmagh, and went 16 mile towards it, mostly on the very wild mountains, The Fews. These Mountains are of a Boggy, heathy Soile, the Road thro' them of a Rocky Gravel ; in all this way meet but one house, and nothing like Corn, Meddow, or Enclosures. We baited on them at the Second House, which is called black Ditch, where is also a small foot Barrack, but without any Soldiers. Here was miserable Entertainment, not so much as tolerable Grass within two mile of 'em. From hence two or three miles brings you to the End of the Mountains, and then you enter into a pleasant Enclosed Corn Countrey, which in 5 or 6 miles brings you thro' very new made Roads to Ardmagh.

ARDMAGH is a very pretty Town and Burrough situated on a Hill. The Cathedral, which is yet in the same place where St. Patrick first fixed his See, stands at the highest part of the Town, and from whence you have all round you a very beautifull prospect of as well an Improved and enclosed Countrey as can be. The choir of this Cathedral has been Lately rebuilt and much adorned by the Dean Drelincourt, who has wainscotted and painted it all at his own Cost, so that it is now, I think, handsomer than any in Dublin. Here is also a very handsome free School now building, and good Barracks. Cousⁿ Dopping was this Evening Sworn a Burgess of yᵉ Town, and I was complimented with my freedome.

TUESDAY.

We went to my Estate at Castle Dillon, and so to Legacorry, which is a very pretty Village belonging to Mr. Richardson. From hence Mr. Chichester, a Relation of my Lord Donnegall's, invited us to dine with him at the house where he lives, belonging to one Mr. Workman, within half a mile of Portadown,   miles from Ardmagh. Mr. Workman shewed us here vast plantations of Fir Trees of All different ages from the seed. They thrive here mighty well, and this Gentleman makes a considerable Gain in this way. After Dinner we proceeded on our journey towards Belfast, where Mr. Chichester promised to accompany us. We passed thro' Portadown, a pretty village situated on the River   , and where so many protestants were drowned in 41 Rebellion by the Irish. Here our horses passed over in a wherry, the Bridge which they were then a Building, very Large and handsome, being not yet finished. From hence we went on thro' a mighty pretty English-like enclosed countrey, and well planted with Large Trees, to Mr. Brownlow's Town, Lurgan, miles from Ardmagh, situated within half a mile of the South Banks of Lough Neagh. This Town is at present the greatest mart of Linnen Manufactories in the North, being almost entirely peopled with Linnen Weavers, And all by the care and cost of Mr. Brownlow, who on his first Establishing the trade here, bought up everything that was brought to the market of Cloath and lost at first considerably; but at Length the thing fixing itself, he is now by the same methods a considerable Gainer. This Gentleman is more curious than ordinary, and has by him several old Irish Manuscripts which he can Read and understand very well. He shewed me one in Parchment of the Bible (as I remember), pretended to be written by St. Patrick's own hand, but this must be a Fable. This Gentleman is not satisfyed about the Petrifying Quality of Lough Neagh waters, and seems rather to esteem the Stones found on its Banks to be *Lapides sui Generis* than Petrifactions. Having Supped with him we lay at an Inn.

WARINGSTOWN.

WEDNESDAY.

We went altogether towards Lisbon *(sic)*. About 2 or 3 miles from Lurgan is a village called Maherlin, where liveth the Bp. of Dromore. Here I stoped to a visit to my old Tutor, Mr. Redman, who lives with his Uncle Cuppaidge, Ministr of the Place. From hence I followed 'em, and passed by Moyragh, a fine seat belonging to Sr Arthur Royden's Family, Leaving Warrenston and Hillsborough to the Right, thro' the fine Improved County of Down, which, with Ardmagh, are the finest Counties in the North, to Lisbon, miles. Here we designed to have waited on the Bp. of Down, who lives within a small mile to the Town; but he being not at home. we spent our Time in viewing the Miserable Ruines of the Late Fire which happened here, and not a house in the Town Escaped. If the story of the Phœnix be ever true, sure 'tis in this Town. For here you see one of the beautifullest Towns perhaps in the 3 kingdoms—all Brick houses, slated, of one bigness, all new, and almost finished, rising from the most terrible Rubish that can be Imagined. When I stood in the Church Yard, I thought I never had seen so dreadfull a Scene before, all round me the church burnt to the Ground, The tombstones all cracked with the fire, Vast Trees that stood round the Church Yard Burnt to Trunks. Lord Conway (to whom this town belongs)—his House, tho' at a distant from all the rest in the Town, burnt to Ashes, and all his Gardens

BURNING OF BELFAST CASTLE, 1708.

in the same condition, with the Trees in the Church Yard. 'Tis scarcely conceivable such dismall Effects should arise from so small cause and in so short a time as they relate. Only Some Turf Ashes thrown on a Dunghill, which a brisk Wind blowing towards the Town Raised and threw on the Shingles of the next house, which, being like Spunk, by a long Drought of Weather which had then happened, took fire, and the Wind continuing what it had begun, the whole Town, in half an hour, was irrecoverably in Flames, insomuch that this accident happening whilst they were at Church on a Sunday morning, by 4 the fire was extinguished, And not a house and but a few of their Goods Remained in being. Its Rise is likely to be as suddain as its fall. Lord Conway has renewed all the Leases, for a year or two, Rent free; gives them as much Wood as they please to cut of his own Woods, which are near, and obliges them to build Regular, so that if the story of the Phœnix be ever true, sure 'tis in this Town. This Town was formerly the greatest Linnen manufactory of the North before the Fire; now much removed to Lurgan and other adjacent places. However, I do not doubt but when 'tis quite rebuilt, 'twill be rather in a more thriving condition than before. From hence we went on   miles to Bellfast, thro' a Countrey,

LISBURN.

all the way from Ardmagh, Extreamly pleasant, well Improved, and Inhabited by English. Belfast is a very handsome, thriving, well-peopled Town; a great many new houses and good Shops in't. The Folks seemed all very busy and employed in trade, the Inhabitants being for the most part merchants, or employ'd under 'em, in this Sea Port, which stands, conveniently enough, at the very inner part of Carrickfergus. Thro' the Town there Runns a small Rivulet, not much better than that they call the Glibb in Dublin, which, however, is of great use for bringing their goods to the Key when the Tide serves. Here we saw as Dismall Effects of another Fire as that at Lisbon, which here, in the night, had Lately burnt a house belonging to the Lord Donnegall's Family (whose Town this is), with three Young Ladys, sisters to the present Earl, It stands seperate from the Rest of the Houses, which as it prevented the Flames going further, so it cut of timely Relief in the midst of courts and gardens, which are an Extreamly noble old Improvement, made by old Sr Arthur Chichester, who was, about 100 years ago, the Establisher of this Family, and Indeed of the whole Kingdome, Especially the North, by planting English Colonies and civilizing the Irish. These Improvements are all Inclosed in a kind of Fortification, being Designed for a place of

Strength as well as Pleasure, and is a lasting Monument of this kind of the greatness of its
founder.   Here we saw a very Good Manufacture of Earthen Ware, which comes nearest
Delft of any made in Ireland, and really is not much short of it.   'Tis very clean and pretty,
and universally used in the North, and I think not so much owing to any Peculiar happiness in
their clay, but rather to the manner of beating and mixing it up.   Here they have Barracks
for   we lay here this night, And the next day—

THURSDAY—

Dined with the Soveraign, Mr. McCartney, where we were made free of the Town.   After
Dinner we went on towards Carrickfergus, about two or three mile from Town.   We struck
off from the Road, which runs all Long the Sea, to view a Park here belonging to the Lords
of Donnegal.   Here they carryed us up a pretty high Hill, where is a very pleasant Fountain,
well shaded with Trees, and from whence you have a very fine Prospect of Carrickfergus, the
Bay, and Belfast, which from'hence makes a very good shew.   Returning to the Road, about
half way to Belfast, we parted with Mr. Chichester, and continued our journey to Carrickfergus.

SHANE'S CASTLE.

FRIDAY.

   CARRICKFERGUS is a place of good natural strength, situated on a Rocky Promontory
which runs out into the Sea ; not so big, clean, or thriving a Town in any wise as Belfast.
It has litle in't remarkable but Ld Donnegall's monument in the Church, which is very rich
and great ; the great Castle belonging to the Crown, and a most noble old house of Lord
Donnegall's Family built by Sr Arthur Chichester, Extreamly great and noble, but wanting
the Gardens at Belfast, which, were they joyned, would make beyond comparison the finest
Improvement in Ireland.   It has a fine situation fronting the Bay, all the Grand^r and
regularities of a modern building, and shews the great spirit of the builder ; but What he set
up is now making hast to fall to the Ground.   From Carrickfergus we went thro' a wild
country in about 4 hours to Antrim ; we passed thro' Castle Norton, a small village.
   ANTRIM is a pretty good Town situated on the North East Banks of Lough Neagh.   It
enjoys a considerable Linnen Trade at present.   Here Lord Mazarreen has a pretty good
house, and good Improvements about it, where he lives.   We saw here the Largest piece of
Lough Neagh Stone that I have ever seen ; 'twas as thick as one's body, Irregularly shaped,
perfectly like ye Root of a Tree, the Trunk and Small branches of the Root Loped off.   This
piece, not only for its bigness and shape, but also for the grain of it too, appeared the most
like Stone of any I have seen.   His Lordship assures me there are several such like sticking
in ye Banks of the Lough, and that he does not doubt but that this Lough has this petrifying

Quality ; Nay, that he could have shewn me, had he been at Antrim when I was there, a piece of which half is a Stone, and half is yet perfect Wood. Mr. Maclean, Minisr of the Town, gave me here certain Stones of a whitish Brown Colour, of a gritty Substance, much the biggness and shape of a Potatoe, save that they all have litle perturbance, by which, he assures me, they stick in the Banks of this Lough near the surface of the Water, the rest standing clear out, and that they there are found to grow till their Weight, and the Water washing away the Earth where they stick, they fall to the bottome. Of these stones the Arch Bpe of Dublin gave me several before, and related the accoᵗ of them.

Having seen in the minuts of the Dublin Society an accoᵗ of Fish called Dolleyn, a sort of Herring or Trout peculiar to this Lough (which also is mentioned in *Giraldus Cambrensis Topog. Hiber.*), I Inquired for it At Antrim, but could not get the sight of one, tho' this was the Season of Catching them, and they told me there had been several Boat Loads brought in there the Market Day before, but were bought up for drying. From Antrim we went to Shane's Castle—Mr. O'Neill's—a very antient building about one mile from Antrim, situated on the very Banks of Lough Neagh, so near that it and yᵉ Garden Walls are washed by the Water, and from hence arrived in 4 or 5 hours thro' a miserable, wild, Barbarous, boggy countrey, to as bad a Lodging in a poor Village called Maghereoghill.

GIANT'S CAUSEWAY, CO. ANTRIM.

SATURDAY.

Having Passed the Night but ill, we were Soon on our journey, and arrived early thro' a wild, open Countrey at Ballymony—a pretty, clean, English-like Town belonging to the Earl of Antrim, who has here in possession a prodigious scope of Land, I believe of some 30 or 40 miles in Length. Here we tooke a Guide to the Gyant's Cawsey. The Land about it, & particularly the head Land under which it Lyes, is very good Sheepwalk, and lies very high, so that you have from hence, as indeed you have from most of the hills in this Easterly part of the North, a fair prospect of several parts of Scotland and the Isle of Man. You go down to the Cawsey by a very narrow path along the side of the Hill. I carryed along with me the print of the Cawsey after Mr. Sandy's Draught from the *Philosophical transactions*, as also Dr. Molyneuxe's *Discourse of it in a Letter to Dr. Lister*, also in the *transactions*, and compared them both on the place as strictly as I could. The Draught is pretty well as to the Cawsey itself, but not so Exact in the face of the Hill and the Organs or Loomes as it should be ; and indeed it does not represent yᵉ Cawsey itself to run from the Hill so as it does. I think it would be as necessary and usefull to have a plan of it as well as a prospect as for the accoᵗ on't in *Dr. Lister's Letter.*

Having taken a sufficient view of the Gyant's Cawsey, we mounted again in order to go to Colrain. We rid here a good way along the North Shore on great sands, where I am

told are Warrens of a prodigious Length of Excellent Rabets. About three mile from
y⁵ Cawsey you come to a Fameous old place called Dunluce. This was an old Castle, formerly
the seat of y⁵ Earls of Antrim. Its situation is very romantick and out of the way. 'Tis
built on a Large Rock, Entirely separated from the Land. It has been a vast Large Pile, and
covers the whole Rock, so that you can spit out of most of y⁵ Windows into the Sea, which
is a Vast depth under you. However, the Natural or Artificial hollows in this Rock are such
that I am told the sea beats into all the Cellars. In high tides 'tis Entirely surrounded with
water, but the precipice by which 'tis divided from the shore is so terrible that this Castle
seemes to me innacessible on all sides at the Lowest water, and was certain when in Repair
a most inexpugnable place to the Instruments of War used in those dayes. They tell you
here that one part of the house and Rock which hung over the sea, being the Kitchin and
part of the Great Hall, fell down during a great Entertainm⁵ into the Sea, and Several
Persons were lost. The only passage into it was by a Bridge over that precipice, of
which there now Remains only one wall to go over by; but it was too windy weather
when I was there to Venture this Passage without y⁵ help of a Rope stretched across
to hold by. The Court belonging to this house is on the Land, but I could not observe
any remains of Gardens or Grown Trees, nor do I think it possible to have any such in this
bleak situation. From hence 2 hours ½ brings you to Colrain, which is a good, large,
compact, well-built Town, sittuated on the Fine River Bann. It looks like a clean, pretty
Town as you go thro' it, but the Inn in which we Lay was the most drunken, Stinking
Kennel that ever I smelt or saw. About a small mile up the River is the Famous Fishery of
Colrain. This has nothing Extraordinary in its Contrivance, and has been wholly to an
accident that it was ever made. There is here a fall in the River, and a Gentleman in the
neighbourhood having occasion to bring Down some Timber down the River, makes at this
fall Cut of a matter of 10 or 20 foot over, to Let his Timber down. The Cut Remains, and
the Salmons, at those seasons of the year they go up and down the River, finding this the
most Easy passage, Come up and Down in great Shoals, which the Fishermen observing,
built here a Wire Enclosing some 40 foot in Length of this Cut, and with some Fish-boats
that Fish at the River's mouth, takes the vast quantity of Fish that is here taken, which I
think is not owing to any peculiar artifice in the Fishery, but the Love the Fish have to that
water, and the great Quantity of Waters that are above, the whole River, which is no small
one, much Larger than the Liffey, from Colrain to the great Lough Neagh, the whole Lough
itself, and several Rivers that run into it. In the high season of the year the Fish pass here
in such Shoals that the whole cut will be sometimes so full the Fish shall force one another
above water. Insomuch that in one day (which the Bspe of Derry has) there have been
taken sometimes to the value of 400⁵ and we were assured 'tis actually sett for
200⁵ pʳ Ann. From a Hill the Road here passes over going to Derry we have a fine
Prospect of the River and Town below the Road, and of a pretty Improvem⁵ of one Mr.
Jackson's joyning the Town. This River has between Colrain and the Lough two very
narrow falls, which in Winter do not Discharge near so much water as the Rains make, which
causes the Lough to overflow some 1,000⁵ of Acres. This might be helped, I hear, for 5 or
6,000 pounds, so as to make the River navigable also to the very Lough to boats
of 30 or 40 Ton.

SUNDAY.

From this to near Newtown, which is half-way to Derry, is all a most Excellent, new,
artificially-made Cawsey in dismall, wild, boggy mountains. It runs for Some miles in an
Exact Straight Line, and it makes a pretty figure to see a work so perfectly owing to Art and
Industry in So wild a place. 'Twill cost 600⁵ We arrived at Newtown Lemnavaddy, where
Mr. Connelly lives, in about 4 hours. Newtown is a very clean, English-like Town, a
Burrough, well planted with English and Scotch Inhabitants. Mr. Connelly is here building
a Park, which will be Extreamly beautifull and well watered by the River that runs thro' the
Town, which Mr. Connelly told me will sometimes swell so as entirely to cover a Bridge
over it in this place, which I could not Esteem Less than 30 foot from the Water. There is
here gathered a kind of black Slate on the Rocks of Magilligan, which they tell me is found
to be an Excellent Medicine in Several disorders. Some other Natural Curiosities are here
talked of, but none very Remarkable. They tell you of Solomon's Porch, which by the
description I could Learn to be no more than an odd figured Rock on the sea shore ;
of a clock maker in this Countrey that has made several attempts for the Perpetual
Motion ; of Mr. MacSwyne's Gun in County Donnegal, which, as I hear, is a hole in the
Cliffs of the Rocks from whence there constantly issues a Considerable noise And wind by the
beating of the waves below, Insomuch as to be able sometimes to return with considerable
violence a Stone when you throw it down into it. They shewed me here some very round
Stones found in great Quantityes in a Hill called Bullet hill, in y⁵ C. Derry. At Mr.
Connelly's we stayed all Monday.

TUESDAY.

We were Invited to Dine with Major Genl Hamilton, who lives at a place called within 2 miles of Newtown, on the Road to Derry. Mrs. Hamilton here told me of a very famous Well in 'Enishowen, in C. Donnegall, which is a Vast Peninsula of Land between Loughfoile and Swilly, all belonging to   called Mallinwell. Here the sick come from all parts to be cured by going into it, yet has the Waters of it no particular virtue, for it seems to be only a hollow in a Rock where one may sit and Let the Waves beat clear over you. However, the Coldness of the water has surely had good effects. She told me that she had been in't several times, but has not found much benefit. From hence, we went, after Dinner, thro' a good, pleasant countrey, and a small village called Muff, to Derry. Almost all the way from Colrain to Derry you travell on the Land belonging to the Corporations of London, to whom it was given by Patent for planting Colonyes and building these two Towns. From Newtown you have the great Bay called Lough Foile to the Right; and here, as we travelled, we saw the great shell Banks which last for 6 or 8 mile here, and are in no likelyhood of being Exhausted, tho' the Boats are continually at work to carry them away for Manure. This being almost the only Manure used within 30 mile from Scotland, they would willingly give a Boat of Coal for as much Shells, but these are more valuable.

WEDNESDAY.

Derry is situated of a steep hill formed by a Turn in the River Foile, which half surrounds it, and washes the suburbs for a great way ; it is here so great a River that they have not yet made a Bridge over it.

It so [happens] that there is no getting into the place from Colrain but by Boat, of wch there are one or two constantly in use. However, the Town spreads, so that there are a few good houses got on Colrain side the River.

Derry is a good, Large, Compact, well-built Town. The old houses have Suffered much by the Siege of it, as well as ye Inhabitants by the Famine caused there. Yet I am assured, by Persons then in the Town, that this much talked of Siege ammounted to no more than a firm blockade. The Irish army Lay Incamped on opposite Hills at one side, while a Boom stretched across the River hindred help from abroad. Neither do I hear that [there] were ever any regular aproaches made but once, when they took a Small height, which indeed commands the Town at the side called Wind Mill hill ; and even this they had not in possession, but were repulsed in 6 hours' time. However, the Artificial strength of this place is so litle, the Wall and Ditch so old and out of repair, and so ill provided with Artillery, rather in a worse condition than Galway or Lymerick, that I could scarce believe any Army could appear before it without reducing it. As to ye Famine, upon enquiry they tell me that there were Indeed no provisions to be bought or gotten in the Town for a Considerable time, so that all the Strangers who had come in to take Sanctuary there, were reduced to miserable difficulties ; but the settled people of the Town, who foresaw things, and had opportunities of Laying Stores in beforehand, were in a much more Easy Condition. The compactness of this Town and Colrain I take to be owing to their having been built at once by the Londoners. They have a handsome, well-adorned Cathedral Church here, built on the Ruins of their old Cittadel ; a good, handsome Town House, built by King William and Queen Mary ; and also a handsome Large Free School, with a good house for the Master, and a Large Chamber above for a Library. This is now building ; when Finished, the Books will be placed in't, which are a Collection of Divinity and Cannon Law Books, with some History, given by Wm., Late Lord Bpe. of Derry, now Bpe. of Dublin. The Houses are many of them good, new-built houses. Since the Siege, however, it does not seem to be a place of much business, Riches, or Trade. Severall of the Inhabitants have several litle pretty Improvements near the Town, particularly the Dean of Derry. Dean Bolton shewed me a place of his called   , about two miles from Town, wch is pretty enough, and lyes halfway to Culmore Fort, which we went to view, or rather its Ruins, being entirely rased ; in the Rubbish there are yet two or three pieces of Cannon. This Fort stood on the Banks of the River, nearer the sea than Derry, at a narrow part, so as to command the Passage. The Rooms was stretched very near this place, nearer the Town, under the Cannon of the Fort ; however, they found means to break thro' it, and thereby Relieved the besieged. We Lay in Derry at Mr. Norman's, an Ingenious man, An Alderman of the Town, and were Civilly Entertained at the Bpe.'s and Dean's. We Stayed here till Thursday.

THURSDAY.

After Dinner we went along the Fine River Foile, thro' an open sort of Countrey, for about 4 hours, and arrived at Lifiard, which is a very nasty, ugly Town, the County Town of Donnegall. Across the River lyes Strabane, wch is Somewhat better Town in Tyrone, belonging to Ld Abercorn, who has here something of the Linnen Manufacture.

FRIDAY.

We left Strabane ; two hours brought us to Newtown Steward, a small village belonging to Ld Mt Joy ; two more, thro' a very woody Countrey, to Omagh, which is but a small ordinary Town For the County Town of Tyrone. From hence, thro' a wild Countrey enough, to Clogher. Here we lay at the Bp's house, tho' he was abroad. This is a Burrough, but a most miserable one, having not above three or four houses in it, and not even the remains of any one, tho' 'tis certainly a very antient See.

SATURDAY.

Left Clogher, and came in about four or five hours by a Short way thro' the miserablest wild uncultivated mountains that can be seen to Monaghan, which is a very pretty, thriving Village—a great many new and handsome houses. Sr Alexander Cairns, to whom the Town and adjoyning Estate belongs, has a very pretty Improvement making near the Town. Round Monaghan is a very pleasant Improved well Inclosed Countrey. From hence we went to Castleblaney, which is a Small Village and Seat belonging to the Lord Blaney, in a pleasant woody Situation near a fine Lough, Here we lay at a Tolerable Inn. From hence,

SUNDAY,

Thro' Ardee to Knouth, and from thence,

TUESDAY,

HOME.

THE SITE OF CON O'NEILL'S CASTLE, CASTLEREAGH.

Depositions in the case of the Island Magee Witches, 1710.

COUNTY ANTRIM.

THE EXAMINATION OF JOHN SMITH, OF LAIRNE, IN Y^E S^D COUNTY, TAKEN AT CARRICKFERGUS, 21 MARCH, 1710,

Who, being duly Sworn and Examined, Saith that Mrs. Mary Dunbar, who has for this Long time been in a most unusual manner tormented and afflicted (as shee Saith, and as by all that see her do verily believe) by witches and Witchcraft, having since the Confinement of Jannet Liston, Janett Meane, and Jane Miller, whom she affirms to be her Tormentors, declared that she was troubled only with one young woman, whom the aforesaid women, when about her And tormenting her, did call Mrs. Ann, but that the said young woman told her that she should never be discovered by her name as the rest were, the Said Mary Dunbar, having given Exact marks and Description of one Margret Mitchell, whom she, this Ex^t doth verily believe, the Said Mary never had seen before the Said Marg^t Mitchell was brought to her, and that the Said Mary assured this Ex^t and others that the Said Marg^t was the young woman that did Torment and afflict her, And that she never saw her before but when she was tormenting her; and that after the Said Marget was set at Liberty, the Said Mary fell into a most violent fit, in which the Said Ex^t heard her say—"For Christ Sake, Let me alone, and I won't discover you." And after being Recovered out of the Said Fitt, was asked to whom she spoke. The Said Mary told them that the Said Marg^t Mitchell was then afflicting her, and told her she would have this Exam^t James Blithe's Picture made & roast it like a Lark, and that they should not Catch her, for she wou'd turn herself into a Hare, and further Saith that the Said Mary did remit Several Pins, buttons, and horse Hair, and further Said not.

THE EXAMINATION OF MARY DUNBAR, TAKEN 12TH MARCH, 1710,

Who, being duly Sworn and Examined, Saith that during these Severall weeks she has been in a most grievous and violent manner tormented and afflicted with Witches; that Several whom she never had known, or to her knowledge seen before, did frequently appear to her (tho' invisible to her keepers and attenders), who make her fall very often into fainting and tormenting fitts, take the Power of Tongue from her, and afflicts her to that Degree that she often thinks she is pierced to the heart, and that her breasts are cut off; that she heard the Said women (when about her) name one another, and that called one Jannet Liston, another Eliz. Cellor, another Kate McCamont, another Jannet Carson, another Jannet Mean, another Latimore, and another Mrs. Anne, and the Said Jannet Liston, Eliz. Cellar, Kate McCamont, and Jannet Carson being brought to her, att their first appearance she knew them to be four of her Tormentors, and that after they were taken into Custody the aforesaid Latimore and Mean did very much Torment her, especially when Mr. Sinclare, the Dissenting Minister, was praying with and for her, and told her they would hinder her of hearing his prayers; but if she would do as they would have her, she soon would be well, and that Jannet Latimore and Jannet Mean being brought to her, she likewise knew them to be other two of her Tormentors, and that since the confinement of the said Jannet Liston, Eliz. Cellar, Kate McCamont, Jannet Carson, Jannet Mean, and Jannet Latimor, none of them has troubled her, neither has been so much tormented as when they were at Liberty, and that there do now only two appear to her (vizt.), the aforesaid Mrs. Ann, as they called her, and another woman, blind of an eye, who told her when Mr. Robb, the curate, was going to pray with and for her, that she should be little the better for his prayers, for they would hinder her from hearing them, which they accordingly did.

THE EXAMINATION OF JOHN SMITH, TAKEN 14TH MARCH, 1710,

Who, being duly Sworn and Examined, saith that, upon the within-mentioned Mary Dunbar giving an acco^t that there was a woman blind of an eye that did torment her, three severall women blind of an eye were brought to her, but she, the Said Mary, declared they never troubled her, and that she had nothing to say against them or Lay to their Charge; and one Jane Miller, of Carrickfergus, who is blind of an eye, being likewise sent for to come to the Said Mary, that as soon as she drew nigh the house where the Said Mary was (the Said Mary did not know of her coming), she became very much afraid, faintish, and Sweat, and as soon as shee came into the Roome where the Said Mary lay, she, the Said Mary, fell into Such a violent fit of pains that three men were Scarce able to hold her—cryed out, "For Christ's Sake, take the Devil out of the Room;" and being asked, Said the blind woman, meaning the Jane Miller, for she was the woman that did Torment her, and shee had seen her too often in her fitts, and the Said Miller being taken from the House, the Said Mary came to her Right Senses, and Declared that the Said Jane Miller was the woman blind of an eye that did afflict her, tho' she did not know her name, nor never had seen her before, but when in her fitts aforesaid, and the Said Jane Miller being brought into her again, shee assured them that shee was the woman that did afflict her, and being brought in the third time into the Roome unknown and unseen to the Said Mary, as he does verily believe, the Said Mary fell into her violent fitts, and begged of the People to take her, the Said Jane Miller, out of the Room.

M

Bryce Blan, Constable, Deposeth that after the said Jane Miller was delivered to him and brought from the said House, he privately, and unknown to the Said Mary, brought her into the Room where she was again, and before the Said Mary saw her, shee fell very ill in violent fitts, and prayed them to take the Devil out of the Roome.

THE EXAMINATION OF H. WILSON (ISLAND MAGEE), TAKEN 10TH MARCH, 1710,

Who, being duly Sworn and Examined, saith that on the 6th Instant he was in the house of Ja. Haltridge, in the Said Island, Gent, and Saw Mary Dunbar in a very ill condition, being, as is supposed, tormented with witches, and one Jannet Latimore, who being often Said by the person grieved to be one of her Tormentors, tho' she never had seen her in her life, but when shee appeared, as she Said, to her in her affliction, came near the House, became very uneasie and faintisb, and much disordered, and became worse and worse, notwithstanding the Said Mary Dunbar, nor none of her keepers or attendants knew of the Said Latimor's coming or being there, and being desired by Some there in the House to go in and see the Said Mary, which she did, amongst several others, and when she appeared to her, the Said Mary fell into Desperate violent fitts, and when she got the Liberty of her Tongue (which was often taken from her), Said that woman Latimore was one of her Tormentors, and that she knew her face full well, tho' shee had never Seen her before, but in her tormented fitts appeared to her. And further saith that one Jannet Menn, wife to one Andrew ffergusson, near Billycarry, in the Said County, was brought by a Warrant, but privately and unknown to yᵉ Said Mary Dunbar, and among very many more came to see her, and at her first appearance Shee, the said Mary, became as before, in her most desperate fitts, and both the Said Mean and Latimore being taken apart from the said Haltridge's house to another house, to be Examᵈ: that after Examination the Said Mean's Husband would not be Satisfied that the sick person would anyway alter at the appearance of his wife. It was agreed that shee Should appear to the Sick person again, and that as Soon as she entred the Roome Doore where the Said Mary lay, she became distracted, tho' Sober ere her entrance ; and further saith that yᵉ said Mary is most tormented when prayed with or for, Save when they personally appear to her, and she Saith that since the Confinement of Jannet Liston and her Daughter Cat: McCamont and Jannet Carson, none appeared to her but the Said Jannet Mean and Jannet Latimore, and appears most to her when prayed for as aforesaid, the Said Mary being, when out of her fitts, very sensible.

THE EXAMINATION OF CHARLES LENNAN, GENT., TAKEN Yᴱ 10TH OF MARCH, 1710,

Who, being Duly Sworn and Examined, Saith that the 5th and 6th Instant he was in the House of James Haltridge, of Island Magee, Gent., where lies in a most Desperate Condition Mary Dunbar, of or about the age of 17 or 18 years, being, as Concluded by all that See her, tormented with Witches and Witchcraft. and his Examination agreeth word for word with the 10th in Examination, and further Saith that when Mr. Sinclare, the Minister, was praying with the said Mary Dunbar, that the Said Mary Said Jennet Latimore and Jannet Mean told her that they would hinder her of hearing his prayers ; but both Said to her if she would do as they would have her to do, she would soon be well. The Ext. further Saith that when the Said Mary was taken or helped out of the Roome she lay in that she fell as dead on the Threshold, and at her Desire the Threshold and floor about was dug up, And in so doing there was a strong Smell as (as was Concluded) of Brimstone, and when done the Said Mary went out of yᵉ Said Roome without any trouble, and in Some hours after, when Mr. Sinclare prayed with her, shee fell into violent fitts, and said she Saw the Said Mean and Latimore, who Said to her that shee should not get so well out of the Door again, whereupon it was agreed that she should try ; accordingly she did, and fell into more violent fitts than before, both at her going out and Returning to the Said Roome.

THE EXAMINATION OF WM. FENTON, OF ISLAND MAGEE, 3D OF MARCH, 1710,

Who, being duly Sworn and Examined, Saith that for sometime past the House of James Haltridge, of Island Magee aforesaid, hath been haunted with Evil Spirits (as he is credibly Informed), and that Mary Dunbar, being now in the Said house, is in great Disorder, and very much tormented both day and night by Witches ; And by the description the said Mary Dunbar gave this Ext. and others of the Witches, they did verily believe that Jannet Liston and Eliz. Cellar were persons Guilty of the Same, upon which, on Friday Last, they Sent for the Said persons, and when the said Jannet Liston and Eliz. Cellar came into the Roome where yᵉ Said Mary Dunbar was. Shee the Said Mary fell into a violent fitt of Pains, and Said that as Soon as she Saw them she was Stung to yᵉ heart, and declared that the Said Jannet and Elizabeth were Devils, and continually with Several other women about her bed troubling her, and further Saith that there were a great many more of other women present when the Said Mary Challenged the Said Jannet and Elizabeth, whom she never Saw in her Lifetime before her trouble aforesaid.

JOHN WILLSON, OF ISLAND MAGEE AFORESAID,

agreeth with the above, word for word.

JAMES BLYTH, OF BANK, IN THE COUNTY OF ANTRIM,

Who, being duely Sworn and Examᵈ. agreeth Verbatim with the aforesaid Examⁿˢ. and further Saith that the Said Mary Dunbar Said she heard her Tormentors name one Katty among them, upon which one Katherine McCamont was sent for ; and as Soon as She came into the Said

Mary's Roome, the Said Mary Dunbar fell into such violent fitt of pains that three persons were not able to hold her, and that the Said Mary Dunbar Declared that the Said Katherine was one of her tormentors, and further Saith that as soon as the Said Katherine entered the House, tho' unseen to the Said Mary, her pains Seized on her with a great Sweat.

James Hill Deposeth that the first Instant, he being in the House of Wm. Cellar of Island Magee, one Mary Twmain (*sic*) came into the Said House and called out Jannet Liston to spenk to her, and that after the Said Jannet came in again shee fell a trembling, and told this Depon[t] that the Said Mary had been desiring her to go to Mr. Haltridge to see Mary Dunbar, but declared she would not goe for all Island Magee, except Mr. Sinclare wou'd come for her (and Said)—If the plague of God was on her, the Said Mary Dunbar, y[e] Plague of God be on them altogether; the Devil be with them, if he was among them. If God had taken her health from her, God give her health. If the Devil had taken it from her, the Devil give her it. And then said—O, misbelieving ones, eating and drinking Damnation to themselves, Crucifying Christ afresh, and taking all out of the hands of the Devil. *Capt et Jurat v[o] Die Martij, 1710.*

William Hatley deposeth that after the aforesaid Mary Dunbar was recovered o[u]t of one of her fitts, and in her Right Senses, she declared that Jane Carson was one of the tormentors.

COUNTY ANTRIM.

THE EXAMINATION OF HUGH DONALDSON OF ISLAND MAGEE, IN THE SAID COUNTY, TAKEN THE 5TH MARCH, 1710,

Who, being duly Sworn and Examined, Saith that the 28th of February, he being in the house of James Haltridge of Island Magee afores[d] he Saw Mrs. Mary Dunbar afflicted in an unusual manner, falling into fitts as if she had been dead, and did not know what any about her said, in one of which fitts he heard her say So and So after she was recovered, and very Sensible was asked what it was She Said in the Said fitt, shee answered, there was a woman came to the bed side, and asked her, Molly Dunbar, how do you do, and the Said Mary, giving the marks of one Jannet Liston, whom shee never had seen in her life, as shee said when out of her fitts, upon which the Said Liston was sent for, and at her approach the Said Mary affirmed that was the woman, and fell into extream torment during the Said Liston's aboad in the Roome, so that Scarce two or three men were able to hold her. She likewise, in her other fits, said shee heard her Tormentors name one another, and that they called one of them Jannet Carson, another Katty, another Jannet Mean, and another McAlexander, all who threatned to kill her if she told their names, upon which the Said Janet Carson was Sent for about the first Instant, and as soon as shee appeared, the Said Mary fell into a great agony during her stay, as also during the abode of one Eliz: Cellar, whom she had given a Description of, and declared to be one of her Tormentors, and that the aforesaid Mary Dunbar declared she never Saw any of the aforesaid women before her affliction aforesaid, and further Saith that about thirty other women were Severally brought into the Roome where she was, and that she never was disturbed in the Least during their Continuance, and Said they were none of her afflictors, still averring that the aforesaid women were her tormentors.

COUNTY ANTRIM.

THE EXAMINATION OF JAMES HALTRIDGE, OF ISLAND MAGEE, GENT., 24TH MAR., 1710,

Who, being duly Sworn and Examined, Saith that his house, situate in Island Magee aforesaid, which for this considerable time past has been haunted with Evil Spirits and Witches, and in which house one Mrs. Mary Dunbar (who is now removed from them to bank in the said County) was afflicted and tormented by witches, as she Saith, whom she discovered by giving Exact marks and account of the most of their names, tho' she never had Seen of them in her life before (as she declares) but when by them tormented ; since yᵉ Confinement of Margt. Mitchell, whom the Said Mary affirm to be the only one that did afflict her since the Confinement of Jannet Liston, Eliz. Cellar, Kate McCamont, Jannet Carson, Jannet Mean, Jannet Latimore, and Jane Miller, who were all sent to and still do Remain in Gaoll, upon her discovering them as aforesaid to be her tormentors, hath never been troubled or molested in the Least, and that the Said Mary Dunbar told this Examᵗ that Since the Confinement of the Said Margaret Mitchell, whome she assured him that she was very Certain was her only tormentor after the Confinement of yᵉ aforesaid persons, she the said Mary has not been tormented or afflicted, and that none of them has appeared to her, but she has been very easie ever Since, Save Some things she thought was in her Stomack, which she would be glad to Vomit, and further Saith not.

Capt et Jurat cor me
die Annoque Supradict.

EDWARD CLEMENTS, *Copia Vera.*

(Pinkerton MSS.)   *(MS. I. 1-3, T.C.D.)*

THE LOUGH and HARBOUR of BELFAST

VIEW OF BELFAST LOUGH FROM WHITEHOUSE ABOUT 1750.

Extracts from Correspondence of Robert Greene, Agent of the Donegall Estates, from 1718 to 1726.

Belfast, ffeb. 5th 1725.

D^{R.} SIR,

Yours the 27th Should have been answerd before had I not expected considerable Sums from two Gent^s both Wilsons, one our late Sherriff, and other Clerk of the Crown and peace, who, instead of paying, unexpectedly hurry'd to Dublin without paying what they promised. Both are expected here by the end of the next week I would more willingly pay than you receive were itt in my power. I shall not forgett your letter till ye money is paid. So soon as these Gentlemen return you shall hear, and I hope effectually.

S^r your friend and humble servt.,

To mr. Thomas Gill, att the
Custom-house, Dublin.

ROB. GREENE.

(EARL OF BARRYMORE.) *April 2^d 1726.*

MY LORD,

I am told its believed by Phisicians and others that Dr Macartney our Sovereign cannot live till midsummer. If your Lordship thinks fitt a Leett may be sent worded to this purpose :—Whereas I, Arthur Earle of Donegall, Lord of the Castle of Belfast, am informed that James Macartney, Esq^{r,} sovereign of the Corporation of Belfast afores^{d,} is very ill, and that its thought he is not likely to live till midsummer, I the s^d . . . . Earle of Donegall, do in case of his Death nominate . . . . . . three Burghesses, one of which to be chosen to supply the s^d sovereign's place in case he shall happen to dye, and this nomination is given under my hand & seale in april, 1726. Such a Leett may be needfull, and one for midsummer Election if he so long live, but its thought he cannot live till the end of this month. I hear mr. Banks began his Journey to my Lady Donegall & mr. Chichester on tuesday last, and that he purposes to see y^r Ldship. I long to hear that ye partys concerned are agreed to gett an act for raising rents & money by setting leases. Nothing can tend more for ye benefitt of my Lord & his family in this town. Then trade will begin to increase & the town will flourish. I desire to know if y^r Lordship approves of erecting a Woollen Manufacture which will be of great advantage & profit to this town & Country as I can easily demonstrate. I beg your Lordship's answer, and am, &c.,

R. G.

(EARL OF BARRYMORE.) *Belfast, aprill the 9th 1726.*

MY LORD,

By severall letters I have told your Lordship that our Sovereign's life is not like to last long ; he is daily prayed for, and grows very weak. Since my last a lease acquir'd by the Death of one ashmore, the former rent and Duty was 1^{li} 19^s 6^{d.} it will now sett for 5^{li} by which there will be an increase rent of 3^{li} per annum. This day I rec^d a letter from Doctor Scot of ye 2^d instant, directing me to send him a bill for 320^{li} English for my Lord's use against the first of May, which will be above 350^{li} and perhaps near 360^{li} of Belfast money. Your Lordship's orders in this and all other affairs is humbly desired by, &c.,

ROBERT GREENE.

(EARL OF BARRYMORE.) *Belfast, april 16th 1726.*

MY LORD,

Our late Sovereign was buried last night. His Death and the discontinuance of my Lord's Courts by mr. Banks being in England causes a great cry amongst the people. My Lord is like to loose above 60^{li} by the want of Surveyors to require the six days' labour. Mock Courts are kept ; one was held yesterday, and Warrants dated the 15^{th,} signed Tho: Banks, are issued to Summon tenants, under tenants, and servants to a Court leet to collect head Money, tho' very illegall. . . . &c.,

R. G.

(EARL OF BARRYMORE.)   *Belfast, aprill 25th 1716.*

MY LORD,

    Yesterday, tho' Sunday, mr. Skeffington, Brigadier Price, our Coll[r] mr. Byrt, & mr. Clugston mett here, and, as I am told, have elected mr. Robt. Byrt sovereign for y[e] Remainder of the year. Its thought, notwithstanding the agreemt. by which it is mr. Clugston's turn, that on midsummer day they purpose to choose him again for y[e] next year. He, as its said, hopes to be town Clark, which, as I take itt, is to be Clark to himself. Having written many Letters without one word in answer, till Honour'd with a few lines, have only to add that I am, &c.,   R. G.

(EARL OF BARRYMORE.)   *Belfast, May 7th 1726.*

MY LORD,

    I have y[e] Hon[r] of your Lordship's the 28th past, and observed y[r] Commands to y[e] Burgesses. The Coll[r] seems well satisfied, and assures me Clugston shall be favoured & indulged by him to y[e] utmost of his power, but thinks its advisable to defer his election till he hath apply'd to y[e] Com[rs] for their consent, and y[e] rather because here is no Constable to swear him. He believes y[e] Com[rs] will refer his request to him as Coll[r] and says he will report in his favour. Mr. Clugston is most thankfull to y[r] Lordship, and seems highly delighted to think of his approaching Hon[r]. All he wants is a book to teach him the law, resolving to read much, as he hears our late Sovereign did, but he understood not what he read, and I believe mr. Clugston's understanding will be abundantly less. Mr. Byrt is much transported to find he is like to be town Clark, tho' if possible would have had both, and made some most unaccountable and presumptuous steps to procure the Sovereignity. Nothing y[t] y[r] Lordship is pleased to direct will meet with the least opposition ; at present all needfull is to take care for y[e] future. The Coll[r] hinted to me that mr. Isaac m'Cartney would quallify if Elected, and said the late Sovereign told him so. Cap[t] m'Cullough formerly offer'd here severall substantial shopkeepers that will, who incline to come over to our church, where they most frequently come. The place may lye vacant till y[r] Lordship's on the Spott. We want some p'sons quallifyd for y[e] Magistracy after Clugston's year's ended. Here is nobody in this town but mr. Byrt, who by being town Clark will be disquallified. This y[r] Lordship will consider, and also that encouragements are needfull to some in the town when severall are going off. . . . &c.   R. G.

THE OLD CORPORATION CHURCH. TOMB OF THE COLLIER FAMILY.
(From drawing by A. Nicholl, R.H.A. Pinkerton MSS.)

Belfast, May 9th 1726.

HON^D SIR,

  The Enclosed Acco^{tt.} given by mr. Macartney I woud have brought, having long purposed to wait on my Lord y^r Brother and you, had I been able. I have a letter from my Lord Barrymore to the same purpose, but a very ill state of health which I att present labour under hath long confined me at home, so as to prevent any more than humble requests that I might be excused, and earnestly desire by all opportunity that my humblest services might be acceptable, with assurance that I shall take pleasure in serving my Lord, Lady, you, or any of your family.

  I desire your friendship therein, and that you may be pleased to Hon^r me with a visit when you come next here, tho' health should not permitt me to perform my Duty or pursue my inclination. In so doing you will most sensibly oblige, &c. ,   R. G.

  To the Honble John Skeffington, Esqr.
   att Antrim.

Belfast, May 14th 1726.

MY LORD,

  I writt to mr. Skeffington, who purposes to be here on tuesday, to elect mr. Clugston. His Election was so long deferr'd that he might have time to apply to ye Com^{rs} for lycence to serve, which I hope he hath gott, tho' I have not seen him these three days past. One Watt, a Master of a ship, is recommended by mr. Mussenden, one of our considerable traders, as an honest man of substance. He is master of one of their ships who hath gain'd and saved money, and offers 37^{li} per ann. for ye 90 acres that became out of lease by the death of Robinson, besides receivers' fees and Dutys, which will be £2 4 :—more he design'd to send his proposall, but being Ord^d by his owners to go for a load Salt, he purposes to wait on y^r Lordship wth his proposall as afores^{d.} which I thought fitt to be laid before you by him who is with ye greatest Duty and respect, &c.,   R. G.

  To Earl of Barrymore, Rocksavage.

(EARL OF BARRYMORE.)   *Belfast, May ye 21st 1726.*

MY LORD,

  On Tuesday last Mr. Clugston was Elected, but cannot Act till some body is Impowered to swear him. Mr. Skeffington did not come to Elect, tho' y^u Collector and I writt to him by an express y^t that I sent. On Thursday night Mr. Jones—who was recommended for a Burgesse—drank hard at Hillshorough, and Rideing home his horse threw him. It was thought he was dead, but he speaks this day and feels pain, wch gives some hopes of his recovery, tho' 'tis fear'd he cannot live. The post of a line is much desired by, &c.,

           R. G.

(EARL OF BARRYMORE.)   *Belfast, May the 23d 1726.*

MY LORD,

  The Coll^r was with me yesterday desiring to lett y^r Lordship know that he purposes to begin his Journey to Wexford Wells on Monday next, and that if mr. Clugston be not Swore before, this town will then have neither Sovereign or Justice to keep peace, adjust differences, or to Settle Army's Quarters. Here is a great cry about itt amongst people of all Ranks in the town. mr. Seymour Sends two Pacquetts, and begs your Lordship's Speedy answer, as doth, &c.,

           R. G.

  I desire directions about the Hawks ; they are expensive and very troublesome.

Belfast, May 28th 1726.

MY LORD,

  The Coll^r begins his Journey to Wexford on tuesday. He desired me to lett your Lordship know that for want of Manor or Town Court the poor people Suffer much, and great Outcrys are daily heard. He hath been told mr. Chichester is going to be Married, and that mr. Banks Stays to attend the wedding. When the Coll^r is gone, for want of a Sovereign or some Justice of the peace in this Town, the Common people will grow very audacious and Licentious, which was thought needfull to be laid before y^r Lordship by, &c.,

R. G.

I have not been Hon^d with a line from y^r Lordship since 28th April.

(EARL OF BARRYMORE.)   *Belfast, June 11th 1726.*
MY LORD,

On Monday last mr. Williams and mr. Banks came to me, and, as mr. Williams said, by your Lordship's order, to examine my Acco^{tts}, take up my Vouchers, and to give me a discharge for the Same, with an attested Coppy of y^r Lordship's order by which he acted, and that mr. Banks was directed his rent Roll to compare with and rectifie mine. After which he wanted a bill of 50^{ll} for his last half-year's salary,and for 37^{ll} 7^s 1½^d costs to mr. Smith, attorney, which bill of 37^{ll} 7^s 1½^d when he had got with a coppy of my Acco^{tts} and book of receipts for Rent & Heriots, &c., he had no (more business with nor any) Receipt for me; but going of I askt if there were any grounds for a report that mr. Banks for his Insolence was to be sole agent & Seneschall. He said he believed itt would be so, y^t he had a power to examine & discharge my Acco^{tts.} I told him he ought to have show'd it, and to have proceeded thereon; that I was ready to acco^t with any p'son empowered to receive my Vouchers and discharge them. On the contrary, mr. Banks would have me take his and dischaige him. I am much surprised at what's done. but find great Satisfaction in knowing I have acted friendly. Justly, and very successfully for ye Service of my Lord Donegall and his family, and that I have deserved much better treatment, which y^r Lordship will allow when you are pleased to consider it, &c.,

R. G.

Belfast, June 23rd 1726.

MY LORD,

I am Hon^d with your Lordship's, in answer to which the Hawks have been taken care of, and are ready to be deliv^d as y^r Lordship shall direct. They have been troublesome to me, who have no convenience for them, and some charge. I humbly desire y^t you may be pleased to order me what due out of the Isle Magee & Maghremorne at all S^{ts} last, I having paid the same. In so doing you will much oblige, &c.,

R. G.

To Lord Hilsborough.

Belfast, Sept. 17th 1726.

D^R SIR,

I am favoured with y^{rs} by this post, and will observe directions. My leggs are yett inflamed, and the Swelling but little abated; the pain in my groin is quite gone. I breath as well if nott better than when you were here, and am no worse if not better in health, but daily perplexed with vexatious proceedings promoted by those who would destroy me if in their power. My most humble service to Doctor Worth; we were once intimate, but I thought he had forgott me. I wish him long life with good health, and the like to Doct^r Robinson, to whom pray make my humblest Service acceptable. You said you had fifty pounds by you; if so, pray pay it forthwith to mr. Hugh Henry on my Acc^{t.} I will repay you on demand with legall interest. I am pincht at present, and shall be for about two months, therefore your assistance now will much oblige,

Dr Will,
Y^r affectionate Uncle,
R. G.

My wife joynes with me in affectionate Services to you and y^r Spouse, and in wishes that y^r wife. you, and y^r Children may long live in health & be most happy. There is a Carrier of this town now in pill lane; pray, by him send me some lemons and Civill orranges.

To mr. William Greene, Surgeon, at y^e
sign Alembeck, on Mercht^s Key, Dublin.

VIEW OF BELFAST NEAR CABIN HILL, RESIDENCE OF DR. DRENNAN.

Extracts from Letters of Mrs. M. M'Tier, of Belfast, to her brother, Dr. William Drennan, between 1776-84.

UR gaiety here continues. Last Friday we had a most elegant ball at Mr. Brown's, Peter's Hill. There was above seventy people. The night before, there was one at Dr. Seeds'. Young Magee has got £500 in the Belfast scheme : it has been ill-managed, by which a great number of tickets remained unsold. Many were subscribed to, and the rest were required by the scheme, which has gained near 18 hundred pounds already.

"The triumph of the few and fears of many begin to decline in regard to the victories in America—from Dublin we hear that there is little credit given to the various accounts of Washington's defeat. Our winter sets out rather gayer than usual ; we have already had three Balls—one, as a house-warming, at Dr. Appesley's ; another at Captain Stewart's ; and a third at Miss Turnly's, by the Wallaces. The officers of the *Arethusa* being here, occasioned their following each other so quickly. We had also a very grand one at the infirmary, the only one I partook of. In the County of Down there is a party formed called a Coterie, occasioned by Mrs. Hunter of Pine Hill giving a dinner and a ball on her son's being of age ; there was at it above forty people of that neighbourhood, and they found it so agreeable that they agreed it should be kept up at each other's houses thro' the winter ; and last week Rainey Maxwell gave the second, but as it was the same night as Hill W.'s, Rainey had the fewest men. Dr. Ross has at length resigned in favour of Dr. Appesley, and quit the stage with decency and fortitude.

"Do you remember Val Pierce in this town? He stayed at Mr. Harrison's, and went to America some time ago. He sold all the goods he had upon Commission, remitted the money, and immediately joined the Provincials. Young Bristow, who was with General Burgoine and lost his all, writes to his brother here that he had heard of his old friend Pierce, and that he was then a Major of Brigade.

"Our volunteer companys make a good figure. Captain Banks' is the most numerous, and he is fond of showing them in marching to Church or Meeting, a parade declined by the others. They, however, I am told, are to fire on Sunday next. Their regimentals are blue, white waistcoats and breeches, and blue cord-laced hats, and it is thought pretty, etc. As J. Gregg resigned when he went to America, there was another Officer to be balloted for his place, and Sam was chosen—a very inconvenient and expensive honor. Rowley wrote from Dublin last post begging leave to join them. Halliday was so much mortified at not being chosen their Captain that he could not disguise it. He had been 1st Lieutenant in the old Belfast Company, a circumstance that was not known by T. Holmes and Sam, who were really the persons who got Saunders appointed, from their opinion of his being a man of knowledge and bravery. Halliday attacked Sam about their choice with great warmth, and was backed by Bamber and all their Patriotism, exclaiming against the appearance of such a wonder as two Vol. Companys in Belfast, and both tory officers. Much was said on both sides.

"Lord Donegall was here: the ladies he paid most attention to were Mrs. Brown and Mrs. Lyon.

"In Belfast we, nor indeed anyone, can now live on a small fortune but in an obscure and, what is worse, a vulgar manner, for a small, genteel house in a tolerable situation is not to be got at any moderate rent, and it is crowded with rich upstarts who, skipping from the counter to their carriage, run one down with force of wealth which sanctions ignorance and vulgarity, and now gives them a lead and fashion who, a few years since, w⁴ have shrunk with awe from the notice of what is called good company.

"Don't you wish to see Miss Brunton? She is very pleasing. I went in to her Juliet, and think she was really Shakspear's; but I am sick of Tragedy, for I have seen it so long that I know each Ha! and Oh! by heart.

"A Nabob of the name of Rankin, son to the dissenting minister, has bought Montgomery's estate near us (Cabin Hill), and builds a great house immediately. Jemmy Crawford is on his return with £60,000. Hull is making a great figure at Drumbo. The Bishop of Down lives elegantly at Purdysburn. Lord Dungannon is expected to settle at Belvoir, and from all parts people are flocking to Belfast.

"The entertainment to the Ld. Lieutenant was most elegant, and conducted with decorum and taste, so as to be much noticed and spoke of by all the noblemen there. Mr. Bristow was determined to please all. He drew up an address for that purpose—merely civil, fixed his toasts, &c. By accident he had omitted to drink Ld. Rawdon, and a note being sent to him from the foot of the table reminding him of it, either a wish to atone for the neglect, or the truth being without caution to his tongue, he drank Rawdon's health and the glorious Camden. This really did receive three cheers. Conscience or recollection struck the company.

"Not but his Lordship, perceiving the danger he was in from the imprudence of the task, and having got the better of a panic which he acknowledged afterwards he felt, he thanked the company, and told them the success of that day was owing to the Harp on his standard and the Irishmen who followed it.

"He supped at Mr. Greg's. Mentioned the Toast, and his distress upon it, from his knowledge of the sentiments of the Belfast people, for which he said he honored them. Mentioned his military enthusiasm being over, and that the war with America was sufficient to affect it; his desire of being active, and for the future hoped it would be in the Cabinet, not in the field, but despaired of it while Mr. Pitt was Minister, as with a man of his duplicity he could never act.

"At Hillsborough Corporation dinner the Governor gave 'the Volunteers.' Ld. H. cried, 'Fy, fy, fy,' and each time knocked his hand on the table—'Do you know, Sir, there is not a toast could be more disagreeable to G'ment.' Ward replyed he would apply to Government for information, and, announcing the toast to the Lord Lieutenant, drank it in a bumper.

"I hear there was a meeting called by Bristow last week to propose subscriptions for raising men for his Majesty's fleet, but M'Cabe and company would not consent. Such men are very useful, and have ten times the merit of their superiors, who dare only to bluster in the private circle of their friends. It is not to such, but to men they look down on that Ireland owes her freedom. I think these sort of expenses ought to be taken in turn, and for this war those who kept free of Volunteer trouble and expense during the last should now step forward, and either guard their Coasts or open their purses. I would be minded, were I an Irish Volunteer, before I would volunteer it either with money or person for George the 3ᵈ.

"The last resolve carried in Belfast is to demolish Bryson's Meeting-House, and build in its stead a new one on the model of the Church. J. Kennedy's name is down for 20 guineas.

"A large number of the Members of the Constitution Club is just passed to C'fergus in order to make a figure for Waddel Cunningham. His friends say he has been offered a seat for Belfast by Lᵈ Donegal if he will give up C'fergus; but this during his Patriotick hour would not do.

"Ld. Donegal is expected immediately, and some fields about the poorhouse a few weeks ago have sold for £10 an acre.

"Belfast has been very gay. Col. Lindsay and his Corps gave the most elegant ball and supper at Sheridan's ever seen in this kingdom. Mrs. Bell Brown gave another last week to 150 people, who all supped in her house. Of this there has been much talk, as it was rather in the tag-rag style.

"Dr. Halliday dined here on Sunday, and shewed me a letter from Lord Charlemont which I think you would like, as it seemed warm from the heart of a good old man zealous in his Country's cause. He tells the Dr. he wishes early to give him an account of his embassy, which

THOMAS M^cCABE DENOUNCING WADDEL CUNNINGHAM'S PROPOSED BELFAST SLAVE-SHIP COMPANY IN THE OLD EXCHANGE, 1786.

has fully answered every purpose he wished from it, and then, I think, uses some words of yours, that *before* the independence of Ireland was only in theory, *now* it's fixed by practise. He raves like a lover of the Prince, and says he knows not how to quit the theme; that till he saw him, he had not an idea of an accomplished prince; that their reception was far more than cordial, and that Ireland may rest assured she has bound by the strongest ties of gratitude the accomplished Prince, who will one day be their King. He asks what the Belfast politics are, laments the fall of Reviews, but says his friends have acted well in determining to do all they could.

"Lord Dungannon is at Belvoir, living in a princely style, and Ld. and Lady Antrim with their 3 daughters. The young man, I believe, is very decent, appears unaffected, pleased with Belfast, and his Mother and sisters. Walks into Town, and attends the public places. He presides at the Côterie next night, his choice Mrs. Rankin, who is much the fashion.

"Of your address to Lord Charlemont I never heard but from yourself. Of Dr. Haliday's politics or any other person's I know little, not having been twice in company since you were here. What Sam hears comes to me, and that is all. By this chance I know that Lord Charlemont wrote to Dr. H., begging he might use his influence to prevent any Volunteers' resolutions about political matters, as it was certain their enemies were upon the watch for some unguarded expressions, which would be eagerly caught on as an excuse for a riot act or some other mode of destruction. His Lordship, you may believe, did not choose to be mentioned in this. I believe his motives were good, as his actions have ever been consistent, and all his words the natural expressions of an honest, affectionate, and anxious friend to the Volunteers of his Country.

"There is in this Town at present a violence of business, if I may say so, which I would think portends something great either in the rise or fall of individuals. Strange it would be in any other man but W. Cunningham, after all the opposition given to the Bank, as a matter hurtful to the public, to declare that next New Year's day he would open a second in Belfast. This, however, he has announced; speaks with contempt of the management, etc., of the present, and looks destruction He has avowed T. Campbell as a partner, but none of the rest. A. Stewart of Newtownards, Carr, Hull, Rankin are spoke of.

"Sam's opinion is that Belfast does not know its strength and power, and that there is business for two Banks, founded I suppose upon the Discount Office having discounted £25,000 a-month even since the Bank opened.

"Websters, Bambers, and Hamills are all going to Belfast to live; but houses are not to be got for the half that want them. In the New Street, £110 is asked as rent.

"Our Linen Hall and New Street is all marked out, and goes back as far as the stone table in the Castle Garden, and quite across the Mall into the exercising field.

"Belmont is sold, and Will Bateson the purchaser.

"Castle Hill is once more going to verify the country people's observation of being unlucky, and often changing its inhabitants. Its present one is embarrassed, and is about selling it to Bunbury, Mr. Isaac's heir.

"Will Bateson keeps Belmont close to himself on his £1,600.

"Atkins has sent a proposal to Mrs. Siddons of £100 for three nights, and Dr. Haliday has wrote to Mrs. O'Neil for her interest.

"Jemmy Kennedy has taken our old Rosemary St. habitation, which has been so much improved by the last tenant that it is really a genteel and most convenient habitation.

"Mrs. Siddons is now here working wonders, and I would really be greatly disappointed if you do not see her. The effects of her Belvedera have done credit to the feelings of the audience. No one disappointed, even the old bigots to Mrs Cibber and Garrick. Haliday swelled; Mattear snivelled; Major Leslie cryed, and damned the play; W. Cunningham rubbed his legs and changed his posture; a Mrs. Aderton was really taken out in convulsions; and Miss Lewis, that was now Mrs. Britt, left the house. Many ladies besides these were much affected, tho' sooner recovered.

"We hear no other subject. Last night in the Unhappy Marriage she is supposed to have reached the height of human powers.

"She was indeed great, beyond all others I ever beheld. Fair ladies were taken out fainting in the last act, and hardly a man could stand it. Sam cried for half-an-hour after he went to bed, and many others who withstood it in the House gave up to tears when they went home.

"The Edinburgh strictures are beautiful and just. As for myself, I can wonder, admire, be chilled, thrilled, &c., &c., but cannot cry—not that I feel too much for tears, but she does not melt me; I believe she is too great. At first I supposed it was my having out-lived these fine enthusiastic feelings of youth; but all ages, all characters yield to her.

"I drop a tear, but it's almost a single one. I am therefore at ease enough to criticise, I see all her perfections, perhaps several little, unassuming, modest beauties not attended to by others. Many, I daresay, have spoke a speech as well, and in great places been as great; but in the delicate minutiæ of character, expressed by a bend, a look, in all those little decencies and graces which are so charming in life that they are to be prized above virtue, or rather are they not the essence of it?—in all these she is perfect, and affords a pleasure to an attentive observer that perhaps was never equalled on the stage unless by Garrick, but in a fine woman they have a finer effect.

"Her behaviour in private company is reserved, elegant, and sensible. She sings charmingly; her sister joins with more judgment, not so sweet a voice. I have not been in company with her; you perhaps may, if you can get here next week, in which there will be the 3 benefits. Whether she stays long is not yet known. A report prevails that Kemble comes down for the sisters' benefits. What the plays are is not yet known.

"And now for the state of the Nation, which at least makes the papers amusing. Much, indeed, and seeming good of the kind, is said on both sides—too much for me to determine—but as to the *heads* of the Party, my admiration, respect, and good opinion has been from the first bestowed on Mr. Pitt.

"His opponent I believe a man of Ability only, whose ambition and fortune tempt to Hereditary Crimes. Ld. Chatham's son, I believe, will be proudly virtuous, neither tempted by vicious pleasure nor broken fortune to sully his or his Father's name, and whose character I daresay it's his ambition to imitate, the praise of which forever charms his ear.

"As I have spent my C'mas with the old ladys I named to you, I cannot retail to you much on the subject of the day worth hearing, except it may be an observation that Sam made to myself. I had not heard anything like it broach'd, and thought if it could be supported it might be, what I am always on the watch for, good subject for your poem, and one which Orrelana might once again come forward as the champion of his country's rights.

"That this was the most fortunate time for Ireland proving indisputably her independence, by voting the Prince Regent from right hereditary, or if England took the other side, then to oppose him, and at any rate *establish* Ireland in her fullest rights. If there is anything in this, why are Irishmen at present so becalmed as scarce to give an opinion, as if they durst not till the matter was fixed for them by England. Were the matter happily weighed, elegantly expressed, insinuatingly conveyed—if truth was its foundation, I would wish you to be the author.

"Much will, no doubt, be said after the Meeting of Parl^ts and by Mr. Grattan in particular, who, I suppose, will be on this occasion a Foxite. Dr Haliday and White are the only ones here.

"There has been nothing here worth relating, as you will see by the insipidity of the resolutions, which were certainly formed so in compliance to Lord Charlemont's desire—at least it was owing to that being made known that there was not an address either here or at Killyleagh, and I believe his Lordship was very anxious that there should not be any from Belfast, as other places, he hoped (and said so), would follow its example. His reason for this was, he *said*, the great trouble he had in answering all these addresses, so much as to make it the only disagreeable matter attending the Review. At the meeting of delegates it was the opinion of all the address, if there was one, should be merely complimentary, and the chief argument against it was that such was not acceptable to Ld. C., who wished to do his duty as a thing of course. Thus the annual proper method of Volunteers making public their political sentiments has been, in my opinion, ungenerously quashed by his L'dship's finding it sometimes inconvenient to declare his own, and this indulgence I would never have granted him, but spoke out to him at the usual times, and never have let even the form die, but at such a time as this to be gagged.

"There was a long debate, but about nothing. Bryson was at first for addressing, but ruined both himself and his cause by a rant of nonsense. He was answered by A. Stewart, and then came about to his opinion. W. Cunningham was for addressing, but not for mentioning politics, yet raged at the proposition, and talked of nothing else; was silenced by Black, who was against addressing. Jones, I believe, never spoke. Bryson drew up a resolution of thanks to Ld. C., and read and proposed it aloud. It was thought cool, and a murmur rose against it. To get rid of it, 'twas proposed a Committee of five should name each other to draw up a complimentary resolution. Sharman, A. Stewart, Isaac, Crawford, and Bryson brought forth the little reptile you see.

"The meeting-house is finished, and meets with great admiration, but is not to be opened till Lord Donegal comes. There is still a large debt, to which the Bishop of Derry very genteely and unasked sent £50.

"Subscriptions are talked of for building an Academy, and Crombie will get every encouragement.

"The Bishop of Down has been staying at Bristow's, and appears to be the modestest and most amiable of Bishops. Crombie waited on him at a time when Trail, Leslie, and many more of the cloth were at court. Among these his L'dship looked like a curate. He received Crombie well, approved of his scheme, etc.; but one of them had the impudence to stagger him by asking if *he* looked on *himself* as the Principal in the affair? To which the pawky carl answered that at present all the trouble and management of the matter devolved on him, but that in future he hoped it would rest on abler persons. Trail supposed considering the matter to the lower branches of education wd. be sufficient for a trading town like this. He was answered these also would be taught in course, and, to their great mortification, they found this intelligence was merely compliment, for that the affair was determined on, and was to meet able support.

"I suppose you have engaged early accounts from W. Bruce of the Convention.

"I think this Country never met so awful, so glorious a day as this. It has been consigned to the delegates by a people who has nobly given them the opportunity and the power of *commanding* justice to be done their Country, for it is in that strain only that they will be listened to. 'Tis by that they will meet with obedience. If they should in the least degree depart from the firm spirit which has hitherto marked them and gained them the confidence of a people, they will lose a moment glorious for themselves and for their Country, perhaps never more to return; such are not frequent. The matter they have to deliberate on is good, and both good and great are divided in their opinions upon it. I would be sorry, however, they would find it so vast as to determine upon nothing, or but a few inferior points. Might it not be better in firm and unanimous terms to demand *one* fundamental right that the rest might grow out of, or time and experience point out.

"I do not hear much politics. There seems to be a timidity about the times creeping over those whose opinions I once thought well of. Some of them are grown old and cold, others have ceased to be volunteers. They are fretted and defeated in their opinions of men they placed too much trust in, and have not candour enough to allow they erred. They are not active in this mighty business, and perhaps thro' envy (a more common vice than is thought) blame and deride those who are.

"Would you give 3ᵈ to know the delegates from Belfast? it is only halfpence a-piece and one over, for we have appointed five. Ld. Bristol, Bishop of Derry; the Revᵈ Mr. Killburn, Presbyterian Minister; Robert Thompson, Mercht., and Henry Joy, Printer; if these are not an aggregate of knowledge, the deuce is in it! If the chusing of Lᵈ Bristol to be a party in what relates to Representation of the people be not wrong, I think these incendiarys (as they are now called) have done very well.

"They have appointed smart men who espoused their cause, and stick to it now that it is out of fashion; for it is really so among all the higher class, and the next, and next, gibe and ape the sneer of their betters, or smile in silence at the list of names which now appear to consider of a Parliamentary Reform and the affairs of the Nation.

"I never was hurt by public matters before; but there is a laugh gone forth and easily kept up by those who, in my opinion, have betrayed a good cause, that once had the voice of a Nation in its favour, and it is not to be borne coming from such. What is become of that torrent of patriotism which, in a rush over the whole land, promised to bear down all before it, till it reached its height? And must it decline so very rapidly—not, surely, without some deep-concealed mine, which, tho' powerful, is yet unsuspected?

"W. Cunningham refused to sign the call for the meeting. He goes to England, so has not time to serve his country in Convention.

"Hill Wilson has set Purdysburn to the Bishop of Down.

"Bruce and Harry Joy are appointed delegates to the Convention from the County of the town of Carrickfergus. Whether these countys will get leave to send them is uncertain; but if any do this will, and I rejoice there is a dissenting Clergyman among them, and that Bruce is he.

"I knew last post you would receive a letter more worthy your attention than mine, and deferred writing till the matter was settled—not from the reason you supposed, for it was known only to one or two that you were to be proposed till the day before the meeting. It was attended by all those who now attend such places, and was flattering to you. Some suppose you will go to Convention; many that you will not. Those who have asked me (among whom were Dr. Haliday) I have answered that I am sure you will be consistent, which could not be the case while you avowed the 'Helot' and refused to attend Convention."

WILLIAM DRENNAN, M.D.
(From the only known Portrait in possession of his grandson, W. H. DRENNAN, ESQ.)

PORTRAIT OF MARY ANN M'CRACKEN.

(From an Oil Painting by W. THOMPSON, *in possession of* G. ATCHISON, J.P.)

Life of Mary Ann M'Cracken, sister of Henry Joy M'Cracken.

By her Grand-Niece, Miss ANNA M'CLEERY.

HE following sketch is a feeble attempt to recall some reminiscences of a life well worthy of a fuller record, whether on account of the excellence of her of whom it treats, who was truly a woman of whom it might be said " she hath done what she could," or because of the stirring events with which she came into close contact.

Miss Mary Ann M'Cracken was born in Belfast, 8th July, 1770. Her childhood was spent in a house in High Street nearly opposite Bridge Street. Her father, John M'Cracken, was captain and part owner of a vessel trading between Belfast and the West Indies, and belonged to a Scotch family which had settled in Ireland. His mother was a strict Presbyterian, stern and uncompromising. On Christmas Day she would sit conspicuously at her spinning-wheel as a protest against the keeping holy of such a time. Her granddaughter, Mary Ann M'Cracken, was wont to say she inspired more fear than love, and was enabled to exercise considerable influence, from the firm conviction, entertained by her children and dependants, that any threatenings she might utter would surely come to pass. Several illustrations were given of this supposed power of invoking judgment, one of which, as it concerns the family, may be related.

In the year 1763 Captain M'Cracken had occasion to spend some months in Liverpool to superintend the building of a new vessel. He proposed to take his wife to reside with him during that time, and to leave their children, two in number, under their grandmother's care. The old lady, not relishing the charge, told her daughter-in-law "she wished she might get a scare before coming back." And truly she did ; for her husband, not wishing her to return in the new and untried vessel, sent her home before him. The ship in which she was encountered rough weather, and was wrecked on the South Rock near Ballywalter. All on board were saved by getting into the boat, but somehow they were unable to bring the boat quite to dry land, and had to wade a long distance in shallow water. To add to Mrs. M'Cracken's fatigue, she carried in her pockets 200 guineas, which had been entrusted to her to bring over, so inconvenient at that time were the arrangements for transmitting money.

Mrs. M'Cracken's maiden name was Ann Joy. She was daughter of Francis Joy, who established the *News-Letter* 1st Sept., 1737 (the third newspaper published in Ireland). The Joys claimed to be of Huguenot descent, three named Joy or Joyeuse having come from France, one of whom settled in the North of Ireland. Mary M'Cracken used to remark that she could trace different nationalities among her ancestry. Her mother's grandfather was Mr. George Martin, of whom she writes as follows :—

"My grandmother Joy was daughter to George Martin, who was Sovereign of Belfast, and a Presbyterian. It was at that time the custom for the Sovereign and burgesses to march in procession to church, and for the Sovereign to hand Lady Donegall into her seat, from whence she had a view of the burgesses' seat. Not seeing the Sovereign there, and, on inquiring as to the cause, finding that he was a Presbyterian, and that when he had performed his official duty he went to his own place of worship, she gave orders that in future none but members of the Established Church should be appointed burgesses ; and at that time there were but eleven who could write their own names. This my mother had heard from her mother, and wished very much to see the book in which their names were recorded, and being acquainted with the Town Clerk, she asked him to get her a sight of the book, which he did, and I looked over her shoulder and saw it written—Hugh (his X mark) Doak, bricklayer, but neglected to ascertain the date. My grandmother Joy's Christian name was Margaret ; she was the youngest daughter of Mr. Martin, and was born in the year 1690, forty years before my mother. George Martin made a present to the town of a piece of ground on which the old Market House was built. He advanced £2,000 to pay the King's troops (he was Sovereign when King William came to the throne), which was never repaid to him or any of his family."

Such was the story related by Mary M'Cracken as a family tradition, but there seems to be some confusion of dates and persons. According to Benn's *History of Belfast*, the only

Geo. Martin whose name appears in the list of Sovereigns held that post in 1649. He did not complete his year of office, as his house and goods were seized by the Parliamentary troops under Venables, and he himself forced to fly to Scotland, because he did not provide accommodation for the soldiers. This Geo. Martin was great-great-grandfather to Henry Joy, and would bear the same relationship to Mary M'Cracken. He had eight sons.

Hugh Doak was Sovereign in 1647. His signature was appended to various public documents, always in initials in printed character (the mode of making a mark frequently practised in those times), the full name having been written by someone else, not always in the same handwriting. His will was signed in the same manner, and shows that he was possessed of considerable property, and that his daughter had been married to a member of one of the best families in the town.

Such an incident as that concerning Lady Donegall and the Sovereign is by no means incredible, as both before and after the Revolution there were laws on the statute book which prohibited dissenters from holding any public offices except the most menial. These laws were not always enforced, but they might be if it suited any one's interest or humour to

CAPTAIN JOHN M'CRACKEN.
Father of Mary Ann M'Cracken.

THE WIFE OF CAPTAIN JOHN M'CRACKEN.
Mother of Mary Ann M'Cracken.

Photo-engraved direct from Miniature in possession of the Misses M'Cracken, grand-nieces of Mary Ann M'Cracken.

demand that they should. There might be reasons why, in Belfast, they should sometimes be allowed to fall into abeyance. Not only were the Presbyterians the most numerous and influential, but the office of Sovereign was one not always coveted in those unsettled times.

That there was much uncertainty in the enforcement of Acts of Conformity would appear from a petition presented to the House of Commons, in 1707, against the return of an M.P. for Belfast. At his election only six burgesses could vote, the others not having received the Sacrament according to the Episcopal form. The six who voted were equally divided; the Sovereign, therefore, claimed to have the casting vote, which he gave in favour of his man. On the petition being presented, one of the opposers of the returned member failed to prove that he had taken the Sacramental test. The M.P. therefore retained his seat, having been returned by three out of twelve burgesses.

Mary M'Cracken was the youngest but one of a large family, of whom four sons and two daughters lived to grow up, and several attained to an advanced age. She was a delicate child, and thought to be in consumption. Contrary to the modern practice, she was kept on low diet for the benefit of her health. However, the treatment does not appear to have been unsuccessful, for, as she said herself, "I have been a long time consuming away." She must have been an active child, since she accomplished the feat of hopping three times across High Street without stopping. She was very fond of animals—a liking she retained to the end of her days.

She went through the usual school routine of the time. The division of subjects would seem strange to the scholar of the present day. There was a school for English, and another for writing. Girls were sent for a time to a sewing and again to a knitting school. In all branches of sewing she was proficient. There was no French teacher in Belfast in her school days, but her father, who had been in France as a prisoner of war, wished his children to learn the language, and engaged an old French weaver, who lived in the town, to come in the evenings to teach them. His English translations were somewhat peculiar—*il faut* was always "it be to be." Mary would generally endeavour to get her lesson said first, that she might get a sleep with her head on the table.

After leaving school she had no idle time. Besides other household work, her share of shirt-making, stocking-darning (her mother knit the stockings), for four brothers, gave plenty of occupation.

When she was past her childhood, the family left High Street, and went to Rosemary Street. Two of the young men married, but remained for a time beneath the parental roof. Their house was known by some as Noah's Ark, and numerous were the inmates, the inferior animals being largely represented.

In course of time Mary M'Cracken, always energetic, proposed to her sister that they should go into business. The project was carried out, and they commenced the business of muslin manufacturers. Mary was the moving spirit, and worked early and late. She has said that so closely confined was she at times, that, when going to the post office before break-fast, she has felt inclined to leap and dance with delight in the fresh morning air. Her chief object in trying to make money was that she might have some of her own to give away as she wished. She was of a very sanguine temperament and did not spare herself, and to some extent she succeeded in her object ; but—perhaps the times were against her—she had much struggling and anxiety, and the ultimate result was disappointing.

Before proceeding further, it may be well to take a glance at the state of the country and the condition of the people. Anarchy had reigned in Ireland for centuries, and even when the times became more settled, the poverty in the rural districts was extreme. Still the mass of the people, ignorant of modern improvements, and prejudiced against innovations, were content to rub along in the old way, particularly those of them who happened to live on the estate of a free-handed resident landlord, who would keep about him an unlimited number of hangers-on, paying little money (for of that he had small share himself), but easy-going in his exactions of service, and dispensing hospitality as lavishly in the kitchen as in the dining-room. But a very little disturbance of the regular order of things—such as a less abundant harvest, a bad potato crop, or anything which reduced ever so slightly the scanty supply of necessaries—brought them to actual want, and any one who demanded money by legal right, be he tithe collector, agent of non-resident landlord, excise or custom-house officer—any messenger of the law—was regarded as a natural enemy to be thwarted and resisted.

The religious element mingled largely with all agrarian troubles, for it so happened that those who were opposed in interests were usually of different creeds. It has ever been the case that religious wars have produced an intensity of bitterness, estrangement, and distrust beyond any others, and Ireland has been no exception to this rule.

It would be tedious even to name the various parties who banded themselves together to resist the law or oppose each other. Their numbers were drawn from the peasantry, or the smaller farmers, who were little better off. Let it suffice to mention a few of the Northern societies—"Oak-Boys" and "Hearts of Steel" between 1762 and 1770; then there were the "Peep-of-Day Boys," from whom were developed the modern Orangemen ; and the "Defenders," who were Catholics. The "Hearts of Steel" came into connection with Belfast on the occasion of a riot in 1770, under the following circumstances :—

Some of Lord Donegall's leases having fallen simultaneously, he asked an increased rent on renewing them. This was by no means unreasonable, because the land had been originally let at a very low rate in the beginning of the century, just after a long period of troublous times ; however, he also desired renewal fines. Some of the prosperous merchants of Belfast were ready to pay larger fines than the tenants had ready cash for, and took some of the farms over the tenants' heads. This was done simply as a speculation for the purpose of sub-letting them, and aroused great indignation in the country. Greatly exaggerated reports were circulated as to the sums Lord Donegall had obtained. Some cattle belonging to a Belfast merchant who had taken land at Ballyclare were maimed, and a farmer from Templepatrick was arrested as a participator in the outrage, and taken to Belfast barracks for security.

The "Hearts of Steel" in the neighbourhood, having assembled, called on the people to release the prisoner, and a crowd marched to Belfast. Being unable to attain their object,

N

they proceeded to the house of another offender, a leading merchant, which they set on fire. They returned to the barracks, but the soldiers fired, and three men were killed. The inhabitants feared the destruction of the town. Negotiations were opened, and eventually the prisoner was released.

While a sort of listless discontent, which on provocation was ever ready to break out into a flame, pervaded the agrarian population, the mercantile portion of the community had likewise their grievances : some of the more important may be noticed.

Previous to the Revolution there had been considerable exportation of wool and woollen manufactures, but in the reign of William III. a law was passed which altogether destroyed the trade. The exportation of woollen goods was prohibited altogether, and only wool might be sent to England. Thus a poor country was further impoverished, and a stimulus given to smuggling—a form of lawlessness already too much practised. In many parts of the island there were facilities for carrying on a contraband trade—a rugged coast, bad roads, and a scanty population, who sympathised with the evasion of laws which were imposed by the stronger country for their own interest with high-handed power. In return for Irish goods, wine and brandy were brought from the Continent. Gentlemen on whose property the landing was effected had their cellars filled at a trifling expense. This ministered to the habits of lavish hospitality which helped to ruin so many families, while it gained for them popularity among their own class, and the devotion of their numerous dependants.

ATTACK ON THE BARRACKS BY THE "HEARTS OF STEEL," 1770.

But smuggling was looked upon as a very venial offence indeed, and was commonly practised. Mary M'Cracken related, as a proof of her father's strict integrity, that he would not smuggle, nor allow his sailors to do so on his behalf, as he considered a custom-house oath as binding on the conscience as any other. Some captains made £200 a-year by smuggling, but her mother made as much by her manufacturing business.

Duties between England and Ireland must have been, to say the least of it, exceedingly troublesome, and were, when possible, evaded. A lady visiting England would buy English lace for herself and friends, and sew it on all her garments, to be taken off on her return.

But to return to the subject of manufactures. When the woollen business was destroyed in Ireland, by way of making some compensation, the manufacture of linen and exporting of it was encouraged. One of the measures taken to promote this object was the sending of Huguenot weavers into the country, to introduce a better manner of weaving.

From time immemorial linen had been manufactured in Ireland, no doubt at first in a very rude manner, but improving with the requirements and appliances of civilisation ; however, it was only about the end of the seventeenth century that it became an article of export.

The manufacture was principally carried on in the North. Spinners and weavers worked in their own houses, and the work when finished was taken to the employers, or to market to be sold. During the eighteenth century the trade in linen increased rapidly, and in the last quarter of the century the cotton manufacture was introduced, and was for a time a considerable business, though it has now left the country.

Belfast had been rising in importance as a commercial town, and had become the chief port in Ulster. Early in the century a brown linen market was held in it, and in 1782 it was proposed to establish a white linen market for the North of Ireland. A subscription was opened to build a White Linen Hall, the foundation-stone of which was laid the following year.

Various other industries were carried on in the town, and as trade with foreign countries increased, and the restrictions upon it became more generally felt, men of business began to find themselves numerous and influential enough to protest against them with some hope of being attended to.

SHOP IN CASTLE STREET, 1790.
(From a billhead in possession of L. M. EWART, Esq., J.P., M.R.I.A.)

In 1779 some partial relief was obtained, and there was great rejoicing in Belfast in March, 1780, when news arrived that an Act had been passed in the British Parliament granting to Ireland "Free trade with America," as it was called. That meant the repeal of a law by which trade with the Colonies could only be conducted through England, so that goods meant for Ireland had to be landed in England and re-shipped, and *vice versa*. The relaxations granted were, however, but partial, and, moreover, rested on an insecure basis. What England was at that time pleased to grant she might withdraw.

When England's resources had been taxed to the utmost by the American War, with France also an enemy, the Irish had been suffered to raise a volunteer army to protect their homes from invasion. When that danger was at an end, the Volunteers turned their attention to home affairs, and, waxing bolder by their first success, assembled in 1782, formulated the wishes of the people, and demanded an independent parliament. The repeal of Poynings' Act was obtained, and the Irish Parliament became, at least in name and form, independent of England. But much more was needed before the hope could be entertained, of obtaining from Parliament the redress of grievances which it was for the supposed interest of the ruling powers to uphold. At that time the so called representation of the people was a mere mockery, and "Reform of Parliament" became the cry. Catholic Emancipation also was maintained to be a duty, but whether it should be asked for in its completeness at once, or whether it ought to be partial and gradual, was a question about which there was much difference of opinion and dissension among the Protestant agitators for reform.

Belfast members of Parliament were chosen by the Sovereign and burgesses, under the direction of the Earl of Donegall. In some of the counties the electors were constrained to return the nominees of their landlords, and even where they were sufficiently independent to send popular candidates to Parliament, these sometimes yielded to the temptation of place or pension, and betrayed the trust committed to them.   No Catholic had a right to vote.

The inhabitants of Belfast were most energetic in endeavouring to secure, in County Antrim (where alone they had any power), representatives pledged to do their utmost to obtain their desires, and to abstain from the acceptance of place or pension.

Reared amid such influences, Mary M'Cracken was from her early years intensely interested in politics; and various political incidents, in which some of her relatives were concerned, became indelibly imprinted on her memory, such as the following :—Her grandfather, Francis Joy, then residing in Randalstown, a very old man, confined to his couch by a disease in his leg, had himself conveyed to Antrim to vote at a Parliamentary election for Rowley and O'Neill, the popular candidates.   His son Robert, meeting him there, said— "What brought you here, sir ?"   "The good of my country," was the reply.   The side for which he voted was triumphant, but the day that the members were chaired he died.

Another anecdote was :—"After reading—

> 'And next the little printer we'll engage:
> Strange that a man so upright and so sage
> Should be perverted by a pageant gown,
> Laughed at by fifteen thousand of the town;
> This man's a contrast to his sons and sire,
> His brother and his sons, whom all admire'—

I asked my sister, ten years older than myself, who were the 15,000 who laughed at my Uncle Harry ; for my Uncle Harry was my mother's favourite brother, to whom she went for advice, and every person esteemed him.   'All the people of the town,' said my sister.'

The lines quoted are from a squib entitled—"In Praise of the Corporation of Belfast : an Heroic Poem."   The principal inhabitants had petitioned Lord Donegall to send Mr. Waddell Cunningham to represent Belfast in Parliament, which he refused to do.   Mr. Cunningham and Mr. Hewitt then contested the seat for Carrickfergus.   The former was returned by a large majority in February, 1784.   In the following month the Sovereign and burgesses appointed Mr. Hewitt M.P. for Belfast.

As Mary M'Cracken advanced to womanhood, the interest in public affairs became more absorbing, and notable events followed in quick succession.

The French Revolution had exerted a powerful influence.   It seemed at the time as if at once the oppression of ages had ceased for ever, and a nation had burst its bonds, and started on a career of progress and prosperity, in which the poor and weak would have a part, and share in the privileges hitherto denied them.

While we associate that great event had not been developed, the enthusiasm was well nigh universal.   On the anniversary of the taking of the Bastille, that and the other events of the period, by which freedom appeared to have been secured, were commemorated in Belfast by processions, assemblies, and dinners, in which the Volunteers took a prominent part.

The war of American independence, and its successful termination, was celebrated with due honour, and the victors held up to admiration.

Ireland, too, had wrongs to be redressed ; and the example set by other nations helped to sustain the energy of those who laboured for their removal.

Some of the Belfast politicians were becoming alarmed at the increasing tendency of opinion towards democracy.   Lord Charlemont was communicated with, and at his suggestion a Whig club was established in the town early in 1790, similar to one which had been founded some years previously in Dublin.

The Volunteers, while they refused to compromise their independence by accepting of any assistance from Government, always professed the greatest loyalty, and manifested their readiness not only to defend the country from foreign foes, but also to lend their assistance to enforce the law at home.

"1786, Nov. 17.—At the request of the sheriff of the Co. Antrim, a party of the Belfast Volunteers, with two six-pounders (one of which belonged to the 1st Compy. the other to the Belfast Blues), marched to Ballymena, to assist in enforcing an execution on a house in that neighbourhood.   On their arrival, the two pieces were drawn up in front of the house (which had been previously prepared for defence), and pointed in order to begin the attack, under the orders of the sheriff, when the defenders fled precipitately, and effected an escape ; after which, possession was taken by the sheriff."

"1792, Ap. 2.—A detachment of Belfast 1st Vol. Compy. with one of the Compy's field pieces, marched, at the request of the sheriff of the Co., to the townland of Derrymore and barony of Upper Massareene, which was forcibly withheld.   After an hour spent in fruitless entreaties to prevail on the intruders to surrender the premises, the sheriff ordered the corps to fire on the house. A hot action immediately commenced, and after a desperate resistance, in which the house was much shattered, the occupiers retired to the rear, and made their escape in different directions. The detachment returned to Lisburn on the same evening, having marched upwards of 32 miles, and arrived in Belfast without the slightest injury having happened to any individual."

The Society of United Irishmen was established in Belfast in Oct., 1791, their ostensible object being to procure "A complete reform in the Legislature, founded on a communion of rights, and a union of power among Irishmen of every religious persuasion."

But every organisation in Ireland, whether for reform, revolution, or rebellion, has been composed of men having different ends in view, who could travel but a short way together. No doubt the ostensible object was the real one of many of the United Irishmen, but it is now well known that some of the organisers aimed from the very first at separation from England.

Theobald Wolfe Tone assisted in founding the first club of United Irishmen, and for that purpose he visited Belfast in the autumn of 1791, accompanied by Thos. Russell. He was invited by a secret committee, who, without obtruding themselves upon public notice, managed the affairs of the advanced political party in Belfast. Tone had espoused the Catholic cause, although he was not a Roman Catholic himself, but appears to have had, in so acting, objects as yet but partially avowed, and, as one who for a time acted with him wrote, "to have been only so far set upon emancipation as it fell in with his ideas of reform upon the French principles."

His advocacy was, however, welcomed by the Catholics; and about half a-year after having organised the United Irishmen's club in Belfast, he was appointed Catholic Agent, under the title of Assistant Secretary, at a salary of £200 a-year.

What were Tone's religious opinions, if he had any, did not very clearly appear even to his contemporaries. Mary M'Cracken, in reply to Dr. Madden, author of *The United Irishmen: their Lives and Times*, wrote—"Tone was not sceptical. There was a society in Belfast of a political kind, all of whose members were sceptics. They would not admit him, because he believed in the truths of religion."

However, he advocated with skill and success the cause of union, and it was uphill work, for distrust of the Catholics was strong among the Dissenters of the North. During Tone's sojourn at this time, there were many discussions and arguments on the subject. Objections such as the following were advanced by the opponents of union :—

1st danger—To true religion. Roman Catholics would, if emancipated, establish an Inquisition.

2nd. To property. By reviving Court of Claims, and admitting evidence to substantiate Catholic titles.

3rd. Of throwing power into their hands, which would make this a Catholic Government, incapable of enjoying or extending liberty.

A newspaper, called *The Northern Star*, was started to advocate the cause of the United Irishmen. The first number appeared 1st Feb., 1792.

The brothers of Mary M'Cracken took their share in the doings of the time. The eldest was a Volunteer; Henry Joy, her favourite brother, two years her senior, and an older one, William, were United Irishmen.

The ladies of the family took a lively, if less active, interest in politics. *The Northern Star* was attentively perused. Miss Mary once exclaimed, on recovering from a fever—"Oh, I have missed so many of the *Stars*."

Paine's *Rights of Man* was read and admired. Tone called it—*The Koran of Blefescu* (Belfast). Mrs. M'Cracken, afterwards hearing of his *Age of Reason*, said it could not be his, but must have been written by some one who attributed it to him to discredit him.

Paine, however, afterwards fell in the estimation of at least her younger daughter, for she spoke of his vulgarity and inordinate self-conceit.

In 1793 the Volunteers were suppressed. A proclamation was issued, 11th March, forbidding armed parties to parade in military array.

When the Volunteers first demanded Reform, all was unanimity. No dissentient voice was heard in Belfast ; but as time went on, differences of opinion arose. Some wished to follow the French example ; others were cautious and moderate, and sought only to improve, not to overturn.

Joy, in his preface to *Belfast Politics*, published in 1794, describes the disunion which prevailed in the town, and the dissatisfaction which was felt on account of its being garrisoned by a large military force. The few adherents of the court who had previously been constrained to keep silence, now ventured to express their opinion, encouraged by the presence of the army. The advanced party took credit to themselves for the change of popular feeling and public measures with respect to the Catholics, and declared their determination to act on the most enlarged principles, and to make no compromise with bigotry and injustice.

The moderate party charged their opponents with having, by imitation of republican principles and language, alarmed the more moderate, and caused distrust on the part of the Catholics; while their affectation of secrecy and policy of bluster had given occasion to the Government to refuse further concessions, and had afforded a pretext for the employment of repressive measures.

In 1795 the Society of United Irishmen changed its character—it became secret, a test was required, and now, without doubt, its purpose was separation.

Henry Joy M'Cracken continued a member in its new organisation. He was employed to induce the Defenders to join with the United Irishmen. He was suited for this work, as he had engaging manners, an agreeable address, and unbounded enthusiasm. The Defenders were Roman Catholics, the United Irishmen mostly Presbyterians.

In the early summer of 1795, Tone paid a second visit to Belfast on his way to America, being compelled to leave Ireland in consequence of his political conduct. During this visit, he and four others met in M'Art's fort, Cave Hill, where they took "A solemn obligation never to desist in their efforts until they had subverted the authority of England over their country, and asserted her independence." One of these four was H. J. M'Cracken.

THE LANDING OF THUROT AT CARRICKFERGUS, 1760.

His beloved sister sympathised with him in his aims, but probably did not know how deeply he was involved in the business. He was for a time manager of a cotton factory in the Falls Road, and resided at the works. In a letter to a friend, she lamented his lonely and isolated position; but it is possible he may have had more occupation for his leisure hours, and even for some of those which might with advantage have been devoted to business, than she or the rest of the family suspected. Indeed, some one wrote to his father expressing dissatisfaction with his attention to business. However, it is impossible to know how these things may have been. Business in general was in a very depressed condition. The cotton manufacture had been introduced, and seemed likely to flourish, but expectations were disappointed. The partnership of the Falls Road concern was dissolved in 1795, and the manager returned home.

Some time afterwards there was a riot, in which some of the dragoons were concerned. They cut down some shop signs, among them a figure of a French and one of an American general. H. J. M'Cracken interfered, and seized one of the soldiers, whom he delivered up to his officer. This affair had the appearance of a drunken brawl, but a deeper political significance was attached to it than appeared on the surface; and M'Cracken went to lodge in Holywood, where Thomas Russell, who had assisted Tone and Nelson in organising the first United Irishmen's Club, frequently bore him company.

On one occasion, Mary M'Cracken asked her brother if he was not afraid to trust the Catholics (at that time there were very few in Belfast). He said—"Would not you trust Betty?" She replied—"I would." Betty was an old charwoman whom their mother had once employed to assist in hiding their silver plate, when it was reported that the French were in Carrickfergus. She was the only Catholic the family knew at the time. The old woman mourned a son who had enlisted as a soldier. "It's not," she said, "the loss of my son, but his taking the oath that's so much against him" (viz., the abjuration of Popery). M'Cracken's special work among the United Irishmen was to organise the Defenders, who were Catholics: he had a command among them. Few of them had education or position to fit them to be officers.

The Government was well informed of the proceedings of the United Irishmen. In 1796 some of those in Belfast were arrested, among whom were Wm. and H. J. M'Cracken. The prisoners were taken to Kilmainham, where they were detained fourteen months. During that time, the Misses M'Cracken twice visited Dublin. Some of their relatives had gone to reside in that city, among others Counsellor Joy. The muslin business was still going on, but does not appear to have been flourishing. Their mother wrote—

"Nov. 16, 1796.

"DEAR MARY,

"I was sorry to find, by John's letter to his wife, that you don't like Dublin, though I was sure it would be the case; but I hoped your seeing Harry, and that you might get some of our muslins sold, would partly reconcile you to it. . . . Our friends are all very attentive to me, and I could do pretty well about your business if I had money to give the weavers; and indeed they behave very well.

"Dear Mary,

"Your affec^{t.} Mother,

"ANN M'CRACKEN."

H. J. M'Cracken suffered in health from his confinement, and was an invalid for some time after his return, but as soon as possible he resumed his labours in the cause. Preparations for the Rising were going on, and the order was expected during March and April, 1798. The coach from Dublin to Belfast was to be stopped as a signal, and North and South were to rise simultaneously; but the courage and resolution for bold action were wanting in the commanders of Co. Antrim ("The cowardly directors," as they came to be designated). They hesitated. The general resigned. The Co. Down general had been arrested. Difficulties arose about a leader. Eventually, H. J. M'Cracken was chosen General-in-Chief. But the opportunity had been lost—everything had become disorganised—the fearful and half-hearted had deserted; many even of the zealous knew not where to go, nor whom to follow. At various places small parties had assembled according to appointment, but finding no leader and no instructions, had no other course open to them but to endeavour to make their way back to their homes as best they might.

H. J. M'Cracken, suddenly thrust into the foremost place, was considered to have shown much skill, but it was a forlorn hope. He and a few coadjutors exerted themselves to the utmost. The battle of Antrim was fought on the 7th June, and the Insurgents completely routed.

H. J. M'Cracken and a small party escaped; they wandered for some days among the mountains near Belfast, their first intention being to join the Wexford men. Mary M'Cracken having heard of the disastrous issue of the fight, went in search of her brother, accompanied by her sister-in-law, who wished to find out something about her husband, also a fugitive. It was soon discovered that William had succeeded in getting back to Belfast. However, his wife would not desert her friend, and the two proceeded on their way. After spending a night in a house of a friend to the cause, they resumed their search, and were at last successful. After giving the information to those in hiding that Col. Nugent knew of their intention to join the Southern rebels, some time was spent in consultation, after which the ladies were led to a poor cottage, where they passed the second night. They had another interview with M'Cracken the following morning, and returned home. Their journey was performed on foot.

Not long afterwards the fugitive was taken prisoner, when on his way to the coast to embark in a foreign vessel, arrangements having been made with the captain to take him on board.

The remainder of the sad story will be best told in Mary M'Cracken's own words. The following are extracts from letters published in Dr. Madden's *The United Irishmen: their Lives and Times* (first edition:)—

"Soon after the former interview, I received the following letter from my brother :—

' Monday, *18th June, 1798.*

'DEAR MARY,

' The clothes came in very good time, as I had much need of a change, having never had that luxury since I left home before.

'H. J. M'C.'

FAC-SIMILE OF AUTOGRAPH OF HENRY JOY M'CRACKEN.
Inscribed in a copy of ' P. TERENTII COMŒDIÆ. MOGUNT. M.D.XXVIII." (In possession of the Editor.)

" Shortly afterwards, I again went to see him at D. Bodle's, beside the Cave Hill, but nearer to Belfast. He was a poor labourer. The girls often rose out of their beds early in the morning to let the fugitives get rest. I had afterwards an opportunity of materially serving that family, and some others who had done similar acts of kindness.

"It was on Sunday afternoon, the 8th July, my birthday, that we got intelligence that Harry was taken prisoner by four Carrickfergus yeomen, one of whom knew him. . . . Immediately on getting intelligence of Harry's arrest, my father and I set off for Carrickfergus, and with difficulty obtained permission to visit him, the officer who accompanied us politely standing at a distance during our conversation. Harry desired me not to use any solicitations on his account ; and, after expressing to me his wishes on many matters, he desired me to tell my brother John to come to him. My mother had sent him a favourite book of his, *Young's Night Thoughts*, and I observed a line from it written on the wall of his cell—' A friend's worth all the hazard we can run.'

"On the 16th he was brought in prisoner to Belfast, in the evening. My sister and I immediately set out to try if we could see him. He was then standing with a strong escort, about a dozen I think, of soldiers, who were drawn up in the middle of what is now called Castle Place. We could not speak to him there. He was then taken to the Artillery Barracks in Ann Street ; and we hastened to Col. Durham, who lodged in Castle Place. We knocked at the door, and just as it was opened, the Col., who had been out, came up ; and when we earnestly requested he would give us an order for admission to see our brother, who was to be tried the next day, he replied that ' if our father, mother, sisters, brothers, and all the friends we had in the world, were in similar circumstances, he would give no such order.' He had by this time entered his hall-door, which he shut against us with great violence. We returned home, and then learned that there was a large party of officers dining at the Exchange Rooms. We hurried there, and sent a message to Col. Barber, who instantly sent a young officer to accompany us to my brother ; and when we apologised to this gentleman for giving him so much trouble, he said he did not consider it any trouble, and would be glad to serve us. . . . When we reached the place of confinement, he very kindly stood at a distance from the door of the cell. . . . Harry desired that Mrs. Holmes, daughter to my uncle, Henry Joy, and Miss Mary Tomb, his granddaughter, might be requested to attend his trial the next day, to prove the fact of their having advised him to leave Belfast, in order that if no material evidence was brought against him, some advantage might be derived from the circumstance of his friends having endeavoured to persuade him to leave town previous to the Antrim business. . . . I rose at six, and set out in a carriage for the place where Miss Tomb was then staying with a lady near Lisburn. I endeavoured to keep up her spirits as well as I could, fearing, from the state of grief and anxiety she was then in, she would be unable to give evidence. She came with me, and on arriving in town, the 17th July, I proceeded to the Exchange, where the trial was just commenced. The moment I set my eyes on Harry, I was struck with the extraordinary serenity and composure of his look. This was no time to think about such things, but yet I could not help gazing on him ; it seemed to me that I had never seen him look so well, so full of healthful bloom, so free from the slightest trace of care or trouble, as at that moment, when he was perfectly aware of his approaching fate.

"I sat very near the table when the trial was going on. Col. Montgomery was President. The first witness called [was Minis]. The other witness [James Beck] knew him by a mark on his throat, which mark was not seen till his handkerchief was taken off.

" Hope informed me that an artilleryman, of the [name of Muldoon], had been on guard the morning of the 17th July, and had told him that the witnesses who had sworn against M'Cracken did not know him ; that he was walking in the yard when an officer pointed him out to them from a window looking into the yard, and told them of the mark on his throat. (This practice of pointing out prisoners to Crown witnesses was by no means uncommon in Ireland at that period.)

" Immediately preceding the examination of the witnesses, my father, who was just recovered from a severe and tedious fit of illness, was called aside by Pollock, who told him

HENRY JOY M'CRACKEN.
(From " Ulster in '98.")

he had such evidence against his son as would certainly hang him, that his life was in his hands, and that he would save it if my father would persuade him to give such information as Pollock knew it was in his power to do, viz., who the person was who had been appointed to command the people at Antrim, in whose place he (M'Cracken) had acted. My father replied he knew nothing, and could do nothing in the matter ; he would rather his son died than do a dishonourable action. The tyrant, however, not content with the trial of his victim, would torture him still further by calling Harry to the conference, and repeated the same offer to himself, who, well knowing his father's sentiments, answered " he would do anything which his father knew it was right for him to do." Pollock repeated the offer, on which my father said—'Harry, my dear, I know nothing of the business, but you know best what you ought to do.' Harry then said—'Farewell, father,' and returned to the table to abide the issue of the trial.

"After I left him, I was told that Major Fox went up to him and asked him, for the last time, if he would give any information, at which he smiled, and said 'he wondered how Major Fox could suppose him such a villain.'

"The proceedings went on, and after some time Henry complained of thirst, and asked me to get him an orange or some wine and water. I hastened home, our house being at a short distance from the place, and on my way back I was accosted by the wife of Wm. Thompson, an Englishman, a calico print-cutter in my brother's employment, who, refusing to give information against my brother, had 200 lashes inflicted on him, on a charge of having engraved a seal with the device of a harp and some popular motto. Mrs. T. enquired of me about the trial that was going on. She said if his life was in danger she would appear as a witness, and swear that she had seen Henry in the street of Belfast on the day of the Antrim fight. She followed me to the Exchange, and repeated the proposal to Harry and Mr. T. Stewart, who was his attorney, who called Harry aside to hear it. They both told her her proposal could not be accepted. . . . . .

"After the examination of the witnesses, I rose and went forward to the table. I stated what appeared to me to be unlike truth in the evidence that had been given by the witnesses for the prosecution, expressing a hope that they would not consider such evidence sufficient to take away life, the testimony of one witness impeaching the character and credit of the approver, on whose statement the charge was mainly dependent for support.

"Harry had taken notes of the trial, and before its termination he said to me in a whisper—'You must be prepared for my conviction.' All his friends could do was to endeavour to get his sentence commuted to banishment. Before the close of the proceedings I hastened home with the intelligence, and my mother went instantly to Gen. Nugent's house and requested an interview, but he refused to be seen. I returned to the Exchange before my mother came back, but found that Harry had been removed.

"I little expected that any efforts to save him would be successful : but I felt I had a duty to perform—to prevent misrepresentation, and to put it out of the power of his enemies to injure his character while living, or his memory when dead. I followed him to the artillery barracks, where I saw Major Fox just going in, and asked his permission to see my brother. He desired me to wait a little, but I followed him, and when he came to the door of my brother's cell I remained behind him at a few paces' distance. The door of the cell was opened, and I heard him say—'You are ordered for immediate execution.' My poor brother seemed to be astonished at the announcement—indeed he well might be at the shortness of the time allotted to him ; but seeing me falling to the ground, he sprang forward and caught me. I did not, however, lose consciousness for a single instant, but felt a strange sort of composure and self-possession, and in this frame of mind I continued the whole day. I knew it was incumbent on me to avoid disturbing the last moments of my brother's life, and I endeavoured to contribute to render them worthy of his whole career. We conversed as calmly as we had ever done. I asked him if there was anything particular that he desired to have done. He said—'I wish you to write to Russell, inform him of my death, and tell him I have done my duty. . . . .' He said he would like to see Mr. Kelburne, who was our clergyman. I told him I feared he would be unable to come (he was ill) ; but that if he wished to see a clergyman, Dr. Dickson was under the same roof, and would come to him. He replied he would rather see Mr. Kelburne, as it would gratify his father and mother. He of course was sent for. . . . In the meantime Dr. Dickson was brought to him.

. . . . . During the early part of the day Harry and I had conversed with tranquillity on the subject of his death. We had been brought up in a firm conviction of an all-wise and overruling Providence, and of the duty of entire resignation to the Divine will. I remarked that his death was as much a dispensation of Providence as if it had happened in the common course of nature ; to which he assented. He told me there had been much perjury on his trial, but that the truth would have answered the same purpose.

"After the clergymen were gone, I asked for a pair of scissors that I might take off some of his hair. A young officer who was on guard went out of the room and brought a pair of scissors, but hesitated to trust them into my hands, when I asked him indignantly if he thought I meant to hurt my brother. He then gave them to me, and I cut off some of Harry's hair which curled round his neck, and folded it up in paper and put it into my bosom. Fox at that moment entered the room, and desired me to give it to him, 'as too much use,' he said, 'had already been made of such things.' I refused, saying I would only part with it in death, when my dear brother said—'Oh! Mary, give it to him ; of what value is it?' I felt that its possession would be a mere gratification to me, and, not wishing to discompose him by the contest, I gave it up.

"The time allowed him was now expired. He had hoped for a few days, that he might give his friends an account of all the late events in which he had taken a part.

THE EXECUTION OF HENRY JOY M'CRACKEN, 17TH JULY, 1798.

"About 5 p.m. he was ordered to the place of execution, the old Market-House, the ground of which had been given to the town by his great-grandfather. I took his arm, and we walked together to the place of execution, when I was told it was the General's orders I should leave him, which I peremptorily refused to do. Harry begged I would go. Clasping my hands around him—I did not weep till then—I said I could bear anything but leaving him. Three times he kissed me, and entreated I would go ; and, looking round to recognise some friend to put me in charge of, he beckoned to a Mr. Boyd, and said, ' He will take charge of you.' Mr. B. stepped forward, and, fearing any further refusal would disturb the last moments of my dearest brother, I suffered myself to be led away. Mr. B. endeavoured to give me comfort in the hope he gave me that we should meet in heaven. A Mr. Armstrong, a friend of the family, came forward, took me from Mr. Boyd, and conducted me home. I immediately sent a message to Dr. M'Donnell and Mr. M'Cluncy, an apothecary, to come directly to the house. The latter came, and Dr. D. sent his brother Alexander, a skilful surgeon. The body was given up to our family unmutilated ; so far our entreaties and those of our friends prevailed.

"From the moment I parted with Harry, the idea which had occurred to me in the morning, that it might be possible to restore animation, took full possession of my mind, and that hope buoyed up my strength, and supported me at the moment of parting with him. Every effort that art could devise was made, and at one time hopes of success were entertained ; but the favourable symptoms disappeared, and the attempt was at length given up.

OLD VIEW OF HIGH STREET.

"I was present when the medical men entered the room where the body was laid, and then retired and joined the rest of the family, awaiting the result with indescribable anxiety. My heart sank within me when we were told all hope was over, and that a message had been brought from the General that the funeral must take place immediately, or that the body would be taken from us. Preparations were made for immediate burial. I learned that no relative of Harry's was likely to attend the funeral. I could not bear to think that no member of his family should accompany his remains, so I set out to follow them to the grave.

"A kind-hearted man, an enthusiast in the cause for which poor Harry died, drew my arm within his, but my brother John soon followed and took his place.

"I heard the sound of the first shovelful of earth that was thrown on the coffin, and I remember little else of what passed on that sad occasion."

Miss Mary M'Cracken thus depicts the character of her brother :—

"Harry partook largely of all the virtues of both his father and his mother. From earliest childhood he was actively and daringly courageous, amounting to fearlessness ; quick as thought in defending a friend, but so good-natured and ready, when at play, to undertake anything that occurred that was difficult or troublesome, that he was a universal favourite with his companions. He had, however, a sort of restless activity, which did not presage the deeply-contemplative character which was afterwards developed. He was particularly distinguished by the utmost quickness of observation, a proof of which was, that when the famous Bristow was here, he detected the secret of almost all his tricks, which he successfully imitated afterwards, to the amusement of his friends. He had the utmost presence of mind, which, added to his manual dexterity, enabled him to be eminently useful on many occasions, particularly when any house in the town took fire, when he was always the first, and sometimes alone, in posts of the greatest danger.

"My brother Harry was joined with a few of the industrious class in Belfast in a Sunday-school in the old Market-House, in which writing as well as reading was taught. In two years a young woman had learned both to read and write. They did not presume to impart religious knowledge, but they taught their scholars how to obtain it for themselves, by which every sect might equally profit.

"It was afterwards found to be practised in England ; and then Mr. Bristow came to the place of meeting with a number of ladies, with rods in their hands as badges of authority, which put to flight the humble pioneers.

"The same party who started the Sunday-school also instituted a cheap public library, on becoming a member of which they advanced one guinea, afterwards half-a-guinea yearly ; and at that time the other libraries charged most exorbitantly for some new publications. I remember one translated from the French so much admired that there were two translations of it, to which different names were given, and for which 10d. a-night was charged, which only the rich could afford."

Mary M'Cracken said her brother gave it as his opinion that "if it had not been for the free quarters and the flogging, there would have been no rebellion after all ; for," said he, "it is not easy to get people to turn out of their comfortable homes, if they have any comfort in them."

The practice in '98 of quartering soldiers on the people where disaffection prevailed, gave opportunities, particularly in country districts, for wanton acts of tyranny and other excesses. Persons were sometimes flogged or half hung to make them confess their own connection with rebellious societies, or to betray others.

James Hope a weaver, one of the most energetic of the United Irishmen, and who, in the interest of the cause, had traversed the greater part of Ireland, working at his trade or taking up some other occupation to support himself and family while doing so, was an active participator in the closing scenes of the '98 movement in the North. He gave valuable information to Dr. Madden for his book, *The United Irishmen: their Lives and Times.* Dr. Madden thus writes—" . . . H. J. M'Cracken was the most discerning and determined man of all our Northern leaders, and by his exertions chiefly the union of the Societies of the North and South was maintained. . . . . . I had an opportunity of knowing many of our leaders ; but none of those I was acquainted with resembled each other in their qualities and their principles, in the mildness of their manners, their attachment to their country, their forgetfulness of themselves, their remembrances of the merits of others, their steadiness of purpose, and their fearlessness, as did H. J. M'Cracken and Robert Emmett."

The eldest brother, Frank, left for Cork to embark for Barbadoes about the latter end of July, 1798. He proceeded thence to America. He was occupied with commercial affairs, but his letters show that he was not much delighted with the country, nor greatly pleased with the mode of transacting business in the United States.

The next incident to be recorded of Mary M'Cracken is an effort to relieve the necessitous ; but, in the first place, it will be necessary to go back to give some account of a person who was intimately associated with H. J. M'Cracken during a part of the time that he was most actively engaged in politics.

It will be remembered that Thomas Russell was one of the founders of the U. I. Club in 1791. He had gone to India as a lad in some military capacity. However, the occupation only lasted five years, when he returned home. He resided several years in Dublin, where he became acquainted with Wolfe Tone. In 1790 he obtained a commission as ensign, and joined his regiment in Belfast. He was very popular, became a member of several clubs, and was admitted to the intimacy of the leading Liberal politicians.

Through his agency Tone was invited to Belfast, introduced to the Secret Society, and the first club of United Irishmen was formed. Russell accompanied Tone back to Dublin to assist in establishing the Society there also.

; An American adventurer was resident in Belfast in 1791, who was possessed of social talents and insinuating address. He professed democratic principles, and had managed to insinuate himself into the confidence of the advanced politicians.

Tone, when visiting the town, had been particularly attracted by him. This man was arrested in the autumn of '91 for a debt of £200, and Russell was induced to go bail for him, though advised not to do so. The consequence was that he was left to pay the debt, and, not having the means otherwise, was under the necessity of selling his commission.

He had now no means of support; but having some interest, by the end of the year he was made a magistrate, and obtained the situation of Seneschal to the Manor Court of Dungannon. In about nine months he felt himself bound, from conscientious feelings, to resign his situation, as he had differed from his fellow-magistrates concerning the mode of deciding questions between Catholics and Protestant Dissenters.

He then returned to Belfast, where he was indebted to the kindness of a friend for support, who, after entertaining him for a considerable time, procured him the appointment of Librarian to the Belfast Library. The salary was very small, and it is difficult to understand how he contrived to live on it; perhaps he made something by literary pursuits. He wrote for the *Northern Star*, and other periodicals of similar politics. He kept up the old intimacy with his former associates, among whom was H. J. M'Cracken. He also occasionally visited Dublin. Tone mentions a Council in Dublin, Jan. 23rd, 1793, at which were present Jas. Plunket, Ed. Sweetman, and Thos. Russell, who agreed to a strong address to the nation on the subject of Catholic Emancipation.

VIEW OF BELFAST FROM CROMAC WOOD, c. 1780.
(From an unpublished proof engraving in British Museum.)

In May, 1795, Russell, on the occasion of Tone's approaching departure for America, accompanied the latter to Emmett's villa, where Tone's project with respect to France was communicated, and sanctioned by Emmett and Russell. Tone proposed, after taking his family to America, to proceed to France.

Russell returned to Belfast, and was followed by Tone and family on their way to the United States, and during their visit numerous meetings of those whom we may now term the conspirators took place.

Russell was arrested in Sept., 1796, as were also some others in Belfast. They were taken to Dublin, where Russell remained in confinement till '99, when he was sent with the other State prisoners to Fort George, where they remained till 1802. In virtue of a compact made with the Government, they were, in June of that year, permitted to leave the country.

Russell's father died in 1792, leaving three sons and one daughter. The latter was fifteen years older than Russell, and in 1802 she was in very destitute circumstances. Mary M'Cracken, ever ready to succour the unfortunate, proposed to ask the former friends of

Russell to subscribe a yearly sum sufficient for her support, never doubting that they would respond to the appeal. As there had just been a collection taken up for the prisoners at Fort George, she was advised to delay her application, which she did for some months, and was then only able to raise what sufficed for immediate relief. Owing to the delay, the application was made only a short time before Russell returned to Ireland, and she almost got into serious trouble, for a person who got sight of the list of subscribers gave information that she was raising money for the purchase of arms. When this became known, she was advised to go out of the way for a time, but refused to do so, and was not further troubled.

The State prisoners, on their release, were sent to the Continent, and Russell, with some of the others, made his way to Paris. He resided there with an old lady who had settled in that city. Russell's brother, Capt. J. Russell, visited him in Paris, and the Captain's son-in-law, Hamilton, was also there in October. About the same time Robert Emmett arrived at Paris from Amsterdam, where he had been visiting his brother. He was preparing for the rebellion which took place the following year. Russell agreed to take part in it. "They determined to listen to proposals which began to be broached at this time, in a mysterious manner, by persons of rank and influence hitherto supposed to be covert friends of the United Irish system, both at home and abroad."

Robert Emmett arrived in Dublin in November; Hamilton soon followed. Shortly afterwards he was sent back to Paris to bring Russell over. J. Hope was sent by Emmett to a friend for a bill of £100. The greater part of this was given to Hamilton for his and Russell's expenses.

Russell was appointed to the chief command in the North, with the title of General. He paid a brief visit there on his first arrival, and afterwards spent a few weeks in Dublin. He again started northward, accompanied by Hope; Hamilton also co-operated with him. Some proclamations were distributed. Russell met secretly with the Co. Antrim General and some others of those who had been concerned in the former rebellion, and went among the people; but all efforts were fruitless; the people would not rise, and nothing could be done. Russell concealed himself as he could, going from one place to another in Counties Antrim and Down till he should be able to make his way back to Dublin. Once, while on his way from one place of concealment to another, which was the house of a weaver in the Misses M'Cracken's employment, he ventured into Belfast and met with the two ladies at their office, where they awaited him. He also wrote Mary several notes, one of them asking for £10, for payment of which she was to draw upon ——. A woman, in whose house he had found refuge, wrote to Miss M'C. in 1843, when she was procuring information for Dr. Madden :—

"   .   .   .   . All who knew Russell, knew him to be enthusiastic in the cause in which he had embarked, but few knew so well as I did how incredulous he was as to the hopelessness of it at that time. At first he would not believe any of the communications he got from Belfast; he said it was impossible; but when he was assured from the newspapers that Emmett was a prisoner, he was convinced. He immediately resolved to go to Dublin, as, he said, he was certain if there he would find means to release him. . . . You yourself provided the money that took him there. My husband got two men in Bangor to take him round in an open boat. He gave them five guineas. . . . ."

He thus got to Drogheda, and from there to Dublin, where he was shortly afterwards taken prisoner, and sent to Downpatrick for trial.

Hamilton, after wandering about for some time, and concealing himself with difficulty, was at length taken, and detained in prison till 1806, but was never tried.

Russell was tried in Downpatrick on the 20th October, 1803. His trial lasted from 10 a.m. till 8 p.m., and he was executed the following day. So confident had he been of the success of the cause, that he had a letter in his pocket written in case he should fall in battle, in which he said—"No doubt the nation would support his sister."

In a letter to Mary M'Cracken from Russell, a few days before his trial, he wrote—"To the more than friendship I owe you and your sister it is impossible to be sufficiently grateful. . . . What I was engaged in with the immortal hero who has fallen, is considered as perhaps wild; yet I *could show*, and it *will be showed*, that the failure was alone surprising. . . . My intention was to have employed no counsel; but Mr Ramsay informs me that the other men, whose trials are to come on afterwards, may be benefited by the cross-examination in mine, which is the first. . . ."

Mary M'Cracken made every possible effort to save Russell. She went among her own and his friends to procure money for his defence; but, in the short time at her disposal, was unable to collect the large sum required, and was obliged herself to raise the greater portion, in part from her own resources, and in part by borrowing on her own responsibility.

Concerning this she wrote :—

"   .   .   . but the fact is, that what I did on that occasion was neither entitled to praise or blame; it was merely obeying a call to duty of such sacred importance that no person similarly situated could have resisted ; for how was it possible to shrink back when told that human lives were at stake, which my exertions might be instrumental in saving, and that no other person dared make the attempt? Would it not have been to incur the endurance of self-reproach through life? And though I had never seen or known any of the party but Mr. Russell, yet even had he not been of the number, I would have felt it my bounden duty to go forward in the business, and, once having undertaken it, there was no question of drawing back from pecuniary risk . . . . to save such a life as Russell's—one of such importance to the country—who, in the changes that were still expected, would not have used every exertion to stop the effusion of blood and to prevent all possible suffering? Who would have hesitated to supply the means when within their reach? There was then no time for deliberation. As if Providence favoured the plan, we had received near £90 that day from a man whom we had sent to sell muslins through the country, business in Dublin being quite at a stand? Thus situated, we were led on alike from a sense of duty and of inclination. I say we, as my sister and I had but one heart, though she always kept in the background and left me to act—frequently on her suggestions—although considerably my senior in years and much my superior in understanding. I had also a dear enthusiastic friend, a sister of ——, to stimulate me, had it been necessary. Pardon my egotism, as it is alike due to truth to disclaim either undue praise or blame. . . . "

Russell has been described as a tall, handsome man, with military bearing, fascinating address and manners, and a strong sense of religion. He was a member of the Church of England.

Mary M'Cracken once remarked to her brother, when Russell was present—"If you fail, you will lose your lives." He replied—"Whether we fail or succeed, we expect to be the first to fall." Russell, interrupting, said—"But of what consequence are our lives, or the lives of a few individuals, compared to the liberty and happiness of Ireland."

Miss Russell was quite destitute. She tried to earn something by teaching young children, some pitying friends paying her rent, while Mary M'Cracken sent her contributions from time to time. She lived for a time with her niece, Mrs. Hamilton, whose husband had taken part in the rebellion; but she too was in difficulties, till, in 1821, Miss M'Cracken, with the assistance of a friend, procured her admission into Drumcondra Retreat. In her latter years she received assistance from her niece's son, who, in a distant land, was pursuing an honourable career, a loyal subject, and a faithful servant of the Government against which his uncle and his father had struggled. By remittances sent through Mary M'Cracken he ministered to the comforts of his mother and aunt.

Mary M'Cracken continued to take an interest in many of those who had been concerned in the rebellion, and to those who needed it she was ever ready to afford help.

A number had emigrated to the United States, either to escape being taken, to follow near relatives who had been under the necessity of leaving the country, or because their business had become deranged from the troubles of the time.

One family in Co. Antrim, who had been deeply implicated, and had suffered proportionably, had been by that means brought into acquaintanceship with her. On one occasion the youngest, a lad of 15, had gone on a night expedition with some young men. From youth or heedlessness, he neglected to blacken his face. He was recognised, taken, and hanged. His mother was a widow.

An elder brother escaped to the United States, where he went into business and made some money, which, at his death, was left to his relatives in Ireland, Mary M'Cracken being appointed executor. It was a troublesome and tedious business, for the money came in by degrees, and, as time went on, the legatees became more numerous, and the sums smaller. They were of the farming class, and the following extract will show that the land question had then, as now, complications, and that the position of a go-between in money matters is by no means desirable :—

"1st Dec., 1829.

"DEAR SIR,—Recd. £349 15s. od. from ——. The remittance is come in very good time for some of the legatees, who would otherwise have been much distressed, as from a new regulation adopted by some of the landlords here, the poor tenants are obliged to pay the half-yearly rent in less than a month after it falls due, which very few of them are prepared for. Of course they had become very impatient. . . .

"M. A. M."

The next shows how Tone's *Life* was received by some :—

" . . . . Frank had got Tone's book a few days before I heard from you, and is in great delight with it. We only got looking over a little of it, as he lent the 1st vol. as soon as he had finished it, and is deep in the 2nd. There are various opinions respecting the work ; some consider it trifling, and others find fault with the author for being so great an egotist, and so vain, without considering that it was not intended for the world, but for his wife and children, to whom nothing would appear trifling that respected one so dear to them ; and what could he have written about that would have interested them half so much as what concerned himself ?"

Mary M'Cracken was such a thorough patriot, and had been so closely connected with political affairs at a time when dissatisfaction with the English Government was very general, that it is interesting to discover her feelings with respect to such things years after the country had settled down in quietness after the sad times of rebellion :—

" 28th Oct., 1835.

" MY DEAR ———,—I send you with this the *Whig* of Monday, that you may see an account of the Lord Lieutenant's visit to Belfast. . . . . All present seemed quite delighted with all they saw and heard, with very few, if any, exceptions. Some indeed complained of the smell of the meat, others of being hungry ; but I was too much gratified with the present to feel any annoyance—not merely with the gaiety of the scene, but in looking forty years back, and in thinking, too, of those who were gone, and how delighted they would have been at the political changes that have taken place—which could not possibly, in their day, have been anticipated by peaceable means—and of the improved prospects of their country, now that the English in general, and particularly the present Ministry, have such just feelings towards Ireland and Irish people. . . . [paper torn] about a year later the last to assist in its completion. and even five years after, Russell was still confident of its ultimate success. . . . . It was a pity that Paine's *Age of Reason* had so soon succeeded his *Rights of Man*, as notwithstanding the latter had much effect on many of natural good understandings, but not in the two last-mentioned, and many who had been led astray by the infidel publication recovered from their delusion.

" And now a better day has dawned. The old prophecy—' That these countries should never be well ruled until a virgin queen should come to the throne '—seems to be realised, as there have been greater improvements in the laws since she came to the throne than for a much longer period before ; and she is so truly amiable and feminine that she is universally beloved."

" May, 1832.

" . . . . Only think of the Reform Bill being lost after all, when every one was sure of it being passed ! It is confidently affirmed that Wellington is to be made Minister in place of Lord Grey, whose party have all resigned, and that there is to be a reform notwithstanding (no doubt a partial one). One can hardly wish (much as reform is to be desired) that Wellington should have the credit of it yet. As Harry used to say—' If the good be done, it is no matter who gets the credit of it.'

" The people here are much more interested in the matter than I expected they would be—nothing what they are in England ; but all, I hope, will in the end turn out for the best."

To those who from this period could look back half-a-century, the peaceful and settled state of the country must have compared favourably with its condition as indicated by the following note written early in the century :—

" MY DEAR MRS. M'CRACKEN,—The pleasure we experienced last night when seated round your social table beguiled us to so late an hour that we narrowly escaped witnessing the horrors of a guard-room. We were stopped at the Bridge for some time ; but my father pleaded so earnestly to allow the ladies to pass, that a sentinel (a countryman of my mother's) permitted us to go, with the remark—' It would indeed be a shocking thing for young women to spend the night in a guard-house.' We joined him with some fervour you may suppose, and drove off, leaving my father and George with the soldiers. They followed in an hour. . . . .   "———,

" Mount Pottinger."

It seemed best not to interrupt the political record, so that we must now go back a little. In the year 1813 Mary M'Cracken suffered from a tedious and painful complaint, which had lasted many months, and in the summer of that year she was advised to go to a Spa for its relief. She chose Ballynahinch as being the nearest, although informed that some other might be more speedily efficacious ; but she wished to be where she could be quickly summoned home, should necessity arise, as her mother was then aged and in precarious health (her father had died in 1803), and business anxieties caused her concern.

She returned with her health almost re-established. Her mother died the following year, and not long afterwards the sisters quitted business, on which occasion she thus writes :—

"MY DEAR MRS. ———,—I hope you do not impute my silence and seeming neglect to unkindness or indifference. I have, indeed, been daily thinking of you, and reproaching myself for not writing to you these several months past; but my time has been so entirely occupied, and my mind so perplexed in winding up our affairs, that we may quit a business in which all who have been engaged these two years past have lost heavily, that I could not command a tranquil half-hour in the four-and-twenty, and now that we are getting clear by degrees, I trust that the little which we got by my dear mother will enable us to pay all we owe, which is a great comfort, even if we should have nothing left. Doubtless, if riches would have contributed to our ultimate happiness, they would have been bestowed on us; and while Providence is pleased to bless us with health and a capacity for industry, we should be thankful and contented; but the sphere of a woman's industry is so confined, and so few roads lie open to her, and those so thorny, it is difficult to fix on any. . . ."

In a printed bill setting forth the grievances of the weavers, but undated, the following passage occurs :—

"But to the great credit of the Miss M'Crackens, they kept the set on full six months after the rest took it off; and if they were under the necessity of paying them in notes, they always paid the discount with it."

The elder Miss M'Cracken was a good housekeeper in every sense of the word, and their orphan niece was becoming able to assist; so that household occupations did not afford to the younger sister scope for her irrepressible energy. She soon became engaged in what was from this time forth her life work—labouring for the poor.

She thus wrote :—

"MY DEAR ———,—Ever since I received yours of 7th I have daily intended writing to you, but was obliged to delay it from day to day owing to want of time. I have allowed my out-of-door avocations to increase so much, that I have less command of time now than when I was occupied with business. I am not sure whether that is quite right or not. I fear that undertaking too many things prevents me from doing anything as it ought to be; but somehow one gets entangled unawares, and cannot draw back, particularly if they think that they are usefully employed."

Of charitable institutions, the one with which she was connected from her earliest years, and which she continued to visit as long as strength permitted, was the "Old Poor-house," or "Belfast Charitable Society." The building of this house was commenced in 1771, and of it she wrote when more than 90 years of age :—

"There were no men in Belfast esteemed more highly than my two uncles, and I believe they were very deserving of the high opinion the public entertained of them. They were both very charitable; but their feelings were exercised in different ways. . . . . My uncle Robert was one year younger than my uncle Harry. He projected our 'Old Poorhouse,' the first in Belfast, for a shelter for the poor. Before that time, rich men who were charitable would leave large sums to be distributed to the poor by their clergymen, lists of which are now to be seen hung round in the hall of our Old Poorhouse at the head of Donegall Street. My uncle Robert paid his last visit to it, when unable to walk, in a sedan chair. From its erection, as long as health was spared him, it had been his constant study to promote the comfort of the inmates in every respect. The husband and wife were not separated, but had curtains round their bed; and he studied to give them variety of food, and in various ways to promote an increase to the means of support, one of which was a shower-bath, and anyone, by paying one guinea a-year, might use it whenever they pleased. The room that is now the girls' school-room was then a ball-room, in which there was a ball once a-month, and for some time concerts once a-fortnight, by the band of the 1st Volunteer Company; but one of the members having died of consumption, which was attributed to his playing on a wind instrument, the music was discontinued, but the dancing for some time went on.

"My father had a garden in the neighbourhood, and as soon as I could walk, my mother took me with her to the garden, and we often visited the Poorhouse.

"Bab was my most beloved cousin, nine months younger than I. She was very benevolent, and most usefully so. . . . . About our Old Poorhouse children, she said she never was muffling her own children on a Sunday morning that she did not think of the Poorhouse little girls. At that period there was but one public collection in the year for our old Poorhouse, and the girls had no additional clothing to what they wore in the house in winter. It was scarcely so much, for in the house they had a bedgown which came up to the neck; but in going to the Meeting-house or Church they wore a frock made of linen, woven in the house, and dyed a drab colour, the sleeves of which did not cover the elbow, and did not come above the shoulder. All the additional clothing they had was a small single calico shawl. The way Bab undertook to obtain funds was to go about asking only for the small sum of 10d., which she thought nobody would refuse; but many might not wish to have their names for a small sum when the one next it might perhaps be

O

for large, and those who wished to give liberally might give as much as they pleased in the names of all their family or any names they chose. There was only one man in all Belfast who refused, and the whole amounted to £9. The thickest and strongest green stuff which could be got was purchased and cut out. The frocks had long sleeves down to the wrists, and they were made up by various young ladies. It was suggested that as straw bonnets were expensive, it would be better to have the girls taught to plat the straw and make the bonnets, which would be a means of support for them when they should leave the house. We followed this advice, and found that it answered very well."

The following, written in 1838, tells of her long connection with another Institution, and also gives her ideas on a much-disputed question :—

" MY DEAR SIR,—I delayed replying to the message you left for me with my niece until I should have an opportunity of reading your sermon, which I procured on my return from Bangor, and have perused twice very carefully ; and I regret to find, that although there are many parts of your sermon in which I perfectly agree with you, yet there are others which appear in such a very different point of view to you from what they do to me,

BATTLE OF ANTRIM, 7TH JUNE, 1798.

that I could not conscientiously undertake to disseminate the work. A variety of circumstances contribute to the formation of our opinions, and when they become matured and confirmed for a number of years they are not easily overturned. There are some things, however, in which, though we disagree, our opinions lead nearly to the same results. Believing, as I do, in the immediate superintendence of an infinitely wise and good Providence, I must so far acknowledge that monarchs reign by Divine appointment so long as they are permitted to reign ; and though I think that there are many evils under which we live, I do not think we are thereby authorised to take up arms against the Government, but consider it a duty to wait with patience till the great Ruler of all events shall bring about a change through the progress of public opinion.

" I have been visiting the Lancasterian School for the last twenty-five years, generally once a-week, and I find the children taught there for the last two or three years much better acquainted with the Scriptures than the scholars of any former period. The master is certainly a very superior man, whose heart and soul is devoted to the business ; and so well is the school conducted, that, although they have enough of Catholic Bibles and Testaments, yet the Catholic children, when sent to the press to take books for themselves, generally take the Protestant translation of their own accord, and there never is a word of disagreement among them. The extracts they read at the schools, should they see no more of the Scriptures there, would tend to excite their curiosity to read the whole. Those whose parents and guardians permit, have access to the entire volume ; and I remember when pious Protestants would have considered it a profanation of the sacred volume to see it made a common school-book of, and our religious feelings were quite shocked to hear it all read and half the words spelled. It was required to be read in a serious and solemn manner, as if felt and understood."

In the Famine year, 1847, an association was formed for the relief of the poor, and an industrial school for girls established, being "the first Ragged School in Ireland." The Frederick Street building (then unused, except for the Sunday School) was granted for the purpose. In the twentieth report, dated 17th March, 1867, is written :—

"We have to record this year the death of a beloved friend and associate in our work, Miss M'Cracken, who was connected with the school from its foundation, and whose place was never vacant at our weekly meetings as long as she was able to attend.

"We know not how to speak of the worth that no words can express, and the loss too little felt, perhaps because it came so gradually. But though the loss may never be repaired, we trust she has left a precious legacy that will never perish from this place of her habitation, in the memory of a life so rich in all good works, and a spirit so full of love.

"When we would think of 'those things that are pure, and lovely, and of good report,' let us remember her who was so long among us, her ardent charity, her large and tender sympathy, her sweet humility and self-forgetfulness."

In the forty-seventh report of the Belfast Ladies' Clothing Society, 1867—"the late Miss M'Cracken was a most energetic collector of its funds."

For the Destitute Sick Society she collected, and sometimes took part in visiting and distributing ; but she used to say the ladies would not let her visit, for she would give too much, and would tell of cases in which she had been imposed upon. It was a hard trial for her to refuse any who seemed in distress.

She was one of an association to prevent the employment of climbing-boys in chimney-sweeping, and was long a member of an anti-slavery society. She abstained from sugar for many years, which must have been a great privation, as she was fond of it. But it would be tedious to enumerate all the public associations in which she took part, and her private charities were innumerable. Besides giving freely to people in necessitous circumstances, she collected money for various private cases of distress. There was one family for whom she was constrained again and again to solicit aid, yet so disagreeable was the task, that she has said she felt it sometimes a reprieve when told that the person for whom she had asked was not at home. She was for many years a total abstainer, and recommended the practice to others, particularly the young ; but, tolerant in that as in everything else, she would not seek to prohibit stimulants to elderly people who had been accustomed to use them, and thought they were required. To such people she would even, with old-fashioned hospitality, offer them.

She took an interest in everything which she believed to be for the good of her fellow-creatures, and all that might serve to promote the welfare of her native land.

Mr. Edward Bunting, the collector and publisher of Irish tunes, had come as a lad to Belfast, where he long resided. He was a close friend of her younger brother, and very intimate in the family. She warmly encouraged him in his work, both when, at the close of last century, he was entrusted with the charge of a publication of Irish music, and at a subsequent period when, on his own account, he travelled about the country collecting tunes, which he afterwards arranged and published. She regarded this preservation from oblivion of an evidence of an ancient civilisation as a patriotic work.

For many years she was accustomed to spend the mornings in some out-of-door occupation—collecting for some charity, attending some meeting, visiting the poor, or in paying friendly visits. After dinner, she took a nap in her chair by the fire, a position she much preferred to lying on a sofa. She would awake refreshed, and her evenings were frequently occupied in letter-writing, as she had a large correspondence.

She was, however, always ready to engage in friendly converse, for she greatly enjoyed social intercourse, or even to attend a public meeting until a late period of life. She was light and active, enjoyed good health, and was able to take a good deal of exercise.

She was a regular attendant on the ordinances of religion, had been brought up in connection with the Third Presbyterian Congregation, and the greater part of her life took part in the services and engaged in all the charitable work of the congregation. For a short time she attended a nearer church, but impaired hearing and failing strength soon caused that to be given up.

She was a constant reader of the Scriptures, enjoying most the devotional portions and the simple gospel narratives. In her latter years, when memory was somewhat failing, she seemed always to turn to that portion of John's gospel contained between the 14th and 17th chapters. She frequently spoke of them, and of the parable of the "good Samaritan," who, though his religion was mingled with error, acted up to the little light he had, as the better-instructed Jews failed to do, and was commended for his love and active benevolence.

She taught for many years in a Sunday School held in Frederick Street Schoolhouse, which was conducted on the system of being unconnected with any church, and having teachers of different Protestant denominations. She even continued her attendance for some time after removing to a considerable distance.

A Roman Catholic servant who lived in the house for many years she taught to read and write, and when sufficiently far advanced she bought her a Douay Bible, and every evening one or two chapters were read, each with her own Bible.

In personal habits she was scrupulously clean, but indifferent about her dress, unwilling to spend money on it, and gave it little thought.

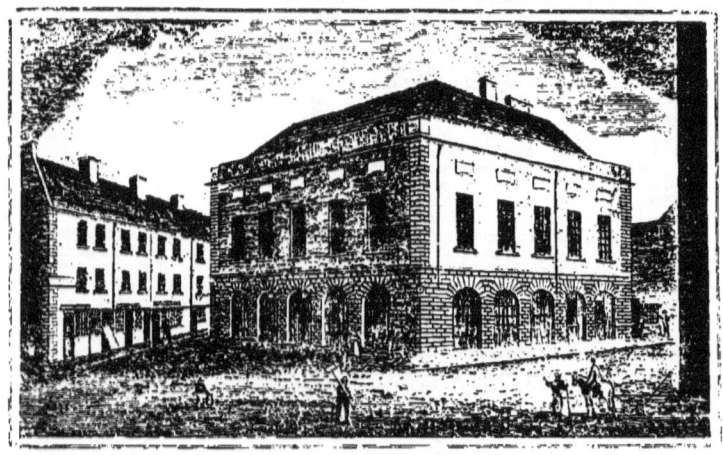

OLD EXCHANGE ROOMS (NOW BELFAST BANK).
Where the Trial of Henry Joy M'Cracken took place. (*From "Town Book of Belfast."*)

She liked to read the newspaper, and always spent some time in doing so, but for other reading she had little leisure. When she did read a novel or hear one read, it was to others as great a treat as the book to hear her comments, how she entered into the story and discussed the characters with such thorough enjoyment, such child-like feeling of reality. In her later years she used to relate anecdotes of family and local incidents, and reminiscences of her youthful days; these, told in her lively and pleasant manner, were listened to with pleasure. Sometimes, but more rarely, and usually when she had only one hearer, she would speak of the graver and sadder events in which she had been concerned, but evidently with such sorrowful remembrance that a listener had not the heart to urge her to continue the theme, intensely interesting though it might be.

She was accustomed to say that people ought not to pride themselves on their ancestors, and should not be valued for what their forefathers had been or done, but only for what they themselves are, and would quote the lines on the moon—

> " I with borrowed lustre shine ;
> What you see is none of mine."

Nevertheless, she took most unmistakable pride and pleasure in some of the doings of her ancestors. The way in which she used to relate anything which gave evidence of a generous and unselfish description was not to be forgotten by those who heard her.

She had naturally a quick and hasty temper, though evidence of this was rarely seen ; but even when at an advanced age, if a helpless person were wronged, or an animal cruelly treated, it was startling to see how her eye would flash, and to hear her hot, indignant words.

She had a talent for figures, which developed early, and it is recorded that she surprised older people by doing difficult sums before she was able to write down the figures. Sufficient money passed through her hands to keep this talent in exercise. She retained her fondness for calculations, but seemed to dwell on the details, and did not appear to take a mental grasp of a financial affair in its entirety. She would take into consideration a sum of money, reckon several things it would do, and then apparently conclude it might be sufficient for all. This may, however, have been only when she was past her prime ; but she was so much more able for a number of things than many younger women, that people were apt to forget she had come to an age when mental vigour usually declines, particularly as she herself felt the elasticity of youth. An old and intimate friend rallied her on this subject in one of his letters in 1841—"We had a good laugh at your expense in reading that part of your epistle where you say ' *we* middle-aged women.' This for an old lady of 70 years is pretty well (meaning yourself). Indeed, you are so strong and healthy, I don't wonder at your claiming the title of middle-aged, though the years on your head are against the assumption."

Her decay was very gradual. She was compelled by degrees to give up her accustomed occupations, till at last she was confined to the house. Walk for walking's sake she would not. As she became unable for other work, she took up the occupation of knitting. Her sight was wonderfully good ; her hearing was so much impaired as to prevent her taking part in general conversation ; but she was always able to converse with one person comfortably for both. She delighted in seeing a large party round the table, and when a laugh went round, she with beaming face and happy smile would join in the mirth, and sometimes say—"Well, I don't know what you are laughing at, but I like to see you enjoying yourselves."

In the autumn of 1865 she had an attack of bronchitis, from which she recovered, but mind and body had become weak. She faded peacefully and gently away, apparently contented and happy, without weariness or pain, until, after some hours of unconsciousness, she breathed her last on the 26th of July, 1866, having completed her 96th year on the 8th of the month.

It was supposed by many that Miss M'Cracken possessed many interesting documents connected with the Rebellion. This belief was not shared by those who had heard her lament the loss of some relics of that sad time.

Still, it was disappointing to find, on examining her papers, an almost total absence of anything of the sort. This is accounted for by the fact that any she had formerly had she had entrusted to people who proposed to write a history of the time, or given to relatives who she believed had a better right to them.

She lent some manuscripts to a man named M'Skimin, who had written a history of Carrickfergus, and proposed writing a more pretentious work. Except perhaps in some contributions to one of the ephemeral periodicals of the day, the papers were not used, as the proposed book never was published, and they were not returned to Miss M'Cracken, though she made frequent applications for them, till she lost sight of the man. It is an evidence of her liberality and toleration that she knew M'Skimin to be a strong opponent of the political party with which she was connected. Indeed, James Hope, a United Irishman who knew him (both were weavers, and mainly self-educated men), described him as almost a monomaniac on the subject.

There were other persons who obtained documents from her, among whom was Mr. Teeling, who wrote a narrative, and also articles which were published in pamphlets or periodicals. To Dr. Madden she gave what remained ; he also obtained some of those Mr. Teeling had, and she procured for him much information from others.

Towards the close of Miss Mary Ann M'Cracken's life, friends requested of her that she would write her remembrances. She endeavoured to comply with their repeated solicitations ; but, while remembering past events, and able to relate them, she had from failing memory lost the power of composing a sustained narrative, and never got beyond preliminaries. Besides, little of what she wrote was of the kind desired, for she was the least egotistical of human beings, and could not be made to understand that it was her very own individual experiences in which her friends were especially interested.

Talking lately with a friend, we regretted that the request had not been made sooner ; but most probably it would have been equally without avail, as hers was a busy life. As long as she was able she was constantly employed, principally in works of charity, and a great part of her evenings or other spare time was occupied in letter-writing.

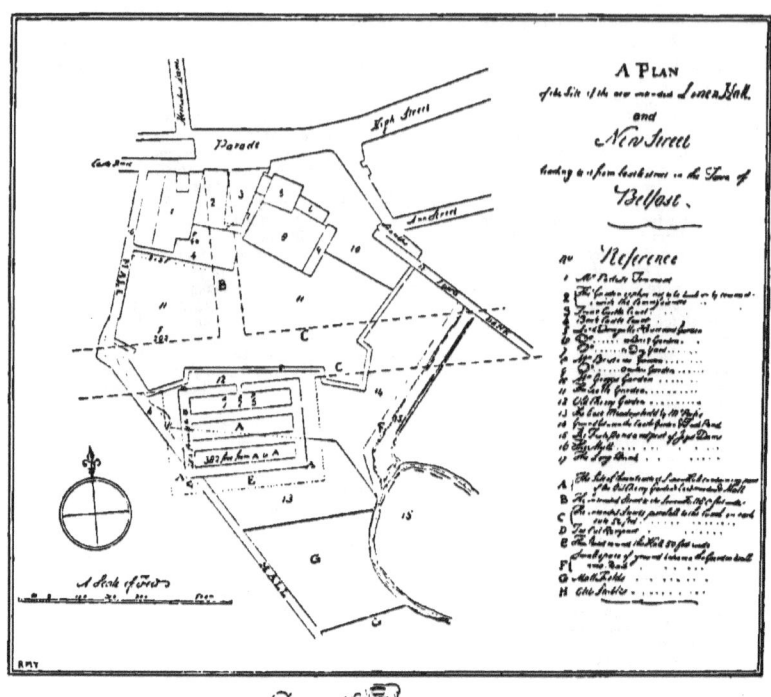

MAP ON THE ORIGINAL LEASE OF THE WHITE LINEN HALL, BELFAST, SURVEYED IN THE YEAR 1783.
Reduced from the copy in the possession of E. H. CLARKE, Esq.

GENERAL OWEN ROE O'NEILL.

A Narrative

of the Wars of 1641

by

Friar O'Mellan, O.S.F., of Brantry, Co. Tyrone,

Chaplain to Sir Phelim O'Neill.

Translated from the Original Irish MS. in possession of Viscount O'Neill,
by Robert Macadam, Belfast.

With Notes by John O'Donovan, LL.D. (J. O'D.),
and J. W. Hanna (J. W. H.),

and now first printed from the Copy in the Grainger Collection,
Belfast Free Public Library.

With additional Notes by John Salmon (J. S.).

The Irish words collated with O'Curry's transcript in R.I.A. by the
Rev. Denis Murphy, S.J., LL.D.

Edited by Robert M. Young, B.A.

BENBURB CASTLE.

Friar O'Mellan's Narrative of the Wars of 1641.

BRANTRY FRIARY.

HE Friary of Brantry, so often alluded to in the following manuscript, O'Mellan the author being one of its members, was situate in a small territory of that name in the townland of Gort-tamlaght-na-muck, now simply called Gort, lying on the south-east of the Barony of Dungannon, in the County of Tyrone. The larger territory of Munterbirne* lies to the south. The name Brantry† is still preserved as that of a new district parish formed out of the parishes of Clonfecle, Aghaloo, and Carnteel. Gort itself formed part of the Manor of Caslan, granted to Tirlagh O'Neale of that place by James I., 9th December, in the 12th year of his reign. The principal part of this estate was afterwards under the Act of Settlement passed to Lord Caulfield. In that townland, about four miles south-west of Dungannon and three miles east of Carnteel, in the bosom of an almost perfect amphitheatre, surrounded by vast hills to the east, south, and west, and within the last 80 years having a dense wood cresting the north, lies the "Friary Lough," shaped like a rose leaf, where, on a knoll or natural breastwork a few perches south of the lake, and lying under and sheltered by Gort Hill, stood the old Friary. Banished from their parent house in Armagh, the expelled friars, under the protection of the O'Neills of Castletown, chose this lovely and secluded spot as their new homestead, and erected a house with proper dormitories, chapel, &c., as also a small brewery at a little distance, the site of which is still called the Brewery Field. To the west stretch the hills of Carrowcashel, where tradition points out a ravine, in which, in periods of great persecution, the Friars celebrated Mass. To the east, in the townland of Drumnamonless, is a high hill called Stoney-Batter, running precipitately to the lough, covered with boulders of freestone and immense tracts of wild gorse ; while southward is Gort Hill, terraced to the top, a plateau crowned with an earthen fort, flat and bald-like, from which apparently it derived the name, Sliabh-na-maol, the bald or *moiled* mountain. It is far and away the highest hill in the district, and on a clear day a circuit of forty miles can be embraced by the naked eye, taking in Lough Neagh, and portions of the counties of Down, Armagh, Fermanagh, and the mountains of Donegal and Derry. Tradition reports that when the friars were at length suddenly compelled to abandon their new home, they sank their most costly and sacred vessels in the lough, and, since that, various but fruitless attempts have been made by the neighbouring peasantry to recover these buried treasures. On one occasion a peasant lad fished up a silver chalice, and numerous other relics of antiquity have been found from time to time. It is said that after the Cromwellian dispersion the surviving friars, with new brethren, returned to the old house of their adoption.

J. W. H.

* Now Minterburn.—EDITOR.
† Brantry takes its name from ꝏꞃꝭꜿ, stinking, putrid, and ꞇꝭꞃ, land, country, region. There is a Brantry in County Donegal, and another in County Clare.—J. S.

SPEED'S MAP OF IRELAND, 1627.

HE chiefs formed a plan to seize upon all the October, 1641. fortified towns and strong places of the English and Scotch throughout Ireland in one night. The day fixed was Friday, being the last day of the moon. First, as to Dublin, there went there from the province of Ulster, Lord Enniskillen (Conor Maguire M'Brian M'Conor, etc.), and Hugh Og M'Brian M'Hugh Og M'Hugh M'Shane Boy (ᴠᴜɪᴠᴇ), and M'Mahon and Rory O'More from Upper Orior (Oɪⴌᴇᴀɪ ᴜᴀᴄᴛᴀɪᴀᴄ). There were likewise some from Meath, from Leinster, and from Munster, &c. But the plot was betrayed by Owen Connolly:[1] the gate of Dublin, (Aᴛ ᴄʟɪᴀᴄ) was closed, the city bells were rung, and the houses were searched. M'Mahon and the Earl of Enniskillen[2] were taken: the rest made their escape.

Sir Felim O'Neill was chosen General in the province of Ulster, that is, M'Turlough M'Henry Og M'Henry M'Shane M'Quin M'Henry

---

1. In the House of Commons, Nov., 1641, it was resolved:—"That Owen Connolly, who discovered this Great Treason in Ireland, shall have 500l. presently paid him, and 200l. per annum Pension untill Provision be made of Inheritance of a greater Value, and to be recommended to the Lord Lieutenant of Ireland for some Preferment there." (See Nalson's *Impartial Collection*, 1682, ii. p. 524.)—J. S.

2. Maguire was only *Baron* of Enniskillen. (See Carte's *Ormonde*, i. p. 156, and Nalson's *Impartial Collection*, ii. p. 888.) M'Mahon was executed, 22nd Nov., 1644; Maguire, 20th Feb., 1645. (See Lingard's *England*, viii. p. 41.) Before suffering at Tyburn they escaped from the Tower of London, and were in hiding for some time in Drury Lane, where they were re-taken. (See, for their adventures, the British Officer's *Irish Warr of 1641*, pp. 11, 12: and Sanderson's *Compleat History of the Life and Raigne of King Charles*, p. 768.)—J. S.

M'Owen, &c. He took Charlemont (Seplimonc) and the Governor of the town, Lord Caulfield, and all who were there from him downwards.[3] Dungannon ('Oungeannunn) was taken, and its Captain, namely Parsons, and all the inhabitants from him down, by Randal M'Donnell (Mac'Ooṁnaill), that is, the son of Ferdoragh (Mac an Fip ooṗéac) M'Owen, &c., and by Patrick Ⅿoɴaṗṗa (the gloomy) O'Donnelly.[4] The great garrison of Mountjoy (Mⴟⵏɼeoᵹ)[5] was seized, with all the soldiers, by Captain Turlough ᵹⵏaṁóa (grim) O'Quin, and Lord Caulfield's Castle in Ballydonnelly (baile i oonn-ᵹoile) was taken by Patrick Ⅿoɴaṗṗa (the gloomy) O'Donnelly. The manor house of Moneymore[6] (Mⴟⵏ́ne móṗ), that is, Sir John Clotworthy's town, was seized on by the Governor Cormac O'Hagan, and Mr.   's[7] (Fuiṗleiṗ) town, in Killeter (Coill ⵏoḋḋaṗaⵏᵹ), that is, Ballyscullion (baile iⵏ ṫ́pⴟalⵏⵏⵏ), was taken by Felim ᵹⵏaṁóa (the grim or morose) O'Neill M'Felim the dumb (balḃ).[8] The garrison of Liscallaghan (Lⵏoṗ ceallaḋaⵏ) was taken

Oct. 23, 1641.

. . . Donnell M'Shane of the curses (ⵏa mallaḋt)[9] and by . . . and the English soldiers who were in it were captured. The strong garrison town of Tandragee (Con ṗe ᵹaeiⵏṫ) was taken by Patrick Og O'Hanlon, and he was killed himself the same day.[10] Newry (an ⵏⴟ̇baⵏ) was seized by Con Magennis (Mac'oⵏᵹⴟṗa), that is, the son of Lord Iveagh (Ibeaḋaḋ), and also the great castle.[11] Dundalk (ṗṗaḋboⵏle ounoelᵹan) was taken by the Lieutenant General Brian M'Hugh Boy (aoò buⵏòe) O'Neill M'Turlough M'Henry Na Garthan (ⵏa ᵹaṗḋan) and by the clan of Hugh (Clannaboy).

<hr/>

3. Sir Phelim O'Neill was on a visit of hospitality to Lord Caulfield's sent at Charlemont when he seized it. (See Carte's *Ormonde*, i. p. 172.) On all subsequent occasions O'Mellan calls Charlemont by its *Irish* name, Aḋaò aⵏ oa ḋaṗaò, *i.e.*, "the field of the two weirs." —J. S. Some vestiges of the old earthworks are still visible.—EDITOR.

4. Carte (*Ormonde*, i. p. 172) and all the later historians represent Sir Phelim O'Neill as seizing Dungannon himself.—J. S.

5. Captain Blaney commanded the garrison at the time. (See Carte's *Ormonde*, i. p. 172.) Mⴟⵏⵏ́peoᵹ represents "Mountjoy" moderately well. O'Clery (*Life of Hugh O'Donnell*, pp. 232, 278) makes an attempt at this English name, in a combination of Irish and Roman characters —Mⴟⵏḋyoy and Mⴟⵏⵏḋioy.—J. S.

6. See Reid's *History of the Presbyterian Church in Ireland*, i. p. 312, note 18.—J. W. H.

7. Bellaghy or Castledawson.—J. W. H. [This blank is filled in as Mr. "Fuisler's town," in a quotation from this *Journal* in the Rev. Geo. Hill's *Montgomery MSS.* (p. 152). Query "Whistler"? baile, a town, often implies no more than a seat or residence.—J. S.]

8. A better rendering of balḃ would be the "Stammerer." Elsewhere it is the one adopted by the translator. Compare the Latin *balbus* and *balbutiens.*—J. S.

9. By an *Inquisition* at Augher, 22nd Sept., 1 Charles I., Donald M'Shane Mallatt O'Nealle, formerly of Shraghgrom, in P. of Donaghmore, B. of Dungannon, died 9th April, 1616, seized of Shraghgrom. Eugene M'Donnell M'Shane Mallatt O'Nealle was his son and heir, and 30 years of age.—J. W. H.

10. Tandragee was held at this time by a troop of Lord Grandison's horse under Captain St. John. (See Carte's *Ormonde*, i. p. 172.) The O'Hanlons (O'h-Anlunin) possessed East and West Orior, Co. Armagh. (See the *Leabhar na g-Ceart, or Book of Rights*, p. 148.) They were the ancient hereditary royal standard-bearers of Ireland north of the Boyne, an office claimed by Col. O'Hanlon, and ceded, when George IV. came to Ireland, in 1821. (See O'Daly's *Tribes of Ireland*, p. 62.)—J. S.

11. Sir Arthur Tyringham was its governor. (See Carte's *Ormonde*, i. p. 172.) There were 70 barrels of gunpowder there when the place was seized. (See Nalson's *Impartial Collection*, ii. p. 516.)—J. S.

On Sunday was taken Desert Martin (ᴏɪᴘᴏɪᴛ mᴀᴘᴛᴀɪɴ) and the Oct. 24, 1641.
manor house of Magherafelt (Ⅲᴀᴄᴀɪᴘᴇ ᴘᴀ́ ᴘɪᴏᵹᴀᴅ) by the Governor
Cormac O'Hagan.[12]

Armagh (ᴀᴘᴏmᴀᴄᴀ) was seized by the General Sir Felim. There Oct. 26, 1641.
were a good many English in the great Cathedral, and plenty of
provisions with them. They could have defended themselves,
but they surrendered.

Sir Felim made an expedition to Bellaghy (bᴀɪʟᴇ ᴀᴄʜᴀᴅ). He Nov., 1641.
sent a messenger to demand the town from Mr. Conway[13] (Conᴘᴀɪᵹ),
but he refused to capitulate. The town was then entirely burnt, together with the haggarts. The master at length surrendered, on
condition of being sent safe across the Bann to Massareene (Ⅲᴀᴘ ᴀ
ᴘᴇᵹnᴀ). Then were burnt the Court of Bellaghy and the town of Sir
William Nugent (Ⅱᴜmnᴘᴇᴘ), and on the same day the court of
Magherafelt.

We shall now make some mention of Colonel Reilly, that is, Nov. 29, 1641.
Philip M'Hugh M'Shane Roe. The O'Reillys, on crossing the Boyne,
received information that a party of soldiers were coming from Dublin
to Drogheda. Philip fell in with them at Julianstown (bᴀɪʟᴇ ᵹᴏʟʟᴀn),
and although his men were but indifferently armed, he attacked them,
and actually killed 700 of the enemy without losing a man. Having
obtained a supply of arms and ammunition, the fruit of this day's
exploit, they placed a guard on the bridge of Drogheda until the
coming of the ensuing spring.

Charles Coote, the accursed scourge and merciless persecutor of May, 1641.
the Gaels, fell in the town of Trim[14] (bᴀɪʟᴇ ᴀᴛᴀ ᴛᴘᴜɪm). It is not
known by whom he was slain, whether friend or foe. Also the bloody ? Feb., 1641.
tyrant Simon Harcourt, knight and third commander of his regiment
(ᴄᴜɪᴅᴇᴀᴄᴛ), was wounded at the White Rock (Cᴀᴘᴘᴜɪᴄ mbᴀɪnᴇ), and

---

12. *Inquisition* at Augher, 22nd Sept., 1 Charles I., Eugen Oge O'Hagan M'Owen Evistan,
formerly of Moneymore, parish of Derry (?), B. of Dungannon, died 4th Nov., 1622, seized in his
lordship of Mullenecor (now   ) and Aghnecreagh (now   ), Cormac O'Hagan,
his son and heir, being then 22 years old and married.—J. W. H.
["Mullenecor" is "Mullinagore," near Dungannon, entered in Ambrose Leet's exhaustive
Directory to the Market Towns, Villages, &c., in Ireland (p. 303), as then (1814) in the possession
of Thomas Hamilton, Esq. "Aghnecrengh" I fail to trace.—J. S.]

13. "Mr. Conway" was Henry Conway. The following is the account of this transaction given
by the late Charles H. O'Neill in his Papers on the O'Neill of Clanaboy from the MSS. depositions
of the Revd. Chas. Anthoney of Bellaghy, dated 12th June, 1642, in Trinity College, Dublin. Mr.
Anthony stated "that on the breaking out of the rebellion in 1641, the inhabitants of Bellaghy
rose in arms for their own defence by the persuasion of Henry Conway, Esq., who lived in the
Castle. The inhabitants repaired to the Castle, and several of Magherafelt likewise. Henry
Conway obliged all these to take the oath of allegiance. That Conway was playing a double
game, for, while he appeared resolved in these preparations, he carried on secretly a correspondence with Anthony O'Mullan and the O'Hagans, all of whom were rebels. The object was that
he, Conway, might be permitted to carry off certain valuables without molestation if he would
deliver up the Castle. A parley was held, Mr. Thomas Dawson acting for the besieged, and
O'Hagan and Sir Phelim O'Neil for the rebels, in which it was agreed to deliver up the Castle on
condition of marching out with liberty and goods, but that, as Conway had got off with
his trunks, the rest were plundered, and the town and Castle burned.—J. W. H.
[See the Rev. Geo. Hill's *Montgomery MSS.* p. 155.—J. S.]

14. Coote was killed, 7th May, 1642, at Trim. (Lodge : *Peerage*, ii. p. 67.)—J. W. H.
[Of Coote, Prendergast tells us (*Cromwellian Settlement of Ireland*, p. 58)—"His soldiers
had orders to spare no infants above a span long." Carte (*Ormonde*, i. p. 318) says—"The
manner of his death was variously reported, and it remained uncertain whether the fatal shot came
from the enemy or from one of his own troopers."—J. S. Coote was made a free Stapler of
Belfast in 1640. See *Town Book of Belfast*, p. 248 and note.—EDITOR.]

died the following day, breathing forth blasphemies against God and the Saints.[15]

June 24, 1641. The Catholics took the fort of Limerick, which was in the possession of King Charles.

March, 1641. A party of Catholics had an engagement with the enemy at
?Feb., 1641. Killsallaghan (Cill SaUgann), where Captain Rochford was killed, together with several officers and a great many soldiers of his regiment, and they were forced against their will to go back to Dublin.[16]

The persons who held the situation of Justices, at this time, in Dublin, were Sir William Parsons, Master of Chancery, and Sir John Borlase, two brutes without feeling or mercy.

Colonel Reilly collected together all the English from Cavan, Ballyhayes, Belturbet, and any other towns throughout that part of the country, and sent them all under an escort to Drogheda.

Colonel Reilly besieged Croaghan[17] (Cruacán mic Tigeapnain) and Kileigh[18] (Cill acaiò), where there were collected 500 persons. They remained thus under blockade for 13 weeks, during which time 300 persons died. Then Sir James Craig and Sir Francis Hamilton and the remaining 200 capitulated, and were all sent off to Drogheda.

A party of 140 horse came from Trim and succeeded in taking great quantities of plunder. Mulmurray MacEmuinn was near the place with 33 horsemen, and perceiving the Creaghts flying he pursued the plunderers. He came up with the troop of cavalry at (Ag Liop na heavapmaròe), and, hearing the noise of the fight, he rushed in on them and compelled them to retreat, and the very last man of them was killed entering the gate of Maperath (pat an mapaoi). Captain Carson was taken.

An army was raised by Sir Charles Vavasour in Ormond, to take the town called Cloghleigh[19] (cloc Liat). The town was surrendered to him, the garrison having a bad supply of provisions. They took

---

15.—Sir Simon Harcourt was mortally wounded in March, 1642, at the attack on Carrick-mines Castle, Co. Dublin. (See Prendergast's *Cromwellian Settlement of Ireland*, p. 37).—J. S.

16. In a letter written by "Ed. Loftus," dated Feb. 27, 1641-2, ordered to be printed by the English Parliament, 7 March, this event is thus given—"The Rebels were gathered at Kil-shalghann, within seven miles of Dublin, above 2,000 men, where they were settled in a verie strong wood. My Lord of Ormond carried out part of our Armie, and killed above a hundred of them, without any considerable losse of our side, onely Captain James Rochford, a most gallant and courageous Gentleman."—J. W. H. There is some discrepancy in several of the dates here.—EDITOR.
[The Irish, under Hugh Byrne and MacThomas, numbered 3,000 men at "Killsalghen," as Carte (*Ormonde*, i. p. 283) calls it.—J. S.]

17. Croaghan, near Killeshandra.—J. O'D. [This was the place where the O'Rourke was inaugurated Prince of Breffny. See the *Four Masters*, iv. p. 808.—J. S.]
"Croaghan." There is a townland of this name, otherwise Coolnashinny (Ordnance Sheet 19), Parish of Kildallon, Co. Cavan, containing a Presbyterian Meeting-house; the river of the same name runs through the Parish. Another townland of the name lies in the Parish of Muntercon-naught, Barony of Castlerahan, in same county (Ord. Sheets 39-43).—J. W. H.

18. In the precinct of Tullaghconche (now the Barony of Tullaghonoho, Co. Cavan) Sir James Craigg, Kt., held the proportions called Drumheda and Killagh, on which there was built a Bawn with a strong and large Castle. (See Pynnar's *Survey*, in Harris's *Hibernica*, p. 154.)—J. W. H.

19. Cloghleigh, P. of Kilworth, Co. Cork. (See Lewis's *Topographical Dictionary of Ireland*, ii. p. 220; also Smith's *Cork*, i. pp. 140, 143; Lodge's *Peerage*, i. 297; and Carte's *Ormonde*, i. p. 431.)—J. W. H.
[Cloghleigh was surrendered 3rd June, 1643, according to Carte's *Ormonde*, i. p. 431.—J. S.]

quarter on condition of their lives being spared : but this condition was not adhered to, for 80 of them were executed. A number of Munster-men came to succour the town and their friends, but to their astonishment found the place burnt. They then attacked Sir Charles's people with such fury that they did not leave, out of 3,000, more than about 300 ; and they took their Colonel prisoner.

For love of this Charles, the daughter of the Earl of Cork, Sir Richard Boyle, gave a bottle of poison to her own husband, that is, the great Barry (báṁṁaċ móṁ).

The forces of Lord Moore and Richard Grenville, amounting to 1642. 4,000 men, surrounded the Court and Castle of Gerald Lacy[20] (Leiṁiṁ) while Gerald himself was absent. Only 30 men formed the garrison of the Castle : yet, in the course of five days they killed 700 of the enemy. The lady of the town and her family received quarter. The garrison collected together all the plate, brass, iron, guns, clothes, wheat, and other valuable things into the Court and burnt them. The besiegers now pressed round the Bawn, and broke down the iron gate. At first one of them came in and demanded a pistol from one of the garrison. " Here it is," said he, when immediately the fellow shot him with two bullets through the breast. Upon this the rest were seized, and bound two and two ; one young man, however, though severely wounded in the scuffle, contrived to escape from them, and made his way to the Castle of   (Co Caiṁlen Ṁiocaiṁo Sl   naṁ). Thus, then, were 29 soldiers put to death. In the County Louth, Lord Moore caused to be put to death 150 persons, between men, women, and children.

At the instigation of the daughter of George Garlan, 248 persons were killed by the garrison of Dundalk (baile ṁic buain), along with the Parish Priest, Turlogh M'Rory ; and yet all these had previously received quarter from Lord Moore.

The Earl of Ormond and a body of Catholics met in battle at Morva. The heretics were routed and one cannon was taken. Colonel Cullen (Cuṁluiṁ) and Colonel Preston were made prisoners, and many were slain on both sides.[21] The Irish came that night to Ross[22] (ṁoṁ mic Ṁṁuin), and on the morrow the enemy came after them to the same place ; Colonel Fox attacked them with five muskets, so sharply that they fled and deserted their camp. Behold them in full flight from us to Dublin !

A detachment under Lord Moore made an incursion on Ṁiaṁlaioṁ of Meath, and in revenge burnt their houses, Kells, and four mills situated on the river near it. Upwards of 60 people were killed in the French mill (Ṁuillionn na Ṁṁancaiṁ). Robert Cusack received quarter, but was killed immediately after by order of Sir Henry Tichbourne (Ṁioṁboiṁn), and also his son without any order.

20. Qu. Lacy, Qu. Lynch's Knock, Co. of Meath, now Summerhill.—J. W. H.

21. Carte (*Ormonde*, i. p. 405) mentions that Capt. Cullen was made a prisoner in this engagement, March 18th, 1643, but says nothing about Preston's capture.—J. S.

22. In Co. Wexford.—J. O'D. [New Ross, Co. Wexford, has this name—not Old Ross in the same county. See the *Four Masters*, iv. pp. 731-2.—J. S.]

Observe here, that from the first till the sixth year of the war, 60,000 Englishmen, Scotchmen, and soldiers were carried off by a pestilence, as the records (Leaḃaṟ oiṟiṟ) of Dublin, Drogheda, and Cork testify. For they state that it was found necessary to appoint new burying-grounds outside the towns on account of the terrific deaths of the people. And it is probable that this bitter lot befel them through the miracles of God, and the decree of that righteous Judge, Christ : for they never observed any engagement or promise of quarter, or protections made by them to the Irish, but shamefully violated them, contrary to the law of nations. They used to murder women and unbaptised children, old men and the sick, both young and old. The truth of this account is evident in the instance of the town of Timolin, in the County Kildare. It is also exemplified in the massacre of their prisoners by the English at Knock (Cnoc a Leṡiṟṟiṡ), where they slaughtered ten or twelve thousand persons, although fettered, and after quarter had been granted to them. They murdered all these, nor did they attempt to palliate the deed, but when questioned in Dublin, merely said that they had fought furiously against them, and that they took care to prevent their doing the like again. But it was out of their power to say that the Irish ever violated a promise of quarter made to them, while they broke engagements with Henry O'Neill the son of Owen, and with Phelim O'Neill, son of Tuathal, in the battle of Scarve Sollus[23] (a maṟóm na Sṡaiṟbe ṟoluiṟ), and the defeat at Kilkenny above-mentioned.[24]

As for the Governor, upon their crossing the Bann there was a Captain of his people, namely William Taafe, left behind him. About the time that he was approaching Movanagher[25] (Maṡ beannciṟi), the people of Coleraine (Cul ṟaċain) came to the Route (Ruta) and Killyquin[26] (Coill o cuinn) in search of plunder, in number 1,100. In Killyquin (Coill o cuinn) there happened to be encamped James M'Alister, the scabbed (Mac Alaṟtṟiṟinn caṟṟaiṡ), James M'Cullagh, and two of the sons of Con Ciotach (left-handed) before them ; so they sent a message to William Taafe to wait in Glenquilly[27] (gleann coilleaṫ) near the Bann till the Scotch should come near them, and when they would see them approach to unfold the banners and beat the drums. This was done, and the M'Donnells fell into the

23. Query Sṡaiṟḃ ṟolaiṟ, Sgairbh Sholais (Scarriffholis) on the Swilly, Co. Donegal ?—J. S.

24. There is no account of any battle at Kilkenny in the whole *Journal*.—J. S.

25. Movanagher Castle ruins are still extant in a townland of that name in the Parish of Kilrea, Barony of Coleraine and Co. of Derry. It lies about 12 miles south of Coleraine, and 1½ miles north of Kilrea, on the west side of the River Bann, which at this place runs over a shoal, having a crooked fall of 12 feet in summer, whence that part of the river is called Movanagher Rapids.—J. W. H.

26. In the *Ulster Inqn.*, 51, 55, 56, Chas. I., there are several grants of lands in Antrim from the Earl of Antrim to Henry, Turlogh, and Philomy O'Quin, of Killoquine.—J. W. H.
In 1641 Donnell Gorm MacDonnell resided in Killyquin, which seems to have included Rasharkin and the four towns of Craigs. See Reeves's *Ecclesiastical Antiquities of Down, Connor, and Dromore*, p. 331.—J. S.]

27. The Rev. James O'Laverty, P.P. (*History of the Diocese of Down and Connor*, iv. p. 126), identifies the locality here called "Glenquilly" as "Glenstall."—J. S.

snare.[28] The Scotch endeavoured to retreat, but they were nothing the better for that, for 948 of them were killed at Bundooragh (ⱱon ⱱⱷbↄoⱰↄⱱ).[29]

As for the Governor,[30] Turlogh O'Neill M'Turlogh M'Henry Og, he went towards Masareene. Two of his Captains were killed, namely, John O'Hagan M'Henry M'Rory Boy (ⱷⱷⱳⱯ) and Captain O'Hara. Leaving the town, they burnt all the corn of the country as far as Larne (LⱯɕↄpⱯↄ), and they set on fire all the Scotch and English towns in their way.

As for the General, he ordered many of his Captains to follow him to Drogheda (ⱱpↄↄƷↄↄⱱ). He ordered a fat ox, a meddar of butter, and four shillings of money to be levied off every Ballyboe[31] from Glassdrummond[32] (Ʒlↄp ⱱpↄⱷⱳⱯↄⱷ) to Tullaghog[33] (Ƈⱷlↄɕ óƷ). Having left Charlemont (ↄɕↄↄⱷ ↄⱷ ⱱↄ ɕↄpↄⱷ) he went to Armagh, and, having hanged and beheaded six persons there, he left that place in revenge of the death of Lord Caulfield,[34] and went to Newry, to Dundalk (pⱷↄɕ ⱱoↄlↄ), and to Bewley in Louth (ⱱↄↄɕↄlↄⱷ). It was here that the General's camp was. He placed four Captains over the Boyne, namely, Niall Og M'Neill M'Turlough M'Quin the lame (ⱱↄɕↄɕ),[35] Patrick O'Donnelly, i.e., the gloomy (ⱷoⱱↄppↄ), Felim O'Neill of the war (ↄⱷ ɕoƷↄⱱ), and Turlogh O'Quin the grim (Ʒↄⱷↄⱷↄ). A detachment of the English came from the City with a cannon on a cart among the troops. The Irish immediately made a brisk attack on them, and slew 40 of their enemies, with a loss of only six men on their side. Captain Niall O'Neill retreated into a walled enclosure which was near

28. *Inqn.* Carrickfergus, 24 Aug., 1635, Alexr. M'Donell, of Killconway, died 14th May, 1634, James M'Donell, his son and heir, being then ten years of age.—J. W. H.

29. Bundooragh, parish of Ballymoney, Co. Antrim.—J. W. H.
[The "Bunderaga" of the British Officer's *Irish Warr of 1641*, p. 22.—J. S.]

30. This was Turlogh O'Neill of Ardgonnel Castle, brother of Sir Phelimy.—J. W. H.
["Tirlagh O'Neil, Brother of the said Sir Phelimy, his chiefest Councellor, and is a very sad Man, well seen in the Laws of England, which he Studied in Lincoln's Inn, and was of good repute there." See Nalson's *Impartial Collection*, ii. p. 888. The British Officer, in his *Warr of 1641* (p. 20), describes Turlogh as "more a Mercurian than of Mars's traine."—J. S.]

31. A Ballyboe was sufficient land to graze 21 cows, with, in addition, a certain quantity of forest, and enough meadow land to provide winter fodder. (See Sullivan's *Introduction* to O'Curry's *Manners and Customs of the Ancient Irish*, i. p. lxxxix.) Dr. Reeves conjectures that "the ancient ballyboe may be estimated as a fifth larger than our present townland;" and the Ordnance Survey gives 228 townlands, each averaging about 406 acres. (See *Primate Colton's Visitation*, p. 130.)—J. S.

32. There are six Glasdrummans, Co. Armagh, one of them near Newry, but the one here alluded to is probably Glassdrummond in the parish of Aghaloo, Co. Tyrone, near Caledon.—J. W. H.

33. The inauguration stone of the O'Neills was at Tullagh oge till 1602, when Mountjoy "brake down the chair wherein the O'Neals were wont to be created, being of stone planted in the open field." (See *Fynes Moryson*, ii. p. 197.) By the *Four Masters* it is called Lↄↄɕ ↄↄ pↄⱷƷ, "the flag stone of the kings." It is said that a piece of it were to be seen in the glebe-house orchard, Desertcreaght, till 1776, when the last fragment was carried away. (See O'Donovan's *Four Masters*, iv. p. 887.)—J. S. A plan of the Fort is given in *Ulster Journal of Archæology*, vol. v. p. 235. EDITOR.

34. This fact strengthens the evidence brought forward by Prendergast (*Cromwellian Settlement of Ireland*, p. 63) to show that Sir Phelim O'Neill has been unjustly charged with murdering Lord Caulfield. Dean Bernard, a contemporary, whose account is not noticed by Prendergast, states that, as Lord Caulfield was walking, "a Fellow came behind him, and with a Brace of Bullets shot him quite through the Back." (See his *Siege of Drogheda*, p. 70.)—J. S.

35. *Inq.* at Augher, 22 Sept., 1 Chas. I., Nealle O'Quyn of Ballenslouge, in the P. of Kildress, of which he was seized, died 5 Octr., 1621. Nealle Oge O'Quyn, his son and heir, was then 32, and married.—J. W. H.

at hand, and closed the gate after them. They brought the cannon along with them in order to break it, but the cart on which it was broke down, and they were a long time mending it. The day closed in on them, and so, having buried the bodies of the dead in the bogs, they repaired to the city (ꝺon caṫṁaiġ), and the Irish came over the Boyne and to Bewley (beťelın) to the camp of Sir Felim, the General.

It was reported to the enemy that General O'Neill would be in the camp of the M'Mahons and M'Kennas on the 5th of March about noon. Accordingly a troop of Cavalry and 100 Infantry came towards the camp of the M'Mahons. They were opposed for some time ; however, Art Roe (the red-haired) M'Patrick M'Art the bald (maol) was wounded and taken prisoner, and his brother Rory was killed. Many of our men were slain. This was beside Tullyallen (ċulaċ alaın).[36]

March 1, 1642.　　On the first Sunday in Lent, a sermon was preached by the Guardian Paul O'Neill in Armagh, another by Father Henry O'Mullen in the Chapel of Carnteel (Caṕn ċSıaṫaıl),[37] another by Father Edmund Roe Mac Cathmaol in Clonfecle[38] (Celuaın Ḟıacla), and one by Father Joannes a Sancto Patricio in the Court-house of Dungannon. Part of the loft fell under them ; some persons were killed, and others had their bones broken.

March 6, 1642.　　Colonel Turlogh M'Art Og M'Turlogh Luineach[39] (Luınıġ) marched according to orders which he received to Tyrconnell (Ṫırconnıll), and displayed seven banners along the Finn (ċoıṕ Ḟınn). There was a body of Scotch, with ten standards, on the opposite side of the Finn. The Connollys (Conallaıġ) were about Magherabeg, and [Sir Ralph Gore][40] with a large part inside, and the Scotch came over to assist him. The Clann of Art Og and the people of Art O'Neill marched after them.

Mar. 26, 1642.　　General O'Neill brought three cannons from the Bridge[41] (Ꝺroıġeaꝺ) to Dundalk (boıle mıc buaın).[42] Along with him was Alexander

---

36.　Tullyallen is north of Drogheda.—J. W. H.

37.　Carnteel is a little village about four miles from Caledon.—J. W. H.

[Carnteel (Caṕn ṫ-Sıaṫaıl or Caṕn ṫ-Sıaġaıl) signifies the carn of Sedulius or Sheil. See O'Donovan's *Four Masters*, iii. p. 297 ; v. p. 1366.—J. S.]

38.　Clonfeakle, a parish in Co. Armagh, is written Cluaın Ḟıacna by the Four Masters. Jocelyn calls it *Cluain-ficail*. In the *Taxation* of 1306, and the *Registries* of Archbishops Sweteman, Swayne, Mey, Octavian, and Dowdell it appears as *Clonfecyna, Clonfekyna, Clonfeguna, and Clonfekina*. (See O'Donovan's *Four Masters*, ii. p. 749.) It means St. Finchna's lawn or meadow.—J. S.

39.　Turlogh, son of Sir Arthur O'Neill (who died 28th Oct., 1600), who was the son of Turlogh Lynagh O'Neill.—J. W. H.

[Lynagh (Luinench) implies fosterage by O'Luinigh (O'Looney) of Muintirlooney, in the Barony of Strabane.—J. S.]

40.　Sir Ralph Gore. I supply the name from Reid's *History* (i. p. 344), where it is stated that Sir William Cole, of Enniskillen, and Sir Ralph Gore, of Magherabeg, in Donegal, received commissions from Charles I. in the latter end of 1641 to raise 500 men each.—J. W. H.

41.　From Drogheda.—J. O'D.

[Drogheda is sometimes simply called "the Bridge," an Ꝺroıċceaꝺ, without the addition of aṫa, "of the ford." See O'Donovan's *Four Masters*, iii. p. 349.—J. S.]

42.　The strand near Dundalk was anciently called Traigh Bhaile Mhic Buain, *i.e.*, the strand of Baile the son of Buan. (See O'Donovan's *Four Masters*, iii. p. 349.)—J. S.

Hovenden's party, and Hugh [the yellow] Kelly (buróc). Lord Moore[43] (Mnbap) fell on them, together with Sir Henry Tichburne[44] (Cpopbipn), eleven flags and three troops of horse, upon the Saturday before Passion Sunday. They came to Warren's Gate (ξebtα an mappnnξ)[45] in the South quarter. They were driven from the town twice, and their men were left stretched on the plain. The Heretics (heipncnξ), that is, the people of the yellow coats,[46] resolved to return at daybreak : they brought a field cannon with them and broke down the gate. They then rushed in on us, and filled the town. The General and his people retreated,[47] having killed upwards of 300 men of the English, while he had only a loss of four killed and six wounded. This was the day when the General's Musician, Thomas Skinner [?] (Sξmep), was killed in Dundalk (rpno b).[48]

As to the General, a great multitude marched with him to Dundalk (cpnc baile), together with the Lieutenant-General of the Army, who was trained up in the army of King Philip, and Colonel Turlogh M'Henry M'Turlogh M'Henry M'Felim Roe ; and they took up their quarters behind Dundalk. Here they lost a good horseman of their troop, Tobias O'Quin.

The General sent his letters to Colonel Turlogh O'Neill, to the descendants of Art, to the Clan of Shane Og O'Neill, and to Art M'Quin M'Shane, directing them all to meet him at the Finn with their detachments of the army.

He sent a message from Tullagh-og (Culác óg) to Ballymoney (Pnpo monaξ)[49] that the soldiers should come to meet him at Kilcronaghan (Cill cpnnecán) to be reviewed : and on the 20th April he himself was in Moneymore (Mnnmn móp), in the house of the Governor, Cormac O'Hagan. The second night he was in a house

<hr>

43. Bernard says Lord Moore and Tichbourne left Drogheda on the 21st of March with 1,000 foot and 200 horse, burned Slane a second time, took "Atherdee" on the 23rd, and that they had only 750 foot and 200 horse when they attacked Dundalk, and that there were 3,000 of the Irish.—J. W. H.
[See Dean Bernard's *Whole Proceedings of the Siege of Drogheda*, 1736, pp. 86, 87, 93. *Bernard* was ordered to be printed in 1642.—J. S.]

44. Tichbourne entered Drogheda as governor, 4th Nov., 1641. Lord Moore arrived there with his troop of horse, 26th Oct. (See Bernard's *Siege of Drogheda*, pp. xvi. 10.)—J. S.

45. It must be the name of a gate at Dundalk.—J. O'D.
[Unknown now.—J. S.]

46. This alludes to the soldiers' buff coats. Captain Grose (*Military Antiquities*, ii. p. 323) says—"The buff coat or jerkin, which was originally worn under the cuirass, now became frequently a substitute for it."—J. S.

47. Bernard says he retreated that night to Ballymaskomlin, "a faire castle of Lord Moore's, of which he burned a part."—J. W. H.
[See Bernard's *Siege of Drogheda*, p. 92. Ballymaskomlin is Ballynascanlan, not far from Dundalk.—J. S.]

48. Cpnξ baile.—J. O'D.
[Spno baile, street town, is the modern name of Dundalk.—J. S.]

49. Vow Ferry, on the River Bann, about 11½ miles south of Coleraine, in the Parish of Aghadowey, Co. Derry. The Bann here forms a deep pool between Carnroe shoal to the north and Movanagher rapids to the south. In the townland of Vow, Parish of Finvoy, Barony of Kilconway, Co. Antrim, on the east side of the Bann (whence this ferry derives its name), is a circular graveyard. (See Reeves's *Eccl. Ant. Down, Connor, and Dromore*, p. 384.)—J. W. H.

P

belonging to Crosby (cɲoɾbɪ), a good Catholic in Culmore[50] (Caʟʟ moɲ), and was well entertained. The General proceeded to Coleraine (Cúl ɲaċaɪn),[51] in the Parish of Kilcronaghan.

April, 1642.

To this Assembly there came from Tullagh-og (Cuʟaċ óᵹ), Felim O'Hagan, the grim (moɒaɲɲa), a captain; Shane O'Hagan M'Cormac, a captain; Niall O'Quin, a captain; Hugh O'Hagan M'Teague, a captain; Patrick O'Mellan M'Rory the freckled (baʟʟaċ), a captain; Rory Murray O'Devlin, a captain; Felix O'Neill, the grim (ᵹɲuama), a captain; Cormac O'Neill from Oghtleydan (Uċc Leaċaɪn), a captain; Donald O'Neill M'Culadh M'Shane (mac cu uʟaɪɒ), a captain; Art Og O'Hagan M'Donnell M'Hugh, a captain; Brian O'Neill M'Carry (mac aɲ ɟɪɲ ɒoɲċa), a captain; Art M'Hugh M'Shane   a captain; and William Taafe, a captain. A thousand men of them were appointed to guard all the country between that and Derry (ʙoɪɲe), and Newtown-Limavady (Léɪm aɲ ṁaɒɲaɒ), Artikelly (Aɲɒ aɲ ċoɪʟʟɪɲ), and Coleraine (Cúl ɲaċaɪn), and to protect it from the incursions of the boats of Lough Neagh (Loċ eaċaċ) out of Claneboy (Cʟaɲɲ aoɒa buɪɒɪ). The General went himself with a troop to Strabane (cɲɲaċ bán), where the Lady of the son of the Earl of Abercorn (Apɲacoɲɲ) was, and she a widow.[52] They attacked the Scotch, and M'Rory the Anglicized (ᵹaʟɒa) was killed that day. The General brought the lady from her town to Charlemont (Aċaɒ aɲ ɲá éaɲaɒ), and left a garrison in Strabane, namely, the Divins (muɪɲcɪɲ ɒuɪbɪn), and Shane M'Namee over them. Three days after, the Scotch of Lifford (Leɪċɲɪɲ) came over to Strabane. The garrison fled, and were all slain, except such as escaped by running. The Scotch came into the Court. . . . . they found gunpowder, lead, pikes, and swords, meat and drink there for them.

As to the General: he sent a Franciscan Friar, Patrick O'Hamill, to convoy the lady to Munster, where Sir George Hamilton then was, and sent a company of horse with her. She had refused to marry the General, saying that she had taken a vow of celibacy for five years; for his own wife died in the preceding harvest, namely, the daughter of Lord Iveagh. Edward Monroe[53] (boɲɲoo)

---

50. See Sampson's *Statistical Survey of County Londonderry*, p. 28. Culmore in Kilcronaghan.—J. W. H.

51. *From* the parish of Kilcronaghan.—J. O'D.
[Coleraine is in the parish of Coleraine and partly in that of Killowen.—J. S.]

52. Lodge (*Peerage*, v. p. 114) says he brought her to his Castle in Tyrone. We prefer the statement in the text. Reid states this to have been in December, 1641. Strabane Castle was placed in charge of Captain Hugh Murragh O'Divin, with 100 choice musketeers and 100 pikes. The Lagan forces took it and put all the men to the sword, placing O'Divin a prisoner in Derry Gaol. They left in the Castle a garrison commanded by Captain Wisher, under the command of Sir Wm. Hamilton. Colonel Audley Mervyn's *Exact Relation*, &c., presented to the House of Commons in England, 4th June, 1642, cited by Reid (*History of the Presbyterian Church in Ireland*, i. p. 361).—J. W. H.

53. *Recte*, Robert Monroe. M'Skimin (*Carrickfergus*, p. 48) states that Monroe landed at Carrickfergus, 15th April, 1642, with 2,500 men. Carte (*Ormonde*, i. p. 309) gives the same number.—J. S.
Sir James Turner's *Memoirs* give a vivid account of the Scotch forces. He says that Monroe's severity had not the success he anticipated, for, "instead of terrifying the rebells from their wonted cruelties, it enraged them, and occasioned the murthering of some hundreths of prisoners whom they had in their power."—EDITOR.

arrived with 4,000 men from Scotland.   They landed in Trian May 1, 1642.
Congal[54] (Tjian Congail).

They burnt and pillaged the Irish until they came to Newry
(a mubap cinn tpaga). Hugh M'Donnell Og M'Eamuin Magenis
was captain of Newry and its Castle, and he surrendered the
Castle to Monroe, in which there was abundance of provisions, arms,
and clothing.[55] Five hundred men were left in Newry,[56] and 3,500
were sent through Trian Congail (Tjian Congail) to sack that
country. A monk of the order of St. Bernard, and Rory O'Sheal, a May 1, 1642.
priest, were hanged, and thrown over the bridge of Newry into the sea
at high water. Edward Monroe[57] sent a message to the Earl of
Antrim (Antjiom),[58] Randal Og, and the Earl invited him to Dunluce
('Oún Libji). The consequence of the invitation was that the Earl
was taken, and the town : a garrison was left in the town, and the
Earl kept a prisoner.

The General sent Paul O'Neill to Galway (Gaillm) to buy Gun- May 2, 1642.
powder. He staid away 40 days, and brought a quantity with him of
that article.[59]

Armagh was burnt ; the Cathedral with its steeple[60] (clogaj') and May 6, 1642.

54. Trian Congal extended from Glynn, near Larne, to Movilla, near Newtownards.
Reeves, *Eccl. Ant.*, p. 344 and note.—J. W. H.

[" Clannaboy (the whole, or the greater part) was more anciently called Trian Congaill."
(See Joyce's *Atlas and Geography of Ireland*, p. 18) A note in Connellan's *Four Masters*, p. 258,
is inaccurate in so far as it does not state that Trian Congail extended into Co. Down. It says:—
" *Trian Congaill* appears to have been a large territory in the southern part of the county of
Antrim, of which the O'Neills of Claneboy were lords, as stated in the course of these Annals."—
J. S.] There is a valuable unpublished map of this district, *circa* 1580, in Carew MSS., Lam-
beth Palace.—EDITOR.

55. Carte (*Ormonde*, i. p. 309) states that the Castle of Newry was surrendered on the 3rd
May, and that it contained " only half a barrel of powder and sixty muskets, not above a dozen
of them fixed : so utterly unable were the Rebels to provide for the defence of that important
place."—J. S.

56. According to Carte (*Ormonde*, i. p. 309), 300 men, under Lieutenant-Colonel Sinclair.
—J. S.
Sir James Turner was there, and describes a storm that arose in the beginning of May. He
says it was attributed " to the devilish skill of some Irish witches."—EDITOR.

57. *Recte*, Robert Monroe. The Earl of Antrim was confined six months in Carrickfergus,
and then made his escape. He was taken again by Monroe in May, 1643, and incarcerated
in the same place. He was assisted to escape from this second confinement by Col. Gordon, of
Monroe's army. (See Hill's *Montgomery MSS.*, p., 426; *Macdonnells of Antrim*, pp. 261-5;
and M'Skimin's *History and Antiquities of Carrickfergus*, pp. 49, 51.) The Rev. Geo. Hill (*ubi
supra*) places the Earl's first captivity in June, 1642.—J. S. [See note concerning Monroe,
Town Book of Belfast, p. 312.]—EDITOR.

58. Antjium.—J. O'D.

59. According to Carte's *Ormonde* (i. p. 307), Sir Phelim had only a firkin and a-half of
powder remaining in April, 1642. Father Paul O'Neill was a most active partisan. In the
Judgment against Sir Phelim O'Neill he is referred to as " yt postilinn ffryer or popish Prest who
went 13 times for you to Brussells in halfe a yeare." (See *Appendix*, Meehan's *Confederation of
Kilkenny*, p. 318.)—J. S.
In the *Pinkerton MSS.* is an interesting note on the difficulty of getting gunpowder, experienced by the Irish in all their wars, as they were quite unable to make it. Pinkerton attached
great importance to this fact, and says it contributed much to their defeats.—EDITOR.

60. Steeple, *i.e.*, Round Tower.—J. O'D.

[Steeple was the name commonly applied by the settlers to a Round Tower. It is still that
which is popularly used in reference to the Round Tower of Antrim. How soon after O'Mellan's
time the Round Tower of Armagh completely disappeared is not known. Its conical cap,
Oenocobap vo Cloiceach Apoa Macha, was blown off in a great storm in 1121.
See O'Donovan's *Four Masters*, ii. p. 1012.—J. S.]

with its bells, organs, and glass windows, and the whole city, with the fine library, with all the learned books of the English on Divinity, Logic, and Philosophy. The weather was very warm, and there was an East wind, so that the flames reached the Cathedral. Lough-gall (baile loc gall), Tandragee (con ɲe Ɡaoiꞇ), Hy-Nialand (iḃ niallan), Lurgan[61] (iḃ ḃꞃeꞃail), Toaghie (ꞇuaꞇ eacḣaé), Maydown[62] (Maꞟ an oin), and Portmore (Poꞃꞇ móꞃ).

The General gave orders that the troops should be assembled at Tandragee to meet the Scotch, namely, Colonel Monroe (ḃoɲꞃoo). About 2,000 men came.

May 21, 1642. A troop came from Dundalk (ꞇꞃꞃaꞇ boile) to the Fews (Ꝼeaḋa), and to Sliabh Fuaid.[63] They took some plunder, but were deprived of it by Turlogh M'Art M'Turlogh M'Henry, and their Captain and 14 horsemen of the troops were killed. Next day a troop arrived out of Dundalk, and a large number of foot soldiers, with a set of horses laden with arms, to place a garrison in the Castle of Glass-Drummond (Ꞡlaꞃ oꞃomuɲe). Shane O'Neill happened to be in that Castle, and having set fire to the upper part of it, he and his party left the Castle in flames, and went off among the bogs. The soldiers, seeing the Castle on fire, returned to Dundalk (Ouɲ ꝺealꞡan).

Donnell Gimley[64] (Ꞡeimleaé), that is, the son of O'Cahan, arrived from Spain at Charlemont (Aéaḋ an ꝺá éaꞃaḋ),[65] where the General was.

May 27, 1642. The Scotch of Massareene (ꞇílaꞃ aꞃꞡna) came over Lough Neagh. Captain O'Hagan met them; four of them were killed and six wounded. They returned immediately over the lake.

May 29, 1642. A great multitude of Scotch arrived from Scotland at Trian Congal (Tꞃiaɲ conꞡaill), so that the Irish (Ꞃeꞃmoɲɲaꞡ) fled over to the Countess of Antrim (cuɲꞇaoꞃ Aɲꞇꞃoim), Sir James M'Allister the scabbed (caꞃꞃaé), James M'Cullagh, James M'Goffrey M'Henry, the

May 31, 1642. clan of Colla Ciocaé (left-handed) across the Bann (banna), and Lady Iveagh, Sarah O'Neill, the clan of Turlogh Iveagh M'Artan.[66]

61. Lurgan?—J. O'D. Clanbrassil.
'Clanbrassil was a territory south of Lough Neagh, where the Bann enters the Lough : co-extensive with the present Barony of O'Neilland East. The O'Garveys were its ancient chiefs ; in more modern times, the MacCanns. See the *Leabhar na g-Ceart, or Book of Rights,* p. 148.—J. S.

62. Maydown, opposite Benburb. It is on the Co. Armagh side of the Blackwater.—J.W.H.

63. Sliabh Fuaid takes its name from Fuad, son of Breogan, who came over with the sons of Milesius. (See O'Donovan's *Four Masters,* vi. p. 1923.) The territory known as the Fews, Co. Armagh, has its name from Ꝼioḃ or Ꝼeaḋ, a wood. "Fewes bordereth upon the English Pale within three miles of Dundalk : it is a very stronge Countrey of wood and bogg, peopled with certeyne of the Neyles, accustomed to lyve much upon spoile of the Pale." (See Bagenal's *Description and Present State of Ulster, 1586,* in the *Ulster Journal of Archæology,* ii. p. 150 ; also *The Description of Ireland in 1598,* p. 21, edited by Rev. E. Hogan, S. J.)—J. S.

64. Gimley.—J. O'D.
[Ꞡeimleaé means a captive.—J. S.]

65.—*Atha an da cara,* "The ford of the two friends," was the old name of the passage over the Blackwater where Charlemont now stands.—J. W. H.
["Achadh-an-da-Charadh" (which is the correct form) means "the field of the two weirs." Compare "Clar-atha-da-Charadh," "the plain of the ford of the two weirs," in O'Donovan's *Four Masters,* iii. p. 413, and "Cluain da Charadh" (Cloondacarra, Co. Roscommon), "the meadow of the two weirs." See Joyce's *Irish Names of Places,* i. p. 255.—J. S.]

66. This passage is evidently wrong translated. Trian Congail was another name for the Claneboys. Lady Iveagh was daughter of Hugh, Earl of Tyrone.—J. W. H.

The General marched against the Scotch of Tir-connell. They June 9, 1642. did not remain long inactive in Tir enna⁶⁷ (Ⴀꙗ enn) when they came near them. They erected a sconce⁶⁸ that very night, in which were 2,000 muskets. Quiet and silent were the Scotch during the night, but noisy and talkative the Irish. At break of day they attacked each other. They rushed forward to the contest ; men were scattered and slain. The Scotch retreated to the sconce, and took away the ammunition. The rear of the Irish, that is, the pikemen, were taken.⁶⁹ The General and O'Cahan were in the fight bravely in the face of the enemy. The Scotch gave way in like manner. The General cried out to his own men saying that the Scotch were retreating, but all in vain, for they would not come back to the charge. Shane O'Donnelly the yellow (buıꝺe), a Captain, Felim O'Hagan the gloomy (mouꙗꝑꝑꙗ), a Captain, and Felim O'Neill the grim (ᵹꞃuꙗmꙗ), a Captain, were all killed, and Allister, son of Colla cıotꙗċ (left-handed), was wounded. Many were slain there. Upwards of 140 blind and lame persons were killed. An old preacher, a Franciscan Friar, Ludovicus M'Namee, from Armagh, was slain, together with Priest Maurice M'Cordan. Nial O'Neill, a lame club-footed man, gave a blow of his big staff to one of the troopers who was about to kill him, which knocked him down. He then despatched him, and took away his arms and horse along with him.⁷⁰

Lord Conway (Conꝑꙗᵹ), Lord Blaney, young Lord Caulfield, and July 14, 1642. Lord Hamilton came and pitched their camp near Armagh with a great army. They gathered plunder, and they sent a large detachment of cavalry to carry off the horses of the O'Byrnes⁷¹ (ꙗ cꞃıᵹ Lꙗbꞃꙗꝯꞃ 1leꝃꝑuꙗL). They burnt Dromorragh (Ꝺꞃum oꝑꝑꙗꞃᵹ), the seat of Sir Felim O'Neill,⁷² and all his plate. Kinard (Cıonn ꙗꞃꝓ)⁷³ was burnt precisely on Sunday (ꝺıꙗꝺomnꙗıᵹ ꝺo ꞃunnꝑꙗꝺ).

These great forces came to Dunavally⁷⁴ (ꝺun bꙗLLꙗ) and remained July 21, 1642. there. As to the General, he left Charlemont (Ꙗċꙗꝺ ꙗn ꝺꙗ ċꙗꝑꙗꝺ), along with Con Og M'Quin M'Neill M'Brien Fagartach (Fꙗᵹꙗꞃcꙗıᵹ) of Kinalarty, the Colonel, and O'Cahan, leaving Niall O'Neill with a

67. Tir Enna, or Tir Enda, was "a territory comprising thirty quarters of land in the present County of Donegall, lying south of Inishowen, between the arms of Lough Foyle and Lough Swilly, that is, between Lifford and Letterkenny." (See O'Donovan's *Four Masters*, iii. p. 19.) It received its name from Enda, the youngest son of Niall of the Nine Hostages.—J. S.

68. A "sconce" is a blockhouse or small fort. (See Halliwell's *Dictionary of Archaic and Provincial Words*, ii. p. 712.)—J. S.   For drawing of one near Belfast, see *Town Book of Belfast*, p. 307.—EDITOR.

69. *Were taken*, or, *received the attack.*—J. O'D.

70. In this engagement the Scotch were commanded by Sir Robert Stewart. It was fought, according to the British Officer (*Irish Warr* of 1641, p. 23), "at a place called Glommaquin, in the County of Dungall," *i.e.*, Glenmaquin or Glenmacwin, near Raphoe.—J. S.

71. O'Byrnes. Stillorgan, *i.e.*, cꞃıᵹ Loꞃᵹꙗın.—J. O'D.

72. Dromorragh, near Caledon, the residence of Sir P. O'Neill.—J. W. H.

73. Kinard, *i.e.*, Caledon. In the settlement under James I., Turlogh O'Neill had a grant of Kinard, with 4,000 acres. (See Lewis's *Topographical Dictionary of Ireland*, i. p. 243; also Pynnar's *Survey of Ulster* in Harris's *Hibernica*, p. 211.) Lord Montgomery burned Kinard on 20th June, according to Carte's *Ormonde* (i. p. 310), "and the next day forced the town of Charlemont."—J. S.

74. Dunavally, in which is the old fort of Legar-hill, overlooking Charlemont.—J. W. H.

garrison in Charlemont (ᴧᴄᴀᴅ ᴀn ᴅᴀ́ ᴄᴀᴘᴀᴅ), and they came themselves to Brantry (bᴘᴏnᴄᴘᴜ), to the house of a Friar of Armagh.   There was a guard upon the ford of Portmore (ᴧᴄh ᴀ ᴘᴜᴘᴄ ᴍᴏᴘ), but in spite of this, the English came across and killed two horsemen of Turlogh ᴢᴜᴀᴍᴀ O'Quin's, namely Eneas and Patrick Og O'Quin, sons of Patrick M'Felim the red (ᴘᴜᴀᴅ.)

July 24, 1642.   Captain Richard Codan [? Cowan] (Coᴅᴀn) was placed in the garrison of Dungannon (ᴅᴜn ᴢᴇᴀnᴜᴍ), and the Court of Bally-donnelly[75] (bᴏᴄᴇ ᴅᴏnᴅᴀᴏᴄᴇ), and the outskirts of the town were burnt by Randal M'Donnell, according to the General's orders.

Lord Conway (Conᴘᴀᴢ) and those other Lords sent to the Captain of Charlemont (ᴧᴄᴀᴅ ᴀn ᴅᴀ́ ᴄᴀᴘᴀᴅ) desiring him to surrender the town to them, and promising him the title of Earl of Tyrone.   " I will not July 27, 1642. surrender," was his reply.   They then attacked the place four days successively.   The Lords and their forces then encompassed Dungannon.   The garrison, namely, Nicholas O'Macan, Patrick M'Manus, Lawrence O'Quillan,[76] and the rest, delivered up the town, and all the prisoners who were in it.   They took Captain Cowan to Lord Conway (Conᴘᴀᴢ), and he was hanged, together with his son, and a Dominican Friar.   A Garrison consisting of a troop and some infantry was left in Dungannon.[77]   The Lords with their army then returned 'to Charlemont (ᴧᴄᴀᴅ ᴀn ᴅᴀ́ ᴄᴀᴘᴀᴅ), and were for three days round it skirmishing with the Garrison. They thought they would take it as easily as Dungannon.[78]   They raised the siege, and carried off with them some spoil from Hugh Boy (bᴜᴅᴇ) M'Kelvey ; they murdered old men, women, and children, and took prisoner the upright Priest, and the excellent preacher and singer, James O'Fallagan, and Hugh O'Quin.   Their lives were taken immediately on returning ; their lives would have been spared if they would change their religion.   Letters came from Owen O'Neill M'Art, son of Ferdoragh (ᴍᴀᴄ ᴀn ᴘᴘᴏᴘᴇᴀ), to the General of the Province of Ulster, stating that he should come to meet him at the Castle of Doe[79] (ᴄᴀᴘᴄᴇᴀn nᴀ ᴅᴄᴜᴀᴄ).   Three thousand men accordingly went there on the 18th of July.

They took the garrisons of Dungannon and Mountjoy, and we lost

75. Ballydonnelly, now Castlecaulfield. (See Pynnar's *Survey* in Harris's *Hibernica*, p. 209.) —J. W. H.   There are some drawings of the Jacobean castle in the Macadam MSS.—EDITOR.

[On an old map of Ulster, in the State Paper Office, this place is shown as " Fort and Lough O'Donnellie."   Castlecaulfield takes its name from Sir Toby Caulfield, ancestor of the Earls of Charlemont, to whom it was granted by James I.   It contained 24 ballyboes, as appears from an Inquisition at Dungannon, 23rd August, 1610.   See O'Donovan's *Four Masters*, v. p. 1404.—J. S.]

76. O'Cuilleain.—J. O'D.

77. The British Officer says (*Irish Warr of 1641*, p. 27) :—" Captain Theophilus Jones, of the Lord Conway's Regiment, was left to command it.   At this time our Regiment [*i.e.*, Sir John Clotworthy's] kept Mountjoy,"—J. S.

78. The British Officer (*Irish Warr of 1641*, p. 27) owns that Charlemont "did them more harm than they could do to it."—J. S.

79. Doe Castle, Co. Donegal, the residence of the MacSwynes.   Owen Roe had come from Dunkirk, sailing round the north of Scotland. (See Carte's *Ormonde*, i. p. 311.)   The *Aphorismical Discovery of Faction* (i p. 43) states that he took two prizes on his way, and that the commanders whom he brought with him were " ould-beaten soldiers of his own regiment in Flanders."   " Ould-beaten," *i.e.*, tried veterans.—J. S.

Patrick gruama O'Quin,[80] and three old heroes, Felim balb (the stammerer) O'Muldoon,[81] Turlogh Dubh, and Conor O'Gibbon; our army being away from us in Tirconnell.

They carried off from the borders of Brantry (brentair) at Knock- July 31, 1642.
nacloy[82] (cnoc an ċluiṫe), above 140 cows, and horses with their harness (Fo na malin gṫib), sheep, goats, and accoutrements.

A party of English and Scotch soldiers came from Trian Congal Aug. 4, 1642.
(Trian Congail) to Hy Nialland (Ib niallain) to reinforce the garrisons of Dungannon and Mountjoy. They went up beyond Clandawell[83] (dabaill) and plundered the M'Kennas indiscriminately. Next
day they returned to Dungannon and brought the plunder with them. Aug. 6, 1642.
These forces left Dungannon in the night and went towards the Large[84] (Leargaig), Truagh (Truċa), Clossach[85] (Clossaċ), and the borders of Slieve Beagh (Sliab Beaṫa), as far as Glendavagh[86] (Gleann an deaṁain). A party of the Irish happened to fall in with them near the woods, when a slaughter ensued on both sides. They carried away their plunder to Dungannon that same day, and eight troopers in sacks along with them.

The same forces went to Mountjoy, and having waited for some time near a wood they received intelligence of plunder being beside Sliabh Gallon (sliab callunn). They carried it off and killed . . . . . and his brother Conor. Twelve troopers went to Kilcronaghan (cil cruinneaċain) and Maghera (Maċaire a rá). The Ulster-men followed them, and there was not a great man of them who was not either killed or drowned in the Bann.[87]

80. Edward Bunting, the musician who collected our national airs, claimed descent from Patrick Gruama O'Quin. (See *Notes and Queries*, 1st series, iv. p. 452.)—J. S.

81. The O'Muldoons were a Fermanagh family located in the Barony of Lurg.—J. W. H.
[There are repeated references to the O'Muldoons, Lords of Lurg, in the *Four Masters*, the earliest being at A.D. 1000.—J. S.]

82. Knocknacloy is situate on the west side of the Oona river, at its embouchure into the Blackwater.—J. W. H.

83. Glenaul.—J. W. H.
Glenaul was a large district, the property of the Primate, on the Armagh side of the Blackwater, lying along its side from Caledon to Blackwater town. It is now the name of an Electoral Division in the Poor Law Union of Armagh. (See *Appendix* to *Ulster Inquisitions* for description.)—J. W. H.

84. The "Large." The principal part of this is the town of Aughnacloy, Co. Tyrone. In the Plantation of Ulster the Lord Ridgwaie was allotted 2,000 acres, called Large, upon which, at the date of Pynnar's Survey (1618-19), he had built "a Bawne of Lime and Stone, 160 feet square, 14 feet high, with four flankers, and a House in it of Timber." (Harris's *Hibernica*, p. 209.)—J. W. H.

85. The "Closaghe." (See Reeves's *Primate Colton's Visitation*, p. 126, for a description of this district, which comprised the present parishes of Clogher and Errigal Keerogue, in the County Tyrone.—J. W. H.
[It was also called *Magh Leamhna*. An old map of Ulster, preserved in the State Paper Office, shows it as "the Countrie of Cormac Mac Barone" [O'Neill]. See O'Donovan's *Four Masters*, i. p. 46: also the *Leabhar na g-Ceart, or Book of Rights*, p. 152.—J. S.]

86. Glenadamhain, now Glendavagh, a townland in the parish of Aghaloo, Barony of Dungannon, Co. Tyrone.—J. W. H.
Devil's Glen.—J. O'D.
[This would be the meaning of the old name, but Glendavagh, as Joyce says (*Irish Names of Places*, ii. p. 434), means "a glen having deep pools along its course."—J. S.]

87. Or, *and all their leaders were either slain or drowned in the Bann*.—J. O'D.

Aug. 12, 1642. From Mountjoy the forces returned to Dungannon, in number 4,000 men. They received information that there was plunder in Munter-Byrne[88] (Muinteip bipn) in the possession of Brian O'Hugh, a priest in Glenkeen[89] (Cluain con). They carried it off with them, and seized upon Edmund Finn, a priest. A horseman of the army having turned upon two young men of the Creaghts[90] (Caoineaċt), was attacked by them with a volley of stones, which knocked him off his horse. They then killed him, and took away his horse and accoutrements with them.

All the great plunder above-mentioned was brought from those places which I have stated to Trian Congal (Tpian congail) on [Saint Clare's] day[91] (Lá pan clapa).

Aug. 13, 1642. The General[92] returned along with Owen O'Neill, the O'Reillys, M'Mahons, the inhabitants of Fermanagh, and M'Keowns, with plenty of ammunition (puptaċt monaipion leo), and the English drew back as the General and his forces advanced. The famous, honorable, persevering Commander had arrived through the sea from the north with only a single ship and a company of soldiers, commanded by Captain Antony, the Fleming, an intrepid officer. They landed at the Castle of Doe (caiplean na ttuat).

Aug. 16, 1642. General Leslie[93] and Lord Auchinbreck came from Scotland, and Colonel Monroe met them in Trian Congal (Tpian congail). They marched together with 8,000 men to Coleraine and Ballymoney[94] (Feappao monaig). O'Kane, that is, Donnell Gimley, with a large party came upon them at the Ferry[95] (peappao). The Scotch were defeated, they took to the woods around, and they lost about 150 men, while not a single one of the Irish was killed. The inhabitants of the Barony of Loughinsholin (Loc inip o lunn) and the O'Kanes went to

88. Muintir Birn was a district in the south of the Barony of Dungannon, adjoining the territory of Trough, Co. Monaghan, and Toaghie, now the Barony of Armagh. (See the Leabhar na g-Ceart, or Book of Rights, p. 151.)—J. S.

89. Glenkeen is a townland in the Parish of Aghaloo, Co. Tyrone, between Caledon and Aughnacloy.—J. W. H.

90. The Creaghts were shepherds in time of peace, and drove the cattle-preys in time of war. The word Creaght comes from cpeaċ, plunder, or caopaċu, cattle.—J. S. See note on above, Town Book of Belfast, p. 304.—EDITOR.

91. This is the festival day of St. Muredach, Bishop of Killala. Also St. Clare's; this probably is the correct reading.—J. W. H.
[St. Clare's festival is 12th August. See Butler's Lives of the Saints at that date.—J. S.]

92. Sir Phelim O'Neill. By "the General," Owen Roe O'Neill is meant, in all entries in this Journal subsequent to 29th August, 1642, when Sir Phelim is noticed as resigning in his favour.—J. S. An engraved portrait of the latter, entitled "Sir Phelom O'Neile, Chief Traytor of all Ireland," exists.—EDITOR.

93. General Leslie landed on the 4th August, according to Carte's Ormonde, i. p. 349. By "Lord Auchinbreck" is meant Sir Duncan Campbell of Auchinbreck. He was a cousin of the Marquis of Argyle. See Hill's Macdonnells of Antrim, pp. 73, 74. Auchinbreck's Regiment is mentioned by the British Officer (Irish Warr of 1641, p. 50) as "Collonel Campbell's, alias Aghinbrack's, quartered in the Route."—J. S.

94. This cannot be Ballymoney, Co. Antrim. It is Vow Ferry, on the Bann.—J. W. H.

95. Toome.—J. W. H.
In the Latin Tripartite Life of St. Patrick, Toome is called Fersait Tuama. (See Reeves's Ecclesiastical Antiquities of Down, Connor, and Dromore, p. 293.) Compare Ferlais Tuamma in the Irish Tripartite, i. p. 168. In the Four Masters (ii. p. 951) it is Tuaim.—J. S.

Brantry (ᏏᎬᎬᎪᏂᎢᏌᎥᏋ), to Truagh (ᏟᏂᎥᎤᏋᎪ), and to Sliabh Beagh. The General[96] and Owen O'Neill happened to be in Charlemont (ᎪᏟᎪᎠ ᎪᏁ ᎠᎪ ᏟᎪᎥᎪᎤ). They were shown the forces approaching. The General went to Sliabh na Maol (ᏑᎥᎪᏏ ᏁᎪ ᎻᎪᎤᏞ) and collected 1,000 men, and Owen O'Neill went to O'Neilland (ᎥᏏ ᎻᎪᏞᏞᎪᏁ) and there gathered 2,000. The numerous Scotch forces arrived at Dungannon and fired off their guns in one volley, and I myself heard that tremendous report. They encamped during the night at   (ᎥᎥᏞᎬᏁ ᏟᏌᎵᏌᏁ), near Armagh, and on Saint Bartholomew's day they marched to Newry (ᎤᎥᏁ ᎥᏌᏏᎪᎵ). Aug. 24, 1642. The General pursued them a great part of the way.

The General sent five Captains about Dungannon, on Saint Augustine's day.[97] They brought away upward of 100 cows. Trenches were made round the Castle, and an excavation was made which was brought under the Castle. Captain Jones (ᏚᏟᎬᏁᎵᎪ) capitulated, and was permitted to bring the arms with them and to Mountjoy. The General placed, as a Governor in Dungannon, Turlogh O'Neill M'Art Og, Turlogh M'Shane Og O'Neill, Randal M'Donnell, and Niall Og O'Neill, all Captains—Art M'Hugh ᏏᏌᎥᎠᏟ (yellow) O'Neill made an incursion into Ballyscanlon (Ꮟ Ꭵ ᎵᎦᎪᏁᏞᎪᏁ), and took from the Bawn outside the gate of the Castle 50 cows. One of them died, and there was a sharp fight for her. Aug. 28, 1642.

A day of general meeting was appointed by the nobles of the province of Ulster. The clan of the O'Neills came, together with the General and Owen : also the O'Reillys, O'Kanes, M'Rorys, O'Dalys, M'Mahons, Managhans[98] (ᎻᎪᏁᏟᏂᎪᎦ), and the M'Donnells, with Sir James M'Allister the scabbed (ᏟᎪᎵᎵᎪᏟ), all came to Clones (ᏟᏟᏞᏌᎪᏁ ᏟᎧᎵ), for the purpose of electing a General. Sir Felim resigned the title on condition that it should be conferred on his elder relation Owen—Owen was accordingly nominated General of Ulster, and Sir Felim, President. Aug. 29, 1642.

Soldiers were sent with Lieutenant-Colonel Shane Og O'Neill M'Shane M'Brien of Munter-loony (ᏞᎪᎥᎦᏁᎥᎦ). The enemy came in search of fuel, and had sixteen of their men killed. Sept. 8, 1642.

O'Kane appointed pay for the two sons of Colla ᏟᎥᎧᎵᎪᎥᎦ (the left-handed), namely, Gillespie and Randal :—in the first place, 25 pounds towards the purchase of clothing and coigny on O'Kane's creaghts[99] (Ꮖ ᏟᏏᎻᎻᎬᎪᎠ ᎪᎵ ᏁᎪ ᏟᎵᏋᎥᎠᏋᎪᏟᎢᎪᎥᏏ ᏟᎪᏟᎪᏁᎪᏟ ᎦᎥ ᏟᎧᎦᏏᎪᎥᏞ ᏏᏌᎪᏁᏁᎪᏋᎢᎪ ᎠᎥᎥᏏ). O'Kane went to the place where the General was. The sons of Colla mustered their people, and told the soldiers to carry away from the people of every house who had coigne, their cows and horses, together with their household furniture, their sheep and goats, with their accoutrements. This was done, and they brought the plunder with them to Coleraine. They raised a fortification for themselves.

---

96. Sir Phelim O'Neill.—J. S.

97. St. Augustine's Day and the date of the entry in the *Journal* are identical. "The General" is still Sir Phelim O'Neill.—J. S.

98. The men of Fermanagh.—J. O'D.

99. *Until they should take Bonaght from them.*—J. O'D.
[Coigny and Bonaght, *i.e.*, entertainment and free quarters.—J. S.]

The General sent 1,000 men to protect the Bann from the enemy, for they were numerous in Trian Congail (Τριαη Conʒαιl).

Oct. 3, 1642.   The Earl of Ormond arrived with 4,000 men and laid siege to Carrickmacross (cαρρυιc mαċαιρε αη ιοιρ); Captain Fox and the Garrison fled. Next day the English came to the Court and hanged the Lady Eveleen, wife of Art Og M'Brien the wrestler (ηα mbαιιιοʒ), and daughter of Eiver M'Cooley M'Mahon.

Oct. 17, 1642.   Pope Urban the Fifth[100] sent an army of 500 men to Ireland. Sir Felim went with his part of the Ulster forces to that army. He soon after married the daughter of Thomas Preston.[101] The dowry he received with her was arms for 500 horsemen, 200 muskets, and 3,000 pounds.

Nov. 13, 1642.   It was determined that a Parliament should be held at Kilkenny. Thither the General[102] went.

Dec. 13, 1642.   The Enniskillen soldiers came and plundered the country. They were attacked by the Maguires (ριοl Uιδιρ).[103] We lost that day three Captains, namely, Donaghy M'Cabe the scabbed (cαρραċ), James M'Goffrey[104] M'Henry, and Captain M'Cabe, with other persons not named.

January 6, 1643   The General and Sir Felim came from the Council of Kilkenny to Charlemont (Λέαυ αη υά ċαιιαυ).

April 27, 1643.   The plunderer, that is, Rory O'Haran, and the son of Sir Thomas Philipps, collected the people of the Castles, and a great multitude from Derry. In Ballynascreen (bαιle ηα ρʒιιηε) they fell in with Niall O'Neill. From that they proceeded to Lissan (Leιιαη) and burnt the Iron-mill of Tattynagilta[105] (τατce ηα ccoιlteαċ). They took from Niall Og O'Quin a stud of horses, his swine and sheep, and about 20 guns. Shane O'Hagan and his people were plundered, Rory O'Mellan[106] the speckled (bαllαċ)[107] was taken, and Cookstown (Coιρι cιιoċαċ) burnt.

The Coleraine soldiers fell upon Cormac O'Neill M'Felim Og at Rallagh, and robbed and killed his people, namely, the M'Williams.[108] Thence they went to the Lake of Loughinsholin, and to Moneymore, until the two forces were near one another. They collected a great

---

100. This should be Urban the *Eighth* (Maffei Barberini). Urban the *Fifth* died in 1370. Urban the *Fifth* occurs again in this translation; but it is not probable that Friar O'Mellan was ignorant of the proper designation of the Pope who was reigning in his own time. The mistake must be the translator's. Urban receives his correct numerical designation in the entry, 28th August, 1646.—J. S.

101. She is quaintly styled "a Dutch borne" by the author of the *Aphorismical Discovery of Faction*, i. p. 53. General Preston had acquired much military fame in the Low Countries.—J. S.

102. Owen Roe.—J. S.   For description of his portrait, written by the Rev. J. O'Laverty, P.P., M.R.I.A., see *Ulster Journal of Archæology*, vol. iv. p. 24.—EDITOR.

103. The *Sil Uidhir* were the Maguires, MacAuleys, MacCaffrys, MacManuses, and their correlatives in Fermanagh. (See O'Donovan's *Four Masters*, iii. p. 476.)—J. S.

104. M'Govry.—J. O'D.   M'Henry *O'Kane*.—J. O'D.

105. Tattynagilta, a townland in the Parish of Lissan, Co. Tyrone.—J. W. H.

106. O'Mellan, now Mullan.—J. O'D.

107. Speckled, *i.e.*, freckled.   bαllαċ (*Ballach* or *Ballagh*) is of common occurrence in the names of Irish chiefs.—J. S.

108. M'Williams, a tribe of the Burkes.—J. O'D.

deal of spoil, and the Creaghts fled to Dungannon.   After plundering to a great extent, the English returned to Loughinsholin.   They sent Rory O'Mellan[109] (ballaċ) to demand the Island (an oileán) from Shane O'Hagan M'Keown M'Cammon Og.   It was refused them. They fired three shots from a cannon they had with them, and then left the place.   They returned to their homes laden with spoil.

The garrison of Mountjoy held out in spite of the Irish.   Precisely on Thursday (oaroaoin oo fonnpaú), a reinforcement of 1,000 men having come to the garrison from Massareene, they took from Felim of the war (an coġaiú) O'Neill 30 cows.   They came in the same April 28, 1643. boats next day to M'Cann's fort and took some plunder.   The General's people followed, and killed above 60 of them.   They lost their plunder too, and a great quantity of arms.   The General only lost eight men, together with Art O'Neill M'Cormac M'Turlogh Breasalagh (bpeapalaċ).   Sir Felim came to the besieging army and doubled it ; so that he prevented all egress.   The reinforcing party were obliged to return in their boats for want of provisions.

The soldiers of Tyrconnell, consisting of 3,000 men under the com- May 4, 1643. mand of Sir Robert Stewart, arrived and plundered Clossagh (cloċpaú), and then proceeded to Truagh (Tpioċa).   Five of their horsemen went May 5, 1643. to Largy (Leapġaiú).   Sir Felim and O'Kane happened to be near the place with 100 horse and 100 foot.   Donnell Gimley went to re-connoitre the enemy, and perceived the five horsemen near him. O'Kane spurred till he was between the two forces, and his horse fell with him.   The animal's head happened to be undermost, so that O'Kane found it impossible to raise him on his feet.   He was immediately taken prisoner, and the horse-men were enabled to get off in safety from the fleetness of their horses.   Hereupon Sir Felim said that he would not suffer them to carry off O'Kane.   He set off in pursuit, but in the meantime a Scotch trooper sent a bullet through O'Kane's head : he fell lifeless to the ground, and they carried away his horse and arms.   Sir Felim came to the body, and had it interred in Armagh.

With respect to the enemy, they came to M'Kenna's residence (boile Mec Ciona) and took it, together with much wealth.   They came back plundering all the way, and hanged Priest M'Gilmurry in May 7, 1643. his own parish of Drumragh[110] (Opoim paċa), on Sunday precisely (oia ooṁnaċ oo funnpaú).

Robert Monroe came to Tandragee with 4,000 men, and burnt the May 12, 1643. houses in O'Neilland (ib niallain).   About that time the General's people, his horse and foot soldiers, came upon them.   The Lieutenant of the enemy's cavalry, two Captains, and a number of soldiers were killed there.   Night coming on, the Creaghts fled, namely, the people of Upper Claneboy, Iveagh, and the County Armagh, to Brantry (bpeucop), Oriel (Oipġialla), &c.   However, the Scotch were not without plunder ; they burnt three corn mills.   Sir Felim sent a party

109. This is incorrect.—J. O'D.

110. The Parish in which lies the town of Omagh.—J. W. H.

The old parish church of Drumragh stood nearly two miles south of Omagh.   In 1622 it is reported as ruined, but that there was "hope" and "means" that a new church might be erected in Omagh.   The ancient walls still exist.—W. T. LATIMER, B.A.

to Anasamery[111] (Eanac ꞃampaꞃꞼ), to the house of the General, to bring away whatever arms were there ; and, about three hours after, the enemy came and burnt Anasamery (Eanac ꞃampaꞃꞼ). A great body of the M'Kennas came and carried away much spoil. Sir Felim sent Colonel Thomas Sanford and 300 men to take it from them ; and they killed about 200 of them. They staid three days encamped at Tandragee, and returned with a large quantity of wheat, meal, and corn.

The plunderer (that is, Rory O'Haran) came, and brought Scotch troops from the Castles, and the son of Thomas Philipps from Newtown-limavady, on an enterprise to plunder Art and Tuathal O'Neill, sons of Hugh M'Shane. Along with him also was Alister Roe, the people of Desertcreaght[112] (Oiꞃoꞃꞇ ėꞃnoė), and many more, amounting to upwards of 2,000.

May 20, 1643.   They killed the Priest who was in the Parish of Maghera (Maċaiꞃe aꞃa), Owen Moder (moꞩaꞃꞼa) O'Creely, and his brother, Conor Og, and some others. Sir Felim pursued them with 13 standards and many horsemen, but did not overtake them. The day on which Patrick Moder O'Loughren (O Laoėꞃꞥen) was buried was Sunday (an ꝺomnaė móꞃ).[113]

Thursday, May 24, 1643.   Lord Conway (Conꝼaꞡ), Chichester, Blayney, Hamilton, and Montgomery, arrived with more than 5,000 men and five troops of horse. The Creaghts fled. The General sent two of his horsemen to guard them, and they took two of the enemy's cavalry, one of whom, Rory (ballaė) O'Mellan,[114] was taken away by Sir Felim. These Lords went to Oriel[115] (Oiꞃꞡialla), as they did not like the Owenites. Having halted at Monaghan, they sent their people to gather spoil, and Lord Moore took a great quantity. The manner in which they divided the booty was this : that each party alternately should have a park full of cattle. The Scotch endeavoured to drive and thrust the cows into their own park, and this did not please the English.

May 28, 1643.   Colonel Robert Monroe came from Trian Congail (Tꞃian conꞡail) to Armagh and Benburb. They killed Maurice O'Haghey,[116] an old Doctor, and some others.

---

111.   Eanach-Samer, now Anasamery, between Loughgall and Charlemont, about 1½ miles from the latter. It is now the property of Sir William Verner.—J. W. H.
[Carte speaks of it (*Ormonde*, i. p. 432) as "Annagh Sawry near Charlemont."—J. S.]

112.   A townland and parish in the north of the Barony of Dungannon. The name is written Oiꞃoꞃꞇ ꝺa ėꞃnoċl by the *Four Masters* (iii. p. 432).—J. S.

113.   This sentence is perhaps a mistranslation, and should read:—"Patrick Moder (*i.e.*, moꞩaꞃꞼa the gloomy) O'Loughran was buried *at Donaghmore*." Quoting from this *Journal*, Dr. Reeves (*Primate Colton's Visitation*, p. 12) says, with reference to the O'Loughrans, "one of the family is spoken of as being buried at Donaghmore." Except this passage, there is none to which such a meaning could be attached. The MS. from which this translation was made not being at present available for inspection (though Dr. Reeves seems to have had the use of it), the matter rests between him and Mr. Robert Macadam, the translator, which is right.—J. S.

114.   ballaė, freckled.—J. S.

115.   As far as Belturbet, *Reid*, i. p. 428.—J. W. H.

116.   O'Heachaidh.—J. O'D.

Thomas Sanford, one of Sir Felim's Colonels, happened to meet them, and skirmished with them from Benburb to Charlemont (ἀċἀὐ ἀn ὐἀ ċἀμἀὐ), to Killyman (ċιLL nἀ mbἀn), to Mountjoy and Moneymore. They plundered Henry M'Rory Boy (bυιὐċ) O'Hagan. Many were killed by them throughout Killeter (CυιLL ιοċτἀμἀιġ).[117]

A Council was held by the General of the Ulster army, and by the President, Sir Felim, at [Mullintur] (mυLLἀċ ἀn τυιμ)[118] in Munter Byrne. May 31, 1643. They resolved not to leave the country on any account. That whoever stole a cow or mare, horse or garron, sheep or goat, the value of these things should be levied off his property, if he had any; or, if a poor man, that he should be hanged. Also, whatever persons should go about drinking out of churns, or raising any disturbance, should be cudgelled with staves till their back bones were broken inside of them; and many other good regulations. There are some persons in the country, O'Kanes, Devlins, O'Haras, the Iveagh, and all the Claneboy and the Route (μυτἀ), who eat mares and horses, who steal and carry off from the rear of the Heretics cats and dogs, and eat men.

Sir Felim, with Paul O'Neill, the Guardian of Armagh, and Captain June 2, 1643. Turlogh ʒμυἀmἀ O'Quin, went with horse-carriages to meet the arms which the King of Spain[119] had sent to Ireland. On Friday, Robert Stewart, with 4,000 men, came from Inishowen. They wasted and plundered Clossagh (ἀn cloμἀιġ). As for the General, Owen O'Neill, he had before this (9th June) ordered the Creaghts to go to the County Longford (Lonʒbοιτ), and they were on the way thither. The enemy came June 13, 1643. to Clones (Cluἀιneἀμ) on the day of Saint Anthony of Padua,[120] and neither the General nor any person else perceived them until they were within about two miles of them. The General's regiment, and four troops of horse surrounding it, met the enemy, who advanced suddenly. The alarm was sounded, and Sir Felim's regiment came forward, together with Lieutenant-Colonel Shane O'Neill.[121] The action was very fierce on both sides; however, the enemy prevailed

117. Carte's narrative may be taken in connection with these two paragraphs:—"*Monroe* marched in *May* with great expedition and secrecy into the County of *Armagh* to surprise *Owen O'Neile* in his quarters at *Annagh Savory*, near *Charlemont*. *O'Neile* himself was the first that discovered them, as he was hunting, at the distance of two miles, and about four from his quarters, whither he immediately retired; and, drawing off his small party of 400 men, after an hour's dispute with *Monroe's* whole force in a lane enclosed with quicksets leading to *Charlemont*, made his retreat thither without the loss of a man. *Monroe* seized the passes about that fortress, intending to make what preys he could in the country; but one of his parties being the next day attacked by Lieutenant-Colonel *Sandford*, an hundred of his men killed, and the prey recovered, he thought fit to return into the County of *Antrim*." (See Carte's *Ormonde*, i. p. 432.)—J. S.

118. Mullintur, parish of Aghaloo, Co. Tyrone.—J. W. H.

[Muintir Birn, a district in the south of the Barony of Dungannon adjoining Trough, a territory in Co. Monaghan, and Tonghie, now the Barony of Armagh. See the *Leabhar na g-Ceart, or Book of Rights*, p. 151.—J. S.]

119. Philip the Fourth. Paul O'Neill, *i.e.*, "yt postilian ffryer" mentioned in note 59.—J. S.

120. St. Anthony of Padua's Day, and the 13th June, the date of this entry, are the same.—J. S.

121. "An old officer who had been 25 years in foreign service." (See Carte's *Ormonde*, i. p. 433.)—J. S.

over us.[122]   We lost Colonel Con Og M'Quin M'Neill M'Brien
Faghertach (Ƒᴀᵹᴀꞃᴄᴀċ), and Captain Niall O'Neill M'Turlogh M'Quin
bᴀcᴀċ (the lame); also Captain Eiver O'Neill M'Conolly mᴀc ᴀn
ꞃꞁꞃᴏᴏꞁᴇᴀ (son of the dark man), Captain Brian O'Devlin of the
Cavalry, Captain Edward [Cooley?] (cᴜᴜᴌᴀᴏ) O'Mulhollan.   The
Colonel of the Orielians (ᴇꞁꞃᵹıᴀᴌᴌ) was taken prisoner, that is,
M'Mahon; Hugh M'Art Og M'Art, son of the Baron (mᴀc ᴀn bᴀꞃᴜꞁꞁ),
took to flight.   The following were made prisoners:—Lieutenant-
Colonel Sir Felim[123] O'Neill and Captain Art M'Hugh the yellow (bᴜıᴅᴇ)
M'Turlogh M'Henry.   We all fled from this dreadful battle.[124]   The
poor Creaghts (cꞃᴏıᴅᴇᴀċᴄᴀ) were left behind entirely at the mercy of
the enemy.   Some of them were driven east, some west, up and down
the country.   It was then that Cormac O'Hagan was slain.   Och! och!
a sorrowful tale!—and all this time Sir Felim was at Kilkenny.   Some
of us fled to Breffny, some to the counties of Armagh, Tyrone, and
Louth.   The General returned to Truagh (Ꞇꞁᴜᴀᴅ).   On the second
night he lodged at Brantry[125] (bꞃᴇᴀꞁᴄꞃꞁ), in the House of the Friars,
at Gort-tamlaght-na-muc (ᵹᴏꞁᴄ ᴄᴀṁᴌᴀċᴄᴀ ꞁᴀ mᴜc).   He left that place
early in the morning, and some time after the Scotch came to Brantry
on Thursday precisely (ᴅᴀꞁᴅᴀᴏꞁꞁ ᴅᴏ ꞃᴜꞁꞁꞃꞁᴀᴅ).   They burnt the houses
of the Franciscan Friars, and killed a great many persons.   We were
four Friars at Brantry, namely, Turlogh O'Mellan, a priest, and three
Friars of the family of Loughran (ᴌᴀᴏċꞃꞁᴇꞁ), namely, Owen, Benedict,
and Teague,—the names when night came.   There were during the
night, at Carnteel (Cᴀꞁꞁ ᴄꞃꞁᴀᴅᴀıᴌ) 4,000 foot and six troops of horse,
including the people from Tyrconnell and Enniskillen, and commanded by Sir William Cole (Cᴏbᴀᴌ), Sir Robert Stewart, and Sir
William Stewart.   They had 4,000 cows divided among them.   We
ourselves, the Friars, took three of them, namely, two milk cows and a
dry one.   We killed the latter, but two fellows from the Route (ꞁꞁᴜᴄᴀ)
took the others from us.

June 17, 1643.   They (the enemy) made a forced march till they arrived in the
Counties of Cavan, Longford, and Leitrim, in pursuit of the General.

122.   Owen Roe was nearly taken prisoner in this engagement.   "At which place," says the
British Officer (*Irish Warr of 1641*, p. 30), "Mac Art escaped narrowly, pistolling him that would
lay hands on him, &c."   O'Mulhollan, who was among the slain, is described by the British
Officer as "Cullo Madder Mulhollan, a Stout old Horseman."   Madder, *i.e.*, ꞁꞁᴏᴅᴀꞁꞃᴅᴀ,
the gloomy.—J. S.

123.   *Reid* (i. p. 428), *Carte* (i. p. 433).—J. W. H.
[Perhaps "Lieutenant-Colonel Sir Felim" should be Lieutenant-Col. Shane O'Neill.   Carte
(*Ormonde*, i. p. 433) mentions no Felim as taken, but says:—"Among the prisoners were Shane
O'Neile, Colonel Hugh O'Neile, nephew to the General, Captain Art O'Neile, grandson to Sir
Turlogh Mac Henry, two other Captains, and three Gentlemen of Quality."—J. S.]

124.   Carte (*Ormonde*, i. p. 433) says:—"The Rebels suffered in this action a greater loss
than any they had met with before in Ulster, most of their Arms being taken, and the greatest
part of the foreign Officers, which came over with Owen O'Neile, being either killed or taken
prisoners. . . .   The loss of the English in this battle, which was fought on Tuesday, the 13th
of June, was inconsiderable, there being only six of them killed, and about twenty-two wounded."
—J. S.

125.   The British Officer (*Irish Warr of 1641*, p. 31) says:—"After the Route at Clownish,
Mac Art came that night to the Braniter Woods, and next day rested at Charlemont, and next
night went after the People of Ulster to the County of Cavan, where he gathered them all
again."—J. S.

He encamped a number of soldiers and cavalry round the garrison of Jamestown (Rosscommon) (bαιle ʁemuıp), to guard the Creaghts.[126] .

George Monroe, (perhaps *and*) Lieutenant-General Leslie, collected June 29, 1643. a great host, including the son of Lord Leven[127] (Lαbαıp), and the son of Randal (Rınnel) Stewart. They crossed the River Bann, having along with them Colonel Conolly (eoȝαn), that is, the man who turned informer in Dublin, and through whom Lord Enniskillen was taken.[128] They proceeded to Mountjoy, to Killeter (Coıll ıoċταpαıȝ), to Clanaghrie (Clnαın eαċpe), and to Brantry, so that any of the natives who had remained in the country, and were unable to fly to distant places, lost every thing they possessed. They encamped at Carnteel; on Saint Peter's day they burnt Bally Turlogh O'Neill (boılı τoıp- noαlbαıȝ ı lleıll), called the castle.[129] From that they went to Bally- July 1, 1643. donnelly, and Con M'Art M'Donnell, the accursed (mαc nα mαllαċτ), delivered up to them the island of Ballydonnelly on Saturday. O'Neill M'Felim M'Donnell, a Franciscan Friar, was taken; he was sent to Carrickfergus (Cαppαıȝ ʁeıpʒupα), and was in confinement 17 months.

They proceeded to Dungannon, and demanded the surrender of July 3, 1643. the town, which was refused. Next day soldiers were sent to fire on the town, and again to demand a surrender. Brian buınoe (yellow) Hughes[130] (O hαονα), an old veteran, was taken in Dungannon, and a Franciscan Friar, named Patrick O'Hamill, was the Father Confessor.[131]

A large force under Colonel Robert Monroe, Lord Chichester, Lord July 4, 1643. Conway (Conpαıȝ), Lord Hamilton, and Lord Montgomery, crossed the Avonmore (Blackwater) to Dungannon. They pitched their tents at Gortmerron[132] (ȝopτ Ⅲeαpαnn). Their numbers amounted to 5,000 foot and 1,000 horse.

On seeing so great a force the garrison was seized with fear, and July 7, 1643. surrendered on receiving liberty to carry away their arms and movable effects. On the fifth day after, a Scotch garrison was placed in the town. Brian M'Donchadh bpαoαıȝ (the rogue) O'Hagan delivered up the island of Lough   (Loċ lnıeα), without any necessity for it, to the Scotch. It was resolved by the Council of the forces to pursue the

126. Jamestown, Co. Leitrim, must be meant. Jamestown, County Roscommon, was an insignificant place, but Jamestown, Co. Leitrim, had a castle, built in 1623 by Sir Charles Coote, which was taken in 1645 by the Earl of Carlingford, and again in 1689 by the Enniskilleners under Colonel Lloyd. (See the *Parliamentary Gazetteer of Ireland*, ii. p. 332.)—J. S.

127. Leslie, who was afterwards Earl of Leven.—J. W. H.

128. Conolly, or O'Connolly, seceded to Protestantism in his youth. He eventually became a Presbyterian elder. (See Reid's *History of the Presbyterian Church in Ireland*, i. pp. 310, 311.) He was killed in 1649 by a Mr. Hamilton, whose brother he had murdered. In 1662, £200 per annum was secured, out of confiscated estates, for the support of his orphans, Arthur and Martha O'Connolly. (See Meehan's *Confederation of Kilkenny*, pp. 88, 89.) According to the British Officer (*Irish Warr of 1641*, pp. 93, 94) Conolly killed Mr. Hamilton's brother in a duel.—J. S. Conolly had left the Presbyterian Church before his death and become a "Separatist."—W. T. LATIMER, B.A.

129. Castletown.—J. W. H. Castletown Bawn, or generally "The Bawn."—W. T. L.

130. O'Hay.—J. O'D.
' *O'Haedha.*—"This name is very common throughout the Province of Ulster, but now anglicised Hughes. In the south of Ireland it is variously anglicised O'Hea, O'Hee, O'Hay, and Hayes." (See O'Donovan's *Four Masters*, iv. pp. 1203-4).—J. S.

131. It is not clear what is implied by the concluding part of this sentence. Irish prisoners were not allowed Father Confessors by the enemy.—J. S.

132. Gortmerron adjoins Dungannon.—J. W. H.

General, Owen O'Neill, and to take the Creaghts from him.   One detachment of them was therefore sent off to Truagh and to Clones and Cavan.   A second party went to Kinard,[133] to Monaghan, and Cavan, and thence to Slieve Brus.   Seven hundred horsemen were sent in pursuit of the Ulster-men, and as they did not fall in with them, they returned to Bun (ᵹo bun), and resolved to go back to their own stations.   They were in Monaghan that night.

I may now make some mention of Charlemont (Áċaú an ꝺá ċapaú) where the harvest was now approaching with a large force, composed of English, Scotch, and Irish arrived at this town.[134]   He planted four cannon at Dunavally[135] (Ꝺun ꝺá baLLa) against the place.   There were attacks and skirmishes every day, the Scotch always losing great numbers.   The thought struck Captain Niall O'Neill M'Shane M'Turlogh M'Henry M'Shane that it might be well to scour the roads which were at some distance round the town.   One day they happened upon a company of horse and foot coming from Mountjoy to the besieging army : they immediately attacked them, killed five soldiers and three horses, and wounded two horsemen.   They took from them wine, beer, vinegar, whiskey, two tents, some spades and mattocks, a cart full of meal, butter and cheese, as much as two horses would draw, and a quantity of linen and woollen clothes.   After this capture, the besiegers extended their encampment on all sides of the town, so that no way of egress for the garrison was left.   However, a sally was made in the night-time across the river in boats, and fourteen men were killed before a word was spoken.

As for the General, Owen O'Neill, he placed soldiers between the Creaghts and the garrison of Jamestown.[136]   The garrison of Elphin arrived on a plundering expedition, and carried off with them horses, cows, and captives, and, among the rest, Brian MacCuconnacht.   Some men were killed.

Aug. 2, 1643.   Colonel Richard O'Farrell, of the County Longford, carried off a considerable booty of arms, clothes, money, and   ?
He killed two young horsemen of the O'Quins.

The General brought the Creaghts across the Shannon westward to the top of Brus,[137] in Breffny, and Sir Felim come from Kilkenny to the same place.   The ambassador of Pope Urban V.[138] arrived

---

133.   Kinard, *i.e.*, Caledon.—J. S.

134.   Perhaps this sentence means, that as the harvest was coming on, a force of English, &c., came to Charlemont.   The British Officer (see his *Irish Warr of 1641*, p. 34) may help us to understand it.   "This Harvest," he says, "the Scottish Army, the Lord Conway's Regiment, the Lord Donegall's Regiment, and our Regiment were all in the counties of Ardmagh, Tyrone, and Londonderry, reaping, threshing, and burning all the Grain the Irish sowed, which was plenty, &c."—J. S.   For corn taken by the Irish, see present vol., p. 55.—EDITOR.

135.   On a hill called Leager Hill, in the townland of Corr and Dunavally, overhanging and commanding the old fort of Charlemont, are yet the remains of this position.   It is now a graveyard, but the trench is complete.—J. W. H.

136.   Jamestown, Co. Leitrim.—J. S.

137.   Now Bruise Mountain, in Tullyhunco Barony, Co. Cavan.—J. W. H.
[Tullyhunco was the Mac Kernans' country.   See O'Daly's *Tribes of Ireland*, p. 93.—J. S.]

138.   *Recte*, Urban the *Eighth*. (See note 100.)   The ambassador was the pro-nuncio, Father Pier Francesco Scarampo, priest of the Congregation of the Oratory of St. Philip Neri.—J. S.

from Rome to observe the progress of the war, and bringing some
assistance to the Irish,

Brian O'Neill M'Art Og and Randal M'Donnell (ᵽᾱⲥ ᴅⲟⁱⁿⲛⲁⳑⳑ) ᴬᵘᵍ· ¹⁴· ¹⁶⁴³
delayed behind the Creaghts. Captain Hanly brought a party of the
enemy on them, when Randal was killed and Brian deprived of all his
effects.

A Council of the Ulster Chiefs, with the General, was held to ᴬᵘᵍ· ²⁵·¹⁶⁴³·
determine whether they should come to the province of Ulster, or go
to Meath, to procure corn. They decided at length upon Meath, and
leaving Slieve Brus, they went to the Church of Lurgan (ⲧⲉⲁⲙⲡⲟⳑⳑ ⲛⲁ
ⳑⲟⁱⲅⲁⲛ) to Lough Ramor[130] (ⳑⲟⳓ ⲣⲉⲁⳗⲁⲣ) and [Balgeeth] (ⲟⁱⲟⁱⳓⲉⲁⲛ
ⲃⲉⳑ ⲁⲧ ⳓⲁⲟⁱⲧⲉ).[140] The General sent a messenger to [Cloon] (ⲥⳑⲩⲁⲛⲁ
ⲃⲣⲉⁱⲫⲛ)[141] demanding the surrender of the town, and the garrison,
upon seeing the strength of the besiegers, capitulated, and received
honourable terms.

Inish O'Linn[142] (ⁱⲛⁱⲣ ⁱ ⳑⲩⲛⲛ) was garrisoned by Shane O'Hagan. ᴬᵘᵍ· ¹²·¹⁶⁴³·
The enemy came and called on them to surrender, which they refused.
They then stopped up a stream that ran out of the lake,[143] and turned
the course of another into it, so that they contrived to inundate the
island. The garrison kept watch in the island-house, and one of their
men was killed by a cannon-ball while on guard. However, they
refused to give up the island on any account. One man, in attempting to swim away, got his legs broken. The enemy at last departed.

The Castle of Killallon[144] (ⲥⁱⳑⳑ ⲁⳑⳑⲩⲛ) and the Castle of Balrath[145]
surrendered to Sir Felim, and the garrisons received good quarter, viz.,
their arms, clothes, and effects.

A message from the General was sent to Ballybeg, ordering the
garrison to surrender, but they returned him a refusal. The soldiers
immediately invested the town, and planted the cannon against it.
The cannonade began, and soon the edifice was broken down and
breaches made. The garrison now asked quarter, but were refused, ᴬᵘᵍ· ³⁰·¹⁶⁴³·
and ordered to come forth and submit to mercy. The whole of them
came out, being 180 in number, between horse and foot soldiers. The
son of Sir Henry Tichborne (ⲧⁱⲟⲣⲃⲉⁱⲣⲛ) and Captain Cardiff
(Coⲣⲣⲟⲩⲃ)[146] were taken.

---

139. Slieve Bruise, the parish of Lurgan, and Lough Ramor, all in Co. Cavan. By the
Four Masters (i. p. 10) Lough Ramor is called ⳑⲟⲥⳁ ⲙⳑⲩⲛⲣⲉⲙⲟⁱⲣⵏ.—J. S.

140. Balgeeth, in Meath.—J. O'D.

141. Cloon, in Leitrim.—J. O'D.

[By the *Four Masters* (iii. pp. 348–9) the place is called ⲥⳑⲩⲁⁱⲛ ⲥⲟⲛⲙⲁⁱⲥⲛⲟ.—J. S.

142. The island in Lough-inis-O'Lynn, Co. Derry, barony of Loughinsholin. An O'Lynn is
said to have founded a monastery hereabouts. (See *Primate Colton's Visitation*, pp. 76–7.)—J. S.

143. It is a small lake about 220 yards in length and 179 in width. (See *Primate Colton's
Visitation*, p. 76.)—J. S.

144. Near Old Castle.—J. O'D.

145. Balrath, Co. Westmeath, is called ⲃⁱⳑⲉ ⲣⲁⲧⲁ by the *Four Masters* (iv. p. 1164),
who make the first mention of ordnance in their *Annals* in connection with the destruction of its
castle in 1488.—J. S.

146. Coⲣⲣ ⲟⲩⲃ, the nearest approach that O'Mellan could make to the sound of this
Captain's name, happens to mean *Black Snout*, or *Beak*.—J. S.

Q

Sept. 1, 1643.   The Castle of   (baile Fiaδain ?) was taken, and a son of Sir William Parsons, from Dublin.   At Athboy (boile ath buiδi) were taken by Captain Smith and two gentlemen.   The monastery of Nenagh (mainirtir an aonaiᵹ) and the Castle[147] of [Assoon] (baile earuin) on the Boyne.   The Castle of   (baile juinilep) also was taken and burnt immediately.

Sept. 8, 1643.   On the festival of our Blessed Lady[148] the Creaghts arrived from Kells (ceanannur)[149] along with Sir Felim at Port   , and (   ).   Siege was laid to Portlester[150] (Porc Leartain), one of the enemy's posts, and it was surrendered to the General.

Lord Moore now came in pursuit of the General, his forces, and Creaghts, determined that not a man or beast of them should escape from his troops, for he had collected great numbers of Scotch and English by his promises of great pay and a share in the plunder. There were probably five or six thousand.

The General raised intrenchments at the Earl's Mill Ford (at an muillinn iapla),[151] and the cannon and small fire-arms were got in readiness.   Our enemies advanced confidently to the bank of the ford (ᵹo hur an ata), but were repulsed with great slaughter.   Lord Moore himself[152] fell by a ball from a cannon of Owen O'Neill's, together with 110 men and nine horses.   This great army retreated in great confusion and without plunder.

Three Captains, three Lieutenants, and six Sergeants (of the enemy) declared that if a Sergeant-major and 300 men were given to them of the flower of the army, they would undertake to seize the town in eight days.   All they required was granted.   They assailed

147.   Assoon, in Meath.—J. O'D.

[No doubt this is the same as "Balsonne," mentioned by Carte (Ormonde, i. p. 448) in his enumeration of castles taken by Owen Roe O'Neill—"Killelan, Balrath, Ballibeg, Beckliffe, Balsonne, and Ardsallagh."—J. S.]

148.   The 8th September is the Feast of the Nativity of the Blessed Virgin.—J. S.

149.   Ceanannur, i.e., head fort, or residence.   The Marquis of Headfort takes his title, and that of his seat, from the old name of Kells, translated.—J. S.

150.   In Carte's Ormonde (i. p. 449) Portlester takes the form of "Port-lesterford upon the Blackwater."—J. S.

151.   The Earl's mill ford.   Carte (Ormonde, i. p. 449) speaks of it as "the Earl's milne, at some distance from the ford."   Owen Roe O'Neill, he says, stationed a Captain with 60 men there.—J. S.

152.   This was Charles, second Viscount Drogheda.   Lodge (Peerage, ii. p. 104) says he was slain, 7th August, 1643.—J. W. H.

[The Rev. Alexander Clogy, chaplain of horse, states in his Life of Bedell (p. 176), that he saw the fatal bullet, 6lb. weight, taken out of Lord Moore's body, "being much spent (by grazing) ere it came thither, Sept. 11, 1643." According to Carte's Ormonde (i. p. 449), the attack on "the Earl's milne," and the fall of Lord Moore, took place on the 12th Sept.   The British Officer (Irish Warr of 1641, p. 33) relates that Lord Moore "was viewing what ground to make a Work on, advantageous against the Pass and the Mill : which Mac Art" [i.e., Owen Roe, who was son of Art] "observing, looked through his prospective Glass, after which he levelled a gun with his own hands, and caused a Cannoneer to fire it, which Shot most strangely killed the Lord Moore.   Upon which they put him into a Waggon all mangled, and marched home to Drogheda.   The news of which came not to Mac Art's ears till Night, at which he was highly concerned, as being very sorry for him, at least he seemed to be so."   If we may believe what the British Officer was "credibly told," some of Lord Moore's men who fell in this action were very singularly formed.   See his statement about them.—J. S.

the place confidently, and were convinced that the Irish could not hold out against them. They surrounded the Bawn,[153] and finding no mode of entrance, they turned back and took possession of a sconce[154] which was the wall of an orchard. The country people of the neighbourhood came near to watch the engagement on both sides. The cannons that were within were fired on them, having been charged full with musket balls, and a dreadful havoc was made among them, that is, among the people on the other side of the river, to the north.

The commander of the fort now consulted with his officers on the propriety of giving the besiegers battle. They approved of the proposal, and the soldiers were accordingly sent out under the command of two officers. They marched forward alongside of the sconce, and a fire was immediately begun on both sides. They then drew their swords and long knives (ꞃᵹꞓᴀᴨᴀ), and, falling on the enemy, wounded and stabbed them in all directions. The Scotch at length gave way: the Sergeant-Major, the three Captains, and all the other officers were killed. They fled into the bog, and here it was not a matter of indifference to the Clann Maolin (ᴄʟᴀᴨᴨ ᵯᴀꝍɪʟɪᴨ)[155] who should be foremost. One of them put forward his musket, and had not raised the butt end of it when he was shot in the shoulder blade by the man who was behind him, and tumbled head foremost into the bog. It is the opinion of those who saw them that twenty men did not escape out of the 300 who marched against the Castle. On that day were killed Donald M'Vittie and Magnus O'Corra, an officer, two of the best soldiers in both armies. Leave was granted in the evening to bury their dead.

Sir Robert Stewart, Sir William Cole, and Sergeant-Major Waring encamped alongside the Castle and river in the fields. Their forces amounted to 4,500 men, and they remained in this camp eight weeks. During this period they lost 1,000 men all but three, while the commander of the Castle only lost, between officers and soldiers, eight men.

General Owen despatched letters of truce to the Governor of Charlemont (ᴀᴇᴀꝍ ᴀᴨ ꝍᴀ ꞓᴀᴩᴀꝍ) and to Robert Monroe, stipulating that they should evacuate the country and retire into the towns. The Scotch (in consequence of this treaty) retired to Trian Congail (ꞇᴩᴜᴀᴨ ᴄꝍᴨᵹᴀɪʟ), bringing with them all the grain they could find in the country. Monroe also departed. The Creaghts now, with the General, set off for Tyrone. Garrisons were left by the Scotch in Dungannon, Mountjoy, Arboe (ᴀᴩꝍ ʙꝍ), and Moneymore. The people gathered into the country after the departure of the Scotch, and some ploughing was done, each man a little for himself. They remained there unmolested till summer.

153. Bawn, *i.e.*, a walled enclosure, usually with towers at the angles. Within it was the residence. On Bawns, see Alfred Lee's interesting *Notes* in the *Ulster Journal of Archæology*, vi. pp. 125-135. Dalway's Bawn at Bellahill, near Carrickfergus, is a typical example.—J. S.

154. It seems strange that a "sconce," which was a small fort, should be described as "the wall of an orchard." Perhaps there is something omitted.—J. S.

155. The family of Malone, near Clonmacnoise, Co. Westmeath.—J. W. H.

Feb. 12, 1644. Robert Monroe gave up possession of Dungannon and Mountjoy[156] to Lord Chichester, who came and garrisoned them. Monroe was going at the time to _____ ,[157] but afterwards remained, and he then regretted having given these places up, since he was remaining himself.

May 8, 1644. A written order arrived from the General to the Creaghts, to travel night and day till they came to the County Armagh. The Friars of Armagh came to the Fews (ꝑeꙍbó) with the Guardian, Paul O'Neill. Thence they went to Iniskeen (1ᴨιꝑ cᴀoιn).

May 14, 1644. Colonel Monroe went to Belfast (ꝃeᴀl ꝑeιꝑꞇe) and obliged Lord Chichester to leave the town.[158] His Lordship set off along with his son, Captain Chichester, for Dublin, and nothing with them but their horses.

May 23, 1644. The General, with the cavalry and infantry, came to Lurgan-boy (Luꝑʒᴀn ꝃuιꝃι). All the Creaghts went to Farney (ꝑeᴀꝑnᴀιʒ), to Clonkee (Cloꝰn [ᴀn] Cᴀoιꞓ), and Armaghbreag[159] (ᴀꝑomᴀꞓᴀ ꝃꝑeιʒe).

May 30, 1644. Sir Felim stayed in Charlemont (ᴀꞓᴀꝃ ᴀn ꝃᴀ ꞓᴀꝑᴀꝃ) with a garrison of considerable strength. . . . delivered up Dungannon to him, and he immediately placed a garrison of his own there.

A Commissary, namely, Thomas M'Tiernan,[160] the companion of Donoghy Mor O'Daly, came to the Friars in the Parish of Donaghcloney (ꝰoṁnᴀꞓ Cluᴀnᴀ). Thence he went to the Parish of Donaghmoyne[161] (ꝰoṁnᴀιʒ mᴀιʒen), and then westwards to Armaghbreague (ᴀꝑom ᴀꞓᴀ ꝃꝑeιʒe), to the Creaghts at Kells (Ceᴀnnᴀnꞇuꝑ), and to Navan (1Iᴀṁn), to Ardbraccan[162] (ᴀꝑꝃ ꝃꝑeᴀcᴀιn), and Port Lester (Poꝑꞇ Leᴀꝑꞇᴀꝑ).

July 2, 1644. A Nuncio arrived at Kilkenny from the Pope,[163] and a message came to Sir Felim from the Council, desiring him to leave Charlemont (ᴀꞓᴀꝃ ᴀn ꝃᴀ ꞓᴀꝑᴀꝃ) and to join the army. After setting fire to Dungannon fort he went to Port Lester (Poꝑꞇ Leᴀꝑꞇᴀꝑ), where the General was.

---

156. See Carte's *Ormonde*, i. p. 488.—J. S.

157. Scotland.—J. W. H.

158. See *Reid*, ii. p. 471.—J. W. H.

159. *Armagh breague* is in the Parish of Lisnadill, Barony of Upper Fews, County Armagh.—J. W. H.

[Lurganboy is a townland in Co. Tyrone : Farney, a barony in the south of Co. Monaghan : Clonkee, a barony in the east of Co. Cavan.—J. S.]

160. MacTiernan, now Kiernan.—J. O'D.

[The Mac Tiernans were settled in Tullyhunco Barony, Co. Cavan. That bitter satirist, Æaghus O'Daly, describes them as starvelings, and absurdly states that their fathers, mothers, sons, daughters, horses, hounds, and cats were all blind.—cᴀoꞓ ! See his *Tribes of Ireland*, pp. 52, 53.—J. S.]

161. This is unquestionably the Parish of Donagh, in the County Monaghan, in which lies the town of Glasslough.—J. W. H.

162. Ardbraccan, in Co. Meath. St. Braccan is said to have erected a religious house here. Ardbraccan had a strong castle, which was the residence of the Bishops of Meath in former times. (See the *Parliamentary Gazetteer of Ireland*, i. 50.)—J. S.

163. This was Father Scarampo. (See Moran's *Memoirs of Oliver Plunket*, p. 4.)—J. S.

On Saint John's Eve,[164] 1602, O'Neill burnt Dungannon at the hour of retiring to bed.

On Saint John's Eve, 1644, Sir Felim burnt it at the same hour.

The Earl of Castlehaven arrived from Dublin unknown to the Sassenaghs, for he was a Catholic, and joined the Irish, who welcomed him joyfully. The Council of Kilkenny sent, under his command, 2,000 foot and six troops of horse to the assistance of the General of Ulster against the Scotchmen : and they reached the place in the County Meath where Owen O'Neill and the Creaghts were. The Earl was informed of the enemy's movements : that all the Scotch, English, and such Irish as had received quarter from them in the province, were assembled in one body in order to banish the Irish natives completely ; that they were now in Longford, and had burnt it, together with Granard and Ballyleague[15] (bel ᴀᴄ Lᴀoᵹ) ; that their number amounted to 19,000 men, and that they were now advancing to Finae (Ƒíoú ᴀn áᴄᴀ).[166]

The General and the Little Earl[167] sent three troops of horse and *Aug. 5, 1644.* 200 foot soldiers to guard the bridge of Finae (Ƒíoú ᴀn áᴄᴀ), commanded by Brian O'Neill M'Quin M'Art ɹuᴀú (the red-haired), son of Ferdinand[169] (mᴀc ᴀn Ƒiɹɹoɹéᴀ). The Scotch advanced to the guarded roads and succeeded in forcing their way. However, in the contest, Captain Graham and eight of his relations were killed. On the other side, Brian O'Neill was wounded and two of his troopers slain, and Gerald ᵹᴀɹb (the rough), from Meath, was also killed.

Finae (Ƒíoú ᴀn áᴄᴀ) was the Earl of Meath's town.

These forces proceeded to Kells (Ceᴀnᴀnᴘuɹ), to Navan (Uᴀṁ), and to Ardee (áᴄ ƒiɹ ᴅiᴀú), and, separating from each other at Dundalk (ᴅeᴀlᵹᴀn), part went to Trian Congail (ᴄɹᴀn conᵹᴀil), to the O'Kanes' country[169] (Cᴀᴄᴀnᴀᴄᴄ), to Tyrconnell, to Enniskillen, to Drogheda, and to Dundalk (ɹɹᴀú bᴀile). At this time the M'Garrys

---

164. St. John's Eve, 23rd June. This event is not recorded by the *Four Masters.*—J. S.

165. Ballyleague, Parish of Clunturkert, Co. Roscommon.—J. W. H.

The raid made by Colonel Monroe at this juncture is fully described in a rare Commonwealth tract in the Editor's possession, entitled, "A Full Relation of the Late Expedition of the Right Honourable the Lord Monroe, &c." London: August 27, 1644. It concludes as follows :—"After the writing hereof, advertisement come unto Mr. Major Rawden, that intelligence is this 23 of July, 1644. come unto him that the Irish Army, consisting of 15,000 horse and foot, are upon their march onwards, and as far advanced as Dundalk."—EDITOR.

166. Ƒíoú ᴀn áᴄᴀ.—J. O'D.

167. Castlehaven, called "Little," in contradistinction to the Earl (created Marquis) of Antrim. There was great competition, about this period, between Castlehaven and Antrim in reference to the supreme command. (See Carte's *Ormonde,* i. p. 496.)—J. S.

168. Ferdoragh.—J. S.

169. Barony of Keenaght, Co. Derry, originally held by the O'Conors, who were driven out by the O'Kanes before the Norman invasion. Keenaght is called Cinnachta "of the abundant store," ó Chiᴀnᴅᴀᴄᴀ in ᴄɹiom ᴄhocᴀiú in the *Leabhar na g-Ceart, or Book of Rights,* p. 122. Ænghus O'Daly (*Tribes of Ireland,* pp. 56, 57) slanders the O'Kanes as—

The O'Cahans of the ignoble deeds,
Eirin's idlers—I will satirize.

Cᴀᴄᴀnᴀiᵹ nᴀ ᵹ-céimeᴀnn Lᴀᵹ
Sᵹɹᴀᴄᴀnᴀiᵹ Eiɹeᴀnn ᴀoɹɹᴀú.—J. S.

(ᵐᵘᵘⁿᶜᵢ‖ ᶜᵃ‖‖ᵘᵃᶜ ᵃⁿ ᵉᵃ‖‖ᵃ), who were all fishermen, were killed at the waterfall, Carrickaness[170] (ᵃⁿ ᵉᵃ‖‖ᵃ), near Maydown (ᵐᵃᵘ ᵃⁿ ᵛᵘⁱⁿ).

The General and the Little Earl[171] marched in pursuit of the enemy, and brought the Creaghts along with them to Tyrone, that is, to Portmore.[172] Their forces amounted to 7,000 foot and 1,000 horse.

The garrison of Charlemont (ᵃᶜᵃᵘ ᵃⁿ ᵛᵃ ᶜᵃ‖ᵃᵘ) refused to surrender the town to the army of the kingdom until they should know the will of Sir Felim, who was then in Kilkenny. Finding they could not take the place, they proceeded to Tandragee, and there erected their tents and booths. The General was informed that some of the enemy were at Dromore Iveagh (Oᵖᵘ‖ᵐ ᵐᵒ‖ ⁱᵇ ᵉᵃᵘᵃᶜ). The Earl, with a large detachment, marched towards them on Saint Clare's day,[173] and, attacking them, killed upwards of 200 men, between horse and foot, and took Captain Blair[174] prisoner. They returned the same day. Letters arrived from the Council, and from Sir Felim, authorising them to give up Charlemont (ᵃᶜᵃᵘ ᵃⁿ ᵛᵃ ᶜᵃ‖ᵃᵘ) to the King's Army. The troops left Tandragee and came to Dunavally[175] (ᵛᵘⁿ ᵛᵃ ᵇᵃˡˡᵃ), where they erected tents, booths, and scaffolding. General Owen was seized with fever, by which he was detained here.

Aug. 15, 1644. The enemy approached near Armagh: and sent . . . . to plunder Toaghie[176] (Cᵘᵃᶜ ⁿᵃᶜᵃᵘ) and Lisnafeedy[177] (ᵃᶜ ᵖᵉᵃᵘᵃ). They fell upon the rere of the Creaghts, and carried off Kathleen Hovenden, the wife of Turlogh O'Neill. They brought her with them, together with the horses loaded with baggage.

Aug. 19, 1644. Soldiers were sent to guard the ford of the Blackwater river (ᵃᶜⁿᵃ ⁿᵃ ⁿᵃᵇᵃⁿⁿ ᵛᵘⁱᵇᵉ), between the Creaghts and the enemy. Captain Davis went without orders to reconnoitre the enemy: he was wounded and taken prisoner, and some of his troop were killed.

170. Carrickaness lies opposite Benburb on the County Armagh side. It adjoins May-down.—J. W. H.

171. Castlehaven.—J. S.

172. Portmore, now Blackwatertown.—J. W. H.　　There are the remains of a crannoge here, as Mr. J. O'Neill, C.E., informs me.—EDITOR.

173. St. Clare's day, 12th August.—J. S.

174. Captain Blair taken prisoner, 12th August. *Reid* (i. p. 475).—J. W. H.
[Carte (*Ormonde*, i. p. 515) states that the Earl of Castlehaven lost only six or eight men on this occasion, with some few wounded.—J. S.]

175. The townland "Corr and Dunavally" adjoins Charlemont. In it is a moated rath called Leaguer Hill, now converted into a burying-ground, and from which Colonel Callimot beleaguered Charlemont in 1690.—J. W. H.
The fortifications of Charlemont are well shown in Tindal's *Continuation of Rapin's History:* London, 1744. On the same sheet is the Map of Belfast reproduced on p. 80, *Town Book of Belfast.*—EDITOR.

176. The territory of "Toaghie" is now known as the name of a manor in the Parish of Derrynoose or Madden. It comprised the town of Keady, and is situate in the Baronies of Armagh and Tureny, in the Co. Armagh. In 1609 these lands were found by *Inquisition* to be held by Sir Henry M'Tirlagh O'Neale, Knt., his ancestors being seized by virtue of a gift from the Archbishop of Armagh.—J. W. H.

177. Lisnafeedy is a townland in the district, Parish of Eglish, Barony of Tureny, County Armagh.—J. W. H.
[It takes its name from Lⁱᵒ‖, a fort, and ᵖᵉᵃᵛ or ᵖⁱᵛ, whistling—the "fort of the whistling;" in allusion to the fairy music said to have been heard there. Several places in Ireland owe their names to a similar circumstance. See Joyce's *Origin and History of Irish Names of Places*, i. p. 192.—J. S.]

Henry O'Neill M'Tuathal was sent to the top of Claneboy Aug. 20, 1644. (clann aoóa bnıóı) to waste the country about the mouth of the Stranmillis[178] (ſſnċaın ınLıſ), and he carried off a great many cows and other booty.

Robert Monroe and Lieutenant-General Earl Leslie[179] are at Armagh with 14,000 men, in opposition to the Irish, of whom there were 7,000 in Dunavally (Oun va balla).

Turlogh Og O'Neill came to an agreement with Colonel   to collect the Creaghts between Dungannon and Charlemont (Aċaó an vá ċaſaó), and threatening with the penalty of hanging any one who disobeyed the order. When the Creaghts were assembled, four or five thousand cows were set apart for the Earl of Castlehaven and his men. This flesh meat, however, on account of their scanty supply of bread, injured their health.[180] They were attacked by sickness, trouble (τſeablaoıv),[181] and the flux, which carried off a thousand men.[182]

Sir Felim's people, together with Colonel Sandford, Rory Maguire, Sept. 1, 1644. and the people of Oriel (Oıſſıall), marched against Enniskillen, whence they carried off 204 cows.

A party of the enemy went from Armagh to the Fews (Fıoó) and killed Shane O'Connellan, a Priest of the country; they carried off plunder along with them.

Another detachment from the enemy, under a Colonel named M'Rodin,[183] crossed the Blackwater by night at the mouth of Aghakip[184] (bel aċ cıp) into Munter Byrne (Ulluıncıſ bıſn). There

178.   "Stran-millis" was in the district of Malone, adjoining Belfast, on which was erected a castle by Sir Moses Hill, the ancestor of the Marquis of Downshire.—J. W. H.

["Stranmillis" comes from ſſuſán, a streamlet, and ınLıſ, sweet, pleasant.—J. S.] (See present volume, p. 117, for a full account of it by W. Pinkerton, F.S.A.—EDITOR.)

179.   General Leslie was not made *Earl Leslie*, but *Earl of Leven*. See Malcolm Laing's *History of Scotland*, iii. p. 221. He was illegitimate and illiterate, and is said never to have got beyond the letter G in the alphabet. See Hill's *Macdonnells of Antrim*, p. 60.—J. S.

180.   The British Officer (*Irish Warr of 1641*, p. 35) states that in consequence of the Scotch and English forces having reaped the fields, the Irish "were necessitated to buy their own Grain at dear Rates from the Scottish or British, or want it." The enemy experienced a want of what the Irish had in superabundance—flesh meat. "We," he says, "had Bread enough, but Cows and Butter was scarce amongst us."—J. S.

181.   Cſeablaċτ, trouble, languor, weakness.—J. S.

182.   The British Officer, who mentions the Irish loss from having to eat flesh without bread or salt (*Irish Warr of 1641*, p. 41), censures Castlehaven for marching into "a waste Country, as the County of Ardmagh, Dundeeragee, and Charlemount, and not to the planted Countries where his Enemies lay dispersed in their Quarters, &c." Owen Roe was much blamed as Castlehaven's counsellor. "They said his Ambition was the cause solely, for that he was not well satisfied he had not the Command of the Army to himself—considering himself not to be the worst soldier, with which several old Soldiers does (!) acquiesce."—J. S.   For Boate's account of "Leaguer Sickness," see *Town Book of Belfast*, p. 315.—EDITOR.

183.   *Qu.* George Rawdon, who was a Major in Colonel Hill's regiment of horse. *Reid*, i. p. 488, and *Montgomery MSS.*, p. 163.—J. W. H. See present volume, p. 124, for account of G. Rawdon.—EDITOR.

184.   *Inqn.* at Dungannon in the reign of Chas. I., No. 50, Wm. Lord Charlemont was found seized, *inter alia*, of Clonarbe, Lissendorcloon, Kenigmore, Aghakippa, and Knockroe, which are called by the name of the Grange, Clonarbe. There is a stone cross still remaining here, probably erected by the Monks of St. Peter and Paul, Armagh, to whom the Grange originally belonged. Another *Inqn.*, sped at Armagh, Sept., 1614, gives Guy-bealakipp river as one of the boundaries, and the Blackwater as another, of this Grange, which lies between Caledon and Benburb.—J. W. H.

were five troops of them. They saw a number of cavalry near them, which were the Irish retreating from them. However, a skirmish took place, in which Con O'Neill M'Neill M'Art Og was killed, and Art O'Neill M'Turlogh M'Henry Na Garthan (na ᵹaᵽċann) was taken prisoner and received quarter : but he was murdered, through revenge, by the son of Lieutenant Graham, at the north side of the Lough of Knocknacloy (Loc enme a cluiċe).[185] Alexander Hovenden was slain between that and the Oona-water (Abann na húna). They killed likewise 12 men of the Creaghts, and carried a great deal of booty away with them.

Lewis O'More, a man from Leinster, and some of Castlehaven's horsemen who saw the murder committed, followed the marauders, along with Turlogh O'Neill, son of the murdered man : they killed eight and took prisoners five of the enemy.

The enemy came[186] and took 16 horses from the Earl's guard. They also carried off three or four captives, and they left a certain officer stark naked except his boots.

Whenever the Earl of Castlehaven's men were sent out to plunder, they would scarcely go half way, when they would turn back to their own camp through fear and cowardice, without having done the least service.

About this time the Garrison of Mountjoy came in search of plunder to Clanaghrie[187] (clann eaċne), and were successful, but Felim of the Wars (an éoᵹaᵫ) O'Neill took it from them and killed 12 of them.

Sept. 13, 1644.

As the Earl of Castlehaven perceived that his men were retrograding daily, falling into sickness and weakness, cowardice and death, he resolved to depart to the provinces of Leinster and Munster, and this determination was put in execution.[188] Owen O'Neill offered to supply 300 cows and 700 barrels of corn if they would stay two nights more in the camp : but it was only like tying sand with twigs to ask that of them. The General sent orders to the Chiefs of the Creaghts to withdraw to Sliabh Beagh and to Truagh (Ꞇꞃuoċa).

In the evening, powder and ball were given to the soldiers. They pretended to be drawing faggots to Kishabuoy[189] (ceaᵽaċ buᵫe), as if they were about to attack the enemy that very night. The enemy's

---

185. Knocknacloy is in the extreme south of the Parish of Clonfeele, Co. Tyrone, lying in the fork where the river Oona empties itself into the Blackwater.—J. W. H.

186. The enemy came, &c.?—J. O'D.

187. Clanaghrie was a district in Tyrone, bordering the S.E. of Lough Neagh, containing the present Parish of Clonoe.—J. W. H.
[Pynnar's *Survey of Ulster*, 1618-19, says :—" Sir Francis Ansby, Kt., hath four hundred and eighty acres called Clanaghrie." See Harris's *Hibernica*, p. 210.—J. S.]

188. The British Officer (*Irish War of 1641*, pp. 40, 41) says :—" At this rate Castlehaven was all this time, having at last no provision left, nor no supply suffered to come to him from Leinster or Conaught by our Army, was glad to eat Flesh without Bread or Salt, which so gave the Lax to his men that they were dying, till at last necessity made them stale away in night time, and so they escaped to Leinster and Munster."—J. S.

189. Kishabuoy was a marsh at the end of Charlemont leading to Loughgall. It is still so called.—J. W. H.

scouts perceived all this, and gave warning to Monroe. His people were much terrified at the tidings. They resolved to send a detachment to Tandragee with their baggage-waggons, and to remain themselves to guard the horses and arms. But matters were worse than this (as it turned out), for it was our own people who were flying.

The General and the Earl, in the darkness of the night, marched Sept. 14, 1644. with their forces over the bridge of Charlemont (ᵭᵉᵃᵭ ᴀɴ ᴅᴀ́ ᴄᴀᴘᴀᴅ) to Benburb, Glasslough, through Oriel (ᴏᴘᵹ1ᴀᴌᴌ), and to Ballynacloch[190] (bᴀ1ᴌe ɴᴀ ᵹ-cᴌᴏᴄ́). They got from Philip O'Reilly and the Chief of the O'Reillys 200 cows.[191] From thence they proceeded to Ballyhayes (beᴀᴌ ᴀᴄᴀ hᴀ1ᴘ), through Breffny, and westwards : and on Good Friday they took[192] the province of Ulster.

As for Monroe, he remained in the camp five weeks. Being assured that the Irish army had left the country, he sent messengers to the top of Sliabh na Maol (ᴘᴌ1ᴀb ɴᴀ mᴀoᴌ), near Brantry, to examine all the country round. They returned with the certain assurance that all the army and the Creaghts had departed. Ballyveagh[193] (bᴀ1ᴌe ɴᴀ mbᴉᴀᴄᴀᴄ́) was burned. Monro marched to Tynan (Cᴀoᴍɴᴇɴ),[194] and October, 1644. there encamped. They then gathered in all the corn they could seize to the distance of twelve miles round the camp. Here they stayed till the Festival of Saint Matthew the Evangelist.[195]

After this the army separated, part going to Tyrconnell,[196] to the O'Kanes' country,[197] and to the Route :[198] while Monro himself with

---

190. Sir Bryan M'Mahon, Kt., was seized, *inter alia*, of an annual rent of £13 6s. 8d., payable out of the ballybetagh of Ballenclogh, also Ballysatrossan, in the Barony of Dartry and Co. Monaghan. (*Inquisition*, taken at Monaghan, 29 Oct., 1624.)—J. W. H.

[The ballybetagh (bᴀ1ᴌe b1ᴀᴄᴀᴄ́, a victualler's town) was the largest measure of land, "and generally contained four quarters, which, being very variable in their extent, there was no fixed standard for their complex . . . In the County of Monaghan this denomination generally contained 16 tates. . . . The Tate, or *Tath*, or *Tagh*, varied from 10 to 60 acres." See *Primate Colton's Visitation*, p. 130.—J. S.]

191. The O'Reillys were the chiefs of East Breffny, or Co. Cavan. (See a long note in Connellan's *Four Masters*, p. 76; also p. 159.)—J. S.

192. Took? *left.*—J. W. H.
[In 1644, Easter Sunday fell on 21st April. Good Friday, therefore, was the 19th. See Bond's *Handy Book for Verifying Dates*, p. 274.—J. S.]

193. Ballyveagh, near Tynan.—J. W. H.

194. By the *Four Masters* (ii. p. 900) Tynan is called Cu1ᴏɴᴉᴅᴀ. It is also written Cu1ᵹɴᴇᴀᴄᴀ.—J. S.

195. St. Matthew's Festival, *i.e.*, 21st September.—J. S.

196. O'Donnell's country, Co. Donegal.—J. S.

197. The whole country from the Foyle to the Bann got the name of *Patria de O'Kane*. (See *Primate Colton's Visitation*, p. 28.)—J. S.

198 This extensive territory in Co. Antrim belonged to the M'Quillins (ᴍᴇᵹ U1ᵹ1ᴌ1ɴ ᴀɴ Ruᴄᴀ) from the time of the Norman invasion till they were dispossessed by Sorley Boy MacDonnell, who took forcible possession of the Route about 1554, establishing himself in M'Quillin's fortress of Dunluce. The M'Quillins were Welsh adventurers who came over with the Normans. Their name is believed to be a corruption of Llewellyn. (See Reeves's *Ecclesiastical Antiquities of Down, Connor, and Dromore*, pp. 326-329.) In 1541 the chief of the M'Quillins declared that no captain of his race "ever died in his bed sith the first conqueste of their saide lande." (See *The Description of Ireland in 1598*, p. 17.)—J. S.

his forces retired to Armagh, then eastward to Glenree[199] (ᵹleann ꞃuᵹe), and over Dromore[200] (Oꞃuim muiᵹe coba). Then they separated, retiring into the different garrisons throughout Dalaradia (Dál naꞃaiᵹe) and Dalriada, etc.

Monro sent orders to the Mountjoy garrison to burn that town, and then to march immediately to Carrickfergus. He sent at this time five or six thousand soldiers over to Scotland against the army of King Charles. The battle was gained by the King, 7,000 men were killed, and the Earl of Auchinbreck, with several other leaders, was beheaded.[201]

All the country across from the Bann-foot (bon banna) to the gates of Dundalk (ꞃꞃan baile), and from the great Cairn of Sliabh Beagh to Torrey (Coꞃꞃᵹ) in the north, presented a wonderfully deserted appearance. Only eight persons were at Lough [Leary][202] (Loc Laoᵹuꞃe), and eight more at Loughinsholin[203] (Loc ꞃꞃ o luꞃn). The Earl, on his leaving the country, had appointed the son of Thomas Gerald as Governor of Charlemont, and Captain White (ꝼaoici) from Limerick, with 150 soldiers, were placed there as a garrison. The Earl sent five troops of horse to bring the cannons and other baggage which he had left in Charlemont, over to him in Breffny. One of the troopers said that he would rather suffer himself to be shot, than come to Ulster in that convoy.

Towards the end of the autumn, when the corn was all shed, or burnt, and the houses destroyed, some of the Creaghts ventured to return to the country; particularly the M'Kennas[204] (M. cꞃonaic), namely Niall, of the race of Hugh, came to the Fews (anꝼeaba), Turlogh O'Neill M'Brian to Tureny[205] (cuac cꞃena), Patrick Modartha

---

199. Glenree, the valley of the Newry river.—J. W. H.

[It extended northwards, beyond Scarva, in the parish of Aghaderg, and was the western limit of Ulidia after 332, when Fergus Fogha, King of Ulster, was slain in battle, and the Ultonians driven eastwards by the Collas. (See Reeves's *Ecclesiastical Antiquities of Down, Connor, and Dromore*, p. 253.) O'Donovan mentions an old map of Ulster, in which the Newry river is called *Owen Glanree fluvius*. See the *Leabhar na g-Ceart, or Book of Rights*, p. 37.—J. S.]

200. Maᵹ Coba was a district in Iveagh, Co. Down. (See the *Leabhar na g-Ceart, or Book of Rights*, p. 166; Haliday's *Irish and English Keating*, i. p. 318; Reeves's *Ecclesiastical Antiquities of Down, Connor, and Dromore*, p. 112.)—J. S.

201. By the "Earl of Auchinbreck" is meant Sir Duncan Campbell of Auchinbreck. He was not executed, as apparently implied by O'Mellan, but slain at the battle of Inverlochy, 2nd February (1644-45). "There Achenbrcke was killed, with 16 or 17 of the chief lords of Campbell; their other lowland commanders (only two lieutenant-colonels) all cut off." See Colonel James Macdonnell's *Intelligence from His Majesty's Army in Scotland, to be presented to the most honourable the lord lieutenant of Ireland*, in Hill's *Macdonnells of Antrim*, p. 92. Auchinbreck fell by the hand of Major-General Alaster MacColl, "who, by one blow of a two-handed claymore, swept off his head and helmet together." See Grant's *Memoirs of Montrose*, p. 222. This may be what O'Mellan alludes to when he says Auchinbreck was "beheaded."—J. S.

202. Lough Leary, in Baron's Court demesne.—J. W. H.

203. Loughinsholin. (See *Desertmartin* in Lewis's *Topographical Dictionary of Ireland*, i. p. 456).—J. W. H.

204. The clann cꞃonaic an cꞃuꞃca were settled in the Barony of Trough, Co. Monaghan. A branch of the family removed to the parish of Maghera, Co. Derry, in the seventeenth century. (See the *Four Masters*, iii. p. 533. iv. p. 906.)—J. S.

205. The Barony of Tureny, in the north-west part of the Co. Armagh.—J. W. H.

O'Donnelly, *i.e.*, the gloomy (мouѧрѫ) to Ballydonnelly,[206] and many others.

The Friars of Armagh came to Brantry. Our Guardian went to Montiaghs,[207] [Multifarnham?] (Mоinтe Ғѧрѧnnѧn), Father Henry O'Mellan, Daniel à Sancta Maria Cahill, Bonaventura Quin, Owen O'Loughran (o Lѧoéтрen), Thomas Cѧlѧm (?), and Edward Dowdall to different other places. Our President, Patrick O'Cosy (o Coрр), and eleven other friars along with him, and also Teague O'Loughran, settled at Brantry.

A flying rumour came that the Creaghts had fled from the Counties January, 1645. of Tyrone, Armagh, and Monaghan westward to .[208] The Friars of Armagh immediately fled to the Fews (ѧ ғeѧѫ) and thence to Clonkee. A party from Lisnegarvey came to scour the country, but they found none in the country except the people of the quarter. They took away from Captain Trevor 140 cows, and it is said that it was the Captain himself who sold the cows to the English.

Names of chief personages. The Pope is Innocent the Tenth ;[209] the King, Charles ; the Commander in Dublin, the Earl of Ormond ;[210] General of Ulster, Owen O'Neill ; President of the Kilkenny Council, Lord Butler ;[211] General of the South (Leiṫ mоѫ), Thomas Preston ;[212] Primate of All Ireland, Hugh O'Reilly ;[213] and the Provincial of the Order of Saint Francis, Brian M'Giolla Kenna from Connaught (Соnѧéтѧé).

A party from Breffny, from Oriel (Oiрғiѧllѧiḃ) and from Fermanagh (mѧnéѧiḃ) went off to plunder Enniskillen. They remained two nights on the watch, and seized some booty, but they were forced to give it up again. There were 220 men of the party killed. Mulmurry O'Reilly[214] was wounded, and his horse taken. Five of their gentlemen were made prisoners, and were afterwards ransomed for 600 barrels of meal, 60 barrels of seed oats, and 60 pounds of money.

206. Ballydonnelly, now Castlecaulfield, Co. Tyrone, about two miles from Dungannon.—J. W. H.

[Pynnar's *Survey of Ulster*, 1618-19, says :—" *Sir Toby Caufield* hath one thousand Acres called *Ballidonnell*, &c." See Harris's *Hibernica*, p. 209.—J. S.]

207. The District of the Montiaghs lies beside Lurgan, to the south of Lough Neagh.—J.W.H.
[Montiaghs, *i.e.*, mоinтeѧéѧ, bogs, mosses.—J. S.]

208. *Query*, Breffny.—J. W. H.

209. Innocent the Tenth (Gian Battista Panfili) succeeded Urban the Eighth (the Pontiff previously named in this narrative) in 1644.—J. S.

210. Commander in Dublin, *i.e.*, Lord Lieutenant. Ormonde was sworn in as Lord Lieutenant in Christ Church on 21st January. 1644. (See Curry's *Review of the Civil Wars of Ireland*, p. 260; also the British Officer's *Irish Wars of 1641*, p. 35.)—J. S.

211. Lord Butler, *i.e.*, Lord Mountgarret. (See Meehan's *Confederation of Kilkenny*, p. 25.)—J. S.

212. Sir Phelim O'Neill's father-in-law. General Preston, received £600 per annum for his services, according to Geoffrey Baron's *Booke of Accomptes*, given as an Appendix to Meehan's *Rise and Fall of the Irish Franciscan Monasteries*, p. 320.—J. S.

213. Dr. O'Reilly, the Catholic Primate, was translated from Kilmore to Armagh *circa* 1628. He died 7th July, 1651. (See Renehan's *Collections on Irish Church History*, i. pp. 33, 47.)—J. S.

214. Mulmurry O'Reilly, *i.e.*, Myles.—J. O'D.
[A very common name among the ancient O'Reillys of Co. Cavan. It means "the servant (or tonsured) of Mary." The tribe name of the O'Reillys was Шuinтрр Шѧolmoрѫ.—J. S.]

March 7, 1645.   The O'Hagans burnt O'Lyn's Island (Inıʃ ı Luınn) for want of
provisions, and followed the General westwards. A detachment came
out of Enniskillen which plundered Hugh and James buıṁe (the
yellow) O'Donnelly, Donnel ᵹıııaṁa[215] M'Connell, and the daughter
of Coocy ballaċ[216] M'Ristard O'Kane. They lost more than 200
cows.

The Archbishop of Fermo,[217] that is, the Apostolic Nuncio, arrived
in Ireland from Pope Innocent the Tenth, with gold, silver, and arms.
He advised the Irish not to make peace with the English, unless upon
condition that they should have complete liberty of conscience, and
that the lands should be restored to the Catholic Church.

May 2, 1645.   Sir Felim, with 150 men, came by authority of the Council of
Kilkenny to place garrisons in Dungannon and Mountjoy.   He
May 27, 1645. arrived in Charlemont at Whitsuntide. Upon the third day, he
ascended to the top of the Castle and said that the enemy were
approaching. He then went to the gate, and called out to his own
people who were outside to come within the gate and defend the town.
They accordingly entered. However, Philip ıııaṁ (the red-haired)
O'Reilly, the Governor, was not in the town, and therefore Sir Felim's
men were again obliged to go outside the gate, and provisions were
given them sufficient to support them as far as Breffny.[218]

Seventeen of the enemy fell into the hands of Sir Felim's men.
Nine of them were hanged, and a ransom taken for the rest.   On the
same day they got 15 horses.[219]

Aug. 14, 1645.   On one occasion it happened, while Sir Felim was in Charlemont,
that a Kern (Ceıꜩıoɼınaċ), named Lowry, had brought from Monro five
troops of horse and four companies of soldiers, watching an opportunity of surprising the town. Accordingly, about the end of the

215. ᵹııaṁa, the grim.—J. S.

216. ballaċ, the freckled.—J. S.

217. Archbishop of Fermo. This was Rinuccini, the Nuncio, but he was only Bishop of
Fermo.—J. W. H.

[Mr. Hanna is mistaken. Rinuccini was Archbishop of Fermo. This See was created
an Archbishopric by a bull of Pope Sixtus the Fifth, dated 12th May, 1589. "*Con sua
bolla del 12 maggio dell' anno 1589, che comincia Universis orbis ecclesiis, innalzava al grado
arcivescovile questa Chiesa, &c.*" (See the Abbate D'Avino's *Enciclopedia dell' Ecclesiastico,*
article *Fermo,* ii. p. 174.) Gian Battista Rinuccini ruled the archiepiscopal diocese of Fermo from
1625 till 1654. He attaches his name to those who adhered to the
peace, 15th Oct., 1646, as *Johannes Baptista Archi-Episcopus Fermanus, Nuncius Apostolicus,* &c.
(See Clarendon's *History of the Rebellion in Ireland,* p. 33.) There is seemingly some disarrange-
ment in O'Mellan's MS. at this place. Rinuccini did not reach Ireland till 22nd *October,* 1645.
He arrived in Paris, 22nd May, remaining there till 30th August, when he set out for Rochelle. He
embarked at St. Martin's, 16th October, and reached "Killmair" [Kenmare] on the 22nd. (See
Carte's *Ormonde,* i. pp. 559, 561. See also Smith's *Kerry,* p. 313, where the date of his arrival is
erroneously given as 27th Oct., but is correctly stated in the same author's *Cork,* ii. p. 155. See
also Renehan's *Collections,* i. p. 46, and Meehan's *Confederation of Kilkenny,* p. 133.) A very
interesting account of the Irish, as they appeared to Italian eyes, occurs in the letter written after
the landing by Massari, Dean of Fermo, to the Nuncio's brother, to be found in Latin and
Italian in Meehan's *Memoirs of the Irish Hierarchy in the Seventeenth Century,* Appendix, pp. 463-
475, and in an English translation in Moran's *Persecutions of the Irish Catholics,* pp. 449-63.—
J. S.]

218. Breffny embraced the present counties of Cavan and Leitrim. It was held by the
O'Reillys and the O'Rourkes, and their correlatives. (See a long note in Connellan's *Four Masters,*
pp. 75-78.)—J. S.

219. For July and part of August. See p. 237.—J. S.

night, they attacked the gate and fired a shower of bullets, so that eight men were killed and a number wounded.

General Monro came with a large force from Trian Congail (Τ̇ριαη Aug. 24, 1645. conṡaιl) to Armagh and to Portmore[220] (Ροιϲ mορ). He sent a messenger to Sir Felim commanding him to surrender the town. Sir Felim's answer was that " he would sooner kill himself with his own hand than betray his trust so meanly ; and that if he wished for fighting he should have it."

Monro went off to Glasslough and to Monaghan. The Scotch from Tyrconnell now held a consultation what they should do. " Let us," they said, " send reinforcements to our garrison towns in the province of Connaught." They did so, and the remainder of their forces returned to Tyrconnell and to Trian Congail (Τ̇ριαη Conṡaιl).

We were fourteen days between the Festival of Saint Francis and that of Capistranus[221] without beholding the sun or the stars all that time, and had frost every day.

A boat belonging to the Governor of Massareene was captured by Sept. 15, 1645, Sir Felim, in which were two brass cannon, ten muskets, twelve barrels of salted fish, some sailors, and a company of soldiers. They brought it to the mouth of the river at Charlemont. Some of the men were hanged and some redeemed.

General Monro[222] marched from Trian Congail (Τ̇ριαη conṡaιl) to July 15, 1645. Armagh, to Sliabh na Maol (ṡlιαḃ na maol), to Clogher, and Enniskillen. They burned and plundered all the country on their way, as far as Tober-bride,[223] in Connaught. O'Connor surrendered Sligo to them, and they left there a strong garrison.

The great fort of Lismore (Lιοṙ mόρ) was taken by the Earl of Castlehaven : he took the town from the O'Briens, Magnus O'Kane was slain, that is, Captain M'Coocy the freckled (ḃαllαċ) M'Ristard. They also took nine garrison places from the Baron of Inchiquin (Ιηιṙ i cuιηη). In this army were 1,500 Ulster-men. Captain Kane, viz. Cooey M'Manus the Anglicised (ṡαlτα) was also killed.

The large garrison of Tulsk (Τ̇uιllṙṡc) was taken by Shane Burke, Aug., 1645. Thomas Taafe, and James Dillon.[224] Hugh O'Gallagher, an Ulster Captain, whose men had been mainly instrumental in the capture of the place, was slain. Elphin (Oιl ṙιηη), Jamestown (ḃοιlε Seμuṙ) Castle ? (εṙṡuḃ?), &c., the Abbey of Boyle (maηιṙτιṙ na ḃuιlε) were all taken.

The Connaught army proceeded to Sligo to take it by force from Oct. 26, 1645. the Scotch, but before they were aware, five or six troops of Cavalry from Tyrconnell and from Enniskillen came upon them and drove them back to their encampment. The Archbishop of Tuam was killed by a wound in his shoulder, and also his Priest. The name of

220. Blackwater town.—J. S.

221. The Feasts of St. Francis and St. John Capistran, 4th and 23rd November, respectively. This entry is strangely placed.—J. S.

222. Reid, i. p. 475 ; also Rushworth's Historical Collections, part iv. vol. i. p. 238, et seq.— J. W. H.

223. Now Ballintober, Co. Roscommon.—J. W. H.

224. Tulsk, Co. Roscommon. It was held by Capt. Robert Ormsby, and was stormed, 13th August, 1645. (See Carte's Ormonde, i. p. 536.)—J. S.

the Prelate was Maolshaughlin O'Coyle,[225] a Doctor, remarkable for his learning, his goodness, and the rectitude of his life. They died, but four Scotchmen fell by their hands in that battle. Many of the Burkes and of the other Irish were taken prisoners, and the camp was given up to plunder. The Scotch reinforced the Garrison of Sligo. Burial of the Archbishop.

General Owen came from Kilkenny, from the Pope's Nuncio, with 3,000 men to Carrickmacross, where he plundered some of the enemy quartered there. Thence he proceeded to Ballybay, where he remained a while, and then went on to Breffny.

As for Owen O'Neill, he despatched Colonel Rory Maguire, and Turlogh O'Neill, an old veteran from Spain, of the race of Hugh, along with 500 men, to Lough Erne. They were joined by their scouts (a ᵹuᴄᴅ bᴘᴀᴄᴀ) with two boats, and landed in Illanbabh[226] (ᴀ noiᴌᴇn bᴀb). They burnt and plundered two islands, and carried away from them upwards of 500 cows, and 140 horses with their accoutrements, and 17 stallions. They brought the plunder to near Ballynamallaght (beᴀᴌ ᴀᴄh mᴀᴌᴌᴀᴄᴅ), and, at the rising of the midnight moon, Rory Maguire's people departed with it. Turlogh M'Brian M'Donnell, son of Felim Roe O'Neill, reconnoitred. "Our enemy is approaching," said he; "come to this trench, fire a volley, and let the pike-men stand here." His orders were obeyed, and eight of the enemy, with their Lieutenant of the Cavalry, were killed. But our pike-men gave way, the enemy pressed on us, and we lost Captain M'Quillan and ten men. Captain Eremon M'Swine from Tyrconnell, and Sergeant-Major Turlogh O'Neill, fell in the slaughter.

1646. The Pope's emissary, Johannes Baptista, Archbishop of Fermo, arrived in Ireland, bringing with him to Kilkenny sixty thousand pounds and a great supply of arms.[227]

The General of Ulster waited upon the Nuncio, and engaged to carry on the operations of the war in that province, if he were furnished with pay for the soldiers. "You shall receive," was the reply, " pay for 3,000 men for six months, and add 2,000 more to them yourself at the expense of the country." The name of the Pope was Innocent the Tenth. A proclamation was then issued by the Ulster General,

225. He is generally known as Malachy O'Queely, but is sometimes called by historians Keely or O'Keely. His name in Irish is Uᴀ Cᴀúᴌᴀ. The priest was his secretary, Father Thady O'Connell. There was another priest killed at the same time. (See Meehan's *Memoirs of the Irish Hierarchy in the 17th Century*, p. 118.) "General Taafe sent, on the 27th [Oct.], a trumpeter to ask for the body of the Archbishop : but was refused without a ransom of £30. Bruodin relates that the Scotch army first cut off his right arm and then cruelly mangled the body, cutting it up into small pieces. Among the important papers said to have been found on his person was an authentic copy of the famous private treaty between King Charles and the Earl of Glamorgan." See Renehan's *Collections on Irish Church History*, i. p. 405. Malachy O'Queely gave a Latin Approbation to the *Annals of the Four Masters* in 1636. (See it in O'Donovan's Edition, i. p. lxx, and in O'Conor's *Rerum Hibernicarum Scriptores Veteres*, iii. p. xvi.)—J. S.

226. Boo Island.—J. O'D.

[It is called bᴀúbᴀ by the *Four Masters* (iii. p. 648). Those who speak Irish in the district call it ᴵnᴘ bᴀúbᴀnn or Oiᴌᴇᴀn bᴀúbᴀnn. It is the largest island in Lough Erne, and not far from the northern shore.—J. S.]

227. For the date of Rinuccini's arrival see Note 217.

desiring all the horse and foot soldiers in Ulster to meet him, and that each man should receive three shillings and six pence a-week. They assembled, accordingly, in Breffny : and seventy horses arrived at the April 24, 1646. Castle of Lough Sheelin,[228] bringing from Kilkenny the arms for the troops. The army continued to collect here until the 1st of June.

Seven boats were captured on Lough Neagh by Sir Felim : four- May 8, 1646. teen men were taken and above twenty killed. The boats were brought to the mouth of the river of Charlemont (Aċaḃ an ḃá ċap̄aḃ), and Sir Felim went to the General's camp. Some of the Scotch May 23, 1646. forces came to the Blackwater-foot, where they erected two forts on the banks of the Avonmore, extending chains between them to prevent Sir Felim's people from fishing in the Lough.

The forces of the General and Sir Felim consisted now of above June 1, 1646. 5,000 foot and nine troops of horse, commanded by seven officers, namely, the General, Sir Felim, Colonel M'Neny (an p̄eana), Alexander the son of the Earl[229] (mac an iaṗla), Manus O'Donnel son of Neal Garve (ȝaṗḃ), Rory Maguire, and Colonel Farrell. The nine troops were under the command of the following:—Henry Roe (p̄uaḃ), son of the General, Con ḃacaċ (the lame) Brian Roe (p̄uaḃ) O'Neill,[230] Brian Roe (p̄uaḃ) M'Mahon, Philip O'Reilly,[231] Hugh MacMulmurray, Mulmurray M'Cammon,[232] Hugh Maguire, and Colonel Farrell. This was the assembly of the Ulster forces, the descendants of the great Owen[233] (Eoȝanaċċ Ulaḃ), with the General, Owen O'Neil, at their head.

The report came that Lord Montgomery, with strong forces both of Scotch and English, was at Glenree[234] on the march towards Munster and Kilkenny, to banish all the insurgents. They pushed forward, therefore, to Benburb, where they fixed their encampment and turned the horses to grass. One thousand men and three troops of cavalry were then appointed to guard the camp, for the enemy were now near Armagh.

The force under the command of Lord Montgomery, together with June 4, 1646. Lord Blayney, Lord Hamilton, and Robert Monroe, were joined by reinforcements from Trian Congail (Ċp̄an conȝail), and from the O'Kanes' country near Dungannon, consisting of 80 horseman and 300 foot. Auxiliaries from Tyrconnell also came to Clossagh[235] (Cloṗaiȝ).

228. On the borders of Counties Cavan, Longford, and Meath.—J. S.

229. Alexander Macdonnell was younger son of the Earl of Antrim.—J. W. H.

230. Brian Roe O'Neill was grandson of Sir Cormac MacBaron O'Neill, and on the death of his elder brother, Hugh Roe, claimed the nominal dignity of Tyrone, which, on his death without issue, was claimed by Hugh, son of Henry, son of Owen Roe. (Lodge's *Irish Peerage*, 1st Edition.)—J. W. H.

231. Philip O'Reilly was brother-in-law of Owen Roe.—J. W. H. [He married Rose O'Neill, Owen Roe's sister.—J. S.]

232. Mulmurry M'Cammon. In the Cavan *Inqu.* of 10th April, 1629, there is mentioned Cohonght M'Comen, a mere Irishman. It is probably MacOwen, one of the O'Reillys. (See p. 57.)—J. W. H.

233. The Eoghanacts of Ulster.—J. W. H.

234. The valley of the Newry river. See Note 199.—J. S.

235. For Clossagh, near Clogher, see *Primate Colton's Visitation*, by Dr. Reeves, p. 126.—J. W. H.

Montgomery had now 14 troops of horse and nine regiments. The heretics proposed immediately to attack Benburb from Armagh. Monroe was of a different opinion, and recommended that they should proceed to Tynan, to Athfeada[236] (Ach ꞃeaда), Caledon (cionn aiꞃꝺ), and Knocknacloy[237] (Cnoc an ċluiċe), as the wind and sun would both be in their favour. This plan was adopted, and they left their waggons and provisions in Munterbirne[238] under the charge of 1,500 soldiers. There was there six weeks' provision for every man : many a sack of white canvas,[239] quantities of biscuits, plenty of meal, beer, wine, whiskey, flour, sugar, hens, capons, and a supply of tents. They exhibited through Munterbirne their great silken banners.

The Irish General sent three troops with Brian O'Neill, son of Con Roe, to reconnoitre the auxiliaries who had gone to the enemy from O'Kane's country; he also despatched 100 men towards the enemy's army, who took a cry out of them (i.e., alarmed them), and then made an honorable retreat back to their own people.

The General, then, in the midst of the forces, thus addressed them :—" Behold the army of the enemies of God, the enemies of your souls! Fight valiantly against them this day : for it is they who have deprived you of your chiefs, your children, your life, both spiritual and temporal : who have torn from you your lands, and made you wandering fugitives, &c."

The two armies met at Drumflugh[240] (Oꞃuim ꝼluiċ), and the heretics, after suffering great loss beside the cannons (for they had seven field pieces),[241] retreated. The Irish pressed hard on them, and a general discharge of musketry and cannon took place on both sides. They then seized their pikes and swords, and a terrible butchery commenced. Then arrived in the battle the brave and honorable hero, the magnanimous and gallant warrior, the protector of the people of Pope Innocent the Tenth, Owen O'Neill (Eoᵹan o neill).[242]

236. Athfeada must be the present Lisnafeedy, in the parish of. Eglish, Barony of Tureny, Co. Armagh.—J. W. H.

237. Knocknacloy was the residence of Murtagh O'Quin : he, with Tob. Quin, sold Lisderry, al. Drum, in the Barony of Dungannon, to Marmaduck Shaw, 10 May, 1637, for £137, who granted it to Thos. Lench for £100, 8 Feb., 1656.—J. W. H.

238. The Territory of Muinterbirne, now the name of a Presbyterian congregational district, includes the present parishes of Aghaloo and Carnteel, on the west side of the Blackwater, having the Oona river to the north, as also Brantry district.—J. W. H. Now Minterburn.—EDITOR.

239. Many a sack of white canvas. Perhaps corn.—J. O'D.

240. There are three different theories regarding the position of the Benburb battlefield— (1) That both armies were on the west side of the Oona; (2) that Monroe on the west side attacked O'Neill on the east side; (3) that both armies were on the east side, and that the first onset took place not more than a mile from Benburb. O'Mellan's statement strongly supports the last theory, as Drumflugh is hardly a mile from Benburb Castle; and the British Officer places the conflict a mile from Benburb. This view is also supported by local tradition, by the fact that the bridge which here spans the river is called the Battle-ford Bridge, and by the additional testimony that musket balls and human bones have been found just where the Scotch army was, according to this theory, driven backwards.—Rev. W. T. LATIMER, B.A. A full account of the battle is given in The History of the Irish Presbyterians, by the same author. Benburb Castle has recently been judiciously repaired by James Bruce, D.L., owner of the estate. —EDITOR.

241. Carte (Ormonde, i. p. 576) says Monroe had four field-pieces. The Nuncio (see Moore's History of Ireland, iv. p. 289) says five—cinque pezzi di cannoni da campagna.—J. S.

242. O'Neill exhibited great military skill. He ordered his men not to fire till within pikelength. The British Officer gives as one reason for defeat—"The soldiers, I mean some that were not strong (enough) in the British Army for his Pike in a windy day, would cut off a foot, and some two, of their Pikes,—which is a damned thing to be suffered."—The Warr of Ireland, p. 49.—EDITOR.

About this time also arrived the three troops which had been sent to Dungannon in the beginning of the day, and the Scotch imagined these to be some of their own people. Moreover, Sir Felim now joined the conflict with ten companies of soldiers, and greatly contributed to confuse the enemy. Lord Blayney was killed, and Lord Montgomery taken.[243] He was deprived of his horse and arms and put into confinement. The heretics now gave way, completely routed. Then did the Irish raise the battle-cry. The General might be seen urging forward his gallant army in the pursuit, sometimes in front, sometimes riding in the midst of them, until they were stopped by the dusk of the evening. Numbers were killed, and a part of the fugitives were drowned in the Avonmore and in the lough of Knocknacloy (Cnoc an clute). The General and the troops returned that night to their encampment, highly elated after their victory. Even those of the enemy who were only wounded did not escape ; scarcely any of them reached their homes, but perished in the wilds. Thirteen horsemen were killed in [Betagh country] (a noutaiʒ biataċ).[244] A Company of the General's, who were coming from Lough Sheelin after the army, killed five and twenty of them. Thomas Sandford, a Lieutenant-Colonel of Sir Felim's, killed twenty-four of them above Armagh. Fifty-seven more were destroyed by Henry O'Neill at the foot of a glen. Many others were found lying dead, without having received any wounds. The Puritans of Tyrconnell sent a message to the General offering battle. He sent the vanguard of the army westwards to Clossagh (Cloʲaiʒ) to meet the enemy ; he remained himself with the main body, and Sir Felim brought up the rear. The enemy fled to Enniskillen and to Tyrconnell. The General then returned the forces to Charlemont, Loughgall, and Tamnamore (Caṁnaċ móʲ). There were killed Magnus O'Donnell,[245] son of Neil Garve (ʒaʲb), and Cu Uladh (cuulað) O'Neill, the son of Ferdoragh M'Brian the scabbed (caʲʲaċ). Above 300 more were either killed or wounded.[246] Sir Felim procured surgical aid at Charlemont for all the wounded men. By the late victory they were now in possession of more than 1,000 muskets, a large quantity of

243. Lord Blaney's body was honourably interred in Benburb Church by Owen Roe, but was afterwards exhumed and taken to Castleblayney. Lord Montgomery was imprisoned in "Cloghwooter." He was released after "about two years." He attended a Council at Lisburn, 14th–15th March, 1647-8. (See the *Montgomery MSS.*, pp. 165, 169.)—J. S.

244. [   ] Betagh Country.—J. O'D.
Ouŧaŧ, a land, a country ; bcŧ, a birch tree, *i.e.*, the birch country. Of the lands in the territory or precinct of Tynan, in the Barony of Tureny, the property of the Primate, were, *inter alia*, Bally-veagh and Gortmorlagh, now Gortmalegg, in the Parish of Tynan. Bally-veagh is now absorbed in some other townland, but it probably was the Duthaidh-beith of the text.—J. W. H.

245. Colonel Manus O'Donnell had been married to Susanna, daughter of Hugh Magennis, Visct. Iveagh, by whom he had a son, Rory, of Lifford.—J. W. H.

246. The Nuncio states that the Irish lost only 70 men, and 100 wounded :—*Dei nostri son morti solamente settanta. . . . Cento soli feriti.* (See Moore's *History of Ireland*, iv. p. 290.) Carte (*Ormonde*, i. p. 576) gives the Irish loss as 70 men, and 200 wounded.—J. S.
A list is given at p. 66 of the additional arms to be distributed among "the 4 regiments of foot that were at Benburb," showing clearly the great loss that had taken place in them. Pinkerton mentions that new entrenching tools had also to be procured, as so many were lost at Benburb.—EDITOR.

R

pikes and pike-axes : also drums, seven field-pieces, and 36 standards. These flags were transmitted by the General to the Nuncio and Council of Kilkenny, as a token of his victory, under charge of the Diffinitor of the Order of Saint Francis, Bartholomew M'Egan,[247] and his servant, Hugh Boy (buιòє) M'Manus. He also sent some extraordinary letters found with the heretics. They had come to the determination on that day not to give quarter to a single man except the General himself. Shane O'Kane and Richard O'Kane, Donald Magenis, son of the Earl of Iveagh,[248] and Rory Maguire, were sent off with 1,500 soldiers to plunder Trian Congail (Cμαn congaιℓ). They sacked and burnt Downpatrick, Saul (ρабаℓℓ), the Bishop's Court, Ballybot[249] (баιℓє nа роμc мιnℓℓιоnn), and Killeagh[250] (Cιℓℓóℓαоċ), and brought away 500 cows to Tamnamore (Cаṁnаċ mоμ), not to mention other plunder. Thomas Sandford, a Lieutenant-Colonel of Sir Felim's, was sent, along with 600 men, to Portadown and Clare[251] (Cℓаμ), both which places they burnt.

The number of the slain between Drumflugh (Oμυιm Fℓιιṁċ) and Lisnafeedy[252] (Δċh ρєаòа) [thanks be to God, for it was He alone that performed the achievement!] was 3,548, and this in a space of three hours, exclusive of those killed in the wilds, such as at Toaghy (сиаċ аċаιò), and in the wood east of Anabeatagh (а mιb єċаċ).[253] Numbers were found dead without a trace of blood on them. The General left Tamnamore (Cаṁnаċ mоμ) and proceeded with the army to Breffny. The Deacon[254] of the Apostolic Nuncio, and the Diffinitor of the Order of Saint Francis,[255] came from Limerick to meet the General of Ulster. The Deacon gave three Rials (one shilling and sixpence) to every single soldier, and more to the officers ; and they were placed to

247. A Diffinitor regulated the affairs of Chapters. (See Fosbroke's *British Monachism*, p. 146.) Bartholomew M'Egan, or Boetius Egan, as he is more generally called, became Bishop of Ross in 1648, and was hanged by Lord Broghill in 1650. (See Meehan's *Memoirs of the Irish Hierarchy in the Seventeenth Century*, pp. 237-38.)—J. S.

248. *Earl of Iveagh.* Correctly, *Viscount.*
Shane and Richard O'Kane were probably related to Lieutenant-General Donnel O'Kane, slain near Clones.
Daniel and Roger Magennis were the two younger brothers of Sir Con Magenis, and sons of Art Roe, created Viscount Magenis of Iveagh, 18 July, 1623.—J. W. H. The Editor has a lease with the latter's signature.

249. Ballybot. ? Ballynewport, adjoining Rathmultan.—J. W. H.

250. Killeagh. ? Killough.—J. W. H.

251. Clare, in P. of Ballymore.—J. W. H.

252. By an *Inq.* of the Primate's property of Clanaule, taken at Armagh, 12 August, 1609, we find Lisnyferrie.—J. W. H.

253. Ana-beatagh. *Qu.* Anaghneveah, now Annagh, p. of Tynan, Barony of Tureny.—J. W. H.

254. This was Massari, dean of Fermo, Rinuccini's secretary. Massari compiled the history of the *Nunziatura*, assisted by Father Richard O'Farrell, probably an Irish Franciscan, and another priest whose name does not appear. The title of the work is *De Hæresis Anglicanæ Intrusione et Progressu et de Bello Catholico Ad. an. 1641. incepto exindeque per aliquot annos gesto, Commentarius.* (See Meehan's *Memoirs of the Irish Hierarchy in the Seventeenth Century*, Appendix N, p. 369.)—J. S.

255. The Diffinitor was Boetius Egan, by whom Owen Roe had sent to the Nuncio, Rinuccini, an account of the battle in a Latin letter dated 9th June, 1646, which is given as an Appendix to Meehan's *Memoirs of the Irish Hierarchy in the Seventeenth Century*, p. 434.—J. S.

guard five counties, namely, the Counties of Monaghan, Cavan, Leitrim, Longford, and Mullingar, until the crops should be ripe. Sir Felim stayed at Charlemont attending to the wounded. He sent six boats to Bunavally (bun an bealaig); the boats were drawn ashore, and soldiers placed between that and the garrison. The boats were then brought to Trowagh Bay (Tpaig oubac), a fort was raised there and soldiers stationed in it, with some fishermen who caught plenty of fish ; the Scotch were thus prevented from leaving Bunavally (bun an bealaig), and they were in great want of provisions.

In Breffny, at Ballyheelin (bel athalian), Brian Roe O'Neill killed June 29, 1646. Hugh M'Art Og M'Turley O'Neill. He shot him with a pistol.

The troops of the enemy came to Munter Birn. They seized Hugh O'Neill, M'Brian M'Henry Og, and carried off four horses and forty cows.

The Council of Kilkenny was now negotiating a peace with the Earl of Ormond, without the permission of the old Irish Chiefs. He was invited to meet them there, which he agreed to do. The Court and Castle were newly decorated for his reception. New gates were erected, splendidly gilt. The Earl arrived with 15 troops of horse and 2,000 foot. The Council of Kilkenny, Lord Mountgarret (Mora goipeao), Donchadh M'Carty, and all the country submitted to him ; and, matters being arranged there, he proceeded to Cashel of Munster, where the people of Munster received him joyfully.

About this time a Chapter was held by the Nuncio at Waterford, where the news reached him that the Earl was in the Country. He immediately dispatched 500 soldiers and letters to the General of Ulster, directing him to leave Breffny with the army.

These letters having reached the General, he sent orders to the Aug. 28, 1646. Captains with their soldiers, and to the cavalry, to meet him this day on Bruise Mountain (sliab bpuip). They accordingly arrived, accompanied by Sir Felim, Colonel of the horse. That night they were in the County Longford, and they made no halt till they were at Ballyskeagh (baile sgeatac). Here 40 horses from Kilkenny met them, loaded with bread, beer, &c.

As for the Earl of Ormond ; hearing, while at Cashel, of the arrival of the Ulster General, he forthwith made his escape with 15 troops and 2,000 foot-soldiers, not to his own place, Kilkenny, but to Gowran (Sabpan). On being informed that the General's cavalry was in the neighbourhood, they fled to Leighlin (Lelinn).[256] In the town they fired a volley of musketry and then all separated, so that upon the Earl's arrival in Carlow he had only with him 12 horsemen. There he alighted and took some bread and wine : the horsemen did not dismount. They then proceeded to Dublin.

The General of Ulster was now at Ballynaskeagh (b. na sgeatan), and pitched his tents and booths beside the Deer-park. Intelligence of this was conveyed to the two Nuncios, one of whom, in the beginning of the war, had come from Pope Urban the Eighth, the other

256. Written Leit glionn by better authorities.—J. S.

from Pope Innocent the Tenth. They both came from Kilkenny to meet the General.[257] He, with Sir Felim and the other chiefs, came into the presence of these holy men and received their benediction.

The General required that the Castle and fortifications of the city should be delivered up to him, and the following hostages from the country and the city, viz., Donchadh M'Carty, Lord of Muskerry (ꝏuᵹⱷ̇aıᵹe), Edmund Butler, son of Lord Mountgarret (ꝏocaᵹaıpeaꝺ), also Beling (belıɴ), the Secretary of the Council, Sir John Begneir, and four others of the principal Gentlemen of the country. These matters were arranged forthwith, and the town and the hostages were taken in charge.

1646.

The General held a review of all his Infantry, who amounted to 14,000 men. Sir Felim, the Colonel of the horse, also mustered the cavalry, consisting of 22 troops. On this occasion all the principal Irish chiefs were present, together with the two Nuncios and the Ambassadors of Spain and France.

The Archbishop of Fermo, one of the Nuncios, passed through the forces, from the west side to the east, giving them his benediction. The soldiers then fired a volley of musketry with one consent, accompanied by a discharge from all the cannons : and on the passing of the Nuncio again from the east side to the west there was a similar universal discharge, in token of honor and glory to God, the Pope and the Nuncio.

The Nuncio then came to where Sir Felim was with the cavalry and blessed them, when they, in like manner, fired a volley from their carbines and pistols. The Review occupied two days. The General accompanied the Nuncios and Ambassadors to the city-gate, taking leave of them, and then returned himself to the camp. The sumptuous feasts which had been prepared in honor of the Earl of Ormond were now distributed among the youths of Ulster, and the whole forces remained encamped at Kilkenny for 10 days without any scarcity of provisions. The golden gate which had been erected for the same occasion was taken down and concealed from the Ulster people. The General gave up the Castle, the town, and the hostages into the hands

Sept. 28,1646. of the Nuncio. Everything being arranged, they received his blessing, and all the troops marched on Monday to Castlecomer (opoıᵹcaꝺ a ꝺeıᵹɴeı) and to (ᵹo baıle peaın mıc Laoıpıᵹ), where they staid four nights. From thence they proceeded to the Hill of Lease

---

257. Both Nuncios, *i.e.*, Scarampo and Rinuccini. It is stated by Dr. (now Cardinal) Moran, in his *Memoir of Oliver Plunket*, p. 4, that Scarampo, Urban the Eighth's envoy, did not, as is commonly represented, remain in Ireland till 1647, but that he returned to Rome in 1645, having received permission to do so by a Brief dated 4th May in that year. O'Mellan, in this paragraph and the next but one, is against the statement of his Eminence. In Rinuccini's letters to Cardinal Pamphili there is evidence that Scarampo was in Ireland as late as February, 1647. A letter dated 21st May, 1646, incidentally mentions that Scarampo [Scarampi] constantly resided in Waterford ; another, 24th May, 1646, notices that *he has often written for leave to depart ;* another, 24th December, 1646, that he has received permission to do so ; in another, 30th December, 1646, Rinuccini writes that he is expecting Scarampo to pay him a farewell visit : in another, 1st February, 1647, he states that Scarampo was in Kilkenny till that day, stress of weather having made him return some little time before: in another, 6th February, 1647, Rinuccini writes that he sends the Cardinal three reports by Scarampo, and one in cipher. (See *The Embassy in Ireland of Monsignor G. B. Rinuccini*, pp. 165, 167, 224, 234, 239, 249.)—J. S.

(boılı na coıllıᵹ a laoıᵹıṗ) and Cullentra Castle (Caıṗlean na Sept., 1646.
cınlentṗoı). The General treated the Captain of the place very
leniently, and placed a garrison of his own there. From this
they went to Maryboro' (poṗt laoıṗ).[258] Before surrounding the
town, Sir Felim, the Colonel of the horse, called on the garrison to
surrender. They replied that they would not, until they saw the
General and the cannon. The troops now arriving, a drummer was
despatched to demand formally the surrender of the place. The
Governor demanded hostages from the General, and, accordingly,
Brian O'Neill M'Quin Roe and Shane O'Neill M'Henry M'Turley, from Oct. 6, 1646.
the wood, were sent. Sir William Gilbert then came to the army, and
on seeing the force and the cannon he agreed to capitulate, receiving
permission for the garrison to carry away all their movables. Port
Lease[259] was given in charge to Felim O'Neill M'Donnell M'Henry.
The army went from thence to Dysart-Enos (oıṗıoṗt). Here Pigot
(an bṗıceanaċ) was ordered through a drummer to surrender the
castle ; but he replied that he would not stir a foot. The General
then commanded Colonel Farrel and Colonel Rory to begin the attack.
The outworks outside the gate were first burnt. They then scaled
the ramparts and made their way into the area, where they burnt the
great hall, the stables, and the great haggart. Upwards of eighty
were killed, along with the Captain and Pigot himself. Colonel Rory
had one Captain killed, namely, Dugald M'Quillan, and five soldiers.
From this place they proceeded to the County Kildare, to Castle
Rheban[260] (Caıṗlen an ṗebaın), which they took ; from that to Athy
(baıle atha hı), which they also took. They then took from the
enemy the Grange of Nurney[261] (ᵹṗaınṗeaċ an ıubaıṗ), Jiggenstown[262] October, 1646.
(boıle ınᵹın), Lyons[263] (boıle lınaın), Castle Martin[264] (caıṗlen maṗtın),
Clane (Claona), the town of Sir John Hay[265] (boıle ṗoṗ ṗeon han),
Ballymore Eustace (boıle na nuṗtaṗaċ), Ballyhenry (boıle henṗı),
and a number of other towns taken from the enemy not mentioned
here. They approached within 12 miles of Dublin, and to the
bridge of Kilcullen (cıll ćınlınn). General Thomas Preston and his
army here joined Owen O'Neill, and they remained thus for a
considerable time.

Let some mention be now made of the people of Lisnegarvey,
Killyleagh, Newry, Rosstrevor (c.tṗeveṗ), of Carlingford, of Dundalk
(ṗṗat baılı), of Drogheda, and of Slane (o boıch ṗlaıne). They all
assembled and fell on the people of Oriel, who fled to the woods of

---

258. Written poṗt laoıᵹıṗı by the *Four Masters* (v. p. 1750).—J. S.

259. Port Lease, *i.e.*, Port Leix, *i.e.*, Maryborough.—J. S.

260. See *Anthologia Hibernica*, ii. 161.—J. W. H.

261. On Petty's Map of Kildare, Nurney Castle is marked on the S. of the Barony of Ophaley.—J. W. H.

262. Jiggenstown, a mile to the west of Naas.—J. W. H.

263. Castle Martin, to the west of Kilcullen bridge, on old map of Kildare. In Petty's Map of Kildare, Castlemartin is marked near the junction of three baronies, Connell, N.W., Naas, N.E., and Kilcullen, S.—J. W. H.

264. Lyons, Co. Kildare, spelled on Petty's Map "Castle lions."—J. W. H.

265. ? Ballyhayes.—J. O'D. ? Ballysonan.—J. W. H.

(ᴏⱼᴜⁱⁱⁱ ᴠⁱⁱⁿ).　They then plundered and burnt their houses and haggarts (ᴀᴈᴀⱼⁱᴄ) as far as the woods of Killaney (ᴄⁱʟʟ ᴀⁿⁿᴀ). They burnt Moybolgue (ᴄ.ᴍⁱⁱᴈᴄ ʙᴏʟᴈ), and destroyed hundreds of pounds' worth of produce.　They returned, bringing with them a great amount of spoil.　They brought with them the soldiers who were stationed at Carrickmacross, and then burnt the place itself.　Sad and sorrowful were the women and the men of Breffny after their departure.

Dec., 1646.　The General was still near Dublin with his forces, but permission did not arrive from the Council of Kilkenny for him to proceed until the month of December came with long and violent rains, and he was then directed to disband the troops for the space of three months. The General accordingly issued orders to the forces to go into quarters, which they did in Munster and Leinster.

The Earl of Ormond, with a strong force, arrived at Trim.　Here he was joined by the Earl of Kildare, the Earl of Westmeath, that is, Richard Nugent (ⁿⁱⁱⁿⁿⱼⁱᴏⁱ), Earl Burke, the Earl of Roscommon, Earl Castlehaven, who had left Kilkenny with the Earl of Ormond, and Sir James Dillon, a Colonel of the Catholics.　He is along with these persons this day, namely, St. Thomas's Day,[266] in the house of Edward Boy (ʙⁱⁱᴠᴄ) Dewitt.　They raised a contribution of two pounds off every ᴈⁱⁱᴏⁱⁱ (*i.e.*, the 12th of a ploughland) in the County of Mullingar, and quarter for the troops and soldiers.

Jan. 15, 1647.　The Earl of Ormond proceeded to Breffny, crossing the country, and collecting the cows, forage, and other property of the people. This was done eight days.　They gathered and tied up everything, killed 38 persons, and carried off from Breffny and Oriel 4,000 cows.

Jan. 18, 1647.　Captain Philip Roe O'Reilly obtained permission from his Colonel, Philip M'Kee, to go with 300 soldiers in pursuit of the enemy.　They came behind a town in which were two troops of them, and towards the end of the night they surrounded the place.　They beat their drums, fired off their muskets, and burnt the houses over the enemy's horses and themselves, killing a number of them.　They had with them 90 horses, which, together with the arms of the cavalry, were brought by the Captain to Ballynacargy (ʙᴄʟ ᴀᴄ[ⁿᴀ]ᴄᴀⱼⁱⱼᴈᴄ).

Jan. 21, 1647.　Sir Felim sent out seven boats and a bark, in which were two field-pieces and a strong crew, upon Lough Neagh (ᴄᴀᴄᴀᴄ).　They burnt two of the enemy's forts in Claneboy and a great haggart belonging to Major Connolly, the person who informed against Conor Maguire, Lord Enniskillen, who was put to death in 1644.[267]　They killed both men and cattle, and brought away with them whatever they pleased in the boats.　They were pursued both by land and water. Sir Felim's people were raising a fort on Trowagh (ⱼⱼᴀⱼᴈ ⁿⁱʙᴀᴄ) in Clan-Bresail, when the enemy surprised them, and killed a number of them, among the rest, Robert Atkinson, a Lieutenant.　Upwards of 20 were taken and some drowned.　Two boats escaped, but the bark and five boats were taken.

266.　St. Thomas's Day, *i.e.*, 21st December.—J. S.
267.　20 February, 1644-45.—J. S.

Shane O'Kane, the Sergeant-Major-General, and Lieutenant- Jan. 26, 1647.
Colonel Felim M'Tuath M'Toole, came to the County of Mullingar,
along with 3,000 foot and a number of horse. They arrived at
Loughcrew (b. Loċa ċṗaoiḃe), and next day had a rendezvous. They
resolved to attack the garrison of Kells (ceananṅcuṗ), where Colonel
Theophilus Jones was stationed with 300 men. They travelled night
and day till they reached Kells. The foot soldiers scaled the walls,
while the cavalry remained outside. Those of Colonel Jones's soldiers
(about 130) who asked quarter were spared ; upwards of 200 were
killed. The people of the town itself were spared. The prisoners
were taken to Finac (Ḟioċ an áṫa), and Theophilus to the Castle of
Lough Sheelin. General Monk, with 3,000 of the Parliamentary
forces and 120 horses, together with their cavalry accoutrements,
arrived in Trian Congail (cṗian conġail) against the Province of
Ulster.

Three thousand soldiers from Parliament arrived in Dublin against Feb., 1647.
Leinster and horses *(cetera desunt).*

NOTE.—Dr. John M'Donnell, Dublin, left some antiquarian notes, now in the Editor's possession. He transcribed the brief notices of Loughinsholin Island in O'Mellan's Narrative, translated
by the Rev. Dr. Reeves in his *Supplementary Observations to Mr. Wilde's Paper on certain
Crannoges in Ulster,* read 11th April, 1859 (see *Proceedings R.I.A.,* vol. vii. p. 157). He has
added the following notice of O'Mellan's MS. without stating his authority :—" Friar O'Mellan
wrote a journal including a period extending from 1641 to 1647. He was of the Franciscan
Order, who had a monastic home in the Co. of Tyrone, Parish of Aghanloo. He is believed to
have been Chaplain to Sir Phelim O'Neill. This journal contains an account of the general
history of the Roman Catholics during the above period. The MS. was sent to the late Earl
O'Neill by the possessor about ten years ago, who presented it to him as descendant (which he
was not) and representative of Owen Roe. It was copied by Eugene O'Curry, and carefully
collated by John O'Donovan, LL.D., by the desire of the Rev. James Henthorn Todd, S.F.T.C.D.,
for the Royal Irish Academy. It was translated by Robert Macadam, of Belfast, for Lord
O'Neill. This translation was sent up to Dublin to Geo. Petrie, who made no use of it. But
the original, borrowed from the possessor, Lord O'Neill, for the R.I.A., was transcribed by E.
O'Curry, and for some time exhibited as a specimen of his caligraphy in a glass case, but of late
years it has been removed. Rev. W. Reeves, Sec. to the Academy, published in the *Proceedings*
the following important extracts." (They are contained in 20 lines of the original.) It may be
added, that in addition to the copy in the Grainger Collection, Belfast Free Library, another copy,
made by the late J. W. Hanna, is in the possession of the Rev. J. O'Laverty, P.P., M.R.I.A.,
who kindly lent it to the Editor.

FINIS.

AFTER THE BATTLE OF BENBURB.

OLD HOUSES TAKEN DOWN AT QUEEN'S SQUARE, BELFAST, IN 1854. (*From a Photograph by* WILLIAM J. YOUNG, *Uncle of the Editor.*)

Appendix.

INVENTORY OF THE *PINKERTON MSS.* SENT BY GEORGE BENN WITH A
LETTER TO ROBERT S. MACADAM, 1872.

(Much condensed here.)

BUNDLE MARKED NO. 1.

1. Short and very good account of the introduction of Printing into Belfast, with list of all the early printers' names. 2. List of Belfast-printed books to the publication of *Belfast Magazine*, 1808. 3. Small MS., with extracts from Hardy, Twiss, and others about Belfast-printed books. 4. Another MS., with an immense list of Belfast books, chiefly reprints by Magee and the Joys. Miscellaneous papers.

2ND PARCEL, MARKED ON BACK, "OLD BELFAST PAPERS, LEASES, ACTS OF PARLIAMENT, WILLS, &C., OF THE DONEGALL FAMILY."

This mainly consists of a large mass of Law papers; offers from tenants for new leases; an Act of Parliament obtained in 1751 to give an enabling power to Earl Donegall and his trustees to grant leases for long terms, as the expression is, to *rebuild Belfast*, then stated to be old and ruinous, some of the inhabitants, it is declared in one of the MSS., being determined to leave the town and settle in Newry or Lisburn if not favoured with such leases; letter of Lord Massareene relative to a Macartney; many documents relating to country parts of the estate—Donegal, Carrickfergus, Antrim, &c.

No. 3. MARKED "MISCELLANEOUS NOTES ABOUT BELFAST."

This parcel contains numerous notes and memoranda referring to documents elsewhere; thus—"Essex's camp; notice about Belfast; important." Amongst more modern papers is a very good account of the origin and history of the Belfast Charitable Society, by the late Mr. Bruce; a good deal about the fords in connection with the Donegall and Templemore lawsuit; and many documents about Turlogh Lynnagh O'Neill and his contemporaries. There are also some printed ballads, and notices of general rather than local interest.

No. 4. REPORT OF THE MUNICIPAL COMMISSIONERS, 1833-34, ON THE BOROUGH OF BELFAST.

No. 5. MISCELLANEOUS. BELFAST.

Several MSS. fastened together, containing about 100 pp., copied from some public depository, but no account of where or what; the dates not clearly referred to, but 1642-1643, and at the end 1647, occur. The papers are taken up with accounts of the wars in Ulster; disputes about corn consequent on the "cessation." A paper in Mr. Pinkerton's handwriting describing the "Old Town Book of Belfast," and which he considers "the most curious and important collection of documents of its kind in Ireland;" followed by a list of early sovereigns and burgesses, oaths of office, fines for non-attendance at church, &c. A bundle of 20 little books containing Mr. Pinkerton's copious extracts from the Record Book of the old Corporation; some already printed, but the greater part, of course, nowhere but in that old Book. Next are four MS. books containing much about the Smiths' attempt to get the Ards in Elizabeth's time. Dealings and letters between the several parties interested, both English and Irish. Also much Scotch seventeenth century history—political and theological. Many documents leading to law or arbitration, connected with settlements, &c., on members of the Donegall family. Many papers and extracts referring to the history of Presbyterianism after the Restoration. Ten little sewed books containing copies of two wills of the Earls of Donegall, notices of the "Key," apparent difficulties between the Corporation and the Donegall family. A satirical poem of 1771, with allusions to the Hearts of Steel. A book with notices of the general wars in Ulster, and at end genealogies of the Joy and Grierson families. Many miscellaneous scraps and loose leaves.

No. 6. BUNDLE ENDORSED "7 BOUND MS. VOLUMES."

No. 1. Extracts from the old Corporation Records. No. 2. Literary quotations about general subjects. No. 3. Marked "Clarke's Correspondence." Much here about King William's proceedings. Belfast introduced, but not prominently. Phillips' account of Carrickfergus, Belfast, Derry, &c. Extracts and Notes on Richard Dobbs' MS. account of Co. Antrim, already known to Rev. George Hill and others. A book containing extracts from *News-Letter*. Notices of books printed in Belfast of the famous schoolmaster, David Manson; notices of maps; calendar of papers referring to Belfast, Antrim, the McDonnells, &c., some scored across, as if Mr. Pinkerton had already given them away or used them elsewhere. A general memorandum book about the Dublin Society, Fishing, Freemasonry, &c. A small book filled with references about the *News-Letter* and Belfast-printed books.

No. 7.

Two bundles tied together. One is labelled, "Port of Belfast," and contains some papers referring to it. The other is marked on back, "Grants, Leases, &c., of the Donegall

Family." It contains copy of original grant of all the estates in Antrim, Carrickfergus, Down, Donegal, Tyrone, and copies of subsequent confirmations, &c., and family settlements of a lengthy nature. Account of the funeral of Sir Arthur Chichester. Notes of interments of other members of the family. Document in large sheets, apparently a confirmatory grant to remedy defective titles from Charles I. to Chichester, with every townland named. These three large books are all in Mr. Pinkerton's handwriting. Very long copy of a deed, dated 1692, between relatives of the Donegalls. A number of loose papers, applications for leases, with small sketch maps. Two books filled with extracts from documents of the Ulster Plantation in Lambeth Palace, beginning with the work done at Dromore, passing to Carrickfergus (building of Joymount there), Derry, Armagh, Monaghan, &c. The notices about Belfast are very interesting. A long document giving a biography of Samuel McSkimin, Crofton Croker, &c.; the genealogy and burials of the O'Neills; the trials, &c., of certain Presbyterian ministers of 1798. A book in Mr. Pinkerton's handwriting containing the proposed transplanting of the Ulster Scots in 1653. Another book filled with proceedings of Convocation in 1729. An Inquisition at Ardquin, Co. Down. Small MS. book of *State Paper* extracts relative to Munster Irish, and the O'Neills of the period. A little book labelled "Forde," containing account of King William's entry into Belfast, Schonberg's proceedings, and the state of the town then. A book containing Smith's Charter in Latin. A book in Mr. Pinkerton's handwriting of miscellaneous gatherings of Chichesters, McDonnells, O'Neills, &c. Allowances to the forces, pedigrees, coats of arms, &c. A large amount of loose leaves and cuttings.

No. 8. MARKED ON BACK, "BERMINGHAM TOWER AND PRESBYTERIANS."

Contains nine small books and a number of loose leaves and scraps. They contain orders of Council, showing the dealings of the Parliament and Cromwell with the Presbyterians; fragments of Scotch history; mentions of the McDonnells and the O'Neills; the petition of Edmund Spenser's grandson to Cromwell, besides many local references.

No. 9.

A book containing an account of the mutiny at Carrickfergus in 1666. A little book about the Customs, Excise, &c., in 1637. A number of references to playing-cards, fishing, &c.

No. 10

Is a very large collection. It contains the full description of Co. Antrim in 1683, by Richard Dobbs, which Mr. Pinkerton intended to publish for private circulation. Several other contemporary descriptions of other counties are in this parcel. Miscellaneous papers.

No. 11. MARKED "MISCELLANEOUS."

A book containing a good many orders, resolutions, letters, &c., relative to the wars of the seventeenth century, with complaints and expostulations from several quarters consequent on Monroe's surprisal of Belfast. Many literary papers of all kinds, on Valentine Greatrakes, the Irish Harp, claims to early civilisation, &c.

No. 12.

This parcel contains eight little books, consisting entirely of extracts from Belfast *News-Letter*, in Mr. Pinkerton's handwriting, down to 1782.

Books relating to Ireland collected by WILLIAM PINKERTON, F.S.A., F.A.S.L., *to aid him in writing a History of the Town of Belfast:*—

ANTHOLOGIA HIBERNICA, 1793-4.
BORLASE, *Reduction of Ireland*, 1675.
CARTE, *Life of Ormonde*, 1736.
CAREW. Reprint, 1810.
DUBOURDIEU, *Survey. Co. Antrim*, 1812.
BOATE, *Natural History of Ireland*, 1755.
BENN, *History of Belfast*, 1823.
BERWICK, *Historical Collections*, 1817.
CASTLEHAVEN'S *Memoirs*, 1753.
AHIMAN REZON (Masonic, 1782), 1795.
CHAMBERS'S *Domestic Annals of Scotland*, 1859.
BRADSHAW'S *Belfast Directory*, 1819.
DUFFY'S IRISH LIBRARY, comprising—
 MITCHEL'S *Aodh O'Neill*, 1862.
 MEEHAN'S *Geraldines*, 1847.
 MEEHAN'S *Confederation of Kilkenny*, 1862.
 MEEHAN'S *Life of Kirwan*, 1848.
 M'GEE'S *Irish Writers*, 1857.
 MACNEVIN'S *Volunteers*, 1853.
 MACNEVIN'S *Confiscation of Ulster*, 1860.
 FRENCH'S *Historical Works*, 1846.
 M'GEE'S *Art MacMurrough*, 1847.
 HAY'S *Insurrection*, 1862.

HARDY'S *Life of Charlemont*, 1810.
HEMPTON'S *History of Londonderry*, 1861.
Belfast Politics, 1794.
Letters between Henry and Frances (Griffiths), 1770.
HARRIS'S *County of Down*, 1744.
GREGORY'S *Highlands and Islands*, 1836.
Historical Account of Election for Co. Down, 1784.
PETTY, *Political Anatomy*, 1691.
PILSON, *History of Rise and Progress of Belfast*, 1846.
M'SKIMIN, *History of Carrickfergus*, 1823.
CALENDAR STATE PAPERS, IRELAND, 1509-73.
RUTTY, *History of Quakers in Ireland*, 1751.
TAYLOR AND SKINNER'S *Maps of Roads, Ireland*, 1778.
HISTORICAL VIEW OF IRISH SOCIETY'S PLANTATION IN ULSTER, 1822.
STORY'S *Wars in Ireland*, 1693.
OLDMIXON'S *Memoirs of Ireland*. 1716.
STUART'S *History of Armagh*, 1819.
KELLY'S *Cambrensis Eversus of Lynch*, 1848.
O'DONOVAN'S *Book of Rights*, 1847.
O'DONOVAN'S *Four Masters*, 1856.
O'CONNOR, *History of Ireland*, 1766.
MILNER, *Catholic Inhabitants and Antiquities*, 1808.

KIRKPATRICK'S *Presbyterian Loyalty*, 1713.
REID, *Presbyterian Church in Ireland*, 1853.
DEVEREUX, *Lives of Earls of Essex*, 1853.
MADDEN, *United Irishmen* (First Series), 1842.
COLBY, *Ordnance Survey, Co. Londonderry*, 1837.
HARBOUR OF BELFAST, 1852.
WOLFE TONE, *Memoirs*, 1827.

TWISS, *Tour in Ireland*, 1776.
TOUR THROUGH IRELAND (*Luckomb?*), 1780.
WRIGHT'S *Giraldus Cambrensis (Bohn)*, 1863.
Letter from Abraham Protest maker, Runner to a Bank in Belfast, 1751.
O'CONNOR, *Ogygia Vindicata*, 1775.
COLLECTANEA DE REBUS HIBERNICIS, 1774.

Pamphlets and tracts selected from a large number as those most likely to be useful :—

IN VOL. I.

Origin of Irish Yeomanry, 1801.
Lord Taafe, Affairs in Ireland from 1691, 1766.
Jebb on a National Circulation Bank, 1780.

IN VOL. V.

Application of Barnel's *Memoirs of Jacobinism* to the Secret Societies of Ireland, 1798.
Report of Committee of Secrecy, 1799.

IN VOL. VII.

Case of W. T. Jones in Jail of Cork on charge of High Treason, 1803.
Detail of Affair of Honour between W. T. Jones and Sir R. Musgrave, 1802.
Letter to the Societies of United Irishmen of Town of Belfast by W. T. Jones, 1792.
To the Magistrates, Military, and Yeomanry of Ireland, 1798.
Letter of Lord De Clifford to Electors of Downpatrick, *n.d.*
Question relative to Petitions from Dublin, Cork, and Belfast for a new regulation of the Portugal Gold Coin, 1760.
Observation on case of Priest O'Neill, 1804.
Meeting of Trustees of Linen and Hemp Manufacture in Ireland, printed by Linen Board about 1803 (curious, useful, and suggestive respecting Linen manufacture).

WILLIAM WARE, c. 1780.
Organist of the Parish Church, and E. Bunting's Master. (From miniature in possession of Editor.)

THE CORPORATION BELLMAN OF BELFAST.

Notes.

Page 1. REPORT BY ROBERT COWLEY

This extract from the *Irish State Papers*, of which a *précis* appears in Hamilton's *Irish Calendar of State Papers*, 1509-73, is printed as an example of the material available for the earlier annals of Belfast and its vicinity. When W. Pinkerton began to collect notices of our local history, of which examples are given at p. 2, the treasures contained in the State Paper Offices were not so easily accessible as since the publication of the numerous calendars now in all large libraries. He gives as the first mention of Belfast, 1551—" Bagenal intends to return to Belfast." In a letter of his addressed to Robert S. Macadam, referring to the death of Edmund Getty in 1857, he mentions the latter had informed him that his proposed work on the "Statistics and Antiquities of the Baronies of Castlereagh, in Down, and of Belfast, in Antrim," was so entitled because there was no historical mention of Belfast as a town before Elizabeth's time. He was anxious to give all the early history he had collected of the district, and therefore chose the wider title. Unfortunately, Getty died before he could carry out his projected work, of which only the prospectus exists. He was well qualified for such an enterprise, as his *History of the Harbour of Belfast* shows. (Pinkerton has left a note on it as follows—" Harbour of Belfast. This was the first of a series of works on the Harbours of the United Kingdom ordered to be compiled by the Harbour Department of the Admiralty. As the names of places were taken in alphabetical succession, Belfast was thus the first. The Admiralty, however, changing their mind, printed no more of the series, and rigidly suppressed this immediately after, if not before, publication. There is no copy in the British Museum! The Admiralty, in compiling the work, were greatly aided by the late Edmund Getty, of Belfast, who presented this copy to his friend W. P. in the Golden Cross, Charing Cross, London, on the 19th June, 1855. This work must consequently be very rare.") His novel, published anonymously, called *The Last King of Ulster*, 3 vols., London, 1841, is almost unknown, but is well worthy to be ranked with Sir Samuel Ferguson's *Hibernian Nights*. Secretary of the Harbour Board from 1837, his antiquarian knowledge was of eminent service in the dispute between Lords Donegall and Templemore in regard to the ownership of the bed and soil of the River Lagan.

Page 1. SAVAGE OF THE ENGLISH CONQUEST

The two chief branches of the great Anglo-Norman family of Savage (originally Le Sauvage) were that of Derbyshire and Cheshire, represented by the Viscounts Savage and Earls Rivers (titles now extinct), and that of Ulster, mainly seated in the Ards, but formerly possessed also of extensive territories in Antrim and in Lecale. The founder of the family was Le Sieur Thomas Le Sauvage, whose name appears in Brompton's *Chronicle* and other documents as having accompanied William the Conqueror from Normandy, A.D. 1066. The founder of the great Ulster branch, the members of which played such a conspicuous part in early Anglo-Irish history, was Sir William Le Savage, who appears to have been a son of Sir Geoffrey Le Savage, of Stainesby, in Derbyshire, who was great-grandson of the above-mentioned Thomas Le Sauvage. Sir William Le Savage accompanied De Courcy in the invasion of Ulster, A.D. 1177, established himself in the Ards, and was subsequently a Palatine Baron. Ardkeen Castle, the chief seat of the branch known as "the Savages of Ardkeen," is referred to by De Courcy in his Charter to Black Abbey in the Ards, A.D. 1180; and Portaferry Castle was no doubt built about the same time. William Baron Le Savage was succeeded by his son, Sir Robert Le Savage, Knt. (living in 1204), who was succeeded by his son, Henry Le Savage (living in 1259, died about 1277), who was succeeded by his son, Henry Le Savage (born August 10, 1270), whose successor was Sir Robert Savage (who died in 1360), a very famous knight, on whom, for his services, Edward III. bestowed very extensive estates in Antrim, and whose Antrim seat was Lisanoure Castle. Sir Robert was succeeded by his son, Henry, Lord Savage, a Baron by writ-of-summons, who was succeeded in the representation of the family by Sir Robert Savage, Knt. (last mentioned in 1389), who was the first sheriff of the Ards, then constituted a distinct county, and who, besides his Ards and Antrim territories, became, through his conflicts with the Irish, possessed also of Lecale. He married Christiana MacDonnell, daughter of John, Lord of the Isles, and granddaughter of Robert II. of Scotland. He was succeeded by Robert Savage (died about 1469), who was succeeded by Patrick Savage (died about 1482), who was succeeded by Sir Roland Savage, Knt., Seneschal of Ulster, who died in 1519. Sir Roland's son and successor was Raymond Savage, surnamed Ferdoragh Mac Seneschal, "the dark son of the Seneschal." Owing to the combination of forces ranged against him, Raymond Savage lost his hold of Lecale. A contention now arose between him and his near kinsman, another Roland, for supremacy in the Ards. The strife was long and disastrous, and at last both parties agreed to refer the subject of dispute to the Lord Deputy and Council; and in A.D. 1559 they appeared before their Lordships and prayed them to "put a quiet and loving end" to their differences. The enrolment of the Treaty established between them is in the Patent and Close Rolls in the Record Office, Dublin, dated 1559. It does not appear that this document confers any actual right of *precedence* upon one party or the other. Roland was to have the rights of "Captain of his Nation" within the lands which correspond to the Portaferry estate, with, clearly, Portaferry Castle as the centre; and Raymond was to have the rights of "Captain of his Nation" within the lands which correspond to the Ardkeen estate, with Ardkeen ("Ardkyne") Castle as the centre. Thus the Little Ards were pretty evenly divided between Roland and Raymond Savage, whose descendants respectively have been known ever since as the Savages of Portaferry and the Savages of Ardkeen. This Roland Savage was not a brother of Raymond, and Raymond was undoubtedly the son and representative of Sir Roland Savage, the Seneschal, who was the representative of the Savage family in Ulster, and the most powerful of the name, in his time. Their adoption of the tanistry custom makes questions of precedency in Irish and Norman-Irish families often very difficult to determine. Raymond was, as we have seen, surnamed Mac Seneschal, "the son of the Seneschal," and his descendants were known always as the "Family of the Seneschal;" and under the Castle Hill of Ardkeen is a little inlet of the Lough still called Seneschal's Port. Montgomery is right in saying that the Savages of Portaferry were (subsequently) styled "Lords Savage," and this was probably through some of them having been, like the common ancestor Henry, Baron Savage, summoned to Parliament by writ (see p. 139). Montgomery was connected with both branches of the family, but more closely with the Portaferry branch than with the Ardkeen branch. The Ardkeen estates were sold in 1837 to the late Mr. Harrison, of Belfast, and are now the property of Captain Harrison, of Holywood, Co. Down. The present representative of the Savages of Ardkeen in the direct male line is Colonel Henry John Savage, son of the late Lieut.-General Henry John Savage, R.E., formerly of Ballygalget (Rock Savage), Co. Down; grandson of Major-General Sir John Boscawen Savage, of Ballygalget (Rock Savage), K.C.H., K.C.H., &c.; and great-great-great-grandson of Captain Hugh Savage, of Ardkeen, who died in 1723. The last of the Savages of Ardkeen who resided in the Ards were the Glastry branch, who are represented by G. F. Savage-Armstrong, Esq., M.A., D.LIT., &c., of Beech Hurst, Bray, Co. Wicklow, and Rushbrooke, Queenstown, Co. Cork, grandson of the Rev. Henry Savage, of Glastry, J.P., Incumbent of Ardkeen, and great-great-grandson (maternally) of Francis

Savage, of Ardkeen, Esq., High Sheriff of Co. Down, who died in 1770. The Savages of Portaferry happily still hold their ancient hereditary estates in the Little Ards, and are represented by Lieut.-General Andrew Nugent, J.P. and D.L., late Lt.-Col. commanding Royal Scots Greys, whose grandfather, Lt.-Col. Andrew Savage, on inheriting a portion of the fortune of his maternal grand-uncle, Governor Nugent, assumed by Royal License the name of Nugent, and claimed the Barony of Delvin. The SAVAGES, now NUGENTS, of PORTAFERRY, are the only Anglo-Norman family in Ulster who still possess and reside upon lands won by their ancestors at the Conquest, A.D. 1177. An admirable and exhaustive history of the Ulster Savages will be found in the sumptuous volume entitled, "The Ancient and Noble Family of the Savages of the Ards," published by Messrs. Marcus Ward & Co., Belfast, 1888.

Page 4. PIERS AND MALBIE

Some account of these Elizabethan soldiers and their exploits is given in Sir Henry Sidney's *Memoir* of his Government in Ireland, edited by H. F. Hore (*Ulster Journal of Archæology*, vol. iii. p. 33). Hill's *MacDonnells of Antrim*, p. 144, contains some reference to Piers, who pickled Shane O'Neill's head in a pipkin, and sent it to Lord-Deputy Sydney. Piers was Seneschal of Claneboy, and also Constable of Carrickfergus Castle. He is frequently mentioned as Mayor in the Town Records of Carrickfergus MS., which the Editor is preparing for publication. A curious entry occurs in 1571, showing that the peasantry were remiss in their military duties. "At a court held on 26 June, 1571, before Richard Sendall, Mayor, and Wolston Elderton and Cornelius Ochan, Sheriffs, in the Town House of Carrickfergus, It was ordered for that the Mayor, sending his officers to warne as well the Husbandmen or Labourers, as also ther Garrons, to be in redinesse for the service of hur Majestye, that the sayd husbandmen for fliing away should paye for the want of every Garron five shill- currant mony of England, and for fliing away of every such husbandman or labourer Twelve pense sterl." In 1575, "Daniell Beggahan and Murto O'Henry, for hiding themselves and their garrons, were fined 7s. 8d." It is mentioned in a letter in the *State Paper* Office, dated 25 September, 1567, at Carrickfergus, that Robert Lyth has arrived in the town, "and has drawn two plats" of it. This was the curious map given in *Ulster Journal of Archæology*, vol. iii. p. 276. It represents this ancient seaport the year before Sir Henry Sydney's visit, and six years prior to its burning by Sir Brian O'Neill. For one of W. Pinkerton's most valuable papers, entitled, "The 'Pallace' of Carrickfergus," with coloured plate, see *Ulster Journal of Archæology*, vol. vii. p. 1.

Page 11. IRISH LINEN YARNS

The history of the Irish linen trade has yet to be written in an exhaustive manner. Many references occur in the *State Papers* which have not yet been utilised. The earliest notice of linen in Ireland is given by Froissart, time of Richard II. Henry Castide, an Italian traveller, told him—"I caused breeches of *linen cloth* to be made for the four Kings of Ireland when I was there." Pinkerton intended to treat of it thoroughly in his *History of Belfast*. Some of his notes are subjoined. "In 1572, Queen Elizabeth granted one Thomas Moore a license to transplant from Ireland three thousand packs of linen yarn in five years. The Mayors of Dublin and Drogheda with others petitioned for the withdrawal of the license, asserting that three thousand packs was a greater quantity of yarn than the whole realm of Ireland could produce in the five years limited.—*State Papers*. [*Note.*—I have somewhere met with the weight or measure of a pack of woollen yarn, but not of linen.] 1550. William Fyan received the grant in fee farm of a nunnery called the Hogges, beside Dublin, annual value £9 13s. 4d., on entering into recognisance to erect and set upon the site of that late suppressed nunnery six looms of linen and woollen yarn in the space of one year (*State Papers*). Oct. 21, 1550. Lord Deputy St. Leger writes to the English Privy Council that he has prohibited the exportation of wool, tallow, butter, linen yarn, &c., from Ireland, as it only encouraged idleness" (*State Papers*). Many other notices might be given besides those cited above.

Sir H. Sydney writes to Secretary Walsingham in 1576, relative to licenses for exporting yarn, that he is "loth to destroy a creature of his own making," and an invention of his own for setting people to work at home, and not to transport the commodity raw and unwrought, as they were accustomed. In Strafford's *Letters* (of which the Editor possesses the late Bishop Reeves' annotated copy), several references to the linen trade occur. He writes to Sir William Boswell, probably Minister in Holland in 1635, from Dublin, "The bearer I send to buy some Flax seed, which I find by this last year's trial to take extremely well in this country; and very ambitious I am to set up a trade of Linnen Clothing in these parts; which, if God bless, so as to be effected, will, I dare say, be the greatest enriching to this Kingdom that ever befel it (vol. i. p. 473)." On Strafford's trial, charge thirteenth was as follows:—" That he monopolised all the flax of the kingdom, and prescribed rules and methods of making yarn and thread which the natives could not practise, and ordering all made in any other manner to be seized, which was accordingly executed with severity, by which multitudes were ruined and many starved."

In the *Treasure of Traffic*, published in 1641, mention is made of Liverpool as a great market in which Irish merchants disposed of their linen yarns.

In an early *Northern Whig*, Samuel M'Skimin gave some notes on the progress of manufacturing by machinery in the County of Antrim. It is noted:—"1741—William Dobbin, Belfast, invented the Beetling Engine for Linen Cloth, which was formerly beetled by hand. 1749—Francis Joy, Randalstown, established a mill for dressing flax, which is thus described at the time, 'A complete new mill for dressing flax was finished and set to work at Randalstown by Francis Joy, which will dress 14 lb. of flax in an hour, fit for the heckle.' 1777—The printing of cotton and linen cloths was established at Greencastle by Nicholas Grimshaw. 1801—The Linen Board offered large premiums to such as would erect mills for spinning hemp or flax by water or steam. The writer supposes that the first spinning mill erected in Antrim was in the vicinity of Crumlin or Stoneyford."

Robert S. Macadam as far back as 1837 had collected "Notes on the History of Belfast Spinning, &c., and probably intended to write about it. Some of his notes are curious. "E. Getty has a letter written by his grand-uncle to his landlord about a farm for keeping cows for giving buttermilk to bleach. He understands that the ancestor of Bradshaw, of Mile Cross, Co. Down, first introduced diapers and damasks, and went over to Holland to get men, &c." He gives the following list of flax spinning mills as at work in January, 1836, in the North of Ireland:—

1. Andrew Mulholland & Co., Belfast.	15. W. Cunliffe, Glynn.
2. S. K. Mulholland, Hind & Co., Belfast.	16. Walker & Co., Carrickfergus.
3. J. & J. Herdman & Co., Belfast.	17. Jas. Murland & Son, Castlewellan.
4. J. & J. Herdman & Co., Francis Street.	18. Samuel Law, Banbridge.
5. John Boyd & Co., Belfast.	19. Dunbar, Stewart & Co., Gilford.
6. John Murphy & Co., Belfast.	20. William Hudson, near Newry.
7. Charters. Coates & Gamble, Belfast.	21. Joseph Nicholson & Son, Newry.
8. Stewart & M'Clelland, near Belfast.	22. A. & J. Davison, Broughshane.
9. Robert Thompson, near Belfast.	23. T. & A. Davison, Laragh, near Castle-
10. Dr. M'Kibbin, near Belfast.	blayney.
11. John Montgomery & Co., Grove, Belfast, Co. Down.	24. H. M'Kean, Keady.
	25. Smith, near Ballymoney.
12. Jas. Grimshaw & Son, Whitehouse.	26. Herdman, Lyons & Co., near Strabane.
13. Edmund Grimshaw, Mossley.	27. W. Cowan & Co., Whiteabbey.
14. R & R. Watt, Doagh.	

Names of the present Bleachers in the Province of Ulster (1839), compiled by R. S. Macadam.

ANTRIM.	Pieces per an.		Pieces per an.
		Isaac Stoney ... ... bleach about	15,000
Jonathan and Jas. Richardson bleach about	35,000	Jno. Christy ... ... ,,	15,000
Jas. W. Richardson & Sons .. ,,	40,000	Benjamin Haughton .. .. ,,	10,000
Coulsons .. .. .. ,,	12,000	W. Nicholson (Donacloney) .. ,,	25,000
Roberts .. .. .. ,,	12,000	Brown ,, .. ,,	20,000
M'Cance .. .. .. ,,	15,000	M'Clelland & M'Murray (Dromore) ,,	25,000
W. Orr .. .. .. ,,	18,000	Jas. Andrews & Sons (Comber) ,,	20,000
Sadler, Fenton & Co. (Springfield) ,,	25,000		
R. Howie & Co. .. ,,	45,000	ARMAGH.	
W. J. Moore .. .. ,,	18,000	Jos. M'Kee (Keady) .. .. ,,	18,000
Thos. Macky & Co. .. .. ,,	10,000	Sam. Kyd .. .. .. ,,	30,000
Jno. F. Ferguson .. .. ,,	25,000	Alex. Kyd .. .. .. ,,	15,000
Michael Andrews (Kilroot) .. ,,	20,000	W. Kirk .. .. .. ,,	30,000
W. Gray .. .. .. ,,	30,000		
W. Chaine & Sons .. .. ,,	50,000	TYRONE.	
Thos. Ferguson & Sons .. .. ,,	25,000	Sproull (Strabane) .. .. ,,	15,000
Miller (Ross) .. .. ,,	12,000	Gunning & Moore (Cookstown) .. ,,	10,000
David Kirk .. .. ,,	15,000	Jonathan Pike .. .. ,,	15,000
W. Johnston .. .. ,,	10,000	Henry Atkinson (Moy) .. .. ,,	5,000
W. Gihon & Sons .. .. ,,	30,000	O'Neill (Strabane) .. .. ,,	5,000
J. & R. Young .. .. ,,	40,000	Gwynne .. .. .. ,,	15,000
J. & D. Curell .. .. ,,	30,000		
J. & A. Barklie (Larne) .. ,,	30,000	DONEGAL.	
,, (Cullybackey) .. ,,	5,000	J. & J. Johnson (Ballybofey) .. ,,	25,000
Smith & Co. (Ballyclare) ,,	15,000		
M'Conkey & Howie (Lambeg) ,,	15,000	LONDONDERRY.	
H. Bragg & Son .. .. ,,	25,000	Smith & M'Clelland (Ardmore) ,,	30,000
Beck (near Antrim) .. .. ,,	5,000	Lyle (Oaks) .. .. ,,	30,000
		Pollock & Smith (Garvagh) .. ,,	25,000
DOWN.		S. Bennett (Coleraine) .. ,,	20,000
Henry Murland .. .. ,,	15,000	Hemphill & Co. (Coleraine) .. ,,	50,000
Crawford .. .. .. ,,	25,000	Bennet & Adams ,, .. ,,	25,000
Mulligan .. .. .. ,,	20,000	G. & A. Barklie ,, .. ,,	25,000
E. C. Clibborn .. .. ,,	15,000	S. & T. Alexander (Derry) ,,	5,000
Richard Hayes .. .. ,,	25,000	Alexander (Newtownlimavady) ,,	10,000
J. Smyth & Co. .. .. ,,	40,000	,, (Maghera) .. .. ,,	10,000
Jas. M'Clelland .. .. ,,	15,000		
Uprichard .. .. .. ,,	15,000		

Page 15. AND HOW SIR BRIAN HATH LATELY BURNT

The Records of Carrickfergus MS. note—"Curia tenta secundo die Junii an⁰ˣ 1573, coram Capitainn Guilielm Pierse Major, Wolston Elderton and Johannem Deere, Vice com⁺ˣ in le Town house of Knockfergus. In this yeare the 2ᵈ day of June was this Towne of Knockfergus for the most part destroyed by fier, by reason of Captaine Smithes departure out of the same with his force, not leaving sufficient force to defend the same, by Sur Brian MᶜPhellime and his co-perteners. In the same yeare abought the 20ᵗʰ of August came the right honorable the Earle of Essex into this land as Lord Governour of the Province of Ulster, accompanied with many a lusty Gentleman, and landed in this Towne of Knockfergus."

Page 16. ANSWER TO THE LORD TREASURER'S OBJECTIONS

The Records of Carrickfergus MS. contain the following reference to this dispute :— "1594. The 10th of June, William Lymsey, Recorder, and Humfery Jhonson, of the Same Town, Alderman, being appointed and chosen by the whole consente of the Towne to be Agents for the obtaynenge of thear Auntyent Lands and Comons, departed the Towne the day and yeare aforesayde for England, for the graunte and passing whearof they obtayned the Quene's letter to Sʳ William Russell, then Lᵈ Deputy, and the Counsell, and from them a Commission under the greate scale of Ireland for the Boundinge and mearinge thearof." There is a small map of the County Palatine of Carrickfergus in the Barony maps of the Down Survey, now in the Bibliothèque Nationale, Paris, showing the Silver Stream as the western boundary, and Coplin Water running down to the town out of Lough Mourne, a lake which derived its name from the M'Mornas, subsequently M'Gillmores.

Page 20. SIR A. CHICHESTER AND ISLAND MAGEE. 1601

Richard Dobbs, in his description of Co. Antrim, 1683, printed in Hill's *MacDonnells of Antrim*, says of Island Magee :—"This Island once belonged to the Earl of Essex, who was beheaded in the time of Queen Elizabeth : his patent was once in my hands." The lease of the island granted by Sir A. Chichester to Sir Moses has very recently fallen in, and the property has reverted to the Marquis of Donegall. Dobbs gives the definition Island Magee from the "Magees that lived here in former times." "John Magie of the Gat" is mentioned in the Records of Carrickfergus as having a quarter share of common land in 1606. "Hugh Magy, of Iland Magee, gent.," was a juror in 1613.

Page 21. LETTER FROM THOMAS WALKER

This curious letter, with its apology for the writer's failure to assassinate the Earl of Tyrone, seems not to have been published. It is printed from a copy in the Macadam MSS. For references to this and other attempts at his assassination, see *Life of Hugh Roe O'Donnell*, by Rev. Denis Murphy, s.j., LL.D. (p. cli.).

Page 23. INQUISITION TAKEN AT ARDQUIN

This is a part of the papers concerning Sir Thomas Smith's grant, which occupy many pages of MS. in Pinkerton's handwriting. They were largely used by Benn, and much of the matter also appears in Hill's *Montgomery Manuscripts*. Pinkerton has the following note relative to the boundary of Smith's territory, taken from this Inquisition :—"Until where the river of Blackstaff falls into Lough Conn, there the mearing between the great and little Ardes proceeds direct through the middle of the river of Blackstaff and by the middle of the ford of Belfast, and on the same river until the river aforesaid emerges from a certain moor called in English the bog of Portabogagh." This was a line following the Lagan to its source, and thence probably to Dundrum Bay, as a stream called the Blackstaff is shown at this point on the ordnance map.

Page 27. TIMBER IN ULSTER

Pinkerton gives no clue about this extract. There is an account of the great wood at Portmore, in Kilultagh, belonging to Sir Fulke Conway, in Johnstone's *Heterogenea*, Downpatrick, 1803. Arthur Stringer, huntsman to Lord Conway, in his *Experienced Huntsman*, Belfast, 1714, gives a graphic account of hunting the deer in this forest of 3,000 acres. (See "An Account of some Notable Books printed in Belfast," by Robert M. Young, in *The Library*, May, 1895.)

Page 28. THE PLANTATION OF ULSTER

This letter affords a valuable insight into the real character of the Ulster settlers. Lord Chichester preferred Devonshire families for his estate about Belfast. The portrait of the great founder of Belfast, as he may justly be styled, is a slightly-reduced *fac-simile* of the very rare engraving published by I. Thorne in 1781, from a copy in Pinkerton's MSS. For an account of Lord Chichester and view of his tomb, see *Town Book of Belfast*, p. 220, *et seq*.

Page 30. ASSIZES HELD IN ULSTER, A.D. 1615

The original Record of the Ulster Roll of Gaol Delivery, 1613–1618, in the Exchequer Record Office, Dublin, was translated from Latin by J. F. Ferguson, and partly printed in

Ulster Journal of Archæology, vols. i., ii. The portion now given was not used by Macadam, but is printed here as an interesting contribution to local history. Mr. C. H. Brett kindly contributes the following legal notes:—

In indictments for homicide, it was usual to express the value of the weapon, although the value was immaterial. This was done because the instrument was forfeited as a Deodand to the King, and the township was liable for its value if it were not forthcoming.

The reason for stating the value of the goods in indictments in cases of larceny was that, until the reign of George IV., there was an important distinction between grand larceny and petty larceny, the former comprising all cases where the goods were above twelve pence in value.

Under the Saxon laws, theft, if above the value of twelve pence, was nominally punished with death; but the prisoner was permitted to redeem his life by a pecuniary ransom. But by 9 Henry I. larceny above twelve pence became a hanging matter, and so continued until 7 and 8 George IV. in England, 9 George IV. in Ireland.

Grand larceny was a "clergyable" offence—*i.e.*, the prisoner was entitled to the "benefit of clergy."

From the pious regard paid to the Church, exemptions of the *persons* of clergy from criminal proceedings before the secular judge were originally granted in a few particular cases. Then the clergy extended the exemptions and persons until they comprehended every little subordinate office belonging to the Church or clergy. Originally, no man was admitted to the privilege of clergy but such as had the tonsure and habit; but in process of time everyone who could read was accounted a *clericus*, and allowed the benefit of clerkship.

When, after the invention of printing, learning became more disseminated, so many laymen claimed the privilege that, by statute 4 Henry VII. c. 13, a distinction was drawn between lay scholars and clerks in orders.

By this statute a person could claim benefit of clergy only once, unless he produced his orders; and all laymen who were allowed the privilege were to be burnt with a hot iron in the brawn of the left thumb.

After this burning, the laity, and before it the real clergy, were discharged from the sentence of the law in the King's Courts, and delivered over to the Bishop, to be dealt with according to the Ecclesiastical Canons.

Then the Bishop set himself formally to make a purgation of the offender by a new canonical trial, held before himself or his deputy and a jury of 12 clerks. Before them, the party made oath of his own innocence; next 12 compurgators swore they believed he spoke the truth; then witnesses *for the prisoner only* were examined, and the jury generally acquitted the prisoner!

This scandalous state of things continued until the time of Queen Elizabeth, when a statute provided that after an offender had been allowed his clergy and been burned, he should be enlarged; but the judge might continue him in gaol for not more than a year.

By a statute of William III., burning in the hand was changed to burning in the most visible part of the left cheek nearest the nose, and this continued till by a statute of Anne it was repealed, and benefit of clergy granted to all who were entitled to ask it without requiring them to read.

LIST OF THE HIGH SHERIFFS OF COUNTY ANTRIM, 1603-1895.

1603. Thomas Pavell, Carrickfergus.
1613. Sir Hugh Clotworthy, ,,
1618. Sir Hugh Clotworthy, Antrim.
1622. Sir Hugh Clotworthy, ,,
1625. Moses Hill, Strandmillis.
1626. Neal Oge O'Neill, Killylagh.
1627. Cormick O'Hara, Creabilly.
1628. William Huston, Craigs Castle.
1629. Alexander M'Donnell, Glenarm.
1630. Robert Adair, Ballymena.
1631. Arthur O'Neill.
1632. Alexander Stuart, Ballintoy.
1633. John Donaldson, Glenarm.
1634. Arthur Hill.
1635. Edward Maxwell, Connor.
1636. John Dalway, Bellahill.
1659. Arthur Upton, Templepatrick.
1660. John Shaw, Bush.
1661. Hercules Langford.
1662. Alexander Dalway, Bellabill.
1663. Thomas Warrin, Belfast.
1664. Richard Dobbs, Castle Dobbs.
1665. John Donaldson, Glenarm.
1666. Anthony Horsman, Carrickfergus.
1667. Francis Stafford, Portglenone.
1668. Patrick Agnew, Ballygally.
1669. Archibald Edmonston, Red Hall.
1670. Sir Robert Colville, Galgorm.
1671. George Macartney, Belfast.
1672. William Upton, Templepatrick.
1673. Thadeus O'Hara, Creabilly.
1674. John Galland, Vow.
1675. Randall Brice, Kilroot.
1676. William Huston, Craigs Castle.
1677. William Lesley, Ballymoney.
1678. Edward Harrison, Kilultagh.
1679. Henry Spencer, jun., Trummery.
1680. Randall Smith, Lisburn.
1681. George Macartney, Belfast.
1682. John Bickerstaffe, Rosegift.
1683. John Bickerstaffe died 20 May; succeeded by Charles Stuart.
1684. Henry Davys, Carrickfergus.
1685. Thomas Knox, Belfast.
1686. Cormick O'Neill, Broughshane.
1687. Cormick O'Neill, ,,
1688. Shane O'Neill.
1689. Shane O'Neill.

1691. Thomas Smith, appointed 20 November.
1692. Thomas Smith.
1693. William Shaw, Bush.
1694. Richard Dobbs, jun., Ballynure.
1695. Clotworthy Upton, Templepatrick.
1696. Sir Robert Adair, Ballymena.
1697. Michael Harrison, Lisburn.
1698. Edmond Ellis, Brookhill.
1699. Andrew Clements, Straid.
1700. John O'Neill, Shanescastle.
1701. John Davys, Carrickfergus.
1702. Benjamin Galland, Vow.
1703. Charles O'Neill, Shanescastle.
1704. Brent Spencer, Trummery.
1705. John Davys, Carrickfergus.
1706. Westerna Waring, Belfast.
1707. Edward Clements, Straid.
1708. Benjamin Galland, Vow.
1709. Arthur Davys, Carrickfergus.
1710. William Shaw, Bush, died 28 June.
      Andrew Clements, Straid.
1711. Andrew Clements, Straid.
1712. Westerna Waring, Belfast.
1713. Brent Spencer, Lisburn.
1714. Robert Green, Belfast.
1715. Edmd. T. Stafford, Mount Stafford.
1716. Edward Clements, Straid.
1717. James Hamilton, Cloughmills.
1718. William Moore.
1719. Hercules Upton, Templepatrick.
1720. Arthur Dobbs, Castle Dobbs.
1721. Francis Clements, Straid.
1722. Henry O'Hara, Creabilly.
1723. William Johnston, Glynn.
1724. Ezekiel Wm. Crombie, Cromore.
1725. Ezekiel D. Wilson, Carrickfergus.
1726. Sir Robert Adair, Ballymena.
1727. Rowley Hill.
1728. John Skeffington, Dervock.
1729. Charles O'Neill, Shanescastle.
1730. Valentine Jones, Belfast.
1731. Alexander Stuart, Ballintoy.
1732. John Moore.
1733. Hector M'Neale.
1734. Hugh Boyd, Ballycastle.
1735. John Huston, Craigs Castle.
1736. Clotworthy O'Neill, Randalstown.
1737. Hill Wilson, Purdysburn.
1738. Edward Smith, Lisburn.
1739. Davys Wilson, Carrickfergus.
1740. William Boyd, Ballycastle.
1741. Conway Spencer, Trummery.
1742. Felix O'Neill, O'Neills' Brook.
1743. George Macartney, Belfast.
1744. William Agnew, Kilwaughter.
1745. Charles M'Daniel, Clogher.
1746. John Cuppage, Ballycastle.
1747. Edmond M'Naghten, Beardeville.
1748. Edward Brice, Kilroot.
1749. Roger M'Neill.
1750. Roger Moore, Cloverhill.
1751. John Dunkin, Clogher.
1752. Conway R. Dobbs, Castle Dobbs.
1753. Robert Adair, Ballymena.
1754. Bernard O'Neill, Triminary.
1755. John Rowan, Bellisle.
1756. John M'Naghten, Benvarden.
1757. Arthur Upton, Templepatrick.
1758. Charles O'Hara, O'Hara's Brook.
1759. James Lesley, Leslie Hill.
1760. Richard Maginnis, Lisburn.
1761. Alex. Boyd, jun., Ballycastle.
1762. Alexander Stuart, Ballintoy.
1763. John Henry, Clover Hill.
1764. Rowley Heyland, Crumlin.
1765. Charles Hamilton, Portglenone.
1766. Alexander M'Auley, Cushendall.
1767. Sampson Moore, Moore Lodge.
1768. Thomas Thomson, Greenmount.
1769. Bryan M'Manus, Mountdavis.
1770. Alexander Legge, Malone.
1771. Lord Dunluce, Glenarm.
1772. John O'Neill, Shanescastle.
1773. Hugh Boyd, Ballycastle.

1774. St. John O'Neill, Portglenone.
1775. Robert Morris Jones, Moneyglass, died in
      Feb., and Sam. Bristow was appointed in
      his room.
1776. Ezekiel D. Boyd, Ballycastle.
1777. William Dunkin, Clogher.
1778. William Moore, Killagan.
1779. Robert Rowan, Bellisle.
1780. William Legge, Malone.
1781. Barthw. M'Naghten, Carringlass.
1782. Alexander M'Manus, Mountdavis.
1783. John Brown, Belfast.
1784. John Crombie, Cromore.
1785. Henry O'Hara, O'Hara's Brook.
1786. John Allen, Springmount.
1787. Robert Gage, Rathlin.
1788. Henry W. Shaw, Ballytweedy.
1789. Charles Crymble, Ballyclare.
1790. Samuel Allen, Allen's Brook.
1791. Richard G. Ker, Red Hall.
1792. Hugh Boyd, Ballycastle.
1793. Edmd. A. M'Naghten, Beardeville.
1794. Roger Moore, Clover Hill.
1795. Stewart Banks, Belfast.
1796. James Watson, Brookhill.
1797. Honble. Chichester Skeffington, Belfast.
1798. James S. Moore, Ballydivity.
1799. James Lesley, Prospect.
1800. Geo. A. M'Claverty, Glynn.
1801. Thomas B. Adair, Loughanmore.
1802. Langford Heyland, Glenoak.
1803. Edward J. Agnew, Kilwaughter.
1804. Hugh Montgomery, Benvarden.
1805. Sir Henry V. Tempest, Glenarm.
1806. Honble. John V. O'Neill, Tullamore.
1807. Francis M'Naghten, Clogher.
1808. William Moore, Moore Lodge.
1809. Sampson Moore.
1810. Ezekiel D. Boyd, Ballycastle.
1811. James Caulfield.
1812. John Campbell.
1813. George Bristow, Belfast.
1814. John Rowan, Larne.
1815. James Agnew Farrell, Larne.
1816. Robert Thompson, Greenmount.
1817. Samuel Thompson.
1818. Right Hon. T. H. Skeffington, Antrim.
1819. John Montgomery, Benvarden.
1820. Edmund M'Donnell, Glenarm.
1821. John Crombie, Cromore.
1822. The Hon. H. R. Pakenham, Langford Lodge.
1823. W. W. Legge, Malone.
1824. Francis Turnly.
1825. George Hutchinson, Ballymoney.
1826. Alexander M'Manus, Mountdavis.
1827. John M'Cance, Suffolk.
1828. Cunningham Greg, Belfast.
1829. Nich. D. Crommelin, Carrowdore Castle.
1830. Richard Magenis, Dirraw.
1831. George H. Macartney, Lissanoure.
1832. Alexander M'Neile, Ballycastle.
1833. Charles O'Hara, O'Hara's Brook.
1834. David Ker, Red Hall.
1835. Hugh Leckey, Bushmills.
1836. Edward Bruce, Scoutbush.
1837. Edmund C. MacNaghten.
1838. James Owens, Holestone.
1839. James Agnew, Fisherwick.
1840. Thomas Greg, Ballymenoch.
1841. Conway R. Dobbs, Castle Dobbs.
1842. Alex. H. Halliday, Cliffden.
1843. John M'Neile, Parkmount.
1844. John M'Gildowney, Ballycastle.
1845. John White, Broughshane.
1846. Thomas M. H. Jones, Moneyglass.
1847. William Moore, Moorefort.
1848. Charles M'Garel, Larne.
1849. James S. Moore, Ballydivity.
1850. Alexander Montgomery, Antrim.
1851. James T. Tennent, Belfast.
1852. Robert Smyth, Gaybrook.
1853. R. A. S. Adair, Ballymena.
1854. James E. Leslie, Ballymoney.
1855. Lord Robert Montagu, Portstewart.

1856. Ambrose O'Rorke, Ballybolan.	1876. Sir Charles Lanyon, Knt., The Abbey.
1857. Robert Grimshaw, Whitehouse.	1877. Sir F. E. Macnaghten, Bart., Dundarave.
1858. Andrew Mulholland, Springvale.	1878. James Owens, Holestone.
1859. George Gray, Graymount.	1879. Edmund M'Neill, Craigdun.
1860. Henry Hugh M'Neile, Parkmount.	1880. James Stewart Moore, Ballydivity.
1861. H. H. Hamilton O'Hara, Crebilly House.	1881. John Casement, Magherintemple.
1862. Fredk. H. Henry, Lodge Park, Co. Kildare.	1882. Anthony Traill, LL.D., Ballylough House.
1863. John Young, Galgorm Castle.	1883. Ogilvie B. Graham, Larchfield.
1864. William Coates, Glentoran.	1884. Wm. Ford Hutchinson, Stranoccum House.
1865. John F. Ferguson, Belfast.	1885. Thomas Montgomery, Ballydrain.
1866. W. T. B. Lyons, Old Park.	1886. Samuel Allen, LL.D., Lisconnan.
1867. Sir Edward Coey, Knt., Merville.	1887. Major-General Henry Cole Magenis, Finvoy
1868. Richard Henry Magenis, Deraw.	Lodge.
1869. John Thomson, Low-wood.	1888. Montagu Wm. Edwd. Dobbs, Castle Dobbs.
1870. Robert Jas. Montgomery, Benvarden.	1889. Capt. James Sinclair Cramsie, O'Harabrook.
1871. Henry Adair.	1890. Wm. Moore, M.D., Moore Lodge.
1872. Robert C. Thomson, Castleton.	1891. John Macaulay, Red Hall.
1873. James Chaine, Ballycraigy.	1892. Geo. Edmonstone Kirk, Thornfield.
1874. Thos. Casement (spring), Ballee House.	1893. Victor Coates, Rathmore.
J. F. Montgomery (sum.), Ballydrain.	1894. Henry Jones M'Cance, Larkfield.
1875. R. J. Alexander, Portglenone House.	1895. Harold Wm. Stannus Gray, Graymount.

The following document from *M'Skimin MSS.* is of much interest as showing the slight importance of Belfast at that time in comparison with Co. Antrim :—

COPY OF GRAND WARRANT FOR LEVYING COUNTY ANTRIM CESS, PRESENTED AT CARRICKFERGUS ASSIZES, AUGUST, 1744.

	£ s d
To James M'Calley for sweeping the House of Correction	2 : 0 : 0
To Jacob Clark for one year's Salary as keeper of the House of Correction	5 : 0 : 0
Assizes, August, 1744—Edmund M'Naghton, Esq., and Nich. Stuart Repairing 640 Perches of Great Road from Glenarm to Broughshane	60 : 0 : 0
To Wm. Henry Blair, Esq., for Repairing the Great Road from Larne to Broughshane	30 : 0 : 0
To Wm. Agnew, Esq., for Full Finishing the Great Road from Larne to Belfast	20 : 0 : 0
To James Webster for Killing Vermin	2 : 8 : 4
To James Allen for repairing 202 Perches of Road from Carrickfergus to Island Magee	30 : 0 : 0
To Henry Burleigh for Repairing Six mile water Bridge	10 : 5 : 0
To Francis Clements, Esq., for Full finishing 381 Perches of Great Road from Belfast to Larne	60 : 0 : 0
To Kennedy Stafford, Esq., for Repairing that Part of the Road from Randalstown to Portglenone	20 : 0 : 0
To John Blizard to Reimburse him sum expended in repairing Bridge Near Ballinderry Church..	2 : 17 : 2
To Mary Reid for Killing One Otter	0 : 5 : 0
To Charles O'Hara for Killing Five Otters	1 : 5 : 0
To Randal Flanagan for Killing Eight Otters	2 : 0 : 0
To Charles Craig for Killing Vermin..	0 : 6 : 0
To Arch. Brown and Wm. White for Killing Two Otters	0 : 10 : 0
To Arthur Hill, Robert Blackwood, Esqs., Rev. Bernard Ward, and Mr. Daniel Mussenden Repairing Belfast Bridge	60 : 0 : 0
To Robert Kennedy and Daniel O'Neill for Repairing 600 perches of the Road from Turnemoyl Hill to Shanescastle	30 : 0 : 0
To Bryan M'Laverty for Killing Vermin	2 : 0 : 0
To Cornelius Crymble and Robert Wilson Carrying on and Repairing Road from Belfast to Broughshane	40 : 0 : 0
To the Treasurer for half-a-year's Salary	10 : 0 : 0
To Rev. Thomas Finley for Relief of Prisoners in Gaol	20 : 0 : 0
To Jeremiah M'Cormack for Killing Vermin..	0 : 8 : 4
To Robert Freer and John Sloan for Killing Vermin ..	1 : 4 : 6
To the Clerk of the Crown for Prosecuting the Overseers of the Highways	5 : 0 : 0
To Andrew Stewart and Pierce Cullen for apprehending and convicting Hugh Kitteagh M'Neill, a notorious Robber	20 : 0 : 0
To Wm. Agnew, Esq., for Transporting Hugh Gallion and John M'Fall to America	10 : 0 : 0
To Wm. Henry Blair for Repairing Inver Bridge	3 : 0 : 0
To Wm. Glass for Repairing the Roof of Shire Hall	10 : 0 : 0
To Samuel Bristow, Esq., for Repairing Roof of Sessions House at Antrim	25 : 0 : 0
To S. Bristow and J. Thompson Repairing 230 Perches of Road from Ballyclare to Antrim	23 : 0 : 0
To Wm. Henry Blair for Repairing the Four Mile Burn Bridge	43 : 0 : 0
To John Hamilton and Thomas Godfrey Repairing the Gaol of this County	2 : 18 : 6
To Anthony Charleton Repairing 300 Perches of the Road from Randalstown to Portglenone	10 : 0 : 0
To Thomas M'Cutcheon for Repairing Carnalogh Bridge	2 : 0 : 0
To the Gaoler for one year's Salary ..	10 : 0 : 0
To Edward Smyth for repairing 1,000 Perches of the Road from Lisburn to Antrim	15 : 0 : 0
	£559 : 9 : 0

Page 31. ROBERT OPENSHAW

He was Dean of Connor, Rector of Carrickfergus, and Chaplain to Lord Chichester. It is noted in the Records of Carrickfergus MS., under 5th July, 1624 :—" It was also ordered, condiscended, and agreed. that the six Pounds which this Towne and Corporacione did allowe and give unto Mr. Openshawe towards the payment of his house rent should be from and after Michaelmas next reduced unto three Pounds ster. per ann., with which three Pounds he is to rest satisfyed and contented in that behalfe, and to have no more from the Towne but 3 ster. yearelye. Note—The 25th Aprilis, 1625, being the assembly daye, this was cancelled with a generall consent."

Page 32. THE ANCIENT GALLOWS CALLED "THE THREE SISTERS," CARRICKFERGUS

Mr. Joseph W. Carey has reproduced the appearance of this once-dreaded place of execution from the description furnished by Mr. John Coates, J.P. See *Ulster in '98*, by R. M. Young : Marcus Ward & Co., 1893 ; 3rd Ed., p. 71.

Page 35. "AC INTERIORA ET MEMBRA SECRETA," &c.

This was the barbarous sentence, "To be hung, drawn, and quartered." The prisoner was brought back to the gaol, his fetters taken off him, and he was led to the gallows and there hung by the neck "ac semi-mortuus ad terram prosternatum ac interiora et membra secreta ejus extra ventrem suum scindantur ipsumque adhuc viventem comburentur, et caput ejus amputetur, quodque corpus ejus in quatuor partes dividatur et caput et quarteria illa disponantur ubi dominus Rex ei assignari velit."

Page 39. ORDER OF THE EXCHEQUER

These grants are more particularly set out in the *Patent Rolls*, James I. Chichester seems to have shown here much consideration for these Northern chiefs. Sir Randal McDonnell was the first Earl of Antrim, an intimate friend and kinsman of King James I. (See Hill's *MacDonnells of Antrim, passim*.)

Page 41. COMMISSION ON WASTE OF WOODS, 1625

The houses built particularly by the English settlers required much oak-wood, as many of them in such towns as Derry, Coleraine, Antrim, &c., were half timbered. Such mansions as Joymount and Belfast Castle, with their massive beams and rafters, could not have been erected except large scantlings of timber were procured. In an old house recently taken down in North Street, the Editor observed a large beam of oak, which may have come from Belfast Castle. In Carrickfergus much old oak is to be met with, supposed by tradition to have been used at Joymount House. It is mentioned in the Records of Carrickfergus MS. that persons are bound to build in the English manner of Cadge work, well tiled or slated. In Phillips' View of Belfast many of the roofs are coloured red to show tiles.

Page 48. DEAN SWIFT

In the *Pinkerton MSS.* are several notices of Swift's connection with Belfast. Benn has utilised these in what he states about Dr. W. Tisdall, Vicar of Belfast. Pinkerton has copied the following extract from a fragment of one of Swift s letters in the Museum of the Dublin Society :—

"Being in a vein of writing epigrams, I send you the following piece upon Tisdal, which I intend to send to all his acquaintances ; for he goes from house to house to show his wit upon me, for which I think it reasonable he should have something to stare him in the face :—

UPON WILLIAM TISDAL, D.D.

"When a Roman was dying, the next man of kin
Stood over him gaping to take his breath in.
Were Tisdal the same way to blow out his breath,
Such a whiff to the living were much worse than death.

Any man with a nose would much rather die,
So would Jack, so would Dan, so would you, so would I.
Without a reproach to the Doctor, I think,
Whenever he dies, he must die with a stink."

Page 49. MONROE'S RAID

This account, with the further dispatch, is apparently unpublished, and was transcribed by W. Pinkerton, probably from MSS. in T.C.D. Library.

Page 55. The CESSATION

A number of letters referring to this event, copied in T.C.D. Library by W. Pinkerton, were printed by Benn as Appendix VII., *History of Belfast*. As to the destruction of corn, see p. 224 of present book.

Page 56. MONROE IN BELFAST

This extract gives a fair example of Pinkerton's more finished pieces of composition. He would, doubtless, have embodied it without much change in his *History of Belfast*. Benn availed himself of it largely. See his *History of Belfast*, p. 163, *et seq*.

Page 64. THE PARLIAMENT AND BELFAST

This excerpt from the *Pinkerton MSS.* throws some light on the position of parties at Belfast in 1645. The Parliamentary party were bitterly opposed by the Scotch, and the King, through the Marquis of Antrim, endeavoured to tamper with the allegiance of the latter to the Covenant. The stranger called M'Donnel was doubtless his emissary. A scarce tract in the Editor's possession, entitled, "Murder Will Out ; or, the King's Letter, justifying the Marquess of Antrim, and declaring, That what he did in the *Irish Rebellion* was by Direction from his Royal *Father* and *Mother*, and for the Service of the Crown : London, 1689," bears out this statement. A curious remonstrance against declaring the Marquis an "innocent," addressed to the King in 1663 from the Council in Dublin, is given at the end of a contemporary MS. of Clarendon's *History of the Irish Rebellion* in the Editor's possession.

Page 65. BELFAST TRADE, &c., 1646-48

Pinkerton had made many notes relative to these and later periods taken from original documents, but unfortunately in most cases without references. Benn has used them largely in his notes on early trade, &c., in his *History of Belfast*. Some of Pinkerton's shorter notices are subjoined :—"John Clugston, merchant, Belfast, to export from Liverpool or Chester to Belfast 12 bags hops, 2 packs broadcloth, 2 packs stuff, 2 packs of small ware, 10 doz. of hats, a bundle of bridle-reins, amounting to £300. David Maxwell and John McDowel, merchants of Newton, licensed to embark from Chester or Liverpool to Strangford, duty free. 3 boxes of apothecary drugs, 12 bags of hops, 2 packs of Yorkshire cloth and friezes, 36 pieces of Norwich stuffs, trimming and furniture for clothes to the value of £40, 40 pair of shoes, 3 doz. sword belts, 3 doz. of spurs, 3 doz. of hats; 20 Nov., 1647. James Hamilton, of Bangor, from Liverpool to Strangford, Bangor, or Carrickfergus, 10 fardels cloth and stuffs, 4 trunks with furniture for the same, 3 doz. of hats for officers, 3 fardels of hardware. Edward Davis, of Carrickfergus, from Liverpool, 15 trunks of broadcloths, stuffs, hollands, trimmings, sword-belts, gloves, buff coats, shammoys, four boxes of hats, rapiers, swords, 3 packs of coarse linens and stockings." Some of the notes refer to military matters in the vicinity of Belfast at the above dates, viz.—"Whereas Sir Jas. Montgomery did willingly part with his quarters in Lecale at our desire for the accommodation of the British forces, we have therefore thought fit and just that he have 20 bolls of meal paid monthly to him. Meal given to prisoners escaped from the rebels, and to guides who assisted their escape—Turlogh Low, the guide, 10 Bolls of meal; 10 Bolls of meal for poor in town of Antrim. By reason of men lying so many months in their clothes, they are worn very bare; extreme necessity for shoes, stockings, sheets. Care to be taken for provision of powder, ball, and matches. No fuel in the country, and it wholly depopulated, and that a magazine of coals be sent out of the sequestered estates in Lancashire and North Wales. The Committee to send over pieces of eight at 5 shillings, so that victuals be better provided, and to encourage the soldiers. A chirurgeon's chest is greatly needed."

Page 67. FIRST ESTABLISHMENT OF A POST

In 1672, Iorevin de Rochford published at Paris his *Travels in England and Ireland*. He passed through Belfast on his way to Scotland, and when at Carrickfergus writes :—" I knew that the common passage for the post and packet-boat was six miles above this town, at a little village called Larne, and that formerly this passage was to Arglas and to Denocadi, villages below Belfast : but for security, and finding an opportunity of passing from Knocfragus, or Karrickfergus, into Scotland, I would wait for proper wind and weather to do it." This extract is taken from the translation of Rochford's Travels in the *Antiquarian Repertory*, 1779, by kindness of Andrew Gibson, Esq.

Page 68. A RELATION OF SEVERAL SERVICES

This is mentioned by Benn as in the *Pinkerton MSS.*, but was not printed in his *History of Belfast* (v. p. 128). In the Descriptive Catalogue of the Collection of Antiquities exhibited in the Museum, Belfast, at the meeting of British Association, 1852, there is the following note :—" From Rev. John H. Jellett, F.T.C.D., Original Miniature of Oliver Cromwell, presented by the Protector himself, together with a grant of land in the Co. Down, to the widow and daughter of James Morgan, an officer of his personal staff, who fell beside him at Drogheda."

Page 75. FOR THE NAMELESS SUPERANNUATED SCOTCH MINISTER

Pinkerton notes that this was Patrick Adair, author of *A True Narrative of the Presbyterian Church in Ireland* (1623-1670). Much generosity was shown at this time by the Parliament to the North of Ireland. Pinkerton notes—"To the poor in the town of Antrim, being (as by Sir John Clotworthy's letter are certified) about 1,000 persons, for whom the Lady Clotworthy doth desire that there be designed £500. There are in Carrickfergus, Belfast, and other parts of Co. Down (by relation of Arthur Hill, Esq.), about 2,000 persons for these £1,000." £12,000 in all given.

Page 77. LETTER FROM THE LORD GENERAL CROMWELL

This and the succeeding letter of Cromwell show the Protector in a favourable light. Neither of them, it is believed, have been hitherto printed. Adair had property at Kinhilt, Wigtonshire, and large estates at Ballymena, the latter still held by Sir Hugh Adair, a lineal descendant. Strafford wrote in 1639 :—"There is one Mr. Adaire, a man of some four hundred pounds land, who went over into Scotland to rebel it there with the rest of that faction, and hath played his part notably and insolently. This fellow I caused to be indicted of treason." Cromwell did not approve of the transplanting scheme of 1653, as Rev. Patrick Adair writes—"For Oliver, coming to the supreme ordering of affairs, used other methods and took other measures than the rabble rump Parliament."

Page 78. THE SCHEME TO TRANSPLANT THE SCOTS

Reid, in his *History of the Presbyterian Church in Ireland*, gives some account of this scheme (vol. ii. p. 177, Appendix V.). Benn prints the first letter of the Commissioners only. This is reprinted here, and the list of Scots to be transplanted is also given, as it differs in several instances from the list given in Reid. The second list is not given by Reid. Pinkerton transcribed the correspondence *manu sua* from the original in Bermingham Tower, Dublin, and attached much importance to it, as showing the animus which inspired the Parliamentarians at that time against the Covenanters. A copy of the Covenant had been signed at Holywood, Co. Down, in 1644 (see *Town Book of Belfast*, p. 315). The list of names of the Scots to be transplanted includes mainly Presbyterians, but also some Episcopalians, such as Lord Montgomery, Lord Claneboy, &c. Space only is available for the subjoined notes on several names by the Rev. W. T. Latimer, B.A. :—

Lieutenant James Lynsey (Antrim Quarters) was no doubt the same Lieutenant James Lindsay *sworn* a ruling elder of Templepatrick in 1646.

Lieutenant Wallace is mentioned as follows in the old Session Book of Templepatrick Church :—"Sep. 7, 1647. It is delated that Lieutenant Wallace hath some Irishes under him who comes not to church. The Session ordains William McCord to speak to the Lieutenant that either he will put them away from him or else cause them to keep the church."

Page 88. COLONEL ROBERT VENABLES

Pinkerton gave a short notice of him (*Notes and Queries*, 3rd S. V.). The Editor has a copy of his *Experienced Angler*. It has an address prefixed by Izaak Walton, and is adorned with some copperplates of fish. Venables writes of salmon in Ireland—"I do not know any River (I mean high in the country) that hath such plenty of them as the blackwater by *Charlemont*, and the broad-water by *Shane's* Castle, both which have their heads in great bogs, and are of a dark muddy colour, and very few (comparatively) in the upper ban, though clearer and swifter than they."

In the *Harleian MSS.* there is a paper in his writing giving an account of his services when commanding the Parliamentary army in Cheshire, 1643-46. He commanded the land forces at capture of Jamaica in 1654. For failure to take Hispaniola, he and Admiral Penn were committed to the Tower. The time and place of his death are unknown.

Page 105. FROM THE CIVIL LIST

Gilbert Simpson was ordained minister of Ballyclare on 9th August, 1655. He was ejected in 1661, but remained among the people.

Thomas Crawford ordained on 28th August, 1655, minister of Donegore.

Henry Livingstone ordained in 1655 minister of Drumbo. He was nephew of the celebrated John Livingstone. He was ejected in 1661, and died in 1697, aged 66 years.

David Buttle ordained minister of Ballymena in 1645. He was imprisoned by the Parliamentarians in 1650. Ejected in 1661, he continued to preach till his death in 1665.

Michael Bruce was grand-nephew of Michael Bruce who crowned the queen of his kinsman, James VI. of Scotland, and who was a lineal descendant of John de Bruce, uncle of King Robert Bruce. Michael Bruce was ordained minister of Killinchy in 1657, and ejected at the Restoration. He fled to Scotland, and was severely wounded in trying to escape arrest. Through the influence of Lady Castlemaine, who heard him preach in prison at London, his sentence was commuted to "banishment to Killinchy in the woods." He remained there till 1689, when he was again driven to Scotland, and died there in 1693. His son James (b. 1661, d. 1730) was minister of Killyleagh. Michael Bruce, of Holywood (1686-1735), and Patrick Bruce, of Drumbo and Killyleagh (1692-1732), grandfather of the first baronet of Downhill, were sons of James. Samuel Bruce, of Dublin (1722-1767), a son of Michael Bruce, was the father of the famous Dr. Wm. Bruce, of Lisburn, Dublin, and Belfast (1757-1841), whose son, Rev. Wm. Bruce, of Belfast (1790-1868), was the seventh member of the family who had been a clergyman of the Irish Presbyterian Church. James Bruce, Esq., D.L., proprietor of the Benburb estate, Co. Tyrone, is a grandson of Dr. Wm. Bruce. He has in his possession some family papers containing letters from James VI., &c., relative to his ancestors.

Page 123. DANIEL O'NEILL

For some account of this remarkable man, son of Con O'Neill of Castlereagh, see an account of D. O'Neill's escape from the Tower of London by the Editor (*Ulster Journal of Archæology*, Sept. 1894). In *Macadam MSS.* there is a curious eulogy of this family, with pedigree, c. 1730. See also Reeves' *Account of Crannoge of Inish Rush* (*Proc. R.I.A.*, vol. vii.).

The Editor has been favoured with some interesting documents relative to the branch of the O'Neills of Castlereagh settled in Lisbon, by Don George O'Neill, Peer of Portugal, &c. His ancestor, Felix O'Neill, fled with James II. to France, entered the Irish Brigade, and

was killed at Malplaquet. His descendants in the male line now resident in Lisbon are—
(1) Joseph Charles O'Neill, b. 1816, head of the family; (2) George Torlades O'Neill, b. 1817, Consul-General of Denmark. His son is George O'Neill, b. 1848; mar. Marie Isabel Fernandez, and have issue, Hugues, George, and Marie Thérése. He resides at a villa adjoining the Royal Palace, Cintra.

Page 127. CONFIRMATION OF THE CHICHESTER PATENTS
This document is in the handwriting of W. Pinkerton, and many others relating to the Donegall family are in the *Pinkerton MSS*. One of these, endorsed " 1692, June 15. Copy Deed between Ld. Longford, the co-heirs of Arthur late Earl of Donegall, Arthur Earl of Donegall, and others," contains the names of the tenants holding several of the town lands, as follows :—

"And as to all that the Castle, Mannor, and Town of Belfast, and the Demesne lands and The parks thereunto belonging, and also the Lands of Tuogh Cinament, And the Cave, the Town and Lands of Skegenearle, and the Quarter of Listillyard, then in the possession of Wm. Warren ; the town And lands of Ballyoghegan, then in the Tenure of Joan Pegg, Widow ; The old park and the new Enclosures adjoining, then in the Tenure of Edward Reynell, Gilbert Wye, Francis Thetford, John Clarke, and Others, by Lease from the said Earl; the Town and Lands of Ballysillan and Outerard, with the Mountains thereunto Belonging ; one half of the Town land of Listillyard, and part of Clough Castle, then the new Park, the other part of the Town and lands of Listillyard, and three parts of the town and lands of Clough castle, then in the possession of George Martin ; the two town lands of Drumnegragh, and the said other Town land, both then lately In the possession of Michael Newby or his assigns ; the two Town Lands of Carentall, then or lately in the possession of William Penery or his assigns, the two Town lands of Ballywinnett and Ballyvaston, then or lately in the possession of George Russell And his Partner ; the two Town lands of Gleneward and Glangormally, then or lately in the possession of Richard Cannon ; as also the Town Lands of Ballyboght, then or then late in the Possession of Thomas O'Killen or his assigns ; as also the Town of Ballymaduffand ; the half town of Ballyhenry, then or then lately in the possession of Doctor Alexander Colvill ; as also the Town lands of White Abby, then or then lately in the possession of Thomas Quaile or his assigns ; as also the White house and town lands of Rantollard, Jordanstown, Coole, Dunany, Ballyvesin, Ballycraggy, Caroferney, and the other half town land of Ballyhenry, and the Mill there upon, then lately in the possession of John Davis, Esqre., deceased ; as also the two Town lands of Monkstown and Ballyhone, then or then lately in the possession of Mrs. Grace Le Squire or her assigns."

Macadam has a note on *Cinament*. He says this word, which occurs in old papers concerning the N.E. of Ireland for a certain division of land, is probably a mistake for *Tinament*, as the letters *c* and *t* were much alike. Ducange gives *Tinamentum*, a district. Spelman says a farm held by vassals of their lord is called *Tinament*. The modern form of same word is *tenement*. Eugene O'Curry says *Siniomon* was an ancient Brehon law term for the produce of land, such as wood and grass ; from river or sea, as fish ; all royalties ; all things found and not claimed. He suggests this as derivation of *Cinament*.

Page 129. TO AN OLD STONE CALLED BALLYROBART
Old stone seems to have been used as a term for an old building, as in the adjoined extract from the finding of a jury in 1601. *Records of Carrickfergus MS.:*—" And we synde that the landes bounded within the meares names and markes of there verdict dothe belonge and hathe of a long tyme bene in the manurance and occupacion of the Inhabitants of the corporacion of C.fergus more than what is exempted by them as belonging to the owld stone called Goodborne, and the hospittall of Spittell." This is further called " a Rewenated and decayed abbaye called Goodborne."

Page 138. DESCRIPTION OF ARDES BARONY
This is one of the accounts of localities in Ireland sent to Mr. William Molyneux, principally by clergymen, in 1683, for publication in the *Grand Atlas* designed to be published by Moses Pitt, a London bookseller. Unfortunately, Ireland was not reached, as, after four volumes appeared, the scheme fell through. This description of the Ards was written by William Montgomery, of Rosemount, so well known as the author of the *Montgomery MSS*. It was printed in 16 pp. folio in 1683, and was so much appreciated that Sir William Petty paid £3 13s. 6d. for a copy. Montgomery wrote it out again in a slightly different form, and sent a copy to his kinsman, Patrick Savage, of Portaferry, in 1701. He writes to him—" This account of ye barrony was more genlly written (long agoo) at ye desire of my kinsmen (Wm. Molineux and G. Ushur, Esqs.), who were collecting materialls to make an atlas or description of Ireland ; you will see ye printed quires [queries?] which are concerning ye same sent herewith to you, wh I received from them by ye post." It appeared in Henry Joy's edition of the *Montgomery MSS.*, printed at the *News-Letter* Office, 1830, of which the Editor has the original as prepared by Joy for the press.

Page 143. PROCLAMATION BY THE DUKE OF SCHONBERG

Pinkerton had collected much original matter on Schonberg's campaign in Ireland, which has afforded nearly all the material for Chapter X. Benn's *History of Belfast*. Pinkerton notes that the Hearth-money of Co. Antrim was let to farm in the following years :—1682, £1,620 ; 1683, £1,662 ; 1684, £1,712 ; 1685, £1,737. Co. Down in the same years was £1,365, £1,408, £1,458, £1,481. The population of Ireland, taken from the assessment of the poll in 1696, was 1,034,102.

Page 146. Y^E K. LANDED AT CARRICKFERGUS

In the preceding year Schonberg had landed at Groomsport, Co. Down, in accordance with a report presented by " Anthony Wild, Belfast ; James Sheares, Donaghadee ; John Magee, Ballyshannon ; and William Mercer, Limerick, masters of ships."—*Pinkerton MSS.* Their report is given in Benn's *History of Belfast*, p. 170. It is probable that the King's advisers consulted Thomas Phillips' Report on the several garrisons of the Kingdom of Ireland, of which several of the beautiful maps are in British Museum, including the view of Belfast, *c.* 1685. Benn gives the date of its execution as 1685, misled, no doubt, by Pinkerton's note-book containing that date on the same page as part of Phillips' report, but it belongs to a note on another subject. As Pinkerton gives no reference to the place where the Report is preserved, and the maps afford no date, the Editor has been unable to determine it. In the Descriptive Catalogue of the Collection of Antiquities exhibited in the Museum, Belfast, 1852, the view is entitled, "Ancient Government Survey of Belfast in 1686." Pinkerton's notes on Phillips are as follows :—" Phillips appointed by Lord Lieutenant to survey and report on the several garrisons of the Kingdom of Ireland ; to report on their present condition, and estimate the expenses necessary to put them and the policy (*sic*) in a state of defence ; and he reports :—

" Amongst all which I do find not above four or five that is capable of being fortified, so as to be made to resist a considerable army, by reason that most of the inland towns were thought strong by being encompassed with bogs and rivers, and as great passes, all of which I do find to be quite contrary, for the improvement of the country hath drained the bogs, and more towns are daily building, making for the benefit of the several counties bordering one upon another, so that it will be no end for his Majesty to be at the charge to secure all passes when that there is no stop or hinderance to be put to the improvement of a Country that is and will be of so great a value to the Crown.

" Carrickfergus as doth appear by its situation to have no command of the channel or river of Belfast which is now the Third place of Trade of this Kingdom, but it having an old strong Castle fit to receive his Majesty's stores in at present. It hath been therefore mentioned to be a place the most fit to be repaired and made a garrison. But I cannot say much to the usefulness of it when it is so fortified, for it is capable of having vessels of any considerable burden come up close to it ; besides, they lie dry at every tide, there being a very large strand before the Castle, as appears in the draught. But above that is one of the most considerable places [Belfast] in the Kingdom, having never less than 40 or 50 sail of ships before it ; the place very rich and numerous, and not well affected, having nothing that can give a check to anything that might happen, either by foreign or domestic attempts. I therefore humbly leave this part of my report to the judgement of those in whose power it is to discern more of the necessity of this affair. I only give my opinion as being upon the place. I cannot think his Majesty should be at any greater expense than to repair the Castle for the present, and put it into a posture for receiving the present garrison ordered for this place, and whenever that money can be spared, to let the most considerable work be done at Belfast. According to the survey and estimate of the repairing of the Castle of Carrickfergus and the purchasing of some houses before the gate, doth amount to £14,703. The building a citadel at Belfast, £42,054."

He was also inspector of ordnance, but did not find any at Belfast, but at Carrickfergus, as he reports that there are one demi-cannon, two culverins, one twelve-pounder, three demi-culverins, two sakers, one three-pounder, fifteen falcons, five pateraroes, and three petards, all brass ordnance. Of iron ordnance covered with brass at the same place he reports one falcon and five demi-culverins, while of iron ordnance there are one eight-pounder, three saker-minions, and one sling-piece.

" Londonderry hath the appearance of a place of strength, it being capable of being made an island, but when that is done it is with the hazard of destroying a most noble river, which is the nourishment of that city ; besides, the hills overlook it so on all sides that there could be no rest there for the inhabitants whensoever an enemy shall attempt it. The place at present is walled round, having several guns mounted, all of which are at the charge of the several companies of London. His Majesty hath a magazine there, with a small quantity of stores, as many as are fit to be trusted in a place of such indifferent force or strength."

Page 148. KING WILLIAM THE THIRD, &C., AT BELFAST.

These unpublished extracts from Clarke's Correspondence are all in Pinkerton's hand-writing, and seem to have been quite overlooked by Benn. The originals of the Proclamations issued at Belfast and Hillsborough were kindly examined for the Editor by Rev. W. Reynell, and are in manuscript. No printed copies have ever turned up, and the idea that printing was executed in Belfast when the King was there is untenable. The Royal gloves and stirrups, &c., illustrated (p. 144), were given by the King to General Hamilton, his aide-de-camp, an ancestor of the Baroness Von Stieglitz, sister of the late Stewart Blacker, D.L., Carrickblacker. At this fine old house, which is built of Dutch bricks in the "Queen Anne style," are preserved many valuable relics and pictures of the period, including an Indenture of 1691 relative to the Corporation losses at Siege of Derry, with signatures of all the leading citizens ; the original of Proclamation against Brass Money ; portraits of William and Mary by Kneller, and of his generals, &c. The bronze stirrups shown in the illustration belonged to Charles I., as they have engraved on them C.R., with a crown, and date 1626. The Editor recently acquired from a London bookseller King William the Third's own copy of the *Book of Common Prayer:* Oxford, 1693; folio. It is bound in old English black morocco, with the Royal monogram and crown in gold on sides and back, and is in good preservation. Valuable matter relative to William's Huguenot followers is contained in *Protestants from France in their English Home,* by S. W. Kershaw, F.S.A.: Sampson Low, 1885.

Page 152. JOURNEY TO Yᴱ NORTH
The author of this original description was the brother of the patriotic William Molyneux, author of the *Case of Ireland being bound by Acts of Parliament in England* (Dublin, 1698), published to arrest the threatened destruction of the Irish woollen trade. Their father was Samuel Molyneux, Master Gunner of Ireland, and son of Samuel Molyneux, Ulster King-at-Arms. Thomas was born in Dublin in 1661, became a graduate of Trinity College, visited Leyden and Paris, and was elected F.R.S. He was created a baronet, and died in 1733. A paper on this tour was read by Mr. W. H. Patterson, M.R.I.A., on 27th January, 1875, before the Belfast Natural History and Philosophical Society, and a few extracts from it were published in the Society's proceedings of that year, otherwise it has not been printed. Sir William Wilde wrote a life of Dr. Thomas Molyneux in *Dublin University Magazine,* vol. xviii.

BOOK-PLATE OF EARL OF DONEGALL, 1739-99 (CREATED MARQUIS 1791).

Page 155. LORD DONNEGALL'S FAMILY
The following document indicates the large establishment kept up at that time at Belfast Castle :—

'A LIST OF SERVANTS' WAGES AND SALLARYS.

	£ s. d.
Mr. Finiston	30. —. —
,, Bristow	50. —. —
John Fordice	10. —. —
Mr. Sharman	11. —. —
The Cook	20. —. —
The Porter	5. —. —
Three foot men	15. —. —
Coachman	8. —. —
Postellion	5. —. —
The helper	3. —. —
The Grooms	21. —. —
Hugh McCashon	3. —. —
Mr. Galtry	5. —. —
John McClatchy, Gardner	5. —. —
George Fielding	5. —. —
Andrew Wallace	3. —. —
Henry Oldfield	6. —. —
John Duffin, the Park	3. —. —
Thos. Hill	11. —. —
Thomas Lindsey, Bayliff	5. —. —
John Butterworth	5. —. —
John Crafford	3. —. —
Brought over,	£233. —. —

	£ s. d.
Brought over,	£233. —. —
Bayliff in the Grange	1. —. —
Mrs. Robison	5. —. —
Mrs. Bell, my Lady's Maid	6. —. —
Wingford, my Lady's chambermaid	4. —. —
Two housemaids	4. —. —
Derry maid	2. 15. —
Kitcheon maid	2. —. —
Mrs. Violett	5. —. —
Master Arthur's maid	2. —. —
Master Hungerfurd's maid	2. —. —
Master John's nurse	10. —. —
Two nursery maids	4. 10. —
Old Tear Mark yᵉ hen wife	2. —. —
Mrs. Anderson	13. —. —
	£296. 5. —
A new Gardner to come.	
Patrick the Baker	£8. —. —
John Clark the Miller	10. —. —
Mᵈ That Mr. Galtry is but £5 or £7 other side, wher it ought to be 7 Pounds added	2. —. —

Page 156. CARRICKFERGUS

The Corporation of this ancient town assumed more dignity than that of Belfast, as the following extract from the Records of Carrickfergus MS. shows:—" The Manner how war was proclaimed against the King of Spain on Monday, the 5th of Nov[r.] 1739 (it being agreeable and according to the Antient Custom of the Corporation of C.fergus proclaiming War), in the Mayoralty of Henry Gill, alderman.

" The Mayor called an assembly of the Aldermen and Burgesses, as also caused all the different Corporations or Trades to be warned ; and when the Aldermen, Burgesses, &c., were assembled, the Mayor, attended by the Recorder, Sherriffs, Aldermen, Burgesses, Sword Bearer, Town Clerk, &c., all on horseback in their formalities, proceeded to the Castle Gate, and there caused the Proclamation to be read by the Town Clerk ; after the Proclamation was read, the Sword of Honour was drawn, each Gentleman in company drawing his sword ; after this they went to the Tholsell, North Gate, and West Gate, where the Proclamation was read. After each reading the People, who attended in great multitudes, gave three Huzzas ; when the ceremony was ended, the Mayor invited the Gentlemen that attended on the occasion to his house, where many loyal healths were drank, particularly success to his Majesty's arms by Sea and Land, at which time the Great Guns at the Castle were fired. N.B.—After the Sword of Honour was drawn, the Mayor carried it until the Ceremony was ended, and before that carried the Rod of Mayoralty."

Page 156. HERE THEY CARRYED US UP A PRETTY HIGH HILL

This hill was the Cave Hill, on whose eastern slope stands Belfast Castle, the finely-situated residence of the Countess of Shaftesbury. Her Ladyship, with her invariable consideration for the people, has recently formed, at great cost, a new pathway to the cave and the summit of the hill, which has already proved a source of innocent enjoyment to many. The fountain mentioned was, no doubt, the spring known afterwards as the Volunteers' Well, and resorted to on Easter Mondays long ago, when the townspeople flocked to the Cave Hill in thousands.

John Kirkpatrick, M.D., in his poem entitled the "Sea-Piece" (London, 1750), gives the following legend of the cave in the Cave Hill :—

" Here, as Tradition's hoary legend tells,
A blinking piper once, with magic spells,
And strains beyond a vulgar bagpipe's sound,
Gathered the dancing Country wide around ;
When hither as he drew the tripping rear
(Dreadful to think, and difficult to swear !)
The gaping mountain yawned, from side to side,
A hideous cavern, darksome, deep, and wide ;
In skipped th' exulting dæmon piping loud,
With passive joy succeeded by the crowd ;

The winding cavern, trembling as he played,
With dreadful echoes rung throughout its shade ;
Then firm, and instant, closed the greedy womb.
Where wide-born thousands met a common tomb.
Even now the good inhabitant relates,
With serious horror, their disastrous fates ;
And, as the noted spot he ventures near,
His fancy, strung with tales, and shook by fear,
Sounds magic concerts in his tingling ear ;
With superstitious awe, and solemn face,
Trembling he points, and thinks he points the place."

Page 157. THE PRINT OF THE CAWSEY

This was the first view published of the Causeway. It is a folding copper-plate, well engraved, and giving also details of some polygonal columns. The finest engravings are the two published by Boydell in 1777, executed by Vivares from drawings of Susan Drury. In a volume of MS. poems by Robert Watson Wade, 1795, in the Editor's possession, is a ballad entitled, " The Unfortunate Travellers ; or, a Trip to the Giant's Causeway." Some verses are subjoined :—

From Derry my brother and I both set out
The Causeway to see we'd heard so much about.

At Newtown we stopt, and a dinner we had ;
If you've ever been there, you may swear it was bad.

To Coleraine we got safe in most dreadful bad weather,
For it rained as if heaven and earth came together.

We had not long sat till a Justice in came,
His name was McNaghten, and well known to fame.

No sketch of our supper I here need to give ;
We had it at Cordner's, 'twas had you'll believe.

And early next morning our Journey pursued,
And with wonder the giant's fam'd Causeway review'd.

&c., &c., &c.

Page 159. THAT THIS MUCH TALKED OF SIEGE

The annexed document in the Editor's possession would bear out this statement of Molyneux :—

Whereas a Quantity of Salmon belonging to me, John Lord Visct. Massereene, was lying at Culmore Fort, and the same being seised and eaten by the Protestant army in and about London Derry at the time of the Seige there, which being by His Maty[s] Commissioners of the Treasury, their Order of Reference, and the Report of William Harburd, Esq., Vice-Treasurer, to whom the Value of the said Salmon was referred, computed at fifteen Pounds Per tun, as by the said Report bearing date the fifteenth day of Augt., 1689, may more fully appeare, I do hereby assigne and sett over all my Right and Demand from his Maty for the Said Salmon So computed at fifteen Pounds Per tun to the Sume of nine hundred Pounds unto Mr. John Railey, Treasurer to the Honble the Irish Society. As witness my hand and seale this two and twentieth Day of May, 1690. MASSEREENE.

Page 161. ISLAND MAGEE WITCHES, 1710

This extraordinary case was published by Joseph Smyth, Belfast, 1822. but without these depositions. The trial took place at Carrickfergus, March 31, 1711, before Judges Upton and M'Cartney, and the prisoners were found guilty. A curious account of the trial, written by Dr. W. Tisdall, Vicar of Belfast, who was present, is given in an appendix. He affirms that "these extraordinary facts, proved upon oath in the course of the evidence, were all preternatural ; not to be performed by the common course of second causes, nor soluble by any human reason." Pinkerton found amongst T. Crofton Croker's papers in British Museum the following ballad and note, evidently sent by Samuel M'Skimin, the historian of Carrickfergus, relative to a later case of witchcraft at Carnmoney, concerning which Mr. W. F. M'Kinney, Carnmoney, has collected curious notes, including another version of this ballad, in which *Butters* is given as the witch's name.

THE CARNMONEY WITCHES, 1807.

From Miscellaneous Anglo-Irish Poems collected by T. Crofton Croker, fol. 63, Addl. MS. B.M., 20,096.

In Carrick town a wife did dwell,
That did pretend to conquer Witches ;
Auld Barbara Cools, or Lucky Bell,
Need not lang to come through her clutches.

A woeful trick this wife did play
On simple Sawny, our poor taylor ;
But she's mittimus'd the other day,
To lie in limbo with the jailor.

Simple Sawny had a Cow,
She was as sleek as any other ;
But it happened for a month or two,
When that they churn'd they got no butter.

With Roun-tree tied in the cow's tail,
And Vervain gleaned about the ditches,
But a these did nought avail,
Tho' They blest the Cow, and cursed the Witches.

The neighbour wives were gathered in,
In number near about a dozen ;
They were Kate M'Cart, an Mary Linn,
An Elspie Doe, the taylor's cousin.

Ay they churn'd, and churn'd away,
Their aprons pinned, and cast their *mutches* ;
But still there was no butter came,
And then they sent for Mary Butlers.

Mary Butlers when she came,
She strait sat down by the fire,
And the Taylor was sent to stand all night
With his waistcoat turned in the byre.

Then the chimney it was stopt,
And every crevice where it smoaked ;
But long before the break of day,
The *guid* folk in the house was choacked.

Had Sawny summonced all his wits,
And sent away for *Hughy Martin*,*
He would have galled the Witches' guts,
He cured the *kye* for Nanny Barton.

But the taylor lost his son and wife,
For Mary Butlers did them smother ;
But as he hates a single life,
In four weeks' time he got another.

If Mary Butlers be a Witch,
It's right the people all should know it,
For if she can the Muses touch,
I'm sure she soon will destroy the Poet.

But I think she is no Witch—
She is only but a mere pretender ;
She has ne'art to raise the *deil*
Like the *auld* wife, the Witch o' Endor.

* A celebrated curer of cows that are bewitched.

NOTE.—In the latter end of July, 1807, a cow of an Alexander Montgomery, tailor, parish of Carnmoney, though she continued to give milk as usual, there was no butter on her milk when churned; in consequence she was supposed to be bewitched! Various spells and schemes were tried to discover the witch ; but these failing, it was agreed to send for Mary Butlers, Carrickfergus, to "cast her cantrips and gie them advice." Her first operation was churning some of the cow's milk, which, as usual, produced no butter, and some persons who afterwards drank of the milk were seized with sickness and a violent vomiting. Mary Butlers then informed the family that after nightfall she would try another spell, which could not fail ; and about ten o'clock she gave orders to old Montgomery and a young man named Carnaghan to go into the cow-house and to *turn their waistcoats inside out*, and in that dress to stand by the head of the cow until sent for by her, while Montgomery's wife, his son, and an old woman remained in the house with the sorceress. She then caused the out door to be closed, the chimney to be stopped, and every crevice that could admit air to be carefully stopped up ; what other measures she used has been but partially ascertained.

Old Montgomery and the person sent to the cow-house remained there until daylight, when, becoming alarmed, they knocked at the door, but receiving no answer, they looked through the kitchen window, and beheld the four persons within stretched out on the floor as if dead. They immediately broke open the door, when they found the mother and son dead, and the woman nearly so. The latter soon after expired ; and Mary Butlers, being thrown out on a dunghill, where she received some hearty kicks, soon after recovered, and was sent to prison.

The house had a strong sulphureous smell, and on the fire was a large pot in which were some milk, needles, pins, and crooked nails.

Mary Butlers was acquitted at the assizes. She still lives in this parish, and occasionally is called upon to cure cattle *that are bewitched!*

She says the three persons in Carnmoney were killed by a Black man with a huge *club*, who also knocked over herself.

N.B.—Such was the origin of the annexed homely ditty.   S. M'S[KIMIN].

Addressed to "T. Crofton Croker, Esq., Admiralty, London."

Page 165. ROBERT GREENE

For some other extracts from his letters in the Editor's possession, see *Town Book of Belfast*, p. 329. He had a lease of lands at Skegonearle (as he spells it in his receipts book) which expired in 1753, as the following document in *Pinkerton MSS.* shows :—"Xbr 8th,

1753. John Gordon beggs leave to Represent to Ld. Donegall's Trustees that at November last, 1753, the ffollowing Leases of Lands and Tenements Expired :—

> Harrison's Leases, now Vall Jones, Esq., 2 Townlands and many houses in town.
> Thetford's, now Dobbins and Junis, Townparks and many houses in town.
> Thetford's, now Wm. Holmes, Townparks and some houses in ye End of ye town.
> Hamilton, for the Lands of Legoneill and some Tenements in the Town.
> Geo Macartney, Two Tenements in Town and three Acres Town parks.
> Edmond Ellis, for the town land of Clough Castle.
> Mr. Reynolds, for the town Land of Bellynamoney.
> Charles Crymble, for the Lands of Carntall and Belly Earl.
> Woods, now John Charlye, 33 acres of Bellyffenieghy.
> John M'Cance, for ffarm Lands in Dunmurry.
> Robt. Hyrt, now Wm. Hyrt, 3 leases of a great many houses in town.
> Fusty (sic), now Cha: Young, A tenement in town.
> Chads, now Mr. Rainey, a Tenement in town.
> Higger, now Mussenden, Higger, and Burgess, a Tenement and Some parks.
> Green, the Townland of Bellyaghigan, and 1/8 part of Listilliard.
> Nath: Wilson, for the Lodge and a part of the old Park.
> ffletcher, now Dawson, Two leases of Lands, part of them town parks.
> Gurner, now Lewis, 2 leases—one of Hellygarry, one a tenement and 28 acres land.
> Mankins, now Banks and Rainey's, 18½ acres town parks, and having Tenements in Town.
> Letitia Smith, now James M'Alexander, a Tenement in North street.
> Carr, now Lyons, 2 leases, with part of the Old Park.

And he further Represents that he has been for Severall months past, and will be for Some months yet to come, constantly Imployed in treating and settling with the people who live on these lands and Tenements, and at present he has aggreed with a great number of them for one year; and if the Trustees have no Objection to the Rent Aggreed upon, they are to continue and get out leases. That in a few months he will be able to show what Advance rent will arise from Each of these leases, distinctly and Seperately the one from the other; and that the greatest part of the Tennants on Said Lands and Tenements have their proposals for their respective holdings upon promise he has made them of being accepted off as my Lord's Tennants on reasonable Terms, and taken from under the oppression of Petty Landlords."

Page 166. TO OUR CHURCH

This was the old Corporation Church in High Street, where St. George's now stands. In the adjacent burying-ground were interred almost all the prominent Belfast families down to 1800, when the Borough Act of that year provided the following clause :—" No Dead Bodies shall be buried in old Church Yard. 5l. Penalty for digging a Grave therein, and 20l. for ordering it." It also says—" And whereas the Water from the Sea occasionally overflows the said Yard, and the burying of dead Bodies therein by the Reason and Means aforesaid, is become a public Nuisance, for Remedy whereof the late Marquis of Donegal granted a Piece of Ground above the Poor-House and Infirmary of said Town, but notwithstanding, several dead Bodies are from Time to Time buried and interred in the old burying-Ground, be it Enacted," &c., ut supra.

Amongst the numerous monuments which adorned the old churchyard, that of the Collier family was conspicuous. The drawing from which the illustration is reduced is in pen and ink, an unusual medium for A. Nicholl. Its interest lies in the fact that it is perhaps the only representation preserved of a relic of the Corporation Churchyard, where so many were "interred in a private, genteel manner," as the old *News-Letters* expressed it.

Page 167. MR. MUSSENDEN, ONE OF OUR CONSIDERABLE TRADERS

He was leading partner in the firm of Mussenden, Bateson & Co., whose offices were in Winecellar Court. A page from their ledger (in *Macadam MSS.*) is given below. It shows that the old Belfast men appreciated a variety of wines, like Lord Castlereagh (see *Ulster in '98*, p. 92).

Belfast, March 20, 1726/7. 351

Posted ..	100	Sold and delivered Thos. Shortrigs, of Portoudown, 68½ galls brandy at 4/9 p.	16	5	4½
		1 Empty hhd		4	6
		permit 6 ..	16	9	10
Posted ..	70	Sold and deliver'd James Dixon in town 2 bottles claret		2	4
Recd. ..		Sold a quart Tent		2	6
Posted ..	70	Recd from Widdow Woods p. Alex. Ure	15	18	11
		abated a hhd		4	
			16	2	11

Posted ..	74	Sold and deliver'd Francis Atchison in town p. alex*r* McKinny, 2 gallons Rum						13		
Posted ..	111	Sold and deliver'd John Hall, Cooper in town, p. alex*r* McKinny, 12 Benecarlo Butts						2	8	
		Sold and deliver'd Samuel Groves, of Dawson's Bridge, p.								
		30 gallons Claret						6		
		15 gallons white wine						2	5	
		6 gallons Rhenish wine						1	12	
		3 gallons Canary						0	16	
		6 gallons Shirry @						1	10	
		21 doz. and 3 bottles						2	2	6

Page 169. EXTRACTS FROM LETTERS OF MRS. M'TIER

These have been kindly copied from the original letters by Mrs. Adam Duffin, her grand-niece. The portrait (page 173) was photographed with difficulty by Mr. Swanston from the original sketch in oils painted at Edinburgh when Drennan was a student. Mrs. M'Tier died in 1837, aged 95, having survived her famous brother 17 years. A letter to her husband, by T. W. Tone, is given in *Ulster in '98.*

Page 170. BUT M'CABE

Thomas M'Cabe was a watchmaker in North Street. He erected the first cotton mill in Ireland, with Henry Joy and Capt. J. M'Cracken as partners. When asked to sign the contract with other Belfast merchants for embarking in the slave trade, he used these remarkable words—"May God wither the hand and consign the name to eternal infamy of the man who will sign that document." The scheme therefore fell through.

Page 175. HER FATHER, JOHN M'CRACKEN

A few papers relative to him are amongst the *M'Cracken MSS.* Some extracts are subjoined. The first is a business letter from George Black, of Stranmillis, his employer at the time, and a Belfast shipowner. His father, John Black, grandfather of the famous Dr. John Black, the chemist, married Jane Eccles, whose father entertained William III., when on his march from Belfast to Hillsborough, at Orangefield, now Cranmore. The Editor recently presented to the University Library, Edinburgh, Dr. John Black's own copy of his treatise on Linen Bleaching, corrected for a second edition, which was picked up in Smithfield. An interesting pedigree of the families of Black, Eccles, Legge, Jones, and Clarke, the latter lineal descendants of Bishop Jeremy Taylor on the female side, has been drawn up by Henry Wray Clarke, Esq., M.A.

LETTER FROM GEORGE BLACK TO CAPTAIN JOHN M'CRACKEN.

Belfast, 3d *May, 1763.*

DEAR JACK,—I suppose last week's very bad weather has retarded Mr. Oakall's launching the two Vessells, so that you have got little or nothing done yet, excepting the draft and moulds, which, no doubt, are finished by Mr. Sutton ere this; and who knows but that the bad weather might induce him to make the small model we spoke of, as he could do no work without doors. Tom Black will tell you what great matters we have been doing here, haveing, on a quarter of an Hour's deliberation, bought a ship of 200 Tons and freighted one of 70. This was on receiving an order from London for the transporting the french prisoners here and at Castle Dawson, in number abt 420, to france, and finding M. Auld was not lyke to appear, we freighted Bob Moore to go to Bordeaux in his place, and he is to carry about 90 or 100 prisrs. The ship we bought of Ts Greg, and is the *Prince of Wales,* from Boston, Capt. Trail, which you saw. She cost us above one thousand Britt: but this is her first Voyage. tho' but indiff'ly found. She is a coarse, stout, full-built carrier. Capt. Eager goes in her to Bourdeaux, when she may be sold perhaps.

LETTER FROM FRANCIS JOY, HIS FATHER-IN-LAW, TO CAPT. JOHN M'CRACKEN.

(Written on paper with his own watermark of F. Joy.)

Teehoge, 26 *May, 1760.*

SON M'CRACKEN,—I congratulate you on your safe arrival. It gave me much ease and pleasure after my reading a Paragraff in the News Paper of Sevl Ships from the West Indies being taken by the French on the coast of this Kingdom, finding the account of your arrival inserted.

Such good Providences demand our reasonable and religious Acknowledgments.

I am, with affectionate Compliments to your kind and good Mother, my Daugr. yr Wife and Child, yr affece father, FRANS JOY.

PARCHMENT DEED RELATIVE TO A PEW IN ROSEMARY STREET PRESBYTERIAN CHURCH (THIRD CONGREGATION).

THIS INDENTURE, made the twenty-ninth day of September, in the year of our Lord One thousand Seven hundred and sixty-three, BETWEEN John Clark, of Belfast, in the County of Antrim, of the One part, and John M'Cracken, of Belfast aforesaid, Mariner, of the other Part, WITNESSETH That the said John Clark, for and in Consideration of the Sum of Eleven Pounds Sterling to him in hand paid by the said John M'Cracken, the Receipt whereof is hereby acknowledged, Hath granted, bargained, sold, aliened, released, and confirmed, and by these Presents Doth grant, bargain, sell, alien, release, and confirm unto the said John M'Cracken in his actual possession now being: All that the Seat or Pue in the Third or new-erected Meeting-House of Protestant Dissenters in the Town of Belfast aforesaid, Number (1) below Stairs, with the Appurtenances hereunto belonging, To HAVE AND TO HOLD the same unto the said John M'Cracken, his Heirs and assigns for ever. AND the said John Clark the said Seat or Pue, unto him the said John M'Cracken, his Heirs and assigns, against him the said John Clark, his Heirs and assigns, and all every other person and persons what-

soever, shall and will warrant and for ever defend by the Presents. IN WITNESS whereof the said Parties have
hereunto interchangeably set their Hands and Seals the day and year first above written.

Signed, sealed, and delivered   JOHN M'CRACKEN.   Seal.
in the presence of
     BEN: THETFORD.

Received from the above-named John M'Cracken eleven Pounds
sterling in full of the Consideration Money above-mentioned,
the day and year first above written.

     Witnesses present :   JOHN CLARK.
     BEN: THETFORD.
     Witnesses present :   I approve of the above.
     MAY GARNET.   JANE CLARK.

Page 177.   THE BUSINESS OF MUSLIN MANUFACTURERS

It would appear that Mrs. M'Cracken was engaged in this business as early as 1779, as
the following letter (in *M'Cracken MSS.*) in her handwriting shows. It is endorsed, "To
Mr. Thomas M'Cabe, for Mr. M'Cracken, Dublin " :—

Belfast, May 1, 1780.

DEAR SIR,—I send you the Inclosed Affidavit to make of it what use you may think proper, either with
the Dublin Society or others. The Deponent cou'd have declared much more if our *Delicacy* had not prevented. Such as that Mr. Twigg, his Sister-in-Law, and Wife, at several times after he had wove the third
piece of Muslin for me, tempted him to quit my Employ to weave a piece for them by promising him Double
Wages and a Premium from Parliament. And this he is ready to, if there be occasion. Sir, Your Hble. Servt.
I forgot that they Seduced his Journeyman, who gave them Instructions and prepared the work, which
knowledge he acquired by Insight from Burnside.   ANN M'CRACKEN.

[COPY OF AFFIDAVIT.]

County of Antrim,) This day came before me, one of his Majesty's Justices of Peace for said County, Thomas
    to wit.   ) Burnside, of Belfast, in said County, Cambric and Muslin Weaver, who made oath that,
being employed as a Weaver by John McCracken, of Belfast, aforesaid, he wove and, about the 10th Day of
January, 1779, Nine, finished a piece of fine Muslin, measuring nine yards, value four shillings and four
pence per yard. That he hath since that time to the present wove for the said John M'Cracken two yards of
the same—part of which of a finer and part of a coarser Texture than the former.
That he verily believeth that the Piece first mentioned was the first of the kind ever woven in the said
Town of Belfast or its vicinage.

           Sworn before me at Belfast this 1st Day of May, 1780, Eighty.
Thos. Burnside.   STEWART BANKS.

Page 177.   THE HEARTS OF STEEL

The following extracts relative to this organisation are copied from the *M'Skimin MSS.*
Benn's account of the taking of David Douglas from the Belfast Barracks was taken from the
above, but it is here printed *literatim* :—

"A general spirit of discontent and tendency to insurrection had manifested itself for some time before, excited by the stagnation of commerce and manufactures ; and an idea had prevailed that the general rise of
rents, which had recently taken place on Lord Donegall's estate, would reduce the tenantry to beggary. This
opinion proved totally unfounded, as shortly after it appeared that the estate in question was let on fair
terms, and that there was hardly a farm that, at the new rent and fine, would not sell a profit to the lessee.
. . . Meetings began to be held about the country, and some excesses were committed. The first act of
violence was entering the gardens of Clotworthy Upton, Templepatrick, and throwing down some ornamental
statues in it. The first house burnt by them was that of John Gill, Ballymartin, on the night of 23rd July,
1769. On the night of Dec. 5th, same year, they also burnt the house of Andrew McIlwaine, of same parish.
On the 7th the house of John Douglass shared the same fate, followed by the dwellings of John Busby and
James McAlister, in the townland of Ballypallady. Feb. 16, 1770, a house was burnt in Ballykeil, Island
Magee, and in March seven head of cattle, the property of William Crawford, Ballysavage, Dunagore, were
maimed. About the same time the farmhouse of Craigs, Ballyclare, was burnt. On 17th August twenty-
three head of cattle, the property of Thomas Gregg, Belfast, were houghed on the lands of Lisnalinchy, parish
of Ballylinny. About the same time persons went openly through the country collecting money for the support
of the *Hearts of Steel,* who were going to lower rents, cess, and tithes. At the same time numerous sums of
money were collected by letters sent to persons, threatening them with instant destruction if they neglected to
lay a certain sum at a particular place by such a time. The sums thus ordered were usually complied with,
and the arrival of the *Hearts of Steel* at the place where the money was to be deposited was announced by a
discharge of small arms. By these means the well-disposed persons in the community were for some time completely overawed, and the civil powers being weak, and the country without any military force, save a few in
Belfast, the system spread rapidly over the entire county and into Co. Down.
"1770. Friday, December 21st. David Douglas, farmer, Templepatrick, reputed to be a leader, and
charged with aiding and assisting in houghing Mr. Gregg's cattle, was taken prisoner in Belfast by Waddel
Cunningham, and for security lodged in the Barrack, where there was about forty soldiers ; a rescue being
apprehended if he had been sent direct to prison. The capture of this person excited no little commotion, and
it was immediately determined to effect his liberation. On the morning of the 23rd an assembly of persons,
avowedly *Hearts of Steel,* met at Templepatrick for this purpose, and proceeded to the Dissenting Meeting-
House there and warned the people out, many of whom obeyed their summons, and assisted to gather others
at different meeting-houses, and proceeded towards Belfast, armed with guns, pistols, swords, scythes, pitch-
forks, &c. The grand randevouse (*sic*) was held at a house on the shore called the Stag's Head, when their
number amounted to about 1,200 men, chiefly from Templepatrick, Doagh, Ballyclare, and Carnmoney. Here
they were formed into regular order by an old soldier called Nathaniel Mathes, or Mathews, who afterwards
gave them the slip on their entering Belfast. In their march from hence, in front was a man named Gorly
Crawford, on horseback, carrying before him several Iron crows rolled up in hay ropes, for the purpose of
forcing open gates or doors. On their approach to the town, Stewart Banks, Sovereign, and about 25
other gentlemen, took refuge in the Barrack and closed the gate. On their arrival in Belfast, they surrounded
the Barrack, and sent in a written message demanding the release of Douglas, their prisoner. Stewart Banks,
Sovereign, gave a direct refusal, on which the mob fired many shots at the Barrack gate and over the wall ;
but failing of the desired effect, a party of them flew to the house of Waddel Cunningham, broke it open, and

were in the act of destroying the furniture, when Dr. Halliday, an eminent physician of Belfast, actuated by compassion, and dreading lest the town might be destroyed, mingled with the crowd assembled at Mr. Cunningham's house. After expostulating with them in vain, he was taken prisoner by them, and sworn that he would immediately repair to the Barracks and procure the release of the prisoners, or failing in having it effected, he would return and surrender himself an hostage. The Doctor had just reached the Barrack on this embassy, pressing through an immense multitude, consisting of the people from the country intermixed with those of the town, when the gate was thrown open by the military, who fired upon the mob, and killed five persons and wounded nine others. Amongst those killed were Wm. Russel, Carnmoney; Andrew Cristy, Dunagore; and J. Sloan, Falls. By the Doctor's humane intercession further firing was prevented. In the meantime, the party who were destroying the house of Mr. Cunningham (a William Adair broke Mr. Cunningham's clock), growing impatient at the Doctor's delay, and conceiving that he had deceived them, set the house on fire, whereby the safety of the town was in the utmost danger. Under the same deception they threatened to destroy Dr. Halliday's house, and fired some shots into Mr. Gregg's, the partner of Mr. Cunningham. To prevent the destruction of the town, it was deemed expedient to give up the prisoner to the insurgents, which was accordingly done about one o'clock in the morning, on which the insurgents retired, and the fire was happily extinguished without spreading further.

"Soon after, several were taken prisoners charged with being in this riot, and the Government offered large rewards for the apprehension of the leaders of these outrages, viz. :—James Barber, Doagh; Paul Douglass and John Douglass, Ballymartin; Hugh Love and Stafford Love, Ballyclare; Samuel Douglass, Ballyheartfield; John Patten, Ballypallady; Thomas Dickey, Templepatrick; John Richey, Parkgate; and Andrew Shaw, Carnmoney. Rewards were also offered for Hugh Wilson, Ballyclare; Robert Cunningham (*alias* Captain Firebrand), of the same place; Nat Mathews, and James Gillespie. A fresh series of outrages took place in 1771. In April, 1772, many persons were tried for acts done as *Hearts of Steel*, and George MacKeown, John Campbell, John Clark, and James M'Neilly were executed on 9th May. Hugh McIlpatrick, John Blair, Thomas Stewart, and Thomas West were found guilty, and executed on 16th August. On 19th Sept., John Blair, a leader of the *Hearts of Steel*, was executed, and a few transported. At the Down Assizes, Hugh Jamison and —— Clenigan were convicted as *Hearts of Steel*, and executed. The county remained in confusion from the numerous military searches, and numbers fled to America, where they settled, and were afterwards conspicuous in the Revolutionary War for their rancorous hostility to the English Government. On Christmas night, 1773, inflammatory papers were put up on Cullybackey Meeting-house, exciting the people to acts of violence and rebellion."

In the Pinkerton Collection is a poem called "The Weaver's Lamentation; or, a Farewell to Ireland." It was everywhere sung as a common ballad, to the tune of "Lochaber," at the time. A verse runs as follows :—

> " Since things, when at worst, if they alter must mend,
> We may hope that our miseries will soon have an end;
> For, whate'er may betide me, wherever I go,
> Greater ills than the present I hardly can know.
> Then weep not, my darlings! O dry up those tears,
> And, trusting in Providence, banish your fears!
> AMERICA's sons, both *industrious* and *free*,
> Will welcome an honest, good workman like me."

Ships advertised in *Belfast News-Letter* to sail from Belfast with passengers for America in 1773 :—

Time.	Ship's Name.		Tons.	Bound for—
Jan. 15	*Friendship*	..	300	Philadelphia.
Feb. 5	*Agnes*	..	200	Charlestown.
" 9	*Peggy*	..	200	Philadelphia.
April 20	*Yaward*	..	350	St. John's Island.
June 11	*Two Brothers*	..	200	Baltimore.
July 6	*New Betty Gregg*	..	200	Philadelphia.
" 9	*Friendship*	..	300	ditto.
" 20	*Lord Bangor*	..	200	Wilmington.
" 27	*Charming Molly*	..	250	Baltimore.
Aug. 6	*Liberty and Property*	..	250	Charlestown.
" 20	*Betty*	..	200	Philadelphia.
" 31	*Catherine*	..	300	ditto.
	Waddell	..	450	Charlestown.

13 Ships, 3,400 Tons.

There also sailed from Newry, 8 Ships, 2,150 Tons. From Londonderry, 14 Ships, 4,050 Tons. From Larne, *James and Mary*, 250 Tons, for Charlestown; *Lord Dunluce*, 400 Tons, for do.

The following unique relic is now first printed :—

COPY OF A THREATENING LETTER SENT BY THE "HEARTS OF STEEL."

Endorsed—

To

madam bready, of greainge,
by thee True harts of steel X

Castle Town office, *March 12th*, in the yr of 1772.

MADAM,—I command you To set your Land To the old Tenens which now is in it at a resonable rent. To be sure, we harts of steel knows that you are a Lonly woman, and dis not Ceair for horting you, for we will alow you a prosaper rent for it, which I think 6s. 6d. a aker is sefisent for it, and a 11s. 4½d. for Each Leas, and we alow your Tenands To be obligen to you, and you most Take Ceair To anser our requist in seting your Land, or if you do not, you may Expect bad Treitment from us soon, and that is what we do not Disier, if posable we could shun it. S(o) be cure To Take our advise at the furst, and we will be your friend and homble Sarvants. C see justice and C fierbrand.

God save King georg the third
and his subjects the True harts of steel.

Page 177. SOME OF LORD DONEGALL'S LEASES

A satisfactory explanation of these leases is given by Benn (*History of Belfast*, p. 613). Belfast owed mainly to the wise benevolence of this unjustly maligned nobleman its rapid progress in the latter part of the eighteenth century.   He built, at his own cost, the Exchange and the Parish Church, gave the site and contributed largely to the Old Poorhouse, greatly assisted the erection of the White Linen Hall, built the Brown Linen Hall, and was the chief promoter of the Lagan Canal.   A notice of his coming to Belfast in 1788 contains the following lines—"His Lordship has the satisfaction to find that the town of which he is the *sole* proprietor has, within these fifteen years, increased in population, commerce, and manufactures in as rapid a manner, proportionably to its size, as any city or town in the three kingdoms.   Within this short space its port duties have experienced an augmentation of from £60,000 to about £112,000 annually.   From being extremely defective in public edifices, it has, of new erections, an elegant church, an exchange, a poorhouse, a dissenting meeting-house, a white linen hall, and a bank; in manufactures its improvement has kept pace, particularly in those of cotton."   The population was reckoned at 17,000.   He was a patron of letters and the Fine Arts, and formed a notable library of beautifully-bound books, some of which are to be met with occasionally.   Two finely-carved and gilt console tables formerly in his possession are now at Rathvarna.   His book-plate is figured on p. 265, from an example kindly given the Editor by the well-known collector, Robert Day, Esq., F.S.A., J.P.

BOOK-PLATE OF THE BELFAST LIBRARY, 1765.

BOOK-PLATE OF REV. J. MACKAY (BEFORE 1765).

The two examples of local *ex libris* annexed (from the Editor's collection) illustrate respectively the plate of the first local Library Society and the earliest private book-plate, both, so far as is known, of Belfast origin.   The subject of Belfast book-plates and their owners will form a section of a volume on Irish Book-Plates by John Vinycomb, Esq., M.R.I.A., F.R.S.A., a leading authority on this fascinating branch of art history.

Page 180. ON THE ANNIVERSARY OF THE TAKING OF THE BASTILLE

This commemoration of the French Revolution was held on 14th July, 1791.   The Editor is indebted to James Johnston, Esq., Seaview, for a copy of a letter written by a Belfast lady, August 3rd, 1791, which contains the following reference to this event :—

And so my friend did not wish to come to the Review ; neither did I, and yet I went. We had a very agreeable day ; indeed, the Review was over by three O'clock. When the Volunteers came into Town they were join'd by the Gentlemen of the Town and Neighbourhood, with the emblematick Paintings and Flags. They then March'd thro' Principal Streets ; their march terminated in Linenhall Street, where the Volunteers fired 3 grand *feu de Joy's.* They then went into the Hall, as many as it would hold, and made their declaration, held their debates, and settled the Affairs of the Nation; it was eight o'clock before they got to their Dinners. There were a number of Publick Dinners thro' the Town, but the Grandest was the Celebration Banquet at the Donnegall Arms ; there they had all the grand Toasts, Celebrated Songs, &c., and paid half-a-Guinea each man. There were a number of Dublin Gentlemen here : among the rest was the celebrated James Napper Tandy that, I suppose, you have often heard of. I suppose there never was such a Number of People in Belfast at once ; the Grand Review was nothing to it. . . . And so you must have an account of the Harpers too. I was hearing them one day ; I like them very much. The Harp is an agreeable soft musick, very like the notes of a Harpsichord ; would be very Pleasant in a small room. There were eight men and one woman, all either Blind or Lame, and all old but two men. Figure to yourself this group, indifferently dress'd, sitting on a Stage erected for them in one end of the Exchange Ball Room, and the Ladies and Gentlemen of the first fashion in Belfast and its Vicinity looking on and listening attentively, and you will have an Idea of how they look'd. You can't imagine anything sweeter than the Musick ; every one play'd separately. The money that was drawn during the four days that they were here was divided among them according to their merit. The best Performer got ten Guineas and the worst two, and the rest accordingly. Now, how do you like the poor old Harpers ?

Mr. Felix B. Simms, grandson of Robert Simms, who was one of the leading Volunteers at this celebration, has the originals of the following accounts relative to timber for the representation of the Bastille, which was put up in the Exchange :—

1791. Mr. Robert Simms to Wm. Wilson, Dr.	
July 12—To 4 Larg Sqrs. for the Frame of the Bastille	2 8
To 8 pleates for Do.	2 8
To 1 Hook and Ey for the Ponle ..	1 0
To 4 Hooks for Holding it in the Excheang	0 8
	£0 7 0

These Articles were provided by Mr. Wilson for the Celebration of the 14th July, 1791. Samuel Neilson. Recd. the above. Wm. Wilson.

An Count of work and Timber for the Bastille.

	£. s. d.
To 2 once Cut Dales, at 1s. 3d. pr. pice ..	0 2 6
To 14 feet of Plank, at 4½d. pr. foot ..	0 5 3
To Sawyr's Bill	0 0 9
To making the same .:	0 11 4½
	0 19 10½

Reced. the above in full.

Robert M'Mullan.

Page 183. The French were in Carrickfergus

This was at the time Thurot captured the town in 1760, of which a full account is given in M'Skimin's *History of Carrickfergus.* The following old ballad on the event is believed to be unpublished :—

Three gallant ships of War
Came anchored in our bay,
Hoised up English colour and landed at Kilroot,
And marched up to Carrickfergus without further dispute.

Colonel Jennings being there at the very same space,
His heart it was a-breaking for this beautiful place.
He could not defend it ; for want of powder and ball,
Aloud unto his enemy for quarter he did call.

As Thourot lay in Hammock he dreamed a dream ;
A voice came unto him and named him by name,
Saying, Thourot, you are to blame for lying so long here,
The English they will be in this night, the wind it does blow fair.

Thourot jumped out of hammock, and called on his men,
Weigh your anchors, brave boys, make all the haste you can,
We'l go in the night-time, and make all the haste we can,
We'l steer soon and consort towards the Isle of Man.

As daylight did appear, Elliott spied Monsieur,
Which gave to him great cheer,
And to his men did say,
Yonder's Thourot, boys, we'l show him some play.

Thourot from the deck to the cabin ran down ;
Then he got his spy-glass and viewed them all round.
When he saw the English preparing themselves in swarm,
Oh, my boys, says Thourot, this place will be too warm.

We'l lose our gallant names, and they'l have it for to say,
The bonnie ship, *Belisle,* was took by English play.
Come, hoist your hooks (*sic*), we'l take them without doubt.
The first that came up was Elliott, without doubt.

Up came one of Elliott's ships, saying, pray, be not so fast,
Give her a galeant broadside, cut off her mizen mast.
Up came the other two, gave her fire round ;
Oh, my boys, says Elliott, this is not in Carrick town.

Up came Monsieur Thourot with his visage pale and wan ;
Strike your colours, brave boys, they'l sink us every one ;
Their weighty shot comes on so hard from sea,
Won't you strike your colours, boys, they'l sink us in the sea.

Before they got their colours struck great slaughter there was made ;
Many a galeant Frenchman on Thourot's decks lay dead.
They came tumbling down in swarms, and on Thourot's decks they lay,
While our brave English heroes cut their booms and yards away.

And as for Monsieur Thourot, as I hear the people say,
He was carried off by Elliott's men and buried in Ramsey Bay.

Here's a health to Elliott's men, and Thourot's men likewise
May all that does invade us be served that same way.
The Irish beat them off by land, the Englishmen by sea.

T

Page 183. THE PRISONERS WERE TAKEN TO KILMAINHAM

In the *Northern Star* their names are given as follows :—" In Newgate—Mr. Thomas Russell, of Belfast; Mr. John Young, do.; Mr. Rowley Osborne, do.; Mr. Samuel Musgrave, Lisburn; Mr. In Kilmainham Jail—Mr. Henry Hazlett, of Belfast; Mr. Samuel Neilson, do.; Mr. Daniel Shanaghan, do.; Mr. Samuel Kennedy, do.; Mr. Charles Teeling, Lisburn; Mr. Barclay, Craigavad."

Page 183. COUNSELLOR JOY

Henry Joy was Mary A. M'Cracken's cousin, an able Q.C., afterwards Chief Baron. The annexed letter in the *M'Cracken MSS.* is endorsed in Mary A. M'Cracken's handwriting—" 1801. From Henry Joy respecting information about the Battles of Ballynahinch and Antrim, which I declined procuring him." Possibly her knowledge of Thomas Russell's inflexible purpose, consummated in 1803, influenced her decision.

LETTER FROM HENRY JOY TO MARY ANN M'CRACKEN.

DEAR MARY,—I did expect you would, as I hoped you cou'd, be the means of assisting me to facts respecting at least the Battles of Ballynahinch and Antrim, and any time previous to them, that might be communicated with propriety. *Secrets* I don't wish to know anything about; but what can be mentioned with truth and propriety you will, I trust, still endeavour to do.

With respect to Antrim I have very imperfect accounts, therefore on that subject I hope you will be particular.

What was the plan of the Battle? In what points did it fail, and in what manner? Numbers engaged; and how was it connected with any general plan, had it been successful? How did it happen that the North did not move when the South did? When Antrim did step forward, what was the cause that Down did not? Why did Down, at the time it did? Were those actual leaders Leaders on the field, who were appointed by any higher power to be the leaders? What description of Leaders *did* appear, and what *did not*? and why did they not? These are some of the Questions that I would wish to have resolved; and as their answers require no names, nor the disclosures of any secrets that can in possibility injure any one, there will be the less reasonable objection to the answers. Had Antrim been successful, what was to have followed? and Down in like manner.

I am, Dr Mary, expecting your assistance in this,

Friday, 11 Dec., 1801.   Yrs. truly,

     H. JOY.

Page 183. COL. NUGENT

Major-General Nugent, who commanded the Northern district, is evidently meant. The following curious letter, now first printed, was recently given to the Editor by W. J. Fitzpatrick, LL.D., F.S.A., Dublin :—

Bangor, *August 24th, 1798.*

DEAR GENERAL,—I cannot resist troubling you with the Case of John Allen, now under Sentence of a Court-Martial for being concerned in taking arms out of the house of A. M'Cleland this Parish. When called on trial, either through ignorance or from being badly advised, he told the Court he had nothing to say against the charge, and threw himself at the Mercy of the Court. Tho' there were several respectable people waiting to give him a character, and three creditable persons had lodged affidavits with the clerk for the Prosecutions, stating that he had acted under the orders of one of their Captains of the name of Robinson. I enclose copies of the affidavits, which Mr. Connor has given to Allen's wife, a paper which, though dirty, I know to be the signatures of several very honest and Loyal men. I rather think he is a man not very fit for service, and if sent he will leave a wife and family totally destitute of support. I should therefore beg leave to recommend him as a fit object for mercy, and remain,

Dear Sir, your very obedient, very humble servant,

Major-General Nugent, Belfast.   ROBERT WARD.

The annexed permits afford some idea of martial law at this dreadful time :—

" Permit Mr. David M'Tear, of Hazlebank, near the white house, in the County of Antrim, or his servant, Alexander Neilson, going into Belfast for the assistance of Doctor James M'Donnell, to pass and repass at all hours.   " THOS. GOLDIE,

" This pass to be in force till Mrs. M'Tear gets her Bed.   *M·Genl.*"

" Permit Mr. Dav^d Mattear to have in his Possession One Gun for the Protection of his Property.   " G. NUGENT,

" Belfast, *May 22d, 1798.*   *Major-Genl.*"

Page 183. THE CO DOWN GENERAL HAD BEEN ARRESTED

In spite of this arrest of Rev. W. Steele Dickson, Henry Monro was declared Adjutant-General in his place. A premature attack was made by the insurgents on Saintfield on the 9th June, which is described in the following letter from the *Gordon MSS.* :—

LETTER OF ENSIGN SPARKS TO CAPT. PAYNE, BROADSTONE HOUSE, DUBLIN.

Downpatrick, *23d June, 1798.*

MY DEAR SIR,—I suppose you are surprised at my not having answer'd your letter sooner, but from the day I recd it to this I could not say that a moment was my own; even now we are ordered to keep all our Camp Equipage and Intrenching tools loaded on Cars so as to be ready to march at an hour's notice, yet I believe we shan't stir for some time.

On Saturday, the 9th June, we had a severe engagement with the rebels near Saintfield. Our force (illegible) of about 270 of our Regt. 50 Yeoman Infry. 30 Yeoman Cavalry, and two Field pieces (6 pounders). The Rebel force we then estimated at about 7,000, but, as we have since learnt, they exceeded 10,000, about

1,200 of whom were armed with muskets, the remainder with pikes. The engagement commenced with our Light Comp³. who were on the right flank of our advanced guard. They received the Rebels' fire, and returned it with great gallantry, tho' with the loss of their Capt. till our main body came up, when the Battle became more general. The ground the rebels had chosen to engage us on was the most advantageous to them that could possibly be immagined—so much so, that I could not, during great part of the Action, bring either of my two Guns to bear on the right, and was obliged to remain idle, exposed to an heavy fire for some minutes. At length a strong column of rebels advanced on our left, attempting to turn our flank and surround us. I waited till they came so close that I must make sure work, and then poured on them a heavy fire of Canister shot, which soon put that column to flight with dreadful slaughter. At that instant their party on our right made a desperate attack on our ranks where I was with the guns, and also on our baggage, and then it was that Dr. James and Lieut. Unite fell. The broken columns of the Rebels were rallied under cover of a young but close wood on our left, from which I soon dislodged them by a few discharges of Canister. Our main body, with the two guns, now pushed forward, and drove the enemy from the strong ground they occupied on our right, where they were completely covered by strong ditches and banks. On this the enemy fled in every direction ; but seeing that we halted on the hill, a great number of them again assembled on another height about ¾ of a mile distant ; but a few Round shot which I threw amongst them, and which we could perceive made lanes through them, soon sent them scampering. Having but a few Cavalry, and being very uneasy for the fate of the wounded (our surgeon having run away panic struck at the beginning of the action), Col. Stapylton thought it prudent to return to Comber, where we arrived about *12 o'clock*, and next day marched into Belfast. At the time the rebels made the principal attack on our centre I was very nearly being taken off. One fellow ran furiously at me with a pike, but I had the good fortune to ward off the thrust with my sword, and instantly laid the villain dead at my feet. Another fired a musket within 3 yards of me, but by chance I then happened to leap on the gun limbers to take out some Canister shot, and the ball just grazed my hand. I rec⁴ a slight cut of a pike over my right eye, and a trifling wound from a ball on my right hand, but neither of them were such as to require surgical aid, or to prevent me from doing my duty ; therefore they are not set down in any return. Several others of our officers and men who have been slightly hurt are not in the returns.

Our Victory, tho' glorious, was very dear bought. I send you a return of the killed and wounded on our side. That of the rebels were not less than 500, 300 of whom were killed on the spot, and the fields for Two miles round were covered by the [illegible] who attempted going off, but who died [illegible] ditches and fields from loss of blood and fatigue.

I shall long to hear from you ; direct to this place. Give my most affte regards to Mrs. P. and all the family ; to Mr. and Mrs. Evans, &c., &c.

Believe me, Dr Sir, yours most truly,

MIKKELL J. SPARKS.

My Spectacles were knocked off by a pike just as I was pointing one of the Great Guns, and one of my glasses broke without doing me any further damage.

RETURN OF KILLED AND WOUNDED, 9th JUNE.

York Regt { 3 officers, 4 Sergts. 2 Drummers, 34 privates killed.
{ 1 officer, 1 Sergt. 1 Drummer, 36 privates wounded.
N:T:Ards Cavalry—1 Sergt. 8 rank and file, 7 Horses killed.
N:T:Ards Infty—3 rank and file wounded, 4 volunteers killed, 1 wounded.

Total—3 officers, 5 Sergts. 2 Drummers, 42 privates, and 4 volunteers killed.
1 officer, 1 Sergt. 1 Drummer, 46 privates, and 1 volunteer wounded.

4 off.   6 S.   3 D: 88 p.   5 v.

There was an Engagemt between the troops and rebels at Ballynahinch, the 13th inst. Gen. Nugent commanded in person ; the troops suffered little. The rebels lost 700, and were finally dispersed. The rebellion is over in this country.

On the back of Sparks' letter is the following :—

On the 13thn, part of our Regt. part of the Monaghan, and a troop of Dragoons, with one Curricle 6-pounder, under the command of Col. Stapylton, were posted so as to cut off the retreat of the rebels to the Ards ; we intercepted some of their supplies. Our situation was such as to prevent us having any share in the engagement. Our dragoons, however, fell in with some of the broken and flying army, of whom they killed about 50. I was not engaged, being stationed with gun, which I commanded, to guard the pass.

Page 188. JAMES HOPE, A WEAVER

This remarkable man, whose political ideas were much in advance of his time, wrote an account of his life, which, somewhat modified by Madden, is given, with a portrait, in the first edition of *The United Irishmen* (third series, vol. i. p. 218: Dublin, 1846). It is strange that the biographies of James Hope, Henry Joy M'Cracken, and Henry Monro, which appear in the first edition of above, are suppressed in the subsequent one, although they are of peculiar interest, especially to Ulstermen. Hope was in the full confidence of H. J. M'Cracken, and till his death was also a warm friend of his sister. Amongst her MSS. are two poems, endorsed in her writing, "James Hope ; given me shortly before his death." One of these poems is a political fable in the form of a long dialogue between a shepherd and a thief, but is not of much merit. The other is subjoined, and is given as originally written :—

POEM BY JAMES HOPE.

Com, Don't Let us caper with history on paper,
While Bankruptcy Marshals its Terible Train ;
The day Must Arive when Nothing can thrive
But the tender of value for value Again.
So Neighbours be wise, Tak your Hands from your
      Eyes,
Let your Enemy feel that your Vision's Corect,
And Nip in the bud Every wish to shed Blood ;
Let Idle declamers and profligiat schemers
Get on with there bother and blind one another ;
The Time is departed when peace they could smother,
      On Patrick's day, &c.

Some say that from England we want seperation,
The very Reverse we are Ready to prove.
We want closer connection in Mutual Afection,
But what separates us we Mean to Remove.
The chain of opression that feters us both,
To shiver in pieces we'l Never be loth ;
We'l unite Holyhead to our own Hill of Howtb.
By our Interest that's common and cripled by no
      one,
A Tide waiter, water-guard, Jailer, or yeoman,
With *Cead Milla Failud* for all but the foemen.
      On Patrick's day, &c.

The following letter of Hope to Mary Ann M'Cracken is endorsed in her writing, "from Jas. Hope." *N.B.*—"Mr. John" was her brother John :—

Nov. 28th, 1808.

DEAR MISS MARY,—I wished to have called on you this some time past, But never had time when you would be at Leisure, and now write to tell you that on Saturday Evening I was obliged to tell Mr. John that I must Leave his Employment for want of wages, not being able Longer to support my family out of my small salery ; and now, in Consequence of the interest you have allwise in my wellfare, I will Describe to you what has Been the nature of my situation since I went to my present place. For the first year I was treated by Mr. Plunket (whom I Consider to be a blunt, honest man) with the Greatest Rigor, under the Idea that, having been an old Sufferer, I was what he Calls a follower of your family, and might be Corrupt Enough (as he had observed several others) to take improper Liberty. However, by a subordination that Required some strength both of Body and mind, I Conquered his prejudice, and completely secured his friendship and Confidence. But as to Mr. John, although he never Checked me much, he allwise treated me (when Ever I spoke to him about my own Situation) with a silence which in another I would have taken for Contempt ; but imputing it to his natural temper and press of business, and Coniceous of never having given any Cause for it, I over Looked it as a thing for which I Could not fully account, and which time Certainly would. I have at Lingth, through all the bustle and inconvenience of the place in which I was obleeged to do business, acquired such improvement in the practice of writing and Keeping accounts as will Enable me to a considerable Share of Business in any office where I may hereafter find Employment. This last assertion is the only one that I would Expect Mr. John to Contradict ; unless he would consider that if he was me and I somebody else, he Could not at all times answer for his own Correctness. As to my future views, there is but one Employment at present in my Reach, which is to apply to the men who Conduct the Cart Business for Belfast and Dublin to Employ me as Guard, which, although it will aford me a Considerable salary, is a Long Road to Either Ease or Credit, and an Employment as different from my Inclination as many others I have thought of, but if I could stand it for one year, I hope I am still possesed of Resolution to save what money will Discharge a few small accounts which I ow, and Enable me again to Join my Little family with the fair Chance of another tradesman, without being troublesome to any one whom I call friend ; and this being at present my higest ambition, I will Risk the last power of my Constitution to attain it. One thing more I mention, and I hope it will not hurt your feelings. I thought between winding and warping to have paid what I am indebted to you, which, although I know you do not think of it, does not make me forget. I think my word is entitled to some Credit, and I can assure you that the piece that was warped in our house was finished and taken off the mill by my own hand, and if I was on my oath could freely disclose that it is my Belief there was not a broken or Latched End in it Leaving our house, what Ever may have been said to the Contrary. Let no friend of mine grieve at my situation ; it is a Little hard, but does not discourage me. I am determined to deserve success. Dr Miss Mary, your Much Obliged Well-wisher,

JAMES HOOPE (*sic*).

Page 190. RUSSELL WAS TRIED IN DOWNPATRICK

By the kindness of Miss Gordon, Saintfield, the Editor has in his possession many original documents relative to Russell's abortive attempt, including the indictments, verdicts, &c., recorded. To Mr. Thomas Standfield he is indebted for the original of Russell's Proclamation, dated Head Quarters, July 24th, 1803. This was in the possession of his father, James Standfield, a well-known philanthropic citizen of Belfast, and a personal friend of Harry Monro and Mary Ann M'Cracken. The latter gave him the document which Russell had given her.

Page 191. A NUMBER HAD EMIGRATED TO THE UNITED STATES

Robert Simms (p. 273) received many letters from "'98" emigrants. The following are of special interest as written by Robert Emmet's brother.

Extract from a letter of Thomas Addis Emmet, New York, to his friend Robert Simms, Belfast (1st June, 1805).

I rejoice, My Dear friend, to think that the resolution you have taken of settling yourself and family here will withdraw you from scenes which I cannot but suppose must be extremely irksome, and from a Country the future prospects of which appear to me extremely gloomy. Believe me, it is with pain I find that you are determined to defer your voyage for one year more. The determination to quit one's native home, natural connexions, and antient friends is so serious and important, that I would scarcely venture to advise it to any man ; but you have taken the resolution, and as your choice is made, I may say I do not believe you will ever repent it, and I may urge that every moment which you unnecessarily delay the execution of your plan is so much thrown away out of your happiness in this Country. As for myself, you will I am sure rejoice to learn that my good fortune here has been so complete. The exertions of my friends have procured me the permission of following my profession here, tho' an Alien, and not qualified by performing the usual preliminary studies within the State. And my prospects in business are to the full as good as my most sanguine expectations ever conceived. Within this fortnight or three weeks I have received a very large and troublesome addition to my family by the arrival of my three youngest boys from Dublin. They are in perfect health, and so much the harder to manage. I am now surrounded by eight children, equally divided as to sex—the three eldest, your old fellow-prisoners, are extremely well, and very fine children—your favourite, Margaret, tho' inferior in beauty, is perhaps the best and most valuable ; they all remember you with very lively affection. The little Scotch lassie is a great beauty and a greater pet, and the eighth is a brave American Girl of only two months old. I had another lovely little girl who died of the Chin Cough shortly after we left France. So much for my children. Mrs. Emmet, who is as eager as I can be to see you, and desires the most affectionate remembrance to you, would be very tolerably if she did not persevere in nursing, which never agreed with her; but we are at this moment also labouring under the most crying grievance of America—the badness of servants—of which and the enormity of their wages you can scarcely form an idea. When you come out, if there be any servant really attached to you and your family, that would accompany you from affection and not from speculation, jump at the proposal. Be so good as to present my respects to Mrs. Simms, though I do not enjoy the pleasure of her acquaintance personally, and to your Brother, who I hope has not forgotten me; and believe me, My Dear friend, very sincerely yours,   T. A. EMMET.

ROBERT SIMMS, Esq., OF BELFAST.

New York, *Novr. 2nd. 1807.*

DEAR SIMMS,—I was extremely gratified by the receipt of yours of the 22nd of August last, and particularly so by finding that you approved of the steps I was induced to take here in politics. I have been compelled by a sense of duty, and the foolish scurrillity of the federalists, to make myself very prominent by my controversy with Rufus King. Their malignity (if they had succeeded) would have pursued me with as much fury and effect as that of the Orangemen in Ireland—but thank God they are powerless. Even beaten as they are, they combined to do me every professional injury in their power, but finding the combination of no avail, a sense of individual interest forces them to abandon it. Rufus King is placed in public opinion just where he ought to be; and unless the federalists possess the power of reviving the dead, I hope and believe he will never again do much mischief; but that they can do a great deal too much is manifest from the issue of Burr's trial. That man, whom they hated while he appeared to be a Republican, whom they never tolerated till he became a Renegade, and never openly upheld until he attempted to sever the Union and establish a monarchy within the territory of the United States,—that man is acquitted by their intrigues and interference, by their partiality and exertions, tho' his guilt is fully developed, and no man affects to doubt it. It is very possible, however, that his acquittal will do good —it will cause a revisal of some defective parts of our criminal law, and perhaps an investigation of the conduct and opinions of some of our Judges, who stand at the head of the federalists, and continued in office notwithstanding the overthrow of their Party. Jefferson's administration is, I think, entitled to all your praise, and as he will not serve again, I think his probable successor (the present Vice-President) will equally claim your approbation for his uprightness, and, what in these times is very necessary, for his decision and firmness. On the subject of war, most people judge here differently from what I apprehend you do in Europe—we expect it. The calamities it will produce are known to every body—universally spoken of and admitted; the ruin of our commerce, and of every occupation connected with it, is held up in the strongest point of view by the English Agents and factors, and under-rated by no one; but nevertheless (except the English and factors) almost every one is ready and willing to bear his share of those inconveniences and calamities. With the English Agents and factors must be counted the leading Mercantile federalists in the commercial cities—if in truth they are not the same thing with different names—but the other federalists in the Country parts partake very much of the general spirit. The claims of Great Britain to the right of search and impressment might have remained undecided upon, but for the affair of the Chesapeak and the report of the West India Committee, which insists upon the necessity of destroying almost all neutral commerce with belligerents; these have now brought into discussion the whole of her pretensions, and awakened the remembrance of all her conduct towards America since 1793. The result is that the most moderate feel the necessity of repressing those pretensions and resenting that conduct at some period; and the most reflecting imagine that no period can promise better than the present. The first consequences of the war are admitted and calculated upon, but the ultimate effects of it on the colonial system, manufactures and commerce of England, and even upon her naval strength if she should fail in the Baltic and be unable to supply herself with naval stores from thence, are anticipated as fully equivalent to the misfortunes of its commencement. French politics have nothing to say to these sentiments, tho' undoubtedly, in the event of a rupture, America would endeavour to turn to the best advantage the alliance with France; and in the West India seas the two powers united, and the ports of each open to the cruisers and ships of the other, would embarrass England much beyond what she has ever experienced in that quarter. Adieu, my good friend. Mrs. E. and my three eldest unite in the most affectionate remembrance with yours very sincerely,   T. A. EMMET.

I request you will remember me most kindly to your brother, and such of my old friends as still feel an interest for me.

Page 195. Mr. EDWARD BUNTING

This well-known musician was a pupil of William Ware, who was organist of the Parish Church, and editor of a collection of anthems dedicated to the Marchioness of Donegall. Bunting was an enthusiastic collector of Irish airs, which he published in three volumes in 1796, 1809, and 1840. His daughter, Mrs. R. A. Macrory, Dublin, writes the Editor that " her father spent a fortune in collecting these airs." Mary A. M Cracken, her brothers John and Frank, and Henry Joy also assisted him. The M'Crackens sent Patrick Lynch to Connaught in 1802. He writes—" I stayed in Castlebar ; had good success ; got near 50 songs, and chiefly from the Mechanicks. I found it expensive—it cost me 2 guineas. I returned to Louisborough, and heard of a Blind piper. I went to a Dancing ; I took down six good songs from the Blind man, and I never found any one who had so great variety of good old songs and tunes. He sings well, and has a great memory—in short, he would be more useful to Mr. Bunting than any man in Connaught. However, I could not stay by him, for I was out of money, and had to return to Westport, where I am running in debt and getting no songs. Lord ! how long must I be confined this way !" The annexed estimate of the cost of production of 1,000 copies of his book is taken from a letter of Bunting's addressed to Frank M'Cracken. Campbell is the poet Thomas Campbell :—

1st. Campbell	..	..	..	..	£50
2nd. Harp engraving (paid for)	..	..	..	10
3. Frontispiece, " Hempson"	..	..	..	15
4. Title ..	..	..	..	..	15
5. Title for the outside in same manner as Moore & Stevenson's..					8
6. Paper as from £3 10s. to £4 0s. 0d. per ream for 50 reams, which will only print 96 pages per 1,000 copies					200
7. Engraving Music plates with Irish titles, &c., 90 plates at 12/6					62
8. Working off at press at 5/- per hundred ..					50
					£400
Allowance to Music dealers, 33 per cent.	..		..	..	300
					£700 without the letterpress.

The following unpublished minute of a preliminary meeting relative to the great gathering of Irish Harpers in Belfast, July 10th, 1792, is taken from *Macadam MSS.* It contains the first mention of Bunting's name in this connection. (For an account of the Harpers' meeting, see an article by the Editor's father, Robert Young, J.P., C.E., *Ulster Journal of Archæology*, Jan., 1895.)

At a meeting of several Subscribers to the scheme for assembling The *Harpers* (By Public Advertisement) in Belfast, the 23d of April, 1792, . . It was agreed—

That a Committee of five subscribers be appointed to forward and receive subscriptions—to circulate by advertisement in different News Papers and other ways the period and objects of the meeting, And to regulate and conduct the subordinate parts of the scheme. That Mr. H. Joy, Mr. Robt. Bradshaw, Mr. Robert Simmes, Doctor Jas. M'Donnell, and Mr. John Scott Be the Committee. That Mr. Robert Bradshaw be appointed Treasurer to the fund, and Secretary. That a Committee be now appointed as Judges for appreciating the merits of the different performers on the *Irish Harps* who may appear at Belfast on Tuesday, the tenth day of July next. That the following Ladys and Gentlemen be appointed to that committee :—

Reverend Mr. Meade.	Honble. Mrs. Meade.
Reverend Mr. Vance.	Honble. Miss De Courcey.
Mr. Rainey Maxwell.	Mrs. M'Kenzie.
Mr. Robert Bradshaw.	Miss Catherine Clarke.
Mr. Henry Joy.	Miss Grant.
Doctor Jas. M'Donnel.	Miss Bristow.
Mr. Thos. Moris Jones.	Mrs. John Clarke.
	Mrs. Kennedy.

That the premiums be adjudg'd (in proportion to the funds rais'd) in the following gradations :— 1st premium, £....; 2nd, ditto ; 3rd, ditto ; 4th, ditto ; 5th, ditto, with smaller gratuities to others in aid of their expenses. That the airs to be perform'd previous to the Adjudication of the premiums be confined to the native music of the Country—the music of Ireland. In order to revive obsolete airs, It is an instruction to the Judges on this occasion not to be solely governed in their decisions by the degree of execution or taste of the several performers, but, independent of these circumstances, to consider the person entitled to additional claim who shall produce Airs not to be found in any public Collection, and, at the same time, deserving of preference by their intrinsic excellence. It is recommended to any Harper who is in possession of scarce compositions to have them reduced to Notes. That the Reverend Mr. Andrew Bryson, of Dundalk, be requested to assist, as a person versed in the language and antiquities of the Nation ; And that Mr. William Weare, Mr. Edward Bunting, and Mr. John Sharpe be requested to attend as practical Musicians. That notification of the meeting on 10th July and an Invitation to the Harpers be published in the two Belfast papers and in *National Journal*, and in one of the Cork, Limerick, Waterford, Kilkenny, Galway, Sligo, and Derry papers.

Page 197.   ON EXAMINING HER PAPERS

A number of interesting MSS. formerly in her possession have been kindly given to the Editor by Christopher Aitchison, Esq , J.P., Elmswood, Loanhead, N.B., who also generously presented to the Belfast Museum part of the uniform and the sword worn by Henry Joy M'Cracken at the Battle of Antrim. Amongst the MSS. are several poems by Miss Balfour, many letters of Edward Bunting on Irish music, and letters written by Mary Ann M'Cracken to her brother Frank ; also several from the Rev. Sinclair Kelburne, Henry and Francis Joy, &c.   The following examples may be of interest :—

This was written after reading " The Sword of my Harry," by Miss Balfour.

'Twas thus the cause the Hero fell,
  Who vainly with oppression strove,
But yet his Country's sorrows tell,
  Who dared not act can yet approve.

They tell that still the spark remains
  Which kindled once the hallowed flame,

And that again on Erin's plains
  Her sons the patriot's meed shall claim.

So, when black clouds and stormy wind
  Obscure and darken o'er the skies,
One beam that lingers still behind,
  Shows that again the sun will rise.

THE SEVENTEENTH OF JULY.   Written by Miss Balfour.

O'er the cold grave where Erin's Hero sleeps,
The despot triumphs and the patriot weeps,
While round the spot with liberal hand he spreads
Fresh leaves still glist'ning with the tears he sheds ;
For e'en amidst this desolated land,
Where, scarce extinct, still smokes the fatal brand,
Where vile oppression's tool and faction's slave

Bear down and trample on the good and brave,
Some hearts with freedom's tide yet fondly swell,
Some lips yet dare the hero's worth to tell—
Dare to repeat with just and noble pride
His name, who bravely for his country died—
Dare still to boast, with emulation fired,
How Erin's son in Erin's cause expired.

The subjoined poem is endorsed in Mary Ann M'Cracken's writing, " Papers from Miss Templeton."   The incident referred to is probably the execution of four privates of the Monaghan Militia at Blaris on 16th May, 1797.

When bid to take aim at the Irishman's heart,
The stout Caledonian recoiled with a start :
" The first of my country; the first of my clan,
Ever ordered to fire on a blindfolded man !
You'll find fitter tools to perform such a deed—
By Irishmen's hands let the Irishman bleed :
In the spirit of Cain let them murder each other,

And the united fall by his *united* brother.'
So the Irish went first, and the Irish went last,
And, guarded by Irish, the prisoners past,
On their coffins knelt down, took their silent
  farewell,
The united men fired, the united men fell.

Page 197.   A MAN NAMED M'SKIMIN

Samuel M'Skimin was a native of Ballyclare, and came to Carrickfergus about 1798, where he held some subordinate position in connection with the yeomen.   It is said that his reason for so doing was his idea that he was a " marked man."   Soon afterwards he started a small shop, and commenced to collect material for his famous *History of Carrickfergus*, the first edition of which appeared in 1811.   Local tradition says that the credit of gathering information and procuring original documents to copy was his ; but that a schoolmaster named O'Beirney, and another friend called Hagan, lent their aid in putting his material into a literary form.   He seems to have been careless with other MSS. besides those lent to him by Mary M'Cracken, as it is mentioned that the Carrickfergus records had been lent to him, and were not forthcoming at the inquiry held by the Municipal Reform Commissioners, 1833-4. A second edition, much enlarged, of his *History of Carrickfergus* was published in 1823, and a third in 1829.   Some Addenda were printed in 1833, and an Appendix added in 1839. He contributed also to the Dublin *Penny Journal*, the *Northern Whig*, &c.   He corresponded with several well-known antiquarians, including T. Crofton Croker, Dr. R. R. Madden, Dr. James M'Donnell, Dr John O'Donovan, and Robert S. Macadam.   His death occurred in 1843, and he was buried in the graveyard of St. Nicholas' Church, Carrickfergus. He collected a good deal of material relative to '98, which was published as a small history of the rising in the North, entitled *Annals of Ulster*, in 1849   He was a Presbyterian, and a member of the congregation of the Rev. James Seaton Reid, D.D., author of the *History of the Presbyterian Church in Ireland*.   After his death, his collection of MSS. was disposed of by his son ; part became the property of the Rev. James Seaton Reid ; a portion was purchased by the Rev. Classon Porter of Larne ; and some of the most curious, including an annotated copy of the autobiography of Newell the informer, came into Dr. R. R. Madden's possession
Mr. John Coates, J.P., informs the Editor that he has often seen the historian of Carrickfergus serving his customers in his little grocer's shop in Irish Quarter West, and then retiring to his desk at the end of the counter to add a few lines to his work.

MISCELLANEOUS NOTES FROM *PINKERTON MSS.*, &c.

FINES AND FORFEITURES DURING STEWART BANKS' SOVEREIGNSHIP,
1778.

Light bread value	£5	14	10
Fines for profane swearing	0	13	0
Fines levied off butchers	1	3	3½
A sum forfeited	1	3	10
Produce of condemned yarn	3	16	6
ditto of false weights	8	9	6½
ditto of a sack of potatoes forfeited	0	7	0½
Fresh butter seized, 61½ lbs.	1	10	0
As weigh-master, half produce of condemned butter	23	5	10¼
Flax seized, 36½ lbs.	1	8	0
	£47	11	10½

Besides two carcases of mutton and a quantity of beef.

The figures subjoined for comparison have been kindly supplied by Robert M'Henry, Esq., Chief Clerk of Petty Sessions Court, Belfast :—

1894.

Amount of fines imposed	£3,409	11	11
Amount of fees (denoted by stamps) received ...	1,504	2	0

Number of cases, 33,112.

ORANGE BALLADS COLLECTED BY W. PINKERTON.

THE ORANGEMEN OF BELFAST. (c. 1813.)

Last Twelfth of July, as you quickly shall hear,
The bold Orangemen of Belfast did appear,
With their Flags and their Colours together did join
To commemorate the deeds done at the Boyne.
            Down, down, &c.

With their Drums and their Colours they marched away
To the Church of Lisburn, as I heard them say ;
Reverend Doctor Cupples, loyal and sincere,
He preached them a Sermon when they came there.

He's Grand District Master of Lisburn Town,
He's a true Orangeman, and a Friend to the Crown,
With brave Captain Verner, near Belfast does dwell,
They inspected our true Orange Heroes right well.

Sure there was Three Thousand in sweet Lisburn town
Of stout Orange Heroes incircled around ;
They all joined their hands, and three times they did
            cheer,
Then they parted in love, and homewards did steer.

But when they drew near to the end of the town,
The Croppies of Belfast began for to frown ;
Both hedges and ditches were lined along,
And with Courage they marched through the Rebel
            throng.

But as they were marching through Hercules Street,
A great opposition they happened to meet
From turn-coat Croppies, became Ribbonmen,
For to murder our Orangemen they did intend.

Belfast District Master, brave Woods is his name,
He bid them all return from whence they came .
To their different Lodge Rooms, and have a due care,
If they were assaulted, no Rebel to spare.

So when he dismissed them they all marched away,
But two of those Lodges they met a sad fray ;
When they entered North Street the Rebels did
            throng,
Both brick bats and stones upon them were thrown.

Brave Calwell and Lynns deserve great applause,
Like true sons of William they supported our cause ;
Carrying the Colours, they were three times knocked
            down,
But they fought their way through and maintained
            their ground.

From every entry and from every lane,
The brick bats and stones in showers they came ;
But the Lord still preserv'd them, their lives did secure,
Till they safe arrived at bold Thompson's door.

When they entered their Lodge Room, refreshment to
            take,
The Croppies another attack they did make ;
Those cowardly Rebels to racking did fall,
Throwing stones thro' the windows to murder them all.

God prosper brave Carroll, and Morgan also,
And likewise M'Mullen, wherever they go,
For they fired out upon them, they loaded with ball,
And three of those Rebels before them did fall.

Those cowardly villains they scatter'd and fled
At the cries of the wounded and sight of the dead ;
The valiant stout Lettens deserves great applause,
For they bravely supported the Protestant cause.

Success to bold Ritchy, the public can tell,
He fought like a Lion those Rebels to quell
Thro' Rebellious Belfast, which still was the seat
Of Traitors and Rebels, a den of deceit.

God Prosper those true Orange Sons of the light,
May all their actions for ever shine bright ;
Likewise Captain Verner and his Yeomanry,
Who made all those damn'd Croppy Ribboumen flee.

Here's to Captain Verner, long may he live well,
The peace for to keep, and the Rebels to quell ;
When he puts on his regimentals, it puts me in mind
Of the Glorious King William when he crossed the
            Boyne.

So now I conclude with a toast at the last—
God prosper the true Orange Sons of Belfast,
Likewise Brother Reed, who employed me to pen
These lines to the praise of the bold Orangemen.

5

MISCELLANEOUS NOTES. 281

TRIBUTE TO THE MEMORY
OF WILLIAM QUAIL, LATE OF BELFAST.
BY A MEMBER OF No. 337 (ABOUT 1815).

You Orangemen of Ireland, I pray you lend an ear,
While I relate a tragic tale as ever you did hear,
The most atrocious of the kind ere acted in our land,
Committed on the body of a Loyal Orangeman.

The ninth of January, it being the Lord's Day,
The Orangemen of Belfast town did meet without delay;
Strict orders had been issued to assemble without fail
For to inter a Brother, his name was William Quail.

He being a Yeoman of the town, a party did attend,
A Solemn Dirge was played along, the scene was truly
grand.
The procession moved in order till we came to Friar's
Bush.
Where, with military honours, his body was laid in dust.

The Funeral Rites being over, we march home without
delay,
No opposition did appear for to impede our way;
Those sons of Baliel (sic) did not think it right for to
appear
For to oppose our Orangemen, whose hearts were void
of fear.

But Night's sable curtain scarce was drawn, burning
with Hellish rage,
Those savage monsters sallied forth, their wrath for to
assuage.
In Friar's Bush they instantly assembled without fail,
And, shocking to relate, they raised our brother,
William Quail.

O'er bedge and ditch they hauled him to satiate their
rage,
Until they came to Ormeau bridge, and there they did
him leave,
With horrid imprecations from the most bloody clan,
Because he was one of William's sons, and a true
Orangeman.

Ye Friends of Religious Liberty, are these your pious
deeds?
Why so provoke the mighty God to pour vengeance on
your heads?
Although you have raised his body, thus led on by
hellish wrath,
The mortal part you could not hurt, his soul was gone
aloft.

THE ANTRIM HUNT. *Panegyric Stanzas thereon.* BY WILLIAM PERCY, 1826.

See Doagh throng'd with grandeur, see Farrell's great
Inn,
Where our fine Antrim Hunters festivity win ;
Where a pattern's afforded, admired by all,
Of the generous landlord in good Donegall.
Hark away ! hark away ! whilst we fervently pray,
That our kindest of landlords may still hear the sway.

The Earl of Belfast I shall now compliment ;
May he learn from his father, in levying his rent ;
May he ne'er, with mad factions, his mind e'er
embroil,
But be brave in the army, like great Arthur Moyle.

Should the Marquis of Downshire your hunt ever grace,
He'll present you a cup, to bring on a fine race ;
'Mongst the highest, he's high—patriotic he's still ;
God prosper for ever the family of Hill.

Now the son of a lord, who Shane's-Castle did own ;
Whose death at old Antrim, all Irishmen moan :
Still possessing a princely estate by entail,
Pray who can be meant but the great Lord O'Neill?

And the Gen'ral, his brother, once Colonel. you know,
Your hunt would embellish, and add to your show ;
He is gen'rous at home, in the army he's brave,
And will ne'er be corrupted to act like a knave.

The noble Macartney next comes for my theme ;
The heir of Lord George, a most honoured name—
Ambassador lie, to the sports of the Chinese court—
His heir must rank high in the midst of your sport.

The race of the Pakenhams now I shall sing,
Who fought, and who died, for their country and king :
When retir'd from the army, and levees of court,
They too, would add lustre, and brighten your sport.

The graceful MacDonnell, who lives at Glenarm,
In person and manners his lady must charm.
Whether sporting at home, or your 'semblage he grace,
There is much that is noble display'd in his face.

Does Bateson, Sir Robert, e'er visit your hunt ?
If he do, you'll respect him as always your wont.
The great Earl Moira you know he succeeds ;
May you all learn from Moira political creeds.

The next is great Watson, a Nimrod by name,
The first of all hunters, and horsemen of fame—
Commodore was his father, on India's old station ;
The pride of his king, and the boast of his nation.

I now feel quite happy in chosing my air,
And melodiously singing to praise good Adair ;
I received his kindness full seven years since,
And conceive him possess'd of the heart of a prince.

I now, with best feelings, smooth numbers advance
The high estimation of Suffolk's M'Cance ;
I hope be just knows that I'm still on the globe,
Would bow to his honour, but shabby's my robe.

John Sinclair, Esquire, I now must advance,
At least to an equal with comrade M'Cance
In the sports of the field few can either excel,
And proud is the minstrel their praises to swell.

A FEW OF THE LOCAL ANECDOTES COLLECTED BY ROBERT S. MACADAM. *(MACADAM MSS.)*

Some excavations were made at a place called Carnaghliss, near Belfast, with the hope of finding coal. A woman there one day inquired of the diggers whether they expected to get English or Scotch coal !

During the time of the Rev. Sinclair Kelburne's ministry in the Third Presbyterian Congregation, Belfast, it happened one Sunday that the Sovereign (chief magistrate) of the town was present at service. His worship was a notorious card-player, and had been engaged at his favourite occupation the night before until a late hour. His pew was in the gallery, and during the service, while leaning over the front, he pulled his handkerchief out of his pocket, and along with it a pack of cards, which scattered and fell down into the house. The minister pointedly remarked that somebody's psalm-book was badly bound !

The first steam engine erected at Belfast was at the Springfield Cotton Mill, belonging to Messrs. Stevenson, and was actually used for pumping up water to drive a water-wheel.

A well-known Belfast merchant, in the beginning of this century, was in the habit of exporting various goods to a port in Spain, where they were sold by an agent. The goods were usually provisions, but sometimes the cargo was made up of linens and other commodities. As was customary, the agent, in sending back his Account of Sales, always made several deductions, such as breakages, damage by sea water, &c.; but one invariable item was "*Eaten by the Rats*," so much. It happened on one occasion that the Belfast merchant sent out a large quantity of *nails*, which were then made at Newtownbreda. In due time the Account of Sales arrived from Spain, and, to his great astonishment, a deduction was made as usual for "Eaten by the rats."

A Belfast hardware merchant, about the same period, whose knowledge of geography was not very extensive, was encouraged to send out a consignment of goods for sale to the West Indies. It is a positive fact that among them were included a quantity of skates and warming-pans! The skates turned out a bad speculation, but, strange to say, the warming-pans were sold at a large profit. The agent in the West Indies, by a slight change in their form, was able to pass them off as improved skimmers for sugar-pans.

In many of the white limestone quarries in the Counties of Antrim and Down there are frequently found curiously-shaped large masses of flint, all nearly similar in size and form, and bearing a rude resemblance to a human head and trunk. Geologists suppose them to be organic remains, and know them by the name of *Para moudras*. This has all the appearance of a Greek word, but no one has been able to point out its derivation. The fact is, there is no Greek in it at all, and the real origin of the name is this—An English geologist (Dr. Buckland, I think), being in the North of Ireland, and hearing of these singular fossils, visited the large limestone quarries at Moira, and saw a number of them there. The quarrymen were at work, and he asked one of them what name they gave to these stones. "We call them *Para moudra*," said the man. The doctor was astonished at hearing such a fine Greek-sounding name, but it simply means in Irish "Ugly Paddy."

Shortly before Mr. Godwin ceased to be the engineer of the Ulster Railway, he wished to try some experiments with *anthracite* coal, and to use it in the locomotives instead of coke. Anthracite has not only a hard name, but is very hard to burn; and very likely the stoker who tried it was tired enough of it when he got back from his journey. Some of his acquaintances who saw him cleaning out his fire-box on his return, in very bad humour, said to him—"Why, what's wrong with you, to-day. Jack?" "Wrong," said he, "everything's wrong. Mr. Godwin wants me to burn this —— *Antichrist*, but I might as well try to burn the devil himself!"

A retired bookseller of Belfast [Tom Ward] built for himself a villa in the neighbourhood, in one room of which appeared, of course, a number of well-bound books. It is highly probable, however, that Tom's acquaintance with books in general was only confined to their titles, if we may judge by one little fact. Finding that he had no medical works, he selected what he considered the most useful, and actually ordered *Buchan's Domestic Medicine* and *De Lolme on the Constitution.*

The same bookseller, speaking of the library in his new villa, said it was so retired that he could read there all day long and nobody be a bit the wiser.

When Ibrahim Pacha paid a visit to Belfast in 1846, he arrived on a Sunday morning, and put up at the Royal Hotel. Being desirous of making good use of his time, and not knowing that the Sunday would make any difference, he forthwith sent out a messenger to seek a gentleman for whom he had a letter of introduction. This was the representative of the linen-house of Richardson & Co., Mr. Valentine, who at the time had just gone to church. The messenger followed him there in great haste, and told the sexton his errand, and that he must let Mr. Valentine know at once. The sexton accordingly went in, and, going forward to the pew, addressed him literally in these words :—"Mr. Valentine; sir, if you plaze, the King of Egypt's wantin' you."

A certain Belfast clergyman was frequently the butt of some of his acuter brethren. One of them actually made a wager with another that the person referred to could not tell whether William the Conqueror or William the Third reigned first. He was told there was a difference of opinion between them on this point, and that the matter was left to his decision. He looked very wise for a few moments, and then gave the following oracular response :—"Well, gentlemen, in my opinion there is a good deal to be said on both sides."

NOTE ON BELFAST CHARACTERS.

The "street characters" of Belfast sixty years ago were numerous and remarkable. Some account of them is given in T. Gaffikin's lecture on "Belfast Fifty Years Ago." "Cocky Bendy" was the favourite itinerant fiddler. Gaffikin writes—"Cocky Bendy was a very little bandy-legged man, who knew the tune to play at every house in the locality he frequented. 'Garryowen,' 'Patrick's Day,' and the 'Boyne Water' were his best paying airs." "Black Sam" was a negro who had performing dogs, great favourites with the children of that period. The fame of Tantra Barbus has survived to the present day. Pinkerton gave an account of him in *Notes and Queries*; but the fullest and most authentic life of this strange being is found in a rare chap-book, entitled, "The Life || of || William Scott, || *alias* || Tantra Barbus, || with || numerous anecdotes connected with || that eccentric character, || together with || an Elegy || written on his death by a Gentleman in Belfast. || Belfast : || printed for the Hawkers. || 1833." From this pamphlet it appears William Scott, better known as Tantra Barbus, was born near Ballynahinch about 1778. Although "thick witted," he had amassed at one time, by peddling hardware, the sum of £60. The story of his gains got wind, and called forth a swarm of competitive vagrants, who offered more substantial treats to the country people in the form of cheap sweets, pictures, toys. &c., in exchange for rags, broken glass, buttons, and old metal, to the ruin of Scott and themselves. By this stagnation of business, Tantra was obliged to use his hoard, and took to drink and begging. He was accused of acting as a spy during the rebellion, and for years after never visited Co. Down. Honesty was not one of his strong points, as the following extract indicates :—"Pewter kitchen vessels at this time supplied the place of delf, and, as this material always found a ready sale, the natural greed of Tantra could not withstand the temptation of appropriating the tempting ornaments of the dresser to his own use. Woe betide the housewife who, when Tantra was her guest, indulged in the luxury of a morning nap, for Tantra was up with the lark, and ten to one but her nicely-scoured pewter plates were converted into cordial before sunset." He also was an adept at pilfering brass rappers. Gaffikin notes—"Tantra Barbus was a man who would have danced for buttons, or swam across the river at the Long Bridge on the coldest day in winter for a few coppers." His picture, engraved by John Thomson, is the largest copperplate he executed.

OLD GLASS-HOUSE, BALLYMACARRETT.

COCKY BENDY,

a well known character in Belfast

INDEX.

Adair, Robert, his petition, 96.
Aitchison, C., MSS. from, 279.
Anarchy and poverty, 177.
Antrim, battle of, 183; cut of, 194; Earl of, 211.
Appendix, 249.
Ardes Barony, description of, 138-143, 263.
Ardkeen, Castle at, 23; Church of, 141.
Ardquin, inquisition taken at, 23, 256.
Armagh burnt, 211, 213.
Army, rules for marching, 148.
Assembly at Kilcronaghan, 210.
Assizes in Ulster in 1615, 30, 256.
Assessment for Ulster, 74-77.

Bagenal, Marshal, letter from, 15.
Balfour, Miss, 279.
Ballyboe of land, 207.
Ballyrobert, 129, 263.
Ballybeg surrenders, 225.
Bangor, Custom-house, 44; ancient bell at, 45.
Barracks, attack on, 178.
Bastille, anniversary of taking, 180, 272, 273.
Belfast, fortified, 5; captured, 56-59; trade of, in 1646 1648, 65-67, 261; Lough and Harbour of, 147, 164; view of, 169, 189; Castle of, old, 146; Charitable Society of, 193.

Belfast Lough, Chart of, 147; and Harbour, 164.
Bellingham, Col. Thomas, diary of, 144-146.
Bellman of Belfast (cut), 252.
Belturbet, seal of, 74.
Benburb Castle, view of, 200; battle of, 63, 240, 241, 247.
Black, Sir Samuel, portrait.
Blackstaff, river of, 256.
Bleachers in 1839, 255.
Blyth, James, examination of, 162.
Book-plates, 272.
Books relating to Ireland, 250.
Borrowe, Capt. Thomas, 3.
Boyne, battle of, map, 153.
Brantry Friary, 200.
Brewing, 9.
Broags, 10.
Brown, Capt. Thomas, 3.
Bruce, Rev. Michael, 262.
Bunting, Edward, 195, 278.

Carleboy, 4.
Carlingford, 69.
Carnmoney witches, 267.
Carrick-a-Rede (cut), 40.

Carrickfergus, lands reserved for garrison, 5, 256 ; petition of agents for, 18-20 ; King landing at, 146, 264 ; Custom-house, 45 ; Corporate Seal of, 163 ; Corporation of, 266 ; the French in, 183, 273.
Carrickmacross burnt, 246.
Castlereagh, 2 ; Con O'Neill's castle at, 160.
Castle Street, shop in, 1790. 179.
Catholic Emancipation, 179.
Cave Hill, 130, 256, 266.
Cessation, the, 1643, 55, 260.
Chancery, suit in, 41.
Charles the First, 56.
Charlemont, 52, 214, 224. 236.
Chichester, Sir A., 20, 21, 256 ; Lord, 28, 29, 256 ; patents confirmed, 127-138, 263.
Church, old, in High Street, 102.
Church, the Old Corporation, 166, 268.
Civil List, 100, 105, 262.
Claneboy, 1542, 2, 3.
Claneboy, Lady, 64.
Clones, battle at, 221, 222.
Cocky Bendy, 282, 283, (cut) 284.
Coleraine, 28.
Collier Family, tomb of, 166.
Commissioners for Ireland, 61-64, 86.
Commonwealth and North of Ireland, 73-108.
Conformity, Acts of, 176.
Conn's water, 42 ; bridge at, 44.
Connaught, arms of, 89.
Conway, Lord, 213, 214.
County cess, 1744, 259.
Connolly, Owen, 201.
Conway, Dame Amy, 41 ; Henry, 203.
Corn, account of, in 1643, 55.
Corry, John, account of, 109. 116.
Covenanters tear their colours, 60.
Cowley, Robert, Master of the Rolls, report by, 1, 252.
Creaghtes, the, 5, 220-228, 232, 234, 235.
Cromwell in Ireland, 70 ; letter from, 97, 261 ; portrait of, 98.
Customs, Excise, &c., in Ireland, 1637, 42-48, 100.
Cypher, 9.

"Defenders," 177, 182, 183.
Deputy, Lord, the (L.D.), 2, 3, 9 ; and Council to the Queen, 12, 13.
Derry, gateway in walls of, 85.
Dissenters excluded from public affairs, 176.
Doak, Hugh, 176.
Donaldson, Hugh, examination of, 163.
Donegall Family, arms of, 127, 265 ; Lady, 175, 176 ; leases of, 272.
Drennan, Wm., M.D., residence of, 169 ; portrait of, 173.
Drogheda, St. Lawrence's Gate, 69.
Dromore, battle at, 70-72.
Drumflugh, battle at, 240, 241.
Dublin, council at, 74 ; arms of, 74.
Dunbar, Mary, her examination, 161.
Dundalk, battles at, 53, 208, 209.
Dungannon, arms of, 36 ; besieged, 49, 51 ; taken, 214, 223 ; burnt, 229.

Dunluce, view of, 10.

Earl's Mill Ford Castle, 226, 227.
"Eaten by the Rats," 282.
Elizabeth, Queen (cut), 7 ; her arms, 11.
Emmett, Robert, 190 ; T. A., 276, 277.
Enniskillen, arms of, 32.
Essex, Earl of (cut), 20.
Exchange Rooms, Old, 196.
Exchequer, order of the, 39, 40, 260.
Exporting, articles for, in 1572, 11.

Felim O'Neill, 213, 217, 218, 220-222, 225. 228, 230, 236, 241, 244.
Fenton, William, examination of, 162.
Fermanagh, inquisition at, 32, 33.
Ford of Belfast (cut), 1.
Frederick Street Schoolhouse, 196.
Free trade with America, 179.

Gallows, ancient, 32, 260.
Galway city, plan of, 99.
Gaol delivery in Ulster, 256, 257, 266.
Garmoyle, 42.
Gerrard, Sir Thomas, 2.
Giant's Causeway, view of, 157, 266.
Glass-House (cut), 283.
Glenarme or Glanarme, 5, 7.
Green, Robert, correspondence of, 165-168, 267, 267.

Haltridge, James, examination of, 164.
Hand-loom, 12.
Harpers, Irish, 273, 278.
Hearts of Steel, 177, 178, 270, 271.
High Street, Belfast, old view of, 187.
Hill, Arthur, 120.
Hillsborough, Earl of, 120.
Hillsborough Fort, 122.
Hollywood, 44.
Hope, James, 188, 275.

Ibrahim Pacha, 282.
Imports, 65-67.
Ireland, Speed's map of, 1627, 201.
Ironworks, 41.

Joy, Francis, 175, 180, 181 ; Henry, 274.

Kells captured, 247.
Kelburne, Rev. S., 281.
Kilkenny, arms of, 77 ; Parliament at, 218 ; Council of, 243.
Kylwarling, 3 ; felling oaks in (cut), 41.

Lagan, lock-keeper's house on the, 118.
Leinster, arms of, 91.
Lennan, Charles, examination of, 162.
Leslie, Earl, Lieut.-General, 223, 231.
Letters, postage of, 68.
Lifford, inquisition at, 34.
Linen Hall, 179 ; plan of, 198.
Linen yarns, Irish, exporting, 11 ; manufacture of, 178, 179 ; history of, 254, 255.
Lisburn, view of, 155.

Lisnagarvy, 49, 60, 72.
Lock-keeper's house on the Lagan, 118.
Londonderrie, inquisition at, 34–36 ; arms of, 34 ;
    view of, 35.
Loom, hand, 12.
Lord Deputy, 2, 6, 9, 12, 14.
Lord Treasurer's objections, answers to, 16–18, 256.

MacAdam, Capt. John, 59 ; MSS., 281.
M'Art's Fort, Cave Hill, 182.
M'Cabe, Thomas, 170, 269.
M'Cracken, Mary Ann, portrait of, 174 ; life of,
    175–197, 269 ; Captain John, 176, 269; wife of,
    176 ; her schooling, 177 ; Henry Joy, 183–188.
M'Cammond, Wm., portrait, xii.
M'Donnell, Dr. John, notes by, 247.
M'Felim, Sir Brian, 2, 3, 8.
M'Skimin, Samuel, 197, 279 ; MSS., 129, 258,
    273, 279.
M'Tier, Mrs. M., extracts from letters of, 161–
    173, 269.
Maiming of cattle, 177.
Magee, Island, 20, 21, 161, 256, 267.
Martin, George, 175, 176.
Maryboro' capitulates, 245.
Masareene, village of, in 1851, 31.
Meal mills wanted, 6.
Mercator's map of Ulster, portion of, 43.
Meredith, Major, relation by, 68–72, 261.
Ministers, Scotch, 76, 101–105, 261.
Molyneux, Dr. Thomas, Journey to y⁰ North,
    152–160, 265.
Moncke, Charles, report by, 42–46.
Monk, General, 247.
Monroe, Major-General, in Newry, 49–56, 260 ;
    in Belfast, 56–64, 237, 260, 274 ; at Lisne-
    garvy, 60 ; at Carrickfergus, 61 ; his petition,
    88, 99 ; Colonel George, 223, 227, 233, 234,
    237.
Montgomery, Viscount, 41, 239 ; Colonel, 184.
Mountjoy, 214, 215, 219, 234.
Mourne Mountains, view of, 49, 52.
Mullintur, Council at, 231.
Munster, arms of, 89.
Muslin trade, 177, 183, 270.
Mussenden, Mr., 167, 268.

Neagh, Lough, 239.
Newry, Monroe's raid on, 1643, 49–55. 69 ; arms
    of, 72 ; surrendered, 211.
News-Letter, the, established, 175.
Northern Star, the, 181.
Nugent, Colonel, 183, 274.

Oaks, felling, in Kilwarlin (cut), 41.
Oge, Randall, 5 ; Alexander, 8.
O'Hara, Teig. his case, 101.
O'Mellan's, Friar, Narrative of the Wars of 1641,
    200.
O'Neill, Con, his castle, Castlereagh, 160.
O'Neill, Daniel, certificate by, 1663, 123, 262 ;
    General, 208, 240.
O'Neill, Tirlagh, 6, 9, 207 ; Hugh, Earl of
    Tyrone, 22 ; Owen, 8, 224, 238, 240 ; Daniel,
    362.

Openshaw, Robert, 31, 259.
Orange ballads, 280.
O'Reillys, the, 203.
Ormond, Earl of, 218, 243, 246.

Para moudras, 282.
Parliament, the, and Belfast in 1645, 64, 260 ,
    an independent, 179.
Peep of Day Boys, 177.
Pensioners, 101, 106.
Pestilence, 206.
Piers and Malbie to the Queen, 4–10.
Piers, Mayor of Carrickfergus, 254.
Pinkerton MSS., 56, 124, 249, 251, 280.
Pinkerton, William, ix.
Plan to seize fortified towns, 201.
Poorhouse, the Old, 193.
Pope, the, Ambassador from, 224 ; Nuncio from,
    228, 236, 238, 244.
Portadown burnt, 242.
Portaferry Castle, ruins of, 139.
Portmore Woods, keeper in, 126.
Post first established, 67, 68, 261.
Princes in Ulster, 1.
Privy Council, correspondence with, 73–77 : reply
    to Commissioners, 84.

Quail, William, tribute to memory of, 281.
Queen Square, Belfast, old houses at, 248.
Quern, the, 120.

Ragged School, first in Ireland, 195.
Rawdon, Sir George, account of, 124–127.
Richard, Protector, 106.
Russell, Thomas, 188–191, 276 ; Patrick, his
    petition, 123, 124.

Saintfield, battle near, 274, 275.
Sarleboy, 9.
Savage, family of, 253 ; crests and arms of, 24.
Seal of the Commonwealth, 73.
Servants' wages, 265.
Schonberg, Duke of, proclamation by, 143, 263,
    264.
Schoolmasters, 106.
Scotch ministers, 75, 103, 104, 261.
Scott, William, 283.
Scots, the, to be expelled, 5, 10, 29, 30, 45 ;
    in Belfast, 58–63 ; scheme to transplant, 78–
    96, 261, 262.
Sgian, ancient Irish, 36.
Shane's Castle, view of, 156.
Sheriffs, High, of Co. Antrim, 1603 to 1895, 257–
    259.
Ships advertised to sail, 271.
Silver tankard, 1681, 113.
Simms, Robert, 273.
Smith, John, of Lairne, his examination, 161.
Smith's grant, 24–26.
Smith, Sir Thomas, portrait, 26.
Smuggling, 178.
Sorley Boy, 3, 9.
Spain, King of, sends arms to Ireland, 221.
Spinning mills in 1836, 255.
Spinning wheel, 13.

Squib, political, 180.
Strabane, 210.
Stranmillis, 60, 117-123, 231.
Steam engine, first in Belfast, 282.
Swift, Dean, 48, 260.

Tandragee, 202, 219.
Tantra Barbus, 283.
Taxation, mode of, in 1637, 46-48.
Thurot landing at Carrickfergus, 182.
Timber in Ulster, 27, 41, 42, 256, 260.
Tir-Connell, battles at, 213, 219
Tone, Theobald Wolfe, 181, 182, 188, 189.
Town lands, bounds of, 19.
Travers, Sir John, 2.
Trinity College, Dublin, Library of, 59 ; silver salver in, 108.
Tuam, Archbishop of, 237.
Tyrone, Earl of, 22 : inquisition at, 36-39.

Ulster in 1538. 1 : plantation of, 28 ; assizes held in 1615, 30-39, 256 ; arms of, 75 ; campaign in, 76.

United Irishmen, 181-183.

Venables, Colonel R., *Experienced Angler*, 88, 96, 97, 262.
Vinycomb, John, 272.
Volunteers, the, 179-181.

Walker, Thomas, letter from, 21, 256.
Ware, William, portrait of, 251.
Waringstown, view of, 154.
Wars of 1641, narratives of, 200-257.
Waterford City, arms of, 94.
Waterworks, old, Stranmillis, 116
Welton, Lt.-Col., 63.
Whig Club in 1790, 180.
Whiteabbey, view of, in 1800, 129, 263.
William III. and his Court at Belfast, 148, 264 ; gloves, stirrups, and horse trappings at battle of the Boyne, (*cut*) 149 ; proclamations by, 150-152.
Wilson, II. II., examination of, 162.
Witches in Island Magee, 161-164, 267.
Woollen trade prohibited, 178.

BLACK SAM, A BELFAST STREET CHARACTER, *c.* 1830.
(From a water-colour in possession of R. S. Birch, Esq.)

JOHNSTON'S
Umbrella and Walking Stick Manufactory.

BELFAST ART AND INDUSTRIAL EXHIBITION, 1895.

Irish Blackthorns mounted in Gold, Silver, Ivory, Connemara Marble, &c.

Plain Irish Blackthorns, wholesale, from 9/- per dozen. Undressed Irish Blackthorns, from 20/- per 100.

Nearly 10,000 Real Irish Blackthorns were used to complete this Cottage.

Re-Covering IN 30 MINUTES.

From 1/- to 21/-.

No extra charge is made for doing small repairs (including broken ribs), re-polishing Sticks, adding New Tassels, etc., to **Umbrellas** and **Parasols** being re-covered, which are thus made equal to new, and delivered in Belfast in one hour, or sent to country Post Free.

PATTERNS ON APPLICATION.

31, HIGH STREET, BELFAST.

THE CITY OF BELFAST, FROM THE CASTLEREAGH HILLS.

From a Drawing by J. Vinycomb, M.R.I.A.

Other Works by Robert M. Young.

THE TOWN BOOK OF THE CORPORATION OF BELFAST. Edited from the Original, with Notes and Chronological List of Events. With Maps and Illustrations. Marcus Ward & Co., Limited, Belfast. 1892. Edition de Luxe, quarto, £2 2s.; octavo, £1 1s. *(Out of print.)*

"This is one of the most beautiful of recent books, and is probably the masterpiece of a firm noted for the artistic character of its publications. . . . The editor, whose painstaking and patience cannot be too highly praised, is to be congratulated on having performed his work with such thoroughness that every archaism of orthography and punctuation is reproduced. To this quaintness, and the extreme beauty of type and paper, the volume owes its charm."—*Athenæum.*

"The editor has done his work admirably, elucidating many points of interest by notes which are full of learning and acuteness."—*The Speaker.*

"Does great credit to the industry of its editor and the taste of its well-known publishers."—*Times.*

"The work forms a noteworthy addition to the literature of the primary sources of municipal history.—*Scotsman.*

ULSTER IN '98: Episodes and Anecdotes now first printed. Illustrated. 3rd Edition. Belfast: Marcus Ward & Co., Limited. 1893. Price 1s.; cloth, 2s.

"Every Irishman, of whatever religion or politics, should have this book in his library."—*Irish Times.*

"For many reasons this little book is welcome. We owe, therefore, a debt of gratitude to Mr. Young for collecting in handy form unwritten traditions and ballads of the time whih have been handed down by Presbyterian Croppies."—*The Speaker.*

"Every endeavour has been made by the editor to authenticate the episodes and anecdotes which now appear for the first time."—*The Bookseller.*

"I wish that in all parts of Ireland reminiscences of this kind could be collected."— *W. E. H. Lecky, Esq.*

BELFAST: MARCUS WARD & CO., LIMITED, PUBLISHERS, ROYAL ULSTER WORKS; ALSO AT LONDON, NEW YORK, AND SYDNEY.

Manufacturing Goldsmiths and Silversmiths,
DIAMOND MOUNTERS, JEWELLERS, MEDALLISTS,
Watch and Clock Makers, Opticians, Engravers, Electro-Plate Manufacturers,

Gold, Silver, Copper, and Nickel Platers.

COPIES OF ANTIQUE PLATE MADE ON THE PREMISES.

Family and Antique Plate repaired and renewed, with all old characteristics preserved.

ARMS, CRESTS, MONOGRAMS, AND INITIALS ENGRAVED ON PLATE, &c.

OLD AND WORN ELECTRO-PLATE REPLATED AS NEW.

WATCHES, CLOCKS, AND JEWELLERY OF ALL KINDS REPAIRED.

ALL WORK DONE ON THE PREMISES.

Our extensive Works, employing upwards of fifty hands, using 85 feet of shafting and 350 feet of belting, the motive power being supplied by an Otto Gas Engine of 26 horse power, are open to the inspection of our Customers.

113, ROYAL AVENUE, BELFAST.

www.ingramcontent.com/pod-product-compliance
Lightning Source LLC
Chambersburg PA
CBHW020808060726
47498CB00017B/955